DALLAS

DALLAS

The Complete Story of the World's Favorite Prime-Time Soap

★ Barbara A. Curran ★

Foreword by David Jacobs, creator of *Dallas*

Introduction by Victoria Principal

CUMBERLAND HOUSE

NASHVILLE, TENNESSEE

DALLAS: THE COMPLETE STORY OF THE WORLD'S FAVORITE PRIME-TIME SOAP
PUBLISHED BY CUMBERLAND HOUSE PUBLISHING
431 Harding Industrial Drive
Nashville, Tennessee 37211

Previously published as *25 Years of Dallas* by Virtualbookworm.com Publishing, Inc.

Cover design: James Duncan, James Duncan Creative
Book design: Mary Sanford

Library of Congress Cataloging-in-Publication Data
Curran, Barbara A., 1961–
    [25 years of Dallas]
    Dallas : the complete story of the world's favorite prime-time soap / Barbara A. Curran ; foreword by David Jacobs ; introduction by Victoria Principal.
        p. cm.
    "Previously published as 25 Years of Dallas by Virtualbookworm.com Publishing"—Copyright p.
    Includes bibliographical references and index.
    ISBN 1-58182-472-6 (pbk. : alk. paper)
    1. Dallas (Television program) I. Title.
    PN1992.77.D3C87 2005
    791.43'72—dc22

                                                                        2005018978

Printed in Canada
1 2 3 4 5 6 7—11 10 09 08 07 06 05

For Tim, Jack, Annabel, and Boo

★ CONTENTS ★

FOREWORD

So here they are again. The Ewings of *Dallas*, their colleagues, their lovers and enemies, their partners in deception and guile. For a time they intrigued us, then they obsessed us, then they became part of our lives and stayed there, and stayed there. They hung on—or maybe *we* were the ones hanging on—as they became tired, more routine than they'd once been. Don't we all? Even after they left the weekly television schedule they didn't completely leave; they came back in one form or another—a TV movie, reruns on cable, newly mastered DVD with commentary. Soon they'll be coming back with new faces on the big screen at a theater near you.

But never has their return been as complete, as pervasive as it is in the book you're holding in your hands. Here are all the Ewings all the time, beginning to end, the family and everybody around them, all their doings and misdoings, names and dates given. Here's everything you want to know, need to know, don't care to know but might someday in the future—for the record.

Barbara Curran's book answers all your questions about the storylines, ratings, and cast and crew of *Dallas*, plus some questions you didn't know you had. What I like best about it, though, are a couple of things beyond its formidable collection of facts, figures, names, and dates. First, it sets straight some of the contradictions that exist in the mythology of *Dallas*'s conception, development, and evolution; and second, it *doesn't* set all the contradictions straight. For while this is a book of hard information, it's also a book about memory. Probing the recollections of so many of those who were there, Barbara Curran has discovered what journalists and historians inevitably discover about memory: that it's not pure science; it's not pure fact; it's not pure anything, except memory.

Memory is the recreation of what happened as each of us remembers it, colored by our own assumptions and imaginations and wishful thinking. For people who like to tell stories, memory is also a fine foundation to build a story on. And real storytellers, remember, are driven first and foremost by the impulse to make any story the best possible story, even if it means improving it a little.

As the great director John Ford put it, when fact and legend are in dispute, print the legend. Tell the better story.

That advice has gotten me into a lot of trouble with my wife and kids over the years. "Dad," my daughter might say after I tell an anecdote from our recent vacation, "I didn't say that; *Mom* said that."

"Really?" I'm always surprised until I dip more deeply into my recollection or ask others who were present and learn she was right. I gave the line to her because the story works better if she says it. Even thus exposed, nine times out of ten it's the revised version I'll store in my repertory.

There are lots of early *Dallas* errors that have worked themselves into legend because they seem to make a better story. For example, over the years it's often been written and said that when the first five episodes of *Dallas* were broadcast, the initial episode drew a modest rating but the numbers grew every week, finally getting to the point where a pickup for a full season was earned. Good story—a story in the spirit of that great racehorse Silky Sullivan, who invariably broke last, trailed for a while, then gained, gained, gained—caught up in the stretch and won at the wire. But as Barbara Curran's immaculate research reveals herein, the Silky Sullivan scenario's not true of *Dallas*.

When the *Dallas* pilot, "Digger's Daughter," originally aired on April 2, 1978, it earned a 37 share. Those were days when only three networks dominated television, and cable was still inconsequential as far as original programming was concerned. A hit was a show that won the timeslot and was seen by at least one-third of the audience watching television at that hour. A mere 30 share meant you were "marginal." (The first show I ever worked on, *The Blue Knight*, was cancelled with a 31 share because it was such a weak second to ABC's *Charlie's Angels*, which was winning the timeslot with 39s and 40s.) Today a 12 share will keep you on the air if the demographics are good.

Dallas's debut with a 37 share was very good. In its second week, however, it aired against an NBC movie starring Fred Astaire and Helen Hayes and got a 26 share. That number and especially the 11 point drop-off from week one seemed to spell doom. Although in weeks three and four the NBC miniseries *Holocaust* won the hour, *Dallas* did manage to climb up over the 30-share mark, keeping hope alive. The future of *Dallas* came down to the fifth and last of the first episodes, "Barbecue."

"Barbecue" won the hour with a 39 share, which guaranteed a pickup for a full season.

Personally, I like this story, which happens to be the truth, better than the slow-growth story. It's better dramatically—a story of initial success followed by apparent failure, followed by the slow recovery of dignity but not certainty, with the triumphant climax saved for the last possible moment. I like it for a self-serving reason, too. (Isn't memory also a tool for making ourselves look good?) It seems that "Digger's Daughter" with its 37 share and "Barbecue" with its 39 were the two episodes among the first five that I had written. The truth, of course, is that weaker competition on the other networks, not the name of the writer on-screen, is what made those two episodes the most successful, but who cares why? Facts are facts, and this book bears them out, so I'm happy to take the credit.

There's plenty of credit to go around for the birth and success of *Dallas*, and, as you'll see in these pages, plenty of credit taken, so in the interest of complete disclosure, here are a few more facts that may color my version of certain contro-versies. I created *Dallas*. I created the premise and format and characters. I wrote four of the first seven episodes (and edited or rewrote the other three). But . . . I didn't run the show. Leonard Katzman did.

And after *Dallas* was launched, I went off with Mike Filerman, the Lorimar executive who'd found me and shepherded *Dallas* and our other projects through the development process, to create more shows together, which we would run our-selves.

When *Dallas* caught on, then took off, I was surprised and delighted, but my delight was experienced from a distance. I wasn't in charge; I didn't read or com-ment on the scripts; I had nothing to do with casting or budgeting or the plotting of story. Which explains why the pleasure I experienced from its success was a slightly guilty pleasure: I wasn't *doing* anything.

Today I am perfectly happy to admit that *Dallas*'s evolution proceeded with-out my guidance. You are free to take my judgments of later developments in *Dallas* history with a grain of salt.

But when it comes to the early history—the history of the show's conception, development, and first appearances—I'd trust me.

For instance, you sometimes hear or read that *Dallas* was never intended to be a series; that the success of the miniseries lit lightbulbs over the heads of CBS ex-ecutives and the series idea was thus illuminated. Not true. The "miniseries" was always meant to be a trial series, a full-fledged series always the goal.

The first draft of the *Dallas* pilot script was dated December 10, 1977, and sent in to CBS the next day, in time for Bud Grant, then CBS's entertainment chief, and Bob Daly, network president, to take it with them on the CBS plane flying to New York. Bud read it first, laid it aside and told Bob that he thought it was a promising idea, but he didn't see what they would learn by merely shooting a pilot. The cast was an ensemble, and one sixty-minute episode might not be enough to determine if the chemistry between characters was working. Moreover, since there was no franchise—these were not cops or doctors in an environment that itself created conflict and jeopardy—it was difficult to know what kind of story we'd be telling week after week.

Then let's shoot six, Daly said. (That later became five.)

Which brings us to another myth: that the idea of serialization came later, after the show was on the air.

We always knew that *Dallas* would have to be a serial. The problem was *start-ing out* with it as a serial.

Except for *Peyton Place*, many years before, there had never been a successful prime-time serial on television. The belief was that the audience was reluctant to commit to a serial in the first place and wouldn't join it after it was under way. In-deed, the conventional wisdom in television was that the principal characters on an episodic drama should not change. Kojak was always Kojak; Dr. Kildare was always Dr. Kildare. The audience, according to that wisdom, took comfort in the sameness, even the predictability of characters. Moreover, because these characters had franchises—cop and doctor—which provided the plot, the episodes could be aired in any order. An outstanding episode could be saved for a "sweeps week;" and a disappointing one buried when the World Series was scheduled on another network.

Early in the 1970s the appearance of programs without franchises—such as *The Waltons, Little House on the Prairie, Eight Is Enough,* and *Family*—began to erode the rule of changeless characters. They weren't serials, but because the stories on these domestic-situated programs were character-driven, not plot-driven, the characters had to change to reflect their experiences. When John-Boy went to college on *The Waltons,* he became a college boy; he could not next week be a kid again; he couldn't even be living at home. On *Family,* Willie married and his young bride died. After her death, the writers could not write Willie as they had before. He had lived through a traumatic and life-changing experience; he was a different person, and that needed to be reflected in his behavior.

As life-changing, domestic issues affected the characters, episodes had to be aired in chronological order. Still, strict serialization was avoided. Dramatically, each episode had to stand on its own. This was difficult: how do you accommodate a reasonable season-long arc of character change while telling a complete, closed-end story every week? Nigel McKeand, producer of *Family,* on which I worked as story editor in 1977, gave us the formula for each episode: "Resolve the situation; don't solve the problem."

We adopted Nigel's formula to the first episodes of *Dallas.* In the pilot, "Digger's Daughter," J.R. tries to disgrace Pam in order to break up her marriage to Bobby. He fails: situation resolved. End of episode. But in future stories, Pam's problem remains, is in fact worsened: J.R. continues to believe that she represents a threat to his mastery at Ewing Oil, and he tries ever-more cleverly to drive her away.

Even as we made each episode self-standing, we knew that the best way to tell the *Dallas* saga was to serialize it; serialization was always our intention and eventual goal. We couldn't go there, though, until the audience was hooked, until we knew they were coming back every week.

They did get hooked, they did keep coming back, and *Dallas* became a serial, with characters who changed through the drama.

This, I now understand, is the most significant contribution that *Dallas* made to the history of episodic television. The changing character. The notion that events in the lives of characters had to register and change their belief systems and motivations. Mike Filerman and I took it further on *Knots Landing,* where one season's villain—say, William Devane as Greg Sumner or Nicollette Sheridan as Paige—could become next season's hero. It was in the air in the seventies, but it took hold and stuck on *Dallas;* and because *Dallas* was such a huge success, proving that the audience would accept and probably from now on *expect* evolution in the definitions of characters, it changed almost every television program that came after it. Even the old franchises—the cop and doctor shows—were reformulated. *Hill Street Blues, L.A. Law, NYPD Blue,* and *ER* were serials; so were *thirtysomething, The Practice, The West Wing, The Sopranos, Sex and the City, The Wire,* and right on through to *Desperate Housewives, Lost,* and *24.* And so, of course, were the next dramatic form in the evolutionary process, the "reality" shows—*Survivor, The Apprentice,* and all *their* progeny.

And when you think about it, it now seems obvious that continuing drama is television's natural form. For production value, sex, violence, exotica, television can't compete with feature films (which of course show on cable and pay-per-view). But no other medium but television can tell you stories that keep going, unrolling like ribbons, revealing new aspects, new twists and turns, showing you not only the stories but the consequences of stories. Like life. Indeed, alone among dramatic media, whether written or unscripted, television's continuing episodic dramas show you what happens after the curtain comes down.

The stories summarized, the facts and credits all lined up neatly and completely, the slightly out-of-whack memories bashing around like bumper cars at a carnival—all the stuff of *Dallas* can be found in these pages. Read them straight through—a formidable challenge—or take a serendipitous dip whenever the mood comes over you, and you'll see how unremarkable the individual stories were, but how unique and well-defined the characters, how firmly they've lodged in the national consciousness, and most of all how many and how memorable the big, big moments were.

Continuing drama didn't start on *Dallas.* But the enormity of *Dallas*'s success, its long life, its worldwide appeal were so profound that it reversed the conventional wisdom and made change, rather than consistency of character, the motor driving drama.

I did that—along with Leonard and all the cast and writers and production team. We took what Mike and I had created and made it into the first American television program to become a worldwide phenomenon. I still take a lot of pleasure in the audaciousness of *Dallas,* and its global achievement, and its place in our cultural history. The guilt that used to temper the pleasure, I have to admit, has faded a bit. After all, if there had never been a me there couldn't have been a *Dallas.* Of no one else on Earth can that be said with absolute certainty.

And when I think of what sprang from it, of its many progeny, of the straight line between *Dallas* and, say, *The Apprentice* . . . and how it's brought almost J.R.-like fame to Donald Trump . . . maybe some guilt creeps back.

But only a little.

DAVID JACOBS
Hollywood, California
May 2005

INTRODUCTION

It is a pleasure to write the introduction to Barbara Curran's *Dallas: The Complete Story of the World's Favorite Prime-Time Soap*. Barbara is a wonderful writer and an impressively accurate historian. Her book is the ultimate *Dallas* diary. Those of us from the original cast—Patrick, Larry, Linda, Steve, Ken, Charlene, and I, and our welcome addition, Mary Crosby—all relied on it during the press interviews we gave while filming *The Return to Southfork* at the ranch last fall.

Barbara smartly provides facts where they can be provided, yet allows for memories and nuance when they cannot. Patrick wrote to Barbara while she was working on the book, "Please remember that memory serves each one of us that chooses to recall something by fitting itself comfortably into one's own subjective reality. I try to be objective but know at times I may have shaken the snowglobe of my life and the flakes have settled in a slightly different pattern."

By taking this sage advice to heart, Barbara has captured for the ages both the factual and atmospheric histories of our iconic series. This book, like our South-fork reunion show, the *Dallas* DVDs, and the upcoming *Dallas* feature film, marks a public renaissance of our show at the same time it seemed to reemerge in my own life.

Dallas entered the "snowglobe of my life" almost thirty years ago! The difference between that cold winter when we filmed the pilot and all those subsequent sweltering summer on-location shoots is a fitting metaphor for how dramatically the success of *Dallas* changed the lives of its cast. It seemed as though one minute we were working actors, and in the blink of an eye our faces were known in the farthest reaches of the globe.

That level of success, achieved alongside David Jacobs, Lennie Katzman, Phil Capice, and so many other devoted and talented writers, directors, and producers, cannot help but change you. It certainly changed, among other things, our opportunities, our careers, and our relationships. Yet, decades later, the core beings in our group seem not to have changed at all. Patrick is ever my handsome and hilarious leading man. Charlene is still like a kid sister, and Ken, like the older brother I never had. Linda remains a much-respected friend and colleague. Steve is the quintessential cowboy of our generation. And, of course, Larry is always the good-time rascal that is the anchor and the soul of the *Dallas* family.

I know that my beloved Jim Davis, a true father figure to me during those early years, continues, at his heavenly ranch, to have the softest heart wrapped in the most leathery exterior. I have not seen Barbara since I left the show in 1987, but Barbara was endearingly consistent. She is an old-school actress to the core, a kind and considerate lady, and (unlike the demure Miss Ellie) a truly bawdy dame!

Even before Kristin shot J.R., *Dallas* was a huge and noteworthy hit. We broke new ground as the first top ten serial since Eisenhower was in the White House. *Dallas* brought more viewers to Friday night than ever before or since. We were critically acclaimed, winning everything from the Emmy to the People's Choice Award. *Dallas* introduced the cliff-hanger to prime time. And we changed prime time's landscape by way of countless imitators, starting with our own spin-off.

On March 21, 1980, there was "Who Shot J.R.?" and we became a true phenomenon. From that point on, the most difficult thing for us to do artistically was to maintain our success. But maintain it we did, through Lucy's wedding, Sue Ellen and J.R.'s tumultuous relationship, the loss of Jock, Pam and Bobby's divorce, and even through Bobby's infamous death and resurrection. Along the way, we enjoyed the company and privilege of cast members like Howard Keel, Priscilla Pointer, Susan Howard, and Priscilla Presley.

But all things must end. We maintained the quality of our show for years, but eventually we all moved on from *Dallas*, at various times and in various ways. As for me, I loved how Pam's dream allowed us to reunite most of the original cast for one more season and to stage Pam's and Bobby's inevitable second marriage.

I left *Dallas* in 1987. In order for me to successfully pursue the rest of my acting career, I felt it was necessary to maintain a consistent public distance from the show. And I did . . . until Charlene phoned me and convinced me that it was time to come home. Then Patrick invited me to join him and the others in the dining room at Turtle Creek where we stayed while filming the reunion. It was then that I realized that distance—any distance, whether geographical or emotional—has a natural end just as it has a natural beginning. I realized that my distance from *Dallas* had come to an end.

So I made my "Return to Southfork" just as the world seemed to rediscover our old friends, the Ewings and the Barneses. I felt free to go back, and it felt good to go back. From this vantage point, without the craziness of the hype, the brashness of youth, and the unending crush of the glare and pace, I could savor it all the more—the friends, the memories, the personal and professional triumphs and tragedies through which we all lived. My *Dallas* journey did not conclude with a cliff-hanger or a dream, but with a most joyous, happy ending.

This exceptional book will allow you to extend your *Dallas* journey for a lifetime. I hope you enjoy your visit back to *Dallas*!

VICTORIA PRINCIPAL
Beverly Hills, California
May 2005

PREFACE

President Jimmy Carter and his fellow presidential candidate George H. W. Bush made references to it in their campaign speeches. The Queen Mother of England tried to use the authority of her position to find it out. Former President Gerald Ford made his golfing partner stop playing and call a Hollywood studio to learn it. Jimmy the Greek and other bookies from Las Vegas to Europe set headline-making odds about it. People from all walks of life in all corners of the globe waited breathlessly for eight months to have it resolved. Finally, on November 21, 1980, 350 million people in 57 countries gathered in front of their TV screens to learn, once and for all, "Who Shot J.R.?"

And so began the phenomenon of *Dallas*. The international frenzy that greeted the whodunit made the CBS series an instant classic, and the resolution of the "Who Shot J.R.?" cliff-hanger was at that time the highest-rated program in the history of television. That episode was recently chosen as one of the top ten greatest milestones in TV history by voters in an industry poll, alongside President Kennedy's funeral and the 1969 Apollo moon landing. The show ran for an astounding 357 episodes over thirteen years, was nominated for twenty-three Emmy Awards (and won four), made superstars of its cast members, including Larry Hagman, Victoria Principal, Linda Gray, and Patrick Duffy, and was one of the top-two-rated series on American television for half of the 1980s. *Dallas* spawned a whole new genre of prime-time programming, and popularized the plot device still used every spring by serials, dramas, and even many situation comedies: the season-ending cliff-hanger.

Overseas, *Dallas* garnered huge ratings in almost every one of the ninety countries in which it aired. It inspired analytical treatises in several cultures. The Bonn Municipal Theatre in Germany put on a ballet inspired by *Dallas*. Restaurant business in Italy fell when the show aired. Turkish parliamentary meetings were adjourned so members would not miss the show. In Johannesburg, theaters were closed to avoid competing with *Dallas*, and in Israel, where schoolchildren wore cowboy costumes so they could look like J.R., the show was even broadcast on radio. The only country where the show flopped was Japan.

The series went on to experience an afterlife that was just as impressive. The domestic cable TV ratings for *Dallas* reruns were so high in the late 1990s and early 2000s that it was shown three times a day, and it continues to air in more than one hundred foreign countries. There are countless *Dallas* Web sites around the world, one of which claims to receive 100,000 hits a day. The Southfork

Ranch in Texas draws 400,000 visitors annually, making it Texas's most popular tourist attraction other than the site where John F. Kennedy's assassination took place. Ebay offers for auction on a daily basis dozens of *Dallas* collector items, from signed photographs to J.R. beer, and Warner Brothers began releasing *Dallas* on DVD in 2004.

Now, almost thirty years after it began, *Dallas* reruns have been seen in an entirely new rotation on the SOAPnet cable TV network, and, following the recent success of movie versions of such TV classics as *Mission: Impossible*, *Charlie's Angels*, and *The Brady Bunch*, "Hollywood is abuzz that a tremendous big-screen version of *Dallas* is in the works." Major news outlets such as CNN, the Fox News Channel and *Variety* have all recently reported that *Dallas* creator David Jacobs has signed on to produce a big budget, silver screen version of *Dallas*, with the likes of Brad Pitt, John Travolta, Bruce Willis, and Kevin Costner rumored to be in the running to play J.R.

Even in a culture thoroughly saturated with television, very few shows become the blockbuster success or define their era as did *Dallas*. It became part of the fabric of the decade that linked the recession-weary 1970s and the high-tech 1990s. *Dallas* invited Americans living through Reaganomics and the final confrontations with the Soviet Union to revel in a country that was rich and powerful. Audiences from Africa to Europe followed the saga of the Ewings of Southfork, enabling this caricature of western capitalism to seep across all corners of the globe as democracy became a widespread export. True fans of *Dallas* find it only partially coincidental that seven months after J.R. Ewing visited Moscow, the Berlin Wall came tumbling down.

This book seeks to provide the definitive account of this beloved cultural icon, and it is the author's hope that it will illuminate the series for original and new fans alike.

ACKNOWLEDGMENTS

An earlier edition of this book, *25 Years of Dallas: The Complete Story of the World's Favorite Prime Time Soap,* was available through print-on-demand publisher Virtualbookworm.com Publishing in 2004, and I remain grateful to those who helped with that book just as I am grateful to those who helped with this new edition.

I am particularly indebted to *Dallas* star Steve Kanaly for his friendship, resourcefulness, and loyalty. Steve has been an unending source of encouragement and guidance, and neither book could not have been written without him.

Others from the *Dallas* family have also honored me with their time, insights, and talent. I thank Victoria Principal as much for our great chats as for providing the Introduction to this book; David Jacobs not only for writing a wonderful Foreword but for helpful information about the *Dallas* pilot, prequel movie, and upcoming feature film; Larry Hagman for his kind and supportive phone calls and emails; and Charlene Tilton for making the TV and radion promotion rounds with me.

Steve, Victoria, David, Larry, and Charlene are among dozens from the *Dallas* fold who graciously provided interviews, and I deeply appreciate their kindnesses, and those of their agents.

Those from the original pilot cast who gave interviews are Patrick Duffy, Linda Gray, Larry Hagman, Steve Kanaly, Ken Kercheval, Tina Louise, Victoria Principal, and Charlene Tilton.

Subsequent cast members who provided interviews are John Beck, Morgan Brittany, Mary Crosby, Lesley-Anne Down, Steve Forrest, Jenilee Harrison, Susan Howard, Howard Keel, George Kennedy, Audrey Landers, Jared Martin, Leigh McCloskey, Cathy Podewell, Priscilla Pointer, Priscilla Presley, William Smithers, and Sheree J. Wilson.

Dallas guest stars who gave interviews are Christopher Atkins, Barbara Babcock, Joanna Cassidy, Barry Corbin, Barbara Eden, Stephen Elliott, Fern Fitzgerald, Anne Francis, Joel Grey, Alice Hirson, Ed Kenney, Susan Lucci, Monte Markham, Margaret Michaels, Richard Roat, Kathryn Leigh Scott, Joan Van Ark, Kenneth White, Noble Willingham, and Morgan Woodward.

I thank you all!

I am also grateful to Barbara Bel Geddes' granddaughter, Hannah Lerman, for discussing her grandmother, and Barbara Carrera, who, while declining to be quoted, spent time talking about her year as a guest star on *Dallas.*

Writers Brenda Scott Royce and David Hofstede, publisher Bobby Bernshausen of Virtualbookworm.com Publishing, Colin Hunter of the *Ultimate Dallas*

Web site, and writer and comedian James Holmes were also generous with their support and assistance.

Two reference sources that provided invaluable ratings, schedule, and cast information are Tim Brooks and Earle Marsh's *The Complete Directory to Prime Time Network and Cable TV Shows, 1946–Present* and Bruce Morris's *Prime Time Network Serials: Episode Guides, Cast and Credits for 37 Continuing Television Dramas, 1964–1993*. Additional ratings and schedule information was obtained from *Variety*. With few exceptions, these reference sources are not included among the endnotes.

I also owe a debt of gratitude to Mark Thompson and his colleagues at the Southfork Ranch Event & Conference Center in Parker, Texas, for the use of their wonderful photographs of the ranch and grounds and, again, to Steve Kanaly, for the use (twice!) of photographs from his personal collection.

I thank the staff of both the Main Reading Room and the Motion Picture & Television Reading Room at the Library of Congress in Washington, D.C. The Motion Picture Reading Room staff, especially reference librarian Rosemary Hanes, assisted with periodical research and was exceptionally helpful in arranging the screening of episodes of *Dallas* maintained in the Library's collection.

The team at Cumberland House is terrific, and my thanks go to Ron Pitkin, Mary Sanford, Teresa Wright, and Tracy Ford.

Finally, I thank my husband, Tim, who helped with the research and editing of both editions and who claims he never wants to watch an episode of *Dallas* again. (But I know he will!)

BARBARA A. CURRAN
Villanova, Pennsylvania
June 2005

DALLAS

Part I

THE EARLY YEARS

THE PILOT
April 1978—"Digger's Daughter"

DALLAS PREMIERED ON CBS AT 10:00 p.m. on Sunday, April 2, 1978. Its pilot was in the form of five one-hour episodes, each of which aired in the same timeslot on consecutive Sundays through April 30. The pilot was created in late 1977 by writer David Jacobs, then a story editor for the ABC drama *Family*. Before joining *Family*, Jacobs, whose specialties were short stories and children's books, wrote scripts for *The Blue Knight*, a short-lived CBS police drama starring future *Dallas* cast member George Kennedy. Jacobs soon landed a development deal with Michael Filerman, an executive with Lorimar Productions, which produced such hit shows as *Eight Is Enough* and *The Waltons*. At the time, Jacobs was interested in creating a family series that examined relationships. "I wanted to do something good," Jacobs later wrote, "a show that mattered, insightful drama that intelligent people could watch and discuss and be moved by," like Ingmar Bergman's *Scenes from a Marriage*.

Jacobs and Filerman screened *Scenes from a Marriage* and both loved it. Filerman, however, had doubts about basing a TV show on the film and was more inclined towards a steamy soap opera. Jacobs recalled that "there was another movie Mike thought we should take a look at: *No Down Payment*, a semi-sleazy 1950s potboiler. I saw the movie and got the picture. Mike knew television better than I did." Jacobs and Filerman each compromised and came up with what became *Knots Landing*, a drama about four middle-class couples. As Jacobs explained, that compromise "remained the pattern of our working relationship. I wanted to do art, Mike wanted to do trash, and between us we made television."

CBS liked Jacobs's and Filerman's basic concept, but they wanted a more sensational storyline and wealthier characters. The network told Jacobs, "We'd like something a little glitzier. Something a little more of a saga." Jacobs credited Richard Berger, the head of drama development at CBS, with thinking up the show that became *Dallas*. A dramatic saga, Jacobs recalled, "filled the network's need at the moment. Cop shows weren't working, especially with all the curbs on violence. The networks were having trouble developing dramas . . . [and] an upscale, bigger-than-life drama could be highly profitable if it worked." The network also wanted to make the project a star vehicle for actress Linda Evans, who had starred in ABC's *The Big Valley* in the late 1960s and had recently appeared in a short-lived CBS series. That show, *Hunter*, a foreign intrigue drama that co-starred James Franciscus, was canceled in May 1977 after only four months, but Evans was still under contract at CBS.

4

It remains unclear who actually thought of setting what was inartfully called *The Untitled Linda Evans Project* in Dallas. Initially, the show was set in Indianapolis. In an interview he gave during *Dallas's* first season, Jacobs stated that CBS suggested a Texas location. Almost ten years later, however, *Dallas* biographer Suzy Kalter wrote that Jacobs chose the Texas locale since he was then reading Texan Thomas Thompson's 1977 best seller, *Blood and Money: A True Story of Murder, Passion and Power.* More than twenty years after *Dallas's* premiere, Jacobs claimed that, after CBS suggested something more epic than Jacobs's concept, "the word 'saga' brought Texas to mind and I had driven through [the state] once. Quickly we came up with the idea of a family dealing in oil and in cattle in Texas."

Jacobs decided that the best way to create his Texas saga was not to rework his initial idea but to start from scratch. He decided to visit Dallas to get a feel for the city, but Filerman "talked me out of it. Timing is everything. CBS is really hot for this script, he said; let's get it in as quickly as possible; don't give them a chance to cool." So Jacobs created the wealthy Ewing and down-on-their-luck Barnes families without traveling to Texas. The central character, to be played by Linda Evans, was Pamela Barnes, named for Jacobs's old friend from Waco, Pamela Hynds Daley. Jacobs then wrote "a letter to myself about this terribly good-looking, semitrashy lady who marries into a rich Texas family." What Jacobs ended up with was a twelve-page history of the Ewing family, much of which was unrelated to the character of Pam. But Jacobs felt his back story "complicated things too much. We had created a ranch hand who had brought [Pam] out to the barbeque where she met Bobby [Ewing]. We had decided that the family's father was once partner with her father. And so on. There were just too many people in it to concentrate solely on [Pam]."

Jacobs's screenplay mirrored his back story. When the script was completed and it was time to add a title page, Jacobs stuck with *The Untitled Linda Evans Project*, even though the story had clearly become an ensemble piece. Jacobs remembered that he added the title page "and sent it over to Mike [Filerman]. I called him later in the day. I said, 'Did you send it in [to CBS]?' And he said, 'Yeah, but I took off the title page because I don't think this is what they're looking for for Linda Evans. This is too much of an ensemble piece and I called it *Dallas.*' . . . He just picked *Dallas* as 'just for now.' . . . But it became forever." CBS liked the presentation enough to commit to it, but felt that a six-episode pilot would work better than a single one-hour show.

Signed to produce the pilot was Leonard Katzman, a veteran of the television industry who had worked as an assistant director on *Playhouse 90*, associate producer on *Route 66*, writer and associate producer on *The Wild, Wild West*, and writer, producer, and director on *Gunsmoke*, for which he won the Western Heritage Award. He also produced *Hawaii Five-O*, *Petrocelli*, and *Logan's Run*. Katzman produced the first seven seasons of *Dallas*. He was executive producer of *Dallas* for five additional seasons, a creative consultant for one, and wrote and directed more episodes of the series than anyone else. He later said *Dallas* "was not created by me. But I really felt very strongly, from the day I started, that it was my show."

The executive producers of the pilot were Lorimar Production heads Lee Rich and Philip Capice. Rich was a former ad executive who co-founded Lorimar. Capice was a former CBS program executive who later became the president of Lorimar Television. After *Dallas* took off in 1980, Lorimar produced a number of imitators, including the *Dallas* spin-off *Knots Landing*, as well as *Flamingo Road* and *Falcon Crest*. In the late 1980s and early 1990s, Lorimar produced many successful situation comedies, including *Full House*, *Family Matters*, *Perfect Strangers*, and *Step by Step*, which starred *Dallas* alumni Patrick Duffy and Sasha Mitchell.

While Jacobs's intent was that the show would become a serial if it were picked up for a full season, he planned the pilot episodes—now scaled back from six to five—as separate, self-contained stories. He wrote the first and last episodes himself. The script for the first episode, called "Digger's Daughter," was completed on December 10, 1977. Brought in to help with the other episodes were two writers who would stay with *Dallas* once it became a series. Camille Marchetta wrote twelve episodes over the course of the pilot and the first two seasons, and Arthur Bernard Lewis wrote sixty-nine episodes from the pilot through Season 7 and from Seasons 10 through 13, and co-wrote both *Dallas* TV movie sequels. Lewis found it ironic that several New Yorkers were the creative force behind a Texas epic, noting that "we all came from Brooklyn. Leonard was born in Brooklyn. Camille Marchetta was born in Brooklyn. I was born in Manhattan but I lived in Brooklyn. And here three Brooklyn residents were writing a show about Texas. None of us had been there!"

The scripts focused on family problems resolved by Pam, prompting producer Leonard Katzman to nickname the show *Pammy Knows Best*. "Then," Katzman explained, "we began to feel that the show wouldn't have a long life that way, the story of a wife who solves everybody's problems." It was agreed that the scripts should provide more conflict between the characters, and the dominant theme became Shakespeare-meets-modern-Texas. "Digger Barnes, who's Cliff Barnes's father," explained Lewis, "accused Jock Ewing of stealing his oil, stealing his wells, stealing everything. And then Jock's son falls in love with Digger Barnes's daughter. And so that's *Romeo and Juliet*."

The pilot scripts featured six main characters: Pam, the Ewing parents, two Ewing sons, and a wayward Ewing granddaughter. These roles were cast in late December 1977 and early January 1978. Katzman credited the actors chosen to portray the Ewings with the show's ultimate success "I don't think any show will succeed with a cast the audience does not like, no matter how well it is written," he said. "First you have to have a cast the audience buys. And they bought our cast."

The first roles cast were those of Ewing parents Miss Ellie and Jock. Although, according to Katzman, "no one was looking for big-name actors," the producers signed acclaimed stage and screen actress Barbara Bel Geddes to play the Ewing matriarch. Bel Geddes, then fifty-five, was the daughter of stage designer Norman Bel Geddes. She began a successful Broadway career when she was still in her teens, and then moved to Hollywood. Bel Geddes felt she "went out to California awfully young. I remember Lillian Hellman and Elia Kazan told me, 'Don't go, learn your craft.' But I loved films." She was "crushed" when Howard Hughes let her go from RKO after only a few movies, "but thank God he did that, because it meant I went back to the theater." Bel Geddes later returned to films, was nominated for an Oscar for her role in *I Remember Mama*, and costarred in the Jimmy Stewart–Alfred Hitchcock classic *Vertigo*. In 1966, Bel Geddes left acting to be with her terminally ill husband, director Windsor Lewis, who died in 1972. Lewis's illness left Bel Geddes "flat broke." When asked not long after the pilot what attracted her to *Dallas*, Bel Geddes replied, "I needed a job and I needed to make some money."

Cast as Jock Ewing was character actor Jim Davis, sixty-seven, who had starred in 150 movies, such as the westerns *Comes a Horseman* and *Apache Warrior*; appeared in more than three hundred TV shows; and had known Katzman since they both worked on Davis's late 1950s syndicated series *Rescue 8*. According to costar Steve Kanaly, Davis's casting was a perfect match between character and actor, especially after a long wait for such a part. "By the time [Davis] got with us on *Dallas*," Kanaly said, "I think he had been kicking around in the industry for well over forty years. A total professional—perfectly suited for this patriarch, this Jock Ewing character. I mean, just look at him and you go, 'That's the guy. Cast him right now.'" David Jacobs agreed, remarking that "Dynasties require a Big Daddy. That strong father figure to head up things. Usually played by John Wayne. But this is television and you can't afford John Wayne. So you get the inexpensive John Wayne. That usually turns out to be Jim Davis."

The hottest cast member at the time was twenty-eight-year-old Patrick Duffy, who had just starred in a minor hit as NBC's *Man from Atlantis*. *Atlantis* premiered in the fall of 1977 and was canceled after just one season, although it had the distinction of being the first American TV show to appear in mainland China. One week after *Atlantis*'s cancellation, Duffy received scripts for five different projects, including *Dallas*. He was ultimately chosen for the lead role of Bobby by casting director Ruth Conforte, who the year before had cast him in *Atlantis*. Leonard Katzman explained that Duffy was chosen over eleven other candidates because "he fit the part—charming, handsome, open."

Linda Evans was never offered the role of Pam once the show developed into an ensemble piece. Ironically, Evans later played a similar role in the long-running Aaron Spelling series *Dynasty*, which was ABC's answer to *Dallas*. Instead, the role of Pam went to former model, actress, and agent Victoria Principal, then twenty-eight. Principal landed the role over one other finalist, daytime soap opera star Judith Chapman, who had appeared on *Days of Our Lives*, *General Hospital*, *As the World Turns*, *Ryan's Hope*, and *One Life to Live*. Principal was nominated for a Golden Globe in 1971 for her work opposite Paul Newman in John Huston's *The Life and Times of Judge Roy Hill Bean*. She appeared in the disaster movie *Earthquake* before leaving acting to become an agent. Aaron Spelling lured Principal back to acting for the 1977 TV movie pilot of his hit show *Fantasy Island*.

Not long after Principal appeared on *Fantasy Island*, a friend called her about *Dallas* and the "part in it that was written for you." Principal set out to get a copy of the script and arrange a meeting with the producers. Principal got the script "and read it and I thought [my friend] was absolutely right." Principal acted as her own agent and set up a meeting with the producers. Her reputation from her carefree youth, however, preceded her. Explained producer Lee Rich in a 1979 interview, "We had heard all the rumors about Victoria. This is a small town. Victoria's background, her so-called checkered past, was a plus. We felt that she had experienced life and could understand the part."

Jacobs confirmed that Principal was hungry for the role. "Victoria, of all the . . . actors, went after the role the most aggressively and if she didn't like the reading there'd be a phone call," Jacobs recalled. "She wanted to come back and do it again. And that kind of determination just sort of became part of the character." Michael Filerman agreed that Principal "really wanted this role. . . . And she worked very hard to get it. And there's a humanity about her that is very winning. And the camera likes her very much. The camera just loves her. That's real important." Principal's reading left Filerman "surprised. She was better than we expected. I think maybe she's so beautiful we didn't think she would have the depth."

Duffy knew Principal was ideal for the role of Pam as soon as he saw her. He read with the Pamela candidates for executives from Lorimar and CBS. He recalled that one of the finalists "was a remarkably talented young actress from New York . . . [who was] really good. [Later,] in walked Victoria Principal in the tightest jeans I've ever seen and the most unbelievable blouse. I just went, 'Hello, Pam.' I just knew that was going to be Pam Ewing. And thank goodness it was for all that time because it was . . . one of those perfect, magical pairings, the Bobby-Pam pairing."

Ironically, the selection of Larry Hagman for the role of J.R. was such a minor event that when the *Dallas Morning News* reported the filming of the pilot, Hagman was not even mentioned in the article. Hagman, whose biggest success to date had been the role of Captain (and later Major) Tony Nelson on the 1960s NBC hit *I Dream of Jeannie*, won the role of J.R. over Robert Foxworth, who would go on to star in *Falcon Crest*, another *Dallas* imitator that followed *Dallas* on CBS's Friday night schedule. Jacobs, without confirming who Hagman beat out for the role, said that the other finalist found the character too mean, saying, "'Well, why is this guy like this?' We said, 'Well, he's the oldest son of this rich father. He's taken the father's business over. He's increased its value by ten. He's got much more power than his father ever had. It's one of the biggest families in Texas. But his father still likes the little brother better.' And the actor said, 'Okay, . . . but how are we going to make him more sympathetic?' And we sort of all looked at each other around the room and I think I answered. I said, 'I don't think we are.'"

Hagman was the son of Broadway musical legend Mary Martin and Texas lawyer Ben Hagman. He was in the cast of Martin's hit *South Pacific* when it played in London, and he later appeared on the daytime soap opera *The Edge of Night*. In 1965, *Jeannie* made him a TV star, and he later appeared in the movies *Harry and Tonto* and *Superman* as well as a few other sitcoms. Hagman, then forty-six, received the *Dallas* pilot script shortly before Christmas 1977. At the time, Hagman and his wife, Maj, were in New York, where Hagman's mother was appearing in a show with Ethel Merman for the benefit of the New York Public Library.

"Two scripts had been sent to me," Hagman later wrote. "One was *Dallas*. The other was *The Waverly Wonders*, which was about a basketball team. . . . Joe Namath did it ultimately. I started reading *The Waverly Wonders* because it was a half-hour comedy and that was my forte at the time." Hagman "heard a 'whoop' from the other room. And my wife, Maj, says, 'You've gotta read this! You've gotta read it!' 'Well, what is it?' I asked. It was *Dallas*. She started laughing. 'There isn't one redeeming or nice character in the whole show—do it!'" Maj Hagman recalled, "I told him, 'It's got wealth, it's got helicopters, it's got a bunch of gorgeous broads, and it's what television needs—a nighttime soap!'"

Hagman "read the first nine pages. . . . Here was this mean son-of-a-bitch they wanted me to play. I said to Maj, 'That's the kind of TV I want to do.' Maj was sure it would be a hit, but I still wasn't. Despite *I Dream of Jeannie*, I knew the vagaries of TV. Maybe one out of three shows go." Hagman "didn't find it humorous. It was a caricature. Worse than *Giant*. But—Daddy was a scoundrel, Mama was a scoundrel, J.R. was a scoundrel, everybody was a no-goodnik—which made me think it had to be a success. Everybody who cheats on his income tax can identify."

Initially, David Jacobs was not sure that the role was a good fit for Hagman. Jacobs thought, "'Larry Hagman? Larry Hagman's a Major [in *I Dream of Jeannie*].' . . . I didn't think of Larry Hagman as an edgy actor. As soon as we met him . . . and he stood there in the door in his Stetson and boots . . . he was the guy." Hagman was interested in the role and got "on the phone to my agent. What they're offering is ridiculous. No, I am not the star of the show. There are eight 'stars.' Three times I turn them down. They make a 'final' offer. Insulting, but I can live with it. I want to play that part. They tell me [Barbara] Bel Geddes will play the mother. I want to be with Barbara; I don't care how terrible the show is, that lady is somebody I want to act with."

Once Hagman committed, however, he set out to correct what he felt was a problem with the J.R. Ewing he read about. "So this didn't capture the real

Texas?" he later recalled. "I figured to fix that. I knew about these people—they were friends of Pappy's. Larger than life. They money you to death, use it like a club. . . . There was something else [about the role]. My dad knew about stuff like this. Of course, he was not as ruthless as J.R. Yet, in a way, I get to play *him*."

The last of the major roles, Ewing granddaughter Lucy, went to seventeen-year-old Charlene Tilton, a young actress who had made her film debut in the Jodie Foster Disney movie *Freaky Friday* and appeared in episodes of *Happy Days*, *Eight Is Enough*, and *Police Woman*. The producers originally wanted Stephanie Kramer, later of *Hunter*, as Lucy. Tilton, however, knew the role was made for her. "I read about the Lucy part," Tilton recalled. "She was described as a manipulative sexpot and I thought that was a role I could really sink my teeth into, but they refused to see me. They wanted a name actress for the part. So I snuck into the studio every day for two weeks by crouching down beside moving cars and kept begging them to give me an audition."

In the pilot, there were four additional characters—J.R.'s wife, the Ewings' ranch foreman, Pam's brother, and J.R.'s secretary—but they were all minor ones. These parts went to Linda Gray, Steve Kanaly, Ken Kercheval, and Tina Louise, respectively. Gray, then thirty-five, was a former model and veteran of commercials who had a regular role as a transvestite on the short-lived Norman Lear sitcom *All That Glitters*. Gray won the role of Sue Ellen Ewing over Mary Frann, who later played Bob Newhart's wife on the 1980s sitcom *Newhart*. The part of Sue Ellen was so small that Jacobs had to write a special audition scene for Gray and the thirty other actresses reading for the role. The scene involved only four lines of dialogue and had Sue Ellen on the telephone since she was not important enough to warrant a two-actor audition scene.

As she went in to the audition, Gray thought to herself, "'Just let it go!' Tears flowed. And the producers were sitting there, as if saying, 'How did you do that?' I said, 'That's called acting!'" While still in the audition, Gray knew she had won the role. "I just knew it intuitively," she said, "and I sat there, tears streaming, and I knew that I had the role of Sue Ellen Ewing." According to Michael Filerman, Gray got the part because of "her eyes. She had very sad eyes. . . . There was a great vulnerability about Linda Gray."

Thirty-one-year old Steve Kanaly, who, like Victoria Principal, had appeared in *The Life and Times of Judge Roy Hill Bean*, won the role of Southfork foreman Ray Krebbs. Dallas came along after a slow point in Kanaly's career. Although he had made several movies in the early 1970s, Kanaly was making guest appearances on TV by the time he signed on for *Dallas*. He learned about the part of Ray from his agent and thought it was a good role. Since the producers had no concept of how the family should look physically, though, Kanaly realized that he could also be cast as either Ewing brother or as Pam's brother.

At the casting office, Kanaly found a room full of young blondes interested in the role of Lucy. Kanaly knew one of the girls and asked her to do him the favor of sneaking him the pilot script. When Kanaly read that Ray Krebbs was in the hayloft with Lucy Ewing, had been interested in Pam, and conspired with J.R. to break Pam and Bobby apart, Kanaly fell in love with the character. He thought, "I don't care about the brothers. This guy Ray would be a lot more fun to play." Kanaly met with Filerman, who had seen Kanaly in the Sean Connery movie *The Wind and the Lion*, and Leonard Katzman. They invited Kanaly back two days later to read for the role of Ray, and Kanaly returned dressed for the part. Kanaly was offered the role the following day over other actors, including his friend Martin Cove, who later appeared in *The Karate Kid*, and Ken Kercheval.

Kercheval, then forty-two, appeared in the movie *Network* and on such TV shows as *Starsky and Hutch* and *Kojak*. He was a stage actor who had been trained in New York, where he met *Dallas* producer Phil Capice. It was Capice who got Kercheval to audition for *Dallas*. Kercheval wanted to play foreman Ray Krebbs, despite the fact that the role of Pam's brother, Cliff, was also a good role. "I read the pilot series scripts on an airplane and sat there thinking about them, and I said to myself, 'There's not one redeemable character in this show except Cliff,'" said Kercheval. "Cliff is the only one with a sense of morality." But Kercheval still "wanted to play Ray Krebbs. . . . I didn't want to play a lawyer. I said I was tired of playing doctors and lawyers. I wanted to play a cowboy. I read for the Cliff Barnes part, but my stipulation was that I could also read for the other role [of Ray]. I was sure that I could convince them I was just right to play a ranch hand." Kercheval felt he "read the pants off that scene. I really did and then I got a call [from my agent] that I was [going to be] working. And I said, 'Great.' I said, 'See, I told you.' And he said, 'Yeah, but you're not playing the cowboy. You're playing the attorney.'" But, said Kercheval, "The money was good, so I figured, 'What the hell.'"

The role of J.R.'s secretary went to Tina Louise, who had starred on the classic 1964–67 sitcom *Gilligan's Island* as the "movie star," Ginger Grant. Louise, then forty-three, was attracted to the role of Julie Grey because she "liked being a grown-up. I liked the strength of the character and the different colors she had. She was independent and pretty shrewd. . . . She was not boring!" The cast members signed seven-year contracts, and received salaries that were standard for television actors at that time. Filerman recalled that "they got what the regular actors on a series would get. I think it was maybe $7,500. . . . Larry did certainly get more than the other people got, but it wasn't phenomenally more."

Within a week of final casting, the producers scheduled a cast read-through, which took place at Warner Brothers. The producers, director Robert Day, and the cast all attended, and the atmosphere was friendly. Larry Hagman brought a case of champagne. Kanaly arrived late because he was filming a car commercial. He was nervous about the read-through, and found the cast seated and waiting for him when he arrived. Kanaly recognized Victoria Principal from the movie they had made together. He also recognized Hagman, Barbara Bel Geddes, Jim Davis, and Ken Kercheval from their work. He saw a young girl who looked no older than fourteen and quickly realized that he would have to play scenes in the hayloft with her. He thought, "Wait until my mother sees this."

Patrick Duffy recalled that it was Hagman who got the read-through off to a festive start. Said Duffy, "We all came in as good, serious actors ready to do our work. Larry came in in a giant western hat, fringed buckskin pants and shirt, big giant saddlebags thrown over his shoulder, stuffed with bottles of champagne. That was our introduction to Hagman. So, we all drank champagne, got a bit looped, and then read the script. And that initial impression is pretty much the way Larry treated life."

By January 1978, the crew was on location in Texas, where all five pilot episodes were filmed. Kanaly credited Katzman with sensing "immediately that the success of the show would depend largely on being on location. So, we could've shot this on back lots in places in Southern California. But he absolutely insisted on going to Dallas." Katzman had flown to Texas with a studio scout to find the perfect Ewing ranch, but found winter conditions more appropriate for New England. "I flew down there in search of Southfork Ranch, which at that point existed only on paper," Katzman wrote. "I was coming from sunny Los Angeles, where we had received the go-ahead to film our miniseries . . . on location instead of locally. Arriving that day, I found Dallas buried under four feet of snow. My only thought was, 'Oh, Lord, what have we gotten into?'" Despite the unusual Texas winter weather, however, Katzman found his Southfork in Frisco. The Box Ranch, owned by Mr. and Mrs. Cloyce Box, was picked for exterior Southfork scenes. Interior Southfork scenes would be filmed inside a private home on Swiss Avenue in Dallas.

The cast was put up at a Dallas motel called the North Park Inn. By the beginning of February, the crew was ready to start filming. On February 1, 1978, the night before the first scenes were to be filmed, Principal suggested that Kanaly come to her motel room to rehearse their romantic scene. Kanaly did so, and they ran dialogue for several hours. When Kanaly walked back to his room, he noticed that snowflakes the size of a silver dollar were falling. This posed a problem for the crew since one of the scenes to be filmed the next day was a lake scene.

By the next morning, a foot of snow had fallen. While the crew stood around the motel lobby wondering what to do, it occurred to Kanaly that the storyline could take advantage of the snow by having him and Principal frolic in it like Ali McGraw and Ryan O'Neal did in *Love Story*. The lake scene was rewritten to fit Kanaly's idea. Meanwhile, an interior scene in which the Barnes children informed their father that Pam has married a Ewing was filmed at the Night Train Bar across from Union Station in downtown Dallas. The rewritten snow scene was also filmed, and the cast and crew felt that the dailies of the scene were remarkable. CBS, however, refused to air the snow scene since it deviated from the script it had previously approved. After the snow melted, the lake scene was shot as planned.

In looking back on the pilot episode, Katzman recalled:

When we first started filming in that terrible, cold, dreadful winter of 1977 in Dallas, none of us knew each other very well. In fact, it was rather like being in the Army. We were all huddled together, looking at one another, and finally we said, "Well, we're all in this together, so let's do it." And we did. From the very beginning, it has been a very tight-knit family group working on *Dallas*. The actors work as an ensemble group, where each respects one another and is generous with each other as performers. Behind the scenes, we really do have a family whose members love each other, who really care about each other, and I think that quality—which comes through on the screen—is a great part of *Dallas*'s- appeal.

Duffy credited Katzman's leadership for the bond that formed between the company. "We were like little orphans, shunted on down to Texas in freezing cold weather and just abominable conditions to make these five episodes," Duffy recalled. "And we were all just huddled around, like, 'Take us somewhere, Daddy.' And Leonard sort of guided us through those five episodes. . . . And then we trusted him. And so, along with trust comes respect and obedience." Hagman found the group "wonderful," saying, "We all respected each other and loved each other and helped each other." That closeness did not end with the pilot. Charlene Tilton said the following year that, "The people on the show are really my family. Larry is like an uncle. Victoria is always mothering me. Barbara Bel Geddes is a wonderful lady of the theater who is willing to sit down with me and tell me her stories. Linda is the swellest lady in the world; she's my favorite."

During the pilot filming, Principal and Tilton became especially close. As Principal explained, the location shoot was hard on Tilton since she was only seventeen years old and had "never really been away from home. And during the miniseries, Charlene actually spent a number of the nights not sleeping in her own room but on my bed wrapped up in my bedspread. She was my sweet little baby kitten." Tilton caught pneumonia and was almost replaced by another actress. Recalled producer Lee Rich, "We weren't sure she could do it." Tilton joked that "it was cold feet," but saved her job by working with acting coach Jeff Corey and reviewing videotapes of her acting. Principal noted that Tilton "could have slid by on her beauty, but she worked her ass off."

Some of the other cast members, however, were not bonding as quickly with Principal, who struck them as being what Katzman called "the world's most isolated lady." Duffy linked Principal's demeanor to her beauty and her reputation. "She had a lot of protective devices. I think maybe they were just the protective devices of a beautiful woman who had been through some things. . . . She just maintained this distance from the others." Katzman confronted Principal, and was given a different explanation.

The confrontation occurred after Katzman, who purposely arranged to have the cast stay at the same motel so they would have the opportunity to bond, learned that Principal asked for a room away from the others. Katzman recalled, "Everybody was hanging out in Larry Hagman's room. Except Victoria. She would never show up. After a while, I thought, 'Maybe she doesn't like us.' I went to see her. She said, 'No, I like everybody. It's just that I want to feel like an outsider, like Pam Barnes does, being married to a Ewing.' She was working on her role, even in those moments." Principal threw herself into the role in other ways as well. For instance, she reportedly hired a Texas woman to help with her accent.

Hagman owned a van that became famous during the shoot. While Kanaly and the rest of the cast flew to Dallas, "Larry was smart enough," Kanaly recalled, "to bring down what I called his hippie van, which was a large brown step-up van with a dome on the top and Persian rugs and a big stereo system. . . . In the off time we would have, Larry would say, 'Well, come on, get on board this. Let's just go out and get some dinner someplace.'" Hagman would "drive us to the best restaurants. Then he'd walk in and go straight to whoever was in charge and say, 'Hi, how y'all doin'? Remember me, Major Tony Nelson from I Dream of Jeannie? Do you think you have a table for us?' He was a helluva lot of fun."

The five pilot episodes of Dallas were completed in late February 1978, and the company moved on to other projects. Jacobs worked on another proposed series, Married: The First Year, which was the show he and Filerman based on Bergman's Scenes from a Marriage. CBS had green-lighted the project shortly after it accepted the Dallas pilot. The actors also looked for other work since, as Duffy noted, "We'd all been out of work enough times [to know] that there are no guarantees." Kanaly felt "that networks tend to pick up series that are like other hit shows. So, for that reason primarily, I thought that Dallas really didn't stand a chance."

On Sunday, April 2, 1978, three months after filming had begun, the first pilot episode aired on CBS, opposite ABC's Sunday Movie and NBC's Big Event. The TV Guide entry for the pilot appeared as follows:

> Dallas—Drama. Debut: A feud between two contemporary Texas families underlies this five-part miniseries. In the opener, young Bobby Ewing (Patrick Duffy), scion of a powerful oil-and-cattle baron, shocks his family by marrying Pamela Barnes (Victoria Principal), the daughter of his father's enemy Digger Barnes (David Wayne). John Ewing: Jim Davis; J.R. Ewing: Larry Hagman; Ellie Ewing: Barbara Bel Geddes; Lucy: Charlene Tilton.

As Jacobs pointed out, while the pilot episode got little critical praise, it got a lot of critical notice. "The response to Dallas was extraordinary," he said. "The critics were both appalled and intrigued. I don't think Dallas got any good reviews. And yet, it got reviewed everywhere. It caused a lot of talk because it was so audacious and so obviously sexy. And because this family was so clearly dysfunctional." *Variety* reviewed the first pilot episode and found it to be "dull and contrived"— "the TV equivalent of women's-magazine fiction" with "numbing" dialogue. Another *Variety* critic called the pilot "a limited series with a limited future."

According to the A.C. Nielsen ratings, the first episode of the pilot was the eighteenth-highest-rated program of the week. Four of the five pilot episodes scored a share of 30 or above and the last two ranked number twelve and eleven in the weekly ratings, respectively. The five pilot episodes earned *Dallas* an 18.4 Nielsen share, good for forty-fourth place for the 1977–78 season. More importantly, the final two pilot episodes ranked in the weekly top fifteen. These ratings were encouraging enough that on May 3, just days after the last pilot episode aired on April 30, CBS announced that it was adding Dallas to its fall 1978 lineup and was ordering a half season worth of episodes. Hagman thought, "Well, maybe we got a chance at this thing."

THE PILOT EPISODE GUIDE

Regular Cast

Starring:
Barbara Bel Geddes as Eleanor Southworth "Miss Ellie" Ewing
Jim Davis as John Ross "Jock" Ewing Sr.
Patrick Duffy as Bobby James Ewing
Larry Hagman as John Ross "J.R." Ewing Jr.
Victoria Principal as Pamela Jean Barnes Ewing
Charlene Tilton as Lucy Ann Ewing
Also Starring:
Linda Gray as Sue Ellen Shepard Ewing
Steve Kanaly as Raymond Krebbs
Ken Kercheval as Clifford Barnes
Tina Louise as Julie Grey

Technical Credits

Producer: Leonard Katzman
Executive Producers: Lee Rich, Philip Capice
Executive Script Consultant: David Jacobs
Executive Supervisor: Michael Filerman
Music: Jerrold Immel, John C. Parker
Unit Production Manager: Barry R. Stern
First Assistant Directors: Wayne Farlow, Ed Ledding
Second Assistant Directors: James E. Inch, Claude Lawrence
Director of Photography: Edward R. Plante
Art Directors: Ed Graves, Carl Braunger
Editors: Fred W. Berger, A.C.E., Michael McCroskey, Edward Beiry, Graham Lee Mahan

In Charge of Casting: Barbara Miller
Casting: Ruth Conforte, Irene Mariano
Location Casting: Shari Rhodes, Liz Keigley
Set Decorator: Jim Hassinger
Property Master: Gaston G. Gray
Costume Supervisor: Jeanne Malone
Costumers: Donna Roberts, Henry Salley, Kathy O'Rear
Production Coordinators: Andy Ackerman, Vicki Ogonowski
Production Sound Mixers: Bud Alper, Robert Sheridan
Makeup: Jim Kail
Hair Stylist: Brent Plaistowe
Script Supervisor: Joe Gannon
Dialogue Director: Fred Martin
Sound Effects Supervisor: Victor Guarnier
Music Editor: Ken Runyon
Electrical Gaffer: Don Nygren
Key Grip: Wes Tansey
Camera Operator: Robert Jessup
Production Supervisor: Mitch Ackerman
Transportation Captain: Glenn Carter
Location Managers: Michael Phillips, John MacLean
In Charge of Production: Neil T. Maffeo
Main Title: Wayne Fitzgerald

1. "Digger's Daughter"

Written by David Jacobs; Directed by Robert Day; Airdate: April 2, 1978
Special Guest Star: David Wayne (Willard "Digger" Barnes)
Subject: Pam and Bobby elope.

Cast Notes   David Wayne was a Broadway star of the 1930s and 1940s (Mister Roberts, Finian's Rainbow) and went on to appear in the movies Adam's Rib, How to Marry a Millionaire, and The Three Faces of Eve. In the 1970s, he appeared on such TV shows as The Adventures of Ellery Queen and The Good

Life, in which, in a switch of their *Dallas* characters' financial status, Wayne played a millionaire to Larry Hagman's butler. Thus, Hagman and Wayne were good friends long before *Dallas*. Hagman flew on the beach side of his Malibu house a banner given to him by Wayne that read "Laurence of Malibu." ★ Donna Bullock is the first of several actresses to play Bobby's secretary, Connie. Bullock also plays Connie in Episodes 2 and 3. ★ Bill Thurman, who appeared in *The Last Picture Show* and the Steven Spielberg movies *Close Encounters of the Third Kind* and *Sugarland Express*, plays Ewing Oil courier Phil Bradley. Thurman returned to *Dallas* as Alan Murphy in Episode 137. He died in 1995. ★ Digger's drinking buddy Harvey is played by Desmond Dhooge, who reprises the role in Episode 11. Dhooge is also seen as a back alley drinking mate of Sue Ellen's in Episode 193 and a drinking pal of Dandy's in Episode 253. Dhooge appeared in the Ryan O'Neal movie *Paper Moon* and the Sissy Spacek movie *Raggedy Man*. Dhooge died in 1999 in Dallas.

Trivia This episode, which aired against two TV movies, ABC's *High Plains Drifter* and NBC's *Love's Dark Ride*, ranked 18th for the week in the Nielsen ratings, earning a 21.5 rating and a 37 share and becoming *Dallas*'s first top-twenty episode. ★ Digger's attempt to kill Jock is seen in the 1986 TV movie *Dallas: The Early Years*. ★ According to author Fran Wenograd Golden, the first building seen as Ewing Oil was the NationsBank Building. The Renaissance Tower and NationsBank Plaza were later used as the Ewing Oil building ★ Several familiar Ewing cars are first seen in this episode, including Jock's Lincoln Continental with EWING 1 tags, J.R.'s Mercedes sedan with EWING 3 tags and Bobby's red Mercedes convertible with EWING 4 tags. In Season 9, the EWING 1 tags were moved to Miss Ellie's Volkswagen convertible. The station wagon with EWING 2 tags driven by Miss Ellie and Sue Ellen debuts in Episode 3. Ray drives a blue and white pick-up, which was later replaced by a white pick-up. ★ Jim Davis's use of the word *jackass* was the first display on *Dallas* of Davis's colorful language. Explained Katzman, "Jim Davis had a habit of saying his lines and throwing in extra swear words—there were a lot of 'hells' and 'damns' in his natural speech pattern. We ha[d] a pretty strict count of four or five 'cuss words' per show, and Jim could get us off count easily." ★ Robert Day, who directed three of the five *Dallas* pilot episodes but did not direct any subsequent episodes of the show, was a movie director who made many films in the 1950s and 1960s, including *Tarzan*. ★ Larry Hagman and Linda Gray had words after their first scene together. At the end of the day, Hagman drove Gray back to their hotel in his van, telling her, "You were terrible." Gray was devastated and promised to improve. She and Hagman went on to become fast friends. Years later, when Gray saw the scene in a rerun, she realized that she played it pretty well. She asked Hagman if he recalled the scene, and he replied, "Oh yeah, you were great." When Gray reminded him how he criticized her at the time, he explained, "I just told you that to let you know who was boss." ★ According to Victoria Principal, she wore her own clothes in her debut as Pam, at Katzman's request, because "they had never gotten that image of Pam [from Principal's audition] out of their minds." ★ Pam's and Bobby's elopement is not seen in this episode, which begins with their trip back to Dallas afterward, but is seen in a flashback in Episode 230 in Season 9. ★ Charlene Tilton recalled that her hayloft scenes with Steve Kanaly were "extremely shocking. I was seventeen and looked twelve. The scenes that we did, especially with the age difference, there had never really been anything like that and it was pushing the envelope at that time." Tilton also recalled that "several seasons later, we found out that Ray Krebbs is actually Jock Ewing's son. So, oops! We can't show my love scenes in syndication because it gets a little incestuous there!" According to Kanaly, "Charlene was a baby when we started, seventeen years old. She was a very sweet girl and everybody loved her. She grew up on that show. We all took her under our wing." Kanaly also found Tilton to have "the greatest hair of any actress I have ever met." ★ Both Jim Davis and Steve Kanaly smoke in this episode. Hagman, a longtime antismoking crusader, convinced Jim Davis to quit, and tried hard to get Barbara Bel Geddes and Victoria Principal to do the same. Hagman complained that Bel Geddes smoked each morning as the actors went through makeup, and he estimated that one-third of the *Dallas* cast and crew smoked. Hagman carried a pocket-sized fan that he used to blow smoke back at his tormentors. ★ Seven years after filming this episode, Victoria Principal wrote that, "Even now, I can feel a glow when I think about how [Pam and Bobby] married. . . . The courtship reminds me of a line from an old Johnny Cash song, 'Jackson,' in which two lovers 'marry in a fever, hotter than a pepper sprout.' Principal also wrote, "One of my favorite [*Dallas* scenes], in fact, came shortly after their marriage ceremony. Pam and Bobby were driving back to Dallas in the convertible on a frigid day with the top down. Their passion for one another made them impervious to the cold." ★ The Southfork butler and maid are named Raoul and Francesca. ★ This episode makes clear that Miss Ellie's father left Southfork to Jock, which is inconsistent with Episode 19 and numerous other subsequent episodes, which make clear that Miss Ellie inherited the ranch.

2. "Lessons"

Written by Virginia Aldridge; Directed by Irving J. Moore; Airdate: April 9, 1978
Guest Stars: Jeffrey Byron (Roger Hurley); Paul Tulley (Miller)
Subject: Lucy fakes an assault.

Cast Notes   Paul Tulley returned to *Dallas* as Holden in Episode 236. ★ Jo McDonnell plays Ray's date Maureen, and does so again in Episode 5.

Trivia   *Dallas*'s second episode was not as highly rated as its first. It earned a 15.2 rating (down from 21.5) and a 26.0 share (down from 37) and ranked 50th (down from 18th) out of sixty-nine shows for the week. ★ The *Dallas* theme, written by Jerrold Immel, plays in the background during the disco scene. ★ This was the first episode directed by Irving J. Moore, who went on to direct fifty-two episodes of the show. Moore liked the relaxed nature of the *Dallas* set, commenting, "You can get a lot more done on a loose set than you can on a tight one." Moore was Victoria Principal's favorite *Dallas* director and was a veteran director of such TV shows as *Gunsmoke*, *Bonanza*, *The Brady Bunch*, *Petrocelli*, *The Blue Knight*, *Eight Is Enough*, and *Dynasty*. Moore died in 1993. ★ Writer Virginia Aldridge appeared as a Gnome Maiden in the 1967 Disney movie *The Gnome-Mobile*, and on such series as *Star Trek*, *The Rifleman*, and *Wagon Train*. ★ Because the snow at the Box Ranch melted during filming of this episode, fake snow made of gypsum was brought in so the ranch would look consistent throughout the episode. The gypsum, however, looked pink on film and another load had to be brought in. After the color was finally matched, it snowed again. ★ According to the creative mind of *Dallas* creator David Jacobs, three days after this episode, Jock reached out to Digger by writing him a letter. This letter was one of several letters Jacobs says Miss Ellie shared with him while he was doing research for *The Early Years*, the *Dallas* prequel TV movie that aired in March of 1986. Jacobs published excerpts of these letters in a *TV Guide* article which ran the week that *The Early Years* aired. According to Jacobs's article, Jock wrote Digger a letter on April 12, 1978, exactly ten days after Pam and Bobby eloped: "Dear Digger, Any ideas, partner? Who the hell would have expected this? Up to now I've been caught up in the fight your boy and my boy have been fighting. I give them their due: they're better at it than we were. Cliff and J.R. don't just feud: they wage war. . . . What [Bobby's] done now I don't know how to handle. I never expected it, did you? . . . Know what Ellie said? She said Cut it out, Jock: you think this is a fitting way for things to turn out; you're just acting mad because you know you're supposed to be mad. . . . What happens now, Digger? Who do we take our cue from? Your boy and J.R.? Or your girl and my boy?"

3. "Spy in the House"

Written by Arthur Bernard Lewis; Directed by Robert Day; Airdate: April 16, 1978
Guest Star: Norman Alden (Senator "Wild Bill" Orloff)
Subject: Pam is accused of spying.

Cast Notes   Norman Alden was a TV character actor who also provided the voice of TV's animated *Underdog*.

Trivia   This episode scored higher in the ratings than did Episode 2 and aired against Part One of the Meryl Streep miniseries *Holocaust*. It was ranked 40th out of sixty-five shows for the week. ★ Ewing attorney Ed is never again seen on *Dallas*. As of Episode 21, Harv Smithfield is referred to as the Ewings' lawyer (although he is not seen until Season 2) and remains so through Season 13 and the 1996 TV movie *J.R. Returns*. ★ This is the first episode written by Arthur

Bernard Lewis. ★ Julie Grey is the first of J.R.'s many extra-marital lovers. Others included Wanda Frick, Garnet McGee, Kristin Shepard, Serena Wald, Leslie Stewart, Louella, Afton Cooper, Marilee Stone, Holly Harwood, Katherine Wentworth, Mandy Winger, April Stevens, Kimberly Cryder, Laurel Ellis, Cally Harper, Diana Farrington, and Sly Lovegren. There was only one mistress that Larry Hagman did not like. "I remember the first kiss," Hagman said. "The director called cut and took me aside: 'What on earth happened?' he said. 'Have you ever kissed a woman who smokes Churchill cigars?' I said. 'Well, it's an experience.'" Hagman's favorite mistress was Holly Harwood, played by Lois Chiles. ★ J.R. and Cliff shared several women besides Julie Grey, including Sue Ellen, Afton, Marilee, and Mandy ★ The family dinner scene became a staple of *Dallas*. Hagman wrote, "Of all the scenes we play in *Dallas*, the most difficult is the around-the-table dinner scene. In the 'biz,' this kind of scene is called 'exposition' and is meant to give the audience the reasons for further action. It gives no one the chance to 'act' because it is so passive, and trying to give it any emotion takes all our skill."

4. "Winds of Vengeance"

Written by Camille Marchetta; Directed by Irving J. Moore; Airdate: April 23, 1978
Guest Stars: Brian Dennehy (Luther Frick); Cooper Huckabee (Payton Allen)
Subject: The Ewings are held hostage.

Cast Notes Brian Dennehy went on to a successful film and stage career, starring in such movies as *Cocoon* and *Presumed Innocent* and winning the 1999 Best Actor Tony Award for his performance in the Broadway revival of *Death of a Salesman*. When asked to name her favorite *Dallas* guest star, Linda Gray said, "We had such lovely guest stars on *Dallas* that it's hard to choose one. But I remember in one of the first episodes where I was terrified and had to stand up with a bathing suit and Miss Texas banner on to sing "People" a cappella with Brian Dennehy holding a gun to my head! I remember loving Brian. I thought he was so talented and so giving as an actor. He's just one of my favorite actors." ★ Nancy Lydick is one of two actresses replacing Tina Louise and Donna Bullock as the Ewing Oil secretaries.

Trivia This episode aired against Part Two of *Holocaust* and jumped to number 12 out of sixty-eight shows, with a 21.1 rating and 35 share. This was *Dallas's* first top-fifteen episode. ★ Bobby's secretary is now named Jeannie. ★ The hurricane is the first of several natural disasters that plagued *Dallas*. Others included a typhoon, a fire, an earthquake, a rock slide, a tornado, and a severe storm in the gulf. As for the hurricane in this episode, Leonard Katzman recalled, "We couldn't figure out what to call it, a hurricane or a tornado—we just needed a lot of wind." Katzman acknowledged that a hurricane has never actually hit the city of Dallas and that this script was written with the help of a Los Angeles research service, not a Texas-based consultant. ★ Future kidnappings during *Dallas's* run included John Ross (three times), J.R. (twice), Lucy (twice), Sue Ellen, Pam, and Bobby. During the show's run, several of its stars had real-life security concerns. Victoria

Principal had to hire her own security guard and, in 1989, a man who worked at a popcorn company partially owned by Ken Kercheval crashed the studio gate with a gun. The man, Ed Phillips, evidently "thought about kidnapping me," said Kercheval. "The indications are that he came here, indeed, to commit suicide." After getting on studio property, Phillips fired several shots, set his truck on fire and then shot himself. ★ This is the first of numerous episodes in which Jock's friend Punk Anderson is mentioned, although Punk was not seen on *Dallas* until Season 3. ★ This episode was the first to showcase Linda Gray. She recalled, "It was the damnedest thing. In the first episode, I had about two lines, like 'More coffee, dear?' and though I was supposed to be the wife of another then-minor character named J.R., there was nothing in the script to indicate *what* I was to him—secretary, mistress, maybe even just a tennis partner. The main story was a modern Romeo-Juliet version of Bobby . . . [and] Pam. . . . It was all Patrick Duffy and Victoria Principal. Most of the rest of the cast were little more than supernumeraries." Confirmed pilot casting director Ruth Conforte, "All we wanted . . . in those hectic days was kind of a walk-on actress who could look as if she once had been a Miss Texas in the Miss America contest." Gray listened to Hagman's evil lines, however, and realized, "The lady who would marry [J.R.] would have to have a few things going on with her psychologically. So I decided that she was not terribly together. When they shot my close-up, I did something with my eyes that said more than words could say." Specifically, Gray decided to "'give them a look to kill.' I said to myself: 'Watch this.' Venom came out. They saw the dailies in Los Angeles and a phone call came saying do something with that part." Part of Gray's performance resulted from "research into Southern ladies. I found out that they could kill you with a look—smile and chop your head off in the same breath. So I set about creating Sue Ellen." ★ David Jacobs recalled that he wanted to expand Sue Ellen's role and provide her with some form of revenge against J.R., but could not find a way to accomplish that in the pilot. ★ Dr. Miller is never seen again. Dr. Danvers is introduced as the Ewing family doctor in Episode 9, and he remained so through Season 9.

5. "Barbeque"

Written by David Jacobs; Directed by Robert Day; Airdate: April 30, 1978
Special Guest Star: David Wayne (Digger)
Subject: The Ewings' barbeque.

Cast Notes Costar James Canning appears as Pam's cousin, Jimmy Monahan, a character also seen in Episode 6. ★ Irma P. Hall, featured as caterer Telly, returned to *Dallas* as Mark Graison's maid, Rosa, in Episode 167 in Season 7. She went on to a successful career as a movie character actress. She appeared in the 1997 film based on the best-selling book *Midnight in the Garden of Good and Evil.* ★ Telly's catering partner is Sam, played by Craver Haskell, who appeared in the Meryl Streep movie *Silkwood* and in a 1993 episode of *Walker, Texas Ranger.* ★

Lisa LeMole plays Ewing Oil secretary Connie in Episodes 8, 9, 11, and 14, but in this episode is a Ewing secretary referred to as Susan.

Trivia This episode was the 11th-highest-rated show for the week, and earned a 21.8 rating and 39 share. ★ David Jacobs originally planned to kill Bobby off in this episode so that any resulting series would focus on the conflict between J.R. and Pam. He recalled, "When I originally created the story, Pamela was the protagonist and J.R. was the antagonist. I saw Bobby as a playboy type. . . . He was like Brick in *Cat on a Hot Tin Roof*. Then he married Pam, who said, 'Be a *mensch*.' . . . I wanted to kill Bobby off at the end of the pilot and leave Pam to fight J.R. When we finally got down to it, everyone wanted a hero in the story. The network and Patrick both wanted Bobby to be a nice guy, a sympathetic character. In addition, if I killed off Bobby, Pam would get the life insurance and maybe wouldn't want to stay around to fight J.R." Indeed, Leonard Katzman and the other producers thought the show worked better with Bobby, and convinced Jacobs to rewrite the ending to keep Bobby alive. Jacobs did so, against his wishes. Patrick Duffy recalled that Katzman was particularly troubled by the logic of keeping Pam at Southfork without Bobby, and that he asked "a very obvious question. He said, 'Why does Pam stay in the Ewing home?' And they said because she was married to Bobby. . . . He said, 'No, she just got $200 million and she would leave.' And whoever the brain trust was at the network said, 'Perhaps Bobby doesn't die.'" ★ During filming of the barbeque scene, the real-life owner of Southfork, Cloyce Box, explained to Katzman that a woman of Sue Ellen's position would never ride the type of horse provided for Linda Gray, so Box loaned her his own quarter horse, worth $250,000. ★ Victoria Principal thought David Wayne was "brilliant" as Digger, but recalls "that on several occasions I found [him] looking at me in a rather unfatherly manner. I remain deeply grateful and flattered." ★ The barbeque scenes took three days to film because of heavy winds. ★ This is the first of eight Ewing barbeques seen in *Dallas* and its TV movie progeny. Others were seen in Seasons 4 through 7, 9, 10, and in *The Early Years*. ★ The scene in which Pam tells Bobby that she is pregnant is a favorite of Victoria Principal's.

SEASON 1
1978–79—"Survival"

WHEN CBS OPTIONED DALLAS as a regular series in May 1978, Leonard Katzman immediately decided to transport the cast back to Texas for two months of on-location shooting beginning the following month. Although Texas was incredibly hot in the summer, its ranches could never be duplicated in California, so Katzman insisted on filming part of the season on location. Despite the short interval between the airing of the pilot and production of Season 1, some changes were made that distinguish Dallas the pilot from Dallas the series. For instance, the Ewings got a new ranch, one that would be seen in thirteen seasons of Dallas, three TV movies and a cast reunion special and become instantly recognizable the world over as the home of J.R. Ewing. This change was the result of Cloyce Box's decision in June of 1978 that he no longer wanted the publicity generated by filming on his ranch.

After Katzman drove hundreds of miles in search of a replacement for the Box Ranch, he and his staff decided on a 164-acre ranch called Duncan Acres as their new Southfork. Duncan Acres' location at 3700 Hogge Road, in Parker, Collin County, was about thirty miles northeast of Dallas. It was built in 1970 and was owned by millionaire Joe R. Duncan, who lived with his family at the ranch and eventually renamed it Southfork in honor of the series. The main building was the 8,000-square-foot, two-story, white clapboard home with a portico and columns.

Joe Duncan and his wife, Natalie, eventually decorated their den with autographed photographs of the Dallas cast members. Duncan recalled that Natalie "put wine and cheese out in the kitchen for the cast. Sometimes Larry Hagman will shout, 'What's in my refrigerator?' He's not at all like J.R. We talk about books, and he often comes into the living room to read. Steve Kanaly plays our piano. They're all family people, the women in the show included." Interior Southfork scenes were now filmed at the home of Mr. and Mrs. Bruce Calder, located on Park Lane in the Turtle Creek section of Dallas.

While in Texas, the crew filmed the exterior scenes for the first seven episodes of Season 1. Once the on-location shoot was completed in August, the cast and crew traveled to California where, as part of "the network's plan to hold down expenses by re-creating Texas on the studio back lot," they resumed filming at the MGM-Lorimar studios in Culver City, Hollywood. At the studio, exact replicas of the facade of Duncan Acres and the interior of the Calder homes were built, and the J.M.J. Ranch in Hidden Hills, California, was used for exterior scenes set on Southfork's range.

Back in the studio, the cast and crew filmed the interior scenes for the first episodes of the season. This began what future cast member Mary Crosby calls the "schizophrenic" filming sequence that the *Dallas* company followed through Season 11. Typically, after the spring hiatus, interiors for the first six or so episodes of a new season were shot at Culver City. The crew would then relocate to Texas, where exteriors for the first six, and then the second six, episodes were filmed. Upon returning to Hollywood, the company would go back and film the interiors for the second six episodes. The remainder of the season's episodes were then shot in sequential order in the studio, with stock footage inserted for exterior shots.

Stage 23 at Culver City housed the Southfork patio and pool, which included fake bushes and shrubs as well as real ones. During Season 8, it would also house Sue Ellen's office set. The Southfork foyer, living room, dining room, and kitchen were built on Stage 18, which would later house the sets for Pam's house. Stage 18 was connected by a path to Stage 19, where other Southfork sets were built. In later years, Stage 5, a two-story building encompassing 19,000 square feet, housed the sets for the second floor of Southfork. The cast's unmarked dressing rooms lined an alley that led to Stage 5.

According to Bruce Calder, when Lorimar rebuilt the interior of his Dallas home on a Hollywood soundstage, it "duplicated everything. Wallpaper, furniture, even the spool headboard I had moved from my mother's house twenty years ago. They also duplicated those awful brocade drapes. It's a strange feeling to see exact reproductions of your home, down to the last detail. The only differences I can observe on television are the placements of a few light switches." The floor plan of the Calder home was very different from that of the main house at Duncan Acres. As noted by Patrick Duffy, however, fans did not seem bothered by this "strange" discrepancy that "the inside [of Southfork] doesn't fit the outside. Whenever we needed a room, we just invented it and somehow the public accepted that it fit in this little tiny ranch house that you see. It's not a very big house. And we had cellars and attics and all kind of stuff that that house doesn't have—long hallways. We'd be halfway through the pasture if you ever tried to put the inside [seen on TV] in there."

Another change that was made in anticipation of *Dallas*'s debut as a series was the expansion of the roles of Sue Ellen and Ray. Both of these roles were so minor in the pilot episodes that the actors who played them were not even in the pilot's main title. It became clear to the producers during the filming of the pilot, however, that these characters, and their portrayals by Linda Gray and Steve Kanaly, added an important dimension to the show. As a result, Gray's and Kanaly's roles were expanded in Season 1 and they were each added to the show's main title. As Season 1 progressed, Sue Ellen became a major character on the show, and was the focus of the show's first season-ending cliff-hanger. While the producers wanted to highlight Kanaly's role in a similar fashion, they were sensitive to the controversial nature of the affair between Ray and teenager Lucy in the pilot. Katzman and his team began to develop Kanaly's character in Season 1, but they did so slowly in an effort to let viewers forget about Ray's relationship with Lucy.

While Lorimar moved the Ewings to a new ranch, CBS moved them to a new timeslot. *Dallas* was added to CBS's Saturday night line-up, airing at 10:00 p.m. against ABC's *Fantasy Island* and NBC's *Sword of Justice*. *Justice* starred future *Dallas* cast member Dack Rambo, who later recalled that Larry Hagman "came over and did a guest shot on the [*Sword of Justice*] pilot. He told me he'd recently done four or five shows for *Dallas*. He said he didn't expect anything to come of it. He was already back doing other things."

Dallas made its first full season premiere on September 23, 1978. *Variety* reviewed the episode, which was the first of a two-part story that focused on a third Ewing brother, Lucy's father, Gary. The review was not particularly favorable, but it was more positive than *Variety*'s review of the pilot. The trade paper claimed that *Dallas* "seems to have toned down the heavy theatrics that were on display when it debuted [the previous spring], but a single major flaw still remains—the [Ewing] family is not particularly admirable." Within a few weeks, however, it was clear that the Sunday night audience that had placed the final pilot episode in the Nielsen top fifteen had not found the show in its Saturday night berth. By mid-October, CBS returned *Dallas* to its Sunday lineup, a move that likely prevented the show's cancellation. Although by early November *Dallas* was averaging only a 14.5 rating and a rank of 59th, which was still behind the 44th place ranking it averaged the previous spring, the numbers were an improvement over the 12.9 share it earned shortly before it was returned to Sunday night.

By mid-November, an emotional episode in which the Ewings coped with a plane crash involving both Ewing sons put *Dallas* back in the top twenty. *Dallas* hovered near the top twenty into December, and its last episode before the new year earned its highest season rating to date. Then, on January 7, 1979, in an episode featuring Miss Ellie's terminally ill brother, the show fell just one place short of making the top ten. CBS had a growing success on its hands, yet decided to move the show a third time. On January 26, 1979, the network moved *Dallas* to Friday night. Although that night was then considered a graveyard for TV shows, *Dallas* would remain on Fridays until it went off the air twelve years later. *Dallas* was given the 10:00 p.m. slot and followed *The Incredible Hulk* and *The Dukes of Hazzard*. After a one-week drop out of the top thirty, *Dallas*'s audience found it on its new night and, by season's end, the show became a regular in the Nielsen top fifteen.

The last important change to *Dallas* took place just as the show reached the top twenty in November, not quite halfway through Season 1. In Episode 15, entitled "Act of Love," Sue Ellen learns she is pregnant. By adding a pregnancy to the storyline, not to mention a question of paternity, *Dallas* transformed, in accordance with David Jacobs's original vision, from an episodic series to a serial. As Leonard Katzman later explained, "*Dallas* became a soap opera when Sue Ellen found out she was pregnant and did not know if [the father] was Cliff Barnes or J.R. Up to then, we were not doing any continuing stories at all. It was a little bit about this and a little bit about that and a little bit about something else. Once she found out she was pregnant—and we said, 'Fascinating idea!'—we couldn't just abandon the fact that Sue Ellen was pregnant, so we went with it. And the more we went with the continuing story, the more the audience got hooked." CBS, like Lorimar, initially opposed the serial format, and only agreed to it because the fall ratings were somewhat of a disappointment. Soon, the growth in the show's ratings were attributed to the change in format, and that conclusion was only enhanced when the final episode of the year just missed the top ten. "The audience," noted Katzman, "seemed to be thrilled with the idea of a continuing storyline at night."

In keeping with serial fashion, Katzman and his team decided to end *Dallas*'s first full year with a cliff-hanger designed to keep viewers in knots over the summer break. Katzman explained, "We made a conscious effort to do what no one had ever done before—to leave an audience hanging in the air for an entire summer. . . . No show had ever gone off and left us wondering about something very important." Accordingly, Katzman and the writers concocted a season finale in which several storylines came together, culminating in potentially fatal repercussions for the Ewings. The final episode of the 1978–79 season, which aired on March 30, 1979, ended with Sue Ellen and her newborn baby each in a coma following a car crash. It ranked number 11 for the week, giving *Dallas* an overall rank of number 40 for the season, and viewers were left to wonder all summer long whether Sue Ellen and her newborn son would survive. The cliff-hanger was a successful device that brought viewers back for Season 2, but in hindsight, it was a small harbinger of the phenomenon that *Dallas* and its season-ending cliff-hanger would become in future years.

SEASON 1 EPISODE GUIDE

Regular Cast

Starring:

Barbara Bel Geddes as Miss Ellie
Jim Davis as Jock
Patrick Duffy as Bobby
Linda Gray as Sue Ellen
Larry Hagman as J.R.
Steve Kanaly as Ray
Victoria Principal as Pam
Charlene Tilton as Lucy
Also Starring:
Ken Kercheval as Cliff
Tina Louise as Julie Grey

Technical Credits

Producer: Leonard Katzman
Executive Producers: Lee Rich, Philip
  Capice
Executive Story Editor: Arthur Bernard
  Lewis
Executive Program Supervisor: Michael
  Filerman
Story Editor: Camille Marchetta
Creative Consultant: David Jacobs
Associate Producer: Cliff Fenneman
Music: Jerrold Immel, John Parker, Richard
  Lewis Warren, Ken Harrison, Bruce
  Broughton
Unit Production Manager: Wayne A.
  Farlow
First Assistant Directors: John Behm, Alan
  Brimfield
Second Assistant Directors: Claude
  Lawrence Jr., Michael J. Kane, Nicholas
  Batchelor
Directors of Photography: Robert Jessup,
  A.S.C., William Mendenhall, Allen M.
  Davey
Art Director: Charles Zacha Jr.

Editors: Fred W. Berger, A.C.E., John
  Arthur Davies, Irving C. Rosenbaum,
  Lloyd Richardson
In Charge of Casting: Barbara Miller
Casting: Irene Mariano
Set Decorators: Robert Gould, Jack Marty,
  Robinson Royce
Property Masters: Robert J. Visciglia Sr.,
  Bob T. McLing
Costumer Supervisor: Arden Cleeland
Head Costumer: Bob E. Horn
Costumers: Raymond Birdwell, Richard
  Mahoney, Bret W. R. Braughn, Sharon
  Williams, Sharon Ann Thober
Production Coordinators: Andy Ackerman,
  Candis Waters
Production Mixers: Robert Wald, Tommy
  Causey
Makeup: Jerry O'Dell
Hair Stylists: Carolyn Stewart Ferguson,
  Holly Hoffman, Travis S. Dixon
Script Supervisors: Joe Gannon, Faye
  Brenner
Dialogue Director: Fred Martin
Assistant to the Producer: Louella Lee
  Caraway
Sound Effects Supervisor: Victor Guarnier
Sound Editing: Michael Hilkene, John J.
  Jolliffe
Music Editor: Jack Lowry
Production Supervisor: Mitch Ackerman
Transportation Captain: Jim Russell
Location Casting: Shari Rhodes, Li Keigley
Location Managers: John MacLean,
  S. Wade Duncan
Main Title Design: Wayne Fitzgerald
Executive Production Supervisor: Edward
  O. Denault

6. "Reunion" (Part One)

Written by David Jacobs; Directed by Irving J. Moore; Airdate: September 23, 1978
Guest Stars: David Ackroyd (Garrison Arthur "Gary" Ewing); Joan Van Ark (Valene Clements)
Subject: Gary returns.

Cast Notes Joan Van Ark makes her first appearance as Valene, a role she would play on nine episodes of Dallas and on its spin-off Knots Landing from 1979 to 1992. During her time on Knots, Van Ark won two Soap Opera Digest Awards for Best Actress. Van Ark attended the Yale School of Drama and was nominated for a Tony Award in 1971 for her performance on Broadway in The School for Wives. She later appeared on the series Temperature Rising and We've Got Each Other. Van Ark recalls that it was her husband, award-winning TV newsman John Marshall, who convinced her to appear on Dallas. "It all happened so fast," Van Ark explains. "They sent me a script for a [Dallas] two-part guest shot, but I was supposed to be in New York recording TV commercials for Estee Lauder. My husband— much like Larry Hagman's wife, Maj, talked him into playing J.R.—basically talked me into playing Val." Van Ark thought David Jacobs's "script was wonderful, and [Valene] was a wonderful character. But we created her within those two episodes. I remember going to wardrobe and getting a peachy pink waitress uniform, and the shoes. And then I was trying to get that Texas sound, her all-important accent. The first few hours I was in Texas I rode around in a cab and just listened. I just wanted to be with people and listen to get that voice down. And so we created her layer by layer. And then I pinned my hair with a little beret, which people always made jokes about, but Val was in a time warp, and that fit her. So, David Jacobs created the skeleton—and a marvelous one—and once I committed to doing it, and I got down there in that 116 degree heat, we created her layer by layer, and I got to play her for fifteen years, which was unbelievable." ★ This two-part episode marks David Ackroyd's only appearance as Gary Ewing. He was later seen on the spin-off of M*A*S*H, After M*A*S*H. Van Ark found Ackroyd a "wonderful" actor, whose Gary was "more introspective [and] . . . a little darker" than the Gary seen on Knots Landing. ★ Costar Philip Levien replaces James Canning as Pam's cousin Jimmy, who was seen only in Episodes 5 and 6. According to Charlene Tilton, Jimmy was never contemplated as a long-term character. Victoria Principal confirms that the producers did not view Jimmy's relationship with Lucy as another Barnes-Ewing romance. Principal recalls that she wondered about the abrupt end of the Jimmy Monahan storyline and "asked Lenny Katzman [and] . . . Lenny said the story just wasn't going anywhere." While Jimmy Monahan never returned to Dallas, Philip Levien did, as Lee McHenry in Season 8. ★ Texas actor Oliver Seale, who appeared without credit in Episode 1 as "a congressman looking into oil shenanigans," has a credited bit part in this episode. Seale went on to appear as an extra in every Oil Baron's Ball episode of Dallas except one, in which real Dallas socialites from the annual Cattleman's Ball were used as

Oil Baron's Ball extras. Seale recalls, "By the third day [of filming], most of them had left, and they were calling the extras. As one of those real 'oil barons' said to me, 'They must think I'm crazy. I'm getting $40 to stand here all day, and I'm losing a fortune by not being at the office.'" Seale loved being around the *Dallas* cast. "They're such warm and wonderful people," he said. "Larry and Patrick were so funny together. They kidded around all the time. And believe me, after three days of [filming], a little levity helps a lot."

Trivia This episode ranked number 56 in the weekly rating. ★ Starting with Season 1, the first several episodes of each season except Seasons 12 and 13 were filmed on location in Dallas. These episodes were typically filmed from June through August after a two-month hiatus following the end of filming for the previous season. This explains the many pool scenes in the early episodes of each season. ★ Larry Hagman found the Texas summers like "hell fire" but lamented the California winters as well, saying, "Just when the weather gets cool in California, we go back there so we can work in big drafty soundstages doing interiors." Linda Gray recalled once when "Barbara Bel Geddes and I were doing a film in the driveway [of Southfork]. It was blacktop, and it was 120-something degrees. And the director said, 'Action.' We just stood there, and he thought we didn't hear him. He said, 'Action' again. Nothing happened. Our high heels had gone into the blacktop. It was so hot, it melted the blacktop. We were just . . . standing there, going, 'We can't move, we can't move!'" ★ While appearing on *Dallas*, Joan Van Ark, a long-distance runner who has competed in numerous marathons, got her daily run in before filming began at 7:00 a.m. ★ This was the first of many episodes to include scenes filmed on location at the Fort Worth stockyards. Some of the *Dallas* crew did not like filming at the stockyards since fights occasionally broke out among the cowboys there. ★ Duncan Acres Ranch is seen as Southfork for the first time in this episode. The ranch was sold for $7 million in 1984 and was opened to the public as a tourist attraction in 1985. Its name was legally changed to Southfork, but subsequent efforts to operate it as a hotel failed. Now a 41-acre property, it was purchased at auction in 1992 by Forever Resorts for $2.6 million and operates as a tourist attraction and conference center. It draws 400,000 visitors annually, about 40 percent of whom are from outside the United States. According to a spokesman for the Dallas Visitors and Convention Bureau, "If it's an international visitor and you stand at the airport gate and suggest they do something before they go to Southfork, they will walk over you." Visitors can tour the grounds and view such exhibits as "*Dallas* Legends: Facts to Fantasy," (which includes video clips from the series, a Ewing family tree showing J.R.'s fifty-six affairs, the stars' directors chairs from the set and such props as the characters' sterling silver–inlaid custom-made saddles, Lucy's wedding dress, J.R.'s cowboy hat, and the pearl-handled .38-caliber revolver that Kristin used to shoot J.R.) and shop at "Lincolns and Longhorns," (which displays Jock's 1978 Lincoln Continental). While the interior of the house is different from the interior seen on the show, the bedrooms have been decorated in tribute to the characters, including the Miss Ellie bedroom suite and Lucy's Yellow Rose of Texas suite, and the conference center includes the Oil Baron's Ballroom. ★ Jim Davis makes an inside joke in this episode, teasing Barbara Bel Geddes about not beating him at backgammon since February, which is when filming of the pilot wrapped. ★ The Calder home kitchen makes a rare appearance in this episode. The Southfork kitchen set was not seen regularly until Season 4. ★ Duncan Acres would not be mistaken by viewers for the Box Ranch. The former has four columns, whereas the latter has six. ★ Ray's and Lucy's use of binoculars to spy on Gary's arrival at the ranch mirrors their use of binoculars to spy on Pam's arrival at Southfork in Episode 1.

7. "Reunion" (Part Two)

Written by David Jacobs; Directed by Irving J. Moore; Airdate: September 30, 1978
Guest Stars: David Ackroyd (Gary); Joan Van Ark (Val)
Special Guest Star: David Wayne (Digger)
Subject: Gary returns.

Cast Notes Costar Sarah Cunningham, who makes her first of five appearances as Digger's sister, Maggie Monahan, played Nurse Anderson on the 1980s CBS series *Trapper John, M.D.* Victoria Principal recalls Cunningham as "a very gifted actress and we were very lucky to have her, however briefly, on *Dallas*. Ms. Cunningham reminded me of a hummingbird . . . not in her physique but in her nature. She would seemingly fly in and hover, produce an elegant scene and then fly out, never being seen to rest. I don't know if she ever got comfortable on the set of *Dallas*, but my impression of her was that she was warm and kind."

Trivia This episode ranked 59th for the week, *Dallas*'s worst ranking ever. ★ Joan Van Ark enjoyed this episode's confrontation between J.R. and Val, as she did their other scenes on both *Dallas* and on *Knots Landing*. Says Van Ark, "I love Larry. . . . Larry is the perfect example of how an actor melds with a character. Larry and J.R. melded into one person. He was so unique, and he became an icon. To work with Larry was to work with power—power as an actor and power as a character. And you have to play up to the level, like you would if you were playing tennis with a great tennis player. And when Larry crossed over to *Knots* there was always a key scene where Val confronted him, and I always enjoyed that, too." ★ Editor Fred W. Berger received an Emmy nomination for this episode. This was the first of four nominations he would receive for *Dallas*. He won an Emmy in 1976 for Outstanding Film Editing for an Entertainment Program for the "Welcome to Korea" episode of M*A*S*H. ★ Berger's nomination was also the first of twenty-three Emmy nominations bestowed on *Dallas* by the Academy of Television Arts and Sciences between 1979 and 1988 (including two nominations for *The Early Years* in 1986). *Dallas* received at least one nomination in each of its first ten seasons and received six in 1981. Four of *Dallas*'s twenty-three nominations resulted in Emmys:

one for acting (Barbara Bel Geddes in 1980), two for music composition (Bruce Broughton in 1983 and 1984) and one for costume design (Travilla in 1985). ★ Series creator David Jacobs acted as *Dallas*'s creative consultant during Season 1, but Episodes 6 and 7 were the only Season 1 episodes for which he wrote the script. Aside from authoring a single Season 2 script (Episode 43, "Return Engagement," which paved the way for the *Knots Landing* spin-off featuring Gary and Valene), Jacobs was not a part of *Dallas* again until he wrote and co–executive produced the 1986 made-for-TV movie prequel, *The Early Years*. Jacobs explained, "I wasn't responsible for [the show's] evolution. As executive producer, Phil Capice had supplanted development executive Mike Filerman as the executive authority behind the show [and] indefatigable producer Leonard Katzman had replaced me as the 'consciousness' of *Dallas*." Jacobs returned to the ABC series *Family*. "Very early in the history of *Dallas*, in the development, it was obvious that Leonard [Katzman] was taking charge," Jacobs would say later. "I . . . have always felt a little distanced from *Dallas*. . . . But I used to think that if I had been more directly involved, it probably wouldn't be the hit it [became]." Jacobs remained with *Family* until he left to produce *Married: The First Year*, which aired briefly in 1979. He then became the producer of *Knots Landing*, which premiered in December 1979, and later produced such shows as the acclaimed 1990s ABC World War II drama, *Homefront*. ★ After replacing the Jacobs/Filerman team, the Katzman/Capice team ran *Dallas* for seven years. However, Jacobs noted, "I don't think that Phil and Leonard got along that well. Phil was really a very nice man [but he] was very difficult in the office—critical, very tough. Where Leonard was that much closer with the actors, Phil would always keep his distance." As *Dallas* writer David Paulsen explained, "Phil had been an executive at CBS and had a totally different perspective on the making of a show than Leonard did." The tensions between Katzman and Capice would lead, several years later, to Katzman's temporary, and Capice's permanent, departure from *Dallas*.

8. "Old Acquaintances"

Written by Camille Marchetta; Directed by Alex March; Airdate: October 7, 1978
Guest Stars: Morgan Fairchild (Jenna Wade); Peter Mark Richman (Maynard Anderson)
Subject: Bobby's ex-fiancée returns.

Cast Notes TV star Morgan Fairchild was the first of three actresses to play Jenna Wade. She starred in *Dallas* imitator *Flamingo Road* and in the TV miniseries *North and South, Book II*. In 1985–86, she had a recurring role on *Falcon Crest*. ★ Peter Mark Richman played Andrew Laird on *Dynasty* from 1981 to 1984. Several other *Dallas* cast members appeared on *Dynasty*, including Joseph Chapman, Brian Dennehy, Ronnie Claire Edwards, Joel Fabiani, John Larch, J. Eddie Peck, Ben Piazza, William Prince, Dale Robertson, Tracy Scoggins and Geoffrey Scott. ★ Young Laurie Lynn Myers created the role of Charlie Wade, a role that was played by another young actress, Shalane McCall, from Seasons 6 through 10.

Trivia This episode earned only a 12.9 rating and a 22 share, almost six ratings points lower than the pilot's average rating. It ranked 58th for the week. CBS would air *Dallas* only once more in its new Saturday timeslot before returning the show to Sunday. ★ The horsewhip incident is seen in *The Early Years*. ★ Director Alex March was a producer/director who worked on such 1940s and 1950s TV programs as *Studio One Summer Theater* and *Kraft Television Theatre*. ★ Naldo's last name is that of episode writer Camille Marchetta. ★ A new Ewing Oil building—both interior and exterior—is seen in this episode.

9. "Bypass"

Written by Arthur Bernard Lewis; Directed by Corey Allen; Airdate: October 14, 1978
Guest Stars: Ed Nelson (Jeb Ames); John Ashton (Willie Joe Garr); Barbara Babcock (Liz Craig)
Subject: Jock's heart attack.

Cast Notes John Ashton played the campus policeman in the 1979 movie *Breaking Away* and recreated the role for the TV version of that film. ★ Barbara Babcock makes her debut as Liz Craig, a role she played through Season 4. Babcock also appeared on *Hill Street Blues* from 1981 to 1985 as Grace Gardner, a role for which she won the 1981 Best Actress Emmy (over *Dallas* nominees Barbara Bel Geddes and Linda Gray), and later played Dorothy Jennings in the Jane Seymour series *Doctor Quinn, Medicine Woman*. She also appeared in the 1992 Tom Cruise movie *Far and Away*. ★ Dan Ammerman, who plays Ewing family doctor Harlan Danvers in this episode, returned to *Dallas* as J.R.'s doctor, Dr. Auclair, in Episode 56; Farlow family doctor Neil in Episodes 132 and 137; John Ross's custody judge in Episode 202; and Lucy's banker in Episode 289. This was Ammerman's only appearance as Dr. Danvers. John Zaremba took over the role in Episode 14 and played it through Season 9. ★ This is the first appearance of bit player Peyton Park, who was seen in minor roles in episodes filmed in Dallas during Seasons 2, 4 through 6, 10, and 11. His most notable role was Caleb, the Hayleyville Hotel clerk seen in Episodes 284–86.

Trivia Weekly rating: number 52. ★ This is the first episode to focus on Jock, who Jim Davis thought was "a tough old bird who is a pussycat underneath. How can I go wrong with that?" Davis described himself as "Jock Ewing without the money." Katzman saw Jock as "a rough, tough man. . . . He was much more a physical warrior than J.R. is. . . . Jock was driven by many of the same devils that drive J.R. His were more personal, however. He wanted to succeed—he was a striver. I don't think Jock was ever involved really with blackmail, but he would take advantage of weaknesses as J.R. did. But he was much more of a direct, go-ahead, knock-them-out-of-the-way kind of guy than J.R. is." ★ The Store was modeled on Dallas department store Nieman-Marcus. ★ Section 40 was also central to storylines in Seasons 1, 2, and 11. Ironically, "not a single barrel of oil has ever been pumped out of the ground in Dallas County, which by its topography and vegetation is more Southern and Midwestern than stereotypically Texan. The 160-acre ranch called 'Southfork' has no oil." ★ Jock's hospitalization was the first of many seen on *Dallas*. During the show's run, every main character was hospitalized for one reason or another, with Sue Ellen being admitted the most. ★ Steve Kanaly recommended Corey Allen, who directed this episode, to *Dallas* producers. Allen was a former actor who played James Dean's drag race rival in *Rebel Without a Cause* and later won a 1984 Emmy for Outstanding Direction in a Drama Series for the "Goodbye, Mr. Scripps" episode of *Hill Street Blues*. Allen, however, never became a full-time *Dallas* contract director, although he directed four episodes in Season 8. According to Kanaly, directors who became involved with the script were too much for the cast to handle. *Dallas* biographer Suzy Kalter confirmed that, according to crew members, "Directors who tell [*Dallas*] actors how to play the characters don't last long around here."

10. "Black Market Baby"

Written by Darlene Craviotto; Directed by Lawrence Dobkin; Airdate: October 15, 1978
Guest Stars: Talia Balsam (Rita Brigs); Barbara Babcock (Liz Craig); James Whitmore Jr.
(Buzz Conner)
Subject: Sue Ellen wants to adopt.

Cast Notes Talia Balsam is the daughter of actress Joyce Van Patten and actor Martin Balsam. Martin Balsam won a Best Supporting Actor Oscar for *A Thousand Clowns* and later costarred with Hagman pal Carroll O'Connor in *Archie Bunker's Place*. Talia Balsam was at one time married to actor George Clooney. ★ James Whitmore Jr. is the son of actor James Whitmore. Whitmore Sr. played President Harry S. Truman in the stage and movie versions of *Give 'Em Hell, Harry*. James Whitmore Jr. also appeared on *The Rockford Files*; *Magnum, P.I.*; *Hill Street Blues*; and *Beverly Hills, 90210*.

Trivia Weekly rating: number 42. ★ Pam's black Corvette, with EWING 6 tags, makes its first appearance. ★ This was the first Season 1 episode to focus on Sue Ellen. Leonard Katzman explained that, when casting the role, "we were looking for a beautiful lady but at that point we thought of Sue Ellen as all polish and no brains. That she's evolved into a character of depth and dimension is all because of Linda. The more we saw her, the more we knew she could do and the wider we stretched." Katzman conceded that the producers "just didn't realize the gold mine we had. . . . Linda hadn't done much of anything. From the very first show, it was [Larry Hagman's] genius and her instinct that made J.R. and Sue Ellen the more dominant characters. He created the smiling villain for himself. She didn't have many lines, so she did most of her acting with those astonishing eyes of hers. . . . Her facial reactions indicated Sue Ellen was a character with a great range of emotions—understanding her husband's villainy, but caught in a lust-sick relationship that had her go along with him. She certainly saw much more in the character than we did when we started." David Jacobs agreed that "the biggest development of [the first two seasons] was Sue Ellen's role getting bigger." Linda Gray told *Time* magazine, "I was lovingly referred to by Lenny Katzman as 'the brunet on the couch.' I could have been J.R.'s masseuse. I decided that any woman stupid enough to marry J.R. had to have a lot of things wrong with her." Gray also thought a lot of her character's success had to do with the chemistry between her and Larry Hagman. "The magic that exists between Larry and me is absolutely one of those rare finds," she told *TV Guide*. "When they said, 'Action,' we were ready. The sparks flew and all that stuff in our eyes that happened was a surprise to both of us." Gray and Hagman had good chemistry off screen as well. "Larry and I would go out on his little scooter, the kind you pumped with one foot when you were a kid. He would put me on the back and we would be absolutely hysterical, turning into two ten-year-olds. I'd be in my high heels and my Sue Ellen outfit and people would do double-takes when they saw us flying around the back lot. They'd round us up like two naughty kids. Then they'd say, 'Action,' and we would be these fighting maniacal, horrendous people and they'd say, 'Cut,' and we'd jump back on the scooter." ★ With this episode, CBS returned *Dallas* to Sunday night, where it had fared better during its pilot run. It now aired against ABC's *Sunday Movie* and NBC's *Lifeline*. ★ David Jacobs felt that the scene between Ray and Sue Ellen is an example of the ground *Dallas* was breaking in prime-time television. "I think from the middle of the first year," he said, "*Dallas* made it clear that this was not a show where you could expect the expected. . . . [After Sue Ellen's and Ray's provocative dialogue,] we go to a commercial break. In any other show, the implications would have been left in the air. In *Dallas*, we went back and picked up Ray and Sue Ellen. We made it obvious what had gone on. From then on, *Dallas* became a show on which anything could happen." ★ The cast joked that Ray had been with just about every female lead except Miss Ellie. Steve Kanaly and Barbara Bel Geddes remedied Miss Ellie's omission from Ray's love life, however, in a scene included on one of the annual blooper reels put together by the *Dallas* crew to celebrate each season's end. For the blooper reel, Kanaly and Bel Geddes filmed a scene showing Ray and Miss Ellie in a passionate embrace.

11. "Double Wedding"

Written by Jim Inman and Arthur Bernard Lewis; Directed by Paul Stanley; Airdate: October 21, 1978
Guest Stars: Robin Clarke (Eddie Haynes); Charles Hallahan (Harry Ritlin)
Special Guest Star: David Wayne (Digger)
Subject: Pam's ex-husband returns.

Cast Notes Charles Hallahan had recurring roles on The Paper Chase, Hunter, and Grace Under Fire. ★ This was David Wayne's last appearance on *Dallas*. He was replaced by Keenan Wynn in Season 2. Wayne died in 1995.

Trivia Weekly rating: number 48. ★ Aunt Rose was never seen on *Dallas*. ★ When David Jacobs first created *Dallas*, the character of Bobby was conceived as an update of the "ne'er-do-well playboy son in *Cat on a Hot Tin Roof*." Both Patrick Duffy and CBS, however, pressed to make him more likeable. According to Jacobs, "The network's idea was that viewers would root for Bobby [if he were likeable]. But I think it's J.R. we're rooting for. Will he be worse this week than he was last week? I wrote the guy bad but my guy didn't have such a good time being bad. . . . What Larry brought to him was this great lust for evil." As a result, Bobby "was dull. I pictured him like Brick in [*Tin Roof*]. Instead, he was heroic, and therefore dull." Duffy also became disenchanted with Bobby's heroism. At about the time of this episode, he complained to Leonard Katzman, "It's not what I will do. You gotta give this man chinks, allow him to fail, pick himself back up." Several years later, Duffy explained, "When I took the part I really had to fight for my life. My character had all the forcefulness and panache of a three-day-old piece of lettuce. I bemoaned my fate every day, but they told me Bobby had to be the way he was to maintain some sort of equilibrium with the others." ★ Of the episodes produced before *Dallas* became a serial, this is the one Phil Capice liked best. "My favorite one of those," said Capice, "is the one where suddenly Pam has an ex-husband who just shows up and says, 'Hi, we used to be married,' and then by the end of the show he sort of disappears."

12. "Runaway"
Written by Worley Thorne; Directed by Barry Crane; Airdate: October 28, 1978
Guest Star: Greg Evigan (Willie Gust)
Subject: Lucy runs away.

Cast Notes   Greg Evigan starred in *B.J. and the Bear* and costarred with Paul Reiser in *My Two Dads*.

Trivia   *Dallas*'s move back to Sunday nights helped its viewership. This episode ranked 35th and earned a 30 share. ★ This is the last episode of Season 1 filmed in Dallas.

13. "Election"
Written by Rena Down; Directed by Barry Crane; Airdate: November 5, 1978
Guest Stars: Joshua Bryant (Peter Carson); Allen Case (Martin Cole)
Subject: Cliff's campaign.

Cast Notes   Meg Gallagher, who makes her first appearance as J.R.'s secretary, Louella, went on to play Officer Tina Russo on *Hill Street Blues* and Wayloo Holmes on *China Beach*. Louella was named after Louella Lee Caraway, who was the Assistant to Producer Leonard Katzman during Season 1 and for *J.R. Returns*. Caraway was also the Executive Coordinator and wrote numerous episodes of *Dallas* during Seasons 11 through 13. ★ Dick Whittington, who plays Jackson, was a regular on *Rowan and Martin's Laugh-In*. ★ Robert Ackerman makes his first appearance as a cartel member, although his character is not identified. His character may be Wade Luce, the oilman Ackerman is identified as in Episode 25. Don

Starr, later seen as cartel member Jordan Lee, appears in the opening scene of this episode in an unidentified role.

Trivia Weekly rating: number 48. ★ This episode marks a turning point for Ken Kercheval's character. As explained by *Dallas* biographer Suzy Kalter, "In early episodes, Cliff's character was loosely modeled on the spirit of John and Bobby Kennedy, but by the middle of the first year the concept was abandoned." ★ A cast photo from the pilot hangs over the fireplace in the Southfork den.

14. "Survival"

Written by Richard Fontana and D. C. Fontana; Directed by Irving J. Moore; Airdate: November 12, 1978
Guest Stars: Barbara Babcock (Liz); John Zaremba (Dr. Harlan Danvers)
Subject: The Ewing plane crashes.

Cast Notes John Zaremba, who played an FBI agent in the 1953–56 syndicated series *I Led Three Lives*, a drama about Communist spies, takes over the role of Dr. Danvers, a role he played through Season 9. ★ Karen Austin, who has a minor role in this episode, played the court clerk on NBC's *Night Court* in 1984. ★ Andy Jarrell plays reporter Jackson in this episode. Jarrell returned to *Dallas* as Ray's business associate Neil Hart in Episodes 84 and 85.

Trivia This episode was ranked number 18 for the week in the Nielsen ratings, earning a 21 rating and an impressive 38 share, *Dallas*'s highest season numbers to date. ★ Barbara Babcock recalls shooting on location in Dallas early in Season 1: "It was 120 degrees. We finished lunch, and were walking across a parking lot to a set. There were about six of us regulars . . . and they were unsure yet how the show would be received. They all thought it would never go, that a soap at night would never go. Everyone was feeling cynical. But I remember Victoria [Principal] saying, 'Oh, this is going to be a major hit. There is no question. There is no way this is going to fail.' And she didn't say it as an actor who was hoping it would go, but as if she had analyzed it. And then I learned that she had been an agent, and I realized she had analyzed it from an agent's point of view. She was very professional and very nice." Principal recalls this conversation with Babcock, and adds, "It was not the first or the last time I shared with someone my deep feelings about the success of *Dallas*. As an agent, I had to learn to read a script and see it as a whole. In the course of being an agent, I read many screenplays. To this day, I remember exactly where I was and how I felt when I read the script to *Dallas*. When I finished reading it, I put it down on my lap and remember having the exact thought that my life had changed forever. I am happy to say that in fact that was the case." ★ In addition to the Southfork plane, seen in this episode, and the Southfork helicopter, seen periodically since Episode 1, the ranch vehicles also included a station wagon with the Southfork logo.

15. "Act of Love"

Written by Leonard Katzman; Directed by Corey Allen; Airdate: November 19, 1978
Guest Stars: Nicolas Coster (Joe Morris); Barbara Babcock (Liz); John Zaremba (Dr. Danvers)
Subject: Sue Ellen is pregnant.

Cast Notes Nicolas Coster later returned to *Dallas* in Season 2 as Assistant District Attorney Sloane. He was a veteran of daytime soaps and had a recurring role as Blair's father on *The Facts of Life*. ★ Nancy Bleier makes the first of five appearances as Bobby's secretary, Connie, replacing Lisa LeMole. ★ Evelyn Guerrero, who has a minor role in this episode, played Carter McKay's secretary in Seasons 12 and 13. ★ Writer/actress Liberty Godshall appears as J.R.'s mistress in this episode and again in Episode 18. Godshall wrote episodes of *thirtysomething*, *Once and Again*, and *My So-Called Life* and appeared on *Charlie's Angels*, *The A-Team*, and *thirtysomething*.

Trivia Weekly rating: number 41. ★ This is the first episode written by Leonard Katzman, who wrote more episodes of *Dallas* than any other writer. Katzman wrote seventy-four episodes, including the cliffhangers for Seasons 3, 7, 10, 12, and 13; the season premieres for Seasons 8, 9, 11, and 13; and, as co-writer, the first TV movie sequel. According to Steve Kanaly, however, Katzman had a hand in writing each episode of the show no matter who got the writing credit. ★ The Cattleman's Club was the *Dallas* business community's lunch spot of choice through Season 5. From Season 6 through Season 13, the Oil Baron's Club was where the *Dallas* movers and shakers ate. ★ Victoria Principal told *Time* magazine that Pam was like "a little Statue of Liberty. When you have utter evil on one side, you can't have mediocre good on the other." ★ The new Ewing Oil set is seen in this episode. ★ As of this episode, *Dallas* became a serial as opposed to an episodic series. The writers' motto as they went about creating a true soap opera was "Resolve the situation [in each episode] without resolving the problem." A hallmark of *Dallas*'s serialized episodes was the cliff-hanger at episode's end that tried to hook the audience into returning the following week. When asked where the "freeze frames" that ended the episodes came from, Katzman replied, "I just have a feeling that was a Lorimar thing that they had done—on *Waltons*, on *Eight Is Enough*—where they fill in Lee [Rich's] credit when it first started. We always wanted to look for that right frame, that right moment, that right look." ★ Ken Kercheval enjoyed having Linda Gray as a leading lady, and thought she had "great lips!"

16. "Triangle"

Written by Camille Marchetta; Directed by Vincent McEveety; Airdate: November 26, 1978
Guest Star: Kate Mulgrew (Garnet McGee)
Subject: Ray falls in love.

Cast Notes TV veteran Kate Mulgrew played the wife of Peter Falk's Columbo on *Kate Loves a Mystery*, Ted Danson's almost-fiancée on *Cheers*, and Captain

Janeway on *Star Trek Voyager*. Steve Kanaly thought Mulgrew sounded like Katherine Hepburn, who Mulgrew played on the New York stage in 2003.

Trivia Weekly rating: number 39. ★ Director Vincent McEveety directed such movies as Disney's *Superdad* and *Herbie Goes to Monte Carlo* and such TV shows as *Magnum, P.I.* ★ Leonard Katzman initially offered the role of Garnet to Susan Howard, who played Donna Krebbs from 1979 through 1987. It was the second time Katzman tried to recruit Howard for *Dallas*. After Howard turned down his offer to appear in the pilot, he "came to me again. 'Read this script,' he said, 'because there's a role in it for you.'" But Howard did not see herself as Garnet McGee. "I could not see myself as a country-western singer," explained Howard. "It just didn't click." Howard thought Kate Mulgrew "did a marvelous job" with the role. ★ Ray slowly became a nicer character as the show developed. Kanaly recalled that although Ray was initially J.R.'s buddy and henchman, Kanaly himself came up with a different idea about Ray, resulting from "the void on TV of worthwhile American blue-collar characters with a well-rooted moral center." Kanaly "loved such characters since watching John Wayne, Gary Cooper, Roy Rogers, and Gene Autry while growing up, and saw this type of personality as a possibility for Ray." Kanaly believes his character got the lead in this episode, however, since the producers "were not yet totally confident about character development and were constantly testing the waters to see what worked." Kanaly explained Ray as "hardheaded, and sometimes he lets his pride get in the way. It's his only character flaw, though. . . . He ran away from his past and grew up on that ranch, gradually growing into prominence. There's a pride in that, in doing a good job and gaining acceptance from Jock."

17. "Fallen Idol"

Written by Arthur Bernard Lewis; Directed by Vincent McEveety; Airdate: December 3, 1978
Guest Stars: Richard Kelton (Taylor "Guzzler" Bennett); Sandy Ward (Jeb Ames); John Ashton (Willie Joe Garr)
Subject: Bobby's college friend visits.

Cast Notes Sandy Ward takes over the role of Jeb Ames from Ed Nelson. ★ John Petlock plays J.R.'s detective Dan Marsh, and is also seen in the role in Episodes 19, 20, 22, and 23. ★ Guest star Richard Kelton died of a heart attack on November 27, 1978, about one week before this episode aired.

Trivia This episode was number 23 for the week in the Nielsen ratings.

18. "Kidnapped"

Written by Camille Marchetta; Directed by Lawrence Dobkin; Airdate: December 17, 1978
Guest Stars: Stephen Davies (Will Hart); Paul Koslo (Al Parker); Kelly Jean Peters (Fay Parker)
Subject: Bobby is kidnapped.

Cast Notes Ken Kercheval's credit, which had appeared in the closing credits, moves to the beginning of the show with this episode. ★ Kelly Jean Peters played nurse Louise Anderson on M*A*S*H in 1983.

Trivia This episode was ranked number 18 for the week. ★ This episode is one of the few times Ken Kercheval got to appear at Southfork in the same scene with his friend Barbara Bel Geddes, and he "would have loved to have worked with her more." ★ Teresa replaces Francesca as the Southfork maid, and would be seen for the rest of the series. ★ The demise of Al and Will are the first of numerous deaths on *Dallas*. Over the years, the death toll included Garrison Southworth, Julie Grey, Sam Culver, Digger Barnes, Seth Stone, Kristin Shepard, Jock Ewing, Jeff Farraday, Amos Krebbs, Rebecca Barnes Wentworth, Walt Driscoll, Mickey Trotter, Mark Graison, Naldo Marchetta, Veronica Robinson, Mark Scottfield, B. D. Calhoun, Jamie Ewing Barnes, David Shulton, Dr. Herbert Styles, Nicholas Pearce, Rolf Brundin, Tommy McKay, twins Arlen and Atticus Ward, Jordan Lee, April Stevens, Johnny Dancer, Daniel "Blackie" Callahan, and Hillary Taylor. Several other characters, including Bobby, Katherine Wentworth, Sam Barker, Grace, Nicholas, and apparently Sue Ellen Ewing and Jamie Ewing Barnes, died during Pam's dream late in Season 7 and throughout Season 8.

19. "Home Again"

Written by Arthur Bernard Lewis; Directed by Don McDougall; Airdate: January 7, 1979
Guest Stars: Gene Evans (Garrison Southworth); Melinda Fee (Kathy Baker)
Subject: Miss Ellie's brother returns.

Cast Notes Gene Evans was a character actor who appeared in the films *Operation Petticoat* and *Walking Tall* and on TV's *My Friend Flicka* and *Matt Helm*. He died in 1998.

Trivia *Dallas*'s audience continued to grow with this episode, which just barely missed the Nielsen top ten. It was number 11 for the week, earning a 25.7 rating and a 39 share. ★ This episode, like the TV movie *The Early Years*, establishes Miss Ellie's fondness for her father, who loved his ranch. Like Miss Ellie, Barbara Bel Geddes worshipped her father, famed theater designer Norman Bel Geddes, who also had an affinity for the outdoors. Bel Geddes' father separated from her mother, a teacher, when Bel Geddes was five years old. "I didn't see much of my father, but I absolutely adored him," Bel Geddes once said. "He was a man who loved animals and who should have been a naturalist." Once when Bel Geddes walked through the woods with her father, "he lifted up a stone and there was this tiny salamander with black button eyes and orange spots. It was absolutely magical." ★ Garrison's Southfork gravesite is seen in Episode 279. ★ On January 3, 1979, four days before this episode aired, the *Dallas* cast and crew recognized Victoria Principal's birthday by jokingly sending her dead roses with a note that read, "When you walked into makeup, these flowers were fresh." ★ Other characters who came back from the dead on *Dallas* were Dusty Farlow, Rebecca Wentworth, and Mark Graison.

20. "For Love or Money"

Written by Leonard Katzman; Directed by Irving J. Moore; Airdate: January 14, 1979
Guest Stars: Martha Scott (Patricia Shepard); Colleen Camp (Kristin Shepard); Fred Beir
(Ben Maxwell)
Subject: Sue Ellen and J.R. fight.

Cast Notes Martha Scott had the lead in Broadway's *Our Town* and was nominated for an Oscar for her re-creation of the role in the movie version. She also starred in *The Ten Commandments, Ben-Hur,* and *The Turning Point.* On TV, she appeared as Lee Majors's mother on *The Bionic Woman* and costarred in the 1980–81 nighttime soap opera *The Secrets of Midland Heights. Dallas* was not Scott's first experience with a soap opera. "I had a daytime show in the 1950s called *Modern Romances,*" she recalled. "I told a story and it was enacted by a group of actors. We did a complete story every week. I remember they let me out to do *Ben Hur.* The wonderful part of it was that the kids all knew me. I was the last face on NBC before *Howdy Doody* came on. Kids would run up to me and say, 'I know you! You're on before *Howdy Doody.*' The power of the medium is astonishing." Scott died on May 28, 2003, in Los Angeles at the age of eighty-eight. ★ Colleen Camp appeared in Alexander Payne's film *Election,* which starred Matthew Broderick and Reese Witherspoon. ★ This is the first appearance of Fern Fitzgerald, who played Marilee Stone for twelve seasons of *Dallas.* At the time she got the part, Fitzgerald "had no idea it would become a recurring role. . . . It's my nature to appear 'confident and in charge.' Most likely the writers picked up on that and decided to expand the role." ★ Barbara Tarbuck has a bit part in this episode. She returned to *Dallas* as Cliff's secretary, Agnes, in Episodes 24 and 31. Tarbuck later appeared on Broadway in *Brighton Beach Memoirs,* won several L.A. Drama Critic Choice Awards and appeared on many TV shows, including *General Hospital, The Waltons, CSI: Crime Scene Investigation, Judging Amy,* and *Falcon Crest,* on which she played Dr. Randall in 1981 and 1987.

Trivia Weekly rating: number 33. ★ Bobby's support of Sue Ellen is typical of his role as the Ewing good guy. Said Leonard Katzman, "If *Dallas* had a hero, it was Bobby, whose instincts were heroic instincts, as opposed to J.R., who was much more self-involved. . . . Bobby cared more about other people. Bobby was the one who stood between J.R. and total devastation of the Ewing family. Even accidentally, I would say that in that sense he was heroic." Some of the cast, however, felt Duffy had a tough assignment playing the show's hero. Explained Larry Hagman, "Poor old Patrick Duffy . . . he had to be the nice guy, and he had to make apologies for me all the time, and he had the most difficult role on the show. I had the fun." Duffy agreed: "At the start, Bobby was ineffectual—blind to the realities of his own family and his own situation. I said, 'Come on guys. We've got to make him smarter, tougher, more of a realist—or the audience won't side with him.' It's tough to write for the good guys. Bobby got the short end of the stick." ★ Bobby's friendship with Sue Ellen was a development encouraged by Duffy and Linda Gray. Recalled Gray, "Patrick and I always tried—not to have our characters be love interests—but have more of a friendship evolve between Sue Ellen and Bobby. We had great respect for each other and wanted to work more together. I remember I went to Patrick's house one afternoon and we came up with a very interesting script outline that we showed to the producers. We wanted Sue Ellen to have an ally in Bobby, because she was kind of an outcast within the family." ★ *Barnaby Jones*, the 1973–80 CBS series starring Buddy Ebsen, was still on the air when it was referred to in this episode.

21. "Julie's Return"

Written by Rena Down; Directed by Les Martinson; Airdate: January 26, 1979
Subject: Julie Grey returns.

Cast Notes Costar Kenneth White makes the first of two Season 1 appearances as cartel member Seth Stone. White also appeared on *Homefront*; *Beverly Hills, 90210*; and *Melrose Place* and as the sheriff in Norman Lear's 1980 series, *Palmertown, U.S.A.* He returned to *Dallas* as a politician in Episode 208. White does not know why he was replaced by Ed Kenney as Seth in Season 2. ★ Jeanna Michaels takes over the role of Bobby's secretary, Connie. ★ Veteran actor Richard Roat plays Victor, the Cattleman's Club waiter, and remembers "how elegant Tina [Louise] was. I worked with her once before in New York, in a show called *The Doctors*, which I was a regular on. It was great to see that she hadn't changed a bit in ten, fifteen years!" Roat has appeared on *Friends*, *7th Heaven*, and as Carl Crayton on *Dynasty*. He played Mr. Austin to *Dallas*'s Priscilla Pointer's Mrs. Austin on the NBC series *From Here to Eternity* in 1980. Other *Dallas* actors who were *Eternity* regulars were John Calvin, who played Wilson Cryder in Season 10, and Richard Erdman, who played Mr. Willis in Episode 298.

Trivia This was the first *Dallas* episode to air on a Friday night. It ran at 10:00 p.m., following *The Incredible Hulk* and *The Dukes of Hazzard* on CBS and against ABC's *Friday Night Movie* and NBC's *Eddie Capra Mysteries*. This episode finished at number 32 for the week, while the series premiere of *The Dukes of Hazzard* finished at number 29. Two weeks later, *Dallas* jumped to number 18, and its audience continued to grow until it was a top ten show by season's end. Explained Katzman, "In the beginning, *Dallas* was kind of a network stepchild. We premiered on CBS on Sunday nights, then were moved to Saturday, then back to Sunday, and then to Friday night, which was known in the industry as television's 'graveyard.' Historically, it was the lowest night of viewership in the week. But our audience followed us and *Dallas* went on to change the television viewing habits of the entire nation. At the peak of its popularity, *Dallas* had more people watching television on Friday night than on any other night." David Jacobs credited at least some of *Dallas*'s Friday night success to its lead-in show, saying, "*The Dukes of Hazzard* actually gave *Dallas* a really good lead in. And they both started growing together during the season." ★ This episode includes the first appearance of cartel member Jordan Lee, but he is played by someone other than Don Starr, who took over the role in Episode 41 in Season 2 and played the character through Season 13. ★ Director Les Martinson directed such movies as *PT-109* and *Batman* (1966), a feature based on the 1966–68 ABC TV series starring Adam West. ★ This episode includes Tina Louise's favorite *Dallas* scenes: "The scenes I remember are the love scenes with Larry Hagman and the fight with him. I was trying to escape and get him to let go of me. Larry made it easy. He was great to work with. . . . Because of the way he played it, it was easy to react to him. He was so painful, but had that smile." Louise found Les Martinson a "fantastic" director and Jim Davis "just adorable. He was great. The scenes with him were colorful, fun, and emotional." ★ The Seth Stone character only appeared in Episodes 21, 26, and 53 (and was heard on the telephone but not seen in Episode 24), but none of those scenes included Seth's wife Marilee. As a result, Fern Fitzgerald, who played Marilee, never met or even knew who played her on-screen husband.

22. "The Red File" (Part One)

Written by Arthur Bernard Lewis; Directed by Leonard Katzman; Airdate: February 2, 1979
Guest Stars: Sandy Ward (Jeb); John Ashton (Willie Joe); Fred Beir (Maxwell)
Subject: Julie's death.

Cast Notes Costar James L. Brown makes his debut as Sergeant Harry McSween, a role he played through Season 11. Brown played Lieutenant Rip Masters on *The Adventures of Rin Tin Tin*. ★ Costar Jordan Charney, who plays Lieutenant Sutton, played the owner of the restaurant where John Ritter worked in *Three's Company* and had a recurring role as Norton Crane on *Falcon Crest*. Charney also played Dr. Katz on *General Hospital* and appeared in the 1976 Faye Dunaway movie *Network*. ★ This is Tina Louise's final appearance on *Dallas*. According to Louise, the producers "wanted her to stay on . . . [and] I wanted to continue. It became complicated after the pilot." But Louise enjoyed playing Julie Grey, explaining, "She played her angles. She tried to get J.R. by going after his father." Louise admired Leonard Katzman and attributes her "wonderful time on *Dallas* [to it being] very well written . . . [and] very well directed."

Trivia Weekly rating: number 30. ★ Cliff's fondness for Chinese food, which Kercheval recalls was the writers' idea, is seen for the first time in this episode and would be referred to throughout *Dallas*'s thirteen seasons and in the first TV movie sequel. In real life, Ken Kercheval was a connoisseur not of Chinese food, but of ketchup and popcorn. Kercheval produced "Kenny's Ketchup," a homemade ketchup based on his Indiana grandmother's recipe, and "Ken Kercheval's Old Capital Popcorn," made from his 4,000-acre Indiana cornfield. ★ Leonard Katzman was one of Ken Kercheval's favorite *Dallas* directors.

23. "The Red File" (Part Two)

Written by Arthur Bernard Lewis; Directed by Leonard Katzman; Airdate: February 9, 1979
Guest Stars: Charles Siebert (Assistant District Attorney Sloane); Walter Brooke (Cole Young); Sandy Ward (Ames); John Ashton (Garr); Woodrow Parfrey (Doctor); John Harkins (Justice Potter)
Subject: J.R. frames Cliff.

Cast Notes Charles Siebert played Jerry on One Day at a Time and Dr. Stanley Riverside on Trapper John, M.D. ★ John Harkins played an agent from Control in Seasons 12 and 13. ★ Walter Brooke played the district attorney on The Green Hornet. ★ Veteran TV actor Woodrow Parfrey, who died in 1984, played general store owner Ike Godsey in the pilot for The Waltons, The Homecoming: A Christmas Story.

Trivia This episode was ranked number 18 in the weekly Nielsen ratings. ★ Cliff, a lawyer and prosecutor, was arrested five times during Dallas's thirteen years on the air.

24. "Sue Ellen's Sister"

Written by Camille Marchetta; Directed by Irving J. Moore; Airdate: February 16, 1979
Guest Stars: Colleen Camp (Kristin); John McLiam (Wally Kessel)
Subject: Kristin visits.

Trivia This episode was ranked number 23 in the weekly Nielsen ratings. Its lead-in, The Dukes of Hazzard, earned a to-date season high of 22nd place. ★ Jim Davis thought that the Ewings' histrionics were brought on, in part, by their unique living arrangements. "Don't you think all this would happen in any family that lives under the same roof?" he asked. "Why we're all under the same roof is a mystery to me—except it's in the script. It's an unusual situation. We're supposed to have a big spread and so much money that we all want to stay together, I guess. That's TV for you."

25. "Call Girl"

Written by Rena Down; Directed by Les Martinson; Airdate: February 23, 1979
Guest Stars: Veronica Hamel (Leanne Rees); Fred Beir (Maxwell); Claude Earl Jones (Matt Henderson); Barbara Babcock (Liz); Mark Wheeler (Kit Mainwaring)
Subject: J.R. frames Pam.

Cast Notes Veronica Hamel went on to star as Joyce Davenport on the Emmy Award–winning Hill Street Blues. She studied acting under drama coach Charles Conrad alongside Linda Gray. ★ Claude Earl Jones returned to Dallas as Wally Hampton in Episodes 94–95 and Duke Carlisle in Episodes 324–35. ★ This is Paul Sorenson's first appearance as cartel member Andy Bradley, a role he played through Season 9. ★ Robert Ackerman's character gets a name in this episode:

Wade Luce, who Ackerman played through Season 5. ★ Larry Hagman's daughter Heidi plays the attendant at the racquetball court in the first of seven appearances she made on *Dallas*. Heidi's real name is Kristina Mary, but her grandmother Mary Martin picked out the nickname Heidi because it sounded Swedish and was a good marquee name. Heidi also played Linda on *Archie Bunker's Place*, a role she got after her father called his old friend Carroll O'Connor to get her an audition. Heidi's younger brother, Preston, who was named after Mary Martin's father, appears in Episode 249 of *Dallas*.

Trivia Weekly rating: number 37. ★ Like the Ewings, some of the actors who played them enjoyed racquetball. Larry Hagman, Patrick Duffy, and Steve Kanaly frequently played together during the show's early years. ★ Looking back on *Dallas* when it ended in 1991, Larry Hagman called J.R.'s set-up of Pam in this episode the "most dastardly deed" J.R. committed during Season 1.

26. "Royal Marriage"

Written by Camille Marchetta; Directed by Gunnar Hellstrom; Airdate: March 9, 1979
Guest Stars: Mark Wheeler (Kit); Linden Chiles (Bill Mainwaring); Jay W. MacIntosh (Marjorie Mainwaring)
Subject: Lucy's engagement.

Cast Notes Linden Chiles played the father on *James at 15*. ★ This is costar Joan Lancaster's first appearance as Andy Bradley's wife, Linda, a role she played through Season 2.

Trivia Weekly rating: number 20. ★ Says Charlene Tilton about this episode, "My favorite Lucy storyline is when I was engaged to marry Kit Mainwaring, . . . who was homosexual. It was way before *Ellen* and *Will & Grace* and all that. It was really ahead of its time and was so well done. Mark Wheeler was just fantastic." ★ This episode is the first of six episodes directed by Larry Hagman's friend Gunnar Hellstrom, who also appeared in front of the camera as Austrian oilman Rolf Brundin in Episodes 303–305 and 310. Hagman was so loyal to Hellstrom that, in 1980, he flew to the Philippines to do a single day of filming for a movie Hellstrom was directing. Hellstrom was a Swedish actor-director who wanted experiences outside his native land. He landed a bit part on *Gunsmoke*, which led to directing jobs on *Bonanza* and *How the West Was Won*. He died in Stockholm on November 28, 2001, at the age of seventy-three.

27. "The Outsiders"

Written by Leonard Katzman; Directed by Dennis Donnelly; Airdate: March 16, 1979
Special Guest Star: John McIntire (Sam Culver)
Guest Star: Susan Howard (Donna Culver)
Subject: Ray falls in love.

Cast Notes Prior to her long-running role as Donna Culver Krebbs, Susan

Howard played the title character's wife in *Petrocelli*, a show produced by Leonard Katzman. In 1976, Howard was nominated for an Emmy for Outstanding Continuing Performance by a Supporting Actress in a Drama Series for her work on that show. (Ellen Corby of *The Waltons* won.) Katzman tried to talk Howard into joining *Dallas* when the pilot was being cast, but Howard was committed at the time to a pilot for Mary Tyler Moore's production company. Later, Katzman tried to get Howard to play against Steve Kanaly as Garnet McGee, but Howard turned that down, too. "About a month later," according to Howard, she and her husband, Calvin Chrane, "were having dinner with Len, and he came up with another *Dallas* script for me to read. This one he had written himself, and the part was Donna." Katzman told Howard, "I have a script and I've written a part for you." Howard recalls that "Leonard knew me. We were friends, and he knew what I liked and the things I felt good about playing. When I read the script, I thought, 'I can do something with this. It has potential. It is going to go somewhere.'" ★ John McIntire was a veteran TV and movie actor who appeared in the movies *Psycho* and *Elmer Gantry* and on TV's *Wagon Train* and *The Virginian*. He died in 1991 at age eighty-three. Susan Howard found McIntire "wonderful," comparing him to Howard Keel and other *Dallas* actors who "were all out of the good old days of Hollywood. They brought integrity to the scene, and discipline, to the art and craft of performing. They gave you something to rise up to, and you wanted to be better. They had so much to offer, just by the way they carried themselves on the set and their respect for others. With John, humble isn't the right word; meek isn't the right word. He saw acting as a partnership. He was unselfish. And he was fun. He had a great sense of humor."

Trivia Weekly rating: number 28. ★ Upon learning that her character would become an alcoholic, Linda Gray "went back to my old acting-class notes and decided that, because of her background, Sue Ellen would never be sloppy. I wouldn't overdo it: she'd be a sophisticated rummy." ★ Lucy's Porsche with EWING 5 tags is seen in this episode.

28. "John Ewing, III" (Part One)
Written by Camille Marchetta; Directed by Leonard Katzman; Airdate: March 23, 1979
Guest Stars: Ellen Geer (Dr. Crane); Peter Horton (Wayne)
Subject: Sue Ellen is committed.

Cast Notes Ellen Geer returned to *Dallas* in Season 12 as Mrs. Boularis. She played Jimmy Stewart's daughter-in-law on his 1971–72 TV show, and went on to play Mary on *Beauty and the Beast*. ★ Peter Horton, who plays Lucy's drug supplier, starred as Gary in ABC's *thirtysomething*. ★ Sherril Lynn Katzman, who plays the jewelry counter saleswoman at The Store in this episode, was the daughter of producer Leonard Katzman. She later played Jackie Dugan in Seasons 3, 4, and 6 through 13. She appeared in 186 episodes of *Dallas*, more than anyone else except Deborah Rennard, excluding those actors seen in the main title. She changed her name to Sherril Lynn Rettino at the end of Season 6, after marrying John Rettino, who was the *Dallas* property master from Seasons 5 through 11 and an associate producer, along with Sherril's brother, Frank, during Season 12. Sherril died of breast cancer at her home in L.A. in 1995. She was thirty-six years old. ★ Costar Ed Kenney, who appears as Senator Newberry, returned to *Dallas* in Season 2 as cartel member Seth Stone.

Trivia This episode was ranked number 14 in the weekly Nielsen ratings, *Dallas*'s best ratings yet on a Friday night. ★ Larry Hagman says that Sue Ellen's commitment is "my favorite [*Dallas*] scene. . . . It was one of the meanest things I ever did to her and I was repaid in full when my bastard son put me in the loony bin [in Season 12]." Linda Gray, however, hated this "stupid" episode. ★ Gray described Sue Ellen's pregnancy as a "gradual progression of changing funny pillows. I kept forgetting 'the baby.' I'd leave it in my dressing room and one time I even left it in a phone booth. Felt like a terrible mother even before I had it!" ★ Charlene Tilton told *People* magazine that Linda Gray "plays a drunk with such elegance that you feel for her even when she's almost killing her baby. . . . [Linda is] warm, funny, and very, very generous." ★ Although *Dallas* had already become a serial earlier during the season, this episode ends with the line, "To Be Continued."

29. "John Ewing, III" (Part Two)

Written by Arthur Bernard Lewis; Directed by Leonard Katzman; Airdate: March 30, 1979 Guest Stars: Ellen Geer (Dr. Crane); Michael C. Gwynne (Dr. Rogers); Peter Horton (Wayne); Dimitra Arliss (Nurse Hatton) Subject: Sue Ellen's car crash.

Cast Notes Dimitra Arliss played Falconetti's wife in *Rich Man, Poor Man—Book II*. ★ This is the first appearance of costar Karlene Crockett as Lucy's friend, Muriel. Crockett played Muriel in Seasons 1 through 5. Crockett appeared in the TV movies *Return to Mayberry* and *Death of a Centerfold: The Dorothy Stratton Story* and on such TV shows as *Family Ties* and *Fantasy Island*. ★ Costar Alan Rachins played Douglas Brackman Jr. on *L.A. Law* and later appeared as Jenna Elfman's hippie father on *Dharma and Greg*. Elfman's high society father-in-law on *Dharma* was played by Mitchell Ryan, who also appeared on *Dallas*, as Detective Fogarty, in Season 7. ★ Heidi Hagman plays the sanitarium receptionist.

Trivia This episode was ranked number 11 in the weekly ratings. ★ This was the first *Dallas* season-ending cliff-hanger, and Katzman recalled that his office "got a tremendous amount of letters after the first year saying, 'How could you let us go on worrying about that baby?' The reaction to that last show was very strong." ★ Other babies born on *Dallas* were Christopher (to Kristin and Jeff Farraday), Margaret (to Donna and Ray), Lucas (to Jenna and Bobby) and an unnamed baby (to Cally and J.R.). ★ During the summer hiatus which followed this episode, *Film Comment* ran a review of *Dallas* in a special issue devoted exclusively to television.

In the review, author Dave Kehr, who typically avoided TV, wrote, "I watched [*Dallas*] once. I watched it twice, and before I knew it, I was hooked. . . . Perhaps part of my initial fascination came from the tone of the show: tawdry, overheated, low-minded, and without a single perceptible note of social value. *Dallas*, in short, dared to be different. . . . The entire production has a slightly shameful, furtive air, as if the producers were trying to sneak it past the PTA monitors. *Dallas* benefits greatly from its low cunning and under-the-counter attitude, but its most distinguishing quality is its animal energy. . . . Everything happens and everyone changes, to the point where, should you miss a week, it takes two to catch up."

SEASON 2
1979–80—"Power Play"

DURING THE SUMMER OF 1979, while fans of *Dallas*'s freshman year wondered about the fate of Sue Ellen and her baby, and early episodes of *Dallas*'s sophomore season were being filmed at Duncan Acres, the National Academy of Television Arts and Sciences announced the nominees for its annual Emmy Awards. To the surprise and happiness of the cast and crew, *Dallas* got the first two of its twenty-three Emmy nominations when Barbara Bel Geddes was nominated for Outstanding Lead Actress in a Drama Series and Fred W. Berger was nominated for Outstanding Film Editing for a Series for "Reunion" (Part Two). Neither Bel Geddes nor Berger won, however, when the Emmys were presented in Los Angeles on September 7, 1979, almost two weeks before the *Dallas* second season premiere. Bel Geddes lost to Mariette Hartley for her work on *The Incredible Hulk*. *Dallas* also earned the first two of its fourteen Golden Globe nominations a few months later. *Dallas* received nods for Best Drama and Best Actress in a Drama for Bel Geddes. The show lost to *Lou Grant* and Bel Geddes lost to Natalie Wood for *From Here to Eternity*.

Dallas continued to gain an audience as its second season unfolded on September 21, 1979. Viewers tuned in to learn the fate of Sue Ellen and her baby, and with the second part of its two-part premiere, *Dallas* cracked the Nielsen top ten for the first time. *Dallas* now aired against ABC's *Friday Night Movie* and NBC's *Eischied*. A mid-November review by *Time* magazine was glowing. Writer Gerald Clarke, noting that *Dallas* hit number 6 in the ratings after ranking as low as number 58 the previous season, found *Dallas* "irresistible" in its "unashamed appeal to the lower emotions and the exuberant ingenuity of its rococo plot." While Clarke thought the production was "slick," he wrote that most of the performances were not. Exceptions, however, included Barbara Bel Geddes, "who does not even attempt an accent, but she is so good at everything else that no one notices," and Larry Hagman, who "does everything just right. . . . The chief joy of *Dallas* is watching him play an overstuffed Iago in a Stetson hat. Mean? There ain't nobody meaner than this dude. But Hagman plays him with such obvious zest and charm that he is impossible to dislike."

A special two-hour episode that aired on November 16 and focused on Miss Ellie's mastectomy was the number 5 show for the week, Dallas's highest rating to date. According to *People* magazine, "Half of all TV-watching Americans were tuned in, an audience share exceeded this fall only by *Jaws* and the seventh game of the World Series." Against this background, the producers happily continued with the cast and format that had fueled the year-long ratings rise, although several supporting cast changes were made in Season 2.

First, Keenan Wynn replaced David Wayne in the role of Digger Barnes. Wayne declined to return to the role after Season 1 because he was involved in other projects and did not need the work. Wynn, the son of movie and TV star Ed Wynn, was a veteran character actor himself. He had appeared on Broadway and had made many movies, including *Annie Get Your Gun*, *The Absent-Minded Professor*, *Dr. Strangelove*, and *Finian's Rainbow*, in which Wayne had starred on Broadway.

Second, Mary Crosby, daughter of legendary movie actor and singer Bing Crosby and screen actress Kathryn Grant, took over the role of Kristin from Colleen Camp. After producers Lee Rich and Phil Capice decided to bring back Kristin as a semi-regular, they agreed that they needed a "new face." They held the "usual 'cattle call'" for the role, and, as Capice explained to *TV Guide*, "It was clear what kind of young woman she was going to be. We brought in twenty candidates and read them, and Mary was the best of them. After the fact, we realized that with the image the Crosby family always had, we'd better sit her down and tell her where the role was going." Crosby—who had never seen the show before reading for the role of Kristin—confirms that Leonard Katzman "had this discussion with me because they were concerned that if they cast me, the general public—who knew Bing Crosby as Mr. Minute Maid Orange Juice and *White Christmas*—might not accept his daughter doing these nasty and unpleasant things. They just weren't sure the public would embrace Bing's daughter doing such things."

Although she recognized that the producers were taking "a big chance" on her because of her father's image, Crosby "thanked [the producers] but said she was approaching it as an actress and it wasn't going to be a problem." However, Crosby explained that things weren't so easy. "The first few scripts I had," she said, "I used to come home . . . and say . . . 'I can't do this!' . . . . [And my first day filming] was the worst. I had spent my entire career saying, 'No, I will not do bikini shots,' so my first scene with Larry is a bikini shot. I did the entire scene with my towel clutched to my breast. I wasn't going to let go of that towel for anything. But Larry was great. He made sure I felt comfortable and eventually we got the scene."

Finally, Ted Shackelford took over the role of Gary Ewing from David Ackroyd. Shackelford made his debut as Gary in the *Dallas* episode that introduced its spin-off series, *Knots Landing*. Ackroyd was unavailable when *Knots* was being cast because he was at Universal filming the 1979 NBC series *Little Women*. Joan Van Ark, who played Gary's wife, Valene, recalls, "Ted Shackelford and I had just done an episode of *Wonder Woman* together, and David Jacobs and some of the CBS brass called me and said, 'What do you think of Ted Shackelford?' And I said, 'Oh my God, no! That will never work. Ted is just like me; we are both pretty emotional.' I felt we were just too much alike and that it would never work for us to play husband and wife. But I was so wrong. Even now, Ted is still my actor soulmate." Shackelford was cast in the role, and continued to make occasional guest appearances in subsequent seasons of *Dallas*.

Meanwhile, audiences became increasingly taken with the outrageous villainy of J.R., whose never-ending scheming and wheeling and dealing at the expense of his friends and family shocked but entertained fans. As a result, Hagman became the breakout star of *Dallas*. In Leonard Katzman's opinion, "What Larry brought to the part that was never written is his joy in everything he does. Larry brought this wonderful, wicked smile and an enjoyment of everything that J.R. did, no matter how horrible." Patrick Duffy believed that Hagman's portrayal of J.R. gave the ensemble show a much needed focus. "Without a single, really flagship character to draw everything else along point lines of interest and plot," said Duffy, "the show wouldn't have lasted thirteen years. Larry is singlehandedly the reason the show stayed on the air for thirteen years."

Hagman became an offscreen leader as well. Charlene Tilton sought his acting advice. Katzman gauged cast morale through him. As Jim Davis summed up, "Sure, we've got a lot of different-type folks on this show. Larry, he's the glue." Davis found Hagman "just a goddam clown. He's got a lot of the little boy in him, but he's a man of his word, a man of integrity." As for Hagman, he thought the show was "the most fun I ever had and a lot, lot simpler than comedy." He was having fun at work, and it was infectious. Hagman even seemed to enjoy the cast press junkets that were merely tolerated by his fellow castmates, as discovered by TV columnist Jeff Simon in 1978. Simon wrote that Hagman possessed "the cheap grandeur of a carny huckster and the charm of a happy reprobate three short hours away from the gutter," while the rest of the cast had "expressions of tenth-graders about to take their geometry midterm [and] poor Barbara Bel Geddes, in particular, looked at that moment like a woman who might have preferred a nice soothing root canal."

Dallas had become a bona fide top-ten hit, and CBS was thrilled. When the network pressed Lorimar for a spin-off, David Jacobs resurrected the concept for what became *Knots Landing*, the show CBS rejected before he developed *Dallas*, and reworked it so the characters included Lucy's parents, Gary and Valene. *Knots* premiered as a special episode of *Dallas* on Thursday, December 20, 1979. It was the number 2 show in the weekly ratings, and the number 3 show was the following night's regular episode of *Dallas*. *Knots* remained on the air for fourteen years. When *Dallas* ended its thirteen-year run in 1991, Hagman joked that J.R.'s chasing Gary off of Southfork was an act "for which Ted Shackelford should be extremely grateful, since he went on to [play Gary in] *Knots Landing* and it is still on the air."

CBS also asked Lorimar to enlarge its original order of twenty-three episodes of *Dallas* to twenty-five. At the same time, CBS gave Lorimar a full season order for the 1980–81 season, which provided the cast and crew with the greatest amount of job security they'd had since they signed on for the pilot in 1977. Steve Kanaly recalls, "The network said, 'We'd like some more shows. Could you do that?' and the writers had to change the plan to have the season end with Digger announcing on his deathbed that he was not Pam's real father." Writer Arthur Bernard Lewis remembered meeting with the other writers to figure out a plot that would take the characters through two more hours and provide a suitable follow-up to the previous year's cliff-hanger involving Sue Ellen and her baby. "Camille Marchetta, Leonard Katzman, and myself met and we had to try and come up with something," Lewis said. Katzman recalled that Phil Capice was also at this meeting.

The creative team first considered a cliff-hanger scenario in which Sue Ellen decides to kill herself and prepares a glass of water into which she mixes barbiturates. While Sue Ellen is in the nursery saying goodbye to her baby, J.R. comes home and drinks her glass of water. Sue Ellen returns from the nursery to find J.R. drinking the lethal mixture, but she says nothing. According to Capice, this storyline "wasn't as stylish as establishing five or six suspects" and was rejected because "it didn't afford us an opportunity to bring four or five story lines together."

Katzman recalled, "We were sitting around, and Phil Capice says, 'Let's have J.R. get his.'" Lewis could not recall who came up with the shooting idea, but confirmed that "one of . . . us said, 'Oh, my God. Why don't we just shoot the son of a bitch?'" Katzman said, "We didn't know who shot him. We said the hell with it, let's shoot him and figure out who did it later." Capice thought a shooting was a better way "to tie up plot threads. We established a motive in each of the plot lines" and, in Katzman's words, "started with the last scene and built backward. We built two entire scripts backward."

Thus, the writers developed a storyline in which J.R.'s chickens finally came home to roost as, in the final seconds of the season's last episode, he was shot by an unknown assailant. As for the resolution of the whodunit, Katzman's widow, La Rue, confirmed, "When they wrote that episode where J.R. was shot, they had no idea who was going to be the shooter." They did know, though, as did the growing number of Dallas fans, that there was a long line of possible suspects. The audience tuned in in droves on March 21, 1980, to watch J.R. get his, and the season finale was number 1 for the week, making Dallas the number 6 show for the season, with a 25 share. What no one foresaw, however, was that the whodunit would turn Dallas into an international phenomenon; "the public went wild," as Capice observed, and spent the spring, summer, and fall of 1980 wondering, "Who Shot J.R.?"

SEASON 2 EPISODE GUIDE

Regular Cast

Starring:

Barbara Bel Geddes as Miss Ellie
Jim Davis as Jock
Patrick Duffy as Bobby
Linda Gray as Sue Ellen
Larry Hagman as J.R.
Steve Kanaly as Ray
Ken Kercheval as Cliff
Victoria Principal as Pam
Charlene Tilton as Lucy
Also Starring:
Mary Crosby as Kristin Shepard
Susan Howard as Donna Culver
Randolph Powell as Alan Beam
Keenan Wynn as Digger

Technical Credits

Producer: Leonard Katzman
Executive Producers: Philip Capice, Lee Rich
Executive Story Editor: Arthur Bernard Lewis
Story Editor: Camille Marchetta
Associate Producer: Cliff Fenneman
Music: Jerrold Immel, Bruce Broughton, Richard Lewis Warren, John Parker
Unit Production Manager: Wayne A. Farlow
First Assistant Directors: Alan Brimfield, John Behm, Ed Ledding

Second Assistant Director: James M. Freitag
Directors of Photography: Allen M. Davey, Robert Jessup, A.S.C.
Art Director: Charles Zacha Jr.
Editors: Fred W. Berger, A.C.E., John Arthur Davies, Lloyd Richardson
Executive in Charge of Casting: Barbara Miller
Casting: Irene Mariano
Set Decorators: Travis P. Nikon, Jack Marty
Property Master: Anthony C. Thorpe
Dialogue Director: Fred Martin
Costumers: Jack Bear, Meschelle Ravare, Violet Cane
Makeup: Cheri Johnston Minns
Hair Stylist: Linda Sharp
Production Sound Mixers: Richard Goodman, Ronald Curfman, Clarke King
Sound Effects Supervisor: Victor Guarnier
Sound Editing: Mike Hilkene
Sound Effects Editors: John Leveque, Rich Steve, Avram Gold, Tony Zero, Steve Pervis
Music Editor: George Probert
Production Supervisor: Mitch Ackerman
Main Title Design: Wayne Fitzgerald
Executive Production Supervisor: Edward O. Denault

30. "Whatever Happened to Baby John?" (Part One)

*Written by Camille Marchetta; Directed by Leonard Katzman; Airdate: September 21, 1979
Guest Stars: Sheila Larken (Priscilla Duncan); Sandy Ward (Jeb); John Ashton (Willie Joe); George O. Petrie (Harv Smithfield); Woody Eney (Dr. Rogers)
Subject: John Ross is kidnapped.*

Cast Notes Movie and TV veteran George O. Petrie makes his first appearance as Ewing attorney Harv Smithfield. Petrie played the role in this and every future season of *Dallas* and in *J.R. Returns*. He was a veteran of radio, TV, movies, and Broadway. He appeared on Jackie Gleason's *The Honeymooners*, the daytime soap operas *As the World Turns* and *Search for Tomorrow*, the crime drama *Wiseguy* and the sitcom *Mad About You*. He also appeared in the movies *Hud* and *Planes, Trains, and Automobiles*. Petrie died at the age of eighty-five of lymphoma on November 16, 1997. ★ Harv's associate, Alan Beam, was played by Randolph Powell, who appeared in the TV version of the sci-fi movie *Logan's Run*, which was produced by Leonard Katzman. ★ Ken Kercheval was added to the main title as of this episode.

Trivia This episode earned a 35 share and was ranked number 19 for the week. ★ With *Dallas* now a full-fledged serial, the producers and story editors spent the weeks immediately after completing filming for one season planning the next season. Explained Phil Capice, "We spend six weeks or so doing a long-range seasonal bible. Then we break that down episode by episode. We spend hours going over each script in all its variations. You must develop a storyline so that when the main story peaks, another variation takes over. And there is usually an interrelationship between the main story and the variations." By 1986, the bible was about four hundred pages long. Katzman called it a "road map. As we go along, we write in the towns, the cities. Like all roads, it twists and turns and takes unexpected little bends." ★ The Southfork nursery set makes its debut in this episode.

31. "Whatever Happened to Baby John?" (Part Two)

Written by Camille Marchetta; Directed by Leonard Katzman; Airdate: September 28, 1979
Guest Stars: Sheila Larken (Priscilla Duncan); Sandy Ward (Jeb); John Ashton (Willie Joe); John O'Leary (Dr. Freilich); Dennis Patrick (Vaughan Leland)
Subject: John Ross is kidnapped.

Cast Notes This is the first appearance of Dennis Patrick as banker Vaughan Leland, who became a leading suspect in the "Who Shot J.R.?" storyline and returned to *Dallas* during Seasons 4, 6, and 7. Patrick had appeared on *Dark Shadows*, and also appeared on *The Twilight Zone*, *All in the Family*, *Eight Is Enough*, *Gunsmoke*, and *Coach*, and in the miniseries *War and Remembrance*. He died on October 13, 2002, at the age of eighty-four in a house fire in his Hollywood Hills home. ★ Jocelyn Brando, who costars as Mrs. Reeves, is a stage actress and the sister of acting legend Marlon Brando. ★ Jordan Charney returns as Detective Sutton, the role he played in Episodes 22 and 23, but he mistakenly introduces his partner to the Ewings as Sutton and introduces himself as Rollins. ★ Bobbie Ferguson makes the first of several appearances as a Dallas TV reporter. She was also seen as the reporter covering the opening of J.R.'s gas stations in Episodes 115–117 and the Ewing family gala held in Episode 191. Ferguson appeared as Monette on *Designing Women* in 1987 and 1989.

Trivia This was *Dallas*'s first top-ten episode. It was the number 10 show for the week and earned a 38 share. ★ Cliff's new apartment set debuts in this episode and would be seen until Cliff bought a condominium in the Turtle Creek section of Dallas in Season 5.

32. "The Silent Killer"

Written by Arthur Bernard Lewis; Directed by Irving J. Moore; Airdate: October 5, 1979
Guest Stars: William H. Bassett (Dr. Peter Holliston); Georgann Johnson (Dr. Carol
Grovner); Martha Scott (Patricia)
Subject: Digger's illness.

Cast Notes Keenan Wynn makes his debut as Digger, a role he would play until
Digger's death near the end of Season 2. Wynn later appeared on TV in *Call to
Glory* with Priscilla Pointer, who played Digger Barnes's ex-wife Rebecca. He
died in 1986 at the age of seventy. ★ Mary Crosby also makes her *Dallas* debut
in this episode. Before becoming an actress, Crosby was a student at the University of Texas. As for why Colleen Camp did not continue in the role of
Kristin, Crosby says, "My understanding is that the producers wanted to go in a
different direction with Kristin. I know Colleen, and she's wonderful and funny
and talented and sweet. We talked and laughed about our experiences playing
Kristin, and not continuing in the role certainly didn't stop Colleen from doing
wonderfully since." ★ Georgann Johnson was a regular on such TV shows as
Mr. Peepers, *Our Family Honor* (produced by Leonard Katzman) and *The Colbys*
★ William H. Bassett returned as the Barnes's family doctor, Dr. Peter Holliston, in Episode 105. He also played Mr. Gurney, Sue Ellen's divorce attorney, in
Season 11.

Trivia Weekly rating: number 31. ★ Cliff had an older brother, Tyler, and another younger sister. ★ The reason for Jock's negative reaction to the play
about the ghost of a man's first wife becomes clear in Episode 35. ★ Ken
Kercheval recalls that Keenan Wynn "wore a hearing aid, and he always asked
me if I was going over to the commissary for lunch. So I would go with him . . .
but all the sounds of silver and china clanking were too sharp for his hearing
aid. It was too painful for him, so he would turn the hearing aid off. Then he
would proceed to talk and talk and talk. I would answer him, but he couldn't
hear a damn word I said!" Victoria Principal found Wynn's portrayal of Digger
as "equally brilliant" as David Wayne's "but in very different ways. I was very
lucky," Principal says, "to have two very talented fathers." ★ Prior to *Dallas*,
Mary Crosby did not know that Larry Hagman was, like her, the offspring of an
entertainment legend. During her ride back to the hotel with Hagman after her
first day of shooting, Hagman recalled how he got into the business when his
mother asked him to appear with her in *Annie Get Your Gun*. "I thought, 'How
cute—community theater.' I said, 'Well, *how nice*. Your mother, would I have
heard of her?' And he says, 'She's Mary Martin.' I went, 'Oh, my God! You're
one too!'" Hagman noted that their parents appeared together on radio on
Kraft Music Hall early in Martin's career.

33. "Secrets"

Written by Leonard Katzman; Directed by Leonard Katzman; Airdate: October 12, 1979
Guest Stars: Joan Van Ark (Valene); George O. Petrie (Harv); William H. Bassett (Dr. Holliston)
Subject: Lucy's mother returns.

Trivia This episode was ranked fifteenth for the week and earned a 35 share. ★ Says Joan Van Ark of her on-screen daughter, "Charlene was just my little girl! She was great—energetic and enthusiastic. I have a daughter of my own, and I was able to transfer my love as a mother to Lucy, and use that parallel of my own daughter in my own life when Val had a scene with Lucy. Charlene is special, and she was perfectly cast." ★ This is the first of twenty-six episodes that were written, produced, and directed by Leonard Katzman, who also co-wrote, directed, and executive produced J.R. Returns. It was Katzman's ability to do all three that led Patrick Duffy to claim that "Uncle Lennie," as the cast called him, was a "walking genius." Duffy also called Katzman "quality control, he was glue, he was your confessor. And he was an amazing individual to have absolute authority. You would never see Larry snap to attention so much except when Leonard wanted something." Susan Howard felt that Katzman "had a real perception of a vision of where characters could go and how they could go. And he drew a lot of it on people's own personalities." Steve Kanaly calls Katzman "the backbone" of *Dallas*, explaining that Katzman was the driving force of the show. He made the major story decisions; policed situations involving the actors, the network, and Lorimar; was the person everyone in the crew leaned on; was a "workhorse extraordinaire"; and was widely loved by the entire company.

34. "The Kristin Affair"

Written by Worley Thorne; Directed by Irving J. Moore; Airdate: October 19, 1979
Guest Stars: Martha Scott (Patricia); Dennis Patrick (Vaughan)
Subject: J.R.'s affair.

Trivia This episode was number 10 for the week. ★ Mary Crosby recalls that, when filming her first bedroom scene with Larry Hagman (which appears in this episode), "[I] had my hair pulled back and he looks at me and says, 'This is terrible! You look like you're twelve. You think I get bad mail now; what's going to happen after I seduce a twelve-year-old?'" Offscreen, Crosby became very close to Larry and his wife, Maj, who Crosby calls "family. Larry and Maj walked me down the aisle at my wedding and spoke at my wedding. They are the best thing that's ever happened to me from being on *Dallas* because they are part of my family. They are my beloveds. Larry taught me so much about work. I was only nineteen when I got on the show. I was a complete puppy, and he taught me about being prepared, hitting my mark and finding my lines. I remember one scene where he was supposed to grab my backside, and I said to the director, 'Oh, Irving, I'm not comfortable with that.' And Larry pulled me aside and said, 'Darlin', if something concerns you, talk to me about it.' And Larry said to Irving, 'We'll do it this way,' and came up with something that was ten times sexier and that I was completely comfortable with. Larry is a wonderful man and working with him was the best experience of my career."

35. "The Dove Hunt"

Written by D. C. Fontana and Richard Fontana; Directed by Leonard Katzman; Airdate: October 26, 1979
Guest Stars: Robert J. Wilke (Tom Owens); Stefan Gierasch (Ben Masters); John Zaremba (Dr. Danvers)
Subject: The Ewings' hunting trip.

Cast Notes Costar Thomas Calloway, who plays Dan Owens, appeared as Dr. Foster on *Falcon Crest*. ★ Stefan Gierash was a veteran actor of movies (*What's Up, Doc?*, *Jeremiah Johnson*, *Carrie*, and *Dave*) and television (*Gunsmoke*, *The Incredible Hulk*, *Star Trek: The Next Generation*, and *ER*).

Trivia *Dallas*'s ratings continued to climb with this episode, which was number 6 for the week. ★ The Caddo Swamp is where J.R.'s and Bobby's plane crashed in Episode 14. ★ The brawl with the Owenses was the first of several memorable fights on *Dallas*, including the Barnes-Ewing brawl at J.R.'s and Sue Ellen's wedding reception; the fistfight between J.R. and Ray that ignited the Southfork fire; the Barnes-Ewing brawl at the Oil Baron's Ball; and J.R.'s fatal fight with Nicholas Pearce.

36. "The Lost Child"

Written by Rena Down; Directed by Irving J. Moore; Airdate: November 2, 1979
Guest Stars: Jeff Cooper (Dr. Simon Elby); Med Flory (McBride); Ronnie Scribner (Luke)
Subject: Pam's miscarriage.

Trivia This episode finished the week at number 5, earning a 44 share. It was *Dallas*'s first top-five episode. ★ Bruce Broughton, a four-time Emmy award winner who composed music for such shows as *Hawaii Five-O* and *JAG*, was nominated for Outstanding Music Composition for a Series for this episode. ★ By the time this episode aired in late 1979, *Dallas* had spent nearly a year paired with *The Dukes of Hazzard* on Friday nights. The reference to Bo and Luke Middens in this episode might be a nod to *Dukes*, on which the lead characters were Bo and Luke Duke. ★ Out-takes from this episode show that Patrick Duffy donned a Superman outfit while attending to Pam after her fall. ★ Bobby receives a postcard from Luke Middens in Episodes 42 and 76.

37. "Rodeo"

Written by Camille Marchetta; Directed by Leonard Katzman; Airdate: November 9, 1979
Guest Star: Jared Martin (Steven "Dusty" Farlow)
Subject: The Ewings' rodeo.

Cast Notes   Jared Martin makes his first appearance as Dusty, a role he would reprise during Seasons 3 through 5, 8, and 13. Almost a decade later, Martin told *People* magazine that playing Dusty on *Dallas* was "like getting on a rocket ship. I still meet people who call me Dusty." Prior to playing Dusty, Martin was a regular on *Fantastic Journey*, a 1977 science-fiction series that aired on NBC and was produced by Leonard Katzman. *Journey* was cancelled after nine episodes. At the wrap party, Martin recalls, "Lennie didn't say a word, except for goodbye. I never expected to see him again. . . . But I did. He became producer of a show called *Logan's Run*—also science fiction. I believe he cast me in a guest-starring role. I don't remember even speaking to Lennie at this time, although I may have. . . . The next time was a casting call for a show called *Dallas*. Lennie wasn't at the casting session. At the time, *Dallas* was looked at as an unfocused semi-ludicrous stab at the heartland America audience. I had no idea the show would explode into legend. I received a three-show contract. . . . I remember thinking *Dallas* was the one show I wouldn't be working on again. I was as surprised as anyone at the show's success. It was a true sleeper, a meteorite from the far side of the moon. No one saw it coming."

Trivia   Weekly rating: number 15. ★ Despite their on-screen competition for J.R.'s attention, Mary Crosby and Linda Gray got along well offscreen. Crosby describes Gray as "a doll and a sweetheart. She was very welcoming to me and very nice to me." Gray explains, "I adore Mary! Mary . . . had this wonderful, great face. And she could turn with a look—without doing anything, or without doing anything that was obvious—and turn so nasty! She was very chameleon-like. I'd be in a scene with her and watch this metamorphosis and I thought she was absolutely brilliant. And I love her as a human being." ★ The only other Southfork rodeo took place during Season 8, in the show's 200th episode. ★ This episode establishes that the Southern Cross was the family home of the Waynes, Dusty's mother's family. Episodes 144 and 156, however, establish that it was the family home of the Farlows—Dusty's father's family—and that Clayton and Jessica Farlow grew up there. The family names of Dusty's parents, Wayne and Farlow, may come from Wayne Farlow, the First Assistant Director of the *Dallas* pilot and the Unit Production Manger from Seasons 1 through 13 and on *J.R. Returns*. Wayne Farlow was also Leonard Katzman's brother-in-law. As Steve Kanaly recalls, there was a lot of nepotism on *Dallas*. ★ This is the last episode of Season 2 with scenes filmed on location in Dallas. ★ The pilot cast photo previously seen above the den fireplace has been replaced with a current cast photo taken in front of Duncan Acres. ★ Jared Martin recalls that the "rodeo episode at the Dallas Fairgrounds was fun. I never felt comfortable with horses—I'd been dumped twice—painfully—in a summer camp years ago and I made a private deal with myself that horsemanship would be a low priority item in my future life. Imagine my surprise when I was cast as the world champion rodeo cowboy. . . . In the rodeo episode staged at the Dallas Fairgrounds, I was supposed to win the all-around best cowboy award and claim Sue Ellen's heart. I was dead game for everything and had a lot of fun, but I know my attempt to rope a calf is probably still showing somewhere on a blooper highlight reel. There were parts of me that fit well with a Texas image, and parts that didn't. One thing the casting directors didn't catch was the fact that rodeo cowboys average about 5'7"—something about centrifugal force and low center of gravity while on a gyrating bronco. I'm 6'3", and even with superior riding skills I would have been cut in half by these professional rodeo competitors."

38. & 39. "Mastectomy" (Parts One and Two)

Written by Arthur Bernard Lewis; Directed by Irving J. Moore; Airdate: November 16, 1979
Guest Stars: Jared Martin (Dusty); John Zaremba (Dr. Danvers); Jeff Cooper (Dr. Elby); Jane Kean (Mitzi)
Subject: Miss Ellie's mastectomy.

Cast Notes Jane Kean is a character actress who played the schoolmarm in the Disney musical *Pete's Dragon* and who took over the role of Trixi Norton from Jayne Meadows for the *Honeymooners* segments revived by Jackie Gleason on his 1966–70 CBS variety show.

Trivia This episode was number 5 for the week in the Nielsen ratings with a 28.9 rating and a 50 share. It was the first two-hour episode of *Dallas*. Mary Crosby recalls what it was like for the cast to be appearing on a show steadily rising to the top of the ratings: "I don't think anybody had any idea where *Dallas* was going to go. The first time we hit a 50 share everybody was jumping up and down. And each step of the way we were all delighted and surprised, and no one took any of it for granted. It was just a wonderful and exciting time." ★ According to her granddaughter, Hannah Lerman, Barbara Bel Geddes always held this episode "close to her heart" because of Bel Geddes' own mastectomy. Aside from the topic, this showcase for Miss Ellie must have been a relief to Bel Geddes, who was asked in an interview the year this episode aired what her fans had to say about her work on *Dallas*. She replied, "They say, 'You don't say very much. Why don't you ask your producer to please give you more dialogue?'" Nevertheless, Bel Geddes found *Dallas* "great fun" to do, although she "never expected the show would be so successful" and admitted to having a "real kind of love/hate about acting. When I'm not acting, I like to get as far away from it as I possibly can." Linda Gray found *Dallas* to be "much harder on Barbara" because she played a "salt-of-the-earth" role. "[But] Barbara," said Gray, "has been around long enough and is so loved that she just goes about the business of squeezing every ounce out of her role." Patrick Duffy commented that Bel Geddes "always had her little collars on her little dresses. There was no flash and flair. The hair was always the same. It was small in terms of the level of her performance but it was intense and it was riveting. If she raised her voice then it was something to be taken quite seriously." ★ Charlene

Tilton was recently struck by the cutting-edge nature of this episode's subject matter, saying, "They got into if it's passed down genetically. And . . . Miss Ellie was telling Lucy, 'You just have to make sure to check yourself.' You're talking twenty years ago!"

40. "Heiress"

Written by Loraine Desires; Directed by Leslie H. Martinson; Airdate: November 23, 1979
Guest Stars: Laura Johnson (Betty Lou Barker); Jeff Cooper (Dr. Elby); George O. Petrie (Harv)
Subject: Lucy falls in love.

Cast Notes Laura Johnson played Cliff Robertson's wife on *Falcon Crest* during the 1985–86 season. She later appeared on the nurse drama *Heartbeat*, which costarred *Dallas* alumni Kate Mulgrew and Gail Strickland. ★ Walker Edmiston, who plays Roy in this episode, returned to *Dallas* in Episode 135 as Judge Thornby and as Reverend Carson in Episode 191. Edmiston appeared on *The Dukes of Hazzard*, *Little House on the Prairie*, *The Waltons*, and *Gunsmoke*, and provided voices for the Disney animated movie *The Great Mouse Detective* as well as the TV shows *The Smurfs* and *H.R. Pufnstuf*.

Trivia Weekly rating: number 8. ★ Charlene Tilton won the Hollywood Presswomen's Best Juvenile Actress award over Kristy McNichol of *Family* and Melissa Gilbert of *Little House on the Prairie* in late 1979.

41. "Ellie Saves the Day"

Written by David Michael Jacobs and Arthur Bernard Lewis; Directed by Gunnar Hellstrom; Airdate: November 30, 1979
Guest Star: Dennis Patrick (Vaughan)
Subject: J.R. mortgages Southfork.

Trivia Weekly rating: number 13. ★ Cliff's quip about the White House foreshadows his destiny as revealed to J.R. in the series finale. ★ This is Don Starr's second appearance on *Dallas*. As of this episode, he takes over the role of cartel member Jordan Lee, a role he would play in eighty-four episodes between Seasons 2 and 13, making him the most seen of all the cartel members. ★ Writer David Michael Jacobs (no relation to David Jacobs) also wrote episodes of *Kaz* and *The Lazarus Syndrome*.

42. "Mother of the Year"

Written by Rena Down; Directed by Larry Hagman; Airdate: December 14, 1979
Guest Stars: Dennis Patrick (Vaughan); Jeff Cooper (Dr. Elby)
Subject: Sue Ellen and her baby.

Trivia Weekly rating: number 7. ★ This is the first of thirty-two episodes directed by Larry Hagman, who Steve Kanaly found to be "very humorous, very easygoing" in the director's chair. Hagman's favorite *Dallas* directors were Leonard

Katzman and Michael Preece. ★ In a *TV Guide* profile of Linda Gray published a few months before this episode aired, Leonard Katzman stated that Sue Ellen had become "the queen bitch of television." Elsewhere, Katzman called Sue Ellen "a drunk, a nympho, a lousy mother, any number of things—a figurepiece that didn't have a brain in her head, but she had tremendous audience sympathy because she was married to that rat J.R." Gray, however, enjoyed playing the character, noting that "the part of Sue Ellen is a lot of fun. She is quicksilver—sometimes hateful and at other times just pitiful, all confusion and repressed anger. This is a lady who's a lush, has an affair with a deadly enemy of the Ewing family, and almost kills her baby." Gray found that if she "were in a series where I had to be nice all the time, I'd be so bored." ★ As Sue Ellen's popularity grew, so did rumors of tension among the women in the cast. Around the time this episode aired, Gray told *People* magazine that she and Victoria Principal "have a pleasant relationship, but the situation [regarding Sue Ellen] must be hard on Victoria, and there has to be some resentment." In the same article, Principal stated that Gray "can act anyone right off the floor. She is so in touch with her own emotions and priorities." Charlene Tilton maintained that the female cast members got along well. "I know the press people would love to hear that they were fighting," Tilton said. "That the women were cat fighting. That Victoria and I hated each other and Linda—none of that was true." Today, Gray confirms, "a lot of people liked to say that there were catfights. It's so erroneous. On the set, and off, we were all very professional. The thing I liked about Victoria was that she was always prepared, always professional. There was none of that nonsense that you can have with two women playing characters like that. But they like to put the catfights in there."

43. "Return Engagement"

Written by David Jacobs; Directed by Gunnar Hellstrom; Airdate: December 20, 1979
Special Guest Star: E. J. Andre (Eugene Bullock)
Guest Stars: Joan Van Ark (Valene); Terry Lester (Rudy Millington); Andra Akers (Sally Bullock); Ted Shackelford (Gary Ewing)
Subject: Lucy's parents remarry.

Cast Notes Ted Shackelford takes over the role of Gary Ewing from David Ackroyd. Shackelford played Gary during all fourteen seasons of *Knots Landing*. Of her two Garys, Joan Van Ark says, "They were both wonderful, but they each played [Gary] differently." Van Ark feels that Shackelford's Gary "was more wild, and [Ted] is so charismatic." Ironically, David Ackroyd eventually made his way to *Knots Landing*, appearing in a guest star role opposite *Knots* star Michele Lee in early 1982. ★ This is the first of six appearances in Seasons 2, 3, and 5 by veteran character actor E. J. Andre as "Mister Eugene" Bullock. Andre appeared in the 1973 movie *Papillon* (along with *Dallas* cast member William Smithers) and on such TV shows as *Gunsmoke*, *Bonanza*, and *Little House on the Prairie*. He died in 1984 at the age of seventy-six. ★ Terry Lester was an Emmy-nominated star of the daytime soap operas *The Young and the Restless* ("Jack Abbott"), *Santa Barbara*, and *As the World Turns*. ★ Costar Ted Jordan played Nathan Burke on *Gunsmoke*.

Trivia This special Thursday edition of *Dallas* set the stage for the *Knots Landing* spin-off, which would take over the Thursday timeslot as of the following week. It was the number 2 show in the Nielsen weekly top ten, earning a 26.6 rating and 40 share, and outperforming the regular Friday episode of *Dallas* that aired the following night. The episode was written by *Dallas* creator David Jacobs, who pointed out that CBS wanted to get another Jacobs show on the air in the wake of *Dallas*'s success. "It was absolutely because *Dallas* was starting to click," said Jacobs. CBS asked him to rework his two-year-old idea for what became *Knots Landing* into a *Dallas* spin-off. Since *Knots* was about four married couples, Jacobs simply made Gary and Valene one of the couples. ★ While it has been reported that Charlene Tilton was given the chance to join the cast of *Knots Landing* but decided to stay on *Dallas*, Joan Van Ark recalls that CBS had its reasons for keeping Tilton on *Dallas*. "The network," says Van Ark, "initially felt that Lucy should stay on *Dallas* because she was one of several characters who could crossover and help get *Knots* established. Once *Knots* took hold, though, the network wanted to keep the two shows separate, so it backed off of the crossovers. By then, the network wanted to make sure each show had its own identity and could stand on its own two feet." Nevertheless, Van Ark "used to hear so many complaints from fans that Charlene was not more a part of *Knots*." Tilton claimed that there was talk about her leaving *Dallas*, not to join the cast of *Knots*, but for a second spin-off, one that focused on Lucy. ★ Hagman costarred in a 1971–72 NBC sitcom called *The Good Life* with future *Knots* cast member Donna Mills and *Dallas* costar David Wayne. ★ Gary's and Val's nuptials were the first of many weddings seen on *Dallas*, including those of Lucy and Mitch, Ray and Donna, J.R. and Sue Ellen, Miss Ellie and Clayton, Jamie and Cliff, Pam and Mark, Pam and Bobby, Ray and Jenna, J.R. and Cally, and Bobby and April. ★ Joan Van Ark particularly enjoyed this episode because it gave her scenes with Barbara Bel Geddes and Patrick Duffy. Says Van Ark of her *Dallas* costars, "I adore Barbara Bel Geddes. She is a theater actress, and a brilliant one, and I related to her since my roots are in the theater, too. She was special, she was warm, and she carried great weight as the matriarch of this family. She was brilliantly cast. In fact, that was the key to *Dallas*: it was cast so well. One thing I remember about Barbara is that she was fascinated by my lipstick! I never wear one color of lipstick. I always take two or three and mix them together. And no matter what I was wearing, Barbara would say, 'What are you wearing?' or 'Now let me try that.' She always wanted the pink or soft colors. She had a great sense of humor. She was so aware of everything. She was very special—she was extraordinary. Patrick was a gorgeous, loving prankster, and he still is. He did guest spots on *Knots*, and he loves to keep the set light and happy and make the job fun. He was always right there in the scene—spot on, perfect—but in between, he was the prankster. He is a director's dream that way: prepared and professional when it's time to shoot, and not problematic in between. Patrick is just great." ★ Numerous *Dallas* cast and crew members worked on *Knots Landing* during the spin-off's 14 seasons. Larry Hagman, Patrick Duffy, Charlene Tilton, and Mary Crosby appeared on *Knots*; Hagman in five episodes, Duffy in three, and Tilton and Crosby in one each. Other *Dallas* cast members who appeared on *Knots* as original characters included Joseph Chapman, Howard Duff, Jonathan Goldsmith, and Ray Wise. *Dallas* writers who wrote episodes of *Knots* included Calvin Clements, Peter Dunne, Joel J. Feigenbaum, David Jacobs, and David Paulsen. Jerrold Immel, who composed the *Dallas* theme song, composed the *Knots* theme, complete with a brief musical reference to the *Dallas* theme. *Dallas* directors who filmed episodes of *Knots* included Larry Elikann, Larry Hagman, Nick Havinga, David Paulsen, Michael Preece, and Nicholas Sgarro. When Hagman directed *Knots*, he would arrive at the *Dallas* set by 7:00 a.m., film several pages of dialogue, then report to the *Knots* set after lunch and direct several pages of dialogue, which typically took until 1:00 a.m. ★ Shackelford and Steve Kanaly were neighbors who frequently ran into each other in Studio City and compared notes on working for Lorimar.

44. "Love and Marriage"

Written by Leonard Katzman; Directed by Alexander Singer; Airdate: December 21, 1979
Special Guest Star: Mel Ferrer (Harrison Page)
Guest Stars: Barbara Babcock (Liz Craig); Barry Corbin (Sheriff Fenton Washburn); Jeff Cooper (Dr. Elby)
Subject: Pam's job.

Cast Notes Susan Howard's return to *Dallas* after her Season 1 appearance as Donna Culver was not a surprise to her. "I knew from the beginning that I would be back on," Howard explains. "That was Leonard's intent. When he called me about the part, he said he wanted to try something because Ray didn't have any kind of long-lasting relationship. So basically I knew. Depending on whether Steve and I had any kind of magic between us, it was a forgone conclusion that Donna would be back." Howard appeared in three additional Season 2 episodes and became a cast regular in Season 3, playing Donna through Season 9. ★ Actor Mel Ferrer (*Lili, War and Peace*) was married to film legend Audrey Hepburn and produced her 1967 hit *Wait Until Dark*. He later played Jane Wyman's lawyer and husband on *Falcon Crest*. ★ Tom Fucello makes his first appearance as Sam Culver's son, Dave. Fucello would play the role in thirty-five episodes during Seasons 2 through 5, 7, 9, and 10. He died of AIDS in 1993 in Van Nuys, California, at the age of fifty-five. According to Steve Kanaly, Fucello was a private and conservative man who possessed a quiet dignity. ★ Barry Corbin also makes his first appearance in this episode. He played Braddock County Sheriff Fenton Washburn during Seasons 2 and 4 through 6. Corbin is a veteran of movies such as *War Games, Urban Cowboy, The Best Little Whorehouse in Texas,* and *Any Which Way*

You Can and TV series such as JAG, Murphy Brown, and Reba and the 1989 miniseries Lonesome Dove. Corbin starred in the 1990–95 CBS hit Northern Exposure, on which he played chamber of commerce president and former astronaut Maurice J. Minnifield, a role for which Corbin received Emmy nominations in 1993 and 1994 as Outstanding Supporting Actor in a Drama Series. Corbin recalls that when he auditioned for the role of Fenton, "They said they were looking for a tall lean sheriff . . . but they hired me anyway. I wasn't 'tall and lean' by any stretch of the imagination, but I guess I was a convincing enough sheriff. . . . Probably the fact that I'm a native Texan brought a little 'Texas' into it." Said Corbin about his character, "It was implied that I was somehow beholden to the Ewing clan for my job. But I was honest and I'd agonize over this thing, you know, whether or not I'd go easy on 'em. But I always decided not to."

Trivia This episode was the number 3 show for the week, finishing just 0.1 rating points behind the previous night's special episode of Dallas. ★ Director Alexander Singer, who directed such 1960s movies as Love Has Many Faces, won a 1972 Emmy for Outstanding Directorial Achievement in Drama for "The Invasion of Kevin Ireland" episode of The Bold Ones: The Lawyers.

45. "Power Play"

Written by Jeff Young; Directed by Leslie Martinson; Airdate: January 4, 1980
Guest Stars: Laura Johnson (Betty Lou); Michael Prince (Jonas Smithers); Stephanie Blackmore (Serena Wald)
Subject: Lucy's engagement.

Cast Notes Stephanie Blackmore makes her first appearance as Serena, a role she would reprise in Seasons 2, 4 through 7, 10, and 12. ★ Keenan Wynn's credit moves to the beginning of the episode.

Trivia This episode ranked number 2 in the Nielsen weekly top ten.

46. "Paternity Suit"

Written by Loraine Despres; Directed by Harry Harris; Airdate: January 11, 1980
Guest Stars: Jared Martin (Dusty); George O. Petrie (Harv); Stanley Grover (Dr. Miles); Stephen Keep (Barry Lester); Martina Deignan (Deborah Johns)
Subject: Cliff's lawsuit.

Trivia This episode was the second-most-watched show of the week. The Dukes of Hazzard was number 1. ★ Jordan Lee's wife is named Sara Lee, but in Episodes 113 and 299 she is named Evelyn. ★ Director Harry Harris, who directed episodes of Gunsmoke; The Waltons; Magnum, P.I.; and Marcus Welby, M.D., won a 1982 Emmy Award for Outstanding Direction in a Drama Series for the "To Soar and Never to Falter" episode of Fame. Said Harris of his lead star not long after this episode aired, "The temptation to have J.R. do a Machiavellian chuckle as he is about to obliterate a rival is very great. Avoid this. Larry will do it for you in a much more subtle way." ★ Leonard Katzman said that the scene in which J.R. bonds with John Ross was intended to arouse sympathy for J.R. "Among other things," Katzman said, "we needed to remind the audience how caring J.R. is, how important it was to him that it be his son, his blood, his carrying on the Ewing heir that from the first show had been mentioned—'your son.' The soft side of J.R., the love. Very, very important to keeping his character interesting and complete for the audience. Most other shows that have ever tried to do a J.R. character have done very one-note characters who just do things for plot reasons or because they're BAD. I find those people rather dull. The thing that has sustained J.R. . . . is the fact that he is so multi-faceted, that the audience knows he's capable of pain, of laughter. He's also got a lot of little boy charm about him." Arthur Bernard Lewis agreed, noting that the writers "had to find a soft spot for J.R. Otherwise, there's no vulnerability and there's no character. And this was a way of exploring his other side. He had two weaknesses: his Mama and Daddy, and his son." According to Phil Capice, "We never think of J.R. as the bad guy. . . . J.R. is too complex to simply be the antagonist. We've seen enough sides of him so that if he's not always likeable, at least he's understandable." While Hagman now claims, "I can't remember any good things [J.R.] did," Hagman, too, once recognized that J.R. was nice "in a way. He took care of his family. I mean, albeit a very difficult family and dysfunctional, to say the least, but he had values of business and family and wife—not necessarily in that order, and he tried to take care of them in his own way." Charlene Tilton attributed J.R.'s vulnerability to the actor portraying him. "As ruthless as J.R. was," she said, "he was still vulnerable, sexy, needed approval from his father, loved his son, and I think that Larry Hagman really kept J.R. the most interesting character on television for fourteen years." ★ Hagman prepared for this episode's scene with John Ross by tape-recording the scene to help with such things as body movement. Although Hagman was in "high spirits" when the scene was filmed, he blew the first take. The second take was done "with more buoyancy and not a hitch." Hagman was happy with the scene and quipped, "I'm tellin' yuh, it's a license to steal." ★ CBS received more than ten thousand positive letters in response to this episode. ★ This episode's final act remains Jacobs's favorite *Dallas* scene of all time. Said Jacobs, "To me, the best scene in *Dallas* history was after J.R. learned that his son was his. Just a private moment between J.R. and 100 million people, when he went into the bedroom and picked up the child." ★ This episode makes clear that Fern Fitzgerald's character "had taken over Stonehurst Oil from my father (who amassed the fortune). My husband, 'Seth Stone,' was a figurehead," says Fitzgerald, "but I was in charge. It was a nice surprise for me, because now I had somewhere to go, besides 'home to Seth,' as it seemed I said after every [Daughters of the Alamo] meeting! . . . It was a pleasant surprise. What woman in the 1980s was happy just being someone's wife?"

47. "Jenna's Return"

Written by Camille Marchetta; Directed by Irving J. Moore; Airdate: January 18, 1980
Special Guest Stars: Mel Ferrer (Harrison); Don Porter (Matt Devlin)

Guest Stars: Francine Tacker (Jenna); Jared Martin (Dusty)
Subject: Jenna Wade returns.

Cast Notes Don Porter played Sally Field's professor father in the TV series based on the 1959 movie *Gidget*. He died in 1997. ★ Francine Tacker takes over the role of Jenna from Morgan Fairchild. Tacker played Elizabeth Logan on *The Paper Chase*.

Trivia Weekly rating: number 8. ★ Episode writer Camille Marchetta also wrote Episode 8, which featured Jenna's first return to Dallas.

48. "Sue Ellen's Choice"

Written by Camille Marchetta; Directed by Leonard Katzman; Airdate: February 1, 1980
Guest Stars: Francine Tacker (Jenna); Jared Martin (Dusty)
Subject: Sue Ellen's marriage.

Trivia This episode was ranked number 3 for the week and earned a 42 share. ★ Leonard Katzman explained that CBS insisted that Bobby not sleep with Jenna during this storyline. "Early on," said Katzman, "when Pam and Bobby had separated [but not divorced], and he met Jenna Wade again, we were going to have . . . Bobby and Jenna Wade go to bed. [The network] said, 'No, no, no, no! Not while he and Pam are still married! It would be wrong.' And so we pulled back and realized afterwards that they were right." ★ This was the last episode written by writer Camille Marchetta, who had been with the show since the pilot. ★ Jared Martin enjoyed playing Linda Gray's romantic interest. "I loved working with her," he explains. "It spoiled me. We had a mental connection that survived the transition from scripted material to real life and back again. We used our common interests to keep the scenes fresh and edgy. We handled the on-set intimacy and the creep of notoriety about . . . Sue Ellen and Dusty [with] a kind of conspiratorial humor. We shared a mutual perspective about the show and production and set details and people we dealt with every day, and beyond the cocoon of the show we talked and shared about things happening in the real world. We were protective of each other. She was . . . intelligent and well read, curious and open. What really won my heart was her courage in pursuing what she was interested in. We created a safe place for ourselves in which to operate as two fictional characters who were intimately involved and deeply in love. She made the difficult scenes into an adventure, the boring scenes interesting and fresh. Hence the spoilage—if you get one or two working relationships like Linda in a career, you're lucky. I was lucky." As for Gray, she "adored" Jared Martin. "He was kind of the Gary Cooper cowboy of our time and wonderful to work with. He was extremely giving. We'd work on scenes together and really hone them, and that made it work, and people loved [Sue Ellen and Dusty]. . . . He was always very present, always there, in the scene. And that's a huge compliment. He was very giving and present and that's key for an actor. They have to be with you."

49. "Second Thoughts"

Written by Linda Elstadt; Directed by Irving J. Moore; Airdate: February 8, 1980
Guest Stars: Laura Johnson (Betty Lou); Chris Coffey (Professor Greg Forrester); Robert
Rockwell (Mitchell); Stephanie Blackmore (Serena)
Subject: Lucy's engagement.

Cast Notes Robert Rockwell was a TV veteran who played Jor-El, Superman's father, on the syndicated classic *The Adventures of Superman* starring George Reeves. He also played Eve Arden's love interest, Philip Boynton, on *Our Miss Brooks* and Alan Thicke's stepfather, Wally, on *Growing Pains*. He returned to *Dallas* as the minister who married Lucy and Mitch in Season 3 and Pam and Mark in Season 8. ★ Christopher Skinner, Victoria Principal's husband at the time this episode aired, plays Kettering, the student in Lucy's class who begins the discussion of Flaubert's *Madame Bovary*. Skinner and Principal met in late 1978, when Skinner, then twenty-one, first appeared on *Dallas* in an uncredited part. Explained Principal the year after they met, "He had a scene with a girlfriend of mine, and I asked who he was. She told me, and I said, 'Don't ever dance with him again.' Everyone laughed but me. . . . I thought he was a little too gorgeous." Principal and Skinner married in Las Vegas three months after they met. They divorced twenty months later.

Trivia This episode was TV's number 1 show in the weekly Nielsen ratings, the first of fifty-eight *Dallas* episodes to hit number 1 between February 8, 1980, and May 17, 1985. ★ Unlike his unemployed alter ego, Ken Kercheval put long hours in on the *Dallas* set. The producers, however, tried to cut costs by filming all of an actor's scenes consecutively, limiting the number of days the actor would be needed on the set. Like a number of *Dallas* stars, for example, Kercheval was usually needed on the set only two days a week. As a result, Kercheval felt it was sometimes too easy to learn the few scenes in the fifty-three-page scripts in which his character appeared. "It's just not that big of a deal," he said. "You don't have to be a whiz-bang to remember a page-and-a-half of dialogue. . . . I've gone to work a couple of days on *Dallas* and drove off the lot that evening and thought, 'I really walked through that thing.' But that's only happened two or three times, because the feeling is so unsatisfying. The only person you cheat is yourself. The audience probably wouldn't catch it, but I can't do that." ★ Outtakes from this episode show that Jim Davis, while filming the scene where he gives Lucy and Alan their wedding present, had problems recalling the name of Harv's law firm. Davis called the firm Smithfield & Williams, Bennett & Williams, Smithfield & Johnson, and Smithfield & Wesson. Eventually he got it right: Smithfield & Bennett. ★ This was the first of seven scripts written by *Dallas* story editor Linda Elstad, who was also a staff writer for *One Day at a Time* and *Call to Glory* (which starred *Dallas* cast members Keenan Wynn and Priscilla Pointer). Elstad died on November 21, 1997, at the age of sixty-five.

50. "Divorce—Ewing Style"

Written by Leonard Katzman; Directed by Leonard Katzman; Airdate: February 15, 1980
Special Guest Star: Don Porter (Matt)
Guest Stars: Barry Corbin (Fenton); Jeff Cooper (Dr. Elby); Stephanie Blackmore (Serena)
Subject: Sue Ellen and J.R. fight.

Cast Notes Tom Fuller is played by John Christy Ewing, the only real Ewing to ever appear on *Dallas*. Ewing also appeared in the 1983 movie *My Favorite Year* as well as on such TV series as *Homefront; Murder, She Wrote; L.A. Law*; and *St. Elsewhere*.

Trivia This episode was TV's most-watched show of the week, finishing number 1 with a 31.1 rating and a 49 share. ★ Mary Crosby felt Kristin "wants to be in a position where she doesn't have to do anything for anybody but Kristin. I think money is terribly important to her. Control—control over people and their lives in order to get control of hers, in terms of getting exactly what she wants out of life. She'll do just about anything to get it." ★ Barry Corbin's second appearance on *Dallas*, like his first, gave him a scene with Barbara Bel Geddes and Jim Davis, who Barry says "were very nice, friendly people who made me feel right at home."

51. "Jock's Trial" (Part One)

Written by Arthur Bernard Lewis; Directed by Irving J. Moore; Airdate: February 22, 1980
Special Guest Star: Don Porter (Matt)
Guest Stars: Barry Corbin (Fenton); Nicholas Coster (Sloane); Jeff Cooper (Dr. Elby);
Chris Coffey (Greg Forrester)
Subject: Jock's arrest.

Cast Notes Nicholas Coster takes over the role of Assistant District Attorney Sloane.

Trivia This episode ranked number 16 for the week with a 36 share when it first aired. CBS reran the episode along with "Jock's Trial" (Part Two) on October 31, 1980, as part of the network's "*Dallas* Week," capitalizing on the "Who Shot J.R.?" craze. The rerun of the two-hour "Jock's Trial" outscored its original airing, earning a 40 share and 9th place finish. ★ Dusty's parents are referred to in this episode, but Episode 164 establishes that Clayton's wife has been dead for twenty years.

52. "Jock's Trial" (Part Two)

Written by Arthur Bernard Lewis; Directed by Irving J. Moore; Airdate: February 29, 1980
Special Guest Star: Don Porter (Matt)
Guest Stars: Stephen Elliott (Scotty Demarest); Nicholas Coster (Sloane); William Watson (Hutch McKinney); Barry Corbin (Fenton); John Zaremba (Dr. Danvers); George O. Petrie (Harv); Sarah Cunningham (Aunt Maggie)
Subject: Digger's confession.

Cast Notes Victoria Principal plays her character's mother, Rebecca, in this episode. Principal recalls that "it was my idea to play Pam's mother in the 1940s flashback scenes. I was worried that the writers and producers of *Dallas* would find this a little too ambitious, but to my delight, Lenny Katzman concurred and I had a delicious time playing my mother." ★ Stephen Elliott makes the first of fourteen appearances as criminal defense attorney Scotty Demarest, who also appears in Seasons 7 and 9. Elliott was a veteran stage actor who appeared in *The Tempest* and *Gypsy* and was nominated for a Tony Award for his role in *Marat-Sade*. He also appeared in the movies *Arthur* and *Beverly Hills Cop* and on TV's *Chicago Hope* as Judge Harold Aldrick and *Falcon Crest* as Jane Wyman's ex-husband. Elliott got the role of Scotty after reading for Leonard Katzman, and he knew Barbara Bel Geddes from their acting days in New York. Around the time he filmed his scenes for this episode, Elliott was a newlywed: on January 1, 1980, he married future *Dallas* cast member Alice Hirson, who would debut as Mavis Anderson in Season 5. Elliott met Hirson while doing a play in New York in 1964. He died of congestive heart failure on May 21, 2005, at the age of eighty-six.

Trivia This episode improved on the prior week's ratings. It came in at number 6 for the week, with a 45 share. ★ Sepia-toned colors are used during the flashbacks. ★ Cliff visits Digger's grave in Episodes 54 and 321. ★ The week after this episode aired, a *Dallas* writer anonymously confirmed Hagman's acting abilities to *TV Guide*, saying, "I mean, who's going to believe this stuff without Larry to make it work? He is also the best actor. No matter how far-out the script, he never fools with the reality of the character." ★ This episode reveals the name of Miss Ellie's father: Aaron, the same name as creator David Jacobs's son.

53. "Wheeler Dealer"

Written by Barbara Searles; Directed by Alexander Singer; Airdate: March 14, 1980
Guest Stars: Dennis Patrick (Vaughan); Lesley Woods (Amanda Lewis Ewing); Ron Hayes (Hank Johnson); Jeff Cooper (Dr. Elby); Stephanie Blackmore (Serena); Sarah Cunningham (Aunt Maggie); Geoffrey Scott (Dusty look-alike)
Subject: J.R.'s deals.

Cast Notes Ed Kenney makes his only appearance as Seth Stone, a role played by Kenneth White in Season 1. Kenney made several appearances on *Alice*, and was also seen on *Flamingo Road* and *Scarecrow and Mrs. King* and as Uncle Chauncy in the Demi Moore movie *The Butcher's Wife*. Kenney was about fifty years old at the time he played Stone and had just gotten back into acting. He had a costarring role as a senator in Episode 28 of *Dallas* and casting director Irene Mariano liked Kenney's first episode enough that she put him on her list of "preferred actors." A year later, Mariano cast Kenney as Seth Stone. Kenney "remember[s] filming the scene with Larry Hagman and the other cartel members." As they played the scene, director Alexander Singer told Kenney, "'Keep doing what you're doing,' and my character seemed to speak for all of the other [cartel members]." Kenney thought the scene worked so well that he looked forward to additional work playing Stone, unaware that his character would not survive Episode 54. ★ Geoffrey Scott, who plays a man Sue Ellen mistakes for Dusty, played Linda Evans's ex-husband, Mark Jennings, on *Dynasty*.

Trivia This episode finished the week at number 6. When CBS re-ran it on Thursday, November 6, 1980, as a prelude to the Season 3 premiere, it came in at number 9. It was also number 9 when CBS re-ran it on September 12, 1980, during an actors' strike. ★ This episode's scenes between J.R. and Kristin are among Mary Crosby's favorites. She explains, "My favorite scenes were any that I did with Larry. They were so sordid and fun. They were exciting and completely my cup of tea." ★ Cliff's contract is dated 1939, but in *The Early Years*, Digger's and Jock's partnership ended in 1934. Episodes 172, 176–77, and 179 in Season 6 establish that the feud dates back to 1930. ★ Said Larry Hagman about J.R. in a *TV Guide* profile that was published the week before this episode aired, "Oh, he's such a miserable crud, I love him. I really do." A few years later, Hagman said, "I admire old J.R. Ewing. He's the most unmitigated SOB on TV. Nobody calls him Junior except his pappy. . . . J.R. isn't an evil man; he thinks he's doing the right things."

54. "A House Divided"

Written by Rena Down; Directed by Irving J. Moore; Airdate: March 21, 1980
Guest Stars: Dennis Patrick (Vaughan); Ron Hayes (Hank Johnson); Jeff Cooper (Dr. Elby); Chris Coffey (Greg Forrester)
Subject: J.R. is shot.

Trivia This episode was the number 1 show of the week, and earned a 32.7 rating and 52 share. It was the highest-rated regular episode of a series in its normal time-slot for the entire 1979–80 season. It was seen by 50 million viewers domestically and 250 million viewers worldwide, making it second only to the Super Bowl as the season's most-watched program. CBS re-ran this episode in the 9:00 p.m. slot on November 7, 1980, immediately before the Season 3 premiere. In that airing, this episode earned a 31.8 rating and 50 share to finish the week at number 4. ★ Larry Hagman watched this episode at home, as he did all episodes of *Dallas*. ★ Fred W. Berger was nominated for an America Cinema Editors "Eddie Award" for Best Edited Episode from a Television Series for this episode. ★ Leonard Katzman's original thought was to have J.R. shot and fall to the floor as he swiveled around in his office chair to face a late-night intruder. When this episode was filmed, however, Katzman opted to have J.R. shot while walking out of his office into the reception area. Katzman used his original idea four years later when Bobby was shot in the Season 6 cliff-hanger. ★ Katzman reflected that the "most famous ending in television [is] the shooting of J.R., which was not supposed to be the end of our year. The year was going to end two shows sooner, at the funeral when Pam found out she wasn't Digger's daughter, and she could have children and Cliff swore his revenge and all that stuff. Well, the network wanted two more shows, . . . and we said . . . 'Let's shoot J.R.!' . . . After we decided that, without knowing who did it—

at that point we had no idea—we had to go back and construct storylines that would lead to Mary Crosby, to Randy Powell, to Jordan Lee, to Fern Fitzgerald, Don Starr, so that by the time he was shot there would be an acceptable list of possible suspects." Phil Capice recalled, "As *Dallas* was developing, there seemed to be a special audience fascination with J.R., this guy they hated and loved. We kept getting letters asking, 'When is J.R. going to get his?' It seemed like a good idea to explore. We never really considered killing him, but we talked about several ways in which near death could occur and make sense." ★ Larry Hagman addressed his future with *Dallas* in a *TV Guide* interview that was published almost a month after this episode aired. Hagman stated then that he didn't have "the slightest idea" who shot J.R. "The way I have been treating people, it could be anyone. The writers are going to decide that this summer. Then, once they do, they are going to sign an oath not to tell." When asked about the rumors that he was leaving the show, he replied, "I'd be crazy to leave that show." Nevertheless, Hagman risked that very thing. Two months after that *TV Guide* interview, in June 1980, he left the country in the first move of his high-stakes gamble to renegotiate his contract. Meanwhile, Hagman told *People* magazine, "Whether I live or die will depend upon my contract negotiations. The producers figure if I demand too much money, then it's the hell with you, you SOB. Then I'm surely dead next season. Something like this happens only every ten or twenty years in an actor's life, and I mean to cash in on it." ★ Fern Fitzgerald "wasn't watching the show the night 'J.R.' got shot, which was the same night 'Seth' committed suicide. I was at my home hosting a dinner party. My husband in real life, Tom Sweet, was at work. . . . One of my friends . . . Joan Lancaster [who played cartel member Andy Bradley's wife Linda], called and said, 'Your husband just committed suicide!' Since I wasn't watching *Dallas*, you can imagine how stunned I was. Once Joan realized I didn't know what she was talking about, she said, 'I'm sorry, aren't you watching *Dallas?*' So, not only did I miss the episode, . . . I didn't get to see who played 'Seth Stone!'" ★ Meanwhile, Ed Kenney, the actor who played the late Seth Stone, also missed the episode. Kenney explains, "I knew of the 'Who Shot J.R.?' plot, but I never learned that Seth killed himself" or that Seth's wife was a suspect in the shooting as a result. Needless to say, Kenney "never heard from them about coming back on. About a year later, I saw [casting director] Irene Mariano at the studio, in the commissary, and I told her, 'I thought you said I was one of your preferred actors?!' And she told me Seth Stone had killed himself right after my scenes! She told me, 'I never would have cast you as Seth if I had known he was going to hang himself!' . . . Later I learned that his widow and the other cartel members had long runs on the show!" ★ According to Mary Crosby, James L. Brown, who played McSween, had difficulty threatening to arrest Crosby's character for prostitution. Crosby recalled that Brown was "a sweet old man who knew my father—and he had such trouble. He said, 'I can't say these things to Bing Crosby's daughter!'" ★ This episode includes Patrick Duffy's favorite scene with Barbara Bel Geddes. "I saw [this episode] again on the Soap Network and remembered how wonderful the goodbye scene was with Barbara," says Duffy. "She always brought out the very best in all who worked with her. You actually ended up better than even you thought you could be." ★ J.R. had been shot once before (by the Owenses in Season 2) and was shot three more times (by B. D. Calhoun in Season 9, Sue Ellen in Season 10, and Peter Ellington in *War of the Ewings*) during *Dallas*'s run. ★ When *Time* magazine did a cover story on the "Who Shot J.R.?" phenomenon in the summer of 1980, writer Richard Corliss declared that *Dallas* "offer[s] the rarest of series commodities—narrative surprise and character change. . . . *Dallas* does well what American commercial television does best: present the viewer with a family of characters so appealing in their hopes, their failings, their resilience that they will be invited back into the living room week after week. The Ewings may be scoundrels and wastrels, but they are good company. . . . Beneath the glamorous settings and soap-opera situations . . . is a solid, suggestive foundation of conflicting themes and characters. . . . At the hub of virtually every conflict in *Dallas* is that human oil slick, J.R. . . . [He] and Hagman deserve the country's gratitude for lighting up Friday nights with that barracuda smile."

Part II

PHENOMENON

SEASON 3
1980–81—"Who Done It?"

ONCE J.R. WAS SHOT AND the *Dallas* cast and crew were dismissed for their spring 1980 hiatus, the writers set out to draft the Season 3 scripts that would resolve the whodunit. As Leonard Katzman recounted later that summer, "We started eliminating and eliminating until we found the person we wanted." New storylines were quickly written as well, in the hope that the audience that tuned in to see the mystery solved would stay with the show after the assailant's identity was revealed. Phil Capice said at the time, "The ripple effect from the revelation will be minimal. We'll move on to other things quite quickly." Larry Hagman, however, set out to use his growing celebrity to demand a new contract, causing a temporary halt to the producers' planning for the new season. While the furor over J.R.'s shooting put Hagman in the position to "go for broke"—Hagman, in an effort to make up for the royalties he never received for *I Dream of Jeannie* a decade earlier, demanded a huge salary increase, directing assignments and a role in deciding the course of the show—it also raised the possibility that the show would continue without him.

When it was announced that the on-location shoot would begin at Duncan Acres on June 12, 1980, Hagman decided to call the producers' bluff; he left the country three days earlier, on June 9. Even before J.R. was shot, Hagman told a *TV Guide* interviewer, "You seldom get a hit of this magnitude in your life. I've had two. I'm not rich yet. I just think I'm ready." Hagman's original *Dallas* contract gave him $7,500 per episode. Since then, Hagman, noting that he "learned more than my lines from J.R.," had renegotiated his contract twice. On one occasion, he demanded an RV equipped with a bathroom, phone, and driver to replace his dressing room, which he thought looked like "a little wooden shack in the black hole of Calcutta." Lorimar balked, saying, "Well, Larry, there's twelve other stars, and if you get one, they'll all want one too." Hagman offered to withdraw the request in exchange for an additional $250,000, and the producers agreed.

By the show's second season, Hagman was making $25,000 per episode. Once J.R. was shot, however, Hagman had significantly more negotiating leverage, since "J.R. was the most famous person in the world at that time. And so I surprised them: I went to England and wouldn't take their calls. Every time they made an offer to my agents, I'd say, 'Let's go higher.' I bought a white Stetson for everybody at William Morris who was representing me. I told them: 'Wear the Stetsons to all the meetings—or don't represent me.'" Patrick Duffy, who thought that it was appropriate that Hagman considered himself "the dog pulling the sled," recalled that, "So, now there was an additional amount of PR and fervor. And not only 'Who Shot J.R.?' but 'Would J.R. Return? Would Larry come back?'" Hagman acknowledged that the "shooting of J.R. was a double-edged sword: it gave my producers and the CBS bosses a perfect way to get rid of me in case my 'demands' got out of hand."

Hagman knew he was "playing a dangerous game" when he and his agents met on May 12 for a "council of war." Hagman's "good sense told me that to let J.R. die would be throwing away one of the most inspired bits of electronic hyperbole since NBC refused to allow Barbara Eden to show her naval in *I Dream of Jeannie*. I was betting they wouldn't let J.R. expire. But I had to be prepared to go all the way. . . . If I lost, I could find myself out of the business permanently." Thus, at the suggestion of his publicist, who thought Hagman should take advantage of the "J.R. mystique," Hagman flew to London on June 9. While he was gone, his agents carried out negotiations on his behalf. Hagman was at Madame Tussaud's wax museum on June 12 being measured for his wax statue when the cast and crew began filming in Dallas, where the scripts were kept "very hush-hush" and the actors were kept in the dark about the culprit's identity. Pages of key scenes were missing and scripts were distributed on a "need to know" and "for your eyes only" basis. In Hagman's absence, rumors ran rampant that he was in hiding, that he was holding out until his demands were met, and that no one knew where he could be reached. Katzman had the crew shoot around Hagman, using doubles in the over-the-shoulder shots until Hagman returned—or was replaced.

Meanwhile, negotiations with Hagman's agents continued. The "heavy-duty dickering" began on June 17 and continued for days. By June 20, a resolution looked possible. In the June 21 issue of *TV Guide*, a spokesman for Hagman insisted that "a lot has happened to Larry since the show began and his new contract is very complicated. Salary is not the issue. We are talking about such things as merchandising and who owns the name J.R. Everything should be settled shortly."

While in London, Hagman wondered about his cast and crew, and he turned to Patrick Duffy for updates. Recalled Duffy, " I talked with him several times on the phone when he was in hiding and he'd say, 'What's going on?' And I'd say, 'Go for it, buddy.'" The days passed slowly for Duffy and his castmates, who were on pins and needles waiting for any tidbit of news about Hagman's situation. His costars wanted Hagman back and rooted for him against "the suits" from Lorimar and CBS. They did not believe rumors indicating that other actors, like Robert Culp of *I Spy* fame, were being considered to replace him.

Duffy explained that "even though the studio said, 'Oh, we're going to bring in . . . this actor or that actor,' . . . we all knew there's nobody [else that] can do that [role]." And, Duffy said, "the network . . . even knew it. They had to pony up. They had to. . . . That show was popular and making an incredible amount of revenue for the network." Despite Lorimar's claim that it could readily explain Hagman's replacement by having J.R. badly disfigured in an ambulance wreck en route to the hospital, Hagman, too, "knew they couldn't do it. I was too hot and the show was too hot." Hagman also knew Katzman's "sensibility. He was too intelligent to let J.R. die. Even as the studio played hardball by floating rumors about possible new J.R.'s, I believed everything would work out." Hagman listened to the advice of his friend Carroll O'Connor, who had become a pop icon himself as *All in the Family*'s Archie Bunker a few years earlier. O'Connor told Hagman, "Never ask for one more dollar than they're prepared to pay, not one."

On June 21, after the cast and crew had toiled in the hot Dallas sun for almost ten days alongside rumors, gossip, and worries, and with his negotiations almost concluded, Hagman left England and went to a friend's home in the Bahamas. Hagman wanted to be "close enough to Dallas to get on the set within hours of consummating a deal." Duffy, who found Hagman "a consummate professional," recalled, "when that contract in fact was done, he wanted to be able to report to work the next morning. And so he sort of creeped in the back door to get as close to Texas . . . as possible." Eventually, as the world soon learned, Lorimar agreed to pay Hagman a whopping $100,000 per episode, and Hagman, in his inimitable way, thought it was money well spent. "Of course I was worth it," he said years later. "We went on for eleven more years. I mean, everybody did rather well." Even at the time, Hagman thought the offer was fair, explaining that "you have to realize I'm going to be forty-nine soon, and this is my fourth series. It's not going to last forever, and I hope to sit out the next down period with a certain equanimity." Two years later, Hagman told a reporter, "I fight for every cent I've got, but I don't go back on promises. When I renegotiated with Lorimar two years ago, I told them I would not come back with my hat in hand asking for more, and I haven't. Actors have to have self-respect, and they can't always be looking for it from other people."

Duffy was not the only cast member who felt that Hagman's good fortune was deserved. Susan Howard, for example, who was under contract at Screen Gems in the 1960s and appeared in an episode of *I Dream of Jeannie*, thought Hagman was "one of the finest actors that I've ever seen. . . . I think he really got ripped off in *Jeannie* and this [contract renegotiation] was a redemption. And it was an opportunity for all the things he had hoped and dreamed for." Hagman's success may also have helped the rest of the cast. By the time the whodunit was resolved, it was reported that Linda Gray's salary had jumped to $50,000 per episode; only one year earlier, Gray, like Victoria Principal, was making $10,000 per episode. There were salary raises for all of the cast members, and they were provided with air-conditioned motor homes for on-location shoots.

Hagman spent June 22 on the phone in final negotiations and, still in the Bahamas, celebrated that night at a casino with actor Richard Harris. Hagman made it to the set in Dallas the very next day. He returned to the production victoriously, in a spectacular helicopter touchdown by the Southfork pool, arriving to the enthusiastic applause of the entire cast and crew. Hagman later said that, upon his return, he went on to give *Dallas* what he thought was its "best season" ever. Throughout the years there would be many long contract negotiations, but at the time the crew felt that Hagman had taken on Goliath and won.

In the meantime, the "Who Shot J.R.?" craze got so big that, by August, *Dallas* even made the cover of *Time* magazine. The cover illustration featured J.R. and several of the leading suspects, including Pam, Bobby, Sue Ellen, Cliff Barnes, Kristin, and businessman Vaughan Leland. *Time* recounted that the whodunit spawned

> millions of *Dallas* T-shirts, bumper stickers, [and] . . . J.R. novelty records. . . . Politicians have climbed on the bandwagon too. Jimmy Carter, at a Dallas fund raiser, confessed with a grin: 'I came to Dallas to find out confidentially who shot J.R.' . . . At the Republican convention, Reaganites distributed buttons that read A DEMOCRAT SHOT J.R. . . . In Johannesburg, . . . Cabinet ministers refuse speaking engagements [when *Dallas* airs] on Tuesday nights. . . . [In England,] when the BBC broadcast last season's final episode, normally congested roads were clear and pubs empty as 30 million Britons (more than half of the U.K.'s population) stayed home to watch J.R. get his.

The editor of Britain's *Punch* magazine wrote that *Dallas* "has us [British] by the minds, the hearts and the throats; it empties our pubs and our streets; it has taken us over." The University of Texas even added to its curriculum a course called "The Making of *Dallas*." As for critical acclaim, the show was recognized when the 1980 Emmy Award nominations were announced while the company was filming at Duncan Acres. *Dallas* was nominated as Outstanding Drama Series for the first time, and Bel Geddes received her second nomination as Outstanding Lead Actress in a Drama Series. Hagman received his first nomination for Outstanding Lead Actor in a Drama Series, and Bruce Broughton was nominated for Outstanding Music Composition for the episode entitled "The Lost Child." When the awards were presented on September 7, 1980, *Dallas* lost to *Hill Street Blues* and Hagman lost to Ed Asner of *Lou Grant*. Broughton lost as well, but Bel Geddes won, becoming the only *Dallas* cast member ever to win an Emmy for acting on the show. *Dallas* also won the 1980 People's Choice Award for Best TV Show, the first of eight People's Choice Awards the show won over the course of its run.

Neither Bel Geddes nor any of the *Dallas* cast or crew attended the 1980 Emmy Awards, however. By the time the awards were presented in September, the on-location shoot in Dallas had been completed, and the company had returned to Los Angeles to begin filming on the permanent sets at MGM Studios in Culver City. But before the actors ever made it to the Southfork soundstages, the Screen Actors Guild went on a labor strike against the Producers Alliance, and the entire film and television industry was suddenly and indefinitely shut down. Because of the strike, there was an industry-wide boycott of the Emmy Awards. The only actor present to pick up his Emmy was Powers Booth, who starred in the title role in the made-for-TV movie *Guyana Tragedy: The Story of Jim Jones*.

The Guild went on strike because producers were offering very small residual benefits for broadcasts in the burgeoning cable television industry. The producers took the position that cable TV would never attract the viewership that network television did, and thus the actors were not entitled to larger residuals. The Screen Actors Guild disagreed, and was resolved not to give in to the producers' position. So, after surviving the delay and drama caused by Hagman's walk-out, the *Dallas* company—and their long-suffering fans—were now faced with more uncertainty over the new season. The strike was one of the longest in the history of the film industry and caused inestimable hardship on thousands of studio technicians, support personnel, and actors.

During the strike, members of the *Dallas* cast joined their fellow actors at organized rallies at the major studios, where they protested against the producers' unwillingness to negotiate. The entire SAG membership was in solidarity on this issue, and it was a fight to the bitter end. Weeks went by without movement on either side, followed by talks that invariably broke down without hope of a compromise or resolution. The strike caused the production of *Dallas*, like that of all shows, to be suspended for two months. Duffy commented, "The only thing that didn't shut down was the panic and fever about the answer to the question of 'Who Shot J.R.?'" Katzman admitted that he was worried about sustaining interest in the cliff-hanger throughout the summer break and the fall actors' strike. "When you do a cliff-hanger," he said, "people can stay with it or just say, 'Forget it.' We worried terribly about the actors' strike—the fear of losing our momentum with so many reruns."

As the additional weeks of waiting ticked by, the J.R. phenomenon took on a new dimension when the British tabloids, led by the *Daily Mirror*, ran contests on "Who Shot J.R.?" Bookies in Las Vegas also took odds on the culprit's identity. The character of Dusty Farlow, Sue Ellen's lover who was thought dead, became the best bet, as odds favored him at 2-to-1. Sue Ellen was next at 3-to-1, followed by her sister, Kristin, at 4-to-1, Cliff Barnes and Alan Beam at 7-to-1, Bobby, Pam and Miss Ellie at 12-to-1, and Jock at 14-to-1. *People* magazine conducted its own poll, asking readers, "Whodunit?" The winner was Dusty, with 21 percent of the vote, followed by Kristin (14 percent), Vaughan Leland (13 percent), Sue Ellen (8 percent), Miss Ellie (7 percent), Lucy and Alan Beam (tied at 5 percent), Cliff Barnes (4 percent), Dr. Elby and Jock (tied at 3 percent), and Bobby and even J.R. himself (tied at 2 percent). Most lists of suspects also included widow Marilee Stone, whom *Newsweek* called the best long-shot bet. Fern Fitzgerald, who played Marilee, "was hoping I hadn't 'done it,' because I thought they'd lock me up, throw away the key and I'd be off the show." The fascination with the whodunit had now become the world's favorite parlor game, and international magazines and television and radio shows were clamoring for Hagman and other cast members for cover shots, guest appearances and interviews—especially so cast members could be pressed to divulge the answer to the question at hand.

At the time, the cast members dutifully claimed not to know who shot J.R. For example, Linda Gray told an interviewer that she wondered if she shot J.R., and called the producers during the summer hiatus to see if she was the one. "We wouldn't tell you even if you did," they told her, and she claimed that she had to keep watching just like other *Dallas* fans. Gray also said that she and other cast members received blank script pages to keep them in the dark. Gray described filming a scene before which "producer/director Leonard Katzman whispered to me on the set, 'Give an evil look over there—just look evil!' 'At whom?' I asked. 'I don't even know what the evil look is for!'" Ken Kercheval said he "didn't know [and] didn't want to know." Kercheval claimed he did not want the burden of knowing the secret, and felt that the "audience wants to know . . . but they love not knowing." Kercheval also made clear that he hoped to be the perpetrator because he would "be an instant hero around the country." Mary Crosby claimed that she learned the outcome the night the revelation episode aired. Time reported that only about forty people, comprised of a select group of producers, story editors, and executives at Lorimar and CBS, knew the culprit. Leonard Katzman told *TV Guide* that he kept the secret by withholding certain parts of the script that later went directly from the typewriter to the cast on the day of filming. *Dallas* biographer Suzy Kalter wrote that the cast did not find out whodunit until a special dinner and screening held the night the revelation episode aired.

Years later, however, some cast members acknowledged that they were in on the secret earlier than viewers were. For example, Hagman admitted in 1988 that "I knew it was Kristin . . . because I'd seen the final cut [before it aired]." Linda Gray also claimed she knew whodunit, and almost gave the secret away by confirming on national television that one of her children had correctly guessed the identity of the perpetrator. Shortly before the revelation episode aired, Gray appeared on the ABC morning show *Good Morning America*. "They said, 'Do your children know?'" Gray recalled, "And I said, 'No, they don't know, but one of them guessed.' And at that moment my eyes glazed over and I thought, 'Oh my God. What have I just said?' So I called home and I said, 'If anybody from the press calls you, don't say anything!'" Mary Crosby recently acknowledged that "quite a lot of the cast had a fairly good idea" and that she herself "had a pretty good idea that it was me" by the time various cast members were filmed pulling the trigger before production ended for Season 2 early in 1980. "The producers knew," recalls Crosby, "and a very small inner circle around them. Someone from the production office came up to me and suggested I get a good publicist, saying, 'Make sure you're taken care of.' It was very subtle but really clear. And this was before we went on hiatus, so I knew it was me before I was filmed shooting him."

Regardless of when the cast knew whodunit, Lorimar and CBS were successful in stoking interest in the mystery without giving anything away. Katzman told *People* magazine, "The assailant will be someone that the audience has seen or heard about. It won't be somebody that J.R. discovered robbing the Ewing office." Hagman joked that the perpetrator was his *I Dream of Jeannie* costar, Barbara Eden, which became a self-fulfilling prophecy in a way when Eden joined the cast in *Dallas*'s thirteenth and final season as yet another scorned lover seeking revenge on J.R.; instead of shooting him, she bought Ewing Oil out from under him. CBS news' Dan Rather guessed that the assailant would not be a woman, because Texas women stand by their men. Republican Presidential candidate George Bush knew that he could not have done it, saying, "On the day J.R. was shot I was getting killed in New Hampshire."

A Lorimar insider told *TV Guide* that scripts were being written in a way to conceal the perpetrator's identity until airtime. Katzman admitted, "The script works like a Chinese puzzle. The pieces can be arranged at random to alter the outcome, perhaps without even the actors knowing. They will know what scenes they shot, but not necessarily which ones will be used. Believe me, not even James Bond could solve this case." Tabloids and mainstream news outlets claimed that incomplete scripts were issued and decoy scenes were filmed in order to safeguard the secret. *People* magazine reported that the revelation script was stolen from Lorimar's offices but was returned, unpublished, by the publisher of the *Herald-Examiner*, a Los Angeles newspaper. Katzman vowed, "We're going to do everything in our power to keep the audience guessing until the show airs."

The worldwide obsession with the whodunit surprised most of the cast, including at least one who believed the sensation would not involve him since his character apparently died before J.R. was shot. After Dusty Farlow seemed to perish in a plane crash late in Season 2, Jared Martin said,

> [I] left Hollywood and was living in a basement apartment on Queens Boulevard in New York so I could study at Lee Strasburg's master class on 15th Street near Union Square. . . . About that time I got an odd request to be photographed for *People* magazine. I thought they had the wrong guy. We went into Central Park and all the time I'm asking the publicist 'why me?' But she doesn't really know. So I pose before the Wollman Skating Rink in my threadbare winter jacket with a big smile on my face as if I'm looking into the future. But no one really knew what was going on. A few days later someone sent me a clipping of the front page of a London tabloid—the *Daily Mail* or *Telegraph*. Dusty Farlow was on the front page—he'd won the most votes as the most likely suspect in a national 'Who Shot JR?' contest. Britain was aflame with *Dallas* fever and Dusty was a number-one poster boy.

Mary Crosby also recalls being in England. "If it was crazy here," she said, "it was insane there. I was offered 500,000 pounds by a man who sold munitions to

Third World countries if I told him who'd done it. . . . The pressure makes it that much more desirable to keep it quiet; the more they wanted to know, the more successful we were in keeping our mouths shut." Hagman was also offered money for the secret when he was in England that summer. Ken Kercheval wished he had a nickel for every time he was asked "Who Shot J.R.?" and Gray commiserated, "By the end of the summer you thought, 'Oh my God. If one more person asks me that I might have to shoot them!'"

Victoria Principal remembered flying back to Dallas from a one-day vacation in L.A. and hearing the pilot come over the intercom and threaten not to land the plane unless she revealed who did it. According to one report, the wife of a *Dallas* crew member tape-recorded her husband at night in case he talked in his sleep. Even a former president of the United States tried to use his authority to find out the secret. *Dallas* writer David Paulsen recalled Jim Davis telephoning Leonard about the matter. "Jim Davis [said,] 'Listen, I'm on the [golf] links with former President Ford, and he'd like to know who shot J.R.' And Len said, 'Well, you know I can't tell you that.' And there was a minute of silence and muffled conversation. And Jim Davis got back on the phone and he said, 'He says he used to be president of the United States. He can keep a secret.' They never told him!"

The Screen Actors Guild strike ended on October 23, 1980. There was a collective sigh of relief among the *Dallas* company when the settlement was announced. The producers scrambled to assemble the crew and get *Dallas* back into production. The season's first few episodes were finished at a frantic pace, and the show's third season premiered on Friday, November 7, 1980, in the midst of a special "*Dallas* Week" promoted by CBS. Between Sunday, November 2, and Sunday, November 9, CBS aired six hours of *Dallas*: the final four episodes of Season 2 and the first two episodes of Season 3. The third and fourth episodes of the new season aired in the regular Friday night timeslot on November 14 and November 21. As each of the season's new episodes aired, the list of suspects grew shorter. Three days before the November 21 resolution episode aired, Hagman traveled to London to perform with his mother, Mary Martin, at a concert in honor of the Queen Mother's eightieth birthday. Hagman and his mother performed "Honey Bun" from *South Pacific*, one of Martin's signature shows. After the show, Hagman got to meet the Queen Mother, who told him, "Now I want you to tell me, young man, who shot J.R.?" Even though by then Hagman had seen the final cut and knew the shooter's identity, he remained strong, telling the Queen Mother, "Not even for you, ma'am."

Finally, on Friday, November 21, 1980, millions of viewers worldwide gathered to find out the answer to the mystery. As the moment of truth arrived, businesses in South Africa closed and the Turkish parliament called a recess. For years to come, the stars of *Dallas* would meet people who would recount exactly where they were and what they were doing when they watched the long-awaited episode entitled, "Who Done It?" Duffy recalled being told about a friend who "was in an airplane and the pilot on the airplane . . . [announced the outcome]. And the airplane went—pandemonium. Went nuts! And they gave free drinks. They had a party the whole rest of the flight." Steve Kanaly recalls being told about a crew of British submariners at sea in the mid-Atlantic who were radioed the solution to the mystery.

Kanaly was at least one cast member who "did not have the faintest idea who would be the chosen one, and I was relieved to not have to live with the knowledge." He believed that other cast members were similarly kept in the dark by Katzman's "masterful job of concealing the plot resolution . . . in one of the best-kept secrets in the history of television." Kanaly and his wife joined the *Dallas* cast and producers at Chasen's Restaurant in Beverly Hills for an extravagant "revelation" party while the episode aired. His table included the top brass from Lorimar, who had evidently shared the secret with their wives. Kanaly commented politely, "Isn't it fantastic? The whole world is on the edge of their seats wondering who did it!" The executives' wives giggled and said, "Isn't Steve cute, acting as if he doesn't know!"

The crowd at Chasen's, like the rest of the world, watched "Who Done It?" and let out a cheer in the show's final seconds, when it was finally revealed that it was Kristin who shot J.R. Approximately 350 million people in over 57 countries tuned in to watch television history in the making, and the episode became the most watched show in the history of television up to that time. Kanaly recalls that the cast and crew celebrated "the genius of Leonard Katzman, and gave thanks to the television gods . . . while consuming many bottles of the finest champagne." At the party, Mary Crosby joked, "It's nice to leave the series with a bang."

Time magazine's review of "Who Done It?" was typical of the critical acclaim the mystery had achieved:

> Of course shedunit. The coed vamp with a mean streak as deep as her cleavage. The peddler of her own educated flesh. The Mata Hari of Ewing Oil. The counterspy . . . scheming sister . . . seducer. . . . What apter justice? The person who fired the shots heard round the world was the female J.R., Kristin Shepard. The surprise is that they did it: the producers and writers of *Dallas*. They created the world's largest soap bubble and, in the eight months between the shooting . . . and the revelation Friday night, somehow kept it from bursting. . . . In fact, Kristin was always the ideal perpetrator. As Sue Ellen's sweet sister and J.R.'s conniving mistress, she was in the family but not of it; her purging from *Dallas* would set off enough shock waves to surprise the unwary viewer without destroying the basic family unit.

Newsweek wrote:

> In terms of artistry and innovation, the series is unrefined Texas crude. The plots are thick as Pamela Ewing's lipstick, and they have pivoted on the moldiest of melodramatic contrivances . . . [but] they make us care

about what will happen to them next. That is no small achievement. *Dallas* may be trash, but is splendidly crafted trash, rich with character development and surprise, exuberant with hiss-along evil. . . . What makes such rascality so irresistible is the way Larry Hagman, with his cherubic baby blues and ain't-I-naughty grin, plays against the character.

As a result of the revelation episode's astronomical ratings, *Dallas* hit number 1 in the ratings and remained the highest- or second-highest-rated show on television for a half a decade. *Dallas* was the number 1 show on nineteen of the twenty-three times it aired original episodes during the 1980–81 season, and the remaining four episodes hit number 2. Regardless of its future laurels, however, *Dallas* would always be remembered for its famous whodunit. Patrick Duffy predicted that the phrase "Who Shot J.R.?" "will always live," and he appears to have been correct. Indeed, the whodunit was recently chosen as one of the top ten greatest milestones in TV history by voters in an industry poll, alongside President Kennedy's funeral and the 1969 *Apollo* moon landing, and *Texas Monthly* magazine cited the shooting of J.R. as one of the 150 most important events in Texas history in a 1986 issue celebrating the state's sesquicentennial.

In the wake of the "Who Shot J.R.?" triumph, *Dallas* received four Golden Globe nominations, one for Best Drama and three for acting, for Barbara Bel Geddes, Larry Hagman, and Linda Gray. *Dallas*, however, was shut out at the Golden Globes ceremony by *Shogun*. When the yearly Nielsen ratings were tabulated in the spring of 1981, *Dallas* won its first crown as TV's number 1 show, garnering a whopping 34.5 share. That spring, Katzman also contemplated how to out-do himself. He realized that his writers would have to come up with a season-ending cliff-hanger as sensational as J.R.'s shooting. But by then, shooting J.R. had "turned into a monster." Katzman called the shooting, in "television terms, . . . the equivalent of Columbus discovering America—except he didn't have to go out again the next year and find another country. It becomes very difficult to come up with cliffhangers that will tantalize the audience but that they won't outguess you on."

Ultimately, Leonard and the writers settled on a variation of sorts. They decided that the cliff-hanger would feature J.R. in another whodunit—but one that left the audience wondering who the victim was instead of who the perpetrator was. Thus, instead of wondering who may have tried to kill J.R., fans were left to ponder who J.R. may have killed. In the final episode of Season 3, the body of a woman is discovered in the Southfork pool, with J.R. standing nearby. But as the *Dallas* company began its hiatus, it knew that it faced a real tragedy, as one of its stars was fighting a losing battle against cancer.

SEASON 3 EPISODE GUIDE

Regular Cast

Starring:
Barbara Bel Geddes as Miss Ellie
Jim Davis as Jock
Patrick Duffy as Bobby
Linda Gray as Sue Ellen
Larry Hagman as J.R.
Steve Kanaly as Ray
Ken Kercheval as Cliff
Victoria Principal as Pam
Charlene Tilton as Lucy
Also Starring:
Mary Crosby as Kristin
Susan Flannery as Leslie Stewart
Susan Howard as Donna
Leigh McCloskey as Mitch Cooper
Randolph Powell as Alan Beam

Technical Credits

Producer: Leonard Katzman
Executive Producer: Philip Capice
Executive Story Editor: Arthur Bernard Lewis
Story Editors: Camille Marchetta, Rena Down, Robert J. Shaw
Associate Producer: Cliff Fenneman
Unit Production Manager: Wayne A. Farlow
First Assistant Directors: Fred Stromsoe, David Menteer, Jonathan Giles Zimmerman

Second Assistant Director: Glen Sanford
Music: Jerrold Immel, Bruce Broughton, Richard Lewis Warren
Directors of Photography: Edward R. Plante
Art Director: Charles Zacha Jr.
Editors: Fred W. Berger, A.C.E., John Arthur Davies, Lloyd Richardson
Executive in Charge of Casting: Barbara Miller
Casting: Irene Mariano
Set Decorator: Phil Leonard
Property Master: Anthony C. Thorpe
Costumers: Jack Bear, Violet Cane
Makeup: Cheri Minns, Alan Fama, S.M.A., Judith Silverman
Hair Stylists: Linda Sharp, Gregg Mitchell
Dialogue Director: Fred Martin
Location Casting: Rody Kent
Production Sound Mixer: Clark King, C.S.A.
Sound Effects Supervisor: Victor Guarnier
Sound Effects Editors: Stephen Purvis, Richard Steven, Tony Zero
Music Editor: George Probert
Main Title Design: Wayne Fitzgerald
Production Supervisor: Mitch Ackerman
Executive Production Supervisor: Edward O. Denault

55. "No More Mr. Nice Guy" (Part One)

Written by Arthur Bernard Lewis; Directed by Leonard Katzman; Airdate: November 7, 1980
Guest Stars: Ted Shackelford (Gary); Peter Donat (Dr. Pearson); Joan Van Ark (Val); Michael Alldredge (Detective Don Horton); Christopher Coffey (Greg)
Subject: J.R.'s surgery.

Cast Notes Peter Donat appeared in *Rich Man, Poor Man—Book II* and costarred in the soap opera *Flamingo Road*. ★ Michael Alldredge returned to *Dallas* as Steve Jackson in Season 7 and Ray King in Season 13. Alldredge was also a regular on the sitcom *Alice*. ★ Tyler Banks makes his debut as John Ross, a role he played through the end of Season 5.

Trivia This episode finished the week at number 2 with a 38.2 rating and 61 share. It was bested in the ratings only by a special Sunday night edition of *Dallas* that aired two nights later. ★ Parkland Hospital, where President John F. Kennedy was taken after he was assassinated, was used as Dallas Memorial Hospital. ★ A substitute for Larry Hagman plays J.R. during the ambulance scene, since Hagman, who had not yet finished renegotiating his contract, was in London when the scene was filmed. ★ A number of decoy arrest scenes were filmed, including one in which Cliff Barnes was arrested outside Ewing Oil as an unconscious J.R. is placed into an ambulance. ★ Prior to the actors' strike, parts one and two of "No More Mr. Nice Guy" were scheduled to air as a two-hour season premiere on September 19, 1980. ★ The cast found it comforting, given the press frenzy and Larry Hagman's walk-out, to have Leonard Katzman directing the first two episodes of the new season. Katzman was approachable and available to the cast, but kept his cards close regarding the perpetrator's identity. ★ This episode gave Mary Crosby, who normally appeared in scenes with Larry Hagman and Linda Gray, the chance to work with Barbara Bel Geddes and Jim Davis. Crosby says, "It was a joy and privilege to work with Barbara and Jim. They knew so much and were quintessential professionals. Barbara was just a very gracious lady with a quiet presence and a sort of 'Angela Lansbury quality.'"

56. "No More Mr. Nice Guy" (Part Two)

Written by Arthur Bernard Lewis; Directed by Leonard Katzman; Airdate: November 9, 1980
Guest Stars: Ted Shackelford (Gary); Peter Donat (Dr. Pearson); Michael Alldredge (Horton); Royce D. Applegate (Detective Crabbe); Jeff Cooper (Dr. Elby)
Subject: Bobby runs Ewing Oil.

Cast Notes Leigh McCloskey makes his first appearance as Mitch Cooper, a role he played through Season 4 and again in Seasons 7 and 10. McCloskey was cast as Mitch by the same woman who cast him on David Jacobs's 1979 serial *Married: The First Year*, which was also produced by Lorimar and costarred *Dallas* cast members Claudette Nevin and K Callan. *Married* ran for only two months, but the casting director remembered McCloskey and "asked me to come in for a meeting about *Dallas*, and at the meeting they asked me to join the show." While McCloskey had heard of *Dallas* and "Who Shot J.R.?" he had never watched the show. "The phenomenon of *Dallas*," he explains, "was something I was completely unfamiliar with, although *Dallas* was on the mind of everyone, whether they watched it or didn't watch it." McCloskey recalls that the producers created the character of Mitch because "they wanted to flesh out the younger people on the show." At the time he joined the cast, McCloskey had a one-year contract. Prior to *Dallas*, McCloskey had appeared in the miniseries *Rich Man, Poor Man—Book II* and the serial *Executive Suite*, which costarred *Dallas* cast members Stephen Elliott and William Smithers. McCloskey was later seen on *JAG; Beverly Hills,*

90210; and *Murder, She Wrote* as well as the daytime soap operas *One Life to Live, The Young and the Restless, General Hospital,* and *Santa Barbara.* McCloskey is an accomplished artist and happily married family man who spent his breaks on the *Dallas* set playing football with Steve Kanaly. In 2003, Olander Press published McCloskey's *TAROT ReVISIONed,* a book that examines the traditional meanings of Tarot archetypes and includes new drawings of the twenty-two archetypes of the Major Arcana of the Tarot. ★ Janine Turner, who plays one of Lucy's friends, replaced Genie Francis as Anthony Geary's love interest on *General Hospital.* She went on to star in the 1990–95 CBS series *Northern Exposure,* playing Maggie, a role for which she received a 1993 Emmy nomination as Outstanding Lead Actress in a Drama Series. ★ Royce Applegate appeared in the movies *Splash* and *The Rookie* and on the series *JAG* and *CHiPs.* He died on New Year's Day, 2003, at the age of sixty-three in a house fire at his home in Los Angeles.

Trivia This was a special Sunday night episode of *Dallas* that was the final of six episodes promoted as "*Dallas* Week." It was the number 1 show of the week and earned a 40 rating and 59 share, which meant that 59 percent of all TVs turned on at the time were tuned in to *Dallas.* ★ According to Patrick Duffy, J.R. was shot not to provide Hagman with an exit from the show but to make Bobby less of a hero and explore "the corruption of an honest man." J.R.'s shooting, said Duffy at the time, "put [Bobby] in a position to take over Ewing Oil. . . . It's tough to write for the good guy. Bobby got the short end of the stick. Now, he could get tougher. Be more of a realist. Do things a little off-center in terms of legalities—as long as the people on the negative side deserve it, and the right people are going to benefit from it. We're trying to broaden him."

57. "Nightmare"

Written by Linda B. Elstad; Directed by Irving J. Moore; Airdate: November 14, 1980
Guest Stars: Barbara Babcock (Liz); Jeff Cooper (Dr. Elby); Laurence Haddon (Franklin Horner); Christopher Coffey (Greg)
Subject: Sue Ellen's arrest.

Cast Notes Laurence Haddon appeared as the Ewing family banker, Franklin Horner, in Seasons 3 through 5, 8, and 9. He also played the foreign news editor on *Lou Grant.* ★ Jan Jordan, who plays a minor role in this episode, played various nurses on *M*A*S*H.*

Trivia This episode was number 1 for the week, with a 53.5 rating and 56 share. ★ Ultimately, Linda Gray could not believe that Sue Ellen would shoot J.R., saying, "The idea that people think good old Sue Ellen would ever do such a thing is painful. Why, she loves J.R.—or why else would she still be at the Southfork Ranch?" Even as Sue Ellen became a suspect, she remained popular with viewers, to Gray's surprise. "When I first started playing her," she said, "because she was psychotic and a drunk, I expected people to react negatively to her. I didn't expect her to be welcomed into people's homes. So I decided to make her a little more vulnerable. But anything I did was acceptable. People forgave me because I was married to such an SOB. There I was expecting the worst and I wound up getting accolades." As a result, Gray hoped Season 3 would not bring a reformed Sue Ellen. She told *Time* magazine, "I keep saying to the writers, 'Whatever you do, don't make her nice!' I've read the first four scripts of [Season 3], and I'm thrilled. The conflict continues." ★ The cast was grateful to have its trusted friend Irving Moore direct this episode. If Moore knew who shot J.R., he did not let on. All of the actors loved Moore, even though he was more of a man's director. His light sarcasm kept the crew relaxed. ★ This marks the first appearance of Ray's red brick house, which is still standing and can be seen from the back of Southfork. It was a modest house built on a plain, bare lot.

58. "Who Done It?"

Written by Loraine Despres; Directed by Leonard Katzman; Airdate: November 21, 1980
Guest Stars: John Lehne (Kyle Bennett); Laurence Haddon (Franklin); Gregory Walcott (Jim Redfield); Jeff Cooper (Dr. Elby); Tom Fucello (Dave Culver)
Subject: Kristin shot J.R.

Cast Notes John Lehne appeared in the 1976 Alfred Hitchcock film *Family Plot*, and played Andrew Parkhurst on *Knots Landing* in 1981 and 1982 and Jonathan Pope on *Beauty and the Beast* in 1990. ★ Gregory Walcott and Steve Kanaly played navy officers together in the 1976 Henry Fonda film *Midway*, which also featured future *Dallas* guest star Monte Markham.

Trivia More than 83 million Americans and over 300 million viewers worldwide watched this episode, and 76 percent of all television sets in the United States were tuned in to the show. Its 53.3 rating and 76 share made it, at the time, the highest-rated program ever, besting the 51.1 rating and 71 percent share earned four years earlier by the eighth and final part of the miniseries *Roots*. The previous record for a TV series was the 45.9 share earned by the final episode of *The Fugitive* in 1967. ★ The record set by "Who Done It?" held for two and a half years and was finally broken when the last episode of M*A*S*H earned a 60.2 rating on February 28, 1983. However, "Who Done It?" remains the most-watched regular series episode and the second-most-watched TV episode in history, after M*A*S*H and ahead of *The Fugitive*. The next most-watched shows are: the 1993 *Cheers* finale (45.5 rating), the 1998 *Seinfeld* finale (41.3), the 1988 *Magnum P.I.* finale (32.0), and the 2000 *Survivor* finale (28.6). ★ In Chicago, 76 percent of televisions in use were tuned in to *Dallas*. In New York, it was a 65 share and in Los Angeles, it was a 68 share. ★ Advertising for this episode set a record of $500,000 per minute. ★ According to *Time* magazine, Kristin was the favorite among Las Vegas bookies in the week leading up to this episode. ★ Eight years after the "Who Shot J.R.?" storyline, Larry Hagman called it "the best thing we ever did." ★ This episode was preceded by a rerun of the previous episode, "A

House Divided," and was postponed from October 3, 1980 due to the actors' strike. ★ The outdoor patio scene resolving the whodunit was filmed at Culver City, not at Duncan Acres. ★ To further conceal the resolution, several of the suspects, including Bobby, Sue Ellen, Cliff Barnes, and Vaughan Leland were filmed pulling the trigger. So were Jock, Miss Ellie, Pam, Jordan Lee, Harv Smithfield, Lucy's college professor, and Lucy. Mary Crosby recalls, "The great thing was that everyone got to pull the trigger, even the producer and make-up artist and even Larry himself! So if it hit the news that I did it, they could have made it someone else before it aired. We were all filmed shooting him before we went on hiatus, so if the *National Enquirer* said that I did it, they could change it and go with someone else." Fern Fitzgerald, who played Marilee, remembers, "Like every other 'suspect,' I filmed a segment that pointed the finger at me. In my segment, the police led me off in handcuffs." Ray Krebbs, however, was not a suspect, so Steve Kanaly was not filmed committing the act. Jokes Kanaly, "I always said, if Ray Krebbs shot J.R., he would have been dead." ★ Katzman said later, "We really didn't know who shot him when we created the whole thing. We said, 'To hell with it, let's shoot him and figure out who did it later.' Someone had to do it. Then we started eliminating and eliminating until we found the person we wanted. Kristin did it by process of elimination." ★ In an effort to maintain secrecy, the revelation scene was shot in August, two months after the rest of the episode was completed. While each episode of *Dallas* was normally sent to New York one month prior to airtime, the revelation episode did not arrive in New York until its actual airdate. ★ Originally, the pregnancy announcement was part of the succeeding episode, "Taste of Success," which explains Leonard Katzman's statement to *Newsweek*, "When you learn who did it, you won't know why until the next episode. Then you'll receive some startling news." ★ Mary Crosby later reflected, "Looking back on it, I was just very grateful for what had happened and for the fact that I was the one that shot him." ★ When recently asked which of *Dallas*'s 357 episodes is the best, Larry Hagman answered, "The revealing of 'Who Shot J.R.?,' of course."

59. "Taste of Success"

Written by Robert J. Shaw; Directed by Irving J. Moore; Airdate: November 28, 1980
Guest Stars: Barbara Babcock (Liz); Warren Vanders (Harry Owens); Michael Bell (Les Crowley); Jeff Cooper (Dr. Elby); Laurence Haddon (Franklin); Gregory Walcott (Jim Redfield); Tom Taylor (Martin Purcell)
Subject: Bobby's business success.

Cast Notes Michael Bell returned to *Dallas* as Pat Connor in Season 13, and his voice is heard on the Nickelodeon cartoon *Rugrats*.

Trivia This episode was number 1 for the week with a 56 share. ★ Patrick Duffy recognized that, while J.R.'s shooting caused him to lose power at Ewing Oil, it had the opposite effect on Larry Hagman. "By holding out," Duffy explained, "and then giving him what he wanted, [Larry] proved they can't do that show without him. So, it didn't become an ego thing for him. What it became was the final word. And if it got murky and everybody had this opinion, that opinion, he could tell it wasn't the direction that he and Leonard and most of us would have agreed the show should go in, he would say what he thought and that had to be what happened." Katzman confirmed that Hagman would "come in and say, 'What if J.R. lost everything?' 'What if John Ross was kidnapped?'" Katzman frequently put his arm around Hagman on the set and talked with him about story ideas, asking, "What do you think of *this*, Larry?" Hagman, however, says, "I never did suggest anything to the writers during the early years. They came up with all that themselves and I only interpreted it. Sometimes they didn't agree with how I interpreted it but it seemed to work out for everybody." ★ Mary Crosby knew by the summer of 1980 that she was only going to appear in the first five episodes of Season 3. At the time, Crosby told *TV Guide* that she did not mind leaving *Dallas* because if "Kristin were to continue, there would be nowhere for her to go. It's good for me, because I don't want to get pegged as that kind of character for the rest of my life." As for reporters who got notice of her limited Season 3 appearances and tried to guess the "Who Shot J.R.?" resolution by linking Kristin's culpability to Crosby's departure from the show, Crosby "gallantly deadpanned" that her "part was up. They need new people." Later, once she was revealed as the culprit, Crosby explained that she was glad to have been the one: "It made me the answer to a trivia question," she said. "What more can I say?" Now, Crosby says that Kristin's inevitable departure from *Dallas* brought mixed emotions. Crosby explains, "I loved *Dallas*. The people on it were wonderful and Larry was such fun and it was a home for me. So, I was sad to be leaving. But at the same time, I was in a strange and unique position to be the girl who shot J.R., and I was both terrified and excited to see where that would lead. It was bittersweet. But if I'd had my druthers, I would have hung out on *Dallas* for a long time because it was a terrific experience for me."

60. "The Venezuelan Connection"

Written by Leah Markus; Directed by Leonard Katzman; Airdate: December 5, 1980
Special Guest Stars: E. J. Andre (Eugene Bullock); Joanna Cassidy (Sally Bullock)
Guest Stars: William Windom (Amos Krebbs); Morgan Woodward (Punk Anderson);
Richard Herd (John Mackie); Jeff Cooper (Dr. Elby); Ted Gehring (Brady York)
Subject: Bobby's tanker goes down.

Cast Notes Joanna Cassidy replaces Andra Akers as Sally Bullock. Cassidy appeared in the movies *The Stepford Wives*, *Blade Runner*, and *Who Framed Roger Rabbit*. She appears on the HBO series *Six Feet Under* and won a Golden Globe for Best Actress in a Leading Role for a Musical or Comedy Series in 1983 for her starring role in the Dabney Coleman sitcom *Buffalo Bill*. Cassidy was not aware that Sally Bullock had previously appeared on the show and does not know why the role was recast. Cassidy got the role after meeting with Leonard Katzman and

Phil Capice, who were familiar with her previous work. Cassidy "loved being on the show. It was great. The character was fun and Larry Hagman was so funny and outrageous. He was so comfortable in his role and so happy." Cassidy found E. J. Andre "a good old-timer, full of stories about the business. He had been around when the west was won!" ★ William Windom starred in the TV version of the movie *The Farmer's Daughter* and in *My World and Welcome to It*, which won the 1970 Emmy for Outstanding Comedy Series. He also played Seth Hazlett, Angela Lansbury's friend, on *Murder, She Wrote*. Windom was Steve Kanaly's favorite guest star on *Dallas*. The two played tennis together. "In fact, I was playing tennis with [Windom] when I got the call to come home when my second daughter was born," recalls Kanaly. Kanaly found Windom's performance "just perfectly seedy; a very authentic portrayal of a slippery con man." ★ Morgan Woodward makes his first appearance as Punk Anderson, a role he would play through Season 10. Punk Anderson was mentioned in the pilot and Seasons 1 and 2 before finally being seen in this episode. Woodward played Shotgun Gibbs on *The Life and Legend of Wyatt Earp* and played the guard in Paul Newman's *Cool Hand Luke*, which also featured future *Dallas* costar George Kennedy. Woodward was a real Texan, born in Fort Worth and raised in the state. According to Woodward, he "was cast as Punk probably because I had worked for Leonard Katzman before on *Petrocelli* and other shows." Woodward "thought Punk was a good role, especially since he was a friend of Jock Ewing's [and] . . . Jim Davis was an old friend of mine. I had known him for years." In fact, Woodward would have liked to play Jock himself. "After Jim had been cast as Jock, I told him, 'If Leonard had cast anybody else instead of me as Jock, I would have been really ticked off. But it's okay with me. You're perfect for the role.'" ★ Richard Herd played Captain Dennis Sheridan on *T.J. Hooker*. ★ Ted Gehring is a TV veteran who played Ebenezer Sprague on *Little House on the Prairie* and was a regular on *Alice*.

Trivia This episode was number 1 for the week with a 37.3 rating and 62 share. ★ The actors enjoyed filming in Fort Worth and liked to walk the streets of the old cow town during breaks and sneak away to their favorite Mexican restaurant, Joe T. Garcia's, for lunch. ★ Not long after her appearance on *Dallas*, Joanna Cassidy told *US* magazine that she enjoyed playing Sally Bullock because "my sexy side was played up . . . for a change." Cassidy thought J.R. "was attracted to Sally Bullock because he was his exact equivalent—not a kept woman, not a quiet woman, not a mistress. She was the hellbent wife of an oil magnate. . . . It wasn't enough that she persuaded American's favorite villain to blow up a tanker containing Venezuelan oil and collect on the insurance. [She and J.R.] played ball in the bedroom as well."

61. "The Fourth Son"

Written by Howard Lakin; Directed by Irving J. Moore; Airdate: December 12, 1980
Special Guest Stars: E.J. Andre (Eugene Bullock); Joanna Cassidy (Sally)

Guest Stars: William Windom (Amos); Ted Gehring (Brady); John Crawford (Mort Wilkinson)
Subject: Jock is Ray's father.

Cast Notes John Crawford played the sheriff on *The Waltons*. ★ Bit player Harlan Jordan played a Southfork butler in this episode and in Episodes 78, 194, and 253. In Episode 194, Miss Ellie calls him "Harlan."

Trivia This episode was number 1 for the week with a 35.8 rating and 60 share. It was the sixth straight week that *Dallas* held Nielsen's number 1 spot. ★ Steve Kanaly considers this episode his best acting on *Dallas*. It is also his favorite story-line, since it made Ray a member of the Ewing family and enabled him to be in the "living room and dining room scenes." Kanaly recalls that, prior to this storyline, he had become unhappy with his character and thought of leaving the show. By the end of Season 2, Kanaly had realized that most of the storylines involved Ewing Oil instead of the Southfork ranch, leaving Ray's role diminished. Kanaly thought there were lots of other opportunities to take advantage of, but Jim Davis and Larry Hagman talked him out of leaving. Davis felt the show was on the verge of becoming a hit. One day, after having a beer following a game of racquetball, Kanaly and Hagman came up with the idea of Jock and Ray being father and son. Hagman tried to help Kanaly work through his frustration over his character's lack of story-lines, and the two began to throw story ideas out to one another. "Then [Hagman] turned to me and suddenly said, 'You know, Steve, you look more like you could be Jim's son than any of us.' Well, a light went on—Larry and I got the idea at the same exact moment—and we ran right to the producers with it." Kanaly also thought that having Ray marry a Mexican woman would provide an interesting conflict between the Ewing family and the Mexican community, but nothing came of the idea. Phil Capice, however, denied that Hagman and Kanaly thought up the familial relationship between Jock and Ray, claiming that writers wanted to make Ray a more central character, and his parentage was simply a way to accomplish that end. As a result of Ray's new status as a Ewing, Kanaly's salary jumped from $3,500 per episode to $20,000 per episode. ★ According to Leonard Katzman, "Had we thought [Ray] was ever going to be the fourth son, he and Lucy would never have been playing hanky-panky in the hayloft. It was OK because nobody knew in those days that he was [Jock's son]." Kanaly recalls that CBS's concern about an incestuous affair led to a delay in this storyline. ★ This is the first episode written by Howard Lakin, who wrote a total of twenty-three episodes during Seasons 3 through 5 and 11 through 13. Lakin felt that the main character in *Dallas* was not J.R. Ewing, but Leonard Katzman himself. "Every character in that show," said Lakin, "every single one of them, was some facet of Len Katzman himself. The father-brother-son triangle, that was him somehow. It was very, very important to him. And women were—I won't say women were arm charms, but they were close. And often I felt like I was writing his autobiography, in a sense, as I wrote these scripts." ★ Joanna Cassidy enjoyed her scenes with Patrick Duffy, who she calls "a doll. He was helpful and got me filled in and was very generous—all the kinds of things that are unusual. I remember he took me to lunch. He was great."

62. "Trouble at Ewing 23"

Written by Louie Elias; Directed by Leonard Katzman; Airdate: December 19, 1980
Guest Stars: Warren Vanders (Harry Owens); Richard Herd (John Mackie); Michael Bell (Les); Laurence Haddon (Franklin)
Subject: Bobby's oil field is destroyed.

Trivia This episode was number 1 for the week with a 33.8 rating. ★ Susan Howard's earlier appearances as Donna generated much positive viewer mail. Ken Kercheval was glad Howard returned to the cast, and he enjoyed playing opposite her as his character's temporary love interest, finding Howard "a marvelous person." ★ The Southfork front door was rarely used after this episode. Future entrances were made from behind the main staircase.

63. "The Prodigal Mother"

Written by David Paulsen; Directed by Irving J. Moore; Airdate: January 2, 1981
Guest Stars: Morgan Woodward (Punk); Richard Herd (John Mackie); Michael Bell (Les); Priscilla Pointer (Rebecca Barnes Wentworth)
Subject: Pam's mother.

Cast Notes This is the first appearance of Priscilla Pointer as Rebecca Wentworth, a role Pointer would play through Season 5. A veteran actress, Pointer appeared in the films *Carrie*, *Honeysuckle Rose*, and *Mommie Dearest* (along with *Dallas* cast member Steve Forrest). Pointer got the role of Rebecca "on the basis of [a] reading. Certainly they wanted someone with film experience, although I think my extensive theater background may have played a part as well. Plus I looked enough like Ken and Victoria that I could have been their mother." Pointer is also the mother of actress Amy Irving and one-time mother-in-law of director Steven Spielberg. She later appeared on the ABC Cold War drama *Call to Glory* with Keenan Wynn, who played her ex-husband Digger on *Dallas*. Pointer and Wynn had a laugh over their *Dallas* connection. Pointer recalls that "Keenan was always 'on' and had a wealth of stories to tell during our breaks [on *Glory*]." ★ Herbert Wentworth is played by John Martin, who played Hickey in Episodes 253–54. According to Pointer, Martin was cast in Texas for the role.

Trivia This episode was number 1 for the week with a 36.1 rating. ★ This was the first episode written by David Paulsen, who wrote forty-five episodes of *Dallas* during Seasons 3 through 7, 9, and 10. He also directed four episodes, making him the only person besides Leonard Katzman who wrote and directed episodes of the show. ★ Pointer had never seen *Dallas* prior to joining its cast, although she remembers being amazed while traveling "in rural Scotland [where] one would see it in the papers: that burning question [Who Shot J.R.?]!" What Pointer "remember[s] most about making the first episode was that, during the scene in the park with Victoria, it was so hot down in Texas that everyone was running around giving us salt pills so that we wouldn't pass out!" Pointer has a second home in Paris, where she recently came across this episode on French television. Pointer jokes that in "La Mere Prodigue," "my French (being dubbed) was impeccable!" ★ As of this episode, Leigh McCloskey's character became a future member of the Ewing family due to his engagement to Lucy. McCloskey recalls, "When I was first on the show, Charlene was quite young and was just starting her career. I had studied acting and had been at it for several years, so we were on different wave lengths, but she was extremely nice and I got along quite well with her."

64. "Executive Wife"

Written by Rena Down; Directed by Leonard Katzman; Airdate: January 9, 1981
Guest Stars: Joel Fabiani (Alex Ward); Morgan Woodward (Punk); Barbara Babcock
(Liz); Michael Bell (Les); Ted Gehring (Brady)
Special Guest Star: William Smithers (Jeremy Wendell)
Subject: Pam flirts.

Cast Notes Joel Fabiani, a veteran of commercials, played King Galen on *Dynasty.* ★ William Smithers, who appeared as Jeremy Wendell in fifty-three episodes during Seasons 3, 4, and 7 through 11, played David Schuster on *Peyton Place.* He was also an award-winning stage actor who played opposite Olivia DeHavilland on Broadway in *Romeo and Juliet.* Smithers recalls that, during his first few episodes on *Dallas,* he "felt he was searching for the character [of Wendell], but was not that comfortable with it yet. As time went on, and I was asked to do more as Wendell, my confidence grew."

Trivia This episode was number 1 for the week with a 33.9 rating. ★ Leigh McCloskey enjoyed this episode since it gave him the opportunity to act opposite Jim Davis, who McCloskey says "was the heart of the show, the center and the patriarch. Jim and his wife, Blanche, gave grounding to *Dallas.* He really was Jock, and he was loved." ★ This was the last episode of the season with scenes filmed on location in Dallas. ★ ABC's answer to *Dallas,* the Aaron Spelling serial *Dynasty,* premiered three days after this episode aired. Four seasons later, it would knock *Dallas* out of first place in the Nielsen overall season ratings.

65. "End of the Road" (Part One)

Written by Leonard Katzman; Directed by Irving J. Moore; Airdate: January 16, 1981
Guest Stars: Joel Fabiani (Alex); Audrey Landers (Afton Cooper); Barbara Babcock (Liz);
Morgan Woodward (Punk); Harry Carey Jr. (Red)
Special Guest Stars: Anne Francis (Arliss Cooper); William Smithers (Jeremy)
Subject: J.R. plots against Bobby.

Cast Notes This episode marks the first appearance of Audrey Landers as Afton Cooper. Landers played the role through the first episode of Season 7 and reprised it in Episodes 302–06 and 308–09 and in *J.R. Returns*, making her the guest star with the most appearances on *Dallas*. Landers auditioned for the role in a new hairdo and a dress borrowed from her sister, actress Judy Landers of *B.J. and the Bear*, since Landers didn't own an appropriate costume for the role. The following evening, Landers was notified that she got the part, and she was on a plane to Dallas the next morning. She quickly became very close to Leonard Katzman, who told *TV Guide*, "When Audrey started to work on the show, my wife and I more or less adopted her. That should tell you about our relationship. We were looking for a grasping little girl with money in her eyes. You can see that, with Audrey, we were casting *against* type." ★ Harry Carey Jr. is the son of character actor Harry Carey, who appeared in several John Ford westerns from the 1940s to the 1960s. ★ Anne Francis is a veteran of stage and screen who succeeded Angela Lansbury as Broadway's *Mame* and appeared with Barbra Streisand in the movie classic *Funny Girl*. On TV, Francis starred in the *Burke's Law* spin-off, *Honey West*, and on *My Three Sons*.

Trivia This episode was number 1 for the week with a 33.4 rating and 55 share, but was *Dallas*'s lowest season rating to date. ★ Leigh McCloskey enjoyed working with both of the actresses who played Mitch's family members. "Anne Francis and Audrey Landers," he says, "were both very professional. I had a really good time working with Anne. I like Audrey immensely. She and her family were very warm and very delightful." ★ J.R.'s favorite drink was bourbon and branch water. Jock's and J.R.'s drinking binge was a case of art imitating life, at least in one instance. Larry Hagman and Steve Kanaly recall going on Dinah Shore's talk show, *Dinah!*, in 1979, along with Jim Davis, Barbara Bel Geddes, Patrick Duffy, Linda Gray, and Victoria Principal. According to Hagman, "Dinah made the mistake of saying, 'Anybody want a drink before we start?' Jim was drinking straight vodka out of a coffee cup, and we got absolutely bleep-faced." Davis and Kanaly had the last interviews, so they remained in the Green Room enjoying their cocktails. Later, while Shore was interviewing Duffy and Principal, Davis, who was now on stage and was still holding his drink in one hand, put his other arm around Kanaly and said, "You are a great guy, Steve. I am so happy we're working together. You know, this show of ours might be a hit after all." Shore looked over and asked if everything was okay. At that point, Davis got up, stumbled over to her to make an apology on bended knee, and ended up spilling his drink all over Dinah's lap. "You can imagine the mayhem that ensued," recalls Kanaly. Said Hagman, "We were never asked back." ★ A third cast photo is seen over the fireplace in the den, which was a frequently used set in Seasons 1 and 2 but was not seen after Season 3. ★ Audrey Landers "got along very well with Leigh [McCloskey]," and found him "so talented." ★ Anne Francis "enjoyed working with the cast" on *Dallas*. Francis found Barbara Bel Geddes "delightful. Victoria Principal saved my younger daughter, Maggie, when she got caught in the elevator at the hotel we were staying at in Dallas."

66. "End of the Road" (Part Two)

Written by Leonard Katzman; Directed by Irving J. Moore; Airdate: January 23, 1981
Guest Stars: Joel Fabiani (Alex); Audrey Landers (Afton); Barbara Babcock (Liz); Ted
Gehring (Brady); Ted Shackelford (Gary); Joan Van Ark (Val)
Special Guest Stars: Monte Markham (Clint Ogden); Anne Francis (Arliss); William
Smithers (Jeremy)
Subject: Lucy's wedding.

Cast Notes TV veteran Monte Markham starred in a remake of *Perry Mason* and
had recurring roles on *The Six Million Dollar Man*, *Melrose Place*, and *Baywatch*. In
the wake of the tabloid coverage of the *Dallas* cast, Markham did not know what
to expect when he agreed to appear in several episodes as Sue Ellen's college
boyfriend. "We had all heard stories about the *Dallas* set," Markham explains, "but
when I arrived, it was one of the most tightly controlled sets I had been on. It was
very professionally run, and that was all a reflection of Lenny Katzman." Although
Markham did not have many scenes with Larry Hagman, the two knew each other
in the 1960s, when both were working on TV series while under contract at
Screen Gems. "He was doing *Jeannie*," recalls Markham. "I remember him complaining to one of the *Jeannie* directors that he was in this comedy show with a
woman without a navel, and the director told him to settle down and enjoy it.
And he did, and he got rich, and that's the time he started drinking champagne
and he was just having a really good time." Markham had also known Jim Davis,
who Markham thought was underestimated when Davis was first cast as Jock.
"You had the sense," says Markham, "that some people . . . looked down on him
when *Dallas* started because they had wanted a more distinguished actor. But people just came to love him. And after he died, I got a call from a bank in Seattle
that he did voiceovers for, asking me if I was interested. I ended up doing the
voiceovers for that bank, which I enjoyed as much for the indirect connection
with Jim as anything else."

Trivia This episode was ranked number 2 for the week, with a 36.4 rating. It was
the first time all season that *Dallas* was not the number 1 show, a feat it had accomplished the previous ten weeks. ★ Lucy's wedding dress is on display at the
Southfork Ranch. ★ Charlene Tilton was almost was late for Lucy's wedding.
"My marriage to Mitch," she recalled, "was a pretty huge event. Obviously, the
highest-rated show was 'Who Shot J.R.?' and the second highest was my wedding.
. . . On my way to the studio that day, I was in a horrible car accident. A man ran a
red light and crashed into me, totaled my car. And they kept wanting to get para-
medics there to take me and I'm like, 'No, I've got to get to the studio. I've got to
get there. There's all these extras, these cranes, it's a huge day. I can't not show
up.' So, on with the show." ★ All that Leigh McCloskey can remember about
Lucy's and Mitch's wedding "is that I was the groom on the cake. I had nothing to
say, and just had to look good! It was really a monstrous scene to shoot because

there were, it seemed, a thousand people there. We shot way into the wee hours of the morning. We were all trying to keep our eyes open. I think the wedding had a far bigger effect on those that were uninvolved than on those that were involved—we were just trying to get it done!" ★ Audrey Landers recalls, "My first scene ever on the show was the scene in which I seduce J.R.—during the wedding! Larry knew that I was a bit tentative—to say the least. I got under the covers of the bed on the set—with about a hundred crew and cast members on hand. I was wearing a strapless dress, so all you could see was my bare shoulders above the sheets. Larry was already in bed, under the sheets wearing his full wardrobe—except for a shirt. He even wore his cowboy boots. When the director called, 'Action!' Larry leaned over to touch my shoulder, and poured a handful of ice down my back. I couldn't help but laugh. It certainly was a unique way to 'break the ice' and set the tone for a very relaxed and harmonious set." Landers believed that "Afton wasn't just after [J.R.] for the money. She had to really love him to put up with him as much as she did." ★ Mitch's push in the pool is the first of many Southfork pool incidents, including Kristin's drowning, the pool brawl at J.R.'s and Sue Ellen's wedding and vandalism after the Ewing tanker spill. ★ Three days after this episode aired, Victoria Principal appeared on NBC's special *TV Guide: 1980—The Year in Television* and introduced a segment featuring the outtakes of various *Dallas* characters shooting J.R.

67. "The Making of a President"

Written by Arthur Bernard Lewis; Directed by Gunnar Hellstrom; Airdate: January 30, 1981

Guest Stars: Joel Fabiani (Alex); Morgan Woodward (Punk); Noble Willingham (Milton); Jerry Hardin (Elroy Askew); Robert Sampson (Justin); Ron Hayes (Hank Johnson); Ivan Bonar (Senator Bascomb); Jeff Cooper (Dr. Elby); Audrey Landers (Afton)
Special Guest Stars: Monte Markham (Clint); Anne Francis (Arliss)
Subject: J.R. runs Ewing Oil.

Cast Notes Susan Flannery makes her debut as Leslie Stewart. Flannery is a daytime soap opera veteran who won a Golden Globe for Outstanding Acting Debut in a Motion Picture for the Paul Newman movie *The Towering Inferno*. She is a multiple Emmy Award winner for her roles on *The Bold and the Beautiful* and *Days of Our Lives*. ★ Ivan Bonar played Dean Hopkins on *The Adventures of Ozzie and Harriet*. ★ Robert Sampson played Father Mike on *Bridget Loves Bernie* and Sheriff Tobias on *Falcon Crest*. ★ Noble Willingham, who plays the nightclub owner who hires Afton, went on to play saloon owner C. D. Parker on *Walker, Texas Ranger* from 1993 until 1999, when Willingham left the show to run for congress. Willingham was the 2000 Republican nominee for an eastern Texas seat, but lost to Democrat Max Sandlin. *Walker* was produced by Leonard Katzman and starred fellow *Dallas* cast member Sheree J. Wilson (and featured *Dallas* veterans Steve Kanaly, Howard Keel, Ken Kercheval and Cathy Podewell in guest appearances).

Willingham also appeared in the movies *Chinatown*; *City Slickers*; *Good Morning, Vietnam*; and *Ace Ventura: Pet Detective*. He died of natural causes at the age of seventy-two at his home in Palm Springs on January 17, 2004. Upon his death, his manager, Sandy Josephs, recalled that Willingham's "distinctive voice and warmly gruff manner helped him bring authority figures to life." ★ This is the first appearance of Deborah Tranelli as Phyllis, who fills in for a sick Connie in this episode and replaces Connie permanently, without explanation, in Episode 72. Tranelli played Bobby's (and, in Season 8, Pam's) secretary through Season 13. ★ Jerry Hardin returned to *Dallas* as Judge Lowe in Episodes 245 and 246.

Trivia This episode was number 1 for the week with a 34.8 rating. ★ Lucy's and Mitch's Oakside Condo set makes its debut in this episode. ★ Audrey Landers's singing talents were worked into this episode, among numerous others. Her character got a job as a lounge singer and, in a later return appearance, even recorded an album. Landers explains, "The way my character was written into the show as a singer was kind of like an old Hollywood discovery story. It was my first day on the set. When everyone broke for lunch, the soundstage emptied quickly. I was too nervous to leave the set and go to lunch, so I stayed. It was so quiet. I wandered around and discovered an old piano in a corner somewhere. I sat down and decided to work on a song I had been writing—to keep my mind off of being nervous. No one was around, so I knew I wouldn't disturb anyone. Well, apparently, someone was in the studio. The next day, Leonard came up to me on the set and told me that Afton would be written into the show as a singer—and as a 'regular.' I was elated!—not only because I would be able to combine my music and my acting—but also because up until that time, Afton was supposed to be a two-episode character—meant to add a little spice to the wedding!"

68. "Start the Revolution with Me"

Written by Rena Down; Directed by Larry Hagman; Airdate: February 6, 1981
Guest Stars: Joel Fabiani (Alex); Barbara Babcock (Liz); Morgan Woodward (Punk); Len Birman (Claude Brown); Ron Hayes (Hank Johnson); Jeff Cooper (Dr. Elby)
Special Guest Star: Monte Markham (Clint)
Subject: J.R. plots overseas.

Trivia This episode was number 1 for the week with a 31.6 rating and 50 share. ★ In this episode, a movie marquee showing the classic film *Camille* is seen. This was the crew's nod to former writer Camille Marchetta.

69. "The Quest"

Written by Robert J. Shaw; Directed by Gunnar Hellstrom; Airdate: February 13, 1981
Guest Stars: Joel Fabiani (Alex); Len Birman (Claude Brown); Woody Eney (Appleton); Ron Hayes (Hank); Jeff Cooper (Dr. Elby); Audrey Landers (Afton)
Special Guest Stars: Monte Markham (Clint); Anne Francis (Arliss); John Lehne (Kyle)
Subject: Sue Ellen is followed.

Trivia This episode was number 1 for the week, with a 30.6 rating. ★ Anne Francis recalls that "wardrobe did not have [a] budget to give me a change of costume for my last scene in the show, so I went out at lunchtime to a local fabric shop near MGM, bought some silk, and made myself a scarf dress just in time for the scene. [I] sewed it by hand while waiting in the dressing room to be called. It threw them all when I arrived on set and they were a bit worried about who had given me permission for the extra wardrobe change until I explained that it was my own dress! So they let me wear it. Other than that, all went smoothly."

70. "Lover Come Back"

Written by Leonard Katzman; Directed by Irving J. Moore; Airdate: February 20, 1981
Guest Stars: Joel Fabiani (Alex); Morgan Woodward (Punk); Ron Hayes (Hank); Jared Martin (Dusty)
Special Guest Star: Howard Keel (Clayton Farlow)
Subject: Sue Ellen finds Dusty.

Cast Notes This episode was number 1 for the week. ★ It marks the first appearance of Howard Keel as Clayton Farlow, a role he would continue through *Dallas's* thirteenth and final season. Keel was a veteran of many 1950s movie musicals, including *Annie Get Your Gun*, *Showboat*, *Kiss Me Kate*, and *Seven Brides for Seven Brothers*. Keel sang a lot on the set and, with his cheerful disposition, fit in from the start, according to Steve Kanaly. Susan Howard loved Keel, and remembers that on "his first day on the set, I asked him to sing, 'We Could Make Believe,' and he did! But he said, 'Susan, don't you try to do that! You're not a singer!'" Linda Gray also recalls Keel's first day on the *Dallas* set. "I adore Howard Keel," she says. "I grew up in Culver City and we went to our little theater and I would sit and watch Howard Keel and Kathryn Grayson, and I thought he was the most handsome man I had ever seen. And I remember when Mr. Katzman brought him on the set on Stage 5. And Mr. Katzman said, 'I'd like you to meet Mr. Keel.' And I was enthralled, like a gushing fan, saying, 'Oh, Mr. Keel, I saw all your films.' And he told me he filmed those very films with Kathryn Grayson on the very same stage." Keel regaled the crew with stories about his fabled career during the golden years at MGM. According to Kanaly, Keel was not brought on the show to replace the ailing Jim Davis, but was one of several characters created for Davis and Barbara Bel Geddes to play against. He was cast as Clayton after traveling to Los Angeles to appear on *The Love Boat* with Jane Powell. He then "got a call to see if I had any photographs to send over to the people at *Dallas*," Keel recalls. "I went over and met with [Leonard Katzman's secretary, Louella Caraway] who gave me a script, and I told her, 'I don't do readings, but I'm a pretty good actor!'" Keel met with Katzman, and they "hit it off right off the bat. [Katzman] was wonderful, very talented. I miss him terribly."

Trivia This is one of the few episodes that begins with a replay of the final scene from the preceding episode. ★ This is the first mention of Dusty's real name,

Steven. ★ Given Dusty's apparent death in Season 2, Jared Martin was as surprised as anyone to be asked back on *Dallas* during Season 3. Martin explains, "Dusty Farlow was as dead as a doornail after his plane crash. Only the craziness surrounding 'Who Shot J.R.?' brought him back. The writers were as surprised as anyone—although no one was more surprised than me. Stories [about J.R.'s shooting] were charged with speculation about Dusty and Sue Ellen, which naturally translated into speculation about Linda and myself. Somewhere during this time my agent called with a heads-up that I might be returning to the show. I reminded her that Dusty was dead—the plane accident had been gruesome. . . . She corrected me, saying this was television and anything can happen—she told me to sit tight, answer the phone, get a shave and new wardrobe. . . . Soon after this I was signed back on the show. . . . Little did I know that a man who was crippled and impotent was about to become an American sex symbol—something about the desire of a woman to nurse a fallen man back to health. The writers got me out of the wheelchair in the next episode, which I was grateful for. I stayed on crutches for a while—which gave me something to do as an actor. If I was strapped for a response I could wince or let my eyes roll back in my head, and a wave of instant sympathy would sweep through millions of living rooms. I'm not cynical about this. People believed what they watched, which meant we were doing a good job. *Dallas* and its audience had synergy, they moved and breathed and felt together."

71. "The New Mrs. Ewing"

Written by Linda B. Elstad; Directed by Patrick Duffy; Airdate: February 27, 1981
Guest Stars: Joel Fabiani (Alex); Morgan Woodward (Punk); Jeff Cooper (Dr. Elby);
Robert Sampson (Justin Carlisle)
Special Guest Star: Monte Markham (Clint)
Subject: Ray and Donna marry.

Cast Notes   Steve Kanaly was glad Susan Howard's character married into the Ewing family. Kanaly found Howard a desirable addition to *Dallas* since she, like her character, was from Marshall, Texas, and Katzman wanted to add more Texans to the show. Kanaly thought Howard was an excellent actress, one with whom he had "very good chemistry." She became a close friend of Kanaly's, almost "like a second wife." Her addition to the cast created a big change for Ray, who had been the only single male at the Ewing ranch for the show's first two seasons. Says Howard about her costar, "With Steve, what you see is what you get. There is not a deceitful bone in his body. He is a great father, good husband, and great friend." Howard also liked joining *Dallas* as a regular because the show helped change the national attitude toward her home state. She explained, "I was born and raised in Texas. I knew what it felt like when John Kennedy was shot in Dallas. We were president murderers. And all of a sudden this show—this silly show—comes on the air. And between *Dallas* and the Dallas Cowboys and Tom Landry and Roger Staubach, Dallas was redeemed."

Trivia This episode was number 2 for the week and earned the show's lowest season rating to date. ★ It is the first of twenty-nine episodes directed by Patrick Duffy, who became the second *Dallas* regular to direct the show; Larry Hagman made his directing debut during Season 2. Three other cast regulars, Linda Gray, Steve Kanaly, and Ken Kercheval, eventually directed episodes of *Dallas* as well, and Susan Howard wrote the script for two episodes (and, in a switch, *Dallas* director Gunnar Hellstrom later acted on the show). Victoria Principal "admired the aspirations of my castmates [but] chose a different path." While acting on *Dallas*, Principal "successfully wrote and sold two screenplays for movies of the week: *Lady on the Moon* to ABC in 1982 and *Scandal Kills* to CBS in 1984. I began my production company in 1985. My desire was to prove myself in these different venues while working without a net." ★ Steve Kanaly found Duffy "a little more precise" a director than Hagman, but Duffy "was also good natured and easy to work with." Hagman recalls that "Patrick Duffy and Linda Gray were suggested by me to direct shows." As for Duffy, while directing, he "enjoyed finding ways to make the women on the show even more beautiful than they already were. We would try to make gorgeous settings and lighting for them. It was also a relief to go out on location on an episode and make L.A. seem like Dallas." ★ Prior to directing, Duffy made clear that, although he socialized with Larry Hagman and Steve Kanaly, he was not as close with other castmates. "I enjoy all the *Dallas* cast as people; no, I do not get along with all of them," he said. "Let's say there are two categories—friendly and friendly-but-not-friendly. For the most part I respect everyone . . . as people." Several months later, after directing this episode, Duffy said, "You know that friendly competition you get into when you're in a scene with somebody? Now I feel totally different. I'm breaking my goodliness record." In particular, Duffy's directing work changed his relationship with Victoria Principal, whom he had considered "the upstage artist of the world. We were in a constant state of competition. We were very territorial in front of the camera, and it was a strain." But once Duffy directed, "I developed an appreciation for her, and I think for the first time she started to trust me. Some of the best scenes on the show were between Victoria and me, and they happened after we got comfortable with each other." Principal agreed that Duffy's directing brought a professional respect to their relationship. "Whenever Patrick directed an episode of *Dallas*," she said, "something he did two or three times a season—I really counted on his guidance. As a director, Patrick is insightful and tender. He cares about actors. The wonderful thing about working with him was that he encouraged me to stretch." ★ The set for the interior of Ray's home makes its debut in this episode. ★ Steve Kanaly knew Jared Martin from the agency they both used. Martin's return kept Kanaly on his toes; Kanaly knew his job security "was at the discretion of the producer," and he felt pressure to be at his best whenever another cowboy was added to the story. ★ Monte Markham was glad when his character finally consummated his relationship with Sue Ellen. "I kept doing the same scene over and over," Markham explains. "I'd say, 'I need you,' and we did that scene in a café, in a car wash, at the tennis court. And Lenny told me, 'Welcome to soap opera.' But he told me to keep with it, and Clint would finally get together with Sue Ellen. And . . . he finally did." Markham describes Linda Gray as "gold. She was one of the sexiest people I have ever worked with."

72. "Mark of Cain"

Written by Leah Markus; Directed by Larry Hagman; Airdate: March 13, 1981
Guest Stars: Priscilla Pointer (Rebecca); Ellen Bry (Jean); Morgan Woodward (Punk); David Healy (Senator Harbin); Jay Varela (Senator); Joseph Warren (Senator Dixon); Jeff Cooper (Dr. Elby); Joel Brooks (Larry); George O. Petrie (Harv)
Special Guest Star: Monte Markham (Clint)
Subject: Miss Ellie and Jock fight.

Cast Notes Mitch's classmate Jean is played by Ellen Bry, who went on to play Nurse Shirley Daniels on *St. Elsewhere.* ★ David Healy returned to *Dallas* as Chick Harvard in Episodes 303–05. ★ Costar Lance Guest played Lance on *Lou Grant*, Steve Brewer on *Knots Landing* and Michael Romanov on *Life Goes On.* ★ Joseph Warren, who makes the first of five appearances as Senator Dixon, played Officer Steinmetz on *Car 54, Where Are You?*

Trivia This episode was number 1 for the week. ★ Priscilla Pointer heard that she was brought back to *Dallas* because her first appearance in Episode 63 "went so well." Pointer enjoyed playing the Barnes matriarch. "Fortunately, I liked all of my children on the show immensely," she says. "Victoria was extremely helpful [and] when I first came on, since most of my scenes were with her in the beginning and she was so at home in the show and in her role, it made things a lot easier." Principal also held Pointer in high regard. When asked about her favorite *Dallas* guest stars, Principal replies, "There were so many talented and generous guest stars that I had the honor of working with that it is very difficult to narrow it down to one single choice. . . . My heart's choice would be Priscilla Pointer for her multi-dimensional talent on-screen and her multi-dimensional self off-screen. [She] played my (Pam's) mother for several seasons and I am forever grateful for the experience." ★ Barbara Babcock recalls that "Larry directed on one of the episodes I was in, and I liked him very much as a director. We had worked before together on *McMillan and Wife*, where we played husband and wife." ★ Monte Markham and Linda Gray "had a great time" filming this episode's hotel tryst scene. Markham recalls, "Larry directed . . . and he had champagne and caviar on the set!"

73. "The Gathering Storm"

Written by Robert J. Shaw; Directed by Michael Preece; Airdate: March 27, 1981
Guest Stars: Ellen Bry (Jean); Christopher Stone (Dave Stratton); Audrey Landers (Afton)

Special Guest Stars: Monte Markham (Clint); Priscilla Pointer (Rebecca); William Smithers (Jeremy)
Subject: Jock leaves Southfork.

Cast Notes Christopher Stone returned as Dave Stratton in Episodes 166–70.

Trivia This episode was number 1 for the week. ★ This is the first episode directed by Michael Preece, who directed more episodes of *Dallas* than anyone except Leonard Katzman. Preece directed sixty episodes during Seasons 3 through 13, and also directed the 1998 TV movie *War of the Ewings*. Preece was a cast and crew favorite. ★ As of this episode, Priscilla Pointer started playing scenes with Ken Kercheval. Pointer "had seen him perform on stage, so we had that in common. . . . I admired the way he always discovered little things, like specific behavior, that he could use to enhance the naturalness of his acting. And he was funny. Once, after trying to make a particular section of the script work, he told the director 'the only thing I can do with this scene is to have a nosebleed!'" ★ Audrey Landers, who describes her relationship with Leonard Katzman and his wife, LaRue, as "a special closeness," returned to the show after the wedding storyline due to her popularity with *Dallas* viewers and producers alike. Landers recalls that "the network was always concerned with viewer feedback. My fanmail skyrocketed, and they were aware of that. From my standpoint, I don't know if I was a Katzman favorite or not. Truthfully, if I had been then I probably should have had more to do in the show than I did. I was so unaware of any politics at that time. I was excited to be a part of the number 1 show in the world, and I basically just did my job to the best of my abilities, and never crossed anyone—I was truly a 'good girl.'"

74. "Ewing vs. Ewing"

Written by Leah Markus; Directed by Irving J. Moore; Airdate: April 3, 1981
Guest Stars: Craig Stevens (Craig Stewart); Christopher Stone (Dave Stratton); Morgan Woodward (Punk); John Randolph (Lincoln Hargrave); David Healy (Senator Harbin); Jay Varela (Senator); George O. Petrie (Harv); Joseph Warren (Senator Dixon); Audrey Landers (Afton)
Special Guest Stars: Monte Markham (Clint); Priscilla Pointer (Rebecca); William Smithers (Jeremy)
Subject: Miss Ellie and Jock reconcile.

Cast Notes John Randolph was a Tony award–winning actor (Neil Simon's *Broadway Bound*) who played Fritz on Broadway in *The Sound of Music*. He was seen in the movies *Prizzi's Honor, All the President's Men, Heaven Can Wait,* and *Earthquake* and as the grandfather on TV's *Roseanne*. He was a World War II veteran who married Sarah Cunningham (who appeared on *Dallas* as Digger's sister Maggie) shortly after the war. They had one son and one daughter and were married until Cunningham's death in 1986. Randolph died in 2004. ★ Craig Stevens was the real life husband of Alexis Smith, who played Clayton Farlow's sister in Seasons 6 and 12. Stevens and Smith were married from 1944 until Smith's death in

1993. Stevens was a dental student who went on to become a 1940s movie star. He later appeared in the Blake Edwards movie *S.O.B.*, which costarred Larry Hagman. He also appeared on TV as Blake Edwards's *Peter Gunn*. Stevens died on May 10, 2000, in Los Angeles. He was eighty-one years old.

Trivia This episode was number 2 for the week. ★ Jock and Miss Ellie have been married for forty-five years, but the dates referred to in Episodes 172, 176–77, and 179 in Season 7 establish an even longer marriage. ★ During Season 6, when she appeared on *Dallas*, Alexis Smith gave an interview in which she was asked about her long and successful marriage to Craig Stevens. "Craig says if you tell people how long you've been married they want to give you a plaque, or conversation comes to a halt," Smith said. "So he tells everyone we've been married twelve years."

75. "New Beginnings"

Written by Arthur Bernard Lewis; Directed by Irving J. Moore; Airdate: April 10, 1981
Guest Stars: Christopher Stone (Dave Stratton); Craig Stevens (Craig Stewart); Morgan Woodward (Punk); Stephanie Braxton (Alisha Ogden); Audrey Landers (Afton)
Special Guest Stars: Monte Markham (Clint); Priscilla Pointer (Rebecca); William Smithers (Jeremy)
Subject: Kristin's son is born.

Cast Notes This is Jim Davis's final appearance on *Dallas*. According to Leigh Mc-Closkey, "You wouldn't know [Davis] was sick at work. I remember he told me once, 'Son, it's better to go out on top, especially if you know you're on your way out. It's good to have it so good now.' I adored him. He had a centering effect on the whole cast, and there was a different feeling to the show when he was there." ★ Stephanie Braxton was a regular on *All My Children* and *The Edge of Night*. ★ This episode also marks Monte Markham's final appearance on *Dallas*. Markham thought that Irving J. Moore was a "great" director, and that *Dallas* was "one of my better experiences in TV. There was none of the stuff that usually goes on. In an ensemble cast, everyone wants to be treated a certain way, but on that set, if there was a problem, Lenny was right down there on top of it, and it was a wonderfully run set."

Trivia This episode was number 1 in the weekly ratings.

76. "Full Circle"

Written by Arthur Bernard Lewis; Directed by Michael Preece; Airdate: April 17, 1981
Guest Stars: Audrey Landers (Afton); Christopher Stone (Dave); Ellen Bry (Jean); Morgan Woodward (Punk); John Randolph (Lincoln); David Healy (Senator Harbin); Jay Varela (Senator); Joseph Warren (Senator Dixon); Jared Martin (Dusty)
Special Guest Stars: Priscilla Pointer (Rebecca); William Smithers (Jeremy)
Subject: Kristin returns.

Trivia This episode was number 1 for the week. ★ A trip to Paris is used to explain Jim Davis's absence. His character took subsequent trips to New York, Washington, D.C., and South America. ★ Ken Kercheval thought the reconciliation scene between Cliff and Rebecca was a "pathetically poignant" one. "You want to talk about complex? There was a scene that Art Lewis wrote when I, as Cliff, finally agreed to see my mother. . . . I flew into a rage at her and she got up to leave. . . . Then Cliff falls into his mother's arms and starts to cry. Now that's a complex scene." It is also Kercheval's favorite scene from his thirteen years of work on the show, and is a favorite scene of Priscilla Pointer's as well, "since it felt so emotionally fulfilled," says Pointer. "It is also the [scene] that *Dallas* viewers that I have met seem to remember the best. All these years later, I still run into people who ask about 'the licorice scene.'" ★ For such scenes, Kercheval prepared by listening to a relevant piece of mood music on a cassette recorder with headphones. He recommended his method to Barbara Bel Geddes once, but it backfired. After suggesting she listen to a piano version of a Cy Coleman song, Bel Geddes complained to him, "Thanks a whole lot. You just ruined my morning with that sad music when I was supposed to be lighthearted in the scene."

77. "Ewing-Gate"

Written by Leonard Katzman; Directed by Leonard Katzman; Airdate: May 1, 1981
Guest Stars: Audrey Landers (Afton); Morgan Woodward (Punk); David Healy (Senator Harbin); Len Birman (Claude Brown); Jay Varela (Senator); Joseph Warren (Senator Dixon); Byron Morrow; James Hong (Ambassador Lan Thong); Jared Martin (Dusty)
Special Guest Stars: Howard Keel (Clayton); William Smithers (Jeremy)
Subject: A body in the Southfork pool.

Cast Notes Costar Bill Boyett played Sergeant MacDonald on *Adam 12*.

Trivia This episode was number 1 in the weekly ratings with a 32.9 rating and 56 share, out-performing the Season 2 cliff-hanger in which J.R. got shot (that episode earned a 32.7 rating and 52 share) and making this the highest-rated *Dallas* cliff-hanger ever. ★ The Lubbock storyline gave Steve Kanaly the opportunity to act with Morgan Woodward, an actor Kanaly admired very much. Woodward says, "Steve was very, very easygoing and just a really fine gentleman." ★ This episode includes one of Leonard Katzman's favorite *Dallas* scenes, in which "J.R. was chasing [Leslie] and [the character] was tougher than nails, and . . . she kept holding off . . . and finally, when on her last show they went to bed, one of my favorite lines was when he looked at her and said, 'Well, it wasn't worth the wait.' . . . That's J.R." ★ Fred W. Berger was nominated for an Emmy Award for Outstanding Achievement in Film Editing for a Series for this episode. ★ While her character may commit treacherous acts, Audrey Landers pointed out, "I'm very, very different" from Afton, saying, "I've got very old-fashioned values. I would never compromise myself for anything." ★ The week this episode aired, *TV Guide* published a profile of Patrick Duffy in which Victoria Principal said of her costar, "He's very professional, unusually bright and aware of his craft at all times." ★ After filming his Episode 70 scenes, Howard Keel returned to Oklahoma City, and later heard Jim Davis was ill. "It came as a complete surprise. I knew him from way back and liked him a great deal." The producers thought about having Keel take over the role of Jock, but Keel turned them down. "Jim was too good in the role. [I told them,] 'I don't want to do that.'" Instead, they asked Keel to return as Clayton, which he does in this episode. "It was such a stroke of luck," recalls Keel. "I was not working and was a bit down, and it really saved me. It was too bad that it was Jim's illness that created their need for me, but I was happy to play the role. The show was run so ably, and Leonard Katzman was a great producer and director. My wife and I got along great with him and his wife."

SEASON 4
1981–82—"Gone But Not Forgotten"

IN LATE 1980, AFTER SUFFERING from migraine headaches for a number of years, Jim Davis was diagnosed with brain cancer. Despite the diagnosis and the chemotherapy treatment he underwent in early 1981, Davis continued to go to work at the Culver City set. His cancer was inoperable, but he was determined to continue working as long as he could. The chemotherapy made his hair fall out, and affected his memory and his ability to walk. But Davis never asked for help and never complained about his condition, although Lorimar built him a dressing room on the soundstage so he did not have far to walk and provided teleprompters to help him with his lines. Davis was beloved by the cast and crew of *Dallas*, and the producers refused to recast the role of Jock or write the character out of the show while Davis struggled with his illness. Leonard Katzman recognized that Davis's "whole life centered around this show. We kept his character alive so he could read the scripts and have the hope and faith that he would make it back. . . . We felt we were better off keeping alive the character . . . until we knew what was really going to happen to Jim."

Davis was able to appear in all but the last two episodes filmed before the 1981 hiatus. His character's absence from those two episodes was explained by a trip abroad. In early April 1981, he had abdominal surgery for a perforated ulcer. The cast gathered at Davis's home in Northridge, California, toward the end of April. Davis died a few days later, on April 26, at home with his wife Blanche by his side. He was sixty-five years old. Larry Hagman called Davis's death the "hardest blow" to hit the cast and crew during *Dallas*'s long run. Hagman was traveling in Scotland at the time of Davis's death, and released a statement calling Davis, "a great surrogate father, a lovely man to work with, and I loved him. I'm very sad, and I shall miss him." Katzman found Davis to be "the most accessible man I ever met. I never saw him mean or cruel to anyone." To Charlene Tilton, "Jim was really like my granddaddy. He and Blanche were the ones I went to when I was in trouble. Jim was the kindest man I ever knew."

While an airport strike prevented Hagman from getting back from Europe in time for Davis's funeral, he sent a wreath that said, "Goodbye, Goom-ba," which was his nickname for Davis "because before every take, he'd clear his throat and make this horrible noise that sounded like 'goom-ba.'" Others from the *Dallas* company, however, did attend the funeral. Victoria Principal, who was particularly close to Davis, gave one of the eulogies. Although Principal "knew that Jim was dying—we all did," she recalled—she was devastated by his death. Principal had bonded with Davis because he "had a daughter, Tara—his only child—who passed away in a car accident when she was in her teens. And unbeknownst to me, we bore an uncanny resemblance to one another. And so from the time that we began working together, we had a very special paternal relationship. In fact, I know that when Jim died, one of the photographs in his wallet was of me and one of Tara." Tara Davis was born in 1953, died in 1970, and is buried next to her father in Los Angeles.

Davis's costars were deeply affected by his death. Hagman loved their light-hearted "sort of a father-son relationship. I used to joke on the set, and he'd get ticked off at me. 'Goddamn smart ass son of a bitch,' he'd say. 'This is business we're doing here. Stop messing around. Do you hear me, boy?'" Hagman wrote in his memoir, "I still see him every day. The first thing you see when you enter my home is the oil painting of Jim that hung in the living room at Southfork." Princi-pal recounted that Davis would look after her and complained when she had a new boyfriend, "Who the hell is this guy and why haven't I had a chance to look him over?" Linda Gray remembered how, on the first day of shooting the pilot, "he gave me a big hug and made sure that everyone knew I was his friend. And that counted." To Ken Kercheval, Davis was "a dynamite guy. Just an old-fashioned movie star." And for Susan Howard, "In Texas, when you call your daddy 'Daddy' . . . it's a special word. And . . . Jim was Daddy."

Steve Kanaly was also very close to Davis, and fondly recalls Davis marveling at the star treatment he got during a trip to Buckingham Palace in London after filming ended in the spring of 1980. "He came back from his trip and told us how the palace guards told him, 'Mr. Davis, if you could just please step inside the gates here, please, sir.' And he was so excited because he was in his seventies and he said, 'I've finally become a success.'" Kanaly also admired how Davis never turned down a request for an autograph because Davis had worked so long and hard to get to that point in his career. Kanaly considered Davis his mentor, and Davis coun-seled Kanaly to stick with *Dallas* during its second year, when Kanaly became frus-trated with Ray's diminished role and considered returning to movies. Davis recounted for Kanaly how his own career started off with high expectations when he landed a leading role in a Bette Davis film that turned out to be a flop, and he subsequently always just missed getting a part or being in a hit. Davis felt *Dallas* was going to be something, and Kanaly decided to stay.

By the time of Davis's death, the writers were working on the storylines for Season 4, and they were now confronted with how the show should address Davis's absence. "The loss of Jim was terrible," explained Katzman, because "it took away the one thing that made *Dallas* different, the strong father figure." The producers remained resolute that Davis's role would not be recast. Phil Capice ex-plained that Davis "was so identified with the character of Jock Ewing, that there was never any question of replacing him. Out of respect to Jim's memory, we felt it would be wrong to bring in another actor." Writer Arthur Bernard Lewis agreed. "We really agonized over the dilemma," he said. "It would have been a very emotional thing for us to substitute another look-alike actor for Jim, but none of us ever went along with that idea. Jim had achieved something big at the end of his life with this role, and we wanted to leave it that way."

The writers and producers knew, however, that it would take time to work Jock's death into the plot because all *Dallas* storylines built up slowly. "People couldn't suddenly say, 'Guess what! Daddy died!'" Katzman explained. And, as Lewis recognized, they had ended Season 3 "with another death—Kristin's, in a swimming pool—and we couldn't make the death of a really major character, Jock Ewing, just a subplot to Kristin's." Even if Lewis and his writers had a quick solution to the problem, a strike by the Writers Guild prevented them from weaving any explanation about Jock's absence into the completed scripts. Katzman considered the strike delay an opportunity to "plan an appropriate and fitting death for Jock that would bring honor" to both Jock Ewing and Jim Davis.

Katzman, Capice, and Lewis and the writing team eventually decided that Jock would die later during Season 4, and that in the interim, his character's absence would continue to be explained by Jock's overseas trip made at the behest of the federal government. Lorimar felt it found a "graceful demise" for Davis's character, and a studio executive told the *Los Angeles Times* that "no one will be able to accuse us of exploiting this tragedy." Although Katzman described this period as "a hard time for all of us," he was pleased with the way Davis's death was handled, noting that "Jock Ewing died an oilman who was serving his country."

Davis received a posthumous Emmy nomination as Outstanding Lead Actor in a Drama Series, his first. The cast and crew of *Dallas* received five other nominations in the summer of 1981, the most the show would ever receive for a single season. Lead acting nods also went to Barbara Bel Geddes (her third), Larry Hagman (his second), and Linda Gray (her first). *Dallas* was nominated as Outstanding Drama (for the second and last time), and Fred Berger received an editing nomination (his second). The show failed to win any Emmys when the awards were presented on September 13, 1983, however, in a *Hill Street Blues* sweep that included an Outstanding Lead Actress win for *Hill Street*'s Barbara Babcock, who was doing double duty by continuing her occasional *Dallas* role as Liz Craig. Linda Gray, though, went on to win Germany's Bambi award and Italy's Il Gato for Best Actress on Television. Ken Kercheval thought it was "really pretty asinine" that *Dallas* was never recognized as Outstanding Drama, and Steve Kanaly felt that there was an artistic bias against the show because it was a "soap opera" and not what the industry deemed to be more prestigious fare.

Midway through the season, in December 1981, CBS moved *Dallas* from its 10:00 p.m. slot to the 9:00 p.m. slot in order to use its popularity to help establish a new show. *Dallas* still followed *The Dukes of Hazzard*, which was simultaneously moved from 9:00 p.m. to 8:00 p.m., but *Dallas* was now the lead-in for *Falcon*

Crest, a *Dallas* imitator about a San Francisco wine family. *Falcon Crest* was created by Earl Hamner, who gave Lorimar one of its first big hits with *The Waltons*, and starred Jane Wyman and Robert Foxworth, who had almost been cast as J.R. three years earlier. A few weeks later, on New Year's Day, 1982, CBS aired an episode entitled "Barbecue Two," in which the Ewings learn of Jock's helicopter crash. This episode was ranked number 5 in the weekly Nielsen ratings, making it one of the season's two lowest-ranked episodes. The following week, CBS aired an episode called "The Search," which featured the Ewing sons' unsuccessful search for Jock amidst flashbacks paying tribute to Jim Davis. "The Search" was the number 1 show for the week, and earned *Dallas*'s highest season rating to date.

In early 1982, *Dallas* received the same four Golden Globe nominations it had earned the previous year: Best Drama, Best Actor (Larry Hagman), and two for Best Actress (Barbara Bel Geddes and Linda Gray). This time, however, *Dallas* was not shut out, as Bel Geddes won the Best Actress award in a tie with Linda Evans of *Dynasty*. This was the last of Bel Geddes' three Golden Globe nominations. Just as she was the only cast member to win the coveted Emmy, Bel Geddes was the only *Dallas* cast member to win the prestigious Golden Globe.

Dallas remained TV's number 1 show during the 1981–82 season, with a 28.4 rating. It was the number 1 show thirteen out of the twenty-six weeks it aired an original episode and the number 2 show seven times. It also earned a *Time* magazine award as one of the best shows on TV, with *Time* asking, "Will Brave Bobby and Barren Pamela adopt the love child of J.R. and his dead mistress Kristin? Enter the Ewing labyrinth and be hooked or be damned." In accordance with CBS's hopes, *Dallas*'s popularity helped *Falcon Crest* find an audience, and that show finished in thirteenth place for the year and went on to air for eight more seasons.

SEASON 4 EPISODE GUIDE

Regular Cast

Starring:
Barbara Bel Geddes as Miss Ellie
Patrick Duffy as Bobby
Linda Gray as Sue Ellen
Larry Hagman as J.R.
Susan Howard as Donna
Steve Kanaly as Ray
Ken Kercheval as Cliff
Victoria Principal as Pam
Charlene Tilton as Lucy
Also Starring:
Jared Martin as Dusty
Leigh McCloskey as Mitch

Technical Credits

Producer: Leonard Katzman
Executive Producer: Philip Capice
Supervising Producer: Arthur Bernard
Lewis
Associate Producer: Cliff Fenneman
Story Editor: Linda Elstad
Music: Jerrold Immel, Bruce Broughton,
Richard Lewis Warren, John Parker,
Lance Rubin
Unit Production Manager: Wayne A.
Farlow
First Assistant Directors: Fred Stromsoe,
Alan Brimfield

Second Assistant Director: Paul Snider
Director of Photography: Edward R. Plante
Art Director: Les Gobruegge
Editors: Fred W. Berger, A.C.E., John
Arthur Davies, Lloyd Richardson
Executive in Charge of Casting: Barbara
Miller
Casting: Irene Mariano
Set Decorator: Phil Leonard
Property Master: Anthony C. Thorpe
Dialogue Director: Fred Martin
Costumers: Jack Bear, Violet Cane
Makeup: Kathy Agron, Susan Cabral,
Judith Silverman
Hair Stylists: Gregg Mitchell, Generio
Gugliemotto
Location Casting: Rody Kent
Production Sound Mixer: Clark King,
C.S.A.
Sound Effects Supervisor: Victor Guarnier
Sound Effects Editors: Tom Gillis Burke,
Tony Zero, Rich Stevens
Music Editor: George Probert
Main Title Design: Wayne Fitzgerald
Production Supervisor: Mitch Ackerman
Executive Production Supervisor: Edward
O. Denault

78. "Missing Heir"

Written by Arthur Bernard Lewis; Directed by Irving J. Moore; Airdate: October 9, 1981
Special Guest Stars: Priscilla Pointer (Rebecca); Audrey Landers (Afton); Howard Keel
(Clayton)
Guest Stars: Barbara Babcock (Liz); Barry Corbin (Fenton); Bill Lucking (Deputy Mat-
land); Herbert Rudley (Howard Barker)
Subject: Kristin's death.

Cast Notes Susan Howard's credit was moved to the main title as of this episode, and Jared Martin's credit was moved to the beginning of the episode. ★ Herbert Rudley costarred with Eve Arden in the sitcom *The Mothers-in-Law.* ★ Bill Lucking played Colonel Lynch on *The A-Team.* ★ Barbara Babcock explains that she began appearing on *Hill Street Blues* in 1981, making her "the only actor at the time who had a recurring role on two hits."

Trivia   This episode was number 1 in the weekly ratings. ★ The first thirteen episodes of Season 4 were filmed in Texas, making Season 4 the one with the highest percentage (50 percent) of on-location episodes. The season premiere pool scene, however, was filmed in Culver City before filming was completed for Season 3 the previous spring. To keep the drowning victim's identity a mystery, alternate scenes were filmed with Ken Kercheval finding Mary Crosby, Linda Gray, and Victoria Principal in the pool. Mary Crosby recalls that "Linda and Victoria and I were all there on the same day, all in our white dresses, taking our turns in the pool. And we would get in with Ken and he would find us and turn us over. We had to be extremely still, so there were no ripples in the pool. I remember at one point Linda broke us all up when it was her chance to be turned over by pushing her hair off to the side and making like a dead body." The following scene, featuring Fenton, was filmed at Culver City after the spring 1981 hiatus. Barry Corbin enjoyed that scene since he got to act opposite Larry Hagman and Ken Kercheval. He recalls, "I didn't get a chance to know them really well because I wasn't there long, but from the time I spent with them, I can say they were a lot of fun to be around." ★ The ranch used as the Southern Cross was actually located in Forney, Texas, twenty miles east of Dallas and not far from Duncan Acres. That ranch was a 455-acre breeding ranch with a swimming pool, guest house, foreman's house, stock tanks and stables. ★ Despite her character's violent run-in with J.R., Mary Crosby has nothing but praise for Larry Hagman, who she felt "was the show. And I think that anytime people wanted to pretend he wasn't, they got into trouble."

79. "Gone But Not Forgotten"

Written by Arthur Bernard Lewis; Directed by Leonard Katzman; Airdate: October 16, 1981
Special Guest Stars: Priscilla Pointer (Rebecca); Audrey Landers (Afton); William Smithers (Jeremy); Howard Keel (Clayton)
Guest Stars: Morgan Woodward (Punk); Barry Corbin (Fenton); Lane Smith (Ward); Bruce French (Jerry Macon); Bill Morey (Judge); Raleigh Bond; Fern Fitzgerald (Marilee); Herbert Rudley (Howard)
Subject: J.R. plots against Sue Ellen.

Cast Notes   Debbie Rennard, known as Deborah as of Season 9, makes her first appearance as J.R.'s secretary, Sylvia "Sly" Lovegren. Rennard appeared in 191 episodes of *Dallas*, more than any other actor except for those seen in the main title. She played Sly through Season 13 and in *J.R. Returns.* When she was hired, Rennard later told *People* magazine, "Larry told me, 'Never ask for a raise.' Maybe that's why I stuck around so long." ★ Veteran character actor Bill Morey makes his first appearance on the show. He returned as Leo Wakefield in Seasons 6, 7, and 10. He went on to star in *Beggars and Choosers*, a Showtime drama about network programming executives developed by NBC programming legend Brandon Tartikoff, who died of cancer several years before the show premiered in 1999. ★ Lane Smith played Perry White in *Lois and Clark—The New Adventures of Superman*, which costarred *Dallas* castmates Tracy Scoggins and K Callan and was produced in its first year by *Dallas* creator David Jacobs. Smith also played the district attorney in *My Cousin Vinny* and Richard Nixon in TV's *The Final Days*. He died on June 13, 2005, at the age of sixty-nine.

Trivia This episode was number 1 in the weekly ratings, but its 28.4 rating was the first rating below 30 that *Dallas* had earned since Season 1. ★ According to Ken Kercheval, when Afton called Cliff a loser, "it stuck. But he was always coming back to try again. . . . He wore his emotions on his sleeve. If he got angry, he exploded. If he got sad, he cried." In another interview, Kercheval elaborated, "Cliff loses, but Cliff is not a loser. . . . He is the most resilient human being in the world. To take the punishment that this guy has taken, and be willing to come back and face the most formidable foe on television. That's not a loser—not in my book! If I adapted that attitude in my performance, nobody would give a damn about Cliff Barnes. I'm the guy that everybody out there has been. Not too tactful with the ladies sometimes. Not much class. But what can I say?" ★ Jared Martin's return to *Dallas* gave him a newfound insight into the level of celebrity that the "Who Shot J.R.?" storyline gave Larry Hagman. Once, when rehearsing a scene with Hagman in Hagman's trailer, one of the "tour buses that took tourists around Southfork . . . went in the wrong gate, and the people got out and began walking around. We could hear them asking where J.R. was. They were right outside our door, and if they'd known he was inside they would have pulverized the motorhome. Squished it. I remember looking at Hagman and seeing something in his eyes. A hunted look. And I knew that he'd never be alone again."

80. "Showdown at San Angelo"

Written by Leonard Katzman; Directed by Irving J. Moore; Airdate: October 23, 1981
Special Guest Stars: Priscilla Pointer (Rebecca); Audrey Landers (Afton); Howard Keel (Clayton)
Guest Stars: Morgan Woodward (Punk); Bruce French (Jerry)
Subject: Miss Ellie's visit.

Trivia This episode was number 4 in the weekly ratings. ★ This is the first appearance of the Southfork kitchen set. ★ Pam's nightmare joins the pantheon of dreams plaguing the citizens of Dallas. During the show's run, Sue Ellen, J.R., Bobby, April, and Wes Parmalee all had dreams, but Pam's *other* dream topped them all: It lasted from the last few scenes of Episode 191 in Season 7 until the final scene of Episode 222 in Season 8. ★ Because of Miss Ellie's visit to the Southern Cross Ranch in this episode, Jared Martin got to act with Barbara Bel Geddes, who Martin calls "a favorite *Dallas* person. She came from the East, had done an enormous amount of stage, and the rumor had it that we went to the same high school in Putney, Vermont. I remember hearing about her when I was in my teens. I never checked out the story and for some crazy reason don't remember asking her about it on the set. But I felt we had something in common. Barbara was smart, cultivated, emotionally available, a pro to her fingertips, a calming influence in sometimes jumpy circumstances, and loved by everyone connected with *Dallas*. She was literally irreplaceable, as Donna Reed found out several years later. . . . With Barbara, class told. She could dominate a scene by moving a teacup five inches across a counter or by arching an eyebrow. That's what the word 'presence' means. You don't have to try to be, you just are." Bel Geddes indeed attended the private Putney School, and confessed that she was expelled from the school at the age of sixteen for kissing a boy, which the school labeled a "disturbing influence." Bel Geddes was amused that "they're always making me play well-bred ladies. I'm not very well-bred and I'm not much of a lady." ★ Linda Gray also considered Bel Geddes one of her favorite costars, explaining, "I called her 'Mama.' She was the reason I took *Dallas*, because I thought if a classy woman like that was doing the show, it was a pretty solid indication of the quality of the project."

81. "Little Boy Lost"

Written by Leonard Katzman; Directed by Leonard Katzman; Airdate: October 30, 1981
Special Guest Stars: Priscilla Pointer (Rebecca); Barry Nelson (Arthur); Howard Keel
(Clayton)
Guest Stars: Ed Winter (Dr. Waring); Morgan Brittany (Katherine Wentworth); Morgan
Woodward (Punk); Donegan Smith (John Jackson); John Zaremba (Dr. Danvers); Herbert
Rudley (Howard); Liam Sullivan (Judge William Packer); Arthur Malet (Forrest)
Subject: John Ross' custody hearing.

Cast Notes Morgan Brittany makes her first appearance as Katherine Wentworth, a role she would play in Seasons 4 through 7 and 10. As a child, Brittany, under her real name, Suzanne Cupito, appeared in such movies as *The Birds; Gypsy;* and *Yours, Mine and Ours.* She played Ron Howard's girlfriend on *The Andy Griffith Show.* While on *Dallas,* she also starred in the prime-time soap *Glitter* along with *Dallas* costar Timothy Patrick Murphy. Brittany was cast as Katherine after the producers saw her play Vivian Leigh in the miniseries *Moviola.* Recalls Brittany, "When they conceived the role of Katherine, she was originally in only three or four episodes. There was really no direction for her at the time. In fact, when I went in on the audition, the part was written for a sixteen-year-old and the actresses auditioning were quite a group. Blondes, brunettes, short, tall, actresses, models, and all different ages. When I got the role, I was told to be mysterious, not to go in any specific direction." ★ Arthur is played by 1940s MGM star Barry Nelson, who went on to star in the TV version of the Lucille Ball radio hit *My Favorite Husband.* Nelson also costarred with Barbara Bel Geddes in one of her many Broadway hits, the 1961 comedy *Mary, Mary.* ★ Liam Sullivan returned to *Dallas* as a judge in Episode 247 and a lawyer in Episodes 333 and 334. Sullivan was a veteran actor who had appeared on *Star Trek*, *The Twilight Zone*, *L.A. Law*, and *Hawaii Five-O*. He also appeared on Broadway in director Mike Nichols's revival of *The Little Foxes*. Sullivan died on April 19, 1998, at the age of seventy-four. ★ Mitch's mentor, Dr. Waring, is played by TV veteran Edward Winter, best known for his guest role as Colonel Flagg on *M*A*S*H*. He also costarred in a 1984 sitcom spoof of the *Dallas* genre called *Empire*, which costarred Francine Tacker, the second Jenna Wade. Winter died in March of 2001. ★ Arthur Malet, who plays the comptroller in this episode and in Episodes 99 and 101, appeared as the butler in the Warren Beatty movie *Heaven Can Wait*. He reappeared on *Dallas* in Seasons 12 and 13 as Ryan.

Trivia This episode fell to number 5 in the weekly ratings, tying Episode 89 as the season's lowest-ranked episode. ★ This episode opens with an aerial view of the front and back of Duncan Acres, filmed from a helicopter flying above the property. ★ Based on Morgan Brittany's early scenes, Priscilla Pointer "didn't suspect that any child of mine would ever be so villainous. Shame on her. . . . Personally I found [Morgan] charming as well as beautiful. She had a young stunt-man husband named Jack Gill and together they made a striking couple." Gill did stunt work for and was John Schneider's double on *The Dukes of Hazzard* and was stunt coordinator for *Knight Rider*. More recently, Gill, who is president of Stunts Unlimited, has acted as stunt coordinator and second unit director in films, including the 2003 movie *Dr. Seuss' The Cat in the Hat* and the 2002 movie *Austin Powers in Goldmember*.

82. "The Sweet Smell of Revenge"

Written by Linda Elstad; Directed by Irving J. Moore; Airdate: November 6, 1981
Guest Stars: Ed Winter (Dr. Waring); Morgan Brittany (Katherine); Gretchen Wyler (Dr. Dagmara Conrad); Morgan Woodward (Punk Anderson); Laurence Haddon (Franklin); Barbara Babcock (Liz); Art Hindle (Jeff Farraday)
Subject: J.R. plots against Clayton.

Cast Notes Gretchen Wyler was a musical comedy star in the 1950s. ★ Art Hindle appeared in the 1981 movie *Porky's* and David Jacobs's 1985 series *Berrenger's*. ★ Costar Jack Rader returned to *Dallas* as Pete Reuther in Season 12.

Trivia This episode put the show back in the number 1 spot in the weekly ratings. ★ Of her scenes with Barbara Bel Geddes, Priscilla Pointer says, "Barbara and I both came from the theater and were of the same generation, so we enjoyed playing together very much. . . . The closest she came to commenting on our respective roles was to always declare that we were the 'matriarchs!'"

83. "The Big Shutdown"

Written by Arthur Bernard Lewis; Directed by Leonard Katzman; Airdate: November 13, 1981
Special Guest Stars: Priscilla Pointer (Rebecca); Audrey Landers (Afton); Howard Keel (Clayton)

Guest Stars: Edward Winter (Dr. Waring); Morgan Brittany (Katherine); Gretchen Wyler (Dr. Conrad); Morgan Woodward (Punk); Dennis Patrick (Vaughan); Art Hindle (Farraday); Tom Fucello (Dave Culver); Laurence Haddon (Franklin); Phillip R. Allen (Lloyd Bettinger)
Subject: J.R. plots against Clayton.

Cast Notes Phillip R. Allen was a regular on The Hardy Boys Mysteries and Alice.

Trivia This episode was number 1 in the weekly ratings. ★ This episode's explanation of how Amy Farlow died, why Clayton rebuilt their house and where Dusty was born differs from the versions of those incidents provided in Episodes 158 and 160, when Clayton's sister arrives in Dallas and J.R. investigates the Farlows' past.

84. "Blocked"

Written by Arthur Bernard Lewis; Directed by Irving J. Moore; Airdate: November 20, 1981
Special Guest Stars: Priscilla Pointer (Rebecca); Audrey Landers (Afton); Howard Keel (Clayton)
Guest Stars: Gretchen Wyler (Dr. Conrad); Art Hindle (Farraday); Joseph Warren (Senator Dixon)
Subject: J.R. plots against Clayton.

Trivia This episode was number 1 in the weekly ratings. ★ Although Susan Howard "loved it when Lenny directed," Irving Moore was Howard's favorite Dallas director. In addition to being directed by Moore, this episode features one of several confrontations between Howard's character and Larry Hagman's. While Donna often confronted J.R., Howard respected Hagman, who she thought succeeded as J.R. because he "played it tongue-in-cheek. And yet he could also play it deadly, deadly serious. And then he could play it with the tenderness that absolutely disrupted every evil thought you ever [had] of J.R."

85. "The Split"

Written by Leonard Katzman; Directed by Leonard Katzman; Airdate: November 27, 1981
Special Guest Stars: Priscilla Pointer (Rebecca); Audrey Landers (Afton); Howard Keel (Clayton)
Guest Stars: Ted Shackelford (Gary); Gretchen Wyler (Dr. Conrad); Dennis Patrick (Vaughan); Art Hindle (Farraday); Robert Symonds (Martin Porter); Bernard Behrens (Haskell); David Tress (Walter Sherr); Joan Van Ark (Valene)
Subject: Jock divides Ewing Oil.

Cast Notes Barbara Stock, who plays Bermuda Chamber of Commerce staffer Heather Wilson, returned to Dallas as Liz Adams in Seasons 12 and 13.

Trivia This episode was number 2 in the weekly ratings. ★ This is one of seven return appearances made by Gary during Seasons 2 through 5, 8, and 13. ★ Editor Fred W. Berger received two award nominations for this episode: an Emmy award for Outstanding Film Editing for a Series and the American Cinema Editors Eddie

Award for Best Edited Episode from a Television Series. ★ Jared Martin liked this episode's "Cotton Bowl scene because of the helicopter ride. It was an ambitious scene because of its gutsy logistics. All elements had to be in place—the chopper had to arrive on time and touch down at the right spot, the light had to be constant, with no wind, Larry would be standing on the right spot, with the cameras rolling and in focus and if either actor came up dry all the elaborate step-by-step mechanics would need to be repeated—at great cost. On the tight *Dallas* schedule it was a real acknowledgement to the power of the J.R.-Dusty-Sue Ellen triangle that the show would spend a full day on one scene, and more specifically one shot—the helicopter arrival and step-down confrontation on the Cotton Bowl's fifty-yard line. My epiphany came with the ride on the chopper. I'd flown in planes of all sizes and shapes, but never experienced the ride of a small bubble-nosed executive chopper where it feels like there's no floor and you're literally catapulting through air with the ground coming up fast and 90 percent of me is tripping out on the fascination of this sensation and the other 10 percent fighting to hold on to the lines and the character's intention and trying to remember not to miss a step dismounting and fall flat on my face. The scene was done in one long take as were all *Dallas* scenes during my time on the show. There were no safety net cutaways after the first two or four lines when the camera moved to another setup and the actors could start over. *Dallas* editors usually got a full compliment of coverage—the full scene in a master, medium and close up. Anyway—Dusty stepped out of the chopper to be met by a sneering J.R., whereupon both men went through the long scene in one take while the remaining parts of Jared Martin were still landing—stomach, arms, brain, and feet reassembling from the helicopter while the scene concluded. It wasn't my best acting because I was only partly there." ★ The J.R./Afton falling out would allow Audrey Landers to proudly proclaim, "I am the only mistress on the show ever to have dumped J.R." Subsequent mistresses would follow suit, leaving Afton the *first* mistress to dump J.R. Landers found that Larry Hagman was "always very professional, and a lot of fun to work with. He always seemed to be in character."

86. "Five Dollars a Barrel"

Written by Leonard Katzman; Directed by Irving J. Moore; Airdate: December 4, 1981
Special Guest Stars: Priscilla Pointer (Rebecca); Howard Keel (Clayton)
Guest Stars: Ed Winter (Dr. Waring); Ted Shackelford (Gary); Gretchen Wyler (Dr. Conrad); Dennis Patrick (Vaughan); Art Hindle (Farraday); Lee de Broux (McCoy); Robert Symonds (Martin Porter); David Tress (Walter Sherr); Sally Kemp
Subject: Cliff plots against J.R.

Cast Notes Lee de Broux returned to *Dallas* as Ewing tanker captain Jack Bouleris in Episodes 317 and 319. He also appeared on *Magnum, P.I.*

Trivia This is the second week in a row that *Dallas* was number 2 in the weekly ratings. It was *Dallas*'s first episode in its new 9:00 p.m. timeslot. CBS moved the show from 10:00 p.m. to 9:00 p.m. to make room for *Falcon Crest*, which earned a number 8 ranking, 21.8 rating, and 38 share with its series premiere. CBS promoted its new series by asking viewers, "What does J.R. do after *Dallas*? He watches *Falcon Crest*!" *Falcon Crest* went on to follow *Dallas* on Friday nights until shortly before *Falcon Crest* went off the air on May 17, 1990, one year before *Dallas* was cancelled. *Dallas* actors who appeared on *Falcon Crest* included Mark Lindsay Chapman, Stephen Elliott, Morgan Fairchild, Mel Ferrer, and Laura Johnson.

87. "Starting Over"

Written by Leonard Katzman; Directed by Leonard Katzman; Airdate: December 11, 1981
Special Guest Stars: Barry Nelson (Arthur); Howard Keel (Clayton)
Guest Stars: Gretchen Wyler (Dr. Conrad); Dennis Patrick (Vaughan); Art Hindle (Farraday); Laurence Haddon (Franklin); Edmund Gilbert (Paul Winslow)
Subject: Bobby brings Christopher home.

Cast Notes Edmund Gilbert played Shaun Cassidy's and Parker Stevenson's father on *The Hardy Boys Mysteries*. ★ Costar Bruce Gray, who plays Dr. Alan Cosby, returned to *Dallas* as Brian in Episode 234, Richard Mertz in Episode 323, and David Stanley in Episodes 351 and 354.

Trivia This episode was number 2 in the weekly ratings. ★ While Jared Martin returned to *Dallas* for limited appearances in Seasons 5, 7, 8, and 13, this episode was the last of his main run as Dusty. One of the things Martin liked best about the role was working with Howard Keel. Martin found Keel "professional, available, generous, funny. Howard had worked in films almost all his life and was like the Rock of Gibraltar for set steadiness. He enjoyed being on *Dallas* and was fun to be around. He was wry and sardonic but always ultra-professional. In Howard I could always see the stage-struck Illinois kid who made it big in the gee-shucks world of Hollywood musicals. I was a single parent in those days and felt conflicted [about] leaving my young son Christian behind, especially as I had only the summer to spend with him. Howard and I struck up a relationship based on this issue—he said the hardest part is letting them go, while I thought the hardest part is finding time for them. . . . Howard and I went to a few functions in Dallas as a kind of father-son entry. I liked him. What he taught me was hard to transmit, but it was all about being a professional."

88. "Waterloo at Southfork"

Written by Linda Elstad; Directed by Irving J. Moore; Airdate: December 18, 1981
Special Guest Stars: Priscilla Pointer (Rebecca); Audrey Landers (Afton); Barry Nelson (Arthur); Howard Keel (Clayton)
Guest Stars: Gretchen Wyler (Dr. Conrad); Dennis Patrick (Vaughan); Patricia McCormack (Evelyn Michaelson); Herbert Rudley (Howard Barker); David Tress (Walter Sherr); Wiley Harker (Judge)
Subject: J.R. is demoted.

Cast Notes Former child star Patricia McCormack starred in the Broadway and movie versions of *The Bad Seed*. She appeared on TV in *Mama* and *The Ropers*, a spin-off of *Three's Company*. ★ Dan Hamilton makes the first of several appearances as Eric.

Trivia This episode was number 1 in the weekly ratings. ★ Cliff's visit with his nephew is overlooked in Episode 120, when they supposedly meet for the first time. ★ Barbara Bel Geddes and Larry Hagman, like their on-screen characters, had a close bond. Hagman called Bel Geddes "Mama" in real life and even took her to visit his stepmother at the Hagman family home in Weatherford, Texas.

89. "Barbeque Two"

Written by Arthur Bernard Lewis; Directed by Leonard Katzman; Airdate: January 1, 1982
Special Guest Stars: Priscilla Pointer (Rebecca); Audrey Landers (Afton); Howard Keel (Clayton)
Guest Stars: Edward Winter (Dr. Waring); Morgan Brittany (Katherine); Dennis Redfield (Roger); Bernard Behrens (Haskell)
Subject: Jock's helicopter crashes.

Cast Notes Dennis Redfield makes his first appearance as Roger. ★ Bit player Anne Lucas makes her first of forty-eight appearances. She played Oil Baron's Club waitress Cassie during Seasons 6 through 9.

Trivia This episode was number 5 in the weekly ratings ★ Larry from Deltham Catering also catered the Ewing barbeques in Seasons 5 through 7. ★ Cliff drives a BMW with "CLIFF B" tags. ★ Leonard Katzman felt that "one of the great losses when we lost Jock was losing something that may be missing in a lot of American families, which was the very strong father figure who, when he sat at the table, nobody talked unless he talked to them [and] no matter how big the boys were it was 'Yessir,' 'Yes, Daddy.' If they were arguing, he'd stop them. That was an element that originally made the show very successful. I think a lot of people longed for that kind of dominant figure in a family. So there was a great loss when [Jim Davis died]." ★ While Clayton was being embraced by some of the Ewings, Howard Keel felt that becoming a part of the *Dallas* family was difficult. "The cast was all wonderful," he says, "although in some ways I never felt part of the group. It is hard when you come in like that to replace somebody. And the writers didn't do anything to help me! I didn't get to really act. Because I hadn't been known as a 'New York actor,' they weren't aware of what I could do. And strangely enough, they never wrote really good scenes for Barbara and me." ★ While Morgan Brittany's Katherine "really took hold after [Season 5] when the writers decided that the public ate up the 'bitchiness,'" the character's fixation with Bobby is on display as early as this episode. As for her interpretation of Katherine, Brittany explains that she "took the makeup look from the [Disney] Snow White queen. The eyes and lips especially. The bulk of the character I stole right from Anne Baxter in *All About Eve*. Some of my scenes with Victoria were very similar to ones with Bette Davis and Anne. I used a lot of facial expressions in my performance and I really studied Anne Baxter a lot. I actually told her that when I did an episode of *Hotel* and she was really flattered! I think one of the reasons I was cast in the role was the fact that I had a sweet innocent look yet had an underlying evilness just like Eve did."

90. "The Search"

Written by Arthur Bernard Lewis; Directed by Irving J. Moore; Airdate: January 8, 1982
Guest Star: Morgan Woodward (Punk)
Subject: The search for Jock.

Cast Notes George Cooper appears as pilot Lee Evans, a role he would reprise in Episode 108.

Trivia This episode was number 1 in the weekly ratings, and had the show's highest season rating to date. ★ Morgan Woodward, like Howard Keel and Leigh Mc-Closkey, did not know that Jim Davis was sick. Woodward explains, "Jim Davis was a brave guy. If he was ailing, I doubt he would show it. . . . I was in Alabama at a celebrity golf tournament when I got the news [of Davis's death]. We certainly missed him and we talked of him often. He left a real hole in the show." ★ A portrait of the late Jim Davis (as Jock) appeared at the end of this episode with the graphic, "Jim Davis, 1909–1981," and was subsequently seen hanging in the Southfork living room and at Ewing Oil. This painting now hangs in Larry Hagman's Malibu home. ★ Clips from Episodes 9, 14, 16, 29, 35, 55, 61, 64, 65, and 69 were shown in this episode's tribute to Jim Davis. ★ Leonard Katzman thought scenes such as the one where Miss Ellie contemplates Jock's death were revealing, and found Barbara Bel Geddes to be quite adept at them. "The most effective things you do are generally scenes where people do not talk, where their emotions, where things that are not said, are as interesting and, of course, have to be translated visually," he said. "The camera has to be in the right place to see what you want to see. The finest actress I have ever been around for playing scenes like that is Barbara Bel Geddes, who can sit at a table by herself and go through an entire range of emotions—anger, tears, joy, love—without ever saying a word." ★ Katzman thought "Jim Davis represented something we've never been able to recapture. As bad as the boys could be, if he walked into a room and told them to knock it off, they did. I think the audience responded to that strong head of the family and the warm woman at the other end of the table. Much of J.R.'s motivation was looking good in his father's eyes. When Jim died, that motivation disappeared. So we had to transfer it to his son. After that, when he did something terrible, it was to build the empire for his son, as his father had done for him." ★ Bruce Broughton was nominated for an Emmy for Outstanding Achievement in Music Composition for a Series (Dramatic Underscore) for this episode. ★ This is the last episode of the season with scenes filmed on location in Dallas.

91. "Denial"

Written by Linda Elstad; Directed by Victor French; Airdate: January 15, 1982
Special Guest Star: Audrey Landers (Afton)
Guest Stars: Morgan Woodward (Punk); Diane McBain (Dee Dee Webster); George O.
Petrie (Harv); Jim McKrell (Henry Webster); Lindsay Bloom (Bonnie Robertson); Dennis
Redfield (Roger); Stephanie Blackmore (Serena); Peter Brown (Tom)
Subject: The Ewings mourn.

Cast Notes Diane McBain, who plays Sue Ellen's friend Dee-Dee, played Daphne
on Surfside Six. ★ Lindsay Bloom, a former Miss Omaha, Miss Arizona, and Miss
USA, played Robert Urich's girlfriend on Vega$, Stacy Keach's secretary Velda on
Mike Hammer, and Boss Hogg's niece on The Dukes of Hazzard.

Trivia This episode was number 1 in the weekly ratings. ★ Director Victor
French was a veteran TV actor who played Agent 44 on Get Smart, Isaiah Edwards on Little House on the Prairie, and Mark Gordon on Highway to Heaven. He
was recommended to the producers as a potential Dallas director by Steve Kanaly.

92. "Head of the Family"

Written by Howard Lakin; Directed by Patrick Duffy; Airdate: January 22, 1982
Special Guest Star: Howard Keel (Clayton)
Guest Stars: Gretchen Wyler (Dr. Conrad); Diane McBain (Dee Dee Webster); George
O. Petrie (Harv); Jim McKrell (Henry Webster); Lindsay Bloom (Bonnie Robertson);
Dennis Redfield (Roger); Stephanie Blackmore (Serena); Ray Wise (Blair Sullivan)
Subject: Bobby runs the family.

Cast Notes Ray Wise had recurring roles in several prime-time soaps, including
Spiros Koralis on The Colbys, the Dealer on Knots Landing, Judge Jim Stinson on
Second Chances, and Edward Burton on Savannah. He is best known, however, as
Leland Palmer from the critically acclaimed David Lynch series Twin Peaks.

Trivia This episode fell to number 4 in the weekly ratings.

93. "The Phoenix"

Written by David Paulsen; Directed by Harry Harris; Airdate: January 29, 1982
Special Guest Star: Priscilla Pointer (Rebecca); Audrey Landers (Afton); Morgan Brittany
(Katherine); Howard Keel (Clayton)
Guest Stars: Lindsay Bloom (Bonnie); Dennis Redfield (Roger); Fern Fitzgerald (Marilee);
Susan Demand-Shaw (Caroline Carter)
Subject: J.R. returns to work.

Cast Notes Vernon Weddle plays Mr. McGregor, who owned the supply store in
Braddock where the Ewings were longtime customers. Weddle returned to Dallas
as Ewing Oil Midland foreman John Carter in Episodes 225 and 244.

Trivia This episode was number 2 in the weekly ratings. ★ The portrait of Jim
Davis hangs in Jock's office in this episode. It would be moved to the Southfork

living room in Season 5, the Ewing Oil reception area in Season 7, J.R.E. Indus-tries in Season 10, J.R.'s office at Bobby's company in Season 11, and both Bobby's and J.R.'s offices at De La Vega Oil in Season 13. Because Larry Hagman kept the painting after the series ended, the poster-sized version of it that hangs in the liv-ing room at Duncan Acres was used in the 1996 TV movie *J.R. Returns*, where it was seen back in the Southfork living room. According to Audrey Landers, the portrait was one way that the memory of Jim Davis lived on among the cast and crew long after Davis's death. "Even after he was gone, you could feel his pres-ence," she said. "You really could. And maybe it was because of that incredible portrait that was there as a reminder. But it was just maybe the feeling that it all started from him, even though it was just a story. You just felt his presence carrying through." ★ This episode includes the last scene in which all four long-time car-tel members—Andy Bradley, Jordan Lee, Wade Luce, and Marilee Stone—appear together. In Season 5, Luce sold his company, and other cartel members retired in later seasons. Fern Fitzgerald calls the actors who played the cartel members "gems. Not one of them was arrogant or a scene stealer. We always had a good time off camera, telling stories of other shows we worked on. I was particularly fond of and friendly with Don Starr [who played Jordan Lee] and his lovely wife, Beverly. Beverly and I kept in touch long after Don's death."

94. "My Father, My Son"

Written by Will Lorin; Directed by Larry Hagman; Airdate: February 5, 1982
Special Guest Stars: Priscilla Pointer (Rebecca); Audrey Landers (Afton); Howard Keel (Clayton)
Guest Stars: Barbara Babcock (Liz); Morgan Brittany (Katherine); Claude Earl Jones (Wally Hampton); Bruce French (Jerry); Dennis Redfield (Roger); Fern Fitzgerald (Mar-ilee); Ron Tomme (Charles Eccles); Patricia McCormack (Evelyn Michaelson)
Subject: J.R. courts Sue Ellen.

Trivia This episode was number 3 in the weekly ratings.

95. "Anniversary"

Written by David Paulsen; Directed by Joseph Manduke; Airdate: February 12, 1982
Special Guest Stars: Priscilla Pointer (Rebecca); Howard Keel (Clayton)
Guest Stars: Barbara Babcock (Liz Craig); Morgan Brittany (Katherine); Claude Earl Jones (Wally); Jenny Sherman (Geraldine Crane); Lindsay Bloom (Bonnie); Dennis Red-field (Roger); Ron Tomme (Charles Eccles); Patricia McCormack (Evelyn)
Subject: J.R. courts Sue Ellen.

Cast Notes This is Barbara Babcock's last appearance on *Dallas*, and she believes that the Emmy Award she won on September 13, 1981, for Outstanding Lead Ac-tress in a Drama Series for *Hill Street Blues* (over, among other nominees, Barbara Bel Geddes and Linda Gray) caused her exit from *Dallas*. "The night I won the Emmy," explains Babcock, "I saw Leonard Katzman and Phil Capice. I came out clutching my Emmy and was walking towards my car. And they congratulated me and told me, 'Now we have to write you out of the show!' I said, 'Why?' and they said, 'Now you will be much too visible to be on our show.' And that was no fun to hear." ★ Danny Dayton, who plays the Miss Texas emcee, appeared as Hank on *All in the Family.*

Trivia Weekly rating: number 2. ★ This episode establishes that Sue Ellen was twenty years old when she met J.R. in 1967. Because Episode 108 establishes that Sue Ellen and J.R. married in 1974, J.R. must have courted her for seven years. ★ Pam's fascination with aerobics mirrored Victoria Principal's. Principal wrote the 1983 best-selling exercise manual *The Body Principal.* In 1984, Principal wrote "The Principal Work-Out," an article for *TV Guide* that was accompanied by pictures of her doing exercises that could be done while watching TV. A second book, *The Beauty Principal,* was published in 1985, and a third, *The Diet Principal,* was published in 1987. Susan Howard may have inspired Principal's interest in the health craze. Howard recalled, "Victoria and I were talking one day and she said, 'Wow! Look at those legs.' And I said, 'Yeah, I'm running. I'm working out.' And before you knew it, honey, Victoria's working out and she's lifting weights and doing those things. And Victoria was smart because she took it and made a book out of it. . . . Victoria took every advantage she could. Smart. Business-minded. Focused. Driven." ★ Barbara Babcock recalls that "Patrick Duffy loved practical jokes. He loved breaking people up and he was good at breaking me up." Duffy was in fine form during his scene with Babcock in this episode. "I remember we were sitting in a restaurant," says Babcock, "and every time the camera came on me, he would try to break me up."

96. "Adoption"

Written by Howard Lakin; Directed by Larry Hagman; Airdate: February 19, 1982
Special Guest Stars: Priscilla Pointer (Rebecca)
Guest Stars: Art Hindle (Farraday); Lindsay Bloom (Bonnie); Dennis Redfield (Roger); Fern Fitzgerald (Marilee); Ron Tomme (Eccles); Robert Alan Brown (Breslin); Ray Wise (Blair)
Subject: Christopher's adoption.

Cast Notes Herb Vigran, who plays Judge Thornby, was a TV veteran who appeared as a number of villains on *The Adventures of Superman* and as a regular on *The Ed Wynn Show.*

Trivia This episode was number 1 in the weekly ratings.

97. "The Maelstrom"

Written by Will Lorin; Directed by Patrick Duffy; Airdate: February 26, 1982
Special Guest Star: Howard Keel (Clayton)
Guest Stars: Morgan Brittany (Katherine); Bruce French (Jerry); Art Hindle (Farraday); Lindsay Bloom (Bonnie); Dennis Redfield (Roger); Fern Fitzgerald (Marilee); Ray Wise (Blair)
Subject: J.R. plots.

Trivia This episode was number 1 in the weekly ratings. ★ While Steve Kanaly "didn't like the idea of turning [Ray] into a bum in Season 4 and was glad once Ray got 'back on track,'" Kanaly "realized it was an opportunity to show other aspects of my acting ability."

98. "The Prodigal"

Written by David Paulsen; Directed by Michael Preece; Airdate: March 5, 1982
Special Guest Star: Priscilla Pointer (Rebecca); Audrey Landers (Afton); Howard Keel (Clayton)
Guest Stars: Morgan Brittany (Katherine); Art Hindle (Farraday); Dennis Redfield (Roger); Bill Erwin (Abel Greeley); Tom Fucello (Dave Culver); Fern Fitzgerald (Marilee); Ray Wise (Blair)
Subject: J.R. investigates Christopher.

Cast Notes Bill Erwin was a veteran character actor who played the hotel clerk in the 1980 Christopher Reeves–Jane Seymour movie *Somewhere in Time*. ★ Lewis Arquette played J. D. Pickett on *The Waltons*.

Trivia This episode was number 2 in the weekly ratings. ★ Morgan Brittany felt that the nasty Katherine was a far less redeeming character than J.R. Hagman "was very, very smart in making J.R. one of those people that you love to hate," she said. "He wasn't really like my character. People didn't love to hate me, they just outright hated me. You kind of wanted to see J.R. get away with it because he was this tongue-in-cheek villain that you almost thought was doing it as sport. He was doing all these evil, nasty things as a game and he was very, very smart in playing it that way." ★ Howard Keel was happy that Clayton had an interest in Sue Ellen. "I really enjoyed working with Linda Gray," he says. "She was so helpful to me, just a lovely gal. And a wonderful actress."

99. "Vengeance"

Written by Howard Lakin; Directed by Irving J. Moore; Airdate: March 12, 1982
Special Guest Stars: Priscilla Pointer (Rebecca); Audrey Landers (Afton); Howard Keel (Clayton)
Guest Stars: Art Hindle (Farraday); Dennis Redfield (Roger); Arthur Malet (Forrest); Tom Fucello (Dave Culver); Ray Wise (Blair Sullivan); Fern Fitzgerald (Marilee)
Subject: J.R. defrauds Cliff.

Trivia This episode was number 1 in the weekly ratings. ★ Sam Culver is reinvented in this episode as an oilman, even though he was at other times described as a magistrate (Episode 27), attorney (Episodes 174 and 177), and investor (*Dallas: The Early Years*).

100. "Blackmail"

Written by Leonard Katzman; Directed by Michael Preece; Airdate: March 19, 1982
Special Guest Star: Howard Keel (Clayton)
Guest Stars: Dennis Redfield (Roger); Art Hindle (Farraday); Jonathan Goldsmith (Joe

Smith); Fern Fitzgerald (Marilee); Tom Stern (Detective White)
Subject: J.R. blackmails Bobby.

Cast Notes Jonathan Goldsmith returned to *Dallas* as Bruce Harvey in Seasons 9 and 11. He also appeared in a recurring role on *Knots Landing*.

Trivia This episode was number 1 in the weekly ratings. ★ The falling out between their characters did not reflect Barbara Bel Geddes' and Susan Howard's offscreen relationship. Howard recalls that "Barbara and I liked each other. We had a respect for each other that crossed over into the personal. I think Barbara saw a lot of herself in me, her younger days, the way she approached things and played a scene."

101. "The Investigation"

Written by Bruce Shelly; Directed by Irving J. Moore; Airdate: March 26, 1982
Also Starring: Leigh McCloskey (Mitch)
Special Guest Star: Priscilla Pointer (Rebecca)
Guest Stars: Morgan Brittany (Katherine); Dennis Redfield (Roger); Jonathan Goldsmith (Joe Smith); Jack Collins (Russell Slater); Fern Fitzgerald (Marilee); Arthur Malet (Forrest); Tom Stern (Detective White)
Subject: Bobby investigates Christopher.

Cast Notes Jack Collins returns as broker Russell Slater in Seasons 5, 6, and 10. He was a regular on *The Milton Berle Show* in the 1950s and appeared in the 1989 movie *Batman*.

Trivia This episode was number 1 in the weekly ratings. ★ Miss Ellie's new bedroom set makes its debut. Her room had not been seen since Jim Davis's death.

102. "Acceptance"

Written by Will Lorin; Directed by Michael Preece; Airdate: April 2, 1982
Special Guest Stars: Priscilla Pointer (Rebecca); Audrey Landers (Afton)
Guest Stars: Morgan Woodward (Punk); Jonathan Goldsmith (Joe Smith); Bob Hoy (Detective Howard); Tom Stern (Detective White)
Subject: Miss Ellie accepts Jock's death.

Trivia Weekly rating: number 2. ★ Leonard Katzman thought that, for Barbara Bel Geddes, losing Jim Davis "was like losing her own husband again. It was terribly difficult and an emotional time for Barbara." ★ Although he would make guest appearances on *Dallas* in Seasons 7 and 11, this episode marks the end of Leigh McCloskey's two-year run as Mitch. Initially, McCloskey had a one-year contract with the show, but he was later asked to stay for a second year. Toward the end of filming for Season 4, McCloskey was told that Mitch would not be back in Season 5. McCloskey asked the producers why his character was being written off the show. He recalls, "Phil Capice told me Mitch was too nice. I asked why they didn't change Mitch to make him more interesting. I was surprised. I guess they ran out of storylines." McCloskey describes his experience on *Dallas* as a good one. "The people were very nice," he says, "and I learned a lot from doing the show. It was such an interesting phenomenon—something that I'd never seen before or since, and it was an experience to have been a part of television history." ★ This episode's scene between Punk and Miss Ellie is one of Morgan Woodward's favorites. Woodward found Barbara Bel Geddes "a delight." ★ Cliff's embezzlement and power grab was a welcome development for Ken Kercheval, who thought his character was "so nice that I wanted to go to a toy company and market a Cliff Barnes doll; when you wind it up, it bends over to be kicked." Producer Phil Capice felt that "Cliff Barnes always was bad underneath—a lecher, a cheapskate, a manipulator—but no once noticed because he always was contesting with J.R. and losing out to greater roguery. Now, he has come into a lot of money through his long-lost mother, Rebecca, and can fight J.R. on his own super-evil terms. It is such unexpected gimmicks that keep shows like ours going." Kercheval summed up, "Evil, schmevil. Good guy or bad guy, it's just a job."

103. "Goodbye, Cliff Barnes"

Written by Arthur Bernard Lewis; Directed by Irving J. Moore; Airdate: April 9, 1982
Special Guest Stars: Priscilla Pointer (Rebecca); Audrey Landers (Afton); Howard Keel (Clayton)
Guest Stars: Fern Fitzgerald (Marilee); Karlene Crockett (Muriel); Susan Adams; James Griffith
Subject: Cliff attempts suicide.

Trivia This episode was number 1 in the weekly Nielsens, with a 27.9 rating. ★ Despite Lucy's rape ordeal, Tilton enjoyed the storylines "when I got to play scenes where I was drunk or stoned or kidnapped or beat up or something where I could get a little messed up." ★ A few weeks after this episode aired, *TV Guide* writer Bill Davidson did a profile of Ken Kercheval in which Phil Capice stated that "the worst thing anyone can do is to take *Dallas* seriously, which is why we beat out all those *Dallas* imitations in the ratings. We try to have fun with our scripts by coming up with the most outrageous things we can think of. Ken is outrageous, too, which is why he fits in so nicely. Besides, even though I can't make him stick to his lines, he's one hell of an actor." In researching the article, Davidson was allowed on the set, and he watched the cast and crew film a love scene between Kercheval and Audrey Landers. Prior to the scene, Kercheval arrived on the set without his script and appeared not to know Cliff's lines. While an assistant director located an extra script for Kercheval, the actor, within earshot of Leonard Katzman, used a profanity to describe the quality of the script. Katzman pretended not to hear. During rehearsal of the scene, Kercheval kept changing his lines, to the protestations of Audrey Landers. Kercheval told his leading lady that, regardless of any ad-libbing he did on camera, he would get her back to her cues. While "Capice and Katzman have resigned themselves to Kercheval's departures from the script, saying that despite his detours he always manages somehow to capture the sense of the scene, . . . the technique . . . does not endear him to more disciplined actors like Barbara Bel Geddes and Susan Howard." When it was time to film the scene on the sound stage, Kercheval "winged his way artfully" through his lines. ★ Landers says that she and Kercheval "always worked well together." She explains, "It was a challenge and a lot of fun working with Ken. I always rolled with the tide. I quickly learned how to work well with Ken's style of acting, and I think we had a great chemistry on screen. One time we had a scene that was written as a heated argument/fight. We shot the master—wide shot. Then we shot my close-up. I kept the mood we had established, intense and full of heat and anger. Then we shot Kenny's close-up, and suddenly he didn't feel the scene that way any more. He said all of his lines in a very quiet, gentle, and calm manner. I was in shock because we had already filmed me screaming responses to what now was his very reasonable approach to my character's complaints. I guess the result was that it looked as if Afton was having a really bad day! After that, the directors honored my request to shoot my close-up after Ken's." ★ Irving J. Moore, who directed this episode, was one of Kercheval's favorite *Dallas* directors.

SEASON 5
1982–83—"Jock's Will"

THOUGH GONE, PATRIARCH JOCK EWING continued to dominate *Dallas* during Season 5. The main storyline focused on a fight for control of Ewing Oil triggered by Jock's will. Patrick Duffy found that "the interesting thing about it when you realize that [Davis] died so early on in the series [is that] he was present in that series, I'd say, almost up through and to the very end, because everything was still in reference to Daddy. J.R. still performed all his functions with his only compass being that it was for what he thought would be the approval of Daddy in the show. It's really a tribute to Jim's being able to sculpt a person in the form of Jock Ewing in a couple of seasons that would last in the public's mind for thirteen seasons."

Dallas, in its fifth year, aired against ABC's *Greatest American Hero* and NBC's *Knight Rider*. Although it remained the most-watched Friday night show, it was bumped from the number 1 spot by the CBS newsmagazine *60 Minutes*, and it finished the season at number 2 with a 24.6 rating. Five episodes, including episodes about the reading of Jock's will and the Ewing barbeque, reached number 1. Among the episodes that reached number 1 was the one that generated the year's biggest publicity for the show, the episode about Sue Ellen's and J.R.'s wedding. *People* magazine reporter Sue Reilly, who had written several cover stories about the show, was allowed to attend the filming of the nuptials, which took place at Duncan Acres in the summer of 1982.

As the wedding scene was underway in the stifling heat and humidity, a thunderstorm erupted, forcing the entire cast and crew to run for cover in the Southfork garage. Patrick Duffy quipped to Larry Hagman that Hagman didn't "have [his] heart in this ceremony." Hagman replied, "No, just my wallet. I see stormy times ahead." Linda Gray reacted to the weather conditions by stating, "If you believe in omens, this one is rather clear." Reilly wrote that Victoria Principal kept to herself, and surmised that the reason was "press accounts of her breakup with [pop singer] Andy Gibb." Charlene Tilton "sat out the shoot in L.A., awaiting the birth of her child." The wedding scenes were completed the following day, when the thunderstorm gave way to "a sense of excitement." Someone handed the newlyweds a toaster as a gag gift, which Hagman grabbed, causing Gray to lament, "We haven't even gotten married again and already we're dividing the community property!" After vows were exchanged and Katzman yelled, "That's a print!" Hagman told Gray, "Say, honey, what do you say after this here service, you and I get in my mobile home and take a little tour of wine country?" Gray replied, "Sure, honey, but only if we bring my husband and your wife along." Hagman, whose wife, Maj, was also in attendance, retorted, "I wouldn't have it any other way, darlin.'" The cast and crew then popped open several bottles of champagne and celebrated the happy occasion.

Although *Dallas* was a contender in several major categories at the Emmy Awards just one year earlier, it now found itself nominated for just two minor awards: Bruce Broughton for music composition and Fred Berger for editing. *Dallas* lost in both categories. *Dallas*, Larry Hagman, and Victoria Principal were nominated for Golden Globes, but they were shut out by *Hill Street Blues* and actors from *Dynasty*.

After J.R.'s shooting took *Dallas*'s popular and critical acclaim to stratospheric heights two years earlier, the show spawned a cottage industry of successful nighttime soaps which by the 1982–83 season routinely ranked among the Nielsen top twenty. These shows included *Dynasty* (number 5 for the season), *Falcon Crest* (number 8), and *Knots Landing* (number 20). *Dallas* was in some ways a victim of its own success. As more and more serials found an audience, it was difficult for *Dallas*'s creative team to come up with fresh storylines, and especially hard for *Dallas* to compete with the legacy of the "Who Shot J.R.?" cliff-hanger at the end of each season. As Phil Capice put it, "'Who Shot?' was the greatest cliffhanger of all time and created a nightmare for us. We don't try to top that time after time because we can't. That period of television history will never come again, and timing was as responsible as anything else. We were all more unsophisticated then; the viewer hadn't been bombarded with all sorts of cliffhangers, many of which have become letdowns. Back then, it was for the fun of it. Now audiences have a 'show me' attitude, or they've totally lost interest because there have been so many cheats. It's almost cliff-hanger abuse out there in TV land." The Season 5 cliff-hanger was an example of how *Dallas* suffered at the hands of its own imitators: its season finale featured several characters trapped in a fire— just like *Dynasty*'s cliff-hanger. The *Dallas* cliff-hanger was number 2 in the weekly ratings. It was the first time since 1979 that its season finale failed to hit number 1.

SEASON 5 EPISODE GUIDE

Regular Cast

Starring:
Barbara Bel Geddes as Miss Ellie
Patrick Duffy as Bobby
Linda Gray as Sue Ellen
Larry Hagman as J.R.
Susan Howard as Donna
Steve Kanaly as Ray
Ken Kercheval as Cliff
Victoria Principal as Pam
Charlene Tilton as Lucy
Also Starring:
John Beck as Mark Graison
Howard Keel as Clayton Farlow
Jared Martin as Dusty
Audrey Landers as Afton Cooper
Priscilla Pointer as Rebecca Wentworth

Technical Credits

Producer: Leonard Katzman
Executive Producer: Philip Capice
Supervising Producer: Arthur Bernard
  Lewis
Story Editor: David Paulsen
Associate Producer: Cliff Fenneman
Music: Jerrold Immel, Bruce Broughton,
  Lance Rubin
Unit Production Manager: Wayne A.
  Farlow
First Assistant Directors: Fred Stromsoe,
  Alan Brimfield

Second Assistant Director: Paul Snider
Directors of Photography: Edward R.
  Plante, Jack Swain
Art Director: Kim Swados
Editors: Fred W. Berger, A.C.E., John
  Arthur Davies, Lloyd Richardson
Executive in Charge of Casting: Barbara
  Miller
Casting: Irene Mariano, Rody Kent
Set Decorators: Phil Leonard, Bryan
  Thetford
Set Coordinator: Bryan Thetford
Property Masters: John Rettino, Anthony
  C. Thorpe, Ray L. Jeffers
Costumers: Jack Bear, Yvonne Kubis
Makeup: Kathy Agron, Susan Cabral
Hair Stylists: Gregg Mitchell, Generio
  Gugliemotto
Production Sound Mixer: Clark King,
  C.S.A.
Sound Effects Supervisor: Victor Guarnier
Sound Effects Editors: Michael Corrigan,
  Tom Gillis Burke
Music Supervisor: David Franco
Music Editor: Patricia Peck
Main Title Design: Wayne Fitzgerald
Production Supervisor: Mitch Ackerman
Executive Production Supervisor: Edward
  O. Denault

104. "Changing of the Guard"

Written by Arthur Bernard Lewis; Directed by Michael Preece; Airdate: October 1, 1982
Guest Stars: Lois Chiles (Holly Harwood); Fern Fitzgerald (Marilee); Don Starr (Jordan);
Karlene Crockett (Muriel); Paul Carr (Ted Prince)
Subject: J.R. is demoted.

Cast Notes Lois Chiles costarred in the movies The Way We Were, The Great
Gatsby, Moonraker, and Broadcast News. Like her character, Chiles was a native
Texan whose father was in the oil business. Chiles was from Alice, Texas, and her
family operated an off-shore drilling company located in South Texas. Chiles had
never seen Dallas prior to being cast as Holly Harwood. "They dug up a tape fast,"

she explained. "I went down there pretty cold." Recalled Larry Hagman, "Of all J.R.'s mistresses, Holly Harwood was my favorite. Damn, Lois has a wonderful body." Although she did not share many scenes with Chiles, Susan Howard also became a fan. "I really enjoyed Lois Chiles," Howard recalls. "Of course, being a Texan, why wouldn't you?" ★ Roseanna Christiansen debuts as Teresa, becoming the last but longest-running actress to play the Southfork maid. Christiansen played the role from Seasons 5 through 13. ★ This episode also marks the debut of Danone Simpson, another long-time supporting cast member. Sampson played Ewing Oil receptionist Kendall Chapman from Seasons 5 through 13.

Trivia The ratings for this episode got *Dallas* off to a slow start for Season 5. It finished at number 5 with a 22.5 rating and 38 share. It tied Episodes 111 and 120 as the season's lowest ranked. ★ Lucy's pregnancy was written into the storyline to accommodate Charlene Tilton's pregnancy. After Lucy's abortion, Tilton was filmed so that her pregnancy was hidden. ★ Because Linda Gray had her long hair cut short during the summer hiatus, Sue Ellen's hair, which was long in the Season 4 cliff-hanger, was somehow shortened by the season premiere. According to Gray, she wanted to be ahead of the short hair fashion trend. She explained, "When the season ended, I was wearing a sweater, pants, and had long hair. We did a direct cut from that to start the new season. There I was in the same sweater and pants—and my hair is suddenly short. I rationalize it this way: I'm in the hospital and distraught. So, being a typical socialite, I go out while Cliff's in a coma and have my hair cut. . . . Frankly, the producers weren't too happy." Gray refused the producers' requests to wear a wig to correct the problem. Leonard Katzman thought the style "was out of character for Sue Ellen." Gray wasn't the only cast member to give the show continuity problems because of a new hairdo. Priscilla Presley, who joined the show during its sixth season, cut her hair the night after a fight scene was filmed. She recalled, "I got a call the next morning saying, 'We have to redo the scene.' And I didn't have the heart to tell them that I'd had my hair cut. I [was] trying to find hairdressers, trying to find wigs, trying to find anything to make my hair [look], of course, the way it did when we shot the scene." ★ Shortly before this episode aired, *TV Guide* profiled Victoria Principal and divulged that she made "secret" trips to Los Angeles each week during the summer on-location shoot in Dallas to see "the current objection of her affections—a man with whom Principal says she is 'very involved.'" While the article did not reveal the identity of Principal's suitor, it may have been pop sensation Andy Gibb, although *People* magazine reported that Principal and Gibb broke up during the summer. ★ This episode marked the debut of the new Ewing Oil office set. That set was the first of several new or redecorated sets unveiled during Season 5, including the living room, the nursery, and the second floor at Southfork; Cliff's condo; and the Barnes-Wentworth offices. ★ Kercheval felt Cliff "just got beat up so many times but he always would dust himself off and pick himself up and start all over again, which I think was a redeemable quality about him."

105. "Where There's a Will"

Written by Leonard Katzman; Directed by Leonard Katzman; Airdate: October 8, 1982
Guest Stars: Morgan Woodward (Punk); Alice Hirson (Mavis); Robin Strand (John Baxter); Fern Fitzgerald (Marilee); George O. Petrie (Harv); Stephanie Blackmore (Serena); Paul Carr (Ted Prince); Charles Napier (Carl)
Subject: J.R. plots to see Jock's will.

Cast Notes This is the first appearance of Alice Hirson as Miss Ellie's best friend, Mavis Anderson, a role she would reprise in Seasons 6, 9, and 10. Hirson played Ellen DeGeneres's mother on *Ellen*. She also appeared on the soap operas *One Life to Live* and *General Hospital*, as the first lady in the Peter Sellers movie *Being There*, and in the 1980 sitcom *When the Whistle Blows* with *Dallas* guest star Noble Willingham. She was cast as Mavis "because I worked with Michael Preece on *When the Whistle Blows* and he suggested me to Lenny Katzman for the role." Hirson's leading man, Morgan Woodward, recalls that she "was a wonderful actress and we had a good time playing Punk and Mavis."

Trivia This episode was number 2 for the week. ★ This is the only mention of Harv's daughter, Harriet. ★ Fern Fitzgerald was glad that Alice Hirson joined the *Dallas* cast because Fitzgerald "made a friend for life when I met Alice on a flight to Dallas. It was her first time on the show and she noticed me reading my script. When she asked if I was on *Dallas*, I thought she was a fan who was going to ask me a lot of questions. (We still giggle about this). But, by the time we got to our hotel rooms, Alice and I were fast friends. She is a wonderful lady and a fine actress. I wish that we had some scenes together. . . . We continue to laugh about our times together in Dallas. We don't get tired of reminiscing, but I'm sure our husbands have heard all of our stories more than enough times." Hirson calls Fitzgerald "wonderful." ★ Pam's pep talk to Cliff indicates a strong sibling relationship. Once, however, a *TV Guide* reporter visiting the *Dallas* set witnessed an exchange between Ken Kercheval and Victoria Principal that undermined the picture of sibling harmony they created on TV. "Victoria Principal came into the makeup room," the reporter wrote. "Kercheval could not take his eyes off her sumptuous bosom. 'Am I ever going to see anything but your eyelids?' she asked."

106. "Billion Dollar Question"

Written by Arthur Bernard Lewis; Directed by Michael Preece; Airdate: October 15, 1982
Guest Stars: Lois Chiles (Holly); Alice Hirson (Mavis); Kate Reid (Aunt Lil); Fern Fitzgerald (Marilee); George O. Petrie (Harv); Frank Marth (Dr. Grovner); Dennis Lipscomb (Nelson Harding)
Subject: J.R. plots to see Jock's will.

Cast Notes Kate Reid was an acclaimed veteran of Broadway. She played Aunt Lil in seventeen episodes during Seasons 5, 6, and 8. Steve Kanaly says of Reid, "She was a very famous actress from New York, and it was wonderful to have her on the show. She really did an excellent job." Reid died in 1993 at age sixty-two in Stratford, Ontario, Canada, after a battle with cancer. ★ Karen Radcliffe appears as a waitress in this episode. It is the first of numerous roles she would play on *Dallas*, including a nurse in Episode 162, Sue Ellen's sanitarium friend in Episodes 197 and 198, a nurse in Episodes 253–256, and a hooker in *Dallas: The Early Years*. Radcliffe also appeared in the movie *Robocop* and on the CBS series *Beauty and the Beast*.

Trivia Weekly rating: number 12. ★ Dr. Crane appeared in Episodes 28 and 29. ★ Michael Preece was Alice Hirson's favorite *Dallas* director.

107. "The Big Ball"

Written by Leonard Katzman; Directed by Leonard Katzman; Airdate: October 22, 1982
Special Guest Star: Dale Robertson (Frank Crutcher)
Guest Stars: Lois Chiles (Holly); Morgan Woodward (Punk); Kate Reid (Aunt Lil); Alice Hirson (Mavis); Fern Fitzgerald (Marilee); Don Starr (Jordan); Melody Anderson (Linda Farlow); Timothy Patrick Murphy (Mickey)
Subject: The Oil Baron's Ball.

Cast Notes Veteran character actor Dale Robertson played Jim Hardie on *Tales of Wells Fargo*, succeeded Ronald Reagan as the host of the western anthology series *Death Valley Days*, and costarred as Walter Lankershim on the first season of *Dynasty*. ★ Timothy Patrick Murphy played Mickey during Seasons 5 and 6. Steve Kanaly recalls that Murphy "was really good in the role and brought a lot of energy to it. I enjoyed playing Ray's relationship with him because it gave me the chance to be fatherly, which I liked." Prior to *Dallas*, Murphy appeared in the miniseries *Centennial* (as Christian) and *The Seekers* (as Jared Kent) and on the soap opera *Search for Tomorrow* (as Spencer Langley). Murphy went on to costar with Morgan Brittany in the serial *Glitter* and played the young Michael Landon in Landon's 1984 autobiographical movie *Sam's Son*. Murphy died of AIDS in 1988 at the age of twenty-nine.

Trivia This episode was number 3 in the weekly ratings. ★ Punk's real name is Marvin. ★ The mention of the Jock Ewing Memorial Scholarship during this episode was taken seriously by so many viewers that Southern Methodist University received numerous inquiries and established a real scholarship for film students. ★ This was the first of seven Oil Baron's Balls seen on *Dallas*. The others were seen in Seasons 6 through 11. The ball was based on a real Dallas social event, the Cattle Baron's Ball, an annual benefit put on by the Dallas chapter of the American Cancer Society. *Dallas* cast members frequently attended the Cattle Baron's Ball. According to Steve Kanaly, before the "Who Shot J.R.?" phenomenon, real Dallasites "used to say they hated [the show]. They always said they didn't know anybody like J.R." Afterward, "they tell me how realistic it is." Larry and Maj Hagman got involved in raising funds for the Cattle Baron's Ball, and several real-life Dallas society matrons became extras in Oil Baron's Ball scenes on *Dallas* through their contacts with the cast members. ★ This episode was Jared Martin's only appearance during Season 5. Dusty's new wife also appears in this episode, and Martin finds it "most ironic" that the *Dallas* writers named Dusty's new wife Linda, the same name as Martin's *Dallas* leading lady, Linda Gray. Gray confirms that this name choice was an inside joke.

108. "Jock's Will"

Written by David Paulsen; Directed by Michael Preece; Airdate: October 29, 1982
Special Guest Star: Dale Robertson (Frank Crutcher)
Guest Stars: Kate Reid (Aunt Lil); Morgan Woodward (Punk); Timothy Patrick Murphy (Mickey); Alice Hirson (Mavis); Peter Hobbs; Don Starr (Jordan); Kenneth Kimmins (Thornton McLeish); George O. Peters (Harv); Ted Shackelford (Gary)
Subject: Jock's will is read.

Cast Notes   Kenneth Kimmins played Howard on the Craig T. Nelson sitcom *Coach*. ★ George Cooper returns as pilot Lee Evans.

Trivia   This episode put *Dallas* back in the number 1 spot in the weekly ratings. It aired at 9:00 p.m., and was followed at 10:00 p.m. by a special Friday night episode of *Knots Landing*. Ted Shackelford appeared on the *Dallas* episode, and Larry Hagman and Patrick Duffy appeared on the *Knots* episode, which was number 4 for the week. Jock's will was not the last *Dallas* storyline to spill over into *Knots Landing*. Three years later, Bobby's death and Gary's reaction to it were part of the *Knots* storyline. *Knots*, however, never addressed the fact that Bobby's death was later revealed to be a dream.

109. "Aftermath"

Written by David Paulsen; Directed by Leonard Katzman; Airdate: November 5, 1982
Guest Stars: Lois Chiles (Holly); Morgan Woodward (Punk); Ben Piazza (Walt Driscoll); George O. Petrie (Harv); Paul Napier (Harold Boyer); Ray Wise (Blair Sullivan); J. Patrick McNamara (Jarrett McLeish); Kenneth Kimmins (Thornton McLeish); Timothy Patrick Murphy (Mickey)
Subject: The will competition.

Cast Notes   TV veteran Ben Piazza played Dr. Rogers on *Ben Casey* and costarred in the Joe Namath sitcom *The Waverly Wonders*, a project under consideration by Larry Hagman at the time he received the script for the *Dallas* pilot in 1977. Piazza died of cancer in 1991 at age fifty-eight. ★ Carol Sanchez appeared in several minor roles before landing the role of Angela, who replaced Louise as Pam's maid during Season 8. Sanchez later played Carmen, Carter McKay's maid, in Season 11.

Trivia   This episode was number 3 in the weekly ratings.

110. "Hit and Run"

Written by Howard Lakin; Directed by Michael Preece; Airdate: November 12, 1982
Special Guest Stars: Dale Robertson (Frank); Nicholas Hammond (Bill Johnson)
Guest Stars: Morgan Woodward (Punk); Ben Piazza (Walt Driscoll); John Larroquette
(Mr. Colton); Fay Hauser (Annie); Fern Fitzgerald (Marilee); Don Starr (Jordan);
George O Petrie (Harv); J. Patrick McNamara (Jarrett McLeish); Kenneth Kimmins
(Thornton McLeish); Tom Fucello (Dave Culver); Martha Smith (Carol Driscoll); Paul
Carr (Ted Prince); Ray Wise (Blair Sullivan); Timothy Patrick Murphy (Mickey)
Subject: J.R. plots against Bobby.

Cast Notes Nicholas Hammond played Friedrich Von Trapp in the 1965 movie
classic *The Sound of Music* and went on to play the lead role in the TV version of
the comic book series *The Amazing Spider-Man*. Hammond's appearance is not the
only connection between *Dallas* and *The Sound of Music*. Larry Hagman's mother,
Mary Martin, originated the role of Maria Von Trapp in the 1959 Broadway production of the musical, and scenes for Episode 303 were filmed at the same
Salzburg home seen in the 1965 movie. ★ John Larroquette won four back-to-
back Emmy awards as Outstanding Supporting Actor in a Comedy Series for his
role as another lawyer, Assistant District Attorney Dan Fielding, on the sitcom
Night Court.

Trivia This episode was number 4 for the week.

111. "The Ewing Touch"

Written by Howard Lakin; Directed by Leonard Katzman; Airdate: November 19, 1982
Special Guest Stars: Dale Robertson (Frank); Nicholas Hammond (Bill Johnson)
Guest Stars: Lois Chiles (Holly); Morgan Woodward (Punk); Ben Piazza (Walt); Albert
Salmi (Gil Thurman); Alice Hirson (Mavis); John Larroquette (Mr. Colton); Fay Hauser
(Annie); Fern Fitzgerald (Marilee); Don Starr (Jordan); J. Patrick McNamara (Jarrett);
Kenneth Kimmins (Thornton); John Carter (Carl Hennessey); Tom Fucello (Dave Cul-
ver); Timothy Patrick Murphy (Mickey)
Subject: J.R.'s variance.

Cast Notes Albert Salmi was a regular on *Petrocelli*, which was produced by
Leonard Katzman. He appeared in the movies *Escape from the Planet of the Apes*
and *Caddyshack*. He died in Spokane, Washington, on April 23, 1990. ★ John
Carter played Lieutenant Biddle on *Barnaby Jones*. He reprised the role of Carl
Hennessey in Seasons 7 and 9. ★ Josef Rainer appeared in minor roles in eight
episodes of *Dallas* during Seasons 5, 9, and 11. He played Pam's doctor, David Gordon, in Episode 282. He also appeared in *The Early Years* as Sam Culver. ★ Lacy
Wayne was a real-life pilot who flew the Southfork helicopter in twenty-four
episodes filmed on location in Dallas during Seasons 5 through 7 and 9 through
11.

Trivia This episode was number 5 in the weekly ratings.

112. "Fringe Benefits"

Written by Will Lorin; Directed by Michael Preece; Airdate: November 26, 1982
Special Guest Star: Dale Robertson (Frank)
Guest Stars: Morgan Woodward (Punk); Albert Salmi (Gil Thurman); Michael Prince
(John Macklin); Fern Fitzgerald (Marilee); Don Starr (Jordan); Kenneth Kimmins (Thornton); Jack Collins (Russ Slater)
Subject: J.R. and Cliff compete.

Trivia Weekly rating: number 5.

113. "The Wedding"

Written by Will Lorin; Directed by Leonard Katzman; Airdate: December 3, 1982
Guest Stars: Lois Chiles (Holly); Morgan Woodward (Punk); Alice Hirson (Mavis); Parley Baer (Minister Brown); Tom Fucello (Dave); Don Starr (Jordan); Ray Wise (Blair); Timothy Patrick Murphy (Mickey)
Subject: J.R. and Sue Ellen remarry.

Cast Notes Parley Baer played Darby on *The Adventures of Ozzie and Harriet* and Mayor Stoner on *The Andy Griffith Show*. He also appeared in the movies *Gypsy* and *Dave*, on the series *Hogan's Heroes* and *L.A. Law*, and was the voice of the Keebler elf on TV commercials. He was a captain in the Army Air Corps in World War II and earned several battle stars in the Pacific. He died on November 22, 2002, at the age of eighty-eight.

Trivia This episode put *Dallas* back in the number 1 spot in the weekly ratings. This was the show's highest season rating to date. ★ Sue Ellen sports a 13.5-carat diamond engagement ring. ★ Said Linda Gray about her character's remarriage to J.R., "The writers took me away from the ranch and put me in my little town house, and then realized that a key element of the show was Larry's relationship with me. I think they are trying to find a way to bring me back to Southfork. There is no question that my favorite scenes in the show are when Larry and I are together." ★ Morgan Woodward's most memorable *Dallas* scene, from this episode, involved Larry Hagman. "My favorite scene was between J.R. and me," Woodward explains, "when I let him know that if he stepped out of line, I would squash him."

114. "Post Nuptial"

Written by David Paulsen; Directed by Michael Preece; Airdate: December 10, 1982
Special Guest Stars: Nicholas Hammond (Bill Johnson); E.J. Andre (Eugene Bullock)
Guest Stars: Lois Chiles (Holly); Morgan Woodward (Punk); Alice Hirson (Mavis); Fern Fitzgerald (Marilee); Don Starr (Jordan); Tom Fucello (Dave); Parley Baer (The Minister); Jon Cypher; Gerry Gibson (Jimmy); Ivan Bonar; Timothy Patrick Murphy (Mickey)
Subject: J.R.'s and Sue Ellen's wedding reception.

Cast Notes TV veteran Jon Cypher appears as a state official in this episode. Cypher played Chief Daniels on *Hill Street Blues* and Major General Craig on *Major Dad*.

Trivia This episode was number 2 in the weekly ratings.

115. "Barbeque Three"

Written by Arthur Bernard Lewis; Directed by Leonard Katzman; Airdate: December 17, 1982
Special Guest Star: E. J. Andre (Eugene Bullock)
Guest Stars: Lois Chiles (Holly); Morgan Woodward (Punk); Alice Hirson (Mavis); Fern Fitzgerald (Marilee); Don Starr (Jordan); James Karen (Elmer Lawrence); Arlen Dean Snyder (George Hicks); Julio Medina (Henry Figueroa); Timothy Patrick Murphy (Mickey)
Subject: The Ewings' barbeque.

Trivia This episode was number 1 in the weekly ratings. ★ The rarely seen Southfork living room TV is on display in this episode. ★ This is the last Season 5 episode filmed on location in Texas. Alice Hirson recalls that "during those barbeque scenes we all sweated to death in those suede outfits standing out in the sunshine!" The wind also affected the cast while filming "Barbeque Three." Wrote Suzy Kalter, "Afton and Pam wear look-alike hairstyles [in this episode], because the wind was so fierce . . . that all women on camera were required to have up-swept coiffures."

116. "Mama Dearest"

Written by Arthur Bernard Lewis; Directed by Patrick Duffy; Airdate: December 31, 1982
Special Guest Star: Donald Moffat (Brooks Oliver)
Guest Stars: Lois Chiles (Holly); Morgan Woodward (Punk); Don Starr (Jordan); George O. Petrie (Harv); Karlene Crockett (Muriel); Paul Carr (Ted Prince); James Karen (Elmer Lawrence), Julio Medina (Henry Figueroa); Arlen Dean Snyder (George Hicks); Timothy Patrick Murphy (Mickey)
Subject: Miss Ellie considers contesting Jock's will.

Cast Notes Miss Ellie's attorney, Brooks Oliver, is played by veteran actor Donald Moffat, who appeared in the movies Patriot Games and Clear and Present Danger.

Trivia This New Year's Eve episode fell to number 24 in the weekly ratings.

117. "The Ewing Blues"

Written by David Paulsen; Directed by David Paulsen; Airdate: January 7, 1983
Guest Stars: Lois Chiles (Holly); John Reilly (Roy Ralston); Fern Fitzgerald (Marilee Stone); Don Starr (Jordan); Lane Davies (Craig Gurney); Scott Palmer (Farley Criswell); Timothy Patrick Murphy (Mickey)
Subject: Miss Ellie contests Jock's will.

Cast Notes John Beck makes his first appearance as Mark Graison, a role he played in Seasons 5, 6, and 8. Beck played a Bobby Ewing–type character on Flamingo Road, one of several Dallas imitators that appeared in the early 1980s. Flamingo Road costarred several other Dallas cast members, including Peter Donat, Howard

Duff, and Morgan Fairchild. Beck also appeared in the movies *Audrey Rose* and *Rollerball*. Beck's initial contract took him through the end of Season 5. ★ John Reilly was a longtime star of daytime TV's *General Hospital*.

Trivia This episode was number 4 for the week. ★ Composer Bruce Broughton won an Emmy award for Outstanding Achievement in Music Composition for a Series (Dramatic Underscore) for this episode. Also nominated was Jerrold Immel, composer of the *Dallas* and *Knots Landing* theme songs, for an episode of *Knots*. ★ This is the first of three episodes both written and directed by longtime *Dallas* writer David Paulsen. ★ John Beck was happy to join the cast of *Dallas*, especially since he missed a chance to make a guest appearance on the show during its first season. "My agent, who didn't turn anything down without talking to me first, told me, 'I turned down a guest spot on that new soap opera *Dallas*.'" Beck's first scene was with Barbara Bel Geddes, who Beck "always loved . . . I watched her growing up. You wouldn't expect it, but she was a real character, a real pisser. She could do anything the guys could do. She was quite a lot of fun."

118. "The Reckoning"

Written by Will Lorin; Directed by Bill Duke; Airdate: January 14, 1983
Special Guest Star: Donald Moffat (Brooks)
Guest Stars: Morgan Woodward (Punk); Fern Fitzgerald (Marilee); Don Starr (Jordan); Tom Fucello (Dave); George O. Petrie (Harv): Arlen Dean Snyder (George Hicks); Laurence Haddon (Franklin); James Karen (Elmer Lawrence); Julio Medina (Henry Figueroa); Fred Carney (Judge Howard Mantee)
Subject: Miss Ellie contests Jock will.

Trivia This episode was number 4 in the weekly ratings. ★ Director Bill Duke was a character actor who appeared in the movies *Car Wash*, *American Gigolo*, and *Bird on a Wire*. ★ John Beck's first scene with Larry Hagman appears in this episode. Beck calls Hagman "the greatest guy in the world. I had worked with him when I first came into the business and got to say one line on *I Dream of Jeannie* in the mid-1960s. I worked with him again when he played the James Garner role in the pilot for the TV version of the movie *The Skin Game*. . . . Larry was always a lot of fun."

119. "A Ewing Is a Ewing"

Written by Frank Furino; Directed by Larry Hagman; Airdate: January 28, 1983
Guest Stars: Lois Chiles (Holly); Paul Mantee (General Cochran); Charles Napier (Carl); Fern Fitzgerald (Marilee); Don Starr (Jordan); April Clough (Wendy); Arlen Dean Snyder (George Hicks); Timothy Patrick Murphy (Mickey)
Subject: Bobby resorts to blackmail.

Trivia This episode was number 3 in the weekly ratings. ★ Said Larry Hagman about Lois Chiles—the actress behind J.R.'s latest conquest, as of this episode— "She's charming, a soft lady who plays a tough cookie. I just tell her, 'Don't worry about the lines, play the moment. That's what you're selling, not the words.'"

120. "Crash of '83"

Written by Howard Lakin; Directed by Bill Duke; Airdate: February 4, 1983
Guest Stars: Albert Salmi (Gil Thurman); John Reilly (Roy Ralston); Ben Piazza (Walt Driscoll); April Clough (Wendy); Arlen Dean Snyder (Hicks); Charles Napier (Carl); Ken Kimmins (Thornton McLeish); Jack Collins (Russell Slater); Timothy Patrick Murphy (Mickey)
Subject: Rebecca's plane crashes.

Trivia This episode was number 5 for the week. ★ Ken Kercheval found his leading lady Audrey Landers "extremely conscientious and she works very hard and she's too young for me! And my character on the show treats her so badly, she just can't win, the poor girl!"

121. "Requiem"

Written by Linda Elstad; Directed by Larry Hagman; Airdate: February 11, 1983
Guest Stars: Lois Chiles (Holly); Morgan Woodward (Punk); Morgan Brittany (Katherine); Arlen Dean Snyder (George Hicks); Ben Piazza (Walt); Fern Fitzgerald (Marilee); Don Starr (Jordan); Alice Hirson (Mavis); Tom Fucello (Dave); Ryan MacDonald; Richard Kuss; John Ingle (Dr. Pittman)
Subject: Rebecca's death.

Cast Notes Guest star John Ingle returned in Episode 297 as the minister who married Cally and J.R. He has played Edward Quartermaine on *General Hospital* since 1993.

Trivia Weekly rating: number 16. ★ Priscilla Pointer recalls, "My death scene, in all its tragic entirety, was being directed by the master of practical jokes, Larry Hagman. No comedy crept into the scene itself of course. My daughter, Amy Irving, wanted to be there and Victoria said afterwards that her own tears kept flowing throughout the scene because when she glanced at Amy, she too was sobbing! For the 'gag reels' of outtakes that are shown at the annual *Dallas* end-of-season parties, however, Larry had me sit up suddenly in my hospital bed in the middle of the scene, still attached to all the machines, and gaily say, 'Actually, I'm feeling much better now.' . . . The crew was [not] in on the gag, so there was a huge gasp, followed by much laughter." Pointer does not know why Rebecca was killed off, but she guesses that "they felt that this particular plot line had run its course."

122. "Legacy"

Written by Robert Sherman; Directed by Patrick Duffy; Airdate: February 18, 1983
Guest Stars: Lois Chiles (Holly); Morgan Brittany (Katherine); Ben Piazza (Walt); Michael Currie (Sam Reynolds); Fern Fitzgerald (Marilee); Don Starr (Jordan); Ken Kimmins (Thornton); Karlene Crockett (Muriel); Tom Rosqui; Timothy Patrick Murphy (Mickey)
Subject: Pam leaves Southfork.

Cast Notes Mary Armstrong makes the first of fourteen appearances as Louise, the housekeeper who works for Pam while she lives at the Fairview Hotel in Seasons 5 and 6 and in Rebecca's house in Seasons 6 and 7.

Trivia This episode was number 1 in the weekly ratings. ★ This is the first episode in which future *Glitter* costars Morgan Brittany and Timothy Patrick Murphy both appear. Brittany found Murphy to be the "the sweetest, most gentle person you can imagine. We worked together on *Glitter* for a year, and I had the best time with him. He was always upbeat and funny. Also, he was one of the most professional actors I have ever worked with. I remember sitting in the *Dallas* makeup room one morning when we were given our scripts for the next week. Timmy flipped to the last page real fast and breathed a big sigh of relief. 'I don't get in a plane, car, or boat or have a gun in my hand; that means I make it to the next episode!' We all used to laugh about how our characters would make their exit from the show and if we got into any kind of vehicle or had a gun it could signal the end!"

123. "Brothers and Sisters"

Written by Will Lorin; Directed by Larry Hagman; Airdate: February 25, 1983
Guest Stars: Lois Chiles (Holly); Morgan Brittany (Katherine); Ben Piazza (Walt); John Reilly (Roy Ralston); Tom Fucello (Dave Culver); Timothy Patrick Murphy (Mickey)
Subject: Katherine courts Bobby.

Cast Notes Don Diamond is a TV veteran who played Corporal Reyes on *Zorro* and Crazy Cat on the sitcom *F-Troop*.

Trivia This episode was number 2 for the week. ★ Clayton visits the Southern Cross again in Episode 305. ★ John Beck found Victoria Principal "fun to work with. She was a kind of joker, and real go-getter."

124. "Caribbean Connection"

Written by Will Lorin; Directed by Patrick Duffy; Airdate: March 4, 1983
Special Guest Star: E. J. Andre (Eugene Bullock)
Guest Stars: Lois Chiles (Holly); Morgan Brittany (Katherine); Ben Piazza (Walt); John Reilly (Roy); Timothy Patrick Murphy (Mickey)
Subject: Bobby uncovers J.R.'s plot.

Trivia This episode was number 4 for the week.

125. "The Sting"

Written by David Paulsen; Directed by Larry Elikann; Airdate: March 11, 1983
Special Guest Star: Henry Darrow (Garcia)
Guest Stars: Lois Chiles (Holly); Morgan Woodward (Punk); Morgan Brittany (Katherine); Ben Piazza (Walt); John Reilly (Roy); Russ Marin (Matthew); Fern Fitzgerald (Marilee); Don Starr (Jordan); Stephanie Blackmore (Serena); Timothy Patrick Murphy (Mickey)
Subject: J.R. sets up Walt Driscoll.

Cast Notes Henry Darrow starred in the TV western *The High Chaparral*.

Trivia This episode was number 1 in the weekly ratings. ★ Director Larry

Elikann also directed *Dallas: The Early Years*. ★ Episode 291, written by Leonard Katzman's son, Mitchell, was also named "The Sting." This is the only instance of an episode name being used twice on *Dallas*. ★ On March 10, 1983, the day before this episode aired, sixty-year-old Barbara Bel Geddes completed filming for Season 5. Five days later, on March 15, she underwent triple bypass open-heart surgery at Cedars-Sinai Medical Center in Los Angeles.

126. "Hell Hath No Fury"

Written by Arthur Bernard Lewis; Directed by Ernest Pintoff; Airdate: March 18, 1983
Guest Stars: Lois Chiles (Holly); Morgan Brittany (Katherine); Ben Piazza (Walt); John Reilly (Roy); Fay Hauser (Annie); John Anderson (McIntire); Kenneth Kimmins (Thornton); Tom McFadden (Curtis); William Bryant (Jackson); Timothy Patrick Murphy (Mickey)
Subject: Bobby and Ray set up J.R.

Cast Notes John Anderson starred in the TV series *The Life and Legend of Wyatt Earp* and in such miniseries as *Rich Man, Poor Man—Book II* and *Backstairs at the White House*, in which he played Franklin Roosevelt. He returned to *Dallas* as Dr. Stiles in Season 10. Anderson died of a heart attack in 1992 in Los Angeles at the age of sixty-nine.

Trivia This episode was number 3 for the week. ★ Director Ernest Pintoff was an animator who made several animated shorts in the late 1950s and early 1960s. ★ During 1983, while Sue Ellen was having marital problems, Linda Gray was going through a divorce herself. She got through it, in part, because "Larry and Maj [Hagman] have practically adopted me as their daughter. After the divorce, they took me on trips to Europe with them, they found the house in Malibu for me so I wouldn't be alone, and they even played Welcome Wagon lady for me by greeting me in the house with balloons, champagne, and a machine that filled the building with bubbles." Gray recalls that one day during that same period, "there was a knock at the door and I opened it and [Hagman] was standing there in one of his wild hats with a feather in it and one of his odd outfits. And he had a . . . Vespa. And he put me on the back of the Vespa and took me to every merchant in Malibu—the dry cleaner, the library, every place—and introduced me to my new neighborhood." The Hagmans "have been pals and buddies and true friends since the day I met them. They have always been there for me no matter what." Hagman recalled, "When Linda Gray separated from her husband after twenty-something years of marriage, she was living out at the beach near us. Maj and I kind of adopted her. She was here at the house nearly every day. We'd call her first thing in the morning to make sure she was all right, we'd make sure she had dinner every night."

127. "Cuba Libre"

Written by Leonard Katzman; Directed by Robert C. Thompson; Airdate: March 25, 1983
Special Guest Star: Henry Darrow (Garcia)

Guest Stars: Lois Chiles (Holly); Morgan Woodward (Punk); Morgan Brittany (Katherine); Kate Reid (Aunt Lil); John Anderson (McIntire); Alice Hirson (Mavis); Hansford Rowe (Andrew Forrest); Don Starr (Jordan); Brit Leach; Timothy Patrick Murphy (Mickey)
Subject: J.R.'s arrest.

Trivia This episode was number 4 in the weekly ratings. ★ While J.R. was traveling to Cuba, Morgan Woodward spent part of 1983 traveling in Europe. "When I was in England, Ireland, France, and Italy . . . *Dallas* was still huge," he remembers. "Number one in the world. Don't think I didn't have the sense to wear my cowboy hat while I was there! They were quite interested in Punk Anderson and I was treated like a king!"

128. "Tangled Webs"

Written by David Paulsen; Directed by Nicholas Sgarro; Airdate: April 1, 1983
Guest Stars: Lois Chiles (Holly); Morgan Brittany (Katherine); Kate Reid (Aunt Lil); William Bryant (Jackson); Kenneth Kimmins (Thornton); Nate Esformes (Ignacio Perez); Tom McFadden (Curtis); Dennis Holahon (George Walker)
Subject: J.R.'s affair.

Trivia Weekly rating: number 4. ★ Leonard Katzman felt that the character of Mark Graison stood for perfection. "That's what the audience demands for Pam," he said. "He may be more one-dimensional than the other characters but it's only because everyone thinks Pam deserves nothing less." ★ Holly arranging to have Sue Ellen catch her in bed with J.R. was the type of behavior Lois Chiles could not predict. Chiles felt that "it was strange not knowing if Holly was a good or bad girl, or what she'd do next." Chiles received only a single script each week, and was often in makeup by the time she got to review her lines.

129. "Things Ain't Goin' Too Good at Southfork"

Written by Leonard Katzman; Directed by Gunnar Hellstrom; Airdate: April 15, 1983
Guest Stars: Lois Chiles (Holly); Morgan Brittany (Katherine); Kate Reid (Aunt Lil); Kenneth Kimmins (Thornton); Timothy Patrick Murphy (Mickey)
Subject: Sue Ellen's car crash.

Trivia Weekly rating: number 3. ★ The last scene of Episode 128 is replayed at the beginning of this episode. ★ Some of the cast and crew returned to Dallas for on-location shooting for this episode's crash scene. ★ The title of Episode 279 in Season 10 was a take-off on this episode's title; that episode was called "Things Ain't Goin' Too Good at Southfork Again."

130. "Penultimate"

Written by Howard Lakin; Directed by Nick Havinga; Airdate: April 29, 1983
Special Guest Star: Barry Corbin (Fenton)
Guest Stars: Lois Chiles (Holly); Morgan Woodward (Punk); Kate Reid (Aunt Lil); Alice

Hirson (Mavis); John Zaremba (Dr. Danvers); Joe Maross (Dr. Blakey); Timothy Patrick Murphy (Mickey)
Subject: Sue Ellen is investigated.

Cast Notes Eric Farlow makes his first appearance as baby Christopher, a role he would play in 44 episodes during Seasons 5 through 7.

Trivia Weekly rating: number 3. ★ In this episode, Barry Corbin's character has uncomfortable news for Sue Ellen, much like he had for Jock in Season 2 and J.R. in Season 4. Corbin found Linda Gray "very nice and friendly." Corbin points out that Fenton "seemed to remain consistent throughout the run of the show. The writers didn't do much to change him." ★ This is director Nick Havinga's first episode of *Dallas*. He directed twenty episodes of the show during Seasons 5 through 8 and 13.

131. "Ewing Inferno"

Written by Arthur Bernard Lewis; Directed by Leonard Katzman; Airdate: May 6, 1983
Special Guest Star: Barry Corbin (Fenton)
Guest Stars: Lois Chiles (Holly); Morgan Brittany (Katherine); Kate Reid (Aunt Lil); Ben Piazza (Walt); John Zaremba (Dr. Danvers); Timothy Patrick Murphy (Mickey)
Subject: Fire at Southfork.

Cast Notes This is Tyler Banks's last appearance as John Ross, although it was not the last time that his on-screen mother, Linda Gray, saw him. During the summer of 2003, Gray "was at a fan show and a young man said to me, 'Miss Gray, could you sign this for me?' And I did, and then he said, 'And could you sign this photograph, too?' And it was a picture of me holding this little baby. And the man was Tyler Banks—the baby in the picture. . . . And it was amazing. Here he was! He was so cute."

Trivia Weekly rating: number 2. ★ The vacation begun by Miss Ellie in this episode lasts until Episode 143 in Season 6. The trip was written into the storyline because of Barbara Bel Geddes' heart surgery, and the writers were unsure "how steadily she'd be able to work next season," according to Arthur Bernard Lewis. Lewis told *TV Guide* that the writing staff came up with contingency plans in case Bel Geddes could not work a full season. Lewis said, "We're just vamping. If Barbara needs a reduced schedule, we'll have to deal with that in the storyline. If she doesn't, there's always the possibility that Miss Ellie will marry someone else. We flirted with that idea this past season." ★ In *Dallas*'s first episode, Pam moves onto Southfork as a newly married Ewing daughter-in-law. Near the end of Season 5, Pam moves off Southfork, and later divorces Bobby. The five years in between comprise Victoria Principal's favorite Pam storylines. ★ A second Southfork hallway was specially constructed for the fire scenes. The fire blazed more quickly than had been anticipated, but none of the cast or crew were hurt. ★ Editor Fred W. Berger was nominated for an Emmy for Outstanding Film Editing for a Series for this episode. ★ According to Leonard Katzman, "Accidentally burning down a house with that many people in it is not easy. You can't just catch something on fire by accident. So we had to go back two or three episodes and have J.R. and Sue Ellen have a fight and have her throw the wine at him that missed and hit [the wall], so that we could peel things off, so that we could have paint and cloths and all of that stuff lying around, for the last episode when he threw the lamp at Steve, so the house could burn."

SEASON 6
1983–84—"And the Winner Is . . ."

By THE 1983–84 SEASON, THE prime-time soap craze begun by *Dallas* started to peak. Four of the top eleven shows in the Nielsen ratings were serials, including *Dallas* (number 1 for the year); its spin-off, *Knots Landing* (number 11); the show that followed *Dallas* on Fridays, *Falcon Crest* (number 7); and ABC's answer to *Dallas*, *Dynasty* (number 3). Of all of *Dallas*'s rival soaps, the only one that generated enough popular acclaim and media attention to rival that of *Dallas* was *Dynasty*. Like *Dallas*, *Dynasty* was a multigenerational saga about the members of a rich and beautiful oil family, although its setting was Denver. It premiered in January 1981, almost three years after *Dallas*, and was canceled in 1989, two years before *Dallas* went off the air. *Dynasty* starred John Forsythe, Linda Evans, and, after its first season, Joan Collins, whose character, Alexis Colby, was generally regarded as a "female J.R." Collins became *Dynasty*'s breakout star.

During the 1982–83 season, *Dynasty* had become TV's number-five show. The mainstream and tabloid media began to make much of the ratings rivalry between *Dynasty* and *Dallas*, and the *Dallas* cast took note. Morgan Brittany recalled, "On Wednesday mornings, we'd run and get the *L.A. Times* and see if we beat *Dynasty* in the ratings. It was really fun and for a while that was a big deal, battling for that first and second position, between *Dynasty* and *Dallas*." *Dallas* director Irving J. Moore also directed on *Dynasty*, and the *Dallas* actors traded gossip with him, peppering Moore with questions about which *Dynasty* stars had the biggest dressing rooms, who had personal parking spaces, whether Linda Evans was as pretty as she seemed on screen and what Joan Collins was like to work with.

Most of the *Dallas* cast felt that the rivalry was either created by the press or the *Dynasty* crew. Larry Hagman felt that the "talk about *Dallas* vs. *Dynasty* . . . all came from their camp. It never got in my way. I think I've only seen *Dynasty* once or twice. It's very glitzy with some wonderful, funny things in it." Ken Kercheval wondered "what was spent on promotion for *Dynasty* relative to what was spent on *Dallas*. I think I know what the answer to *Dallas* is. Very, very little. I don't know if the media is responsible for this *Dynasty-Dallas* thing, but I don't think the shows are comparable at all. I daresay that *Dynasty* has been more enthusiastic about toppling *Dallas*. I don't think we even think about it. I think *Dynasty*'s real interested in being number 1, and we just go along and do what we do." Steve Kanaly claims that *Dynasty* was the *Dallas* company's favorite competitor, and that the *Dallas* cast and crew actually welcomed *Dynasty*'s success because it established beyond doubt that *Dallas* had forged a new TV genre and would be on the air for many years.

Nevertheless, the press gave the rivalry between the shows great play. *TV Guide* even did a cover story entitled, "*Dallas* vs. *Dynasty*: Which Is Better?" Author Stephen Birmingham framed the question, and answer, this way:

> Which, then, tells the better, more convincing yarn? I guess I'd vote for *Dallas*. Somehow, the continuing saga of the Ewing clan of Southfork Ranch is the more plausible. . . . *Dallas's* J.R. Ewing is a more subtly written character [than *Dynasty's* Alexis Colby]. Alexis is without redeeming social value. But J.R.—even when he knits his brow and squints his eyes, and we know he is plotting to place flies in the ointments of his friends and relatives—is a character we somehow like, and even at times feel sorry for. . . . Of the two shows, *Dallas* seems the more secure and self confident.

Interestingly, J.R. and Alexis had a real-life encounter long before they became TV icons. Larry Hagman claimed he dated Joan Collins in London "when she was seventeen and I was nineteen."

Meanwhile, the soap opera phenomenon ignited by *Dallas* was about to affect the syndicated television market as well, because by early 1984, enough episodes of *Dallas* had been filmed to sell the show to interested buyers. As of February of 1984, 161 episodes of *Dallas* had been completed, and the show went into syndication that August. Prior to that time, CBS showed relatively few *Dallas* reruns since continuing serials did not fare too well in the summer ratings. The exception was the summer of 1980, when CBS capitalized on the "Who Shot J.R.?" phenomenon by rerunning episodes from the pilot and Season 1. CBS tried to alleviate the rerun problem by increasing the number of original episodes. Thus, while fewer than twenty-five episodes of *Dallas* were produced during each of its first three seasons, by Season 5 the order was up to twenty-eight and by Season 6 CBS requested thirty episodes.

One result of the increased episode order was the abandonment of plans to make a movie version of *Dallas*. Lorimar had considered the idea since "Who Shot J.R.?" aired in 1980. As Bob Crutchfield from Lorimar explained, "We kept getting orders from CBS for more episodes. . . . There's just no time to make a movie. We also had the problem that the actors tend not to want to do the same characters in a movie. We found if we wanted the actors it meant a lot of negotiations because a movie deal wasn't in their contracts." A *Dallas* movie was at one time pre-sold at the Cannes Film Festival and would therefore have been made to some extent for the European market. According to Crutchfield, "The European theater people wanted something to get people out of their homes on the night *Dallas* was on." By the show's twenty-fifth anniversary in 2003, David Jacobs had signed to produce, at last, a silver screen version of *Dallas*.

While *Dallas* remained TV's number 1 show during the 1983–84 season, *Dynasty* climbed to number 3, and it also beat *Dallas* for the Golden Globe for Best Drama. *Dallas*'s nomination was the last of its five consecutive nominations for this award. *Dynasty*'s ratings climb would continue the following season, when, on a technicality, it would inch past *Dallas* in the final season ratings for the only time between *Dynasty*'s premiere in 1981 and its cancellation in 1989. Season 6 was *Dallas*'s last season as TV's number 1 show. It aired against ABC's *Lottery* and NBC's *Manimal*, hit number 1 nine times during the season and earned a 25.7 rating for the year.

SEASON 6 EPISODE GUIDE

Regular Cast

Starring:
Barbara Bel Geddes as Miss Ellie
Patrick Duffy as Bobby
Linda Gray as Sue Ellen
Larry Hagman as J.R.
Susan Howard as Donna
Steve Kanaly as Ray
Ken Kercheval as Cliff
Victoria Principal as Pam
Charlene Tilton as Lucy
Also Starring:
John Beck as Mark
Morgan Brittany as Katherine Wentworth
Howard Keel as Clayton
Audrey Landers as Afton
Timothy Patrick Murphy as Mickey Trotter
Priscilla Beaulieu Presley as Jenna Wade

Technical Credits

Producer: Leonard Katzman
Executive Producer: Philip Capice
Supervising Producer: Arthur Bernard
    Lewis
Story Editor: David Paulsen
Associate Producer: Cliff Fenneman
Music: Jerrold Immel, Richard Lewis
    Warren, Bruce Broughton, Lance Rubin
Unit Production Manager: Wayne A.
    Farlow

First Assistant Directors: Fred Stromsoe,
    Alan Brimfield
Second Assistant Director: Frank Katzman
Directors of Photography: Robert
    Caramico, A.S.C. , Bradford May
Art Director: Kim Swados
Editors: Fred W. Berger, A.C.E., John
    Arthur Davies, Lloyd Richardson
Executive in Charge of Casting: Barbara
    Miller
Casting: Irene Mariano, Rody Kent
Set Decorator: Bryan Thetford
Property Master: John Rettino
Costumers: Jack Bear, Ann Lambert
Makeup: Susan Cabral, Joe Hailey
Hair Stylists: Gregg Mitchell, Generio
    Gugliemotto
Production Sound Mixers: Ronald
    Curfman, C.A.S. , Clarke King
Sound Effects Supervisor: Victor Guarnier
Sound Effects Editors: Douglas Grindstaff,
    Tom Gillis Burke, Alan Nineberg, Don
    Higgins
Music Supervisor: David Franco
Music Editor: Patricia Peck
Main Title Design: Wayne Fitzgerald
Production Supervisor: Mitch Ackerman
Executive Production Supervisor: Edward
    O. Denault

132. "The Road Back"

*Written by Arthur Bernard Lewis; Directed by Nick Havinga; Airdate: September 30, 1983
Guest Stars: Kate Reid (Aunt Lil); George O. Petrie (Harv); Kay E. Kuter (Andy Sampson)
Subject: Fire at Southfork.*

Cast Notes   Omri Katz takes over the role of John Ross from Tyler Banks. Katz played the role for the last eight seasons of *Dallas* and in the 1996 TV movie sequel. Of all the children who appeared on *Dallas* during its long run, Katz appeared in the most episodes, appearing in 151 of the show's 357 episodes. In 1984, he won the *Soap Opera Digest* Award for Outstanding Prime Time Juvenile Actor. The fall after *Dallas*'s cancellation, he starred in the NBC comedy drama *Eerie, Indiana*. ★ Kay Kuter played Newt Kiley on *Petticoat Junction* and its spin-off, *Green*

Acres. ★ Arthel Neville, who plays a waitress in this episode, later became an anchor for CNN. ★ John Beck returned for a second straight season as Mark Graison. Beck found the *Dallas* ensemble "very gracious and open" but "tended to feel like an outsider since they had all been together since the beginning and had been through so much together."

Trivia This episode was number 2 in the weekly ratings, earning a 27.5 rating and 44 share. ★ Barbara Bel Geddes was still recovering from heart surgery when filming resumed for the 1983–84 season. As a result, she missed the first third of Season 6. The producers explained her absence, which lasted until Episode 143, with a trip to Takapa. ★ Leonard Katzman's son, Frank, joined the crew as a second assistant director, a title he held through Season 8. He returned to *Dallas* as a first assistant director during Seasons 10 and 11 and was the Associate Producer during Seasons 12 and 13. He was the first assistant director of *J.R. Returns.* ★ Not long after this cliff-hanger resolution aired, Leonard Katzman told *TV Guide* that a cliff-hanger such as the Southfork fire lacked certain things that a whodunit such as "Who Shot J.R.?" or "Who Drowned in the Southfork Pool?" bring to a show. Katzman said that "whodunit[s are] a much easier secret to keep than whether someone lives or dies; that one becomes obvious when people come back to work."

133. "The Long Goodbye"

Written by Leonard Katzman; Directed by Leonard Katzman; Airdate: October 7, 1983
Guest Stars: Kate Reid (Aunt Lil); Joe Maross (Dr. Blakey); George D. Wallace
Subject: Pam's and Bobby's marital troubles.

Trivia This episode was number 2 in the weekly ratings. ★ Pam's desire to forget the last year is fulfilled belatedly in Episode 223, when Season 8 is explained away as her dream. ★ Lucy's room was also seen in Seasons 4, 5, and 11. ★ Shortly before this episode aired, Phil Capice told *TV Guide*, which was doing a profile of Morgan Brittany, that "it's interesting" to have a "beautiful woman, as sweet-looking as [Brittany] is" play "a character who's evil underneath." Patrick Duffy added, "Obviously, [Morgan Brittany is] diametrically opposed to the character she plays. Katherine's an absolute schemer. Morgan is . . . one of those disgustingly likeable human beings."

134. "The Letter"

Written by David Paulsen; Directed by Nick Havinga; Airdate: October 14, 1983
Special Guest Star: Christopher Atkins (Peter Richards)
Guest Stars: Kate Reid (Aunt Lil); Diana Douglas (Dr. Suzanne Lacey); Stephanie Blackmore (Serena)
Subject: Katherine forges a letter from Pam.

Cast Notes Christopher Atkins starred with Brooke Shields in the 1980 movie *The Blue Lagoon*. He joined the *Dallas* cast at the suggestion of his manager. "*Dallas* was at the top of its game," explains Atkins, "and they wanted to keep the pace by adding some spice with a younger man in Sue Ellen's life. Interestingly, it was back when movie stars did not do TV and some felt it was a very bad decision by my manager and part of the decline to my movie career. Ironically it wasn't too far into the future that movie and TV figures would cross the barriers and it became acceptable." ★ Diana Douglas costarred with Jim Davis in the TV series *The Cowboys* and appeared as Professor Tyler on *The Paper Chase*. ★ Tony Garcia takes over the role of Raoul, the Southfork butler, and would play it through Season 11.

Trivia Weekly rating: number 12. ★ Bruce Broughton won the Emmy for Outstanding Achievement in Music Composition for a Series (Dramatic Underscore) for this episode. ★ This episode includes one of the more memorable of the many ploys Katherine used to break Bobby and Pam apart. Morgan Brittany "had a hard time justifying why someone who had everything, money, looks, position, etc. would risk it all unless she had a desperate side to her character." As a result, "as time went on and the character became one of the main storylines," explains Brittany, "I found a desperate vulnerability in her that explained why she did some of the things she did." ★ One of the first cast members Christopher Atkins met after signing up for *Dallas* was Larry Hagman. Atkins found Hagman "a really funny guy. He really cared about his actors. I'll never forget walking on to the show with an armload of clothes for a photo shoot and meeting him. He grabbed the hundred pounds of clothes I had and personally welcomed me to the show and walked me to the dressing room. He was the most intimidating for me but after a moment my fears fell and he was an awesome guy." Atkins based Peter Richards on "my real life days as a camp counselor/sailing instructor back at the American Yacht Club in Rye, New York."

135. "My Brother's Keeper"

Written by Arthur Bernard Lewis; Directed by Leonard Katzman; Airdate: October 21, 1983
Special Guest Star: Christopher Atkins (Peter Richards)
Guest Stars: Kate Reid (Aunt Lil); Glenn Corbett (Paul Morgan); Stephanie Blackmore (Serena); Tracy Scoggins (Diane Kelly)
Subject: J.R. plots against Pam.

Cast Notes Glenn Corbett makes the first of eighteen appearances in Seasons 6 and 8 through 10 as attorney Paul Morgan. Corbett played Linc Case on *Route 66*. ★ Tracy Scoggins, who starred in the *Dynasty* spin-off *The Colbys*, returned to *Dallas* as Harv Smithfield's niece Anita in both *Dallas* TV movies.

Trivia This episode was number 2 in the weekly ratings. ★ Christopher Atkins enjoyed his scenes with Omri Katz. "Omri was a great kid," Atkins recalls, "and had a lot of talent. We pretty much played the whole time. I love kids and still think I'm one."

136. "The Quality of Mercy"

Written by Leonard Katzman; Directed by Nick Havinga; Airdate: October 28, 1983
Special Guest Star: Christopher Atkins (Peter)
Guest Stars: Kate Reid (Aunt Lil); Lois Chiles (Holly); Morgan Woodward (Punk); Joseph R. Maross (Dr. Blakey); Jack Collins (Russell)
Subject: Ray commits euthanasia.

Trivia This episode was number 5 in the weekly ratings. ★ A home once owned by Nieman-Marcus co-founder Stanley Marcus was rented for use as Pam's house.

137. "Check and Mate"

Written by David Paulsen; Directed by Leonard Katzman; Airdate: November 4, 1983
Special Guest Star: Christopher Atkins (Peter)
Guest Stars: Kate Reid (Aunt Lil); Lois Chiles (Holly); Glenn Corbett (Paul); Morgan Woodward (Punk); George O. Petrie (Harv); Kenneth Kimmins (Thornton); Jack Collins (Russell)
Subject: The will contest ends.

Cast Notes Costar John Hostetter, who plays accountant Gerber, played John, the stage manager, on *Murphy Brown*. ★ As Season 6 progressed, John Beck played more and more scenes with Ken Kercheval, who Beck found to be "a real character. He was really enjoying himself, being on a big hit TV show."

Trivia Weekly rating: number 1. ★ This episode includes one of Christopher Atkins's several scenes in which he appeared in nothing but a small bathing suit. Atkins recalls, "The producers asked me to stop stuffing my swimsuit one time which was kinda funny to me and flattering." ★ Katherine and J.R., who toast Bobby's and Pam's divorce in this episode, were not the only ones who enjoyed the end of that union. Morgan Brittany also "really enjoyed breaking up Pam and Bobby's marriage! The mean, underhanded things that Katherine did were brilliant! I loved the double side to the character where she was sooo sweet to your face and then just stabbed you in the back."

138. "Ray's Trial"

Written by Arthur Bernard Lewis; Directed by Michael Preece; Airdate: November 11, 1983
Special Guest Star: Christopher Atkins (Peter)
Guest Stars: Kate Reid (Aunt Lil); Lois Chiles (Holly); Glenn Corbett (Paul); Richard Jaeckel (Percy Meredith); Charles Aidman (Judge Emmett Brocks); Don Starr (Jordan); Fern Fitzgerald (Marilee); Joseph R. Maross (Dr. Blakey); Will Hare; Priscilla Presley (Jenna)
Subject: Ray's trial.

Cast Notes Priscilla Beaulieu Presley, who was married to Elvis Presley from 1967 to 1973, is the third actress to appear as Jenna Wade, a role she played through Season 10. Prior to *Dallas*, she co-hosted *Those Amazing Animals* with Burgess

Meredith. She went on to co-produce *Elvis*, a 1990 TV series about her husband, and she also participated in the production of the 2005 miniseries *Elvis*. She costarred with George Kennedy, who joined *Dallas* the episode after Presley's departure, in the movie *Naked Gun* and its sequel. Steve Kanaly recalls that "we were so pleased to have her be our third Jenna. Patrick and I took her to a Mexican restaurant in Fort Worth over the lunch break on her first day. We had some beers and margaritas and got a bit tipsy by the time we got back. She was great. Very private but loved by all. She was very kind to the crew. Once in a while, she would discuss Elvis. Her acting went through an excellent curve during the five years she was on the show. Her acting ability just got better and better. . . . She had the most beautiful, unusual skin, which photographed just fantastically." ★ This episode marks Lois Chiles' last appearance as Holly. In contrast to Holly's less than complimentary feelings about J.R., Chiles found Hagman a "wonderful" costar, to which Hagman responded, "She has great taste." ★ Costar Steven Williams played Mr. X on *The X-Files*.

Trivia   Weekly rating: number 2. ★ Billy Bob's honky-tonk is located in the Stockyards section of Fort Worth, which was a prime Southwest cattle receiving area in the late 1800s. ★ Priscilla Presley's lack of acting experience almost cost her the role of Jenna. "When my agent submitted my name to Lorimar," she later explained, "they said they weren't interested. I had a tape made of some of the best things I've done and he offered to send it over. Another no. So he brought it over anyway and said, 'Don't you think she at least deserves an interview?'" Phil Capice explained, "She had only been acting a few years and didn't have many credits." Capice then recalled Presley's TV movie appearance with Michael Landon in *Comeback* and "decided to call her in. The first thing that struck me was how beautiful she is. I emphasized how hard the work would be and how much traveling would be involved and I remember her exact answer: 'I wouldn't be here if I didn't think I could do it.'" Presley recalls that she was cast three days after her audition with Capice, and that she never learned why neither Morgan Fairchild nor Francine Tacker were asked to return as Jenna. Presley "purposely never watched the original episodes with the prior Jenna Wades. I wanted to create my own character apart from what they had created." ★ Presley won the 1984 *Soap Opera Digest* Award for Exciting Prime Time Female Newcomer. She found the *Dallas* cast "a very tight little group but I didn't have any trouble. All my life I've always been the new girl on the block." Leonard Katzman said, "It was sink or swim and she swam. . . . [Patrick Duffy] is glib, quick, and funny and if you can't keep up with him, you're in trouble." Duffy thought Presley was "a little nervous and I cut her no slack whatever. I don't believe in tippy-toeing around with a newcomer. . . . [She is] unaffected and not burdened with any actress paraphernalia. She simply does good, clean, honest work." Presley admits, however, that she was worried before meeting her new costars. "There were so many tabloid stories about the cast members. . . . So, I'm walking into this thinking, 'Oh my God. It's going to be a cat fight as soon as I walk in.' So, of course, I'm nervous walking in, thinking, you know, 'We'll never get along. I better keep to myself. I'll just stay in my trailer. I'll do my work. I'll say my lines. I'll get off the set.' And to my surprise, it was nothing like that." Presley credited Larry Hagman with making her feel at home on *Dallas*, and recalls that her offscreen "relationships were mostly with Larry . . . and Linda Gray." Gray thought it was Presley's own personality that won Presley acceptance among the cast. "When someone like Priscilla comes on any set," said Gray, "I think there's sort of that . . . bit of awe, like, 'That's Elvis' ex-wife.' But what happened was, Priscilla was such a treasure." Patrick Duffy agreed that "everybody was walking around on eggshells knowing that Priscilla Presley was going to be on the show and it's like they expected Elvis to walk in right behind her. It's an amazing thing. You learn to appreciate what she has to walk around with on a daily basis. She is so sweet. She is exactly like this almost Southern Belle aristocratic perfect person."

139. "Oil Baron's Ball"

Written by Leonard Katzman; Directed by Leonard Katzman; Airdate: November 18, 1983
Special Guest Star: Christopher Atkins (Peter)
Guest Stars: Kate Reid (Aunt Lil); Morgan Woodward (Punk); Glenn Corbett (Paul); Richard Jaeckel (Percy Meredith); Charles Aidman (Judge Emmett Brocks); Priscilla Presley (Jenna)
Subject: The Oil Baron's Ball.

Trivia Weekly rating: number 2. ★ According to Ken Kercheval, Cliff "did not get the kind of recognition J.R. did, but I do believe [that there would be no J.R. without Cliff]. If that hadn't been true, I wouldn't have continued on the show, and they wouldn't have written it the way they did." ★ The Oil Baron's Ball scenes were the first that Priscilla Presley filmed after she was cast as Jenna. She won the role on a Thursday, flew to Fort Worth on Friday, and filmed three Oil Baron's Ball scenes that Saturday. She recalled, "I was petrified. There were so many lines and I had never met any of the *Dallas* regulars and I wondered what they would think of me. My problem is, people know who I am but they don't know about my work." Presley found Larry Hagman "so big, so intimidating. I had learned my part and I would say my line and then he'd ask, what's my line? I was so serious and he was so casual. It really threw me." Presley felt comfortable enough after a day of filming, however, to complain to Leonard Katzman about "a couple of things I didn't think Jenna would do." Katzman did not think Presley "knew I had also written the script." Nevertheless, he heard her out, agreed with her, and changed his script accordingly. ★ Christopher Atkins found the ball scenes "massive but well organized. They had it down pretty well and it seemed to go fast. I get kind of nervous in those situations where I have to work in front of large crowds so I was glad to get it done."

140. "Morning After"

Written by David Paulsen; Directed by Michael Preece; Airdate: November 25, 1983
Special Guest Star: Christopher Atkins (Peter)
Guest Stars: Morgan Woodward (Punk); Glenn Corbett (Paul); Shalane McCall (Charlie); Joe Dorsey (Ben Kesey); Tom Williams (Joe Clooney); Priscilla Beaulieu Presley (Jenna)
Subject: The Oil Baron's Ball.

Cast Notes With this episode, Priscilla Presley added her maiden name to her credit, now appearing as Priscilla Beaulieu Presley. She later explained, "I simply don't want to be so completely identified with the name Presley. . . . The other day at the airport a woman yelled, 'Hi, Jenna.' I loved it. It made my day. I hope I hear it for years." ★ Shalane McCall makes her first appearance as Charlie Wade, a role she played through Season 10. She won several awards for her work on *Dallas*, including *Soap Opera Digest* Awards in 1984 and 1985 for "Best Youth Actress in a Continuing Primetime Drama Series."

Trivia This episode was number 3 in the weekly ratings. ★ The end of Episode 139 is replayed at the beginning of this episode. ★ Christopher Atkins's and Linda Gray's characters start to become intimate in this episode. Says Atkins, "Linda is nuts. She was a total kick in the pants. There wasn't a day that we didn't seem to belly laugh even in the serious scenes. She pulled this prank on me at our first kiss. She rubbed a tooth numbing solution on her lips for our first kiss. Here I am trying to play it cool and be the greatest kisser for her of all time and she is messing with me. I then took the stuff and kissed Priscilla. Before we knew it everyone was numb! Got to admit, Linda had the softest lips I've ever had the pleasure of kissing and you can quote that!" ★ Three days before this episode's airdate was the twentieth anniversary of the assassination of President John F. Kennedy in Dallas. A Gallup poll taken on the anniversary showed that *Dallas* was helping the city's image recover from the assassination. The poll asked respondents to name the first and second things that came to mind when the city of Dallas was mentioned. Of respondents between the ages of 30 and 49, 27 percent named the assassination and 26 percent named the TV show. Of respondents between the ages of 18 and 29, 23 percent named the TV show while 7 percent named the assassination. The assassination initially gave David Jacobs pause when he thought about setting his story in Dallas. "I may have blanched," Jacobs said, "when I realized I was setting a television show in the town where Kennedy had been killed, but on reflection I decided that fifteen years was long enough to hold the grudge; besides, the Cowboys had won the Super Bowl the year before and that somehow entitled the city to a fresh start."

141. "The Buck Stops Here"

Written by Arthur Bernard Lewis; Directed by Leonard Katzman; Airdate: December 2, 1983

Special Guest Star: Christopher Atkins (Peter)
Guest Stars: Shalane McCall (Charlie); Jack Collins (Russell Slater); Joe Dorsey (Ben Kesey); Priscilla Beaulieu Presley (Jenna)
Subject: Charity rodeo.

Trivia This episode was number 3 in the weekly ratings. ★ Priscilla Presley found Morgan Brittany, whose character became a nemesis of Presley's in this episode, "absolutely beautiful and a very talented actress." ★ The Oil Baron's Club was built on Stage 5 at MGM.

142. "To Catch a Sly"

Written by David Paulsen; Directed by Michael Preece; Airdate: December 9, 1983
Special Guest Star: Christopher Atkins (Peter)
Guest Stars: Shalane McCall (Charlie); Edward Mallory (Stranger); Priscilla Beaulieu Presley (Jenna)
Subject: Sly spies.

Trivia This episode was number 2 in the weekly ratings. ★ The Southfork gym is seen for the first time in this episode, and was seen throughout the remainder of the series. ★ Christopher Atkins found the Texas shoot "fun. Linda Gray and Priscilla Presley were about the only ones I spent any time with and even that was not much. I was new on the show. I'm kind of a loner."

143. "Barbeque Four"

Written by Arthur Bernard Lewis; Directed by Leonard Katzman; Airdate: December 16, 1983
Special Guest Star: Christopher Atkins (Peter)
Guest Stars: Martin E. Brooks (Edgar Randolph); Shalane McCall (Charlie); Alberto Morin (Armondo Sidoni); Christopher Albee (Travis Boyd); Priscilla Beaulieu Presley (Jenna)
Subject: The Ewings' barbeque.

Cast Notes Martin E. Brooks played Dr. Rudy Wells on *The Six Million Dollar Man* and its spin-off, *The Bionic Woman*. He also played Lieutenant Samuels on *Medical Center*. ★ Bit player Mitch Pileggi returned to *Dallas* as Morrisey in Episodes 333–336. He went on to costar as Assistant Director Walter Skinner on *The X-Files*. ★ This is the first appearance of Pat Colbert as Dora Mae, the hostess at the Oil Baron's Club. Colbert played the role through Season 13. She became a Larry Hagman fan during the course of her work on the show, saying, "We all adore him. He and Patrick Duffy keep us in stitches during rehearsal. They're our life preservers when things get tense." ★ This episode also marks the first appearance of Blue Deckert, who played minor roles in eleven episodes of *Dallas* and in *J.R. Returns*. All of Deckert's appearances were filmed on location in Texas. His roles included Grub, the foreman of Dandy Dandridge's oil field in Season 10; Ace Hendricks, Tracey Lawton's billiard hall opponent in Season 11; and Detective

Markham in *J.R. Returns*. Deckert appeared in the movie *The Rookie*; on *Walker, Texas Ranger*; and in *Heaven and Hell: North and South Book III*.

Trivia This episode was number 3 in the weekly ratings. ★ Cliff's over-large handkerchief sticking out of his suit jacket pocket became a trademark during the series. According to Ken Kercheval, he brought humor to the role of Cliff that was not written into the character. An example of this was Cliff's wayward handkerchief, which was Kercheval's idea. ★ This is the last episode of Season 6 filmed on location in Texas. Her recovery from surgery prevented Barbara Bel Geddes from participating in the on-location shoot, however, so her scenes in this episode—her first since Episode 131—are limited to interior scenes filmed in Culver City.

144. "Past Imperfect"
Written by David Paulsen; Directed by Larry Hagman; Airdate: December 23, 1983
Special Guest Star: Christopher Atkins (Peter)
Guest Stars: Don Starr (Jordan); Michael Griswold (Thomas Hall); Alberto Morin (Sidoni); Priscilla Beaulieu Presley (Jenna)
Subject: J.R. investigates Clayton.

Trivia Weekly rating: number 1. ★ Contrary to this episode's physical confrontation between J.R. and Clayton, Larry Hagman and Howard Keel got along well out of character. Keel found acting with Hagman was "quick, precise, and always a pleasure." In more than a decade of working together, Keel recalled only one brief, minor incident in which words were exchanged, and the two quickly diffused the situation with humor.

145. "Peter's Principles"
Written by Arthur Bernard Lewis; Directed by Patrick Duffy; Airdate: January 6, 1984
Special Guest Star: Christopher Atkins (Peter)
Guest Stars: Martin E. Brooks (Edgar); Lee Montgomery (Jerry); Don Starr (Jordan); Fern Fitzgerald (Marilee); David Gale (Melvin)
Subject: Sue Ellen's affair.

Cast Notes Priscilla Beaulieu Presley's credit moves to the beginning of the episode.

Trivia This episode was number 1 in the weekly ratings. ★ Christopher Atkins "didn't think twice about the age difference" between Sue Ellen and Peter, whose relationship is consummated in this episode. "But, yes, it turned out to be highly controversial," admits Atkins. "I don't think the producers knew it would be that big a deal at the time but it certainly became one." ★ Clayton's quip about the singing talents of the actor playing King Arthur in a production of *Camelot* that he and Miss Ellie are attending is an inside joke since Keel was a veteran of musical comedy theater. Keel's singing talents, and those of other cast members such as

Jenilee Harrison and Steve Kanaly, led to a 1985 *Dallas* record album called *Dallas: The Music Story*, released on the Warner Brothers/Lorimar Records label. The album, which featured a photograph of Southfork on its cover, included ten "episodes" (or songs) including three performed by *Dallas* actors. Kanaly, as Ray, performed "Who Killed Jock Ewing?" Keel, as Clayton, sang, "J.R.! Who Do You Think You Are?" And Harrison, as Jamie, sang "I'm a Survivor (From the Women of *Dallas*)." Country and western singing stars also appeared on the album. Crystal Gayle and Gary Morris sang "Makin' Up for Lost Time (The *Dallas* Lover's Song)," which was released as a single. Charlene Tilton's first husband, Johnny Lee, sang "The Loneliness in Lucy's Eyes (The Life Sue Ellen Is Living)." The album also included "The Theme from *Dallas*." The project was conceived, directed, and executive produced by Artie Ripp.

146. "Offshore Crude"

Written by David Paulsen; Directed by Ray Danton; Airdate: January 13, 1984
Special Guest Star: Christopher Atkins (Peter)
Guest Stars: Martin E. Brooks (Edgar); Shalane McCall (Charlie); Armondo Morin (Sidoni); Fern Fitzgerald (Marilee)
Subject: J.R. investigates Edgar Randolph.

Trivia Weekly rating: number 1. With this episode's top ranking, *Dallas* held the number 1 spot for three weeks in a row, the first time the show had accomplished this feat since Season 4. ★ Director Ray Danton was a Hollywood leading man of the late 1950s and early 1960s who specialized in gangster roles but also appeared in the 1961 World War II classic *The Longest Day*. He later directed such TV shows as *Magnum, P.I.* ★ Larry Hagman relished the role of J.R., but not the character's business scruples. The year this episode aired, Hagman gave an interview that made it clear that he would not abide J.R.'s tactics. Said Hagman, "I met a guy on the airplane the other day who really admired J.R. and really thought that he was J.R. He was into aggressive takeovers of companies. And he just thought I was the role model and he was really a despicable kind of person."

147. "Some Do . . . Some Don't"

Written by Leonard Katzman; Directed by Larry Hagman; Airdate: January 20, 1984
Special Guest Star: Christopher Atkins (Peter)
Guest Stars: Martin E. Brooks (Edgar); Shalane McCall (Charlie); Fern Fitzgerald (Marilee); Lee Montgomery (Jerry); Christopher Albee (Travis)
Subject: Miss Ellie breaks her engagement.

Cast Notes Costar Kate Vernon played Lorraine Prescott on *Falcon Crest* and Tony Danza's girlfriend Kathleen on *Who's the Boss?*

Trivia Weekly rating: number 6. This was the lowest-ranked episode of the season. ★ Larry Hagman used to tease Morgan Brittany that once Katherine slept with J.R., her character would no longer be useful to the plot and she would be killed off, as serial characters frequently were. "That was the whole thing on soap operas," said Brittany, "because you never know [when you would be written out of the show]. You did not want to get in the car, you did not want to get in an airplane because you could go over real easily if your character was not long for this world. Larry used to laugh because he'd say the minute you sleep with me, you're outta there!" As it turned out, Brittany appeared in eighteen more episodes after her character slept with J.R. Katherine was finally killed off in Episode 191, although she returned in Episodes 253 and 254 after Season 8 was revealed to be part of Pam's dream. ★ Says Priscilla Presley about Patrick Duffy, whose character once again became Jenna's lover in this episode, "Patrick was a very professional actor and a lot of fun to work with. I don't think I ever saw him miss one line or have more than two takes for a scene. Even though he joked around a lot he always came prepared." Presley felt that Bobby was "the love of Jenna's life. . . . Yes, she married Naldo, but that was because she was so young."

148. "Eye of the Beholder"

Written by Arthur Bernard Lewis; Directed by Leonard Katzman; Airdate: January 27, 1984
Special Guest Star: Christopher Atkins (Peter)
Guest Stars: Martin E. Brooks (Edgar); Barry Jenner (Jerry Kenderson); Bill Morey (Leo Wakefield); Donegan Smith (Detective Johnson); Christopher Albee (Travis); Fern Fitzgerald (Marilee)
Subject: Miss Ellie and Clayton reconcile.

Cast Notes Barry Jenner played Lieutenant Murtaugh on *Family Matters*.

Trivia Weekly rating: number 2. ★ The winter of 1978, when the *Dallas* pilot was filmed, was unusually cold and snowy for Texas, so Patrick Duffy's quip in this episode about the weather when Bobby and Pam eloped is accurate. ★ Pam's joke about the Man from Atlantis is an inside joke about Patrick Duffy's pre-*Dallas* series, *The Man from Atlantis*. ★ This is one of several episodes in which Pam and Bobby seemed headed for a reconciliation. Patrick Duffy recalled, "After the divorce, I thought, 'Boy, Bobby will start dating like crazy.' [The producers] said, no, that I had to be good. But we were always sort of getting back together because the couple was so firmly established in the minds of the audience that the scriptwriters couldn't walk away from it." Principal agreed that "even after Bobby and Pam broke up . . . you could feel the lingering spark of attraction. They always generated an alluring warmth."

Trivia Weekly rating: number 2.

149. "Twelve Mile Limit"

Written by David Paulsen; Directed by Patrick Duffy; Airdate: February 3, 1984
Guest Stars: Martin E. Brooks (Edgar); Joanna Miles (Martha Randolph); Fern Fitzgerald (Marilee); Ray Girardin (Richard); Donegan Smith (Johnson)
Subject: J.R. blackmails Randolph.

Cast Notes Joanna Miles won a 1974 Emmy for Supporting Actress of the Year for her performance in the TV movie *The Glass Menagerie*.

Trivia Weekly rating: number 1. ★ There were several suicides during *Dallas*'s run, including Seth Stone, Walt Driscoll, Mark Graison (who was briefly resurrected during Pam's season-long dream), and Mark Scottfield.

150. "Where Is Poppa?"

Written by Arthur Bernard Lewis; Directed by William F. Claxton; Airdate: February 10, 1984
Special Guest Star: Christopher Atkins (Peter)
Guest Stars: Martin E. Brooks (Edgar); Alice Hirson (Mavis); Glenn Corbett (Paul); Joanna Miles (Martha); Ann Gee Byrd (Dr. Jeffries); Shalane McCall (Charlie); Fern Fitzgerald (Marilee); Donegan Smith (Johnson)
Subject: Sue Ellen's miscarriage.

Cast Notes This is Anne Lucas's first appearance as Oil Baron's Club waitress Cassie. ★ Ann Gee Byrd appeared as Nurse Richardson in Episode 332.

Trivia Weekly rating: number 3. ★ Christopher Atkins found the scenes dealing with Sue Ellen's miscarriage among his most difficult on *Dallas*. "Peter really loved this woman and deep down knew he could never have her," he says. "So close yet so far." ★ Director William F. Claxton also directed episodes of *Gunsmoke*. ★ Punk and Mavis celebrate their twenty-fifth wedding anniversary, although the script initially called for them to celebrate their fortieth anniversary. Upon reading the script, Alice Hirson says she told the writers, "'But I'm not old enough to be married for forty years!' and they said, 'Okay,' and they made it twenty-five." Yet two years later, during Season 8, Punk and Mavis celebrated their fortieth anniversary. ★ Not long after this 150th episode aired, Larry Hagman traveled to Washington, D.C., to donate one of J.R.'s cowboy hats to the Smithsonian.

151. "When the Bough Breaks"

Written by Leonard Katzman; Directed by Nick Havinga; Airdate: February 17, 1984
Special Guest Star: Christopher Atkins (Peter)
Guest Stars: Glenn Corbett (Paul); Daniel Pilon (Renaldo Marchetta); Ann Gee Byrd (Dr. Jeffries); Shalane McCall (Charlie); Fern Fitzgerald (Marilee); Donegan Smith (Johnson); Debbie Rennard (Sly)
Subject: Sue Ellen ends her affair.

Cast Notes Daniel Pilon starred in the 1983 prime-time soap opera *The Hamptons*, created in the wake of the *Dallas* phenomenon by legendary daytime soap opera producer Gloria Monty, who took ABC's *General Hospital* to record popularity in the early 1980s. Pilon's costars on *The Hamptons* included *Dallas* guest stars Leigh Taylor-Young, John Reilly, and Bibi Besch.

Trivia Weekly rating: number 1. ★ Neither Patrick Duffy nor Priscilla Presley remember whether Daniel Pilon's accent was real, and Morgan Brittany recalls that Pilon "was always in character, so I don't know if [his accent] was real or not. Whenever we ran lines or sat together off camera, he had the accent." ★ Miss Ellie redecorates her room, then does so again in Episode 169.

152. "True Confessions"

Written by David Paulsen; Directed by Paul Krasny; Airdate: February 24, 1984
Special Guest Star: Christopher Atkins (Peter)
Guest Stars: Martin E. Brooks (Edgar); Daniel Pilon (Naldo); Tricia O'Neal (Dr. Barbara Mulgravey); Debbie Rennard (Sly); Fern Fitzgerald (Marilee); Shalane McCall (Charlie); Bill Quinn (Percival); Erica Yohn (Mrs. Mulgravey)
Subject: Charlie's father returns.

Cast Notes Bill Quinn played Sweeney the bartender on *The Rifleman*, the college dean on *Please Don't Eat the Daisies*, and Mr. Van Ranseleer on *All in the Family*.

Trivia Weekly rating: number 4. ★ Around the time this episode aired, CBS and Lorimar considered creating a second *Dallas* spin-off, one focusing on the Krebbses and starring Steve Kanaly and Susan Howard. Kanaly says "neither Lorimar or CBS ever talked with myself or Susan Howard directly but I do remember Leonard Katzman mentioning that the idea was being kicked around. I remember at the time that I felt I would be leaving a hit show and going out to the big unknown and possible quick cancellation; it would be like sending characters to Siberia never to be heard of again." Nothing ever came of the idea, which made Kanaly "happy to have stayed on *Dallas* for the next five years, although I think that a Ray and Donna spin-off could have worked if you added some unsavory characters to balance the cast."

153. "And the Winner Is . . ."

Written by Arthur Bernard Lewis; Directed by Nick Havinga; Airdate: March 2, 1984
Special Guest Star: Christopher Atkins (Peter)
Guest Stars: Martin E. Brooks (Edgar); Morgan Woodward (Punk); Alice Hirson (Mavis); Joanna Miles (Martha); Wendy Fulton (Jan); Don Starr (Jordan); Fern Fitzgerald (Marilee); Debbie Rennard (Sly)
Subject: Cliff's contract bid.

Trivia Weekly rating: number 3. ★ This episode establishes that Mavis is Miss Ellie's best friend. In real life, Alice Hirson was friends with the actress as well. "I knew her from my New York days when my then-husband wrote for the Philco TV Playhouse. She's a real talent."

154. "Fools Rush In"

Written by David Paulsen; Directed by Michael Preece; Airdate: March 9, 1984
Special Guest Star: Christopher Atkins (Peter)

Guest Stars: Dennis Patrick (Vaughan); Barry Jenner (Jerry Kenderson); Peter White (Alex Newton); Barbara Cason (Iris Porter); Shalane McCall (Charlie)
Subject: Mark's illness.

Cast Notes Peter White returned to *Dallas* during Season 13 as Breslin. White played Arthur Cates on *The Colbys* in 1985–86. ★ Barbara Cason was married to Dennis Patrick, who plays Vaughan Leland in this episode, as he did in eighteen other episodes in Seasons 2, 4, 6, and 7. Cason died in 1990.

Trivia Weekly rating: number 1.

155. "The Unexpected"

Written by Arthur Bernard Lewis; Directed by Nick Havinga; Airdate: March 16, 1984
Special Guest Star: Christopher Atkins (Peter)
Guest Stars: Dennis Patrick (Vaughan); Wendy Fulton (Jan); Bill Morey (Leo Wakefield); Stephanie Blackmore (Serena); Alexis Smith (Jessica Montford)
Subject: Clayton's sister arrives.

Cast Notes Canadian-born actress Alexis Smith was a movie star of the 1940s and 1950s who made a career comeback when she appeared on Broadway in *Follies* in the 1970s. She appeared in the movie *Jacqueline Susann's Once Is Not Enough* and was married to actor Craig Stevens from 1944 until her death in 1993. She reprised the role of Jessica in Episodes 330, 331, 333, and 334. Craig Stevens appeared on *Dallas* in Episodes 74 and 75. Says Morgan Brittany about Smith, "Alexis Smith was great! I remember her first day with us. She was a true Hollywood star. [She] always came to the set looking beautiful and just brought such an air of class that only 'old Hollywood' can give. I used to love to sit and watch her and Howard Keel work. I could almost imagine what it was like in the 1940s when they were on that very same soundstage back in the day. She was a great addition to the show."

Trivia Weekly rating: number 2. ★ Production for Season 6 ended on March 22, one day before this episode aired. The cast and crew held their annual wrap party on Hollywood's Sunset Strip. The party featured home movies shown by Larry Hagman. ★ Shortly after joining the *Dallas* cast, Alexis Smith was asked how she was picked for the role. She replied that she did not know, but noted that the character was interesting, "wealthy and titled—all the things I usually play." Smith also quipped that "it doesn't hurt that it's the number one show, and they seem to do it better than anybody." Prior to *Dallas*, Smith stayed away from television because she found it "mediocre or worse." Then *Dallas* came along. "I had a meeting with the producers, which was pleasant, but I didn't learn anything about the character or what's coming up," she explained. "It's funny. It's a funny way to work. But it's a wonderful company and I love working with Larry. . . . I think it's interesting that Larry has played this despicable character in such a way that the entire world adores him." ★ Smith was one of several high-profile guest stars to appear on *Dallas* over the years, but Phil Capice once explained the producers' thoughts about casting a well-known star. "We differ," said Capice, "from some of the other shows in casting. I think that other shows go after a big name and then create a part for that person to play and work it into the story. On *Dallas*, the story always comes first. We shy away from a big-name actor who is best known for being himself. We want our audience to accept the actor as the character."

156. "Strange Alliances"
Written by Leonard Katzman; Directed by Larry Hagman; Airdate: March 23, 1984
Special Guest Star: Christopher Atkins (Peter)
Guest Stars: Dennis Patrick (Vaughan); Barry Jenner (Jerry); Denny Miller (Flowers); Shalane McCall (Charlie); Debbie Rennard (Sly); Alexis Smith (Jessica)
Subject: J.R. and Jessica bond.

Cast Notes Sherril Lynn Katzman is now billed as Sherril Lynn Rettino, having recently married the crew's property master, John Rettino.

Trivia Weekly rating: number 1.

157. "Blow Up"
Written by David Paulsen; Directed by Patrick Duffy; Airdate: April 6, 1984
Special Guest Star: Christopher Atkins (Peter)
Guest Stars: Dennis Patrick (Vaughan); Morgan Woodward (Punk); Alice Hirson (Mavis); Barry Jenner (Jerry); Denny Miller (French); Shalane McCall (Charlie); Alexis Smith (Jessica)
Subject: Jessica plots against Miss Ellie.

Trivia Weekly rating: number 1. ★ This episode includes one of Christopher Atkins's scenes with Charlene Tilton, about whom he says, "Charlene was her character. She is an extremely nice person but boy when she put on that Lucy, look out. She could work you like nobody could. When she would get angry as Lucy, I thought she was angry. When she was flirting, I thought, score! She was good."

158. "Turning Point"
Written by Arthur Bernard Lewis; Directed by Gwen Arner; Airdate: April 13, 1984
Special Guest Star: Christopher Atkins (Peter)
Guest Stars: Dennis Patrick (Vaughan); Donald May (Wes McDowell); Denny Miller (Flowers); Shalane McCall (Charlie); Debbie Rennard (Sly); Alexis Smith (Jessica)
Subject: J.R. fights with Katherine.

Trivia Weekly rating: number 3. ★ This episode's script provided Priscilla Presley with one of her infrequent scenes with Victoria Principal. These types of scenes were among Presley's favorites. Presley liked the "scenes when I first came on board. Th[ose] episodes relayed the inner turmoil between Bobby, Pam, and myself. The stories were about our personal conflicts and where we fit into each other's lives . . . [and were] always centered around our intense love triangle." ★ This episode also includes one of several scenes in which Larry Hagman and Morgan Brittany threaten each other. According to Brittany, "Larry and I used to love 'out-eviling' each other. Some of the outtakes are hilarious with our evil looks to each other. We had the crew cracking up." ★ Director Gwen Arner is a former TV actress.

159. "Love Stories"

Written by Leonard Katzman; Directed by Michael Preece; Airdate: May 4, 1984
Special Guest Star: Christopher Atkins (Peter)
Guest Stars: Dennis Patrick (Vaughan); Barry Jenner (Jerry); Denny Miller (Flowers);
Bert Kramer (Lawyer); Shalane McCall (Charlie); Bill Morey (Leo); Alexis Smith (Jessica)
Subject: Bobby's engagement.

Trivia Weekly rating: number 2. ★ Alexis Smith filmed one of her *Dallas* scenes at Sherwood Forest, a frequently used location site west of Los Angeles. While doing the scene, Smith suddenly recalled that she had filmed on location there before, for the 1947 movie *Stallion Road*, which also starred Ronald Reagan and Zachary Scott. When Smith was at a White House dinner in 1983, she and President Reagan reminisced about the film. "He talked about the horse he rode," recalled Smith. "He bought the horse from that picture, Tarbaby. He said, 'Alexis, you won't believe this, but Tarbaby's granddaughter just died.' He always had an interest in horses, but I think it was working on that picture that clinched it." ★ Mitzi's is the diner where Sue Ellen first met Dusty in Episode 37.

160. "Hush, Hush, Sweet Jessie"

Written by David Paulsen; Directed by Gwen Arner; Airdate: May 11, 1984
Special Guest Star: Christopher Atkins (Peter)
Guest Stars: Bill Morey (Leo Wakefield); Don Starr (Jordan); Debbie Rennard (Sly);
Alexis Smith (Jessica)
Subject: Miss Ellie is kidnapped.

Trivia Weekly rating: number 4. ★ During this episode's scene in which Pam confronts Katherine about a forged letter—and slaps her—"Victoria missed my nose by about an inch!" recalls Morgan Brittany. "I felt the breeze as her hands went by and that is why I looked so shocked when I fell onto the bed. Actually my husband was there that day and coached me on how to take a punch. It looked real, didn't it?" This episode also includes one of Brittany's favorite scenes, in which Katherine rejects Cliff's request for a loan. "Ken Kercheval and I used to break up during scenes like that," explains Brittany. "He used to say he felt like such a wimp and I was a HUGE bitch! That particular scene is my favorite because I became Scarlett O'Hara gone over the top. I give Cliff the once-over and make him sweat then turn him down. Such fun!" ★ The Quorum is where the Ewings lived after the Southfork fire and where Naldo Marchetta and Johnny

Dancer stayed. ★ Barbara Bel Geddes won the 1984 *Soap Opera Digest* Award for Outstanding Prime Time Actress in a Mature Role.

161. "End Game"

Written by Arthur Bernard Lewis; Directed by Leonard Katzman; Airdate: May 18, 1984
Special Guest Stars: Christopher Atkins (Peter); Barry Corbin (Fenton)
Guest Stars: Dennis Patrick (Vaughan); Shalane McCall (Charlie); Don Starr (Jordan);
Billy Green Bush (Deputy Rockwell); Bill Morey (Leo Wakefield); John Zaremba (Harlan
Danvers); Debbie Rennard (Sly); Alexis Smith (Jessica)
Subject: Bobby is shot.

Cast Notes Billy Green Bush played Elvis Presley's father in *Elvis*, a biographical series co-produced by Priscilla Presley. ★ This episode is Christopher Atkins's last appearance on *Dallas*. While Atkins has "this thing about watching myself" and has still not watched the show, he says his *Dallas* "experience was awesome. . . . The writers, directors, and cast were some of the most talented people in Hollywood and for that it was a tremendous experience. It was a big family, and I was very grateful to them for accepting me and letting me play with the big dogs. I love that bunch of old hippies!" ★ This episode also includes Barry Corbin's last appearance as Fenton. Corbin recalls, "When I came on the set for [Episode 161], Larry [Hagman] asked me how I thought the show was going and I said something along the lines of 'I don't know, Larry. I never watch it.' As I think back now, that might have been offensive . . . but I just don't much watch TV. I didn't then and I still don't now. If the TV is on, it's usually on the Western Channel, TNT, or the Weather Channel." As for why Fenton never returned after this episode, Corbin says "maybe he died. Or, maybe my . . . comment to Larry sped up his departure . . . ha ha!"

Trivia Weekly rating: number 1 with a 26 rating and 45 share. The season-ending cliff-hanger craze was now at its peak. *Dynasty*'s cliff-hanger, which had Joan Collins's character arrested for murder, finished third for the week. *Knots Landing*, on which Michele Lee's character was shot and Donna Mills's character was kidnapped, was number 7. *Falcon Crest*, which had its entire cast on a doomed flight to Italy, came in at number 8. *Time* magazine, in a story on the cliff-hanger phenomenon, reported that the producers of *Dallas* "filmed four different endings for this week's season finale; not even the actors know which one will be telecast and which are decoys." Indeed, the script for this episode listed sixty-five scenes, but only sixty-one scenes were distributed to the cast. The cast was informed that the remaining four scenes were "to come from director [Leonard Katzman]—verbally." Phil Capice told *Time* that the now standard season cliff-hanger was "good storytelling, and the best manner to hook an audience into wanting to come back." ★ Katzman thought having shots fired into J.R.'s office only to reveal that it was Bobby who was shot "was terrific. Our feeling was the audience was going to look at it and say, 'Agh!! They're not going to do it! . . . Oh, they wouldn't do that again! Oh, boy! They wouldn't do that! . . . ' Then, when Bobby falls, 'Uhhhhh-hhh!' And it worked." ★ Making Bobby central to the cliff-hanger helped beef up the role of Patrick Duffy, who still felt Bobby was too boring. Duffy originally in-tended to stay with *Dallas* only through Season 4, then changed his mind and signed a three-year contract. He tried to get out of his contract at the end of Sea-son 5, but was rebuffed by Lee Rich and Lorimar. During Season 6, Duffy said, "If *Dallas* ran forever, I don't think I would stay with it. I have this year and one more year left on my contract. All things being equal, I would like to get away at the end of that period and do something else permanently. I would go right back in and do another series, but I've done just about all I can do with this character. I'm getting tired of it." ★ Howard Keel felt that "one of the reasons [Clayton] married Miss Ellie is that he acts as her adviser, helps take care of her. He has a great need to give, and to help people. . . . Clayton is a rock and she really needs someone like that." As for his character's wife, Keel said, "Ellie is a real Texas mama. She makes Southfork so warm that no one ever wants to leave it. . . . It's an earthiness; her feet are in Texas, in that ranch. That's what the show is really all about. Whatever strength Ellie has is what she gets from the ranch, from the earth be-neath her." Keel found Jock to be a "tough man. Actually, he was a reprobate. Jock was a tough old wildcatter who made good, but money and success don't change what a person is inside. He taught J.R. everything he knows; he liked for him to play dirty. Clayton's entirely different. I sometimes wish he were more of an SOB. He'd be more interesting to play." ★ Cliff appears to have lost his fortune in this episode, which epitomizes the struggle Ken Kercheval faced playing J.R.'s eternal whipping boy. "There came a time when I got defeated by J.R., and then came a second time, and then a third time. I really got kicked down. So I went to Lenny Katzman and said, 'Turn the other cheek? This is ridiculous! How many cheeks does the guy have to have?' And he said, 'Kenny, you still have two cheeks.' I fig-ured that Cliff would have to have been lobotomized unless he had the ability to laugh it off and pick himself up and keep going. So he took it and took it and took it but was able to laugh it off."

SEASON 7
1984–85—"Swan Song"

ON MAY 22, 1984, FOUR days after the "Who Shot Bobby?" cliff-hanger aired, production on Season 7 began with the filming of interior scenes at Culver City. Barbara Bel Geddes was not required to report to the set since her character was on an extended honeymoon. While Bel Geddes had previously intimated to the producers that she might not return to the show for Season 7, she made her decision official on June 4, when it was announced that she was leaving *Dallas*. Bel Geddes' departure was the first of several cast defections, and one major production staff departure, that were announced during Season 7. Other than Jim Davis's death, her exit was the first change to the core group of players that had been with *Dallas* since it was created in late 1977, and it drastically altered the show that viewers saw in Season 8.

Bel Geddes, who had missed the first eleven episodes of Season 6 as a result of her heart surgery, cited personal reasons for her departure, and the press and the public presumed those reasons had to do with her health and the strain of filming a series. *Dallas* writer David Paulsen, however, claims that the reasons were financial. According to Paulsen, Bel Geddes' "manager wanted more than the show felt they could afford to pay. It was a very tightly run show from a budgetary standpoint and from a pleasantness stand point," Paulsen said. "I know Leonard tried very hard and Phil tried very hard, I believe, to say, 'This is the limit. . . . Understand that we're moving ahead.'" Evidently, Bel Geddes was not open to staying within the producers' limit, and she opted to leave. She told Howard Keel that she was "looking forward to going back east and working on her pottery and other projects."

Bel Geddes' exit shocked Larry Hagman, who "didn't find out about it until it was a fait accompli, which ticked me off no end. I really felt that if I'd just been told, I could have done something about it. Barbara and I have a great relationship. We'll be on location, and I'll have to talk her into going out for a drink, then I won't be able to get her to go home until two in the morning. I was crushed when she decided to leave the show." Hagman confirmed that Bel Geddes felt overworked and underpaid, and he believed that he could have helped her reach a compromise with the producers. "But," he wrote later, "Barbara was following the advice of a business manager, one of those guys who helped her out of a job."

With Jock gone, the producers decided that the Ewings could not afford the loss of a second parent. Phil Capice did not "want to leave J.R. an orphan. . . . Barbara's leaving was a far different situation [than Jim Davis's death was]. We couldn't simply eliminate Miss Ellie—she was the only authority figure left at Southfork—it would have changed the whole chemistry of the show. Without mama around, J.R. would have started running wild. Family devotion—to his mother, to his son—that's what redeems him. So even though we were concerned that the audience might not suspend its disbelief and accept a new actress in the role, it was the only option open to us. We had no good solution to the problem of Barbara Bel Geddes leaving; we just felt recasting was the lesser of two evils."

Katzman and Capice began looking for a replacement for Bel Geddes even before her departure was announced. According to Mary Martin, she was asked by son Larry Hagman whether she wanted to replace Bel Geddes as Miss Ellie, but Martin told him, "No, that's your play." Capice recalled that someone mentioned Donna Reed, the Oscar-winning star of *From Here to Eternity, It's a Wonderful Life,* and TV's *The Donna Reed Show.* "When Donna Reed's name came up, everybody looked at each other and their eyes widened," he said. "Someone said, 'I wonder what she's doing.' She came over with her agent and she was charming." Reed later recalled, "It came as a surprise when they asked me to interview for the role. I've been around too long to interview. But I agreed, not knowing what role they had in mind."

When Reed met with the producers, she still "didn't know for sure it was for [Miss Ellie], although I had heard Barbara might be leaving. And I still didn't know when the meeting ended because they were very sensitive about anything prematurely getting in the papers." Reed was "stunned when they said I was to replace Barbara. I thought they'd planned to have me play a new addition to the series." According to her husband, Reed "lost a few pounds fretting" about the offer, but ultimately felt she "was ready for one more baptism of fire." Reed had watched *Dallas* occasionally, including the last two episodes of Season 6. She "liked Miss Ellie" and "could relate to the pioneer element in her life and the fact that she was essentially a farm woman, like me. I thought it would be lovely to play a woman with a strong attachment to the land and her family. Her marriage last year added a new dimension. There aren't many romances around these days for our age bracket."

On June 4, just after the announcement of Bel Geddes' departure, Reed signed a one-year contract to play Miss Ellie, and Lorimar released a press statement the following day. Howard Keel thought "it was strange to cast Donna because she was so refined and genteel and Miss Ellie is just Miss Ellie—down to earth and a real Texan!" According to Katzman, Reed was chosen because she had the same "authority and gentleness" as Bel Geddes and was in "the same age range. We weren't looking for a [twin], but we didn't want somebody too far off." Katzman approached the recasting with "great delicacy. It would be easy for the audience to resent [Bel Geddes'] replacement. There's going to be some initial shock—but once people see Donna's warmth and strength, they'll accept her."

Because the producers signed Reed so early in the summer, the writers were able to add Miss Ellie, who was on her honeymoon, back into the storyline in time for the season's seventh episode. Reed, who was nervous about replacing a long-time cast member, ran into some of her new castmates at MGM, where she reported for makeup testing. "It was a fearsome thought," she said. "I thought perhaps they might resent me for replacing Barbara. I could understand why they might be disgruntled. I was asked to come to MGM before production began this summer for makeup tests, which helped break the ice. I bumped into Howard, Linda, Victoria, and most of the others. I was warmly received." Reed then joined the cast for the annual on-location filming in Dallas, which took place from June 20 through August 17, 1984. Howard Keel easily adjusted to his new leading lady. While Keel found that "Donna was naturally kind of nervous in the beginning, as anybody would be taking over for Barbara," he found Reed "a pro and I don't think any of us have had significant adjustments to make working with her. There was one story out that the cast was upset about her as the replacement—ridiculous. She's blended in very gracefully."

Shortly after Reed's debut episode aired in November 1984, Lorimar announced that it was dropping Charlene Tilton from the cast at season's end. Tilton learned the news from Katzman. "Leonard Katzman called me and he said they were not going to pick up my contract. And I was shocked," she said. "And he started to cry and he said, 'Look, it's nothing you did. It's just we don't know what to do with your character,' or whatever. You know, I don't know if that was B.S. or what. I mean, to this day, I have no idea." A press agent for Tilton stated, "The termination results from Lorimar's creative decision to no longer expand her character. While Charlene was surprised and disappointed, she looks forward to future projects and will leave amicably." A Lorimar spokesman explained that the "writers didn't feel they could do anything further with the character, so the show's producer, Len Katzman, opted not to do another contract."

At a press party attended by the *Dallas* cast two months later, Charlene Tilton stated, "I don't know how the decision came about. My first feeling was just really shock. I've never had a jolt like that in a million years. The thing that I have to believe is that the end of *Dallas* is not the end of Charlene Tilton. I'm not bitter at all. I'm really not. I respect their creative decision. [Leonard Katzman's] like a father to me. He was very upset. He was crying, I was crying." At the same event, Linda Gray claimed, "I think it's a mistake to change a cast that is familiar to the audience. I think it's bad timing." Larry Hagman agreed, "She's a part of our family. I'm not happy with that at all."

To make matters worse, on November 19, a few days after Tilton's departure was announced, Patrick Duffy's agent, Joan Scott, confirmed that Duffy was also leaving *Dallas* at the end of Season 7, primarily "to go on to other things." The producers tried over several months to change Duffy's mind, but in March, Duffy had a lunch meeting with Leonard Katzman, Lee Rich, and Phil Capice and made his departure official. Capice acknowledged that Duffy's departure was "a problem. We tried to convince Patrick to stay." Lorimar offered Duffy a raise from $40,000 per episode to $50,000 plus more interesting scenes for Bobby. Duffy turned the offer down.

Duffy explained, "I had my problems with Lorimar for a couple of years. They weren't letting Bobby grow or do anything. He was really stuck, and everyone else was chewing the scenery. Absolute purity is not very interesting, as far as I'm concerned. I don't think anybody can compete with Larry's character. You can only have one character like that." In other interviews, Duffy claimed that he was "itchy to leave" since he "never felt appreciated" and "got real frustrated with the static quality of the character I was playing." To Duffy, Bobby remained "boring. There is no place to go with the character. *Dallas* started out to be a pretty energetic show. It had lots of outdoor stuff and barroom brawls. Now it's just talking and kissing—boardroom and bedroom." Duffy, saying he was "the opposite of those people who say they're doing TV only until they get their film career going," hoped to move into another television series.

The producers were left having to decide whether to replace Bobby, like they did with Miss Ellie, or write him out of the show, as they did with Jock. Duffy felt strongly that he did not want another actor to play his role. "I didn't want Bobby to disappear in a fiery ball in the sky and come back as someone different who parachuted to safety," he said. "I would feel terrible looking at someone else doing the part." While it was difficult to kill off a popular character, the producers recalled that, when David Jacobs created *Dallas* in 1977, he envisioned killing off Bobby at the end of the pilot, setting the stage for a series driven by Pam's ongoing conflicts with the Ewings. The producers and writers became intrigued with the otherwise risky idea of killing Bobby because doing so fulfilled Jacobs's original outline. Duffy himself recognized that Bobby was "supposed to die after the first five episodes" because *Dallas* "was supposed to be Romeo and Juliet." There could be endless storylines resulting from widow Pam taking on J.R. and the other Ewings. The producers thought that such a dynamic would breathe fresh life into a series that was going into its eighth year. Accordingly, the creative team agreed that Bobby would die in the season cliff-hanger.

Compounding the departure of Bel Geddes, Tilton, and Duffy was Leonard Katzman's decision to step down as the producer of *Dallas* at the end of Season 7. Like Duffy, Katzman thought of leaving *Dallas* at the end of Season 5, but Hagman and other cast members had convinced him to stay. But by 1984, Katzman had signed to develop and produce for ABC a drama called *Our Family Honor,* which featured future *Dallas* cast member Sheree J. Wilson. While Katzman agreed to keep a hand in *Dallas* in Season 8, during which he was a creative consultant to the show and wrote seven episodes, he knew most of his efforts would be centered around the new series.

Moreover, Katzman had tired of fighting with executive producer Phil Capice over the direction of *Dallas*. Katzman and Capice had battled over creative control since *Dallas* began. Katzman emerged from these struggles with the support of the cast and crew, which was difficult for Capice. Larry Hagman explained that when "people . . . got in [Katzman's] way, . . . he didn't pay a lot of attention to them, to tell you the truth. He's always run the show." Katzman himself concluded that his relationship with Capice was "not a wonderfully pleasant story. . . . Our show works on the premise that if anybody wants an answer to something, they come and see me. We don't work by committee. And that made things very, very difficult for Phil." Years later, Katzman's wife, LaRue, told an interviewer that Katzman's departure was caused by "a disagreement with Phil Capice about the direction the show should go in. I'm sure Lenny had ideas it should go one way and Phil had ideas it should go another way."

Despite the behind-the-scenes turmoil, however, *Dallas* continued to receive critical and popular acclaim. In early 1985, Larry Hagman received the last of his four Golden Globe nominations as Best Actor. *Dallas* easily beat its Season 7 competition, ABC's *Hawaiian Heat* and NBC's *Hunter*. While it dropped to number 2 in the overall season ratings, its 24.7 Nielsen rating put it only 0.3 rating points behind the new number 1 show, *Dynasty*. *Dallas*, however, aired its Season 7 cliffhanger—its highest-rated episode of the season—after the official close of the ratings season. *Dallas* and *Dynasty* see-sawed between the top two ratings spots all season, with *Dallas* hitting number 1 nine times during the year. Two other prime-time serials finished in the top ten; in addition to *Dynasty* at number 1 and *Dallas* at number 2, *Knots Landing* finished the year at number 9 and *Falcon Crest* was number 10. Coming in third behind *Dynasty* and *Dallas*, however, was a new ratings blockbuster, one that signaled that the soap era inaugurated by *Dallas* would not last forever and that the reemergence of the situation comedy was at hand: NBC's *The Cosby Show*, which earned a 24.1 rating and 37 share and became TV's number 1 show for the remaining five seasons of the 1980s.

SEASON 7 EPISODE GUIDE

Regular Cast

Starring:
Patrick Duffy as Bobby
Linda Gray as Sue Ellen
Larry Hagman as J.R.
Susan Howard as Donna
Steve Kanaly as Ray
Howard Keel as Clayton
Ken Kercheval as Cliff
Priscilla Beaulieu Presley as Jenna
Victoria Principal as Pam
Donna Reed as Miss Ellie
Charlene Tilton as Lucy

Also Starring:
Morgan Brittany as Katherine
Jenilee Harrison as Jamie Ewing
Audrey Landers as Afton
Jared Martin as Dusty
Leigh McCloskey as Mitch
Dack Rambo as Jack Ewing
Deborah Shelton as Mandy Winger

Technical Credits

Producer: Leonard Katzman
Executive Producer: Philip Capice
Supervising Producer: Arthur Bernard
   Lewis
Story Editor: David Paulsen
Associate Producer: Cliff Fenneman
Music: Jerrold Immel, Bruce Broughton,
   Richard Lewis Warren, Lance Rubin,
   Angela Morley
Unit Production Manager: Wayne A.
   Farlow

First Assistant Directors: Fred Stromsoe,
   Alan Brimfield
Second Assistant Director: Frank Katzman
Directors of Photography: Robert
   Caramico, A.S.C., Kim Swados
Art Director: Kim Swados
Editors: Fred W. Berger, A.C.E., John
   Arthur Davies, Lloyd Richardson
Executive in Charge of Casting: Barbara
   Miller
Casting: Irene Mariano
Location Casting: Rody Kent
Costume Designer: Travilla
Set Decorator: Bryan Thetford
Property Master: John Rettino
Costumers: Jack Bear, Kathy Monderine
Makeup: Susan Cabral, Joe Hailey
Hair Stylists: Generio Gugliemotto,
   Rebecca De Morrio, Gregg Mitchell,
   Lola "Skip" McNally
Production Sound Mixers: Vince Garcia,
   Ron Ronconi
Supervising Sound Editor: Doug Grindstaff
Sound Effects Editors: Tony Garber, Tom
   Gillis Burke, Dick Friedman
Music Supervisor: David Franco
Music Editor: Patricia Peck
Main Title Design: Wayne Fitzgerald
Production Supervisor: Mitch Ackerman
Executive Production Supervisor: Edward
   O. Denault

162. "Killer at Large"

Written by Arthur Bernard Lewis; Directed by Leonard Katzman; Airdate: September 28, 1984
Guest Stars: Gerald Gordon (Dr. Halperson); Mitchell Ryan (Detective Fogarty); Fern
Fitzgerald (Marilee); Debbie Rennard (Sly); Shalane McCall (Charlie); Dennis Haysbert
(Dr. Forbes); Martin E. Brooks (Edgar)
Subject: Bobby's surgery.

Cast Notes   Police Captain Fogarty is played by Mitchell Ryan, who played Jenna
Elfman's father-in-law, Edward, on *Dharma and Greg.* ★ Casey Sanders, who has a

bit part in this episode, played Wade on *Grace Under Fire*. ★ Guest star Dennis Haysbert appeared in the movies *Waiting to Exhale* and *Far From Heaven* and in the TV miniseries *Lonesome Dove* and *Queen*. He costarred as Dr. Theodore Morris in the CBS series *Now and Again* and as President Palmer on Fox's *24*. ★ Howard Keel and Priscilla Presley were added to the main title as of this episode. ★ This episode includes Audrey Landers's last appearance as Afton until Season 11. Landers "never felt assured that I would be a part of *Dallas* forever, so I needed to pursue other areas. When I got [a costarring role in the movie version of the Broadway hit] *A Chorus Line*, I don't think the [*Dallas*] producers were happy about it, but from my standpoint, I had not gotten a firm contractual commitment from *Dallas*, so I had to take the movie . . . but—when I left *Dallas*—the door was still open to return." ★ Jenny Gago, who plays a nurse in this episode and the next three, returned to *Dallas* as CIA employee Henrietta in Season 9. Gago has also appeared on *JAG*, *The West Wing*, *24*, *Ally McBeal*, as Maria on *Knots Landing*, and as Detective Beatrice Zapeda on *Alien Nation*.

Trivia Weekly rating: number 1, with a 26.4 rating. ★ With the start of Season 7, and the premiere of the Aaron Spelling soap opera *Glitter* on ABC, Morgan Brittany became one of the few actors to appear simultaneously on shows airing on different networks. "I feel very schizophrenic because the two characters are completely different," said Brittany at the time. "I REALLY LIKE *Glitter* better than my *Dallas* character. It gives me the chance to show the public I'm not just a villain." ★ On September 5, 1984, a little more than three weeks before this episode aired, an exhibit of *Dallas* memorabilia called "The *Dallas* Traveling Museum" opened in Dallas. Lorimar sponsored the exhibit, which traveled across the country, to promote the syndication of *Dallas*'s first six seasons. Cast members, including Steve Kanaly, Howard Keel, Ken Kercheval, and Charlene Tilton, made appearances at exhibit stops and participated in question-and-answer sessions about the show. The exhibit included the .38-caliber Smith and Wesson used to shoot J.R., J.R.'s hat and boots, a square foot of land from Southfork, Sue Ellen's sanitarium commitment papers, Sue Ellen's wedding dress, the letter Katherine wrote to break up Pam and Bobby, Sue Ellen's arrest I.D. plate, Ewing Oil office nameplates, a Southfork barbeque invitation, Sue Ellen's Oil Baron's Ball gown, Bobby's belt buckle, Sue Ellen's license plate, and Bobby's and Pam's swimsuits. The exhibit traveled to Los Angeles on September 6, 1984, and opened a four-day run at the Bonita Plaza Mall in San Diego County on October 4, 1984. ★ Ken Kercheval enjoyed having a romance with longtime cartel member Marilee Stone, played by Fern Fitzgerald. Kercheval recalls that Fitzgerald had a "really great sense of humor and a great sense of the character."

163. "Battle Lines"

Written by Arthur Bernard Lewis; Directed by Nick Havinga; Airdate: October 5, 1984
Guest Stars: Dennis Patrick (Vaughan); Mitchell Ryan (Fogarty); Gerald Gordon (Dr.

Halperson); Don Starr (Jordan); Debbie Rennard (Sly); Shalane McCall (Charlie); Omri Katz (John Ross)
Subject: J.R. frames Cliff.

Cast Notes This is Howard Keel's first episode of the season.

Trivia Weekly rating: number 1.

164. "If at First You Don't Succeed"

Written by David Paulsen; Directed by Leonard Katzman; Airdate: October 12, 1984
Guest Stars: Joanna Miles (Martha); George O. Petrie (Harv); Gerald Gordon (Dr. Halperson); Mitchell Ryan (Fogarty); Shalane McCall (Charlie); Omri Katz (John Ross); Bill Morey (Leo); Debbie Rennard (Sly)
Subject: Katherine shot Bobby.

Cast Notes Deborah Shelton costarred in the 1983–84 Cybill Shepard soap opera *The Yellow Rose* and appeared as Marie in the movie *Body Double*. Phil Capice found Shelton "kind, sweet, and anxious to learn. She is not yet a thoroughly accomplished actress, but she responds well to direction." Shelton thought her character was "a fun girl. Laughs a lot, really in control of her life, not somebody's pet. I'm not all soft, but I'm not a bitch. I'm not black or white; I'm kind of a light gray." Larry Hagman described Shelton as "a woman who had no idea how beautiful she was. There was absolutely not an imperfection on that woman." Shelton had "the greatest body I could ever remember," Hagman said. When asked about Shelton, Kercheval replied, "Oh, my God. What a beautiful lady. Just beautiful."
★ Bit player Lee Gideon makes his first of several *Dallas* appearances. He appeared in Seasons 7 through 11 and in *J.R. Returns*, in scenes all filmed on location in Texas. His roles included a Washington lobbyist in Episode 239 in Season 9; investment broker John Cate in Episodes 253, 259, and 263 in Season 10; the Oil Baron's Ball Emcee in Episode 292 in Season 11; and Judge Hooker in *J.R. Returns*. Gideon died in 2003.

Trivia Weekly rating: number 7. This episode, along with Episode 183, was the season's lowest-ranked. ★ Although it was not until this episode that it was revealed that Katherine shot Bobby, Morgan Brittany knew before the cliff-hanger aired the previous spring that she was the one who pulled the trigger. "When Lenny [Katzman] told me that I was going to be the one who shot Bobby," recalls Brittany, "I asked him if he was going for the BIG cliff-hanger again. Of course the answer was yes, but they knew it would never reach the heights that the J.R. ending did. Bobby was one of the great heroes of television at the time and it was the belief that people would be shocked that one of the most beloved characters at the time would die at the end of the season. They knew he would survive, but they went for the shock value." While Christopher Atkins may not have known who shot Bobby, he knew by the end of Season 6 that his character had not. Atkins was under contract to *Dallas* only through the end of Season 6 and could not be extended due to his commitment to appear on Broadway with Gina Lollobrigida in *The Rose Tatoo*. Nevertheless, Atkins felt "it's always cool to be a suspect."

165. "Jamie"

Written by David Paulsen; Directed by Nick Havinga; Airdate: October 19, 1984
Guest Stars: Randolph Mantooth (Joe Don Ford); Kathleen York (Betty); Shalane McCall
(Charlie); Omri Katz (John Ross); Debbie Rennard (Sly)
Subject: Jock's niece arrives.

Cast Notes Dallas newcomer Jenilee Harrison also played a cousin on *Three's Company*, in which her character, Cindy Snow, was related to Suzanne Somers's Chrissy Snow. Harrison joined the *Three's Company* cast after Somers, Patrick Duffy's future *Step by Step* costar, left in a contract dispute. Harrison was cast on *Dallas* by Leonard Katzman. "He saw me at a publicity event," recalls Harrison, "and introduced himself to me. I had also just starred in a feature film called *Tank*, alongside James Garner and Shirley Jones. In that role, I played a young hooker. . . . There were three new roles on *Dallas* available that year, and the two female leads were the roles of Jamie and Mandy, the hooker. I initially read for Mandy and Leonard then asked me to read for Jamie." ★ Randolph Mantooth starred as paramedic Johnny Gage on *Emergency*. ★ This episode marks the first appearances of two minor players who appeared on *Dallas* several times. The first, Alan Ackles, plays Katherine's lawyer in this episode and returned to *Dallas* as a TV talk show host in Episode 234 in Season 9; Pam's doctor in Episodes 255 and 256 in Season 10; and J.R.'s doctor in Episode 282 in Season 11. (Ackles's son, Jensen Ackles, who was born in Dallas, played Eric Brady on *Days of Our Lives* and C.J. on *Dawson's Creek*). The second, Frank Swann, played Oil Baron's Club bartender Mike in Seasons 10, 11, and 13.

Trivia Weekly rating: number 2. ★ With Katherine's confession to shooting Bobby, Morgan Brittany joined Mary Crosby as Ewing sisters-in-law who took aim at a Ewing. Brittany explains, "Mary and I never worked together on the show and we never really talked about [the two shooting cliffhangers] in other situations. A lot of people confuse me with her and think I am the one who shot J.R., but then again, they also think I'm Morgan Fairchild!" ★ TV investigative journalist Morley Safer of *60 Minutes* wrote a tongue-in-cheek article for *TV Guide* as Season 7 got underway, purporting to summarize his investigation into Bobby's shooting. Safer claimed that he interviewed suspects including Bobby's dog, J.R., Miss Ellie, Cliff, Sue Ellen, and even Pam, before alighting on the real perpetrator, CBS Entertainment Division President B. Donald "Bud" Grant, who allegedly explained his motive by referring to the 53 rating generated by the "Who Shot J.R.?" storyline: "I figure Bobby is worth at least a 40." ★ As was the case with the "Who Shot J.R.?" cliff-hanger, alternate resolution scenes were filmed, this time with Sue Ellen and Holly Harwood pulling the trigger.

166. "Family"

Written by Leonard Katzman; Directed by Leonard Katzman; Airdate: October 26, 1984
Guest Stars: George O. Petrie (Harv); Christopher Stone (Dave Stratton); William Smithers (Jeremy); Kathleen York (Betty); Shalane McCall (Charlie); Omri Katz (John Ross); Debbie Rennard (Sly); Fredric Lehne (Eddie Cronin)
Subject: Jamie stays at Southfork.

Cast Notes Fredric Lehne played one of Timothy Hutton's friends in *Ordinary People*, which won the 1980 Best Picture Oscar. ★ This is William Smithers's first appearance as Jeremy Wendell since Episode 85, which aired almost three years earlier. The absence was explained, in part, by Smithers's blackballing in Hollywood after he sued MGM in a breach of contract action. Smithers won a $2.4 million judgment but lost work as a result. Smithers explains, "In 1976, I was a series 'regular' on the TV series *Executive Suite*, produced by MGM and CBS; the show lasted one season. During that time, my contract was violated several times with regard to billing, and when I sought to bring legal action [there was a] threat to blacklist me. . . . Shortly after winning that case, I did not work for several years." It was Larry Hagman who suggested that Smithers return to *Dallas*. "*Dallas* brought me out of it," Smithers acknowledged. Hagman "liked what [Smithers] did [on the show a few years earlier]. I thought he was one of the few men who could stand up to J.R." After returning to *Dallas*, Smithers's career resumed. "In years since, " recalls Smithers, "I've been approached on the street or in a restaurant by some young person who tells me 'Smithers vs. MGM' is being studied in his or her Entertainment Law class."

Trivia Weekly rating: number 2. ★ This episode includes Jenilee Harrison's favorite scene, the "one in which I have just come onto the Ewing Ranch . . . [and] J.R. is implying I am a fraud . . . and I 'slam him' with my wits about oil. Quite fun indeed."

167. "Shadow of a Doubt"

Written by Leonard Katzman; Directed by Nick Havinga; Airdate: November 2, 1984
Guest Stars: Christopher Stone (Dave); William Smithers (Jeremy); Kathleen York (Betty); Rick Jason (Avery Carson); Shalane McCall (Charlie); Omri Katz (John Ross); Debbie Rennard (Sly); Fredric Lehne (Eddie)
Subject: Pam investigates Mark's death.

Cast Notes Rick Jason played Lieutenant Hanley on the TV war drama *Combat*. He also starred in Orson Welles's *The Fountain of Youth* and appeared on the daytime soap *The Young and the Restless*. He died on October 16, 2000.

Trivia Weekly rating: number 1.

168. "Homecoming"

Written by Arthur Bernard Lewis; Directed by Gwen Archer; Airdate: November 9, 1984
Starring: Donna Reed

Guest Stars: Christopher Stone (Dave); Kathleen York (Barry Jenner); Omri Katz (John Ross); Michael Alldredge (Steve Jackson); Fredric Lehne (Eddie) Subject: Miss Ellie returns.

Cast Notes Donna Reed, who watched *Dallas* occasionally before joining its cast, told *People* magazine, "I wasn't looking for a permanent part in a series but Miss Ellie was too good to turn down. . . . [And] emotionally, I needed to work. Doing nothing eventually makes you feel bad." Nevertheless, Reed was "very worried" about joining another series, and knew that "fans will be sad to see that Barbara is no longer on the show. But if they have a choice between having a Miss Ellie and not having a Miss Ellie, I hope they'll be happy to see me." Reed felt "Miss Ellie is a part of our past. She manages somehow to keep her family under one roof, which is really kind of a crazy fantasy these days—nobody does that any more. But I think it does touch people very deeply. Possibly it *was* a little better when American families were less mobile—or were mobile but moved *together*." Reed found the work on *Dallas* to be what the producers promised her when she was hired, saying, "They promised I'd only work three days a week and quit at 6:00 p.m. That's the way it's been so far, and I've loved every minute." After her first week of filming in Dallas in the summer of 1984, Reed told *TV Guide* that she felt "unexpectedly comfortable, *almost* at home. There's something that's just right about this role for me at this time in my life. I'm looking forward to the first time I get a chance to play a scene with J.R. where Miss Ellie just backs him against the wall." According to Reed's husband, Grover Asmus, "Miss Ellie had only one thing to do and that was to raise a coffee mug. Donna wanted to change the character somewhat so that she would be more like the people we knew in Tulsa. The oil men were the potentates of the region and the women were many times the power behind the throne." ★ When Reed joined the cast, Linda Gray publicly stated her respect for Reed's courage in taking over the role of Miss Ellie since fans would constantly compare her to Barbara Bel Geddes. Steve Kanaly thought Reed was a "great" addition to *Dallas* and recalls that "everyone in the cast enjoyed her. She was fun and light-hearted" and "wonderful" in the role of Miss Ellie. ★ Donna Reed's "Starring" credit appears at the beginning of this episode, stating that she was playing "Ellie Ewing Farlow." ★ Rody Kent, who was in charge of location casting for Seasons 3 through 11 and *J.R. Returns*, appears in this episode in a minor role.

Trivia Weekly rating: number 1. ★ This episode's airport scene was the first one that Donna Reed filmed with Larry Hagman. "I'd been warned to expect a lot of hijinks and jokes," she recalled. "Sure enough, when I arrived [at the airport, Hagman and Duffy] were sitting together like a pair of angels with their hands over their mouths in a silent pledge to behave. They both promised to be good sons. At the end of the first day's shooting Larry took me by the arm and escorted me to my dressing room. It was a sweet gesture. They've been a riot ever since, topping each other with one-liners and having fun. It's a very upbeat, warm, integrated cast. They really like each other." Patrick Duffy told an interviewer that, out of deference to "America's perfect mother," he and Hagman also refrained from their normal pranks during the filming of Reed's first family dinner scene, which appears in this episode. Hagman later wrote that Reed "definitely brought a different take to the character. I first noticed it in her very first scene. She'd gotten off a plane and was running up the ramp toward Bobby and me. I remember thinking running was something Mama would never do." ★ Said director Gwen Archer about Miss Ellie's office scene with Clayton, "There are a lot of subtle subtexts for Donna to handle because of Miss Ellie's marriage to Clayton. Her family and Southfork Ranch mean so much to her that she has mixed feelings about bringing a new man into the situation. Donna can show those complicated motivations without talking directly about them or releasing emotions outright."

169. "Oil Baron's Ball III"

Written by David Paulsen; Directed by Michael Preece; Airdate: November 16, 1984
Guest Stars: Morgan Woodward (Punk); Christopher Stone (Dave); Kathleen York
(Betty); William Smithers (Jeremy); Omri Katz (John Ross); Debbie Rennard (Sly); Don
Starr (Jordan); Michael Alldredge (Jackson); Fredric Lehne (Eddie)
Subject: The Oil Baron's Ball.

Cast Notes Donna Reed was added to the main title as of this episode.

Trivia Weekly rating: number 2. ★ While Miss Ellie worked to make Clayton feel at home at Southfork, Reed was trying to fit in there herself. *People* magazine reported some hazing at the start of Reed's stint, but Reed gamely explained that Larry Hagman and his fellow practical jokers were "like a bunch of small boys" but were "very welcoming and supportive." Hagman returned the compliment, saying, "I've always been an admirer of hers—she's an absolute delight." ★ As for the legendary practical jokes that were played on the *Dallas* set, Hagman says, "I don't know how it started, but I think Patrick was the first victim." ★ Phil Capice told *TV Guide* that Deborah Shelton's character was written to make "bells go off for J.R." when they meet for the first time, which they do in this episode. "She has assumed the role of J.R.'s lady and will continue to be that—with some interesting complications." J.R. was not the only one who reacted to Shelton's beauty. "When she first appeared on the set," said Ken Kercheval, "we were kind of overwhelmed, 'cause she's such a pretty lady." ★ Three days after this episode aired, Patrick Duffy's agent confirmed Duffy's intention to leave *Dallas* at season's end. Not long after, Kercheval told a reporter, "What it really comes down to is that while an actor would like to argue that his contribution is indispensable, the bottom line is that it isn't true. . . . It's clear from the incredible response to the show that the audience wants *Dallas*. They've accepted not having the Ewing patriarch here. Jim Davis brought an ingredient that was a real plus to the show. But his death didn't keep us from being Number 1. So, no actor is indispensable to the show, although,

I'm not sure about Larry. I believe it would be impossible to carry on the show if he left." ★ The Oil Baron's Ball scenes were filmed in Dallas. William Smithers found that "getting dressed up in a tux and being in a ballroom full of people in tuxes and gowns is a lot of fun. . . . One day between shots Larry Hagman shouted from across a ballroom filled with actors, 'Geez, Smithers, did they bring you all the way from L.A. to do one line?'"

170. "Shadows"
Written by David Paulsen; Directed by Gwen Arner; Airdate: November 23, 1984
Special Guest Star: Daniel Pilon (Naldo)
Guest Stars: Kathleen York (Betty); Christopher Stone (Dave); Shalane McCall (Charlie); Michael Alldredge (Jackson); Martin Cassidy (Carp); Fredric Lehne (Eddie)
Subject: Jock's portrait.

Trivia Weekly rating: number 5. ★ This episode's claim that Charlie has never met her father contradicts events in Episode 47, when Charlie flew to Italy to visit him. ★ Reed found that her role as Miss Ellie gave her "a far wider range of emotional things to do than I was ever asked to do in films. I'm not always in love with the dialogue—I don't think the producers always feel it's anywhere near perfect— but the emotional range is very satisfying."

171. "Charlie"
Written by Leonard Katzman; Directed by Michael Preece; Airdate: November 30, 1984
Special Guest Star: Daniel Pilon (Naldo)
Guest Stars: William Smithers (Jeremy); Shalane McCall (Charlie); Michael Alldredge (Jackson); Fredric Lehne (Eddie)
Subject: Charlie runs away.

Trivia Weekly rating: number 2. ★ A painting of a nineteenth-century gentleman replaces Jock's portrait in the living room.

172. "Barbeque Five"
Written by Arthur Bernard Lewis; Directed by Gwen Arner; Airdate: December 7, 1984
Special Guest Star: Daniel Pilon (Naldo)
Guest Stars: William Smithers (Jeremy); Barry Jenner (Jerry); Ronnie Claire Edwards (Lydia); Fern Fitzgerald (Marilee); Shalane McCall (Charlie); Omri Katz (John Ross); Fredric Lehne (Eddie)
Subject: The Ewings' barbeque.

Cast Notes Ronnie Claire Edwards played storekeeper Ike Godsey's wife, Corabeth, on *The Waltons*.

Trivia Weekly rating: number 3. ★ Jock's portrait has been moved to Ewing Oil. ★ By the time of the Ewing barbeque, Jamie had been accepted by most of the Ewings. In real life, Jenilee Harrison found that "coming into a show that has already had its ensemble cast for some time is a bit uncomfortable. Fortunately I had already worked with some of the cast of *Dallas*, and Patrick Duffy and I had actually played opposite one another on a *Love Boat* [episode], . . . so we had a nice friendship. I will say, the cast was delightful. There weren't any true 'cliques,' in my opinion, as Victoria Principal opened her arms to me, and Larry Hagman is such a class act to everyone who surrounds him. I was also so impressed by Priscilla Presley, as she has such a 'persona' but is the most down to earth, unaffected, and genuinely kind person. Steve Kanaly was a joy, Linda Gray a sweet person, and Ken Kercheval is an excellent man. I was just real lucky to be in all their company." ★ Fern Fitzgerald "loved whenever Marilee was sarcastic," which got her pushed in the pool in this episode. Fitzgerald "always felt 'Marilee' was laughing at [Jamie]. . . . I treated 'Jamie' as an impulsive punk kid who was just an annoyance to me, even when she pushed me in the pool."

173. "Do You Take This Woman"

Written by Leonard Katzman; Directed by Michael Preece; Airdate: December 14, 1984
Special Guest Star: Daniel Pilon (Naldo)
Guest Stars: George O. Petrie (Harv); William Smithers (Jeremy); Shalane McCall
(Charlie); Madison Mason (Jack Phipps); Fredric Lehne (Eddie)
Subject: Jenna is missing.

Trivia Weekly rating: number 2.

174. "Deja Vu"

Written by David Paulsen; Directed by Leonard Katzman; Airdate: December 21, 1984
Special Guest Star: Daniel Pilon (Naldo)
Guest Stars: James Cromwell (Gerald Kane); Shalane McCall (Charlie); Burke Byrnes
(Pete Adams); Sarah Cunningham (Aunt Maggie); Fredric Lehne (Eddie)
Subject: Jenna marries Naldo.

Cast Notes James Cromwell played Stretch Cunningham on *All in the Family* in 1974 and starred in the 1995 movie *Babe*, which earned him a Best Actor Oscar nomination. ★ This is Sarah Cunningham's last appearance as Aunt Maggie. She died on March 24, 1986.

Trivia Weekly rating: number 4. This episode gave *Dallas* its lowest season rating to date. ★ This is the last episode of the season filmed on location in Texas. ★ *TV Guide* reporter Bill Davidson, who had previously written a profile of Ken Kercheval, was allowed to come to Stage 18 at MGM-Lorimar during the filming of one of this episode's interior scenes as part of a profile of Linda Gray that was published just after this episode aired. Despite attempts to keep him in the dark, Davidson deduced that Jenna was missing on her wedding night. Leonard Katzman told Davidson, "Wherever I go, anywhere in the world, people invariably tell me the one person they want to meet from *Dallas* is Sue Ellen. In most places in Europe and Asia, they don't even know her real name." ★ This episode includes one of the rare scenes between Larry Hagman and Ken Kercheval where their characters are not feuding. Kercheval notes that he and Hagman had about "two confrontational scenes a year," and otherwise rarely worked with each other.

175. "Odd Man Out"

Written by Arthur Bernard Lewis; Directed by Larry Hagman; Airdate: December 28, 1984
Special Guest Star: Daniel Pilon (Naldo)
Guest Stars: Michael McRae (Benton); Omri Katz (John Ross); Tom Fucello (Dave); Burke Byrnes (Peter Adams); Fredric Lehne (Eddie)
Subject: Bobby is depressed.

Trivia This episode put *Dallas* back in the number 1 spot for the first time in seven weeks.

176. "Lockup in Laredo"

Written by David Paulsen; Directed by Patrick Duffy; Airdate: January 4, 1985
Special Guest Star: Stephen Elliott (Scotty Demarest)
Guest Stars: James Cromwell (Kane); Omri Katz (John Ross); Stephanie Blackmore (Serena); Val De Vargas (Judge Langley); Beau Billingslea (Dr. Miller); Fredric Lehne (Eddie)
Subject: Jenna's arrest.

Cast Notes Val De Vargas appeared in the 1976 Disney movie *Treasure of Matecumbe* with Peter Ustinov and on *Barnaby Jones*, *Kung Fu*, *Mission: Impossible*, and *Mannix*.

Trivia Weekly rating: number 3. ★ Stephen Elliott was happy that his first return to *Dallas* since his Season 2 appearances gave him the opportunity to work with the "ever handsome and funny" Patrick Duffy and the "beautiful" Priscilla Presley.

177. "Winds of War"

Written by Leonard Katzman; Directed by Leonard Katzman; Airdate: January 11, 1985
Special Guest Star: Stephen Elliott (Scotty)
Guest Stars: Gail Strickland (Veronica); George O. Petrie (Harv); Shalane McCall (Charlie); Omri Katz (John Ross); Fredric Lehne (Eddie)
Subject: Cliff courts Jamie.

Cast Notes Veronica Robinson is played by TV veteran Gail Strickland, best known as Olive on *Dr. Quinn, Medicine Woman* and as Esther MacInerney in the 1995 Rob Reiner movie *The American President*.

Trivia Weekly rating: number 1. ★ Shortly before this episode aired, Ken Kercheval explained Cliff's motivations to go after Ewing Oil despite his status as an oil baron in his own right. "Cliff has enormous new-found wealth in off-shore oil leases," he said. "He has wealth comparable to the Ewings. But, no, it doesn't satisfy him. He wants more. I don't know that he wants the money as much as he wants the demise of the Ewings. . . . The bottom line is that his father was a down-

and-outer. Cliff is misdirected in his thinking. He has a blind loyalty to his father that's admirable but not too realistic. He aspires to have his father's memory become as famous as Jock's, but society just doesn't glorify down-and-out drunks. Cliff has become as shifty as J.R. He learned from the master. Cliff has become a worthy opponent for J.R." ★ Leonard Katzman both wrote and directed this episode. Jenilee Harrison describes Katzman as "legendary . . . I had no idea what was in [his] head from week to week as he wrote and created that show, and he knew those characters like his own family. . . . We would show up every week and read through the script wanting to know what was happening with everyone, just like the home viewing audience. . . . Leonard Katzman was a master at always bringing up thrilling and unexpected 'twists and turns.'"

178. "Bail Out"

Written by David Paulsen; Directed by Michael Preece; Airdate: January 25, 1985
Special Guest Star: Stephen Elliott (Scotty)
Guest Stars: James Cromwell (Kane); George O. Petrie (Harv); Shalane McCall (Charlie); Dean Santoro (Ferguson); Clyde Kusatsu (Dr. Albert Matsuta); Val De Vargas (Judge Langley); Burke Byrnes (Pete Adams); Beau Billingslea (Dr. Miller); Fredric Lehne (Eddie)
Subject: Jenna's release.

Cast Notes Clyde Kusatsu appeared occasionally on Magnum, P.I. and was a regular on Tom Selleck's 1998 sitcom The Closer.

Trivia Weekly rating: number 1. ★ Stephen Elliott's Texas accent was not real. Elliott was born in New York City. ★ As Dallas coped with the loss of Barbara Bel Geddes, the pending losses of Patrick Duffy and Charlene Tilton, and Dynasty's continued surge in the ratings, its producers sought to generate some press for the show by hosting a party for two hundred TV reporters and people affiliated with CBS stations. Like the previous press bash the producers put on in June of 1980, this one was hosted by Larry and Maj Hagman at their Malibu home. Guests were brought to the house from Culver City by bus. Other cast members attending included Linda Gray, Steve Kanaly, Howard Keel, Priscilla Presley, Donna Reed, and Charlene Tilton. Neither Patrick Duffy nor Victoria Principal, who had not yet renewed her contract, attended. At the party, Larry Hagman discussed his new two-year contract (for $125,000 per episode) which caused CBS to renew Dallas for two additional seasons. Linda Gray also signed a two-year contract, which included an agreement that Gray could direct several episodes of the show. "They fought me," Gray said at the party. "They didn't want me to direct. They were afraid that if I wanted to do it, everybody else in the cast would want to direct, too." As for Duffy's pending departure, Hagman opined, "I don't see how you can recast him." Donna Reed acknowledged the good reviews she received from fans. "The mail, I'm happy to say, has been positive. If anyone disapproves, they haven't had the nerve to write me." Reed found her relationship with J.R. a "little more loving" than Bel Geddes' had been, and she hoped to head "toward stronger scenes and more confrontation. I came to the show with the idea of being very open and straightforward with J.R., and letting the chips fall where they may." Hagman, who said he was now working three-day weeks on the show, complained that J.R. had turned into a "namby-pamby" during the season, and said he was "gonna have to talk" to the writers about that. Around the time of this party, Duffy traveled to Nashville to host an awards show. While there, he vowed that "there won't be another Bobby Ewing on the show" after his departure. "I spent too much time and effort constructing the character," he explained.

179. "Legacy of Hate"

Written by Arthur Bernard Lewis; Directed by Robert Becker; Airdate: February 1, 1985
Special Guest Star: Stephen Elliott (Scotty)
Guest Stars: George O. Petrie (Harv); Kathleen York (Betty); Morgan Woodward (Punk); Rosemary Forsyth (Ann McFadden); Dean Santoro; (Ferguson); Burke Byrnes (Pete Adams); Fredric Lehne (Eddie)
Subject: The Barneses' lawsuit.

Trivia Weekly rating: number 3. ★ Donna Reed gave an interview to *Parade* magazine the week this episode aired. In the interview, Reed acknowledged that she was still "very nervous" about replacing Barbara Bel Geddes. Reed, however, liked her role very much. "I feel comfortable with Miss Ellie, so I hope that comes through. She's one of the few good female role models on television. She's strong and sturdy."

180. "Sins of the Fathers"

Written by Leonard Katzman; Directed by Larry Hagman; Airdate: February 8, 1985
Special Guest Star: Stephen Elliott (Scotty)
Guest Stars: Kathleen York (Betty); George O. Petrie (Harv); Eddie Firestone (Alf Brindle); Shalane McCall (Charlie); Omri Katz (John Ross); John Carter (Carl Hennessey); Harvey Vernon (Judge Harding); Dean Santoro (Ferguson); Beau Billingslea (Dr. Miller); Fredric Lehne (Eddie)
Subject: The Ewings investigate Cliff's claim.

Cast Notes Eddie Firestone played Clayton's friend Robert "Rabbit" Hutch in Season 12. He starred as Eddy Coleman in the 1949 soap opera *Mixed Doubles*. ★ Tony Romano, who has a minor role in this episode, played Poochy Pompio on *Wiseguy*. ★ John Carter reprises the role of Carl Hennessey, which he originated in Episode 111 and played again in Episode 235.

Trivia Weekly rating: Number 4.

181. "The Brothers Ewing"

Written by David Paulsen; Directed by Patrick Duffy; Airdate: February 15, 1985
Special Guest Star: Stephen Elliott (Scotty)
Guest Stars: Eddie Firestone (Brindle); Kathleen York (Betty); Omri Katz (John Ross);
John Carter (Carl Hennessey); Fredric Lehne (Eddie)
Subject: The Ewings align against the Barneses.

Trivia Weekly rating: number 2.

182. "Shattered Dreams"

Written by Arthur Bernard Lewis; Directed by Nick Havinga; Airdate: February 22, 1985
Special Guest Star: Stephen Elliott (Scotty)
Guest Stars: Gail Strickland (Veronica); Kathleen York (Betty); Don Starr (Jordan); Omri
Katz (John Ross); Erik Holland (Conrad); Fredric Lehne (Eddie)
Subject: Jenna's witness dies.

Trivia Weekly rating: number 1. ★ This was the last time a regular episode of Dallas hit number 1. The only subsequent time Dallas finished first in the weekly ratings was when it aired a special ninety-minute cliff-hanger at the end of Season 7.
★ This is the first of three episodes filmed on location in Hong Kong. Leonard Katzman accompanied Victoria Principal and Linda Gray overseas. While it was Dallas's first on-location shoot ever outside of Texas and California, it was not Victoria Principal's first overseas trip for Dallas. In late 1981, she traveled to Tokyo to promote the show. Unlike every other country in which it aired, Japan rejected the show, and it earned a lowly 5 percent share there. ★ Jamie is the first of two girlfriends who share Cliff's passion for Chinese food. Future girlfriend Liz Adams is the other.

183. "Dead End"

Written by Leonard Katzman; Directed by Michael Preece; Airdate: March 1, 1985
Special Guest Star: Stephen Elliott (Scotty)
Guest Stars: Fern Fitzgerald (Marilee); Debbie Rennard (Sly); Don Starr (Jordan); Burke
Byrnes (Pete); Sam Anderson (Detective Howard); Dean Santoro (Ferguson); Ben Cooper
(George Parrish); Erik Holland (Conrad); Fredric Lehne (Eddie)
Subject: Pam's search for Mark.

Cast Notes Sam Anderson played Sam Gorpey on the ABC sitcom Perfect Strangers.

Trivia Weekly rating: number 7. ★ This episode tied Episode 164 as the season's lowest ranked. ★ Sue Ellen's and Pam's trip to Hong Kong was designed to keep the actresses who played them happy. Gray was getting tired of playing Sue Ellen, especially when she learned that Sue Ellen would start drinking again toward the end of the season.

184. "Trial and Error"

Written by David Paulsen; Directed by Larry Hagman; Airdate: March 8, 1985
Special Guest Star: Stephen Elliott (Scotty)
Guest Stars: Rosemary Forsyth (Ann McFadden); Virginia Kiser (Judge Roberta Fernety); Allan Miller (Hoskins); Shalane McCall (Charlie); Don Starr (Jordan); Debbie Rennard (Sly); Dave Shelley
Subject: Jenna's trial.

Cast Notes Allan Miller played Dr. Alan Posner on the sitcom *Soap* and Scooter Warren on *Knots Landing*. ★ Larry Hagman's daughter, Heidi, appears in this episode and the following two as a juror.

Trivia Weekly rating: number 6. ★ The trial scenes were filmed in an unused courtroom at the Los Angeles Southeast Superior Court. There were lots of laughs among the cast and crew while filming these scenes about murder victim "Naldo from Larado."

185. "The Verdict"

Written by David Paulsen; Directed by Patrick Duffy; Airdate: March 15, 1985
Special Guest Star: Stephen Elliott (Scotty)
Guest Stars: Rosemary Forsyth (Ann McFadden); Allan Miller (Hoskins); Barbara Rhoades (Lila Cummings); Michelle Johnson (Rhonda Cummings); Virginia Kiser (Judge Roberta Fernety); Nicholas Pryor (Nathan Billings); Omri Katz (John Ross); Debbie Rennard (Sly); Bill Morey (Leo Wakefield); Victor Campos; Conroy Gedeon (Dr. Finch)
Subject: Jenna's verdict.

Cast Notes Barbara Rhoades is a TV veteran who is best known for her role as Maggie Chandler on *Soap*. ★ Michelle Johnson returned to *Dallas* as Bobby's love interest, Jennifer Jantzen, in *War of the Ewings*. ★ Nicholas Pryor played a fiancé of one of the Bradford daughters on *Eight Is Enough* and the university dean on *Beverly Hills, 90210*. ★ Costar William Phipps played Curley Bill Brocius on *The Life and Legend of Wyatt Earp*. ★ Conroy Gedeon returned to *Dallas* as hotel clerk Emil in Episodes 214 and 215 and Detective Rigg in Episode 302.

Trivia Weekly rating: number 5. ★ Prior to receiving the script for this episode, Priscilla Presley was in the dark about Jenna's fate. "I really don't know what's going to happen," she told the *Associated Press* earlier in the month. "They don't tell us what's coming up. But it looks like Jenna might be going to jail. At this point let's just say I'm out on bail. In acting it becomes very interesting [to not know]. It goes against everything you learned in acting class."

186. "Sentences"

Written by Arthur Bernard Lewis; Directed by Michael Preece; Airdate: March 29, 1985
Special Guest Star: Stephen Elliott (Scotty)
Guest Stars: Virginia Kiser (Judge Roberta Fernety); Allan Miller (Hoskins); Nicholas Pryor (Billings); Shalane McCall (Charlie); Laura Malone (Janice Hopper); Fern Fitzger-

ald (Marilee); Marj Dusay (Bernice Billings); Debbie Rennard (Sly); Dean Santoro (Ferguson); Fredric Lehne (Eddie)
Subject: Jenna's sentencing.

Cast Notes Marj Dusay costarred with James Garner in Bret Maverick, an early-80s updated version of Garner's 1950s TV hit, Maverick. Dusay also played Blair's mother on The Facts of Life. Nicholas Coster, who played Blair's father, appeared in Episodes 15, 51, and 52 of Dallas.

Trivia Weekly rating: number 6.

187. "Terms of Estrangement"

Written by Peter Dunne; Directed by Alexander Singer; Airdate: April 12, 1985
Guest Stars: Gail Strickland (Veronica); Lyman Ward (Norman); Rod Arrants (Schuman); Omri Katz (John Ross); Stacy Keach, Sr. (Waldron); Ben Cooper (George Parrish); Debbie Rennard (Sly); Barry Sattels (Group Leader); Laura Malone (Janice Hopper); Paul Gleason (Lt. Lee Spaulding)
Subject: Bobby investigates Naldo's murder.

Cast Notes Dack Rambo makes his first appearance as Jack Ewing. Rambo and his twin brother Dirk, whose real names were Norman and Orman Rambeau, played Dack and Dirk Massey, the twin sons of movie legend Loretta Young on her 1962–63 show, The New Loretta Young Show. Dack went on to play Walter Brennan's grandson on The Guns of Will Sonnet. He also costarred in the Morgan Fairchild prime-time soap Paper Dolls. Rambo was initially considered to replace Patrick Duffy in the role of Bobby but, as he explained, "It would have been difficult for people to accept someone else in that role." Rambo was happy to play a nice character after playing "ruthless" ones on Paper Dolls and the ABC daytime soap opera All My Children. Steve Kanaly felt Rambo was "a great addition to the show. He did a real nice job. I felt a little bit of competition when he—like Jared Martin, who played Dusty—joined the show because they played cowboys, which is what Ray was." ★ Lyman Ward played Matthew Broderick's father in the movie Ferris Bueller's Day Off.

Trivia Weekly rating: number 6. ★ Writer Peter Dunne wrote nine episodes of Dallas during Season 8, when he also served as supervising producer. Dunne and Philip Capice won the 1977 Emmy Award for Outstanding Special (Drama or Comedy) for the Sally Field TV movie Sybil. ★ Production for Season 7 was scheduled to wrap the day after this episode aired. Several days later, Charlene Tilton married her second husband, entertainer Domenick Allen. Her two-and-a-half-year-old daughter, Cherish, from her first marriage to country singer Johnny Lee, was the flower girl.

188. "The Ewing Connection"

Written by Arthur Bernard Lewis; Directed by Nick Havinga; Airdate: April 19, 1985

Guest Stars: Nicholas Pryor (Billings); George O. Petrie (Harv); Shalane McCall (Charlie); Omri Katz (John Ross); Barry Sattels (Group Leader); John Zaremba (Dr. Danvers); Paul Gleason (Spaulding)
Subject: Jack's offer to help the Ewings.

Trivia Weekly rating: number 6. ★ According to Leigh McCloskey, who began a four-episode return appearance as Mitch starting with this episode, "When I went back [on the show in Season 7], Charlene had really blossomed and matured as an actress. She was more focused, and was really comfortable in her own skin." McCloskey also found that, since he last appeared on the show in Season 4, "the atmosphere [on the set] had changed. It was very strange. It didn't have the same hub. It was more businesslike. When I went on during the 'Who Shot J.R.?' period, it was very buoyant on the set. When I came back, there wasn't the great unanimity they had." ★ By this point in *Dallas*'s run, producer Katzman had "nearly run out of severe emotional problems for [Sue Ellen] to handle." He told *TV Guide*, however, that the mental cruelty displayed by J.R. in this episode was "so heinous that Sue Ellen seemingly has to leave him for good."

189. "Deeds and Misdeeds"

Written by David Paulsen; Directed by Michael Preece; Airdate: May 3, 1985
Guest Stars: Susan French (Amanda Lewis Ewing); John Larch (Wallace Windham); Shalane McCall (Charlie); Omri Katz (John Ross); Debbie Rennard (Sly); Don Starr (Jordan); Paul Gleason (Spaulding)
Subject: The Ewings visit Amanda.

Cast Notes John Larch returned to *Dallas* in Season 12 as twin brothers Atticus and Arlen Ward. ★ Costar Rance Howard, who plays the minister who marries Cliff and Jamie, is the father of Ron Howard, the former child star of *The Andy Griffith Show* and *Happy Days* who went on to direct such movies as *A Beautiful Mind* and *Apollo 13*. Rance Howard played Henry Boomhauer on the sitcom *Gentle Ben*, which costarred his other son, Clint Howard. He also appeared on *Seinfeld*, *Melrose Place*, and *Gunsmoke*, as well as *The Andy Griffith Show* and *Happy Days*.

Trivia Weekly rating: number 3. ★ Ken Kercheval says that he and Jenilee Harrison "had fun together" playing star-crossed lovers Cliff and Jamie. ★ The first seven seasons of *Dallas*, up to the plot of this episode, were summarized in a fictitious biography of the Ewings published in September 1985 by Doubleday under the title *Dallas: The Complete Ewing Family Saga, Including Southfork Ranch, Ewing Oil and the Barnes-Ewing Feud, 1860–1985*, by Laura Van Wormer. The book includes separate chapters summarizing the storylines of the major Ewing characters (Jock, Ellie, Clayton, J.R., Sue Ellen, John Ross, Bobby, Pam, Christopher, Gary, Val, Lucy, Ray, and Donna) as if they were real people, and also includes photographs from many episodes from the pilot through Season 7. It also features chapters on Southfork, Ewing Oil, and the Barnes Family (Digger, Rebecca, and Cliff).

Although the book refers to some late–Season 7 developments such as Lucy's second marriage to Mitch, it overlooks Bobby's death and the outcome of Jamie's lawsuit for a share of Ewing Oil. (In 1986, Doubleday published a sequel of sorts, Van Wormer's *Knots Landing: The Saga of Seaview Circle*). Other titles among the many books published about *Dallas* include Suzy Kalter's *The Complete Book of* Dallas: *Behind the Scenes of the World's Favorite Television Program* (Harry N. Abrams, 1986), a coffee-table book about the production of the show; Robert Tine's *Who Killed Jock Ewing?* (Simon & Schuster, 1985), a fictitious whodunit suggesting Jock's fatal crash was not an accident; Jason Bonderoff's *The Official* Dallas *Trivia Book* (New American Library, 1984), with an introduction by Leonard Katzman; and several novelizations by Burt Hirschfeld of early *Dallas* episodes, including *The Ewings of Dallas* (Bantam Books, 1980), *The Men of Dallas* (Bantam Books, 1981) and *The Women of Dallas* (Bantam Books, 1981).

190. "Deliverance"

Written by Peter Dunne; Directed by Nick Havinga; Airdate: May 10, 1985
Special Guest Star: Daniel Pilon (Naldo)
Guest Stars: George O. Petrie (Harv); John Larch (Windham); Rod Arrants (Shuman); Shalane McCall (Charlie); Dean Santoro (Ferguson); Sam Anderson (Detective Frank Howard); Fern Fitzgerald (Marilee); Debbie Rennard (Sly); Don Starr (Jordan); Harvey Vernon (Judge Harding)
Subject: Bobby solves Naldo's murder.

Trivia Weekly rating: number 2. ★ Said Dack Rambo of Jack Ewing, "At first we didn't know if Jack was a good guy or a bad guy, but I think he's a good guy. There can be only one bad guy in a show like this and J.R. does that brilliantly. Jack really isn't the con man one might have thought. He lives by his wits, yes; he's not good at office hours or big business. . . . Maybe he saw a need for family and that's why he pushed his luck with the Texas branch." ★ Linda Gray was not happy about Sue Ellen's drinking storyline and told the producers, "'I don't want any more of this! That'll be it!' I've told Lorimar that I'm through with drinking in the series. I won't do it! Frankly, I was bored last year. At the time I renegotiated my contract, I complained that all I did was sit around. As an actress it was not challenging or fulfilling." ★ Ken Kercheval thought this episode glorified Jock and overlooked how he took advantage of Digger's drinking problem. "The motivating factor with [Cliff] has always been that he's felt that he would be in a position similar to J.R.'s if Jock hadn't cheated his father," he said. "The issue I'm talking about is justice. In the storyline there is the scene that reveals testimony that Jock had bought Digger's share of their oil company legally. Digger was drunk, though, and you can't in good conscience buy anything from a drunk unless you're certain he's sober. Jock couldn't prove that to me. I think that in this particular episode they were trying to make Jock look honorable, after he was dead. . . . It's not envy. If you're talking about Cliff Barnes, you're talking about one of the few honorable people on this show." ★ Jared Martin returns as of this episode for a thirteen-episode storyline. Martin recalls, "About that time, I'd accepted my hired gun position on the show and didn't have a strong opinion on the storyline. It had been made clear to me that if I wasn't available to return to the show someone else would be inserted in my place—not kill Dusty and find another love for Sue Ellen—but substitute another actor for Jared Martin. I thought I'd do a better job playing myself than someone else so I re-signed once again and reported to Dallas."

191. "Swan Song"

Written by Leonard Katzman; Directed by Leonard Katzman; Airdate: May 17, 1985
Guest Stars: David White (Mark); Shalane McCall (Charlie); Omri Katz (John Ross);
Bobbie Ferguson; Debbie Rennard (Sly); Walker Edmiston (Reverend Carson)
Subject: Katherine kills Bobby.

Cast Notes   David White played Darrin Stephens's boss, advertising executive Larry Tate, on *Bewitched*. ★ This episode includes Donna Reed's last appearance as Miss Ellie.

Trivia   Weekly rating: number 1 with a 27.5 rating and 46 share. Nearly 60 million Americans and 300 million viewers in ninety-eight countries watched this episode. It garnered *Dallas's* highest rating of the year and helped the show finish at number 2 for the season. It was the last time *Dallas* hit the number 1 spot. The ratings outperformed *Dynasty's* cliff-hanger (in which the cast was gunned down by terrorists at a European royal wedding), which garnered a 25.9 rating and 39 share, but *Dallas's* cliff-hanger aired after the official close of the 1984–85 season and was therefore not considered in the year's seasonal rankings. While declining ratings in Season 8 were typically attributed to Patrick Duffy's departure from the show, *Dallas's* ratings had actually started to drop before Duffy's exit. Indeed, in the final third of Season 7, there was a six-week stretch in which the show finished no higher than number 5 in the weekly ratings, which had not happened since Season 2. ★ "Swan Song" aired as a special ninety-minute episode but was edited down to sixty minutes in syndication. ★ Shortly before this episode aired, Patrick Duffy told an interviewer, "The beginning of the end came when they moved indoors. People related to the wide-open Texas spaces. Characters were outdoors, doing what they did before they had money. Now, it's boardrooms and bedrooms." ★ Priscilla Presley denied that Jenna was competing with Pam for Bobby's affections, saying that Jenna's competition, as Jenna "sees it, is with Pam and Bobby's adopted son, Christopher—not with Pam. And she's fighting the hold Southfork has on Bobby." ★ Leigh McCloskey's return to *Dallas* gave him the opportunity to work with his second Miss Ellie. McCloskey thought Barbara Bel Geddes and Donna Reed "both were wonderful actresses. Barbara was like Jim Davis—part of the original cast, and there was a great warmth towards Barbara. Donna always felt outside of things. I also felt that way. It was a tight group. They were both wonderful actresses, but there was a feeling behind the scenes that was different. Donna and I got along well, and I also got along well with Barbara. I liked both of them. It was difficult for Donna because she had to play such an important character." ★ Academy Award–winning fashion designer William Travilla, who joined *Dallas* at the beginning of Season 7 as its Costume Designer, won the last of *Dallas*'s four Emmys for Outstanding Costume Design for a Series for this episode. Travilla designed clothes for Betty Grable and Jane Russell, and designed the famous white dress Marilyn Monroe wore in *The Seven Year Itch*. ★ This episode's quip by Sue Ellen that J.R. would have driven Joan of Arc to drink was recognized by *TV Guide* as one of the 1984–85 season's most memorable lines. ★ The day this episode aired, Larry Hagman appeared in concert with the Dallas Symphony Orchestra, playing the flute with world-famous flutist James Galway. ★ The deathbed scene was filmed on April 3, 1985, and required several takes. Said Patrick Duffy a short time later, "There were lots of real tears. Everyone was involved emotionally. It wasn't because the character was dying—we were all feeling bad about leaving friends. We had established something we knew would no longer exist. . . . I felt a real relief when I realized it was all over. I couldn't be more happy with the way they offed the old guy." After the last take, Hagman presented Duffy with a Colt .45 engraved "To Patrick from his brother Larry Hagman . . . Thanks for the last seven years of your life." According to Patrick Duffy, director Leonard Katzman was so moved by Bobby's deathbed scene that he could not speak in order to yell, "Cut." "Leonard couldn't cut the camera," Duffy said. "He actually couldn't get the words out . . . when I died to even stop the filming. He went over and turned off the camera physically. It was almost as if your real family member died." ★ Morgan Brittany was seven months pregnant with her daughter at the time this episode was filmed, so it was decided that Katherine would kill Bobby by a hit-and-run so Brittany's pregnancy could be hidden from viewers by having her inside a car. ★ The year after Duffy left the show, Victoria Principal said, "Patrick is not at all like Bobby. He is a much more complex man. If you followed him around for six weeks you could not do a thorough investigation. Patrick is very self-aware and very protective of himself and his family." ★ Charlene Tilton's release from *Dallas* seems unfortunate in light of her comment to *People* magazine in 1979, "I'm terrified about what I will do when the series is over. It's tough out in the rest of the world. I can't think of any place to work where it would be as much fun as here." Hagman "could never understand why the producers dropped Charlene Tilton. Good, bad, or indifferent, she was part of the Ewing family. . . . You move the Ewing family out of that house, and it's not *Dallas* anymore." Susan Howard felt that what happened to Tilton reflected the problem with soap operas: "When they run out of things for your character to do, you get dropped—like Charlene Tilton was." Howard faced the same problem herself at the end of Season 9. ★ Duffy liked the storyline of this episode in general and its final scene in particular. He thought that it "fit well with the sort of way that *Dal-*

las was so popular. It was high drama, high tragedy, high rapture. The death of the hero is a great thing to hang a season on if you wanted to. So we killed him. . . . And it was the greatest death scene in the world. Lying in a bed, surrounded by your family, and the hero dies. It was incredible." Duffy "really felt something for Bobby. I wanted Bobby to go heroically and with dignity, and he did." Duffy won the 1985 *Soap Opera Digest* Award for Outstanding Prime Time Lead Actor. ★ The scene in this episode where Bobby proposes to Pam is one of Victoria Principal's favorites. "I can't forget the [proposal] scene," Principal wrote. "[Pam] starts laughing and crying simultaneously because she's so happy." ★ Leonard Katzman finished editing the episode on April 19, 1985, and later that day gave an interview in which he explained that he, like Bobby, was "pulling away" from *Dallas*. "Swan Song," he said, was "different from anything we've ever done . . . I think it's a fitting show for my departure, for Patrick, for Charlene, for all of us." ★ Just before this episode aired, *People* magazine did a story on Bobby's departure which included an erroneous summary of the plot. The article declared that, after Lucy's and Mitch's wedding, "Bobby and several guests go into downtown Dallas [when] a car veers suddenly into the group. . . . Frozen in horror, they watch as . . . [Bobby] steps forward to deflect the inevitable collision of metal and flesh." ★ Hagman found Duffy's exit from the show the most difficult cast departure to handle. "It was the toughest because I knew it was coming," Hagman wrote, "and I couldn't stop him."

Part III

THE DREAM AND
THE MORNING AFTER

SEASON 8
1985–86—"Rock Bottom"

WITH THE EXCEPTION OF THE loss of Jim Davis in 1981, *Dallas* kept its lead cast intact under the creative control of "Uncle Lenny" Katzman for seven years. In that time, the show reached a success unimaginable by the cast and crew when it convened in snowy Dallas in the early days of 1978 to film the pilot. *Dallas* was either the number 1 or number 2 show on TV for five of those seven years and was a worldwide sensation. The *Dallas* seen in Season 8, however, seemed like a different show altogether. A show that originally focused on the competition between the two sons of an oil magnate was now without the patriarch and one of the two sons. Leonard Katzman's guiding touch was absent. The wayward Ewing granddaughter was gone, and the previous year, viewers had seen Miss Ellie's face change, and in Season 8 change back again. With movie star Barbara Carrera playing a murderous villain amidst new international storylines, even J.R. and the show's Texas roots seemed diluted.

According to Leigh McCloskey, who had a continuing role as Lucy's husband in Seasons 3 and 4, "There was a type of alchemy—a combination of elements. Leonard and Patrick [Duffy] were wonderful, and Charlene [Tilton] was one of the permanent people that populated that reality. For all of them to be missing left a hole in the psyche of the show." Viewers noticed these changes and, with ratings falling to their lowest point since Season 1, it looked like *Dallas* was beginning the end of its run. While J.R. may have been off of his game in Season 8, however, Larry Hagman was on top of his. Toward the end of Season 8, Hagman took drastic steps to get his show back on track.

Ironically, preparation for Season 8 got underway with a casting coup when the producers announced that Barbara Bel Geddes was returning to the role of Miss Ellie. Lorimar announced Bel Geddes' return on April 11, 1985, when there were still four episodes of Season 7 left to air. According to Lorimar spokesman Bob Crutchfield, "Barbara all along had hoped to come back, and everyone had hoped so, too. Donna knew this was basically a temporary situation all along, not knowing going in whether Barbara would recover [from heart surgery] enough to return." Another statement released by Lorimar that day said, "*Dallas* executive producer Philip Capice said he spoke for the entire cast and crew when he said we are truly delighted with Barbara's return to our family. All of us owe a debt of gratitude to a fine actress and a very special lady, Donna Reed, whose talents and professionalism allowed us to continue to present *Dallas* without major adjustments during Barbara's absence."

Despite Lorimar's efforts to make it seem like Bel Geddes always planned to return, however, Bel Geddes' departure had been deemed final when she left in 1984. Indeed, in October 1984, before Reed's debut episode aired, Reed's initial one-year contract was extended through 1987. It remains unclear whether Bel Geddes or Capice initiated negotiations for Bel Geddes' return. Although it has been written that the show's producers enlisted Larry Hagman and Linda Gray, two of the cast members closest to Bel Geddes, to call Bel Geddes at her New York farm and persuade her to rejoin the cast, *Dallas* writer Arthur Bernard Lewis recalled that Bel Geddes herself instigated the comeback. Lewis claimed that "when [Bel Geddes] saw Donna Reed on the air in her role, she called and says, 'I want to come back.' She says, 'I can't stand to see somebody else read my lines.'" Howard Keel agrees. "I think Barbara saw Donna playing her role," he says, "and decided 'I want to come back.'" A lawyer for Bel Geddes' former business manager also claimed that after leaving *Dallas*, Bel Geddes "decided she no longer wanted to retire." According to Hagman, he had lunch with Bel Geddes in New York and asked her to come back, unaware that she was already negotiating her return.

While Duffy's departure naturally made the presence of long-familiar faces even more desirable, another factor in Bel Geddes' rehiring was the fact that the audience never seemed to accept Donna Reed as Miss Ellie. Despite the positive face shown to the press upon Reed's arrival, there were some reservations within the cast and crew about Reed as well. Larry Hagman noticed in Reed's first scene that she did not capture the character known so well to the *Dallas* company and viewers alike. "As much as I adored Donna," Hagman later wrote, "she didn't have the strength or edge that Barbara had given Mama." Howard Keel agreed, explaining, "I enjoyed working with Donna and loved her, but it didn't work. . . . I told Lenny that Donna was all wrong for Miss Ellie. She was too sweet, too pretty, too set." *People* magazine reported that the crew deemed Reed demanding for insisting on certain lighting and camera angles. According to Jared Martin, "The cast had become attached to Barbara Bel Geddes, who, quite frankly, had become the mother of the cast offstage as well as on." Reed's husband conceded that Reed had a tough time on the *Dallas* set. "When Donna saw how she was lighted—she called it monster lighting—she was in tears," said Grover Asmus. "She was in tears looking at it. She didn't want anybody else to see it. She went to the cinematographer and asked, 'Where is my key light?' He told her, 'They won't let me give you one.' Now, who 'they' were he would never say. Donna would come back frequently in tears. And I said, 'Look, it's not worth it. Why don't you just quit?' Typical Donna. She said, 'I'm not a quitter.'"

Lorimar did not inform Reed of its decision to release her from her contract, and its efforts to make Reed's departure seem amicable backfired. Filming for Season 7 had wrapped by the time Bel Geddes' return was announced, and by then Reed was traveling in Europe with her husband. Susan Howard, who had become friendly with Reed during Season 7, was also traveling in Europe with her husband, Calvin Chrane, and the two couples met up in France, where Reed's husband had been stationed during World War II. "We spent some weeks together in France," recalls Howard. "She did not even know [she had been released from her contract], and I didn't either. She called me and told me about it once she found out." Reed was in Paris when she learned the news, and she also spoke with Wilt Milnick, one of her agents. Milnick signaled to the press that things were not as clear as Lorimar made them seem. "I really don't want to discuss it right now," Milnick told a reporter. "It's still up in the air. Call me Monday. I may have some more information then."

Reed was "terribly hurt" over her firing, according to Harry Flynn, her longtime press agent. Reed felt she worked hard on the role and integrating with the cast, and she resented being let go and hearing about it secondhand. "After forty-four years in the business," said Flynn, "she feels she hasn't been treated fairly." On May 24, 1985, one week after the ratings triumph of Bobby's deathbed cliffhanger, Reed filed a $7.5 million breach of contract suit against Lorimar in Los Angeles Superior Court. Although Reed lost in her bid to halt production of the show until she could be reinstated in the cast, she settled the suit for more than one million dollars. When Katzman spoke with Reed that summer, however, "that hurt was still there."

Virtually all of Reed's castmates felt she was treated unprofessionally by Lorimar. Even Bel Geddes commented, "I think the way she was told was very unfortunate. You would have thought the producers could have discussed it with her before she went on vacation." Hagman claimed, "I would have sued, too. . . . She was on a vacation, for gosh sake. Some vacation. . . . She's a sweet and wonderful lady." Years later, Hagman, who admitted that he was "ecstatic" when Bel Geddes decided to return, elaborated that he "was sorry for Donna Reed. . . . [The way Reed was told] was unforgivable. Absolutely unforgivable. I'll always regret the way that was handled. Donna was devastated. I don't think she ever trusted anybody after that. . . . Nobody told [her] she was being let go. It went on until it was too late." Ken Kercheval was somewhat more realistic about the nature of show business, saying, "Rejection is just not new. It happens to be a very painful, ungracious ingredient of our business. Donna is not the first person this has ever happened to." Susan Howard agreed that it was "very unfair. But it's Hollywood. I mean, you hear these horror stories all the time. Are they shocking to you? No. And of course, at that time none of us knew that it was really Donna that was sick."

Shortly after her litigation with CBS and Lorimar, Reed suffered a bleeding ulcer. On December 10, 1985, three months after *Dallas* started Season 8 without her, she underwent surgery at Cedars-Sinai Medical Center in Los Angeles. During the surgery, a malignancy was discovered, and Reed was diagnosed with pancreatic cancer. While in the hospital, Reed received flowers from Bel Geddes. Reed was released in fair condition on Christmas Eve. In early January, Reed heard that Howard Keel was in Northridge Hospital Medical Center for double bypass surgery, and she sent him a plant. On January 12, 1986, she phoned Keel in his hospital room from her Beverly Hills home and, according to Keel's manager, spoke for about ten minutes but "never once mentioned her own illness. Howard had absolutely no indication of how sick she was. In fact she was the one who ended the conversation. She didn't want to tax him too much."

Two days later, on January 14, Reed died at her home with her husband by her side. She was sixty-four years old. Leonard Katzman, who had known Reed since the late 1950s, said Reed "was just a lovely person. It hurts a lot. . . . [On *Dallas*,] she was tentative at first, and it was a few days of everybody finding out how they felt about each other. But it wasn't long before she was made welcome by all the cast. She was so open and nice, and didn't play the star at all. She was hurt [by her dismissal] and rightfully so, but decisions are sometimes made in the name of ratings, and I think that was one of them."

Meanwhile, Season 8 got underway amid reports that, in addition to Bel Geddes, the producers were negotiating to get Charlene Tilton back on the show on a periodic basis. Tilton's agent turned down the offer when Lorimar would not commit to a certain number of episodes in advance. The cast and crew of *Dallas* missed Duffy and hoped Tilton would come back, but were optimistic about the new season. Steve Kanaly told a reporter during the summer shoot in Dallas that he hated to see Duffy go, but he liked "the scripts, the new writers, the new producers, the whole new setup. It's good to bring in new blood and shake things up a bit." Linda Gray was also energized by the new storyline and felt the Season 8 scripts were "wonderful. The acting is everything I've wanted forever and never had before." As for Duffy's departure, Gray said, "If the series, now in its eighth year, had been at the bottom of the ratings, I, too, might have thought it was time to leave. But I couldn't see quitting a series this successful." Howard Keel thought that *Dallas* "can go on as long as Larry doesn't get bored. In *Dallas*, Larry Hagman is the man." Ken Kercheval did not feel that *Dallas* was slipping, and suggested that Duffy might have let Bobby get boring, since keeping a character interesting is "the actor's job." Cliff was effectively "lobotomized," but "it's how you interpret the character that makes the difference. I'm the one who has to make him interesting." Only Hagman, who missed Duffy "as a friend, and [for what] he contributed to this show as Bobby," admitted that "the show will suffer for a while" due to Duffy's departure.

In addition to the cast and crew shake-ups, however, Season 8 also felt the effects of the slow fade of the soap era boom. During the 1985–86 season, *Dynasty*, the previous year's number 1 show, fell in the ratings to the number 7 spot. *Knots Landing* slid to number 17 and *Falcon Crest* dropped to number 24. *Dallas* fell to number 6—its lowest overall season ranking in six years—and finished the year with a 21.9 rating. For the first time in over half a decade, another network placed a Friday night show in the top ten as NBC's hip detective series, *Miami Vice*, which aired against *Falcon Crest*, finished the year at number 9.

Despite the ratings decline, Phil Capice was somewhat philosophical about what was happening to *Dallas* with him in charge. Capice reflected,

It's difficult to come up with things that are entirely new and fresh when you've got as many shows as we have on the air. We find ourselves saying often on *Dallas*, "That's good, but we did it two years ago." I think we tended to get somewhat spoiled by those years of spectacular ratings, when the audience tended to be obsessed with the serial form. . . . I think the show is being done with the same quality and care. We are not doing anything terribly different. I think it's the beginning of the end when you become so involved in the ratings that they dictate to you creatively what you should and shouldn't do. We have never responded to audience research. The show has always been successful based on the gut creative feelings of the small core group that [produces] the show. . . . We knew [Duffy's departure] was going to be a tough one. The audience absolutely loved the character of Bobby. I think his absence has affected the show, perhaps more than we anticipated.

Meanwhile, Larry Hagman, who later called Season 8 the show's worst, concluded that *Dallas* was not the same since Katzman and Duffy left, and he set out in early 1986 to get them both back. As writer David Paulsen explained, Hagman "had a major stake in the show [and] he was realizing that if things continued the way that they were at the time, the show would be off the air very quickly. And he didn't want that to happen." Hagman blamed Capice for losing viewers with a focus on international intrigue, and Hagman used this complaint to demand Katzman's return. Hagman felt that Capice "wanted us to be like *Dynasty*, with all the European stuff and the glitz. It didn't work. I told them, 'I don't want to do it this way.' And they said, 'You have to.' Finally, I stood up to them. I said: 'Do you want to make another hundred million dollars on this show? Or do you want to make nothing? This will make me another $20 million personally and I'm not willing to risk that for the guy who's producing the show. So either we do it my way, and you get Leonard Katzman back, or I won't be here. It's up to you.'" Lee Rich, the former *Dallas* executive producer who was by then the president of Lorimar-Telepictures Entertainment, told Hagman, "thank you, but no." Rich felt that "no performer is going to run this show. I just wish [Hagman] would give me an ultimatum. That would be the end of the show. . . . This is none of Larry's damn business."

But the Season 8 ratings slump put Hagman in a position to push his agenda through. Hagman, claiming that "Katzman left because he couldn't take Capice's [bleep] and interference any more," realized that "the only way Katzman will come back now is if Capice is gone." Hagman vowed to "bring Katzman back any way we have to do it." According to actress Sheree J. Wilson, who Katzman cast in *Our Family Honor* and who later spent five seasons playing April Stevens on *Dallas*, Hagman "offered to put up one million dollars of his own money to get Lenny back, if CBS would match it." In the meantime, *Our Family Honor* was cancelled after just thirteen episodes, and Katzman acknowledged that his year away from *Dallas* was "not totally satisfactory" and that none of the other projects he worked on "took off brilliantly."

As a result, Katzman was open to Lorimar's overtures. In April of 1986, less than four weeks after Hagman told a *TV Guide* reporter, "[Katzman]'ll be back, believe me," Lorimar announced that Capice was departing *Dallas* and that Katzman would return, now as executive producer. Capice, who retired shortly after stepping down from *Dallas*, responded that "Hagman and I have never quite gotten along. . . . I remain not very close to Larry Hagman." While Katzman conceded that he, like Hagman, did not get along with Capice, Katzman disagreed that personal relationships were behind the transition. "Phil and I disagreed about a lot of things, continually, and it had been seven years of battling to get what I wanted to do," Katzman recalled. "I think Larry felt the show was in imminent danger of dying without me. It was not a change made because [Larry] and I were buddies. It was made because he felt the show was in danger of going down the old dumper if it continued on the path it was taking." Katzman emerged from the struggle as the sole power behind the show. In time, he would hang in his office a sign with mounted longhorns reading "The Duke of *Dallas*."

Hagman also moved to get his friend Patrick Duffy back in the cast. In the early months of 1986, Hagman, with the consent of Lorimar executive Marv Adelson, called Duffy to invite him to lunch. Duffy biographer Lee Riley writes that it was in February of 1986 that Hagman called Duffy, although *TV Guide* reported that the lunch took place in April. During the call, Hagman told Duffy, "Don't tell anybody I called." Duffy met Hagman an hour later at a Mexican restaurant in Malibu. As they drank margaritas, Hagman told Duffy, "We're in trouble: I've been sent here to bring you back to *Dallas*. The show needs you." Duffy replied, "I don't need the show." Hagman pressed on. "I miss you. I'm bored to tears without you. It will be a lot more fun working with me on *Dallas* than anything you've done this year. Besides, if you come back, they'll give you a lot of money." Duffy told Hagman that money did not drive his decision to leave, nor would it drive a decision to return. Hagman asked Duffy to consider his "top secret" request.

Duffy later acknowledged that Bobby's death left him skeptical that he could return. His first reaction was, "'How the hell can I go back?' I thought I was definitely, certainly, irrevocably gone. I did not expect to ever set foot on [that] set again." However, during his absence from *Dallas*, Duffy discovered that other TV series "would have put me right back in the same position I was in on *Dallas*." Moreover, such opportunities were not as plentiful as he had hoped. "I didn't just jump into a new series," Duffy acknowledged. "That wasn't the reality of the time," he said. Indeed, during his year away from *Dallas*, Duffy's other projects were limited to appearing on ABC's *Hotel*, CBS's *Alice in Wonderland* special, a syndicated movie version of Arthur Hailey's *Strong Medicine* and some commercials.

After his lunch with Hagman, Duffy "never thought anything would come of it until I got another phone call from Larry, saying, 'Well, they say they're serious and they would like to sit down and discuss it with you.' . . . Then we started talking about going back. They told me, 'You have to go back to the show. It's not the same without you.' The ratings said that, too. Lorimar came in and said, 'What will it take to get you back?' And we told them and they said, 'Okay.'" Duffy agreed to return for Seasons 9 through 11 for a $35,000 per episode raise to $75,000 per episode, a $1 million signing bonus, the ability to direct three episodes per season, and control over the storyline resurrecting Bobby.

On April 9, 1986, CBS announced that Patrick Duffy was returning to the cast of *Dallas* as of the upcoming May 16 cliff-hanger. Lorimar confirmed the news, but was already working to build suspense, and ratings, by playing coy about the details of Duffy's return. Said Lorimar spokesman Bob Crutchfield, "All I know is that the way Lorimar wrote its release about his return there's no guarantee about next season mentioned in it. . . . The producers say this will be a really good cliff-hanger, the best since 'Who Shot J.R.?' . . . Lorimar has convinced [Duffy] to come back. I really have no idea what Patrick's character will be or what the storyline is surrounding his return."

Lee Rich stated, "We are extremely pleased to have convinced Patrick to return to the show. He is a fine actor and a good friend of the series. . . . In the tradition of *Dallas*, Patrick's character and the storyline surrounding his character will not be divulged." Duffy himself had hinted about the pending announcement the day before it was made. He was in Dallas for an appearance on behalf of Southwestern Bell when he told a local TV news show that he had "a few surprises up my sleeve and hopefully people will see me back on the air. Not only on the air, but right dead in the center of it. I can't say anything about it now because the surprise factor is always what everybody loves."

Duffy felt vindicated by his new contract. Although "out in the cold, cruel world, . . . nobody wanted me," Duffy had "never felt appreciated" by *Dallas* either. "They thought anybody could play Bobby. Or Pam. Or Sue Ellen. They thought that we were like computer parts. I would leave and Dack Rambo would be put in my place. But it didn't work that way. I think they learned their lesson. . . . Now my job is to save the ratings. Not single-handedly—but I'm here to shake everything up." Shortly after Duffy's return was announced, Hagman told *People* magazine, "I need somebody to bounce off of. We didn't have much fun on the show this season, and it showed in the ratings. We got away from our family format." Hagman summed up, "He missed us and we missed him."

With Katzman back in control of the show and Bel Geddes and Duffy back in the cast, *Dallas* ended Season 8 with its most talked-about cliff-hanger since J.R. was shot six years earlier. In the final seconds of Season 8, Duffy appeared in Pam's shower, and viewers were left to ponder if he was Bobby and, if so, how it was that Bobby was alive.

SEASON 8 EPISODE GUIDE

Regular Cast

Starring:
Barbara Bel Geddes as Miss Ellie
Linda Gray as Sue Ellen
Larry Hagman as J.R.
Susan Howard as Donna
Steve Kanaly as Ray
Howard Keel as Clayton
Ken Kercheval as Cliff
Priscilla Beaulieu Presley as Jenna
Victoria Principal as Pam
Also Starring:
Steve Forrest as Ben Stivers
Jenilee Harrison as Jamie
Jared Martin as Dusty
Dack Rambo as Jack Ewing
Deborah Shelton as Mandy Winger
Marc Singer as Matt Cantrell

Technical Credits

Producer: by James H. Brown
Supervising Producer: Peter Dunne
Executive Producer: Philip Capice
Executive Story Consultant: Joel J.
  Feigenbaum
Story Editors: Stephanie Garman, Hollace
  White
Associate Producer: Cliff Fenneman
Music: Jerrold Immel, Lance Rubin,
  Richard Lewis Warren, Angela Morley
Unit Production Manager: Wayne A.
  Farlow
First Assistant Directors: Fred Stromsoe,
  Alan Brimfield

Second Assistant Directors: Frank
  Katzman, Lorraine Raglin
Director of Photography: Robert Caramico,
  A.S.C.
Art Directors: Walter "Matt" Jeffries, Kim
  Swados
Editors: Fred W. Berger, A.C.E., John
  Arthur Davies, Lloyd Richardson
Executive in Charge of Casting: Barbara
  Miller
Casting: Irene Mariano, C.S.A.
Location Casting: Rody Kent
Wrangler: Jimmy Darst
Costume Designer: Travilla
Set Decorator: Chuck Rutherford
Property Master: John Rettino
Costumers: Jack Bear, Lee Peters, Kathy
  Monderine
Makeup: Joe Hailey, Ralph Gulko
Hair Stylists: Generio Gugliemotto, Diane
  Pepper
Production Sound Mixer: Robert Sheridan
Sound Supervisor: Doug Grindstaff
Sound Effects Editors: Tom Gillis Burke,
  Dick Friedman, Tony Garber, Richard
  Corwin, Michael F. Pignataro
Music Supervisors: Dick Berres, David
  Franco
Music Editors: Dave Cates, Patricia Peck
Main Title Design: Wayne Fitzgerald
Creative Consultant: Leonard Katzman
Executive Production Supervisor: Edward
  O. Denault

192. & 193. "Rock Bottom" (Parts One and Two)

Written by Leonard Katzman (Part One), Joel J. Feigenbaum (Part Two); Directed by Nick Havinga (Part One), Michael Preece (Part Two); Airdate: September 27, 1985
Special Guest Star: Ted Shackelford (Gary)
Guest Stars: Shalane McCall (Charlie); Omri Katz (John Ross); John Zaremba (Dr. Danvers); George O. Petrie (Harv); Don Starr (Jordan); Fern Fitzgerald (Marilee)
Subject: Bobby's funeral.

Cast Notes Barbara Bel Geddes rejoins the cast as Miss Ellie. Patrick Duffy felt that Donna Reed's termination was not handled correctly but that "there was no right way to do it and so it was just done and you just hoped that, in the end, people forgive people. . . . But when Barbara came back, I must say, that Barbara is who that person was. Donna was a great actress and played the part well, but Barbara is Mama and will always be." ★ Costar Joshua Harris joins the cast as Christopher Ewing, replacing Eric Farlow in the role. Harris played the role in 112 episodes through Season 13. ★ Movie and Broadway star Lou Diamond Phillips plays a waiter in the post-funeral reception scene. Phillips played singer Richie Valens in the movie *La Bamba* and costarred in *Young Guns*. He went on to play the title role in the 1996 Broadway revival of *The King and I*, which earned him a Tony nomination for Best Actor in a Musical. ★ Bit player Desmond Dhooge appeared in the very first episode of *Dallas*, in which he played a drunk, as he does in this episode.

Trivia This episode finished at number 7 in the weekly ratings, with a 23.9 rating and 38 share, its lowest ranked season premiere in six years. It was also *Dallas's* first two-hour episode since "Mastectomy" aired in Season 2. CBS went on to air a two-hour episode of *Dallas* in each of the show's remaining five seasons. This episode aired against a two-hour season premiere of NBC's ten o'clock show, the new detective hit *Miami Vice*, which finished at number 8 for the week, just 0.7 rating points behind *Dallas*. *Vice's* competitive performance caused NBC Entertainment President Brandon Tartikoff to say, "We're looking real carefully at the possibility" of moving *Vice* to 9:00 p.m. to air it against *Dallas*, but this would not come to pass for another year. ★ In syndication, Part One of this episode was renamed "The Family Ewing" and Part Two remained "Rock Bottom." ★ Linda Gray, although tired of Sue Ellen's drinking, agreed with the producers that "they had to bottom me out before I could begin to move forward. The first script came in. 'Hmmm,' I thought as I read it. Then the second script, and they had Sue Ellen drinking with a bag lady. 'At least this is acting,' I thought. I've always been someone who would rather play an interesting character than someone who was liked and safe." Playing "a down and out in the gutter drunk" was one of Gray's two favorite Sue Ellen storylines. She explains, "I loved the acting and being down and drunk and thrown in jail and walking around in a Valentino outfit that was ripped and torn. And they would put grease in my hair without any other make-up. I was in and out of make-up in twenty minutes. Normally it took two hours to create Sue Ellen! And so for me, when I got out there without all the Sue Ellen accoutrements, I felt—interestingly enough—more free. I could be a different part of that character, and I loved it." ★ Victoria Principal wrote in *TV Guide* that, for Pam, who always remained in Bobby's shadow, "now the shadow is gone. As an actress, this excites me. As the new TV season progresses, I'm going to be able to develop Pam as an individual, a free and single woman. This is a stimulating challenge—Patrick's last creative bequest to me. I'm thrilled at the prospect of creating this new Pam. It's going to be good for me and good for *Dallas*. . . . Yet a person doesn't cast off an almost-decade-long association so easily. I found this out during the summer. I was on location in Dallas to shoot our exteriors in the steamy July heat when I agreed to do an interview. One of the first questions the interviewer asked was, 'So how is it now that Patrick Duffy is gone?' I started to answer, but before I could get a word out, I began to cry." ★ Larry Hagman recalled that, after this episode aired, Patrick Duffy "sent me a tape. On it, Bobby was being buried, and Patrick was saying in a squeaky voice, 'Hello, Larry, I'm in here. Hey, let me out. It's cold in here. Let me out.' I really didn't have as much fun after he left. I missed him always accusing me of being a cheap son of a bitch." ★ Famed movie and TV art director Matt Jeffries was one of the Season 8 and Season 9 art directors. Jeffries was also art director on *The Little House on the Prairie* and Robert Stack's *The Untouchables*, and he designed the famous Starship Enterprise for the original *Star Trek* series. Jeffries died on July 21, 2003, in Los Angeles. He was eighty-two. ★ The return of Dusty Farlow meant Jared Martin got to have more confrontation scenes with Larry Hagman, as he does in this episode. Recalls Martin, "There was always a buzz when working with Larry. By [Season 3] he was literally the most famous man in the world and his time was precious. Working with him was a pressured circumstance. You didn't want to drop lines or be off-point. He was the franchise—he was why you were there. It was sometimes difficult to see where the character ended and the man began. I admired his Sunday days of silence when he wouldn't open his mouth to speak a word. He must've needed that as a release, to get back into himself. He was enormously funny. A fountain of ribald wit and scathing humor and the character quickly draped itself around his real-life personality. No one could write that stuff. He set the tone and the writers created situations like a mold into which Hagman would pour the character like telegenic maple syrup and things would take off from there. He had tremendous stamina and otherworldly energy. I had a healthy respect for him. . . . [The celebrity] had to take a lot out of him. . . . I think the show was his destiny, and his fate." ★ Pam's near-miss of a bulldozer as she races down a country road foreshadows her crash in Episode 251, which occurs after a similar near-miss.

194. "Those Eyes"

Written by Peter Dunne; Directed by Nick Havinga; Airdate: October 4, 1985
Guest Stars: George O. Petrie (Harv); William Smithers (Jeremy); Laurence Haddon (Franklin); Shalane McCall (Charlie); Omri Katz (John Ross); Don Starr (Jordan); Debbie Rennard (Sly); Fern Fitzgerald (Marilee)
Subject: Sue Ellen in detox.

Trivia Weekly rating: number 3. This episode tied the Season 8 cliff-hanger as the season's highest-ranked episode. ★ The Krebbses' plan for a new house grew out of Susan Howard's and Steve Kanaly's complaints about their characters' lack of growth. We "began to speak out," recalled Howard. "We said, 'Donna and Ray are supposed to be wealthy, so why are they living in what seems to be a one-room trailer? Why don't they have children? They don't even have a bedroom in which they can get children *started!*'" Steve Kanaly recalls suggesting a bedroom scene before quickly realizing that the bedroom set no longer existed; it had been converted into the Southfork gym early in Season 6. ★ Priscilla Presley felt Jenna stayed at Southfork because "she really is part of the Ewing family. She wasn't the outsider Pam Barnes was. She was literally the girl next door." ★ Jared Martin "thought the new-old [Sue Ellen drinking] storyline was redundant. How many times can Sue Ellen go on a bender? Unless the producers were going to kill off her character you kind of knew she'd be cured. But the nature of melodrama is to extract every last emotional twist from a situation, and so she picked up the bottle and started drinking. Dusty's way of helping seemed to alternate between taking his shirt off in motel bedrooms and squiring her to restaurants where alcohol was served so he could try to talk her out of drinking. The detox scenes were dark, and gave J.R. and Dusty another chance to square off. This time in a physical fight, which was kind of fun because rodeo champion Dusty was spending too much time sitting in restaurants. Only at the fairgrounds rodeo sequence and tussling with Hagman in the de-tox ward did the character physically break out. Incidentally Larry Hagman is built like a bull and definitely held his own. Any show that runs more than four or five years is subject to stories about going dry. There was some conjecture at that time that this was happening to *Dallas* and the folks at Lorimar were working furiously to stay ahead of that curve."

195. "Resurrection"

Written by Hollace White and Stephanie Garman; Directed by Michael Preece; Airdate: October 11, 1985
Guest Stars: Alan Fudge (Dr. Lantrium); George O. Petrie (Harv); William Smithers (Jeremy); Laurence Haddon (Franklin); Shalane McCall (Charlie); Omri Katz (John Ross); Debbie Rennard (Sly); John Beck (Mark)
Subject: Mark Graison returns.

Cast Notes Although his character apparently died toward the end of Season 6, John Beck "felt that possibly they would bring me back." With his return in this episode, Beck is listed as a "guest star." In Episodes 196 and 197, he receives an "also starring" credit. From Episode 198 through the end of the season, he is billed as a "special guest star." ★ Alan Fudge was a regular on Patrick Duffy's previous series, *Man from Atlantis.* ★ Costar Bever-Leigh Banfield, who appears as a sanitarium nurse, played forensics expert Lily Morgan on the updated version of the 1960s TV classic *Burke's Law.* ★ Featured actress Lisa Davis was a regular on *The George Burns Show.* ★ Also featured in this episode is Jimmy Darst who, along with his wife Carol, was an animal handler for the show since its early days. It was Darst who suggested that John Ross get a pony after coming across one fit for a Ewing.

Trivia Weekly rating: number 6. ★ This is the first of six Season 8 episodes cowritten by Hollace White and Stephanie Garman. ★ About the time this episode aired, *TV Guide* published an article by Victoria Principal about the post-Duffy era on *Dallas*. In "Life Without Bobby," Principal lamented the "double loss" caused by Duffy's and Bobby's departures. While admitting that "Patrick and I did not have an off-the-set friendship and rarely saw one another out of makeup," she wrote that they nevertheless forged a relationship based on professional respect, especially after Duffy began to direct on the show. Principal recalled how Duffy teased her relentlessly about such things as her real hair color (which was dark, not Pam's red) or a flubbed line. ★ This episode includes a scene between Jack and Jamie, which Jenilee Harrison enjoyed because she found Dack Rambo "a wonderful guy. He was so very sweet, truly humble. Ironically, we didn't work together often, as he was a love interest of others, and thus, his storyline didn't coincide with mine much."

196. "Saving Grace"
Written by Joel J. Feigenbaum; Directed by Nick Havinga; Airdate: October 18, 1985
Guest Stars: Alan Fudge (Dr. Lantrium); William Smithers (Jeremy); Burke Byrnes (Pete); Debbie Rennard (Sly)
Subject: Mark confronts J.R.

Trivia Weekly rating: number 9. ★ Two days after this episode aired, NBC aired a reunion movie version of Larry Hagman's former hit series, *I Dream of Jeannie*. Hagman's schedule prevented him from reprising his role of Major Anthony Nelson. According to costar Barbara Eden, "Larry was told it would just be a cameo role but as the story evolved it became a much larger part. Larry only gets three weeks off from *Dallas* and he wanted to go to London. I don't blame him." Wayne Rogers, who played Trapper John on M*A*S*H, played Hagman's old role. Eden and Hagman would eventually reunite on the small screen when Eden guest starred on *Dallas* in its final season. Hagman also declined to appear in another *Jeannie* movie, 1991's *I Still Dream of Jeannie*. In that outing, Christopher Bolton played Tony Nelson and Ken Kercheval guest starred as a character named Simpson.

197. "Mothers"
Written by Hollace White and Stephanie Garman; Directed by Michael Preece; Airdate: October 25, 1985
Special Guest Star: Martha Scott (Patricia)
Guest Stars: Bibi Besch (Dr. Gibson); William Smithers (Jeremy); Barry Jenner (Jerry Kenderson); Shalane McCall (Charlie); Omri Katz (John Ross)
Subject: Patricia Shepard returns.

Cast Notes It was to Martha Scott's "great surprise" that she was invited back for a second *Dallas* encore, after having appeared in Seasons 1 and 2. "I guess I'm another new kid on the block," she said early in Season 8. "But I'm also the only one in the history of *Dallas* who ever got Miss Ellie told," which happens in this episode. Scott "loved it, even if it did feel very strange. I love Barbara Bel Geddes, and there I was, dressing her down for causing Sue Ellen's downfall. I really gave her what-for." ★ TV veteran Bibi Besch appeared on two *Dallas* imitators: *The Secret of Midland Heights*, costarring *Dallas* cast members Martha Scott and Bea Silvern, and *The Hamptons*, costarring *Dallas* cast members Daniel Pilon, Leigh Taylor-Young, and John Reilly.

Trivia Weekly rating: number 8. ★ This episode's shopping scene is an example of Donna's and Jenna's growing friendship. Offscreen, Priscilla Presley was one of Susan Howard's favorite cast members. "I loved Priscilla Presley," says Howard. "I liked her a lot. She is different than a lot of people would think."

198. "The Winds of Change"

Written by Peter Dunne; Directed by Corey Allen; Airdate: November 1, 1985
Special Guest Stars: Barbara Carrera (Angelica Nero); John Beck (Mark); Martha Scott (Patricia)
Guest Stars: Frances Lee McCain (Dr. Amy Rose); William Smithers (Jeremy); Shalane McCall (Charlie); Omri Katz (John Ross); Don Starr (Jordan); Fern Fitzgerald (Marilee)
Subject: The Oil Baron's Ball.

Cast Notes Barbara Carrera is a former fashion model who appeared in such movies as *The Island of Dr. Moreau* and the James Bond movie *Never Say Never Again*. She also starred in the NBC miniseries based on James Michener's *Centennial*. Not long after arriving on *Dallas*, Carrera told *TV Guide* that Angelica is a "sultry and outrageous match for J.R., and we just use each other endlessly, shamelessly." Phil Capice found Carrera not unlike her character, noting, "She has not volunteered much about herself. She is not easy to understand, just like Angelica Nero." ★ Frances Lee McCain played the mother in the movie *Gremlins*. She also starred in two TV shows in which her husband was played by Ronny Cox: the family drama *Apple's Way* and the prime-time serial *Second Chances*.

Trivia Weekly rating: number 7. ★ This episode marks the beginning of Susan Howard's favorite storyline, "the one about Down's syndrome. We had all those children on the show—they're called 'special people' today—and we adopted the deaf boy. There was a humanity there. And some people thought that is not what *Dallas* is about. But as I have traveled around, the highlight for a lot of people was that storyline. People are always talking about it with me. It changed a lot of attitudes. That season opened up a lot of TV movies of the week and series focusing on such children, and Phil Capice was responsible for that." ★ Patricia's home, supposedly in the Turtle Creek section of Dallas, was actually in the Hancock Park neighborhood of Los Angeles. ★ Deborah Shelton, who liked her character's independence, did not like the ball scene in which Mandy gives in to J.R. "[Mandy] thinks she's very different from all the others," Shelton said. "She has a strong personality and she is very dignified. I hated it when she had to come back to J.R. at the Oil Baron's Ball and tell him she'd be anything to him." ★ Barbara Bel Geddes' beaded gown for the Oil Baron's Ball scenes weighed twenty pounds and cost $5,000. ★ Some of the extras in the Oil Baron's Ball scenes won their appearances on *Dallas* through a Lux soap contest run in Italy. *Houston Chronicle* reporter Ann Hodges was allowed to visit the on-location set at the Dallas Marriott Quorum Hotel where the ball scenes were filmed over three full days in late July of 1985. Hodges wrote about the "ballroom tables . . . draped in gold [with] fine crystal goblets spark[ling] with champagne" and the "bibs [worn by the *Dallas* men] to battle makeup-ring-around-the-collar." Hodges also wrote about the cast members she saw during the filming. Barbara Bel Geddes told Hodges that she was happy "to be home again" on the show, and wore black bowling shoes under her ball gown. Larry Hagman nailed the scene in which he "cut poor Sue Ellen cold . . . in just one take," to the applause of the two hundred extras dressed in black tie and ball gowns, who "all say that Hagman and [Linda] Gray are their favorites." Gray—"the darling of the *Dallas* cast"—laughingly told Hodges, "I'll show you a secret," as she lifted her gown to reveal a skirt lined with plastic bags attached with safety pins. Gray quipped, "At least my bags are from Neiman-Marcus." Victoria Principal spent her downtime reading in the "communal dressing room," explaining, "It's hard to walk. This dress weighs thirty pounds." Barbara Carrera, on her first day as part of the cast, watched the permanent *Dallas* actors pose for their annual cast photo. Carrera told Hodges that she joined the show because it "is number 1, not only in America but in the whole world. That's a powerful position to be in, and this character I play is a way to show women all over the world that women can be just as powerful as men. . . . I think this is a great opportunity, and I hope women everywhere will respond to it." Later, she told Hodges, "My first scene is over. I can relax. They're such nice people. I think this show will be fun to do." Jenilee Harrison approached Carrera and told her, "It's so good to have you here. I know you'll really like it. Our working schedule is good—better than most, really, since the cast is so big." Don Starr joked with Hodges about the slow pace of filming a TV show, quoting the saying, "It's not the time it takes to take the takes, but the time it takes between takes. That's the time that does you in." Extra Jim Thompson, like all extras, had to supply his own wardrobe and got paid $40 a day for his work on the show. Thompson was a corporate pilot from Houston who worked as an extra "because it's fun." Director Corey Allen picked Thompson from the crowd of extras to appear in a scene with Hagman and Deborah Shelton. Hodges also spoke with Dallas jeweler Jorge Miguel, who provided Gray with a million dollars worth of brown diamonds and Carrera with two million dollars worth of diamonds, emeralds and rubies for the ball scenes. Miguel proudly told Hodges that "*Dynasty*'s things are fake; *Dallas*'s are real."

199. "Quandary"

Written by Joel J. Feigenbaum; Directed by Michael Preece; Airdate: November 8, 1985
Special Guest Stars: Barbara Carrera (Angelica); John Beck (Mark)

Guest Stars: Frances Lee McCain (Amy Rose); Merete Van Kamp (Grace); Omri Katz (John Ross)
Subject: Donna's pregnancy.

Trivia Weekly rating: number 11. This is the first time *Dallas* fell out of the top ten since 1979. ★ Barbara Carrera found Angelica "dreadfully ambitious. Greed and a lust for power are the keys to her personality. . . . She uses J.R. and he uses her. This is not only the basis of Greek tragedy but of the universal human condition. We all want to believe we could behave like J.R. or Angelica. Vicariously, we love the villain. We, the audience, are forced by society to be goody-goodies. On the screen we want people who can act out our fantasies." ★ In this episode, Cliff explains his fondness for Jamie. Jenilee Harrison hopes she "brought to Jamie a sincerity, calmness, intelligence, and lovingness that was not anticipated."

200. "Close Encounters"

Written by Hollace White and Stephanie Garman; Directed by Corey Allen; Airdate: November 15, 1985
Special Guest Stars: Barbara Carrera (Angelica); John Beck (Mark); Martha Scott (Patricia)
Guest Stars: Merete Van Kamp (Grace); Omri Katz (John Ross); Shalane McCall (Charlie); Debbie Rennard (Sly); Robert Harper
Subject: The Southfork Rodeo.

Cast Notes Texas governor Mark White, who held office from 1983–87 and appears in this episode, was one of two people to play themselves on *Dallas*. The other was Dallas Cowboys owner Jerry Jones, who appeared in *War of the Ewings*.

Trivia Weekly rating: number 9. ★ The Southfork Rodeo and the appearance of Texas Governor Mark White were written into the script to mark *Dallas*'s two hundredth episode. There was talk of a TV special honoring this milestone, but nothing ever came of the idea. The episode was taped on July 29, 1985. The crew built a full rodeo arena for the filming, including bleachers and chutes that remained on the Southfork grounds permanently. Five hundred extras were used for the rodeo scenes. ★ Larry Hagman found Barbara Carrera "quite cool and businesslike, but very exciting, too, in her interpretation of the role. . . . She is a sexy gal. Everything looks super on her. . . . She's more than a bad gal on the show. She's brought a touch of class to what's a very elegant role." ★ As originally written, Donna decided to abort her baby once she learned it suffered from Down's syndrome. Susan Howard, however, complained about the script to Phil Capice. "We've had two abortions on the show already," Howard said. "Why can't we show the other side—that a Down's syndrome child can lead a productive life with the right guidance and training?" Capice, who found Howard tough, "though always in a ladylike manner," asked her, "If *you* were to become pregnant at this time of your life and found out you were going to have a Down's syndrome baby, what would *you* do?" Howard recalls, "I said, in a small voice, 'I'd have the baby,' and Phil said, 'I'll never ask you to do anything that goes against your beliefs.' Believe me," says Howard, "that's quite remarkable for television." Howard, however, still had reservations once the script was re-written to have Donna lose the baby after falling from a horse. "No five-months pregnant woman in her right mind would be riding a horse," she explained. Howard learned from her years on *Dallas* that keeping a character fresh is "a constant struggle. . . . The problem is that they write one-dimensional characters. The characters don't change and grow, like people do in real life. I think producers believe that audiences don't *want* change. . . . To Phil Capice's credit, he listened [to Steve Kanaly's and my complaints]—and that's how we got underway with this entire sequence involving Donna's pregnancy, the Down's syndrome complication, and so on. Before that, the stories for Donna and Ray never really took root." ★ Arthur Bernard Lewis, however, felt that the show's newfound focus on social issues, more than cast changes or the end of the soap opera fad, was the cause of the show's Season 8 ratings slump. "It became socially conscious and *Dallas* was never socially conscious," he said. "It was outrageous and it was our big cartoon of what Texas oilmen were like." ★ This episode includes one of John Beck's more memorable *Dallas* scenes: the one that required him to ride a bull. "I'll never forget . . . sitting on two thousand pounds of flexing muscle!" recalls Beck.

201. "Suffer the Little Children"

Written by Leonard Katzman; Directed by Michael Preece; Airdate: November 22, 1985
Special Guest Stars: Barbara Carrera (Angelica); John Beck (Mark); Martha Scott (Patricia)
Guest Stars: Merete Van Kamp (Grace); George O. Petrie (Harv); Omri Katz (John Ross); Shalane McCall (Charlie); Burke Byrnes (Pete Adams); Debbie Rennard (Sly)
Subject: Sue Ellen's custody suit.

Trivia Weekly rating: number 10.

202. "The Prize"

Written by Hollace White and Stephanie Garman; Directed by Corey Allen; Airdate: November 29, 1985
Special Guest Stars: Barbara Carrera (Angelica); John Beck (Mark); Martha Scott (Patricia)
Guest Stars: Merete Van Kamp (Grace); George Chakiris (Nicholas); Omri Katz (John Ross); Shalane McCall (Charlie); Burke Byrnes (Pete Adams); Debbie Rennard (Sly); Blake Leonard Conway
Subject: John Ross's custody hearing.

Cast Notes George Chakiris appeared as a dancer in the movie *Brigadoon* and won the 1961 Best Supporting Actor Oscar for his role in the musical *West Side Story*.

Trivia Weekly rating: number 11. ★ The week this episode aired, *TV Guide* did a cover story comparing *Dallas* to its progeny, *Knots Landing*. Writer Stephen Birmingham, who two years earlier did a similar story declaring *Dallas* better than *Dynasty*, extensively quoted his soap opera–addicted hair stylist friend, who found *Knots Landing* "down-to-earth" and *Dallas* "boring." According to Joan Van Ark,

David Jacobs, who created both shows, used to say, "*Dallas* is about 'them' and *Knots* is about 'us.'"

203. "En Passant"

Written by Peter Dunne and Joel J. Feigenbaum; Directed by Michael Preece; Airdate: December 6, 1985
Special Guest Stars: Barbara Carrera (Angelica); John Beck (Mark); Martha Scott (Patricia)
Guest Stars: George O. Petrie (Harv); Merete Van Kamp (Grace); George Chakiris (Nicholas); Omri Katz (John Ross); Burke Byrnes (Pete Adams); Terrence McNally (Sam Parker)
Subject: John Ross returns to Southfork.

Trivia Weekly rating: number 7. ★ This is the last Season 8 episode filmed in Texas. The on-location shoot started on June 17 and lasted for eight weeks. A real-life Southfork wedding took place during that time: on June 25, Victoria Principal married plastic surgeon Harry Glassman at the ranch. While Larry Hagman had in previous summers rented a house in Dallas for his family, in 1985, he joined other cast members at the Dallas luxury hotel The Mansion on Turtle Creek, where Barbara Bel Geddes' suite was around the corner and Linda Gray's was one floor below. Once when Hagman was at the Mansion, an elderly woman who was upset over J.R.'s treatment of Sue Ellen hit Hagman with her pocketbook. While on location that summer, Susan Howard and her mother spent their free time at the Cooper Aerobics Center.

204. "Goodbye, Farewell, and Amen"

Written by Will Lorin; Directed by Linda Day; Airdate: December 13, 1985
Special Guest Stars: Barbara Carrera (Angelica); John Beck (Mark); Martha Scott (Patricia)
Guest Stars: George O. Petrie (Harv); Barry Jenner (Jerry); Merete Van Kamp (Grace); Omri Katz (John Ross); Shalane McCall (Charlie); Don Starr (Jordan); Robert Walker (Harding)
Subject: Sue Ellen returns to Southfork.

Cast Notes This episode marks Martha Scott's last appearance on *Dallas*. She told TV reporter Jerry Buck the month after "Goodbye, Farewell, and Amen" aired that "there are very few parts for, shall we say, older women." Scott liked roles like Patricia, where the character "was the entrepreneur . . . a woman who's trying to guide her daughter's life." Scott also enjoyed the element of surprise involved in a show "like *Dallas* [where] they won't tell the actors anything."

Trivia Weekly rating: number 9. ★ Once, when filming an airport scene like the one in this episode, a British woman who had just landed in the United States saw Larry Hagman and "went through security yelling, 'You bastard. How could you treat Sue Ellen that way? I'm going to get you.' And Hagman said to her, 'Truly, truly, I'm not a bastard.'"

205. "Curiosity Killed the Cat"

Written by Deanne Barkley; Directed by Larry Hagman; Airdate: December 20, 1985
Special Guest Stars: Barbara Carrera (Angelica); John Beck (Mark)
Guest Stars: Merete Van Kamp (Grace); Omri Katz (John Ross); Debbie Rennard (Sly);
Terrence McNally (Sam Barker); Philip Levien (Lee McHenry); Robert Walker (Harding)
Subject: A package for Bobby.

Trivia Weekly rating: number 5. This is *Dallas*'s first top-five finish in eleven
weeks. ★ This is the last appearance of Ray's red brick house.

206. "The Missing Link"

Written by Bill Taub; Directed by Linda Day; Airdate: January 3, 1986
Special Guest Stars: Barbara Carrera (Angelica); John Beck (Mark)
Guest Stars: Barry Jenner (Jerry Kenderson); Sam Melville (Dr. Kenfield); Morgan Wood-
ward (Punk); Shalane McCall (Charlie); Omri Katz (John Ross); Philip Levien (Lee
McHenry); Debbie Rennard (Sly)
Subject: Matt Cantrell arrives.

Cast Notes Marc Singer was best known for his 1977 TV movie *Something About
Joey*, his appearance in *Roots: The Next Generation* and his 1982 movie *Beastmaster*
and its two sequels. According to *The Toronto Star*, Singer's character—"good guy
Matt Cantrell, a boyhood friend of the late Bobby Ewing"—was "planned for several months, [but] the producers had a tough time casting him until Singer came
into the picture." ★ Sam Melville starred as Officer Mike Danko on *The Rookies*.

Trivia Weekly rating: number 11. ★ Deborah Shelton felt that "Mandy really
hates spying on J.R. for Cliff. She tells J.R. and he forgives her. He understands that
she did it from anger and jealousy, it wasn't business to her." ★ J.R. makes a pur-
chase through a man named Fenneman, whose name is likely a nod to Cliff Fenneman, the associate producer of *Dallas* from Seasons 2 through 10, co-producer in
Season 11, producer in Seasons 12 and 13, and writer of five episodes during Seasons 10 through 12. ★ Five days after this episode aired, Howard Keel underwent
elective double bypass heart surgery at Northridge Hospital Medical Center in Los
Angeles. Keel was released on January 28 and recuperated at home before returning
to *Dallas* on February 3. Keel's illness did not halt production of the show since the
crew was able to shoot his scenes after his return and edit them in prior to airtime.

207. "Twenty-Four Hours"

Written by Hollace White and Stephanie Garman; Directed by Robert Becker; Airdate:
January 10, 1986
Special Guest Stars: Barbara Carrera (Angelica); John Beck (Mark)
Guest Stars: Barry Jenner (Jerry Kenderson); Sam Melville (Dr. Kenfield); Merete Van
Kamp (Grace); George Chakiris (Nicholas); Shalane McCall (Charlie); Omri Katz (John
Ross); Russell Johnson (Sheriff Wyatt Mansfield)
Subject: Jack is missing.

Cast Notes Russell Johnson played Roy Hinkley, known as the Professor, on *Gilligan's Island*. Tina Louise was the first *Gilligan's* cast member to appear on *Dallas*. ★ Costar Shirley Mitchell played Kitty on the John Forsythe sitcom *Bachelor Father* and was a regular on *Pete and Gladys*, the successor series to *December Bride*.

Trivia Weekly rating: number 12. ★ Susan Howard was coached in sign language by Todd Rutherford, a teacher of the hearing-impaired. ★ Jamie's injuries, like most storylines, took Jenilee Harrison by surprise. "It was a mystery to me," Harrison says, "how Leonard Katzman and the writers could keep up with everything that was going on on *Dallas* between all the characters and all the storylines. Amazing stuff. Every page was unique, every page had someone doing something that you totally did not expect. That is why people were glued to the show, and still are. It is one of the best written soap operas of all time."

208. "The Deadly Game"

Written by Bill Taub; Directed by Larry Hagman; Airdate: January 17, 1986
Special Guest Stars: Barbara Carrera (Angelica); John Beck (Mark)
Guest Stars: Barry Jenner (Jerry Kenderson); Sam Melville (Dr. Kenfield); Morgan Woodward (Punk); Merete Van Kamp (Grace); Shalane McCall (Charlie); Omri Katz (John Ross); Debbie Rennard (Sly); Don Starr (Jordan); Robert Walker (Harding); Fern Fitzgerald (Marilee)
Subject: Angelica's plot.

Trivia Weekly rating: number 8.

209. "Blame It on Bogata"

Written by Peter Dunne; Directed by Robert Becker; Airdate: January 24, 1986
Special Guest Stars: Barbara Carrera (Angelica); John Beck (Mark)
Guest Stars: Alejandro Rey (Luis Rueda); Barry Jenner (Jerry Kenderson); Merete Van Kamp (Grace); George Chakiris (Nicholas); Laurence Haddon (Franklin); Don Starr (Jordan); Shalane McCall (Charlie); Omri Katz (John Ross)
Subject: J.R. plots against the Barneses.

Cast Notes Alejandro Rey played Carlos on the Sally Field sitcom *The Flying Nun*. ★ Costar Tom Fitzsimmons was a regular on *The Paper Chase*.

Trivia Weekly rating: number 11.

210. "Shadow Games"

Written by Joel J. Feigenbaum; Directed by Roy Campanella Jr.; Airdate: January 31, 1986
Special Guest Stars: Barbara Carrera (Angelica); John Beck (Mark)
Guest Stars: Alejandro Rey (Luis Rueda); George O. Petrie (Harv); Barry Jenner (Jerry Kenderson); Merete Van Kamp (Grace); George Chakiris (Nicholas); Frank Aletter (Floyd Ericson); Don Starr (Jordan); Shalane McCall (Charlie); Omri Katz (John Ross); Debbie Rennard (Sly)
Subject: Pam's trip to Bogata.

Cast Notes Frank Aletter starred in two CBS sitcoms in the 1960s: *Bringing Up Baby* and *The Cara Williams Show.* ★ John Beck was glad that, as Season 8 progressed, his character interacted with Sue Ellen. "When I first joined *Dallas*, I was disappointed that I didn't get to work with Linda, who I had known before and who I have a real soft spot for."

Trivia Weekly rating: number 13. ★ This is the first of two episodes in which Victoria Principal was not seen due to an old back injury. To explain Principal's absence, the producers altered the script to have Pam kidnapped. When Principal healed more quickly than expected, the kidnapping was resolved. During the mule train scenes, a long shot of a stand-in was used, and Principal later recorded voiceovers. Principal's back troubles also prevented her from filming the introduction to the prequel TV movie, *Dallas: The Early Years.* ★ The Lorimar call sheet for Monday, November 25, 1985, the sixth day of filming on this episode, provides insight into how *Dallas* was made. The call sheet indicates that *Dallas* was a closed set, on which no visitors were allowed. The crew and the actors' stand-ins were to be on Stage 5 at 7:30 a.m. to prepare to film Scene 9 from Lorimar Episode #174119, in which J.R. and Grace are seen at Melvin's Bistro. The actors involved in the scene, Larry Hagman, Marete Van Kamp, Robin Bach (as the maître d'), and the extras (the two waiters and fourteen patrons referred to as "atmosphere" characters on the call sheet), were to be on the set at 8:00 a.m. To prepare for their scenes, the lead actors in this scene had varying makeup calls. Van Kamp was scheduled to be in makeup at 5:48 a.m. Hagman did not have to be there until 7:00 a.m., and Robin Bach had a 7:30 a.m. call. The company was allotted from 8:00 a.m. until 10:45 a.m. to film the two and one-half pages of script that comprised Scene 9. At 10:45, the crew turned to Scene 4, in which Sue Ellen and Jerry visit the Exotic Car Showroom. By then, Gray had been in makeup since 8:45 a.m., and Barry Jenner and Conrad Bachmann (as Burt Walker) had followed her there at 10:00 a.m. The company was scheduled to work on Scene 4 (three pages of dialogue) from 10:45 a.m. until the lunch break at 1:00 p.m. After lunch, the crew moved to Stage 19 to Jamie's bedroom set for Scenes 3 and 26. Scene 3 (a little over three pages of dialogue) featured Cliff, Jamie, Jack, a nurse, and two ambulance attendants. Merrill Leighton, who played the nurse, was scheduled to go into makeup at 12:30 p.m. Ken Kercheval, Jenilee Harrison, Dack Rambo, and the ambulance crew, played by J. D. Hall and Chip Heller, were scheduled for makeup at 2:00 p.m. After the scene was completed, Kercheval, Harrison, and Leighton were scheduled to film Scene 26 on the same set. That scene was comprised of a little more than two pages of dialogue. As for other members of the company, the producers had a production meeting scheduled for 9:30 a.m. at the Gable Building. Cast members not needed for the day's shooting—Barbara Bel Geddes, Susan Howard, Steve Kanaly, Howard Keel, Priscilla Presley, and Marc Singer—were in a "hold" status. Victoria Principal was not on "hold" due to her back injury. The call sheet also included an "advance schedule" for the following two days, indicating for the crew what scenes would be filmed, and thus what sets would be needed. Scheduled for filming on Tuesday, November 26, 1985, were additional scenes from "Shadow Games," including Scenes 11 (Bobby's Gravesite), 13–15 (Exterior Stables-Corral Area), and 12 and 20–22 (Exterior Columbia Highlands). Also scheduled for filming on November 26 was Scene 7 (Exterior Colombia Highlands) from Episode 211, "Missing" (Lorimar Episode #174120), the episode after "Shadow Games." Scheduled for filming on Wednesday, November 27, were Scenes 4 (Interior Hotel Corridor) and 5 (Interior Angelica's Penthouse) from "Missing" and Scene A-39 (Interior Southfork Kitchen), a scene added to an earlier show, Episode 207, "Twenty-Four Hours" (Lorimar Episode #174116).

211. "Missing"

Written by Leonard Katzman; Directed by Michael Hoey; Airdate: February 7, 1986
Special Guest Stars: Barbara Carrera (Angelica); John Beck (Mark)
Guest Stars: Alejandro Rey (Luis Rueda); Barry Jenner (Jerry Kenderson); Merete Van Kamp (Grace); George Chakiris (Nicholas); Shalane McCall (Charlie); Omri Katz (John Ross); Debbie Rennard (Sly)
Subject: Pam is kidnapped.

Trivia Weekly rating: number 8. ★ Miss Ellie cooks a product endorsed by Barbara Bel Geddes, who talked up chicken soup in commercials made for Campbell's Soup during *Dallas*'s run.

212. "Dire Straits"

Written by Joel J. Feigenbaum and Peter Dunne; Directed by Bruce Bilson; Airdate: February 14, 1986
Special Guest Stars: Barbara Carrera (Angelica); John Beck (Mark)
Guest Stars: Alejandro Rey (Luis Rueda); Barry Jenner (Jerry Kenderson); Merete Van Kamp (Grace); Robert Pine (Psychiatrist); Shalane McCall (Charlie); Debbie Rennard (Sly)
Special Guest Star: William Prince (Alex Garrett)
Subject: Pam is released.

Cast Notes William Prince starred in *The Mask* in 1954. It was one of TV's first hour-long mystery shows. He also appeared in the movies *The Stepford Wives*, *Network*, and *Nuts*. Prince died on October 8, 1996. ★ Jenna's psychiatrist is played by Robert Pine, who was Sergeant Joe Getraer on *ChiPs*. ★ Tony was played from this episode through Episode 222 by Solomon Samiotto, a deaf student from the Riverside School for the Deaf in California. In September of 1986, Samiotto appeared with Susan Howard at the National Technical Institute for the Deaf in Rochester, New York, to promote Deaf Awareness Week.

Trivia Weekly rating: number 12. ★ Director Bruce Bilson won a 1968 Emmy Award for Outstanding Directorial Achievement in Comedy for the "Maxwell Smart, Private Eye" episode of NBC's *Get Smart*. ★ The week this episode aired,

TV Guide critic Don Merrill reviewed Dallas to see how it was doing "after all these years." He found the veteran cast members were "carrying on in fine style and . . . haven't aged a minute in the past eight years. Larry Hagman still plays J.R. to perfection: a selfish, scheming user whose sole redeeming virtue is his fervent love for his son John Ross. Linda Gray continues to make credible her role as long-suffering wife Sue Ellen, when it could easily become maudlin. . . . Miss Ellie, once again personified by Barbara Bel Geddes . . . [and] lovely Victoria Principal and the other regulars are comfortable with their characters and continue to play them with intelligence and vigor. . . . Angelica Nero [is] played to the hilt—and well beyond—by Barbara Carrera. . . . The thorough professionals who turn out Dallas have mastered the technique of keeping this show fascinating to its audience. Its viewers care about what happens to the people on Dallas, enough to keep it among the top ten shows on television, and that, after all, is the accolade that counts. For what it is, and it's a soap opera pure and simple, Dallas is as good as they come." ★ Several scenes from this episode, including those in which Pam is returned by her kidnappers and Donna works with handicapped students, were filmed at an arboretum in Arcadia, California. ★ Susan Howard won the 1986 Soap Opera Digest Award for Outstanding Prime Time Supporting Actress.

213. "Overture"

Written by Hollace White and Stephanie Garman; Directed by Corey Allen; Airdate: February 21, 1986
Special Guest Stars: Barbara Carrera (Angelica); John Beck (Mark); William Prince (Alex Garrett)
Guest Stars: Barry Jenner (Jerry Kenderson); Merete Van Kamp (Grace); George Chakiris (Nicholas); Shalane McCall (Charlie); Omri Katz (John Ross); Debbie Rennard (Sly)
Subject: J.R. courts Sue Ellen.

Trivia Weekly rating: number 15, Dallas's worst performance of the season to date.

214. "Sitting Ducks"

Written by Susan Howard; Directed by Linda Day; Airdate: February 28, 1986
Special Guest Stars: Barbara Carrera (Angelica); John Beck (Mark); William Prince (Alex Garrett)
Guest Stars: Alejandro Rey (Rueda); Barry Jenner (Jerry Kenderson); Merete Van Kamp (Grace); George Chakiris (Nicholas); Shalane McCall (Charlie); Omri Katz (John Ross); Debbie Rennard (Sly); Peter Fox (Psychiatrist); Phil Levien (Lee McHenry)
Subject: Angelica's plot.

Cast Notes Peter Fox succeeded John Ritter as the preacher on The Waltons after Ritter left to star in Three's Company. ★ According to Lee Riley's 1988 biography of Patrick Duffy, on February 27, 1986, the day before this episode aired, Larry Hagman telephoned Patrick Duffy and invited him to lunch to discuss Duffy's possible return to Dallas. TV Guide, however, reported that the lunch took place in April.

Trivia Weekly rating: number 10. ★ This is the first of two episodes written by Susan Howard, the only *Dallas* cast member to write an episode of the show. Her second effort, Episode 245 in Season 9, was written under her married name, Susan Howard Chrane. Howard recalls that, while the directing bug seemed to catch a number of her costars, her only extra-curricular interest was writing. "From the beginning," she says, "I would rewrite things in the ways of speaking, of attitudes. In the beginning, there was the word! They shape your character and change everything. I realized that Steve and I had specific ideas about Ray and Donna. I saw them as 'the cowboy and the lady.' And that was Steve. He was Gary Cooper and Joel McCrea—that's who Steve is to me. Because Steve and I were not the central characters, we could rewrite and get away with it, and nobody said anything. And people liked Ray and Donna. They were the 'normal ones.' So, when everyone started directing, I went to Phil [Capice] and said, 'I'd like to write an episode.' And he said, 'How do I know you can write?' And I didn't have the guts to tell him I'd been rewriting all along! So I gave him a sample of a few ideas, a few scenes I had written. He said, 'You can write!' And I said, 'I told you!' He said, 'You can write one this year and one next year.'"

215. "Masquerade"

Written by Leonard Katzman; Directed by Larry Hagman; Airdate: March 7, 1986
Special Guest Stars: Barbara Carrera (Angelica); John Beck (Mark); William Prince (Alex Garrett)
Guest Stars: Barry Jenner (Jerry Kenderson); Merete Van Kamp (Grace); George Chakiris (Nicholas); Shalane McCall (Charlie); Omri Katz (John Ross)
Subject: The Masquerade Ball.

Cast Notes Heidi Hagman appears in this episode and the following one as a guest at the masquerade ball.

Trivia Weekly rating: number 13. ★ John Beck recalls that Larry Hagman was a "good director. He wanted to get it done and move on."

216. "Just Desserts"

Written by Peter Dunne and Joel J. Feigenbaum; Directed by Linda Gray; Airdate: March 14, 1986
Special Guest Stars: Barbara Carrera (Angelica); John Beck (Mark); William Prince (Alex Garrett)
Guest Stars: Barry Jenner (Jerry Kenderson); Merete Van Kamp (Grace); George Chakiris (Nicholas); Shalane McCall (Charlie); Omri Katz (John Ross); Don Starr (Jordan); Debbie Rennard (Sly); Fern Fitzgerald (Marilee); Raymond St. Jacques (Inspector Remy)
Subject: Grace's murder.

Cast Notes Raymond St. Jaques was a regular on *Rawhide* and *Falcon Crest*. He also starred as the Drummer in the miniseries *Roots*.

Trivia Weekly rating: number 14. ★ Linda Gray directed this episode, but her insistence on it almost cost Gray her job. While renegotiating her contract after it expired at the end of Season 7, Gray made clear that she wanted to direct an episode in Season 8. Explains Gray, "It was an extension for me. I'd always wanted to direct. I'd studied with Women in Film and a wonderful French woman director. I didn't want to just be on the show and say, 'Let me direct' without being prepared, so I studied with Women in Film on my days off. And when I felt I was ready, I told the producers, 'I'd like to direct an episode,' and they said, 'No.' My contract was up for renewal for the next two years, and I said, 'But I'd like to direct just one episode, and I don't want any money for it,' and they still said, 'No.' And I was fired! I told them, 'I want it to be part of my renewal,' and they said, 'Well, if that's the way you want it, you're not on the show.' And Larry Hagman became my cheerleader. I kept it quiet for awhile, but when he mentioned something about the next season, I told him I wasn't coming back. And he said, 'What?!' So he went in and talked to them, and they agreed that I could direct one episode over the next two years. But they negotiated an option, so that if I directed an episode, they would have me in the cast for [another] year. . . . I ended up directing five episodes. They liked what I did and I was grateful." Gray "was terrified" when it came time for her to go behind the camera. "I did a couple of scenes and found myself in front of the cameras waiting for someone else to shout, 'Cut!' Then it hit me that *I* was the director. . . . [It was] one of the most exciting, challenging things I've ever done. . . . My episode has a different look, I think, from the usual look of the show." ★ Gray also directed Episode 244 in Season 9, Episodes 269 and 280 in Season 10, and Episode 305 in Season 11. ★ According to Gray, Hagman supported the cast and crew in problems great and small. "If a hairdresser had a problem, Larry was the one who had something done about it. Whatever anyone says about Larry, people would have to agree he's devoted to his friends. . . . He's there for people. He would take care of things when the executives did nothing." When Lorimar executives doubted Gray's ability to direct, "Larry said, 'Who are you to say that Linda can't direct? She has talent. She can do it.' I got my chance to direct. . . . When I told the executives that I didn't want my character, Sue Ellen, to drink anymore, that we had exhausted that story, Larry was right there to support me, too. He's always been our leader on the show." ★ Steve Kanaly recalls that Linda Gray was a "fastidious" director. John Beck thought Gray did a "great" job directing. "It was something she really, really wanted to do. . . . She got tremendous help from the crew, which really wanted her to succeed." ★ The 216th episode of *Knots Landing* is also entitled "Just Desserts." It aired on April 14, 1988, was directed by *Knots* star Kevin Dobson, and was co-written by Don Mueller and *Knots* star William Devane.

217. "Nothing's Ever Perfect"

Written by Leonard Katzman; Directed by Bruce Bilson; Airdate: March 21, 1986
Special Guest Stars: Barbara Carrera (Angelica); John Beck (Mark)
Guest Stars: Barry Jenner (Jerry Kenderson); George O. Petrie (Harv); George Chakiris

(Nicholas); Laurence Haddon (Franklin); Keith Charles (Walter); Shalane McCall (Charlie); Omri Katz (John Ross); Don Starr (Jordan); Debbie Rennard (Sly); James L. Brown (McSween)
Subject: J.R. courts Sue Ellen.

Trivia Weekly rating: number 14. ★ In a telephone interview that took place the day before this episode aired, Phil Capice stated that he had "no idea" whether Duffy would be interested in returning to the show. "We haven't addressed ourselves to that," Capice said. "In television, I suppose anything could be possible. I don't see it right now. He in fact died on the show. But stranger things have happened." ★ Toward the end of Season 8, Phil Capice told *TV Guide* that the adoption storyline that resulted from Susan Howard's objections to Donna's abortion "turned out to be a much better story" in the long run. ★ Two days after this episode aired, CBS aired the TV movie prequel, *The Early Years*.

218. "J.R. Rising"

Written by Joel J. Feigenbaum and Peter Dunne; Directed by Linda Day; Airdate: April 4, 1986
Special Guest Stars: Barbara Carrera (Angelica); John Beck (Mark)
Guest Stars: Alejandro Rey (Rueda); Barry Jenner (Jerry Kenderson); Laurence Haddon (Franklin); Shalane McCall (Charlie); Omri Katz (John Ross); Jill Andre (Nan Colton); Hugh Gillin; Penelope Windust (Mrs. Crane); Don Starr (Jordan); Fern Fitzgerald (Marilee)
Subject: J.R.'s deals.

Cast Notes One of the children in Tony's foster family is played by Kellie Martin, who went on to star as Becca Thatcher in *Life Goes On* and as Lucy Knight on *ER*.

Trivia Weekly rating: number 16. This is the first time *Dallas* fell out of the top fifteen since 1979, and it was the season's lowest-ranked episode. Five days after it aired, CBS announced that Patrick Duffy was returning to the cast of *Dallas* for the May 16 cliff-hanger. Despite the growing press clamor for details about Duffy's return, however, news of Bobby's possible resurrection would not propel the show back into the Nielsen top ten until the final episode of the season.

219. "Serendipity"

Written by Leonard Katzman; Directed by Bruce Bilson; Airdate: April 11, 1986
Special Guest Stars: Barbara Carrera (Angelica); John Beck (Mark)
Guest Stars: Alejandro Rey (Rueda); Barry Jenner (Jerry Kenderson); Shalane McCall (Charlie); Omri Katz (John Ross); Jill Andre (Nan Colton); Penelope Windust (Mrs. Crane); Debbie Rennard (Sly); Fern Fitzgerald (Marilee)
Subject: J.R. courts Sue Ellen.

Trivia Weekly rating: number 14. Almost two weeks after this episode aired, NBC announced that it would air *Miami Vice*, now routinely beating *Falcon Crest* in the ratings, against *Dallas* during the 1986–87 season. ★ By the final episodes of Season 8, the press frenzy over Patrick Duffy's return continued to grow. Nine days after this episode aired, it was reported that Duffy would appear in a cliff-hanger scene taking place at Pam's wedding to Mark Graison. By the end of the month, Leonard Katzman gave an interview in which he stated that Duffy's return would be mysterious. "It's going to be more of an 'Oh, my God!'" he said. "The return of Patrick, we think, is going to help [the show] a great deal."

220. "Thrice in a Lifetime"

Written by Peter Dunne and Joel J. Feigenbaum; Directed by Jerry Jameson; Airdate: May 2, 1986
Special Guest Stars: Barbara Carrera (Angelica); John Beck (Mark)
Guest Stars: Barry Jenner (Jerry Kenderson); Keith Charles (Walter); Shalane McCall (Charlie); Omri Katz (John Ross); Jill Andre (Nan Colton); Tuck Milligan (Bomb Expert); Fern Fitzgerald (Marilee)
Subject: Sue Ellen and J.R. reconcile.

Cast Notes Steve Forrest makes his *Dallas* debut in the first of three consecutive episodes in which he plays a Jock Ewing look-alike using the alias Ben Stivers. In Season 9, Forrest's character uses a new alias, Wes Parmalee. Before *Dallas*, Forrest starred in the action series *S.W.A.T.* and in the movies *The Longest Day, North Dallas Forty,* and *Mommie Dearest* (costarring *Dallas* cast member Priscilla Pointer). Forrest explains that he was cast on *Dallas* because he had previously worked with Leonard Katzman on a 1965 episode of *Gunsmoke.*

Trivia Weekly rating: number 11.

221. "Hello, Goodbye, Hello"

Written by Leonard Katzman; Directed by Nick Havinga; Airdate: May 9, 1986
Special Guest Stars: Barbara Carrera (Angelica); John Beck (Mark)
Guest Stars: Barry Jenner (Jerry Kenderson); Morgan Woodward (Punk); Kate Reid (Aunt Lil); Glenn Corbett (Paul); Laurence Haddon (Franklin); Philip Levien (Lee); Jill Andre (Nan Colton); Fern Fitzgerald (Marilee)
Subject: J.R. is kidnapped.

Trivia Weekly rating: number 15. ★ Three days after this penultimate episode aired, CBS entertainment president B. Donald "Bud" Grant added to the furor over Patrick Duffy's return by announcing that Duffy was returning to *Dallas* not as a new character or a Bobby look-alike, but as Bobby Ewing himself. Grant stated that "the big mystery is really how we're going to do it." ★ As Season 8 wound down, John Beck learned that Patrick Duffy's return meant Beck would not be back for Season 9. "Lenny Katzman . . . walked by me, and almost as an afterthought said, 'I need to talk to you.' We moved behind part of the set and he said, 'John, you're not coming back next year.' It was clear that he had a real difficult time talking about this, so he just blurted it out. It was the hardest hit I've taken in my career." When asked about her favorite *Dallas* guest stars, Principal replies, "I would like to single out actor John Beck for his extraordinary grace under pressure and his unending good will."

222. "Blast from the Past"

Written by Joel J. Feigenbaum and Peter Dunne; Directed by Michael Preece; Airdate: May 16, 1986
Starring: Patrick Duffy
Special Guest Stars: Barbara Carrera (Angelica); John Beck (Mark)
Guest Stars: Omri Katz (John Ross); Tuck Milligan (Bomb Expert); Thomas Oglesby; Garret Smith; Robert Rockwell (Minister)
Subject: Pam finds Bobby in her shower.

Cast Notes This is Barbara Carrera's last appearance on *Dallas*. From the start, however, Carrera was open about the fact that she was "not staying with this series for eight or ten years. I've committed myself to one season and nothing more. . . . This is putting me in line to do the next thing."

Trivia Patrick Duffy's return appearance pushed *Dallas* back into the top ten for the first time in three months and the top five for the first time in five months. This episode was number 3 for the week with a 24.9 rating, tying Episode 194 as *Dallas's* best outing of the season. ★ CBS's press release about this episode was silent on Duffy's return, saying, "The happiness on Pam's and Mark's wedding day soon fades as J.R.'s attempt to outwit Angelica may have come too late to save Jack's life and ultimately jeopardizes Sue Ellen's life as well." ★ Prior to this episode's airing, Duffy told a reporter, "Even the people on the show will be taken aback about how I return. I didn't mention returning as Bobby Ewing. I won't mention it. I'm not saying I won't be Bobby Ewing, but I'm not saying I will. Leonard Katzman had this brilliant idea of how I would return." ★ The end credits teased the audience by indicating that "Patrick Duffy starred as _____." ★ On the day the wedding scene was shot, a few weeks before this episode aired, producers told the cast about Duffy's return but offered no explanation. "Nobody on the show knows exactly where the moment comes," explained Katzman. Because Bobby's return was not included in the script distributed to the cast, Katzman said, "There are going to be a lot of surprised actors when the show airs." ★ The week this episode aired, *People* magazine reported that Bobby would appear at Pam's wedding to Mark Graison, quoting a source who said, "Duffy literally appears in a flash at the wedding. Neither the characters nor the audience knows exactly who he is." Katzman stated that, "Without Bobby we lost the white knight to J.R. and the Romeo to Victoria's Juliet. With Patrick back we can return to the family drama that made the show." Katzman added, "We're not above leaking scripts to throw people off." *People* surmised that the producers' options included Duffy returning as a long-lost twin, an imposter, another Ewing brother, or as Bobby himself. As for the last possibility, Katzman said, "Maybe his eyes opened up on the way to the morgue. Don't rule out resurrection." ★ In accordance with Katzman's and Duffy's prediction, Victoria Principal was stunned to see Duffy on-screen when this episode aired since she filmed the scene with John Beck earlier that spring. In a version that Principal and Beck filmed—one of three different versions filmed as decoys—Pam found Mark dead on the shower floor the morning after their wedding. Duffy recalls, "Victoria called me maybe sixty seconds later—after the show was over—screaming! . . . She had no idea that that's how I was coming back or that she was a party to it." John Beck recalls that he and Principal also filmed a shower scene much like the one between Principal and Duffy. For Beck, it was his most memorable scene on *Dallas*. "It was the last day of shooting for the season. Victoria and I got the script for this shower scene, and it didn't have a lot of dialogue. I thought, 'What is this all about?' When we filmed the scene, there was no bar of soap, so someone from the prop department found a potato and peeled it. And that was our bar of soap. Of course, later Patrick was edited in in my place." As for Duffy's return, Beck said at the time that it could "only stretch credibility so far. It can't be shoved down viewers' throats." ★ Katzman, Duffy, and an outside crew secretly filmed Bobby in the shower at an off-site studio, using the ruse that they were doing a commercial for Irish Spring soap. Recalled Duffy, "We did an Irish Spring commercial. We took all day and had cases of Irish Spring. And I turned around in that shower a hundred times, all lathered up, turned around and go, 'Good Morning. And you can have a good morning, too, if you wake up like the Duffys.' And we did this commercial over and over and over again so that they would think it was really that." Katzman "cut out just that one little part [where Bobby says, "Good Morning"] and it was taken to New York by briefcase and put into the master just before airtime." ★ Duffy discussed his departure from *Dallas* with TV reporter Jerry Buck just before this episode aired. Said Duffy, "I wasn't angry or fed up [when I left]. I wanted to set up my own production company. I wanted to do all the things I couldn't do because I didn't have time while doing a series." Duffy did not know "if the drop in ratings had anything to do with [Bobby's departure] or not. The show lost three million viewers [in Season 8]. The only thing they're happy about is it finished ahead of *Dynasty*. They've never been aware of what makes *Dallas* successful. It's the combined chemistry of the characters and the actors playing those roles." Duffy said he was "looking forward to returning. I've never had another working situation like this in terms of camaraderie and support on the set. There's so little competition. I think in the beginning Victoria and I had a little competition but that ended the first time I directed. I could see that it depended on teamwork." ★ Travilla received a second Emmy nomination for Costume Design for this episode. One *Dallas* cast member who Travilla did not design for was Barbara Bel Geddes, whose wardrobe was a frequent subject of complaints from viewers. Bel Geddes had clothes tailor-made by Hollywood legend Jean-Louis. ★ Ironically, fifteen months before this episode aired, Duffy told the *Associated Press* that he would never "use the viewers' loyalty" by taking part in a guessing game over Bobby's fate, saying, "There won't be a 'Will Bobby be back?' under any circumstances" once he left the show.

SEASON 9
1986–87—"Return to Camelot"

PATRICK DUFFY'S RETURN GAVE DALLAS a unique opportunity: a reunion of its lead producer and all but one of the surviving original cast members for the first time in three years. The one exception was Charlene Tilton, who was asked by Katzman to return for thirteen episodes and eventually returned to the show in Season 10. Meanwhile, two great challenges faced the producers, one of which was of their own making. First, a satisfactory explanation was needed for Bobby's return from the dead. Second, Dallas was facing its first direct ratings challenge since it gained an audience during Season 1.

As TV Guide writer Elaine Warren recounted, "It was a summer of unrest in South Africa, discord in Congress over aid to the Contras, fear throughout the world about Arab terrorism. But the really crucial issue that had TV viewers everywhere breathlessly waiting out the long summer months was this: how did Dallas's Bobby Ewing come back from the dead?" As viewers found out in the opening minutes of Season 9, Bobby's return was explained by pretending that he never died in the first place. His death in the final scene of Season 7, and all of the Season 8 episodes, had been dreamed by Pam. According to Duffy, it was his wife, Carlyn, who realized that Bobby could only be brought back if he had never died at all: "One day, she said, 'I know it's crazy but you can do [a dream].' I laughed and told her it was outrageous." A week later, the couple heard Katzman's idea for bringing Bobby back. Katzman said, "Here's my idea. It's going to be a dream and we're just going to erase that year." Duffy and his wife "just looked at each other with the look used by people who have been married for years."

While the "dream resolution" was a less than satisfying plot device, Katzman knew that getting Duffy back on the show was crucial no matter how it was achieved. He felt Duffy's departure "left Juliet without Romeo. It was a big piece missing from the show." Moreover, "Bobby versus J.R. is one of the great male love-hate relationships. You could always count on Bobby to stop J.R., but then they would band together against outsiders. Nobody could break that bond. The loss of Bobby had a drastic effect on the show. If we are skilled enough dramatists, we can pull it off. Everybody says it's a big risk, even my bosses at CBS, but I've been fired from jobs before. It's worth it. There hasn't been as much excitement around here in a long time."

For Katzman, however, pulling off Duffy's return was only the tip of the iceberg. Katzman thought that, Duffy's absence aside, Dallas suffered during Season 8 because of three main problems: too much international intrigue, weakened male characters, and a wimpy J.R. When Katzman rejoined the show as executive producer, he replaced the Season 8 writing team of Peter Dunne, Joel Feigenbaum, Stephanie Garman, and Hollace White with David Paulsen, a writer from Seasons 3 through 7, and Leah Markus, a writer from Season 3, to help fix these problems. Katzman acknowledged that he had a hand in the ill-fated Angelica Nero storyline in his capacity as a creative consultant to *Dallas* during Season 8. He thought, however, that the story took over the season. "The basic story for that was my idea," he conceded, "but it was designed for seven or eight episodes and it ended up playing more than twenty episodes." Katzman also felt that, during Season 8, "*Dallas* had become a women's show." He did not believe *Dallas* should "have weak women, but the men have always been the strong characters in the show. The women have been strong in their own right, but they haven't dominated the men."

The writers, said Katzman, "practically ruined J.R. last year. He was deceived by women. They lied to him. If you diminish J.R., you diminish the series." J.R. "was never, really, in our minds, an SOB. We always thought he was very understandable. He had certain goals, certain things he wanted to do. He had certain needs. He never set out to hurt anyone, as long as they did what he wanted and didn't get in his way. He's very ruthless; he's a constant womanizer." But during Season 8, Katzman complained, "J.R. was whipped at every turn. Everybody was just shoving him around, pushing him around. . . . I did give warnings along the way. I kept saying that we've got the best character on television and we're making a wimp out of him. . . . [In Season 9,] you're going to see the real J.R. again." Writer Howard Lakin recalled that Katzman "couldn't deal with what they had done [in Season 8]. He didn't understand it. He just didn't get a grip on it. And that upset him because he was a very controlling kind of man. So, faced with this, he decided to make the year disappear."

In addition to resolving Duffy's return, *Dallas* had to fend off a potential ratings challenge by NBC's new hit, police drama *Miami Vice*. *Vice* had aired for two seasons and starred Don Johnson and Phillip Michael Thomas. It got little notice during the 1984–85 season, its first, when it aired against *Falcon Crest*. However, during the 1985–86 season, *Vice* caught on with viewers, beat *Falcon Crest* and finished the season at number 9, only three places behind *Dallas*. *Vice* even performed competitively against *Dallas* when their respective two-hour season premieres aired simultaneously on September 27, 1985. That night, Bobby's funeral finished only 0.7 ratings points ahead of *Miami Vice*. Ever since, NBC executives had toyed with the possibility of moving *Vice* to the 9:00 p.m. timeslot and airing it against *Dallas*. As the 1985–86 season unfolded and *Dallas*'s ratings slipped, NBC became emboldened and, on April 22, 1986, amidst the hype over Patrick Duffy's return, the network publicly confirmed that that it was considering airing *Miami Vice* at 9:00 p.m. during the 1986–87 season, directly against *Dallas*. A short time later, NBC announced its decision to do so.

The press made much of the young NBC upstart show taking on CBS's long-time ratings champ, just as it had hyped the ratings race between *Dallas* and *Dynasty* several years earlier, although *Dallas* and *Dynasty* never aired on the same night, let alone at the same time. NBC Entertainment President Brandon Tartikoff claimed, "Our research says *Miami Vice* will beat *Dallas* at nine o'clock," but CBS research vice president David Poltrack felt that "the early-season results will be very close, but by end of season *Dallas* will be the winner. The audience will stay with it." Larry Hagman predicted, "We have such a huge center of the country as loyal, loyal watchers that I don't think *Miami Vice* has that much of a chance. Maybe I'm wrong, but I think we'll bury 'em." Hagman told another reporter that *Dallas* was "back on track. We'll return to that old wink of the eye that people missed. . . . Afraid of *Miami Vice*? Hell, no." Duffy agreed that, for "a tired old show we're doing okay. We got 'em whupped."

The ratings race and Duffy's return caused a press frenzy that *Dallas* had not seen since the days of "Who Shot J.R.?" Hagman stoked the flames in an interview that appeared in *TV Guide* a few weeks after Duffy was seen in Pam's shower. In the article, Hagman called Capice "a no-talent, obnoxious [bleeper]." Hagman complained about *Dallas*'s "lethargy" and "dumb" international storylines. "This show could run for four, five more years if people did the smart things. . . . You would think [Capice] would care about success and security. . . . [Katzman was] the real brains behind the show." When the author of the article pointed out to Hagman that Katzman worked on the bible for Season 8, and remained one of the show's creative consultants, Hagman dismissed the point, saying, "Capice is in control. He does the hiring and he makes the final decisions; and that has always been the problem. . . . And you can see where we've gone with just Capice."

Bob Crutchfield of Lorimar responded to Hagman's comments by saying that they were not a surprise to the company, and he even tried to put a positive face on them. Said Crutchfield, "We were well aware of [the interview] when it was being done. It was set up by Larry's press people. . . . Originally it was supposed to coincide with the cliff-hanger. Any press during that period would certainly have been welcome. Hopefully, people will reread the article just before the fall season starts."

Meanwhile, neither Lorimar nor the network confirmed who Duffy would play once he stepped out of the shower. Katzman jokingly confirmed only that Duffy "will come back clean." Katzman filmed three solutions to the cliff-hanger to keep the resolution a mystery, including scenes in which Duffy played a Bobby imposter. Photographs of Hagman watching Duffy remove facial bandages appeared in the July 1, 1986, edition of the *Star*. *People* magazine tried to solve the mystery by tracking which stars were returning to the show, such as Jenilee Harrison and Steve Forrest, and which stars were not, like John Beck, and figuring out why Victoria Principal was fitted for a $2,300 wedding dress.

Shortly after the *Dallas* crew resumed filming at Culver City in June of 1986,

CBS threw a party for more than 130 TV columnists at the Bistro Gardens in Beverly Hills. Cast members in attendance included Patrick Duffy, Linda Gray, Larry Hagman, Jenilee Harrison, Steve Kanaly, Priscilla Presley, Victoria Principal and Deborah Shelton. One of the chief topics of conversation was Duffy's return to the show. Duffy commented that *Dallas*'s ratings decline was "definitely a motivating factor" on the part of Lorimar, and its financial offer to Duffy was "an incredible incentive" to him. Duffy explained that filming had already begun at Culver City, but four crucial scenes resolving his return had yet to be shot and "won't be filmed with the regular cast members around. They'll be filmed in a very isolated setting." Duffy thought, by Season 8, *Dallas* was "getting stale, absolutely. . . . It's not a show of foreign intrigue. It's a show that could take place over the next fifty years within the state of Texas. I think it took the wrong avenue. It ran the risk and it was not successful."

Victoria Principal agreed. "The show was missing a lot of things this year," she said. "It was missing good writing, good direction, good plot lines, and it had too many outside characters. We're returning to the original formula. The family element. The family group." Priscilla Presley commented on the "thousands and thousands of letters" from viewers "who all wanted Patrick Duffy to come back. It's ingenious how they're doing it." When asked about his friend and costar's return, Hagman simply said, "I'm happy."

By early July, the company traveled to Dallas for the on-location shoot. While there, Katzman told a TV reporter, "If you liked *Dallas* the way it used to be, this is what you're gonna see. We're going back to what was the strength of *Dallas*, which is the relationships in the family. It's the Barneses and the Ewings and a Farlow, and that's it." The strategy behind the public relations offensive was clear. Katzman summarized, "We feel that if we get 'em for that first show, we'll keep 'em hooked. The first show is really kind of all important." Two months later, the on-location shoot wrapped, the company returned to Hollywood and audiences prepared for the fall premiere and long-awaited explanation of what Duffy was doing in the shower.

With its reassembled cast, *Dallas* met NBC's challenge. *Dallas* clobbered *Miami Vice* in the ratings for the first week of the new season, taking the number 4 spot while *Vice* slipped to number 23. *Dallas* also improved on its own Season 8 premiere ratings, earning a 26.5 rating and 44 share; a year earlier, Bobby's funeral earned a number 7 ranking, 23.9 rating and 38 share. These numbers gave *Dallas* its best season premiere rating since Season 6. While *Dallas*'s overall season ranking dropped during Season 9 (*Dallas* finished the year at number 11 with a 21.3 rating, falling out of the top ten for the first time since its first season), *Dallas* was CBS's third most popular show, behind *60 Minutes* and *Murder, She Wrote*. But it was *Dallas*'s dominance over *Miami Vice*—which did not even make the top twenty-five in the overall season ratings during the 1986–87 season—that made the year a triumph. *Dallas*'s performance against NBC's newest hit was even more impressive in light of the continued audience drop-off experienced by the aging prime-time soaps. *Falcon Crest* slid to number 23 for the year, *Dynasty* was number 24, and *Knots Landing* did not even make the top twenty-five. Several years later, Hagman reflected, "*Miami Vice* was a hell of a show and if we are ever knocked off the air then I hope it is by a quality show. If we had been knocked off by *Miami Vice* then that would have been okay." Hagman joked that *Vice* did no such thing, however, because he put a hex on the show.

Dallas's successful cast reunion and ratings victory created a renaissance for the series' cast, crew, and fans alike. But the "Return to Camelot" was short-lived. Halfway through Season 9, on January 28, 1987, Victoria Principal announced that she would leave the show at the end of the season. After finally getting their Romeo back in *Dallas*, Katzman and his team were now faced with the loss of their Juliet. Initially, Principal's departure was reported as nothing more than a "snag" in her contract renegotiation. Even after Principal's spokesman announced her departure from the show, Lorimar indicated that Principal's exit was the result of disagreement over financial terms. It said through a spokesman, "We were unable to reach an agreement on a new contract and the producers are now revising scripts to take her out. . . . She turned down our last offer." Sheree J. Wilson recalls that salary was an issue, saying that Principal "wanted Larry Hagman's salary. But we were all paid a lot and there was no more money. . . . So, we knew she was leaving."

According to Principal, however, the decision had nothing to do with money. Not long before her final appearance on the show, Principal confirmed that Lorimar tried to persuade her to stay by giving her a large salary increase. "We had discussions. Lorimar has always been very generous to me. [But] it was just a sense that this was the time." Principal claimed,

> I've considered [leaving *Dallas*] for two years, and in the last six months, it's seemed real clear to me. I realized my job would become my career if I stayed. Some people stay with a series to the end, you know, and afterward they often have some problems, I think, finding new opportunities. And I wanted a career after *Dallas*. There's great sadness in leaving friends and the show—I was never bored with it—but I'm not at all ambivalent about this. I'm realistic about taking care of myself financially. I didn't walk away blindly without plans. My plans are set. I have a project with a network that is ready to go that I can't talk about yet. It's a drama-mystery.

Principal later elaborated that leaving *Dallas* was the only way she could "find out what I lived in fear of not knowing. I didn't want to look back on my life and say—what I might have done. What I might have been. What I might have been capable of. It was important to me to go out and answer that."

Leonard Katzman telephoned Larry Hagman with the news of Principal's departure the day it was announced. The next day, Hagman gave an interview in which he stated, "I don't like to upset the apple cart. I like to keep my family together. We've been through all this before, from Miss Ellie to Bobby. I really hate it. Her going is a loss to the family." While Hagman admitted that Principal, unlike former departing cast members Barbara Bel Geddes and Patrick Duffy "is not one of my pals," Hagman was upset by the news, and reluctantly acknowledged, "I think it's over. I think she'll finish out her contract, and that's it. We only have four more shows to do for this season, and I don't know what will happen or how it will be handled." One year later, Hagman explained that he understood Principal's reasons for leaving *Dallas*. While Hagman felt that Bel Geddes and Duffy were making a mistake when they decided to leave the show, he felt otherwise about Principal. "The only person I could really understand leaving was Victoria Principal," he wrote. "She wanted out. She felt she'd reached a point where she really wanted to do something else. For an actress, at a certain age, unless you become a great character actress, your career is shorter than an actor's. And looking the way she does, Victoria has another career ahead of her."

Just days before Principal's announcement, Lorimar announced that it was not renewing Susan Howard's contract for Season 10 since her character, in Katzman's words, "had run its course." Howard had hinted to TV reporter Ann Hodges during the summer of 1986 that Season 9 might be her last. According to Howard, her role was being cut back to accommodate the expansion of other roles, such as Priscilla Presley's. Howard began to make plans for other projects, including a movie script. During the course of Season 9, as Howard's character divorced Ray and moved to Washington, D.C., it became clear to Howard that her run on *Dallas* had come to an end as well.

SEASON 9 EPISODE GUIDE

Regular Cast

Starring:

Barbara Bel Geddes as Miss Ellie
Patrick Duffy as Bobby
Linda Gray as Sue Ellen
Larry Hagman as J.R.
Susan Howard as Donna
Steve Kanaly as Ray
Howard Keel as Clayton
Ken Kercheval as Cliff
Priscilla Beaulieu Presley as Jenna
Victoria Principal as Pam
Dack Rambo as Jack

Also Starring:

Steve Forrest as Wes Parmalee
Jenilee Harrison as Jamie
Deborah Shelton as Mandy Winger
Sheree J. Wilson as April Stevens

Technical Credits

Supervising Producer: Calvin Clements Jr.
Producer: David Paulsen
Executive Producer: Leonard Katzman
Associate Producer: Cliff Fenneman
Story Consultant: Leah Markus
Story Editor: Mitchell Wayne Katzman
Music: Jerrold Immel, Richard Lewis
   Warren, John Parker, Lance Rubin,
   Angela Morley

Unit Production Manager: Wayne A.
   Farlow
First Assistant Directors: Fred Stromsoe,
   Frank W. Katzman
Second Assistant Director: Richard R.
   Johnson
Director of Photography: Robert Caramico,
   A.S.C.
Art Directors: Walter "Matt" Jeffries, David
   K. Marshall
Editors: Fred W. Berger, A.C.E., John
   Arthur Davies, Ed Brennan
Executive in Charge of Casting: Barbara
   Miller
Casting: Irene Mariano, C.S.A., Rody Kent
Set Decorator: Chuck Rutherford
Property Master: John Rettino
Costumers: Jack Bear, Nancy Renard
Makeup: Joe Hailey, Ralph Gulko
Hair Stylists: Generio Gugliemotto, Lola
   "Skip" McNalley, Lee Crawford
Production Sound Mixer: Robert Sheridan
Sound Supervisor: Doug Grindstaff
Sound Effects Editor: Tom Gillis Burke
Music Supervisor: Richard Berres
Music Editor: Patricia Peck
Main Title Design: Wayne Fitzgerald
Executive Production Supervisor: Edward
   O. Denault

223. & 224. "Return to Camelot" (Parts One and Two)

Written by Leonard Katzman and Mitchell Wayne Katzman; Directed by Leonard Katzman; Airdate: September 26, 1986
Guest Stars: David White (Mark); Kristina Wayborn (Jack's Date); Shalane McCall (Charlie); Don Starr (Jordan); Fern Fitzgerald (Marilee); Debbie Rennard (Sly) Subject: Pam's dream.

Cast Notes Dack Rambo was added to the main title as of this episode. ★ Featured actor John L. Martin, who plays Hickey, played Herbert Wentworth in Episode 63. ★ Starla Hagman, the wife of Larry Hagman's son, Preston, has a small role in these two episodes. In the summer of 1985, Starla and Preston made Hagman a grandfather when their daughter, Mary Noel, was born. Hagman's family tradition dictated that each girl be named Mary in honor of Hagman's mother,

Mary Martin. ★ Swedish actress Kristina Wayborn played Dr. Greta Ingstrom on *General Hospital*. She also played Magda in the 1983 James Bond movie *Octopussy*, joining Lois Chiles and Barbara Carrera as the only three *Dallas* actresses who were also Bond women.

Trivia Weekly rating: number 4 with a 26.5 rating and 44 share. *Miami Vice* finished 23rd for the week. Excluding the cliff-hanger, this was *Dallas*'s highest ranked episode of the season. ★ This episode aired as a two-hour special. ★ CBS's promotions for this episode teased viewers by asking, "But will a mother know her own son?" and showing a clip of Barbara Bel Geddes saying, "I wonder." ★ Critical derision aside, Katzman thought the "dream" scenario was accepted by the *Dallas* audience "rather well." Indeed, in the first few weeks of Season 9, *Dallas* returned to the top ten and gained about four million viewers. ★ Just as it had done six years earlier with the "Who Shot J.R.?" cliff-hanger, the cast and crew successfully kept the resolution to "Who is in Pam's Shower?" a surprise until the airdate. During the summer hiatus, however, and up until the resolution episode's airdate, certain clues were given by people in the know. In a June interview, new CBS entertainment programming vice president Kim LeMasters told a reporter that a "willing suspension of disbelief" was necessary for viewers to accept Duffy's return. That same month, Duffy attended a party for TV critics and confirmed that he would play Bobby Ewing and not another character. Duffy also said that "there was not a lot of contortion involved" in Bobby's return. Duffy admitted that the audience could very well respond to the way Bobby returned by saying, "Ho-ho! You've gotta be kidding." At the same event, Steve Kanaly thought the storyline "asks the audience to accept a lot." In August, Katzman told Dallas TV critic Ed Bark that "*Dallas* fans want Patrick back anyway we can get him back. They want him back as Bobby, not as someone else obviously, and they're willing to accept almost anything that we do, as long as it's not too painful. . . . You might speculate that if Patrick was going to come back, he would come back at a period when the show was on a peak, instead of in the valley. There is no acceptable way to bring back a character who's died. How do you do that, unless you say, 'OK, for just a moment you've got to go along with us.' And then, bing, the moment is over. . . . Speed is of the essence when you do something like that." Bark guessed from Katzman's comments that "it appears increasingly likely that *Dallas* will bring Bobby back by dreaming his death away." Shortly before "Return to Camelot" aired, Duffy told *People* magazine, "Only three people really know how Bobby comes back. Me; my wife, Carlyn; and Leonard Katzman." *People* reporter Suzy Kalter came pretty close to solving the mystery in her article on the subject. Kalter reviewed the possible resolutions, including: it was a dream; Bobby is really an imposter; or Bobby was revived after apparently dying. She also visited the set to determine which option was the most likely. She witnessed the filming of a pre-wedding scene, which would ultimately air in Episode 230. The scene took place in Sue Ellen's room at Southfork and featured Pam and Jamie Ewing. Victoria Principal appeared in a $2,300 Zandra Rhodes wedding dress. Jenilee Harrison, whose character had apparently died in an explosion in the final seconds of Season 8, told Kalter, "I thought I was dead too." Harrison received word that her contract was not being renewed at the end of Season 8, then subsequently received a telegram reading, "Disregard previous telegram." Principal and Harrison had lines that made it clear that Pam was remarrying Bobby. Further, John Beck, whose character married Pam in Season 8's final episode, did not return for Season 9. Kalter took the obvious conclusion to Leonard Katzman, who would only say, "On a soap opera, anyone who dies off camera has a 50–50 chance of coming back alive. . . . J.R. would lie, cheat, and steal but he would never hurt his mama by letting her think Bobby was dead if he wasn't." Katzman called the resolution "brilliant" and taped several alternate storylines as decoys. Hagman told Kalter that he hoped the "Bobby Never Died" solution would be used, saying, "I do hope that's it. I was terrific in that scene." Howard Keel thought the solution would be the dream scenario, saying it would be appropriate since Season 8 "was a real nightmare." Kanaly just wanted the resolution aired "so people can stop talking about it." Hagman also told Kalter, "Last year I was exhausted. Now I could go dancing. The ladies in the cast all feel better. We've gotten everything worked out. The spirit is back at *Dallas*." ★ Beck told another reporter that, after the season ended, "When I was told I was being let go, I had mixed feelings. It also gave me great freedom. I could do theater or a movie or another series. When you're doing a show you can't do anything else. . . . It can get frustrating." ★ *TV Guide* solicited tongue-in-cheek resolutions of the mystery from such best-selling authors as Judith Krantz (the death was faked by J.R.), Stephen King (the still-dead Bobby has been reanimated by J.R.'s enemies through magic rituals), and Erich Segal (Mark Graison had plastic surgery to please Pam). ★ Katzman's son Mitchell co-wrote this episode with him. Mitchell Katzman went on to write or co-write twenty episodes of *Dallas* during Seasons 9 through 13. ★ TV critic David Bianculli claimed that the "dream" resolution "ranks among the most stupid and spineless plot lines ever presented on television." But, he admitted, it was also, "in its own way . . . an absolutely brilliant move. . . . The viewers repulsed by that cliffhanger cop-out will be more than offset by the *Dallas* fans attracted to what's happened since." The resolution was similarly derided by *TV Guide* ("The Ewing Oil Shaft") and other critics. ★ Writer David Paulsen recalls learning about the "dream" resolution when Katzman "came down to the set and he just looked at me and said, 'It was all a dream.' . . . And it was perfect. It was absolutely perfect." ★ According to Suzy Kalter, although parts of the first twelve episodes of Season 9 were shot by the time "Return to Camelot" aired, few in the cast knew how the scenes all fit together to resolve Bobby's return. Some in the cast were not crazy about the "dream" explanation once they finally learned about it. Susan Howard commented, "Sometimes the less said is best. I liked the storyline about the handicapped child. I felt we were making a contribution to society, and it was successful.

I've got to completely turn around and forget that ever happened." Said Linda Gray, "At the beginning of last year, I finally got to do what I wanted to do—to act. No more victim. For me last year was a high. When Patrick came back to 'save the show,' I was not happy. The show wasn't in trouble, as far as I was concerned. What kind of slap was this?" Priscilla Presley responded, "I'm not complaining, but I liked it when I got to do more scenes with other people." The writers from *Knots Landing* might also have been less than pleased with the dream resolution, since Bobby's death had been incorporated into the *Knots* storyline during the 1985–86 season. Explains Joan Van Ark, "Bobby's death was very much a part of the plot on *Knots*. We even named one of Valene's twins Bobby as a tribute to Bobby, and to Patrick Duffy. Like the whole world, we believed that the character was gone! When Bobby came back, it was very strange and impossible to undo what had been written. We just had to ignore it. It was a little tricky to handle, so we didn't get into it. We just let it go by." ★ Kanaly felt that, "It's nice having Patrick back and it's nice having Leonard back. But that was a nice storyline we had developed with Susan Howard and me, raising children late in life and the problems of the handicapped. It was nicely received. . . . One actor leaving doesn't cause the demise of any particular show." ★ Larry Hagman, Victoria Principal, and Jenilee Harrison were downright optimistic about Duffy's return. Hagman stated, "We have the team that made it a hit back together again. Everybody's feeling good, everything's running smoothly." Said Harrison, "Patrick's return can do nothing but pull us up. Anybody who denies that is being foolish. He's come back to save the show, and that's a fact. He can do nothing but help us all keep our jobs. . . . He can keep *Dallas* around." Victoria Principal claimed, "He fools around all the time. Whenever we do a love scene, he always brings something into the bed with us, a mannequin, an arm, a leg, a frog, a chain. But it's great to have him back." ★ As for Katzman, he later said, "I will go to my grave convinced that was the only way to do it." And Duffy, who had insisted that he was "leaving Southfork permanently" and would never "under any circumstances, come back as Bobby Ewing," also felt the dream scenario was the best way to get the series back to basics. Duffy only watched *Dallas* twice during Season 8, but felt that the show lost viewers because it lost its sense of "family in the sense of where they came from, their shit-kicking background. They're rich, but they throw it around like the Texans do. All of a sudden, the show turned into *Architectural Digest* and *Gentleman's Quarterly*." Duffy agreed that Bobby's return might help turn the show around. "You make a cake," he said, "and leave one ingredient out, and it's not the same cake." He noted that he was "getting more fan letters now than I was last year." Once he returned, "It was like the year really had disappeared. It was like I went to work the next day. . . . I felt not one glimmer of animosity or jealously." Indeed, Duffy was thrilled to be back to a job he loved before—and after—his season off. "I can swear to you," he said, "in thirteen years there was not one day that I wasn't so excited to get to work. . . . I always left the house earlier

than I wanted to just so I could get in the car and get there and start having fun."
★ *Magnum, P.I.* used a variation of the "dream scenario" when the show unexpectedly returned for a final season in 1987–88, after Tom Selleck's title character died and went to heaven in the final episode of the 1986–87 season. Upon the show's return in the fall of 1987, it was explained that Magnum had dreamed that he died. ★ Principal and Duffy spoofed the "dream scene" years later in cameo appearances on the December 26, 1999, episode of *The Family Guy,* a Fox Network animated situation comedy. As Duffy explains, after *Family Guy's* millennium episode, he and Principal appeared in a live action scene "where we reenacted the bed and shower scene and had a fantastic time doing it. . . . I would work with her in a heartbeat again." Duffy had the chance to work with Principal again—and poke fun at the "dream scene" again—in the 2004 reunion show, *The Return to Southfork.* At the end of that show, Duffy wakes Principal who, winking at the camera, claims that the cast reunion that had just been seen by viewers was a dream. ★ The "dream season" was also famously spoofed on Bob Newhart's 1982–90 sitcom *Newhart.* At the end of that show's final episode in May 1990, Newhart woke up not with his *Newhart* wife, Mary Frann (who had been a finalist to play Sue Ellen), but with Suzanne Pleshette, his wife from his former 1972–78 sitcom, *The Bob Newhart Show,* and proceeded to dismiss *Newhart's* eight seasons as a dream. Newhart and Pleshette recreated this scene on the 2003 Emmy Awards show.

225. "Pari Per Sue"

Written by David Paulsen; Directed by Michael Preece; Airdate: October 3, 1986
Guest Stars: George Coe (General Longley); William Smithers (Jeremy Wendell); Derek
McGrath (Oswald Valentine); Debbie Rennard (Sly); Vernon Weddle (John Carter);
Joshua Harris (Christopher)
Subject: Sue Ellen's business.

Cast Notes Derek McGrath was a regular on *Mary,* one of Mary Tyler Moore's comeback vehicles. ★ George Coe, a veteran TV and film actor, was on *Saturday Night Live* during its debut season, which he described as "walking a tightrope."

Trivia Weekly rating: number 15. Although *Dallas's* audience dropped off since its premiere the week before, it still beat *Miami Vice,* which was number 24 for the week. ★ When Leonard Katzman stated publicly that Patrick Duffy's return signaled a return to a show "of strong men—not weak women—but strong men," Linda Gray complained and insisted that Sue Ellen had become a strong character in Season 9, resulting in the Valentine storyline. Explained Gray, "I was offended and frustrated by what [Katzman] said—and took the stand that if that's the way it's going to be, maybe it's time for me to move on. . . . I'm tired of playing the victim. I need to grow as an actress and a woman. And I've made that point very strongly this season. . . . [Sue Ellen] is showing some growth—she becomes conniving and funny. So they are listening to me. . . . I'm almost like a female J.R. this year, but not evil. I'm a little conniving, a little devious, a lot funny. . . . Finally, after nine years, I'm getting to do something I always wanted to do." The Valentine storyline was one of Gray's two favorite Sue Ellen storylines. Says Gray, "I . . . loved when [Sue Ellen] became her own person. She had her own company and could stand up to [J.R.]. I felt it was very empowering for the women who watched." ★ Katzman insisted, however, that he did not take "suggestions" from the actors, saying, "We have been fortunate enough that (a) the actors trust us and (b) our scripts are of a quality that they accept. I think once you let the actors tell you how the storylines should go, you're in terrible trouble, because then there is no creative control among the people who do the creative work. Certainly we will talk to actors about scenes, if they have a thought about a scene, if they want to come to us and say, 'What if I did this later on in the year?' or 'What if I did that?' or 'Wouldn't it be interesting . . . ?'—we're wide open to that kind of thing. But that is only on an if-we-think-it's-right-for-the-show basis." ★ TV critic David Bianculli, who found the dream resolution "too absurd," thought the show immediately recovered. "This season's second installment . . . was the show's best episode in years. The writers, like Pam, have suddenly awakened."

226. "Once and Future King"

Written by Calvin Clements Jr.; Directed by Leonard Katzman; Airdate: October 10, 1986
Guest Stars: Jim Haynie (Gordon); Karen Carlson (Nancy Scottfield); Tom Fucello
(Dave); Shalane McCall (Charlie); Joshua Harris (Christopher); Debbie Rennard (Sly);
Don Starr (Jordan); Fern Fitzgerald (Marilee)
Subject: Parmalee's claim.

Cast Notes Karen Carlson was married to actor David Soul of *Starsky and Hutch* fame. Carlson met Soul while appearing on his previous series, *Here Come the Brides*.

Trivia Weekly rating: number 14. *Miami Vice* was number 22 for the week. ★ The Trammel Crow Center, located at 2200 Ross Avenue in Dallas, was used for on-location scenes set in Sue Ellen's Valentine offices. In Culver City, the set was on Stage 23, alongside the outdoor Southfork set. ★ Writer Calvin Clements Jr. was the supervising producer during Season 9 and wrote five other Season 9 episodes. ★ A new building was used as Ewing Oil as of the Season 9 location shoot. The Interfirst Plaza was chosen to replace the Interfirst II Building because Interfirst II was undergoing renovations. ★ If Miss Ellie seemed to recognize Parmalee, perhaps it was because Barbara Bel Geddes and Steve Forrest worked together twenty-five years earlier. "We had fun talking about that," Forrest recalls. "She and I had worked together in the Martin Ritt movie *Five Branded Women* that was filmed in Italy." ★ Ray's new home makes its debut in this episode. The white house was located in the Plano area, not far from Ray's old red brick house, which could been seen across the field from the white one. Like parts of Southfork and the red brick house, parts of the white house were recreated on the Culver City set.

227. "Enigma"

Written by Leah Markus; Directed by Michael Preece; Airdate: October 17, 1986
Guest Stars: Morgan Woodward (Punk); Laurence Haddon (Franklin); Jim Haynie (Gordon); Hunter Von Leer (B. D. Calhoun); Omri Katz (John Ross); Joshua Harris (Christopher); Debbie Rennard (Sly); Don Starr (Jordan)
Subject: Miss Ellie wonders about Parmalee.

Trivia   Weekly rating: number 8. *Miami Vice* was number 26. TV columnist John Horn said of *Dallas*'s ratings wins over *Miami Vice*, "At first, it looked as though the serial's dream sequence was going to produce a nightmare, and possibly final, season. More than four million viewers, perhaps feeling cheated by the farfetched *Dallas* cliff-hanger, abandoned the program after its first week. The program quickly skidded from fourth place to fifteenth place in the A.C. Nielsen Co. television ratings. NBC's *Miami Vice* . . . was gaining ground. . . . The killjoys claimed that *Dallas* had finally done itself in. The program, surviving for seven seasons on a sequence of improbable gimmicks, had gone too far, they said. The audience wasn't going to be manipulated anymore. Yet, in typical *Dallas* fashion, there was a twist. The reports of the program's death had been greatly exaggerated. In the last two weeks, *Dallas* has regained its footing and is well on its way to another strong season. In the most recent ratings, *Dallas* attracted four million more viewers than *Miami Vice* and appears to be pulling away. . . . [CBS research vice president David] Poltrack said that *Dallas* is as strong as ever, and that the cliff-hanger did not backfire. 'The resolution came in the first five minutes, yet people stayed and watched the full two hours. There was no drop-off. . . . It's very encouraging. We got back to the basic storyline that we left last year.'" ★ While Steve Forrest's run on *Dallas* required him to play a white-haired man who dyed his hair brown, in reality Forrest was a brown-haired man who had to dye his hair white. Forrest "knew Jim Davis and did not want to try to imitate him" but he agreed to dye his hair white for the role. He recalls that "when I went to my wife's hairdresser to get my hair bleached, in came Arnold Schwarzenegger, . . . so I got to meet the now-governor of California!" Forrest felt he had "natural similarities" to Jim Davis because "we were both Southern boys."

228. "Trompe L'Oeil"

Written by Leonard Katzman; Directed by Leonard Katzman; Airdate: October 24, 1986
Guest Stars: Morgan Woodward (Punk); Hunter Von Leer (B. D. Calhoun); Debbie Rennard (Sly); Omri Katz (John Ross); Joshua Harris (Christopher)
Subject: J.R.'s overseas plot.

Cast Notes   Jack's former—and Bobby's future—wife, April, is played by Sheree J. Wilson, a model who appeared in the 1985 CBS miniseries version of Jeffrey Archer's bestseller *Kane and Abel*. She also appeared in *Our Family Honor*, the 1985–86 series produced by Leonard Katzman. In *Honor*, a drama about the mob starring Eli Wallach and Ray Liotta, Wilson played mob wife Rita Danzig. After *Honor* was cancelled, Katzman "called me into his office," Wilson recalls. "I was told he wanted a meeting, and he told me, 'I am going back to *Dallas*, and I'd like you to join the cast. The show is a mess. They have ridiculous characters that have nothing to do with the core of the family, and it's too hard to follow. It's not *Dallas*. The only way to get it back is to make [Season 8] all a bad dream.'" Katzman went on to tell Wilson, "J.R. needs a nemesis—more than his typical mistress, but a real nemesis who is a thorn in his side." Katzman then told Wilson about April, the role he created for her, and she accepted the offer on the spot. Wilson "first played April like my character on *Our Family Honor*, a sassy little character, a spitfire. At that time in my life, everything off the set was smooth, and so I loved playing a bitch on wheels with a whip on *Dallas*! Then I could go out and be so sweet in my real life!" Katzman told a reporter that he found Wilson "a young lady with a wonderful sense of humor. It's a marvelous trait and you hardly ever see it." Duffy said Wilson "was a little tentative at first, but then she relaxed and began to have fun. Everyone wants to be on our show but some don't fit in. Sheree does." Ken Kercheval thought upon first seeing her, "God, she's cute. I hope she can act. . . . She can prank with the best of them." Not long after Wilson's debut as April, fan mail "cascaded" in. Wilson loved the show. "We don't work all the time and when we do, we're prepared," she said. "You know your lines and do your thing and then you can play and have a good time." Wilson went on to star in a third Leonard Katzman series, *Walker, Texas Ranger*, in which she played Assistant District Attorney Alex Cahill.

Trivia Weekly rating: number 12. *Miami Vice* was number 20. ★ While Mandy's Valentine ad outraged J.R., Katzman liked the poster well enough to hang it in his office at the Dallas hotel used by Lorimar during the on-location shoot. ★ Despite the friction between their characters, Steve Forrest and Howard Keel were old friends and played a lot of golf while Forrest was on the show. "We shot *Dallas* at Metro," Forrest says, "where I first went into the business when I got out of UCLA. Howard and I were filming on the stage next door to where he and I acted and where he took voice lessons."

229. "Territorial Imperative"

Written by David Paulsen; Directed by Michael Preece; Airdate: October 31, 1986
Guest Stars: Alice Hirson (Mavis); George O. Petrie (Harv); Hunter Von Leer (B. D. Calhoun); Derek McGrath (Oswald); Jim Haynie (Gordon); Shalane McCall (Charlie); Joshua Harris (Christopher); Debbie Rennard (Sly); Don Starr (Jordan)
Subject: J.R.'s mercenary.

Cast Notes Featured player Kerry Scott Knerr was the Property Master during Seasons 12 and 13. She also appeared in a minor role in Episode 203 in Season 8.

Trivia Weekly rating: number 13. *Miami Vice* was number 24. ★ This episode aired on Barbara Bel Geddes' birthday, an occasion that is recognized annually by her fans. According to Bel Geddes' granddaughter, Bel Geddes "loves that she still has fans and she loves that they still remember her. I told her about a birthday tribute to her on the *Ultimate Dallas* Web site. I said, 'Grandma, I wish you had a computer so you could see all of your fans wishing you a Happy Birthday.' And she got excited as I described it to her, and she said, 'Well, that's absolutely wonderful.' It made her day."

230. "Second Time Around"

Written by Calvin Clements Jr.; Directed by Leonard Katzman; Airdate: November 7, 1986
Guest Stars: Jim Haynie (Gordon); George O. Petrie (Harv); Hunter Von Leer (B. D. Calhoun); Derek McGrath (Oswald); Debbie Rennard (Sly); Omri Katz (John Ross); Shalane McCall (Charlie); Joshua Harris (Christopher)
Subject: Jenna's pregnancy.

Trivia Weekly rating: number 9. *Miami Vice* was number 23. ★ Jenna's pregnancy was easy to work into the storyline because Priscilla Presley was pregnant in real life by writer/director Marco Garibaldi. Said Presley, "It was a shock to everyone. . . . The character was supposed to be pregnant and it was a great opportunity to get pregnant." Jenna's pregnancy "came first . . . and it just so happened [that] I wanted a child so badly and so when I heard quite a few months before that they were thinking of Jenna getting pregnant, [I thought,] 'Okay, well, here's my opportunity.'" Steve Kanaly admired his costar for "work[ing] through a pregnancy on camera, [which she did by] wearing loose clothes and standing behind couches." ★ Despite Jamie's troubles with Cliff, as seen in this episode, Jenilee Harrison "cared about Ken [Kercheval], on and off the camera. It's easy to 'act' in those scenarios when it is 'straight from the cuff.'"

231. "Bells Are Ringing"

Written by Leah Markus; Directed by Michael Preece; Airdate: November 14, 1986
Guest Stars: Jim Haynie (Gordon); Hunter Von Leer (B. D. Calhoun); Laurence Haddon (Franklin); Joshua Harris (Christopher); Debbie Rennard (Sly); Don Starr (Jordan)
Subject: Pam and Bobby remarry.

Trivia Weekly rating: number 10. *Miami Vice* was number 28. ★ Said Priscilla Presley of J.R.'s efforts to come between Pam and Bobby, "[Jenna's] very aware of the manipulations J.R. uses—she's known his number since childhood. But J.R.'s always been on her side, she's never had to deal with his wrath the way Pam did." ★ Steve Forrest recalls that while filming this episode at "the Dallas Museum of Art, . . . we were right by a metallic sculpture. There was a lot of background noise, which there usually is on location, and it makes the scene difficult to do. I had most of the dialogue. We had a tough time with the scene, but once we finally got it, I was so elated, I walked over to that metallic sculpture and gave it a thump—a thump out of sheer exuberance that we got the scene. Well, the museum staff came down on me like a flood!" ★ Late on November 18, 1986, four days after this episode aired, Patrick Duffy's parents, Terence and Marie Duffy, were murdered by two teenagers at "The Lodge," the tavern they owned in Boulder, Montana. Duffy traveled to Boulder upon learning of the tragedy the following day. Production of *Dallas* shut down briefly on November 19, out of respect for Duffy, even though he was not scheduled to be on the set that day. Duffy, however, insisted that filming continue and shooting resumed that afternoon. Because the crew was ahead of its schedule, it was able to continue to shoot around Duffy during his absence. Duffy later recalled that, on the set of *Dallas*, "everything and everybody was just so supportive. And when I came back it was . . . the type of thing that when they're real good friends there's never a difficult moment. There was never, 'Oh, can we talk? Can we do this, that?' It was like we're all members of the same family. So they all went through it, to a certain degree, with me." On March 19, 1987, nineteen-year-old Kenneth Miller was convicted of felony charges resulting from the murders; nineteen-year-old Sean Wentz pleaded guilty to homicide on May 5, 1987. Recalled Duffy, "The good thing was the two boys who killed Mom and Dad were caught immediately. They were tried immediately. And they went to prison immediately. And the press pretty much just said, 'Well, that's the end of the story.' . . . People think that I (a) didn't have a good relationship with my parents or (b) was not affected by the deaths or . . . didn't care, or any variation of those themes. It has to do with . . . the Buddhist concept of what life is actually all about and the eternity of life. I am probably closer to them now in terms of my thought process because I chant for them every day. And so they're part of my morning and evening prayer."

232. "Who's Who at the Oil Baron's Ball"

Written by David Paulsen; Directed by Leonard Katzman; Airdate: November 21, 1986 Guest Stars: Morgan Woodward (Punk); Alice Hirson (Mavis); William Smithers (Jeremy); Derek McGuire (Oswald); J. A. Preston (Leo Daltrey); Jonathan Goldsmith (Bruce Harvey); John Zaremba (Harlan); James Ray (Paul Deacons); Shalane McCall (Charlie); Debbie Rennard (Sly); Fern Fitzgerald (Marilee) Subject: The Oil Baron's Ball.

Cast Notes   J. A. Preston played the military judge in the Tom Cruise–Jack Nicholson courtroom thriller *A Few Good Men*. ★ James Ray played Kevin Bacon's father in the 1988 John Hughes movie *She's Having a Baby*, in which *Dallas* cast members William Windom, Paul Gleason, and Bill Erwin also appear.

Trivia   Weekly rating: number 13. ★ Alice Hirson recalls that "for the ball scenes, we all looked so serious, but there we were all pinned up with clothespins and a bunch of safety pins and ribbons keeping it all together in the back!"

233. "Proof Positive"

Written by Calvin Clements Jr.; Directed by Michael Preece; Airdate: November 28, 1986 Guest Stars: Tom Bower (Mancuso); George O. Petrie (Harv); Jonathan Goldsmith (Bruce Harvey); Shalane McCall (Charlie); Debbie Rennard (Sly) Subject: Parmalee takes a polygraph.

Cast Notes Tom Bower played Dr. Curtis Willard on *The Waltons*. ★ Costar Jeff Kaake, who appears as Mandy's movie costar, played Chas on *Melrose Place*.

Trivia Weekly rating: number 7. *Miami Vice* was number 28. Excluding the season premiere and season-ending cliff-hanger, this was *Dallas*'s highest ranked episode of the season. Wrote TV critic Ed Bark the week after this episode aired, "ABC's *Dynasty* and NBC's *Miami Vice*, both top ten series at the end of last season, are television's big dippers through nine weeks of this season. . . . *Vice* is languishing in twentieth place and has been no match so far for CBS's *Dallas*. Like *Dynasty*, *Vice* also is down to a 17.4 rating. *Dallas* has slipped from sixth place last season to tenth so far this fall. But the show's 22.4 rating, against far more formidable competition, is slightly higher than last season's 21.9 average." ★ This episode provided Priscilla Presley and Victoria Principal with another confrontation scene, but their offscreen relationship was less complicated. Presley explains that she sees Principal "from time to time" and "like[s] her a lot." ★ Of all her *Dallas* directors, Jenilee Harrison "loved Michael Preece. He was a lovely, down to earth, and funny man, and one heck of a director. *Dallas* had a handful of their favorite directors, who visited often, and Michael was one of them. He worked with the actors in a subtle yet encouraging manner, which I thought made for the best weeks of work." ★ As this episode makes clear, Sheree J. Wilson's character initially played off J.R., Jack Ewing, and Cliff Barnes. Wilson "felt like the Black Widow, playing a femme fatale who picked off the characters one by one."

234. "Something Old, Something New"

Written by Leah Markus; Directed by Leonard Katzman; Airdate: December 5, 1986
Guest Stars: William Smithers (Wendell); Jim Haynie (Gordon); J. A. Preston (Daltrey); Hunter Von Leer (Calhoun); Jonathan Goldsmith (Bruce Harvey); Tom Fucello (Dave Culver); Shalane McCall (Charlie); Bruce Gray (Brian)
Subject: Miss Ellie visits with Parmalee.

Trivia Weekly rating: number 9. ★ Miss Ellie's carriage ride with Parmalee was filmed in the historic West End area of Dallas. Steve Forrest "had a lovely time" filming his love scenes with Barbara Bel Geddes. "It wasn't too hard to get sweet with Barbara," he says. "She had such a warm quality."

235. "Barbequed"

Written by David Paulsen; Directed by Michael Preece; Airdate: December 12, 1986
Guest Stars: Jim McMullan (Senator Andrew Dowling); Morgan Woodward (Punk); Alice Hirson (Mavis); William Smithers (Wendell); Derek McGrath (Valentine); James Ray (Paul Deacons); Tom Fucello (Dave Culver); Deborah Rennard (Sly); John Carter (Carl); Bruce Gray (Brian)
Subject: Parmalee leaves Dallas.

Cast Notes Jim McMullan played Dr. Terry McDaniel on *Ben Casey*.

Trivia Weekly rating: number 10. ★ This is the last episode of the season filmed in Texas. The crew began the shoot on July 1, 1986, and it lasted for eight weeks. Because of a directors' strike in 1987 and a writers' strike in 1988, the 1987 and 1988 summer location shoots were moved to the spring and fall of those years, respectively, and the *Dallas* company did not return to Texas to film after 1988 (except for the TV movies and the reunion special). As a result, the filming that took place in July and August of 1986 was the last of the series' nine consecutive summer shoots in Texas. ★ As for whether Leonard Katzman considered having Parmalee turn out to be Jock, Forrest felt Katzman "was going to wait and see how my character was received before he decided. . . . I had it in my mind that they did want me to join the cast permanently." Forrest, however, had to leave *Dallas* to film a *Gunsmoke* reunion movie, resurrecting the villainous character of Will Mannon, which he created in a 1965 episode that ended with Mannon going to jail. In the 1987 telemovie, *Gunsmoke: Return to Dodge*, Will Mannon had just been released from prison. Forrest recalls that Katzman "tried to get me to stay longer," but Forrest was already committed to *Gunsmoke*. ★ Like Parmalee, Jamie left town in this episode, although she was not killed off until several episodes later. Of her time on *Dallas*, Jenilee Harrison says, "Sure, I wish it would have lasted for the entire run, as how many actors get the opportunity to work on a hit show? . . . I also learned from the best. We had the best writers, the best actors, the best crew, the best location (home in Hollywood and in Dallas on Southfork) and we all had a lot of fun and got paid big bucks to do it." Harrison adds, "In summation, *Dallas* was a great gig for me." Dack Rambo's Jack Ewing also leaves Dallas as of this episode, although he returned later in Season 9.

236. "Fire Next Time"

Written by David Paulsen; Directed by Patrick Duffy; Airdate: December 19, 1986
Guest Stars: Jim McMullan (Senator Andrew Dowling); Morgan Woodward (Punk); William Smithers (Wendell); Laurence Haddon (Franklin); J. A. Preston (Daltrey); Shalane McCall (Charlie); Deborah Rennard (Sly); Paul Tulley; Omri Katz (John Ross); Joshua Harris (Christopher); Tom Fucello (Dave Culver)
Subject: J.R.'s mercenary.

Trivia Weekly rating: number 12.

237. "So Shall Ye Reap"

Written by Leonard Katzman; Directed by Jerry Jameson; Airdate: January 2, 1987
Guest Stars: Jim Haynie (Gordon); Glenn Corbett (Paul); William Smithers (Jeremy); Tom Bower (Mancuso); Hunter Von Leer (Calhoun); Deborah Rennard (Sly); Joshua Harris (Christopher); Don Starr (Jordan)
Subject: J.R. is stalked.

Cast Notes Judith Jordan, who had a featured role in this episode, played Miss Switzer on *The Beverly Hillbillies*.

Trivia Weekly rating: number 9.

238. "Tick Tock"

Written by Mitchell Wayne Katzman; Directed by Patrick Duffy; Airdate: January 9, 1987
Guest Stars: William Smithers (Jeremy); Jim McMullan (Andrew); J. A. Preston (Daltrey); Hunter Von Leer (Calhoun); Deborah Rennard (Sly); Shalane McCall (Charlie); Omri Katz (John Ross); Joshua Harris (Christopher)
Subject: J.R. is stalked.

Trivia Weekly rating: number 12.

239. "The Night Visitor"

Written by Calvin Clements Jr.; Directed by Larry Hagman; Airdate: January 23, 1987
Guest Stars: William Smithers (Jeremy); Glenn Corbett (Paul); Jim McMullan (Andrew); Hunter Von Leer (Calhoun); Shalane McCall (Charlie); Omri Katz (John Ross); Joshua Harris (Christopher); Clarence Felder; Mark Withers (Private Investigator); Michael Champion; Deborah Rennard (Sly); Tom Fucello (Dave)
Subject: Sue Ellen is kidnapped.

Trivia Weekly rating: number 12. ★ The day after this episode aired, the *Dallas Morning News* reported that Susan Howard was leaving *Dallas* at season's end to "take on other acting challenges." The *Associated Press*, however, reported a short time later that Howard was being let go because, as Leonard Katzman told her, "her character had run its course. Now that Donna and Ray Krebbs are no longer together, her connection to the Ewing family is severed and consequently [so is] her involvement in the plots." To make matters worse for *Dallas* fans, within days of this report, Victoria Principal announced that she, too, was leaving the show.

240. "Cat and Mouse"

Written by Leah Markus; Directed by Michael Preece; Airdate: January 30, 1987
Guest Stars: Jim McMullan (Andrews); William Smithers (Jeremy); Glenn Corbett (Paul); Hunter Von Leer (Calhoun); Shalane McCall (Charlie); Omri Katz (John Ross); Joshua Harris (Christopher); Deborah Rennard (Sly); Tom Fucello (Dave); Brenda Strong (Cliff's date)
Subject: Calhoun stalks J.R.

Trivia Weekly rating: number 11.

241. "High Noon for Calhoun"

Written by David Paulsen; Directed by David Paulsen; Airdate: February 6, 1987
Guest Stars: Jim McMullan (Senator Andrew Dowling); William Smithers (Jeremy); Charles Cyphers (Pogue); Hunter von Leer (Calhoun); Omri Katz (John Ross); Joshua Harris (Christopher); Debbie Rennard (Sly)
Subject: Calhoun's death.

Trivia Weekly rating: number 12. ★ Howard Keel's singing talents are on display briefly in this episode's scene in which he serenades Barbara Bel Geddes with

"Don't Get Around Much Anymore." While Keel agreed to sing to Bel Geddes to cheer up Miss Ellie (whose cold landed her in bed and ruined Clayton's first vacation since their honeymoon in Episodes 161–67), Keel on another occasion refused Phil Capice's request that Clayton serenade Ellie in bed, a protest of the Farlows' lack of a physical relationship.

242. "Olio"

Written by Leonard Katzman; Directed by Steve Kanaly; Airdate: February 13, 1987
Guest Stars: Jim McMullan (Senator Andrew Dowling); William Smithers (Jeremy); Derek McGrath (Oswald); J.A. Preston (Daltrey); Charles Cyphers (Pogue); Shalane McCall (Charlie); Omri Katz (John Ross); Joshua Harris (Christopher); Deborah Tranelli (Phyllis)
Subject: Jamie's death.

Trivia   Weekly rating: number 16. ★ This is the first of three episodes directed by Steve Kanaly. He directed one episode each in Seasons 9 through 11, the last of which was after Kanaly left the cast. ★ Says Jenilee Harrison about her character's untimely demise, "It was somewhat customary on *Dallas* that new characters would show up, and then after a few years, they would die off and new ones would come on. Dack, Deborah Shelton, . . . and myself were the new kids on the block [in Season 7] and we relatively all 'died' off around the same time. Oh, I would have loved to have stayed on *Dallas*. . . . [But] writers always need new plot twists, the element of surprise, in order that the audience does not get bored. . . . Thus, new characters come and go. I feel extremely lucky to have had 'my shot.'" ★ April Stevens's mother is referred to in this episode, and is finally seen during Season 12.

243. "Death in the Family"

Written by Mitchell Wayne Katzman; Directed by Michael Preece; Airdate: February 20, 1987
Guest Stars: William Smithers (Jeremy); Glenn Corbett (Paul); Derek McGrath (Oswald); Shalane McCall (Charlie); Omri Katz (John Ross); Joshua Harris (Christopher); Amy Yasbeck (Mary McCall); John Millford; Cheryl Anderson (Miss Gordon); Bill Cort (Lancaster)
Subject: Jamie's will.

Cast Notes   Amy Yasbeck went on to star as Casey Davenport on the sitcom *Wings*, and was married to *Three's Company* star John Ritter until his death in 2003. ★ Costar Judith Ledford played Carla on *The A-Team* in 1986. ★ Bill Cort returned to *Dallas* as Sawyer in Episode 283.

Trivia   Weekly rating: number 17. This is the first episode to drop out of the top fifteen since April, 1986. It tied Episode 244 as the season's lowest-ranked episode. ★ Composer Angela Morley received the first of two *Dallas*-related Emmy nominations for her work on "Death in the Family."

244. "Revenge of the Nerd"

Written by Calvin Clements Jr.; Directed by Linda Gray; Airdate: February 27, 1987
Guest Stars: Glenn Corbett (Paul); Derek McGrath (Oswald); J. A. Preston (Daltrey);
James A. Watson Jr.; Frederick Coffin (Alfred Simpson); Vernon Weddle (John Carter);
Bill Cort; Cheryl Anderson (Miss Gordon); Debbie Rennard (Sly); Tim Wise
Subject: Cliff's inheritance.

Cast Notes James A. Watson Jr. was a member of the repertory company on the
1972–74 ABC comedy anthology Love, American Style and played District Attorney Jim Barnes on NBC's Quincy, M.E.

Trivia Weekly rating: number 17. ★ This is the second episode directed by Linda
Gray, who noted, "One of my pet peeves is that on Dallas they don't move the
camera enough, so within the confines of what I had to do on my script, I wanted
the camera to move and I moved it, which I think is much more exciting. I told
the actors, 'I don't want you sitting at a desk and have to come in close for a tight
shot.' It bores me. I've looked at our show—as an audience, as an actress, as a camera, as a director. I moved the camera as a director . . . [which] makes the audience
feel like a participant. You feel like you're really there when the people are eating
breakfast."

245. "The Ten Percent Solution"

Written by Susan Howard Chrane; Directed by Michael Preece; Airdate: March 13, 1987
Guest Stars: Jim McMullan (Andrew); Karen Carlson (Nancy Scottfield); William
Smithers (Jeremy); J. A. Preston (Daltrey); Jonathan Goldsmith (Bruce); Jerry Hardin
(Judge Lowe); Frederick Coffin (Alfred); Shalane McCall (Charlie); Omri Katz (John
Ross); Joshua Harris (Christopher); Amy Yasbeck (Mary); Deborah Rennard (Sly); Gerry
Gibson (Banker); Tom Ligon; Fern Fitzgerald (Marilee)
Subject: J.R. frames Cliff.

Cast Notes Bea Silvern, who plays Andrew Dowling's maid, Patty, returned to
Dallas in Season 12 as Sarah Ewing. Silvern starred in Secrets of Midland Heights. ★
This is the second episode of Dallas written by Susan Howard. In her writing
credit for this episode, Howard uses her married name, Susan Howard Chrane.

Trivia Weekly rating: number 16, with an 18.6 rating, the show's lowest to date
for Season 9. ★ Shortly before this episode aired, the Dallas crew filmed Victoria
Principal's last scene on the show. Principal had already announced that she
would not be returning to the show for its tenth year, and said as her final scenes
approached, "I know my heart will be beating a little faster in those scenes that include everyone. It will be strange. It's been the only thing I've known for quite a
while. . . . I'm excited, but it's still a breathless thing, leaving the place that made
you, you know?"

246. "Some Good, Some Bad"

Written by Louella Lee Caraway; Directed by Larry Hagman; Airdate: March 20, 1987
Special Guest Star: Stephen Elliott (Scotty)
Guest Stars: Jim McMullan (Andrew); Karen Carlson (Nancy Scottfield); William
Smithers (Jeremy); Derek McGrath (Oswald); Jerry Hardin (Judge Lowe); Frederick
Coffin (Alfred); David Crowley (Detective); Shalane McCall (Charlie); Deborah Rennard
(Sly)
Subject: Jack returns.

Cast Notes Tim O'Connor, who has a featured role in this episode, played Elliott
Carson on *Peyton Place*. ★ David Crowley returned to *Dallas* as Pete Johnson in
Episode 338.

Trivia Weekly rating: number 13. ★ Stephen Elliott's final two episodes as defense attorney Scotty Demarest gave him the opportunity to work with Ken
Kercheval, who Elliott describes as a cast "favorite of everyone."

247. "War and Peace"

Written by Leah Markus; Directed by Dwight Adair; Airdate: April 3, 1987
Guest Stars: Jim McMullan (Andrew); George O. Petrie (Harv); Stephen Elliott (Scotty);
Karen Carlson (Nancy Scottfield); Derek McGrath (Oswald); Jonathan Goldsmith
(Bruce); Frederick Coffin (Alfred); Tom Fucello (Dave); Shalane McCall (Charlie); Lew
Brown (Harrigan); Liam Sullivan (Judge)
Subject: April's lawsuit.

Cast Notes This episode, the second of two consecutive episodes which include
Jack Ewing's brief return to Dallas, is Dack Rambo's final appearance on the show.
Rambo died of AIDS at his home in Delano, California, in 1994. He was fifty-
three. Hagman later wrote that Rambo "was openly bisexual and outspoken about
having AIDS. Dack accused me of getting rid of him because I was homophobic.
Until then, I liked Dack, but his charge was so far-fetched it wasn't worth arguing
about in the press."

Trivia Weekly rating: number 15. ★ Donna's move to Washington is not her first
time there. She and other Dallasites, including Jock, J.R., and Bobby (and Cliff in
the series finale's fantasy sequence) traveled to the nation's capital during the
show's run. In real life, *Dallas* counted among its loyal fans one of the ultimate
Washington insiders, Meg Greenfield, the late Pulitzer Prize–winning *Newsweek*
columnist and *Washington Post* editorial page editor. According to *Washington Post*
publisher Katherine Graham, Greenfield was "devoted" to *Dallas* and spent "many
hours" watching it.

248. "Ruthless People"

Written by Mitchell Wayne Katzman; Directed by Patrick Duffy; Airdate: April 10, 1987
Guest Stars: Jim McMullan (Andrew); George O. Petrie (Harv); William Smithers (Wendell); J. A. Preston (Daltrey); Karen Carlson (Nancy Scottfield); Frederick Coffin (Al-

fred); Derek McGrath (Oswald); Lew Brown (Harrigan); Deborah Rennard (Sly); Shalane McCall (Charlie); Omri Katz (John Ross); Joshua Harris (Christopher)
Subject: Wendell plots against Ewing Oil.

Cast Notes Costar Troy Evans played Sergeant Pepper on China Beach and Artie on Life Goes On.

Trivia Weekly rating: number 13. ★ According to Deborah Shelton's agent, Mandy was brought back to the show after CBS was "deluged with angry mail" when she was written out earlier in the season.

249. "The Dark at the End of the Tunnel"

Written by Calvin Clements Jr.; Directed by Larry Hagman; Airdate: May 1, 1987
Guest Stars: Jim McMullan (Andrew); George O. Petrie (Harv); William Smithers (Wendell); Derek McGrath (Oswald); Jonathan Goldsmith (Bruce); Tom Dahlgren; Deborah Rennard (Sly); Shalane McCall (Charlie); Vince Howard
Subject: Ewing Oil is investigated.

Cast Notes Larry Hagman's son, Preston, appears as April's masseuse. ★ Veteran TV actor Vince Howard played Lieutenant Joe Taylor on Barnaby Jones.

Trivia Weekly rating: number 8. This is the first time Dallas cracked the top ten in twelve weeks. ★ A new set showing the hallway at the top of the main staircase at Southfork is seen for the first time in this episode.

250. "Two Fifty"

Written by Leonard Katzman; Directed by Michael Preece; Airdate: May 8, 1987
Guest Stars: Macon McCalman (Gorman); Jim McMullan (Andrew); George O. Petrie (Harv); William Smithers (Wendell); Karen Carlson (Nancy); Frederick Coffin (Alfred Simpson); J. A. Preston (Daltrey); Derek McGrath (Oswald); F. J. O'Neil; Kenneth Tigar (Dr. Gordon); Deborah Rennard (Sly); Shalane McCall (Charlie); Tom Lacy
Subject: The federal government closes Ewing Oil.

Cast Notes F. J. O'Neil played Mr. Wainwright on Perfect Strangers from 1989 to 1992.

Trivia Weekly rating: number 11. ★ TV Guide writer Susan Littwin was allowed to visit the Dallas set during filming of this episode's hospital scene as part of a profile she was doing on Steve Kanaly. On February 25, 1987, Littwin visited a vacant and unheated Veterans Administration hospital in Los Angeles, which doubled as the hospital where Clayton was admitted. Littwin reported that Howard Keel, lying in a hospital bed, barked, "What was that —— line?" as he kept forgetting his dialogue. "Can I see those damn lyrics again?" he asked. Barbara Bel Geddes was less annoyed when her memory lapsed, saying, "I'm sorry. My line just dried up." Director Michael Preece complained that the extras tasked with walking past the hospital room door "look like they're walking through puddles." The assistant director tried to bring calm to the set by chastising the extras in the hallway, "I'm getting p—— off now, and I'm going to send some of you home." Kanaly discussed the scene with Priscilla Presley, who was due with her baby any day. Patrick Duffy arrived on the set in dark sunglasses and leaned against the wall, apparently bored with the shooting. Bel Geddes asked Presley, "Isn't this a wonderful time of life? I loved being pregnant!" Littwin found Kanaly to be the cast member who "never falters. He does his bit of business flawlessly, take after take." The actors made it through the scene after Keel asked for some silence so he could collect himself. "That was a nice rehearsal," Kanaly told his costars. Four days later, on March 1, Presley gave birth to a son, Navarone Garibaldi, in Southern California. ★ By the time this episode aired two months later, the cast and crew were in Dallas filming on-location scenes for Season 10. During the evening of May 7, 1987, the night before this episode aired, the hosts of CBS's *The Morning Show*, Mariette Hartley (who beat Barbara Bel Geddes for the Best Actress Emmy in 1979) and Rolland Smith, commemorated *Dallas's* 250th episode by filming a salute to the show to air on the following morning's broadcast. Appearing on the salute, which was filmed on the grounds of Duncan Acres, was most of the *Dallas* cast. Those interviewed by Hartley and Smith included Patrick Duffy, Linda Gray, Larry Hagman, Steve Kanaly, Howard Keel, Ken Kercheval, and Priscilla Presley. The segments were filmed after shooting for *Dallas* ended for the day and darkness fell, even though those involved gamely acted as if it were morning since that was when the show was going to air. The salute filled all two hours of *The Morning Show's* broadcast the next day. On Friday, May 8, as "Two Fifty" aired, Lorimar threw the cast and crew a private party at Duncan Acres to celebrate the milestone. The party featured a large white cake in the shape of Texas. On the cake was written in icing: "Dallas 250th Episode." The cast in attendance at the party included Barbara Bel Geddes, Patrick Duffy, Larry Hagman, Joshua Harris, Omri Katz, Howard Keel, and Sheree J. Wilson.

251. "Fall of the House of Ewing"

Written by David Paulsen; Directed by Leonard Katzman; Airdate: May 15, 1987
Guest Stars: Macon McCalman (Gorman); Jim McMullan (Andrew); George O. Petrie
(Harv); William Smithers (Wendell); Karen Carlson (Nancy); Jonathan Goldsmith
(Bruce); Kenneth Tigar (Dr. Gordon); Deborah Rennard (Sly); Mark Schneider; Omri
Katz (John Ross); Joshua Harris (Christopher); Frank McCarthy (Richard Taylor)
Subject: Pam's car crash.

Cast Notes This episode marks Victoria Principal's final appearance on a regular episode of *Dallas*. Patrick Duffy commented at the time of Principal's departure from the cast, "She's very open today, almost to the point of being uncomplicated. Since I began directing episodes, I've had a better chance to observe her and my appreciation has grown. The protective devices are gone now." ★ Principal's departure did not mean that Pam was not seen again on *Dallas* and that Principal was not seen again at Southfork. Pam was seen again in Episodes 252 through 256, though hidden by bandages, and in Episode 282, when she was played by Principal look-alike Margaret Michaels (and Principal reprised the role herself in a brief cameo appearance with Patrick Duffy on the Fox Network's *The Family Guy* on December 26, 1999). Principal was seen again at Southfork in 2004's *The Return to Southfork*. Principal returned to TV in 2000 on the Aaron Spelling soap *Titans* and has had much business success with her Principal Secret skin-care products. ★ This episode also marks Susan Howard's final appearance on *Dallas*, and she did not appear in either of the two TV movie sequels or in *The Return to Southfork*. After *Dallas*, Howard went on to follow in one-time presidential candidate Pat Robertson's footsteps as host of *The 700 Club*, a syndicated religious program. She lives in her native Texas, where she serves as a commissioner on the Texas Parks and Wildlife Commission and as a member of the NRA Board of Directors.

Trivia Weekly rating: number 3. This was *Dallas*'s highest-ranked episode of the season. ★ This episode features one of several show-down scenes between Larry Hagman and William Smithers. Smithers remembers one of the *Dallas* producers telling him that he made "Jeremy seem always unflappable in any situation." But Smithers has "'nerves' during performance like most actors, but . . . in [the] conflict scenes—most of which were with J.R.—once the camera started rolling, I felt as though I, as Jeremy, could pretty much hold my own with anyone in front of me." ★ On May 16, 1987, the day after this episode aired, CBS re-ran *The Early Years*, which had first aired fourteen months earlier. ★ One of Victoria Principal's favorite things about the Pam-Bobby relationship was that "it was one of the few TV marriages that wasn't sterile. Physical love was important to Pam and Bobby. Since the episode in which they first came together, things were torrid." ★ Perhaps the person most professionally disappointed by Principal's departure was Ken Kercheval, who told a reporter, "You know, 90 percent of the scenes I did, I did with Victoria. So I went to the producers and said, 'Who the hell am I gonna talk to next year?'" Kercheval feels he and Principal had "a very, very good relationship."

Above: The Cloyce Box Ranch in Frisco, Texas. The Box Ranch was seen as Southfork in the five-episode *Dallas* pilot that aired in April 1978. When *Dallas* returned as a regular series in September 1978, the producers chose Duncan Acres as the new Southfork. *Below: Back row:* Linda Gray, Brent Kanaly, pilot property master Gaston Gray, Steve Kanaly, Patrick Duffy, Tina Louise; *Front row:* Barbara Bel Geddes, Charlene Tilton, and Larry Hagman at the North Park Inn in Dallas, in front of the infamous "hippie van" that Hagman drove to Texas while filming the pilot in January and February 1978.

Above: Director of Photography Edward R. Plante and the camera crew during the filming of Episode 5, "Barbecue," at the Box Ranch in Frisco, Texas, February 1978. *Below:* The mansion at Southfork Ranch and Conference Center, Parker, Texas, formerly the Duncan Acres Ranch. The mansion was seen in Seasons 1 through 13 of *Dallas* (although only stock footage was used in Seasons 12 and 13), the TV movies *The Early Years, J.R. Returns,* and *War of the Ewings,* and in the cast reunion, *The Return to Southfork.*

The Southfork gate.

Above: The view from inside the Southfork gate. *Below:* The rear of the mansion, which includes the patio and pool where many scenes were filmed during the on-location shoots that occurred annually from the summers of 1978 through 1986 and in the spring of 1987 and the fall of 1988. The pool was covered up for *The Early Years,* which, like *J.R. Returns*, *War of the Ewings,* and *The Return to Southfork* also included scenes filmed on the patio. The pool and patio were recreated at the Culver City studio.

Above: The Southfork kitchen and doorway to the patio. While the kitchen was never seen on *Dallas,* many scenes filmed outside showed cast members going in and out of this doorway. *Below:* The Southfork patio.

Above: Steve Kanaly, Brent Kanaly, Larry Hagman, Barbara Bel Geddes, Charlene Tilton, Stefan Gierasch (who guest-starred in Episode 35, "The Dove Hunt"), Carlyn Duffy, Padraic Duffy, and Patrick Duffy in front of Folse House in Dallas in July 1979, en route to a Fourth of July party. Padraic Duffy appeared on four episodes of *Dallas* in 1990 and 1991, joining his brother Conor, Linda Gray's children Kehly Gray Sloane and Jeff Thrasher, and Larry Hagman's children Heidi Hagman and Preston Hagman as children of *Dallas* regulars who appeared on the show.

Steve Kanaly and Susan Howard (with a tour staffer) on the Mount of Olives east of Jerusalem during a March 1982 publicity tour in Israel, where *Dallas* was a top-rated show. Audrey Landers and Leigh McCloskey were the other cast members on the tour, which also included *Dallas* executive producer Philip Capice. The Israeli Tourism Ministry advertised the visit with the slogan, "Follow the Ewings to Israel," and Kanaly, Howard, Landers, and McCloskey filmed a promotional segment for the Ministry during their tour. The cast members met with Prime Minister Meachem Begin, who joked about J.R. that "Shakespeare could not have invented such a scoundrel."

Audrey Landers and Steve Kanaly in Jerusalem during the 1982 Israel tour.

Patrick Duffy,
Brent Kanaly,
and Steve
Kanaly in
1982.

Susan Howard and Steve
Kanaly outside a Texas
courthouse during the
on-location shoot in the
summer of 1982.

Steve Kanaly and Timothy Patrick Murphy at the Southfork horse barn, 1982.

Larry Hagman in Malibu, California, in 1983 (taken by
Steve Kanaly).

Maj Hagman, Brent Kanaly, and Larry Hagman at a ranch in Dallas at the 1984 Cattle Baron's Ball, a fundraiser for the American Cancer Society.

Howard and Judy Keel speak with Leonard Katzman at a 1984 Vietnam veterans awards luncheon in Dallas honoring Vietnam veteran Steve Kanaly.

Charlene Tilton and Howard Keel at the 1984 veterans' luncheon in
honor of Steve Kanaly.

Steve Kanaly and Victoria Principal at a 1986 celebrity tennis tournament at the La
Costa Resort and Spa in Carlsbad, California.

The living room at Southfork, seen in *War of the Ewings* and *The Return to Southfork*. A private home in the Turtle Creek section of Dallas was used for interior Southfork scenes from Seasons 1 through 11 and in *J.R. Returns*. A reproduction of that home was constructed at the MGM-Lorimar studios in Culver City, California, and was also used for interior Southfork scenes from Seasons 1 through 13.

Steve Kanaly and Patrick Duffy in Texas on the set of *War of the Ewings,* fall 1997.

Steve Kanaly and Patrick Duffy on a "catch and release" sturgeon fishing trip on the Frazier River, British Columbia, Canada, in 1999.

Above: The Southfork exhibit "*Dallas* Legends: Facts to Fantasy," which includes video clips from the series, a Ewing family tree showing J.R.'s fifty-six affairs, the stars' director's chairs from the set, and such props as the characters' sterling silver inlaid custom-made saddles, Lucy's wedding dress, J.R.'s cowboy hat, and the pearl-handled .38-caliber revolver that Kristin used to shoot J.R. *Below:* Jock's 1978 Lincoln Continental, with EWING 1 tags, seen in the Lincolns and Longhorns store at Southfork.

Part IV

THE FINAL YEARS

SEASON 10
1987–88—"The Lady Vanishes"

THE DALLAS CAST REUNION OF Season 9 was short-lived. Victoria Principal and Susan Howard announced in early 1987 that they would not return to the show for its tenth year, starting a parade of cast defections that would continue through the end of the series. Priscilla Presley announced midway through Season 10 that it would be her last, and Steve Kanaly's character was written out along with Presley's. Linda Gray left after Season 11. Charlene Tilton, who rejoined the cast late in Season 10, and Barbara Bel Geddes each made their second and final departure from the show after Season 12. In some instances, the departures were voluntary. In others, the decision was made by Lorimar, which announced in 1987 that it was making "dramatic cast reductions" on *Dallas*, *Knots Landing*, and *Falcon Crest* as part of the company's "budget overhaul." While Lorimar did not specify how the cuts would affect *Dallas*, it stated its intention to trim the *Knots* cast from seventeen to ten and the *Falcon Crest* cast from twelve to sixteen actors down to eight to ten actors. Lorimar felt that these actions would ease the shows' budgets and also make the storylines better and plots easier to follow. As Howard Lakin noted, at the time, *Dallas* "was the most expensive show on television. And it was only expensive because . . . Len [Katzman] took care of [the actors]."

One of the most significant of the cast changes was Principal's defection, since she was the show's "Juliet" and had only a half-season earlier remarried her "Romeo." To avoid having to perform a second resurrection in the event that Principal later returned to the show—"we would be very careful about killing anyone else," Leonard Katzman told a reporter at the time—the producers decided not to kill off Pam, and instead had her flee Dallas after being disfigured in a car accident seen in the last seconds of Season 9. This explained Pam's absence, kept the door open for her return, and freed Bobby up for new storylines in the meantime. Although two other actresses, one wrapped in bandages, would appear briefly as Pam in early Season 10 and the first episode of Season 11, Principal never returned to *Dallas* after the spring of 1987, and did not appear with her *Dallas* costars again until the 2004 cast reunion, *The Return to Southfork*. *Dallas* used several guest stars to off-set the dwindling number of original cast members. TV regular Jack Scalia, former *Peyton Place* star Leigh Taylor-Young, movie veteran Howard Duff, and TV actor Andrew Stevens all made extended appearances during Season 10.

Toward the end of Season 10, Priscilla Presley announced that she was leaving the show. Presley explains, "I originally was signed to do the show for one year and ended up on the show for five years. To be honest, I wasn't happy where the storyline was headed and felt the show was taking a turn in another direction. I had aspirations to do films and wanted to try other projects, which eventually led me to the *Naked Gun* series and . . . to producing films." Lorimar then announced that Steve Kanaly, whose character was now married to Presley's, was leaving the regular cast. Kanaly returned to the show for five episodes of Season 11, the series finale in Season 13, 1998's *War of the Ewings* and 2004's *The Return to South-fork*—and also directed a Season 11 episode—but Season 10 was his final year as a regular cast member.

According to Kanaly, he was let go after Season 10 as a part of the corporate downsizing that affected *Dallas* and other Lorimar productions. Kanaly learned his fate during a conversation with Leonard Katzman. The show had reduced its licensing fee and Lorimar had to find ways to compensate. As a result, Lorimar let go some of the more expensive cast members in favor of newer actors who commanded much more affordable salaries. Kanaly feels that Lorimar made a terrible mistake in not renewing the contracts of longtime audience favorites. In his opinion, the error cost the show its run. He was not happy about being let go, but he believed Katzman's justification and felt no animosity towards the company. The timing of his departure was ironic; Season 10 was Kanaly's favorite year on the show since "Ray matured, . . . [and] had a new romance, and his own ranch."

In its tenth year, *Dallas*, which now aired after CBS's *Beauty and the Beast*, finished the season ranked at number 22 with a rating of 16.8. It beat *Miami Vice* for the second year in a row, causing NBC to return *Miami Vice* to its original 10:00 timeslot in the 1988–89 season. *Dallas*'s other one-time ratings competitor, *Dynasty*, was no longer in TV's top twenty-five. *Dallas* also beat its ABC Friday night competition, *Max Headroom*. Despite its own ratings decline, *Dallas* remained CBS's fourth most popular show, behind the network's powerhouse Sunday night lineup of *60 Minutes*; *Murder, She Wrote*; and the *CBS Sunday Night Movie*. Larry Hagman and Steve Kanaly received personal laurels during Season 10, when each won *Soap Opera Digest* Awards presented at a ceremony at the Aquarius Theater in Hollywood in January, 1988. Hagman was named Outstanding Prime Time Villain (he previously won the same award in 1984, 1985, and 1986, and he won it again in 1989; he also won a second trophy in 1986 for Outstanding Prime Time Lead Actor) and Kanaly won the award for Outstanding Prime Time Supporting Actor (an award he also won in 1984 and 1985).

SEASON 10 EPISODE GUIDE

Regular Cast
Starring:
Barbara Bel Geddes as Miss Ellie
Patrick Duffy as Bobby
Linda Gray as Sue Ellen
Larry Hagman as J.R.
Steve Kanaly as Ray
Howard Keel as Clayton
Ken Kercheval as Cliff
Priscilla Beaulieu Presley as Jenna
Also Starring:
Morgan Brittany as Katherine
Karen Kopins as Kay
Bert Remsen as Harrison "Dandy" Dandridge
Jack Scalia as Nicholas Pearce
Andrew Stevens as Casey Denault
Leigh Taylor-Young as Kimberly Cryder
Charlene Tilton as Lucy
Sheree J. Wilson as April

Technical Credits
Supervising Producer: Arthur Bernard Lewis
Producer: David Paulsen
Executive Producer: Leonard Katzman
Associate Producer: Cliff Fenneman
Story Consultant: Leah Markus
Story Editor: Mitchell Wayne Katzman
Music: Jerrold Immel, John Parker, Richard Lewis Warren, Angela Morley

Unit Production Manager: Wayne A. Farlow
First Assistant Directors: Frank W. Katzman, Fred Stromsoe, Richard R. Johnson
Second Assistant Directors: Richard R. Johnson, Gene La Due, Joe Adamson
Director of Photography: Robert Caramico, A.S.C.
Art Director: David K. Marshall
Editors: Fred W. Berger, A.C.E., Ed Brennan, John Arthur Davies
Executive in Charge of Casting: Barbara Miller
Casting: Irene Mariano, C.S.A.
Set Decorator: Chuck Rutherford
Property Master: John Rettino
Costumers: Jack Bear, Nancy Renard
Makeup: Joe Hailey, Ralph Gulko
Hair Stylists: Generio Gugliemotto, Lola "Skip" McNalley
Location Casting: Rody Kent
Production Sound Mixer: Robert Sheridan
Sound Manager: Doug Grindstaff
Supervising Sound Editor: Thomas Gillis Burke
Music Supervisor: Richard Berres
Music Editor: Patricia Peck
Main Title Design: Wayne Fitzgerald
Executive Production Supervisor: Edward O. Denault

252. & 253. "After the Fall" (Parts One and Two)
Written by Arthur Bernard Lewis (Part One), David Paulsen (Part Two); Directed by Leonard Katzman (Part One), Michael Preece (Part Two); Airdate: September 25, 1987
Special Guest Star: Morgan Brittany (Katherine)
Guest Stars: John Calvin (Wilson Cryder); Shalane McCall (Charlie); Omri Katz (John Ross); Joshua Harris (Christopher); Deborah Rennard (Sly); Don Starr (Jordan); Fern Fitzgerald (Marilee); Derek McGrath (Oswald); Tim Donoghue (Ralph Combes)
Subject: Pam is hospitalized.

Cast Notes Episode 253 marks Morgan Brittany's return to *Dallas* for the first time since her character apparently died with Bobby in Episode 191. But Katherine's death, like Bobby's, was part of Pam's dream, and after Patrick Duffy agreed to re-turn to *Dallas* at the end of Season 8, Leonard Katzman sought to bring Morgan Brittany back on the show as well. "When Lenny called me a year [after Bobby and Katherine died] and asked me to come back I was flabbergasted!" recalls Brit-tany. Brittany, however, had been content with the way her character was closed out on the show, and liked being at home with her newborn daughter. "I knew that this was a great ending for my character and I was happy with the fact that I could stay at home and be with my baby. . . . I had moved on by that time and had my sights set on other things. " Yet, when Katzman called Brittany about appear-ing in Season 10, Brittany "agreed to help out the storyline. He told me that Vic-toria wanted to leave and the only character to get rid of her was Katherine, so I agreed to do it." Brittany's return to the show, however, was for only two episodes because Brittany "was working on a lot of other things and really couldn't sign on for any length of time." ★ This episode marks Jack Scalia's *Dallas* debut. Says Linda Gray about Scalia, "I love Jack. I thought he was sexy and adorable. And women loved him." ★ Burt Remsen was a veteran TV character actor who once appeared opposite Mae West on Broadway. He found *Dallas* "terrific! I like TV se-ries work. I just love doing a character I can play with and develop over a period of time." Ken Kercheval suggested that Remsen stay in the storyline as "an older sidekick for Cliff." Kercheval had worked with Remsen years earlier, and found him "a delightful man and we had a lot of fun doing that storyline." Remsen died on April 22, 1999. ★ Several early Season 10 episodes include Pam, although she is covered in bandages as a result of her car accident. Patrick Duffy cannot recall who "was under the wraps," but Morgan Brittany believes that Pam was played in these episodes by "a local girl from Texas who never got any credit." In addition to this uncredited actress, three other people played the role of Pam: Victoria Princi-pal in the pilot and Seasons 1 through 9; Margaret Michaels in Episode 282 in Season 11; and Andrea Wauters in *Dallas: The Early Years*.

Trivia Weekly rating: number 26, with a 16.9 rating. This two-hour episode was *Dallas*'s lowest-ranked season premiere since its first season and the first episode that failed to crack the top 25 since 1979. Nevertheless, *Dallas* still outperformed *Miami Vice*, which came in 33rd for the week. *Dynasty* finished at number 29. ★ In syndication, Part One was renamed "Ewing Rise" and Part Two was renamed "Digger Redux." ★ Morgan Brittany felt she "brought [a desperate vulnerability] to Katherine and towards the end, when she finally went over the edge, you actu-ally felt sorry for her." ★ This episode's scene between Bobby and April is an ex-ample of the transformation of April's character that Sheree J. Wilson describes as going "from the nemesis to Julie Andrews!" ★ When Leonard Katzman filmed Part One of this episode, he filmed all scenes except those that gave clues to the resolution of Pam's Season 9 finale car crash. In a bid to maintain plot secrecy, those scenes were filmed later and edited into the episode prior to airtime. ★ This episode, unlike the season premieres for Seasons 1 through 9, was not filmed during the summer. As early as January of 1987, the producers of *Dallas* contemplated moving the summer location shoot for Season 10 to March in case the Directors Guild of America followed through on its threat to strike on July 1, 1987. By March, Lorimar made the decision official, and canceled the spring hiatus to begin filming the first twelve episodes of Season 10. The producers of *Knots Landing*, *Falcon Crest*, and *The Equalizer* made similar schedule adjustments. As a result, the cast and crew of *Dallas* traveled to Texas in March soon after completing filming for Season 9. The on-location shoot was scheduled to continue through June 5, roughly three weeks before the threatened strike date. ★ During the shoot in Dallas, Larry Hagman was honored as the 1987 Communicator of the Year by the Dallas Communications Council. On May 30, 1987, the Council held a gala awards dinner in Hagman's honor at the Fairmont Hotel, which was seen and mentioned on *Dallas*. Among the eight hundred guests in attendance were Barbara Bel Geddes, Linda Gray, Leonard Katzman, Ken Kercheval, Mary Martin, Jack Scalia, Amy Stock, Leigh Taylor-Young, Sheree J. Wilson and Hagman's two-year-old granddaughter, Mary Noel, and her parents, Preston and Starla. Master of Ceremonies for the event was Patrick Duffy, who told the crowd, "We're here to honor Larry and his work. . . . Larry's more than a friend. He's someone who is equal to or better than a brother." ★ As of this episode, the thirty-second episode introduction was replaced with a thirty-second summary of the previous episode.

254. "The Son Also Rises"

Written by Leah Markus; Directed by Leonard Katzman; Airdate: October 2, 1987
Guest Stars: John Calvin (Wilson Cryder); Shalane McCall (Charlie); Omri Katz (John Ross); Joshua Harris (Christopher); Deborah Rennard (Sly)
Subject: Christopher visits Pam.

Cast Notes This episode marks Morgan Brittany's last appearance on *Dallas*. Says Brittany, "It was a great experience and I wouldn't trade it for anything." ★ Andrew Stevens, the son of movie star Stella Stevens, appeared on the TV soap *Emerald Point N.A.S.* Not long after joining the cast of *Dallas*, Stevens told a reporter, "I'm having a lot of fun working with Larry Hagman. He knows how to play scenes with twists and under-currents. . . . When *Dallas* came up, I hadn't yet left [the play *Bouncers*]. But I decided the contribution to my artistic self had depleted my savings. . . . Here I am walking into a top-ten show with a great role I'm having fun doing."

Trivia Weekly rating: number 24. ★ Exteriors for Bobby's new office were filmed at Fountain Place, located at 1445 Ross Avenue in Dallas. ★ Casey Denault has the same last name as Edward O. Denault, who was the executive production supervisor of *Dallas* from Seasons 1 through 10. ★ Around the time this episode aired, Victoria Principal told an interviewer, "I can't imagine any circumstances that would take me back [to *Dallas*]. I was very ready to leave. Perhaps in the future I'll get to where there's a sadness and longing for the people who are there, but come back? No. . . . I used *Dallas* as a learning ground. I took chances there, but it was like taking chances with a safety net. Now I don't have a safety net. . . . It's scary, but it's exciting." A short time later, Linda Gray reflected on Principal's departure from the show, saying, "She wanted to go, and I respect what she wanted to do. In a family such as ours there is always a void when one leaves, just as there would be in any normal family. But Victoria is doing very well, and I'm glad for her." Patrick Duffy recently recalled, "Once Victoria left *Dallas* there were several times when for PR reasons they asked if we all could get together for something and she would decline. I believe she wanted to concentrate on her other business interests and movies and maybe figured being related back to *Dallas* might hinder that. She and I did do a [December 1999] episode of a cartoon [*The Family Guy*] . . . and had a fantastic time doing it. So I know it is not a feeling of negativity that exclude[d] her."

255. "Gone With the Wind"

Written by Mitchell Wayne Katzman; Directed by Michael Preece; Airdate: October 9, 1987
Guest Stars: Kenneth Tigar (Dr. Gordon); Shalane McCall (Charlie); Don Starr (Jordan);
Fern Fitzgerald (Marilee)
Subject: Pam is missing.

Trivia   Weekly rating: number 6. This is *Dallas*'s highest-ranked Season 10 episode, and the only one of the season to make the top ten. Said Linda Gray after seeing these ratings, "After ten years on the air, that is something! And Sue Ellen is getting stronger, richer, and more powerful every day." ★ While Victoria Principal's departure from the show initially made Ken Kercheval concerned about his character's future, Kercheval's role actually increased in Season 10. In an interview he gave while filming the first episodes of the 1987–88 season, Kercheval agreed that Cliff could be "one-dimensional," but still maintained that Cliff's resilience proved that he was not a "loser." Kercheval conceded that he was "in a position of having to like Cliff. I have to. If I didn't, you would see that. But I admit the justification for some of his behavior sometimes baffles me. I look at scripts sometimes and I say, . . . 'He's not gonna do that!' . . . I never take for granted that I'm a very lucky man. There aren't many people who get the opportunity to make the kind of money we make in our position."

256. "The Lady Vanishes"

Written by Leonard Katzman; Directed by Leonard Katzman; Airdate: October 16, 1987
Guest Stars: Robert Colbert (Parker Ellison); Thomas Ryan (Tom Marta); Stephanie
Blackmore (Serena); Deborah Rennard (Sly)
Subject: Pam leaves Dallas.

Cast Notes   Robert Colbert, who plays Parker Ellison, appeared as James Garner's brother Brent in *Maverick*.

Trivia   Weekly rating: number 23. ★ With its 256th episode, *Dallas* knocked *The*

Love Boat from third place on the list of TV's longest running hour-long series. *Dallas* bumped *Bonanza* from the number-two spot when *Dallas*'s 319th episode aired on December 15, 1989. Despite continuing for 357 episodes, *Dallas* never reached the number-one spot; that is still held by *Gunsmoke*, which ran for 402 episodes. While *Knots Landing* outlasted its parent show by one season (*Knots* aired for fourteen seasons to *Dallas*'s thirteen), there were only 344 episodes of *Knots*, thirteen fewer than *Dallas*'s 357 episodes. ★ A scene for this episode was filmed in The Palm restaurant, located at 1321 Commerce Street in Dallas. On-location filming was also done at The Palm for several Season 11 episodes, and scenes for both *Dallas* TV movie sequels were filmed there. The *Dallas* crew filmed at The Palm because it was allowed to do so for free. ★ Shortly before this episode aired, Colonia Inc. launched a men's cologne called "Dallas," an "herbal woodsy, mossy blend" inspired by the show. To mark the occasion, Colonia threw a party at the Cadillac Bar in Dallas. Attendees included Patrick Duffy and Leigh Taylor-Young, who made her debut as J.R.'s new mistress four episodes after "The Lady Vanishes." Taylor-Young heard the cologne was "handsome and full-bodied," and joked that she wished J.R. would use it. Three years earlier, Charles of the Ritz introduced a *Dynasty*-based perfume called "Krystle Forever," and it introduced a "Carrington" men's cologne one year later.

257. "Tough Love"

Written by Arthur Bernard Lewis; Directed by Michael Preece; Airdate: October 23, 1987
Guest Stars: John Calvin (Cryder); Shalane McCall (Charlie); Omri Katz (John Ross);
Joshua Harris (Christopher); Stephanie Blackmore (Serena); Fern Fitzgerald (Marilee);
Amy Stock (Lisa Alden)
Subject: Bobby mourns.

Cast Notes Future *Dallas* regular Kimberly Foster, who played April's sister Michelle in Seasons 12 and 13, appears in this episode as Nicholas's lover. Foster also appeared on *Hotel, Knight Rider, thirtysomething,* and *Paper Dolls.* ★ Amy Stock was discovered on *Star Search*, a 1980s syndicated talent show hosted by Ed McMahon.

Trivia Weekly rating: number 16. ★ Sheree J. Wilson was happy to be back for a second season on *Dallas*. Initially, her Season 9 contract "was for only six months, and there were too many peripheral characters, so they were getting rid of a lot of people. But Larry and Leonard decided that they liked me, and we all got along so well. It was just like I stepped into this exciting family and they embraced me completely. I was at Larry's house every weekend, and we all even vacationed together. But I knew if I was staying that I could not be J.R.'s mistress or a bad girl forever. . . . The question was: who was I going to pair up with? Not J.R. or Cliff, and without Pam, Bobby was the natural choice." ★ The Galleria is a mall located at 13344 Noel Street in Dallas.

258. "Last Tango in Dallas"

Written by David Paulsen; Directed by Jerry Jameson; Airdate: October 30, 1987
Guest Stars: Morgan Woodward (Punk); Alice Hirson (Mavis); Robert Colbert (Parker El-
lison); Shalane McCall (Charlie); Joshua Harris (Christopher); Deborah Rennard (Sly);
Stephanie Blackmore (Serena); Amy Stock (Lisa Alden)
Subject: The Oil Baron's Ball.

Trivia Weekly rating: number 19. ★ While Priscilla Presley was fond of Steve Kanaly, whose character becomes Jenna's lover in this episode, Presley felt that the *Dallas* writers should have kept Jenna with Bobby. "Steve Kanaly," says Presley, "was very laid back, cowboy-ish and very much a family man. I enjoyed working with him. However, working with Patrick was truly where this storyline should have remained." ★ Jack Scalia, like Nicholas Pearce, who is seen jogging with April in this episode, liked to run to stay in shape. Scalia ran in several marathons and also competed in thirty triathlons. He liked being on *Dallas* because its large ensemble cast provided him with days off on which he could train. Scalia, who is also a former minor league baseball pitcher, found that "as an actor, idle time gives me a lot of frenetic energy, and I'm finding real joy in running."

259. "The Mummy's Revenge"

Written by Mitchell Wayne Katzman; Directed by Michael Preece; Airdate: November 6,
1987
Guest Stars: Sharon Wyatt (Marvelle Reed); Kenneth Tigar (Dr. Gordon); Fern Fitzgerald
(Marilee); Shalane McCall (Charlie); Omri Katz (John Ross); Joshua Harris (Christo-
pher); Amy Stock (Lisa Alden)
Subject: Pam divorces Bobby.

Cast Notes Sharon Wyatt played Tiffany on the ABC daytime soap opera *General Hospital*.

Trivia Weekly rating: number 20.

260. "Hustling"

Written by Leah Markus; Directed by Jerry Jameson; Airdate: November 13, 1987
Special Guest Star: Leigh Taylor-Young (Kimberly Cryder)
Guest Stars: Fern Fitzgerald (Marilee); George O. Petrie (Harv); John Calvin (Cryder);
Elaine Wilkes (Mary Lou Lassiter); Shalane McCall (Charlie); Omri Katz (John Ross);
Joshua Harris (Christopher); Deborah Rennard (Sly); Amy Stock (Lisa Alden)
Subject: J.R. plots his comeback.

Cast Notes Leigh Taylor-Young, the one-time wife of movie actor Ryan O'Neal, appeared in movies in the late 1960s and early 1970s and on TV in *Peyton Place*. She left acting to raise her family, and returned in such movies as 1985's *Jagged Edge*. In 1994, she won an Emmy Award for Outstanding Supporting Actress in a Drama Series for her role as Rachel Harris on *Picket Fences*. Taylor-Young liked working on *Dallas* because she was able to provide input in the development of her character. "The bottom line on [a nighttime soap opera]," she said, "is that you are really hired to express [the producer's] vision, and you just hope you get an opportunity to contribute. Fortunately, on a show like *Dallas*, they're not closed to ideas." Taylor-Young also enjoyed the opportunity to "change jobs and play new characters and meet new people." She reprised the role of Kimberly Cryder for one episode in Season 11.

Trivia Weekly rating: number 20. ★ Angela Morley received an Emmy nomination for Outstanding Achievement in Music Composition for a Series (Dramatic Underscore) for this episode. This was her second nomination for *Dallas* as well as the show's twenty-third and final Emmy nomination.

261. "Bedtime Story"

Written by Leonard Katzman; Directed by Michael Preece; Airdate: November 20, 1987
Special Guest Star: Leigh Taylor-Young (Kimberly Cryder)
Guest Stars: Irena Ferris (Tammy Miller Kent); Richard Beymer (Jeff Larkin); Paul Lieber (Larry Doyle); Shalane McCall (Charlie); Joshua Harris (Christopher); Bill Morey (Leo Wakefield); Don Starr (Jordan Lee); Amy Stock (Lisa Alden)
Subject: Bobby dates Tammy.

Trivia Weekly rating: number 26 with a 15.7 rating. This was *Dallas*'s first ratings loss to *Miami Vice* in Season 10. *Miami Vice*, which aired a special episode in which Don Johnson's character got married to guest star and Scottish pop singer Sheena Easton, earned a 16.8 and 24th place finish for the week.

262. "Lovers and Other Liars"

Written by Arthur Bernard Lewis; Directed by Jerry Jameson; Airdate: November 27, 1987
Special Guest Star: Leigh Taylor-Young (Kimberly Cryder)
Guest Stars: Shalane McCall (Charlie); Omri Katz (John Ross); Joshua Harris (Christopher); Deborah Rennard (Sly); Amy Stock (Lisa Alden)
Subject: Sue Ellen and J.R. court others.

Trivia Weekly rating: number 24. ★ April's and Bobby's penchant for oversized greeting cards is seen in this episode and in Episode 265. According to Sheree J. Wilson, these cards were not part of the actors' ad-libbing, but were part of the scripts written by Arthur Bernard Lewis and Mitchell Wayne Katzman, respectively.

263. "Brothers and Sons"

Written by David Paulsen; Directed by Michael Preece; Airdate: December 4, 1987
Special Guest Star: Leigh Taylor-Young (Kimberly Cryder)
Guest Stars: Paul Lieber (Doyle); Elaine Wilkes (Mary Lou Lassiter); D. David Morin (Mr. Hawk); Shalane McCall (Charlie); Omri Katz (John Ross); Joshua Harris (Christopher); Deborah Rennard (Sly); Don Starr (Jordan); Amy Stock (Lisa Alden)
Subject: Ray and Jenna marry.

Cast Notes Jack Scalia and Leigh Taylor-Young costarred on the Rock Hudson series *The Devlin Connection*. ★ Kehly Gray and Jeff Thrasher, the then twenty-one-year-old daughter and twenty-three-year-old son of Linda Gray and her former husband Ed Thrasher, appear in minor roles in this episode. Kehly, initially using her mother's last name and later using her married name, played Sue Ellen's secretary, Kelly, in Seasons 10 and 11. Gray thought the role was "a great way to break her [daughter] in" to show business. Kehly was Miss Golden Globe during the 1987 Golden Globes ceremony. Jeff was interested in cinematography, so his mother got him a job on the set.

Trivia Weekly rating: number 19. ★ This is the last Season 10 episode filmed on location in Texas.

264. "Brother, Can You Spare a Child?"

Written by Leah Markus; Directed by Patrick Duffy; Airdate: December 11, 1987
Guest Stars: Morgan Woodward (Punk); Alice Hirson (Mavis); John Calvin (Cryder);
Glenn Corbett (Paul); Elaine Wilkes (Mary Lou Lassiter); Jack Collins (Slater); Shalane
McCall (Charlie); Joshua Harris (Christopher); Amy Stock (Lisa)
Subject: Christopher's aunt.

Cast Notes Leigh Taylor-Young's credit is moved to the beginning of the show with this episode. ★ Future superstar Brad Pitt costars as Randy, a role he played in three other Season 10 episodes.

Trivia Weekly rating: number 26. ★ This was Morgan Woodward's last appearance on *Dallas*. Woodward "knew when they asked me for two episodes [for Season 10] that it would be my farewell performances on *Dallas*. The ratings were down and they were getting rid of people all the time. A lot of the family members were gone. I was also doing *Days of Our Lives*." But Woodward "loved working with all of [the *Dallas* cast]. It was a great experience. There was not a bad apple in the bunch. It was a delightful seven years." Woodward's *Dallas* leading lady, Alice Hirson, says, "Morgan was a dream, a swell guy." ★ Ken Kercheval notes that his scene with Barbara Bel Geddes on a park bench, where their characters discuss the Barnes-Ewing feud, "was the only real scene we ever had together." Bel Geddes used to tell Kercheval, "Oh, Kenny, if you were only three or fours years older and I were three or four years younger!" ★ Priscilla Presley enjoyed episodes, such as this one, that were directed by *Dallas* cast members, although she found that, by the time she joined the cast in Season 6, the production of the show was almost routine. "When I came to *Dallas*, the show pretty much ran itself. The cameraman would set up most of the scenes." Nevertheless, Presley found most of the *Dallas* directors "wonderful and very helpful."

265. "Daddy's Little Darling"

Written by Mitchell Wayne Katzman; Directed by Larry Hagman; Airdate: December 18, 1987

Special Guest Star: John Anderson (Dr. Styles)
Guest Stars: Glenn Corbett (Paul); Alice Hirson (Mavis); Elaine Wilkes (Mary Lou Lassiter); John Howard Swain (Arlo Howard); B. J. Ward (Krauser); Shalane McCall (Charlie); Omri Katz (John Ross); Joshua Harris (Christopher); Amy Stock (Lisa)
Subject: J.R.'s takeover attempt.

Cast Notes Dr. Styles is played by John Anderson, who appeared as McIntire in Episodes 126 and 127.

Trivia Weekly rating: number 31. This is the first episode to fall out of the top thirty since 1979, and was Dallas's lowest-ranked episode of the season. ★ Halfway into her second year as April, Sheree J. Wilson knew that she "was accepted on Dallas . . . during a kissing scene with Bobby. Larry Hagman was directing. We clinched and the kiss went on and on and instead of calling, 'Cut,' Larry just walked away. The crew began shuffling around. Finally somebody yelled, 'Isn't anybody ever going to stop this?' When the big guys play jokes on you, you're home free." Wilson also got along well with her female costars. "Priscilla seems very polite. And who wouldn't love Linda Gray? And I certainly think Victoria was very brave to leave the show the way she did."

266. "It's Me Again"

Written by Leonard Katzman; Directed by Leonard Katzman; Airdate: January 8, 1988
Special Guest Star: Annabel Schofield (Laurel Ellis)
Guest Stars: John Calvin (Cryder); Elaine Wilkes (Mary Lou Lassiter); John Howard Swain (Arlo Howard); B.J. Ward (Krauser); Shalane McCall (Charlie); Omri Katz (John Ross); Joshua Harris (Christopher); Deborah Rennard (Sly); Charles Tyner (Bovay); Charles Grant (David Shulton); Amy Stock (Lisa)
Subject: J.R.'s and Sue Ellen's marital problems.

Cast Notes Charles Tyner, who plays Farmer Bovay, is a veteran character actor who appeared on TV's Little House on the Prairie spin-off, Father Murphy. He also played Merle in the 1977 Disney musical Pete's Dragon, which featured several other Dallas actors, including Jane Kean, Jack Collins, and Al Checco. ★ Annabel Schofield was the first foreign actress to join Dallas as a regular.

Trivia Weekly rating: number 20. ★ This was another episode both written and directed by Leonard Katzman, who Sheree J. Wilson says "was the show." Wilson adds, "With Lenny back [in Season 9], the show came back. Lenny was Dad. He created it from his own personal experiences. He had these characters in his mind. I remember one episode where he brought in an outside writer, to give him a shot. The script was terrible! And Linda and Larry went to Leonard and said, 'We can't shoot this! How can we let this pass?' And Leonard looked at it and said, 'Go back to your trailers for some R&R and I'll see you in an hour.' He sat down at his typewriter and cranked it out. He fixed the script and they shot it one to two hours later."

267. "Marriage on the Rocks"

Written by Arthur Bernard Lewis; Directed by Larry Hagman; Airdate: January 15, 1988
Special Guest Star: Annabel Schofield (Laurel Ellis)
Guest Stars: Alice Hirson (Mavis); Don Hood (Vaughn); Shalane McCall (Charlie); Omri Katz (John Ross); Joshua Harris (Christopher); Deborah Rennard (Sly); Amy Stock (Lisa)
Subject: J.R.'s and Sue Ellen's marital problems.

Trivia Weekly rating: number 25.

268. "Anniversary Waltz"

Written by David Paulsen; Directed by David Paulsen; Airdate: January 22, 1988
Special Guest Stars: John Anderson (Dr. Styles); Annabel Schofield (Laurel Ellis)
Guest Stars: Alice Hirson (Mavis); Derek McGrath (Oswald Valentine); Paul Lieber (Larry Doyle); Deborah Rennard (Sly); Tom Fucello (Dave Culver); Charles Grant (David Shulton); Shalane McCall (Charlie); Omri Katz (John Ross); Joshua Harris (Christopher); Amy Stock (Lisa)
Subject: Miss Ellie's and Clayton's anniversary.

Trivia Weekly rating: number 21. ★ David Paulsen wrote and directed this episode, which featured a guest appearance by Alice Hirson. Hirson had Paulsen to dinner during *Dallas*'s run, and Paulsen told her, "'I love this house.' And," Hirson recalls, "I told him there was one for sale across the street and now he's my neighbor." ★ Priscilla Presley announced her departure from *Dallas* the week after this episode aired. Presley decided to leave the show to spend more time with her newborn son. "I really wanted to be with him," she said, "and felt too guilty. I mean, I was having him come to the set. I was nursing him on the set." Presley first considered leaving *Dallas* a few seasons earlier, but after she and Hagman had lunch and discussed how Duffy had regretted leaving the show, Presley decided to stay.

269. "Brotherly Love"

Written by Leah Markus; Directed by Linda Gray; Airdate: February 5, 1988
Special Guest Star: Annabel Schofield (Laurel Ellis)
Guest Stars: Alice Hirson (Mavis); Paul Lieber (Larry Doyle); Shalane McCall (Charlie); Omri Katz (John Ross); Joshua Harris (Christopher); Deborah Rennard (Sly); Bill Morey (Leo Wakefield); Tom Fucello (Dave Culver); Charles Grant (David Shulton); Amy Stock (Lisa)
Subject: J.R. blackmails April.

Trivia Weekly rating: number 15.

270. "The Best Laid Plans"

Written by Mitchell Wayne Katzman; Directed by Patrick Duffy; Airdate: February 12, 1988
Special Guest Star: Annabel Schofield (Laurel Ellis)
Guest Stars: Alice Hirson (Mavis); Mark Lindsay Chapman (Brett Lomax); Glenn Corbett

(Paul Morgan); Tom Fucello (Dave Culver); Don Starr (Jordan Lee); Shalane McCall (Charlie); Omri Katz (John Ross); Joshua Harris (Christopher); Deborah Rennard (Sly); Amy Stock (Lisa)
Subject: J.R. plots against Sue Ellen.

Cast Notes Mark Lindsay Chapman played Charley St. John on *Falcon Crest* and appeared as a crew member in James Cameron's Oscar-winning epic *Titanic*.

Trivia Weekly rating: number 18.

271. "Farlow's Follies"

Written by Louella Lee Caraway; Directed by Steve Kanaly; Airdate: February 19, 1988
Special Guest Stars: John Anderson (Dr. Styles); Annabel Schofield (Laurel Ellis)
Guest Stars: Karen Kopins (Kay Lloyd); Alice Hirson (Mavis); Glenn Corbett (Paul Morgan); Charles Grant (Shulton); Tom Fucello (Dave Culver); Shalane McCall (Charlie); Omri Katz (John Ross); Joshua Harris (Christopher); Deborah Rennard (Sly); Charles Bateman (Senator Troutt); Robert Phalen (Senator Wynn)
Subject: Clayton flirts.

Cast Notes Charles Bateman, who played another senator in Episode 348, played a detective in the syndicated police drama *Manhunt.* ★ Karen Kopins reprised the role of Kay during Season 12. She is a former Miss Connecticut (1977) and veteran of TV commercials who also appeared on *Full House*, *The A-Team*, *Knight Rider*, and *T. J. Hooker* and in the 1989 Shelley Long movie *Troop Beverly Hills*.

Trivia Weekly rating: number 18. ★ The three children in the cast, Joshua Harris, Omri Katz, and Shalane McCall, appeared in this episode, which was good news for director Steve Kanaly. Kanaly "liked directing the kids on the show. That was a big thrill. Most of the directors overlooked the kids and made no effort with them."

272. "Malice in Dallas"

Written by Arthur Bernard Lewis; Directed by Larry Hagman; Airdate: February 26, 1988
Special Guest Star: Annabel Schofield (Laurel Ellis)
Guest Stars: Joseph Campanella (Joseph Lombardi Sr.); Mark Lindsay Chapman (Lomax); Donna Mitchell (Angela Larkin); Alice Hirson (Mavis); Glenn Corbett (Paul Morgan); Charles Grant (Shulton); Omri Katz (John Ross); Joshua Harris (Christopher); Deborah Rennard (Sly); Marlena Giova (Anna Lombardi); James Avery (Judge Fowler); Amy Stock (Lisa)
Subject: Christopher's custody hearing.

Cast Notes Joseph Campanella played Lou Wickersham on *Mannix*, occasionally appeared as Bonnie Franklin's ex-husband on *One Day at a Time*, and was a regular on *The Colbys.* ★ The judge is played by James Avery, who starred as Will Prince's rich uncle in *The Fresh Prince of Bel-Air.* ★ This is Glenn Corbett's last appearance on *Dallas*. He died of lung cancer in San Antonio, Texas, in 1993.

Trivia Weekly rating: number 19. ★ Alice Hirson's last episode as Mavis includes her favorite *Dallas* scene. "Mavis was always Miss Ellie's pal," Hirson explains. "But they never really gave Mavis any great scenes until one time after Jock died and Howard had come on the show, and we had a scene in a restaurant where we talked about marriage and losing one's spouse and love and life—it was very nice." Hirson found director Larry Hagman "a wonderful and imaginative director."

273. "Crime Story"

Written by David Paulsen; Directed by Patrick Duffy; Airdate: March 4, 1988
Special Guest Stars: John Anderson (Dr. Styles); Annabel Schofield (Laurel Ellis)
Guest Stars: Joseph Campanella (Joseph Lombardi Sr.); Mark Lindsay Chapman (Lomax);
Karen Kopins (Kay Lloyd); Charles Grant (Shulton); Shalane McCall (Charlie); Joshua
Harris (Christopher); Deborah Rennard (Sly); Marlena Giova (Anna Lombardi); Amy
Stock (Lisa)
Subject: April is kidnapped.

Cast Notes Bee-Be Smith, who plays a restaurant hostess in this episode, was a regular cast member on *A Different World*, the spinoff of *The Cosby Show*.

Trivia Weekly rating: number 24. ★ Two days after this episode aired, Jack Scalia and Pat Colbert competed in the City of Los Angeles Marathon. Scalia also ran the race in 1986 and 1987.

274. "To Have and To Hold"

Written by Leah Markus; Directed by Larry Hagman; Airdate: March 11, 1988
Special Guest Star: John Anderson (Dr. Styles)
Guest Stars: Karen Kopins (Kay); Erich Anderson (Stranger); Shalane McCall (Charlie);
Omri Katz (John Ross); Joshua Harris (Christopher); Deborah Rennard (Sly); Felice Or-
landi (Eddie); Bruno Marcotulli (Al); Tim Rossovich (Max)
Subject: Clayton leaves Southfork.

Cast Notes This is the first appearance of Deborah Marie Taylor, who played a minor role in this episode and the next, and then played Oil Baron's Club waitress Debi (known as Debbie beginning in Season 11) from Episode 279 through *Dallas*'s final episode. ★ Erich Anderson played Ellen's husband on *thirtysomething*.

Trivia Weekly rating: number 24. ★ The adolescent antics of Jenna's teenage daughter, on display in this episode, ultimately provided the explanation for Priscilla Presley's and Steve Kanaly's departure from *Dallas*. Offscreen, Presley found young Shalane McCall "very sweet and so willing to be her character. She was going through her own adolescence during the same time she portrayed it on the show."

275. "Dead Reckoning"

Written by Mitchell Wayne Katzman; Directed by David Paulsen; Airdate: March 18, 1988
Guest Stars: Charles Grant (Shulton); Elaine Wilkes (Mary Lou); Michelle Scarabelli

(Connie Hall); Erich Anderson (Sal Lombardi); Shalane McCall (Charlie); Omri Katz (John Ross); Joshua Harris (Christopher); Deborah Rennard (Sly); Bill Morey (Leo Wakefield); Earl Boen (Doctor); Tim Rossovich (Max)
Subject: Clayton is arrested.

Cast Notes Michelle Scarabelli appeared on Alien Nation and played opposite Steve Kanaly in the 1993 African adventure series Okavango: The Wild Frontier, in which Kanaly played J. D. and Scarabelli played Jessica.

Trivia Weekly rating: number 29.

276. "Never Say Never"

Written by Leonard Katzman; Directed by Cliff Fenneman; Airdate: April 1, 1988
Special Guest Stars: John Anderson (Styles); Annabel Schofield (Laurel); Howard Duff (Senator Harrison Henry O'Dell)
Guest Stars: George O. Petrie (Harv); Mark Lindsay Chapman (Lomax); Michelle Scarabelli (Connie Hall); Omri Katz (John Ross); Joshua Harris (Christopher)
Subject: Bobby negotiates to get Ewing Oil back.

Cast Notes Howard Duff starred in B action movies in the 1950s and 1960s and later appeared in the movies Kramer vs. Kramer and No Way Out. He was married to frequent costar Ida Lupino and was a regular on such TV series as Felony Squad and Flamingo Road. He also played William Devane's father on Knots Landing. He died of a heart attack in 1990 at the age of seventy-two. ★ Bit player J. T. O'Connor, who is a police officer in this episode, was in eight episodes of Dallas during Seasons 2 through 4, 7, 10, 11, and 13.

Trivia Weekly rating: number 17. ★ This is the first of three episodes in which Priscilla Presley does not appear while Jenna is out of the country. They are the only three episodes of Dallas without Presley from her debut in Episode 138 to her final appearance in Episode 281. ★ This episode was considered Dallas's tenth anniversary episode, since the first pilot episode aired on April 2, 1978. In noting the occasion, Leonard Katzman said that Dallas's long run was "a blessing, but it's also similar [to]: 'If I'd known I was going to live this long, I'd have taken better care of my body.' We wouldn't have used up all our great material. How often can Sue Ellen and J.R. split up, then come together?" Nonetheless, Katzman recognized that Dallas "has a kind of mythic quality. There are certain things that the audience takes for granted about Texas—that the men are all macho and strong, that the women are all beautiful, there's money aplenty and everybody lives on huge ranches. Our show is not very hip, not very with it. We don't do voguish things, trendy things. We don't have real-life characters. We've created our own fictitious city of Dallas within the city of Dallas." Katzman told another interviewer, "It all seems like yesterday and a hundred years ago." Katzman said there was discussion of a ten-year Dallas retrospective special, but nothing came of the idea. ★ Larry Hagman wrote in People magazine's look back at ten years of Dallas,

"I would have thought by now *Dallas* would have petered out somewhat. But I hope we can get a couple more years out of it. I know a lot of TV actors get terrified of getting trapped in a hit show. Maybe I'm lazy, but I'm happy doing what I do." ★ Victoria Principal told *USA Today*, which did an article on the show's anniversary, "I have the sweetest memories of the [pilot] miniseries. Those are still my five favorite shows." Principal admitted that, over her years on the show, "The more virtuous [Pam] became, the less interesting I found her." As to reappearing in the role, she said, "I have absolutely no intention of going back. I'm sure everybody has a price, but I don't think my price could be found."

277. "Last of the Good Guys"

Written by Arthur Bernard Lewis; Directed by Michael Preece; Airdate: April 8, 1988
Special Guest Stars: John Anderson (Styles); Annabel Schofield (Laurel); Howard Duff (Senator Harrison Henry O'Dell)
Subject: Bobby negotiates to get Ewing Oil back.

Trivia Weekly rating: number 16.

278. "Top Gun"

Written by David Paulsen; Directed by Michael Preece; Airdate: April 15, 1988
Special Guest Star: Annabel Schofield (Laurel)
Guest Stars: Michelle Scarabelli (Connie Hall); Warren Munson (Richard Barker); Deborah Rennard (Sly); Tom Fucello (Dave Culver); William Smithers (Wendell)
Subject: J.R.'s takeover attempt.

Cast Notes Warren Munson also appeared in Episodes 52 and 68.

Trivia Weekly rating: number 21.

279. "Things Ain't Goin' Too Good at Southfork Again"

Written by Leah Markus; Directed by Dwight Adair; Airdate: April 29, 1988
Guest Stars: Michelle Scarabelli (Connie Hall); David Haskel (Mr. Bradley); Deborah Rennard (Sly); Tom Fucello (Dave Culver); Tom McGreevey (Mr. Ballard); Omri Katz (John Ross); Joshua Harris (Christopher); William Smithers (Wendell)
Subject: Ray is stalked.

Trivia Weekly rating: number 19. ★ Miss Ellie's mother's headstone establishes that her name was Anna, but in *The Early Years* her name was Barbara, perhaps in a tribute to Barbara Bel Geddes. ★ This episode's title is a play on the title of Episode 129 in Season 5. Like that episode, this one was the third-to-last episode of the season and set the stage for the cliff-hanger two episodes later.

280. "Pillow Talk"

Written by Mitchell Wayne Katzman; Directed by Linda Gray; Airdate: May 6, 1988
Guest Stars: Michelle Scarabelli (Connie Hall); Deborah Rennard (Sly); Omri Katz (John Ross); Joshua Harris (Christopher); Bill Morey (Wakefield); Tom Fucello (Dave Culver);

Ken Smolka (Manny); Fredric Cook (Mo); William Smithers (Wendell)
Subject: Ray is stabbed.

Cast Notes Charlene Tilton returns as Lucy in this episode, and stayed through Season 12. When Lorimar announced her return in January of 1988, Katzman explained that when Charlene had left in 1985, "we thought we'd done as much as we could with her character. She was no longer the teen-age vamp and she wasn't a full-grown woman either. Now the character and the actress have matured. [Now there's] trouble in her paradise." Katzman and Tilton discussed bringing Lucy back to Southfork two years earlier, in the wake of Pam's dream, but they couldn't come up with an appropriate storyline for the character. Said Katzman at that time, "If we could think of a really good storyline for Charlene, we would love to bring her back. But we wouldn't do it just to have her sit around and answer the phone and be a pouty little girl." Despite Katzman's efforts over the years, it was Larry Hagman who was "instrumental" in arranging for Tilton's return in this episode. Lorimar attorneys started negotiating with Tilton's attorneys in the fall of 1987, when Tilton was in rehearsals for Larry Shue's play *The Foreigner*, which was running at the La Mirada Civic Theatre. Said Tilton, "They have to want me back bad enough to give me the storylines I'm looking for. I want Lucy to be more responsible this time around and I wanted her to be older and wiser because I'm older and wiser. And I don't want her to be a victim anymore." Lorimar announced Tilton's return in January 1988. As of Tilton's return, her character was listed in the opening credits as "Lucy Ewing-Cooper."

Trivia Weekly rating: number 18. ★ Judge Hooker was also seen in *J.R. Returns*.

281. "The Fat Lady Singeth"

Written by Leonard Katzman; Directed by Leonard Katzman; Airdate: May 13, 1988
Guest Stars: Elaine Wilkes (Mary Lou Lassiter); David Sage (Senator Walter); Deborah Rennard (Sly); Joshua Harris (Christopher); John Posey (Alan Bodine); Tom McGreevey (Ballard); Don Starr (Jordan); William Smithers (Wendell)
Subject: Sue Ellen shoots J.R.

Cast Notes This was Priscilla Presley's last episode as Jenna and Steve Kanaly's last episode as a regular cast member. ★ At the start of Season 10, Kanaly told *TV Guide*, "I always thought I had the best character on the show, but he was never used effectively." When asked how he was able to stay with a role for so many years while some of his colleagues left theirs, Kanaly replied, "They weren't in the jungle." Kanaly's years in Vietnam left him better able to appreciate the stability of a long-running hit like *Dallas*. Said Leonard Katzman about Kanaly, "He's a devoted family man. He's content to be part of an ensemble where no one works more than three or four days a week and to lead a normal family life."

Trivia Weekly rating: number 12, with a 17.3 rating and 30 share. While this was *Dallas*'s second-highest-ranked episode of the season, it was its lowest-ranked cliff-hanger to date, failing to surpass Season 1's cliff-hanger, which earned an eleventh-place ranking and a 40 share in 1979. ★ Just as the Season 8 cliff-hanger end credits teased the audience by omitting the name of Patrick Duffy's character, this episode teased the audience by momentarily freezing the action during Nicholas's fall before continuing with the shooting scene.

SEASON 11
1988–89—"Comings and Goings"

THE DALLAS CAST EXODUS CONTINUED during Season 11, when Linda Gray announced that she was leaving the show. On February 21, 1989, Gray confirmed her departure, saying, "I'm excited and looking forward to the future." That same day, a day on which Gray's presence was not required on the set, she sent a letter to Leonard Katzman. According to Gray, the letter "said that I would like to leave with a lot of dignity. I don't want to die, and please, no showers, no auto crashes, no 'disease of the month.' I said I would like one last shot at J.R." Katzman responded to the letter by stating that "it caught us all by surprise. We haven't had a chance to talk to Linda. . . . It's hard to imagine the show without her." Katzman phoned Larry Hagman with the news and said that Hagman "was as shocked as I was. I don't think he thought it would come to that." In another 1989 interview, Gray explained her departure as stemming from the fact that "I wasn't used to my capacity. I felt very frustrated and I didn't know what to do and they weren't writing for me and it was definitely a male oriented show. . . . [T]he scripts were geared towards Larry, Patrick, and the male stars on the show. And women were kind of fillers."

To some extent, however, Gray's exit was not entirely her own decision. On February 24, 1989, just three days after she announced her departure, Gray gave an interview to TV reporter Ed Bark in which she stated that it was "absolutely ludicrous" for Katzman to feign shock at the news. "My contract is up April 7," she said. "They all knew that, and no one had ever approached me about renewing it." Gray explained to Bark that maybe the others in the cast "think I'm holding out for more money, which is always everyone's first impression. And that couldn't be further from the truth. . . . They were planning for me to walk into the sunset with Ian McShane, but no one had ever come to me and asked, 'How do you want to depart?' After eleven years, I thought that was quite uncaring." Steve Kanaly confirms that Gray, like Kanaly himself, was let go as part of an effort to cut the high cost of producing *Dallas*.

Gray had hoped for a happier end to *Dallas*. Almost eighteen months earlier, she said "one of these days, we'll all leave. When the time comes, we'll all know it. It's my feeling that *Mary Tyler Moore*, M*A*S*H, *Carol Burnett*, all lasted eleven years, and they went out in style. There just comes a saturation point where you say, 'But I've done all this before.' Then it's time to move on. Ideally, my feeling is that it will be a group decision. We'll all get together and say, 'Well, we did it, and we did it well, and thank you for watching us.'" As for the character she played for over a decade, Gray commented that Sue Ellen had gone "every which way that she could go. . . . I've had an absolutely splendid job, but you know that it's time to move on."

Hagman knew that Gray was fed up with playing Sue Ellen as a victim, but also realized that Katzman was not going to change his vision of the show. Hagman claimed that he had "many dinner parties . . . where I begged her not to go" and that he "would've used every bit of my clout if she wanted to stay." He called Gray his "favorite female costar. She was the greatest leading lady I've ever worked with. She was here for twelve years. There was a lot of electricity and a lot of subtle work between us. We would always find pieces of the story that weren't written into the script. She was the best so far in my life."

Katzman and his team countered the gradual cast changes by keeping Charlene Tilton, who had appeared in the last few episodes of Season 10, on the show as a full-fledged regular. In addition, Oscar-winning actor George Kennedy joined the cast as the new Ewing nemesis, a role he would play through the end of the series and in the 1996 and 1998 TV movies. Katzman also took cast members Hagman, Duffy, and Sheree Wilson and newcomers Kennedy and Cathy Podewell to Europe, where several episodes were filmed on location in Vienna, Salzburg, and Moscow in March of 1989. It was the first time that *Dallas* filmed overseas since Victoria Principal and Linda Gray filmed scenes for Season 7 in Hong Kong. Given the collapse of communism that swept across Eastern Europe in the late 1980s, a highlight of the trip was the visit to Moscow, where Hagman "walked around the city unrecognized."

The *Dallas* crew filmed on location in Red Square and the Arabat pedestrian mall and used several local actors, including well-known Russian actor Alexander Potapov. Potapov, like the other Russian actors who appeared, were unbilled. Potapov had never heard of *Dallas* prior to the shoot but said, "It seems to be about noble and honest people. There are legends about Hollywood, so it's nice to have a chance to experience this." Katzman, who directed these scenes, found that the Russians "aren't geared up for the fast pace that is necessary for a television series. But if you persist, you eventually get what you want." Katzman loved the idea of filming in the then–Soviet Union. "We think it's a great audience grabber," he said. "The Ewings go to Moscow."

Another significant change that was discussed for Season 11 never materialized. During the second half of Season 10, Lorimar and CBS considered changing *Dallas* from a serial back to the episodic show it was in the pilot and the first half of Season 1. Katzman denied that the change was the result of declining ratings but a result of "the show . . . getting long in the tooth" and needing a new direction. "I'm not sure that the form has necessarily run its course," he said, "but all the shows that are in that genre that are on now have been on for quite a while, and you necessarily use up a lot of material. . . . How many times can you have Bobby and Pam move in and out of Southfork?"

It was thought that this change would rejuvenate *Dallas*, cut costs, and make the show more attractive for syndication. Katzman also liked the format because it would enable him to use guest stars for a single episode. He thought that contained storylines might improve the characters' depth. As an example, he envisioned an episode where Bobby's high school basketball coach dies, and Bobby must locate the coach's daughter to give her the news. Katzman suggested the idea to Lorimar, and the studio and CBS considered the new format for *Falcon Crest* as well. According to Barbara Brogliatti, a Lorimar vice-president of corporate communications, "We tested [the idea] with audiences and they loved it. We think it's a very creative idea that everybody is excited about." CBS even considered renaming the show *The New Dallas* to reflect the change in format, but in the end CBS changed neither the format nor the show's title.

Dallas finished Season 11 outside the Nielsen top twenty-five for the first time since Season 1. It aired against NBC's *Something Is Out There* and ABC's *Mr. Belvedere* and *Just the Ten of Us*, and finished the year at number 30. *Dallas's* ratings drop did not result in cancellation, however, because CBS had so few other hits on the air. During the 1988–89 season, the network placed only two shows in the top twenty-five, *60 Minutes* and *Murder, She Wrote*. *Dynasty* was not as lucky; its dropping ratings resulted in its cancellation in the spring of 1989. As for the other serials, *Knots Landing* surpassed *Dallas* for the first time in the seasonal ratings, finishing at number 28, and *Falcon Crest* finished at number 54.

SEASON 11 EPISODE GUIDE

Regular Cast

Starring:
Barbara Bel Geddes as Miss Ellie
Patrick Duffy as Bobby
Linda Gray as Sue Ellen
Larry Hagman as J.R.
Steve Kanaly as Ray
Howard Keel as Clayton
Ken Kercheval as Cliff
Charlene Tilton as Lucy
Sheree J. Wilson as April
Also Starring:
George Kennedy as Carter McKay
Audrey Landers as Afton
Ian McShane as Don Lockwood
Cathy Podewell as Cally Harper
William Smithers as Jeremy Wendell
Andrew Stevens as Casey Denault
Leigh Taylor-Young as Kimberly Cryder
Beth Toussaint as Tracey Lawton

Technical Credits

Supervising Producer: Arthur Bernard
    Lewis
Executive Producers: Leonard Katzman,
    Larry Hagman
Co-Producers: Cliff Fenneman, Mitchell
    Wayne Katzman
Music: Jerrold Immel, Richard Warren
    Lewis, Angela Morley, John Parker,
    Lance Rubin
Unit Production Manager: Wayne A.
    Farlow

First Assistant Directors: Frank W.
    Katzman, Richard R. Johnson
Second Assistant Director: Amy
    Rosenbaum Jacobson
Director of Photography: Rick R. Gunter
Art Director: David K. Marshall
Editors: Fred W. Berger, A.C.E., John
    Arthur Davies, Lloyd Richardson
Executive in Charge of Casting: Barbara
    Miller
Casting: Irene Mariano, C.S.A.
Set Decorator: Chuck Rutherford
Property Master: John Rettino
Costumers: Jack Bear, Nanrose Buchman
Makeup: Joe Hailey, Bob Jermain
Hair Stylists: Generio Gugliemotto, Lola
    "Skip" McNalley, Rebecca De Morrio,
    Julia L. Walker
Production Sound Mixer: Andrew Gilmore
Sound Manager: Doug Grindstaff
Supervising Sound Editor: Thomas Gillis
    Burke
Music Supervisor: Richard Berres
Music Editor: Patricia Peck
Main Title Design: Wayne Fitzgerald
Location Casting: Rody Kent
Executive Coordinator: Louella Lee
    Caraway
Executive in Charge of Production:
    R. Robert Rosenbaum

282. "Carousel"

Written by Leonard Katzman; Directed by Michael Preece; Airdate: October 28, 1988
Guest Stars: Dakin Matthews (Detective Kane); Deborah Rennard (Sly); William H. Bassett (Attorney Gurney); Omri Katz (John Ross); Joshua Harris (Christopher); Margaret Michaels (Pam Ewing)
Subject: J.R. is hospitalized.

Cast Notes George Kennedy makes his debut as Ewing nemesis Carter McKay. Kennedy won the 1967 Best Supporting Actor Oscar for *Cool Hand Luke* (with

Morgan Woodward) and also appeared in *Airport*, *Earthquake* (with Victoria Principal), and *Naked Gun* (with Priscilla Presley). According to Kennedy, he was cast as McKay because "Leonard Katzman needed someone strong to butt heads with J.R. I was his billy goat for three years." ★ With this episode, Kehly Gray is credited as Kehly Sloane. She was married on October 31, 1987. ★ Charlene Tilton's and Sheree J. Wilson's credits were moved to the main title as of this episode. ★ Victoria Principal look-alike Margaret Michaels appears as Pam. Michaels appeared on the soap opera *Santa Barbara* and was frequently told that she looked like Principal. Michaels got the role of Pam accidentally. Although she had heard that the *Dallas* producers were conducting a search for a Principal look-alike, it never occurred to her to audition. One day, Michaels was running errands with her friend Linda Howard, the wife of actor Ken Howard and the president of a stuntwomen's association. One of their errands was at a studio. "Patrick Duffy and Loni Anderson were filming a movie," Michaels recalls. "As we got to the set, Patrick came over to me and said, 'Please tell me you're an actress.' And he set up an appointment with Leonard Katzman, who set up a reading and sent me a script." Michaels traveled to Dallas to film the episode, and had "the nicest week" with the cast and crew. She recalls being taken to lunch by Howard Keel, who Michaels calls "the sweetest person on the planet."

Trivia Weekly rating: number 20, with a 17.4 rating and 30 share, an increase over the Season 10 premiere's twenty-sixth place ranking and 16.9 rating. ★ Larry Hagman was promoted to co-executive producer as of Season 11, a title he shared with Leonard Katzman. As a result, Hagman now earned $300,000 per episode. Hagman felt he "had it easy. I didn't have a secretary. I didn't have a separate office. I didn't write the scripts—well, of course, I always rewrote some of my dialogue on the floor. It was just a ploy to get me to come back to the show for more money. I made a lot more money. And I deserved it." ★ Pam's engagement to a doctor may have been an inside joke about Victoria Principal's second marriage to plastic surgeon Harry Glassman. Ironically, Margaret Michaels's husband is also a plastic surgeon, and he knows Glassman. ★ The October season premiere date was the result of a five-month strike by the Writers Guild of America from April 1988 through August 1988. Said Larry Hagman as the strike wound down in early August, "I haven't been out of work this long in twenty-five years. That's a long time. We don't have any scripts to go. I mean none, zero, zilch." But Patrick Duffy was not worried, claiming, "I don't think it's going to be a scramble. *Dallas* is probably the easiest show to produce and get started and continue than anything I've seen before. There are no conflicts of interest or personality problems. We'll roll." As a result of the strike, the two-month on-location shoot that typically took place in Texas during the summer was postponed to the fall of 1988. Since *Dallas* did not return to Texas for on-location filming in Seasons 12 and 13, the final scene of the Season 11 on-location shoot was the last scene filmed in Texas for the series. That scene featured Hagman and Kennedy, took place at the Million Dollar Saloon on Greenville Avenue in Dallas and was filmed in November 1988. ★ Margaret Michaels thought Ken Kercheval was a "fabulous" actor to work with, and of the Season 11 and Season 12 episodes she appeared in, her scene with him from this episode is her favorite. She found the scene "very emotional and Kenny was just terrific." She also felt that director Michael Preece "did not give us too much direction. He has ideas. He's very thorough. He sits down with the actors and goes through it, but he let it ride once we were doing the scene."

283. "No Greater Love"

Written by Simon Masters; Directed by Russ Mayberry; Airdate: November 4, 1988
Guest Stars: Irena Ferris (Tammy Miller); Leigh McCloskey (Mitch); William Cort
(Sawyer)
Subject: John Ross returns to Southfork.

Cast Notes This single-episode guest appearance marks Leigh McCloskey's final episode of *Dallas*. Recalls McCloskey, "If they considered bringing Mitch back to stay longer [in Season 11], they didn't tell me about it. I usually came back to get Lucy back on [the show] or take her away. I used to joke that I was the 'Hello, I Must Be Going' character. Once I went upstairs to wait while Lucy made her decision. I thought I should come back down the stairs with cobwebs in my hair as I said, 'Have you decided?' Mitch was the most known of Lucy's relationships, which is why I was the one who came back for those type of scenes." ★ This is James L. Brown's final appearance as Harry McSween. Brown died in 1992 at the age of seventy-two.

Trivia Weekly rating: number 18. This was Season 11's second-highest-ranked episode. ★ Russ Mayberry was a director from the John Huston era in Hollywood. He also directed nine episodes of *Magnum, P.I.* between 1984 and 1988.

284. "Call of the Wild"

Written by Jonathan Hales; Directed by Michael Preece; Airdate: November 11, 1988
Guest Stars: Cliff Potts (Boaz Harper); Sherman Howard (Japhet Harper); Gerrit Graham
(Fred Hughes); Omri Katz (John Ross); Joshua Harris (Christopher); Deborah Rennard
(Sly); Don Starr (Jordan Lee)
Subject: The Ewings' hunting trip.

Cast Notes Cathy Podewell makes her first appearance as Cally, a role she would play almost continuously through *Dallas*'s final episode in May of 1991. Podewell had appeared on the TV series *Growing Pains* and *Valerie*. Podewell was cast as Cally "through a regular audition. Initially, the part was for a couple of episodes. . . . I read with the casting director. At the second interview, after one hundred girls were narrowed down to ten, I met with the casting director and Leonard Katzman. At the third interview, I met with the casting director, Leonard, and Larry. At that point, there were four of us. I heard it was down to another girl and me. I got a great vibe from Larry—we just had chemistry. And then I was in Cleveland with my husband's family and got a call that they were so torn between two of us that they wanted to see the two of us again. I was in the Cleveland airport the next day getting ready to fly back to L.A. when I got a page over the loudspeaker. I called my manager who told me I got the job, which was great—and unbelievable!" Hagman found Podewell "a pretty great mistress" for J.R. He bragged that, in his new capacity as co-executive producer, he was the one who picked Podewell to be his "new leading lady. . . . I auditioned all the women and selected Cathy Podewell. She's a joy." ★ Sherman Howard appeared as Lex Luthor in a syndicated version of *Superboy*. ★ Cliff Potts played Ted McCovey on *Lou Grant*.

Trivia Weekly rating: number 22. ★ Carter's girlfriend is called simply "The Red-head" during her five appearances in Season 11. When she returns in Episode 311 of Season 12, however, she gets a name: Rose Daniels. ★ Hagman claimed that he had a role in creating the Hayleyville storyline. "I wanted to get the show back to the family," he said. "The reason Bobby and J.R. went to Arkansas, where J.R. ended up getting married, was to get us out and doing something physical. It got us out of sitting around the boardroom, making deals."

285. "Out of the Frying Pan"

Written by Mitchell Wayne Katzman; Directed by Russ Mayberry; Airdate: November 18, 1988
Guest Stars: Cliff Potts (Boaz Harper); Sherman Howard (Japhet Harper); Warren Kem-merling (Sheriff Hanks); William H. Bassett (Gurney); Omri Katz (John Ross); Joshua Harris (Christopher)
Subject: J.R.'s arrest.

Cast Notes Joseph Chapman, who appears as the businessman who buys Valen-tine lingerie from Sue Ellen, played villain Mark St. Claire on *Knots Landing*.

Trivia Weekly rating: number 31. ★ Cathy Podewell "loved" the Hayleyville sto-ryline and "thought it was hysterical."

286. "Road Work"

Written by Arthur Bernard Lewis; Directed by Michael Preece; Airdate: December 2, 1988
Guest Stars: Sherman Howard (Japhet Harper); Gerrit Graham (Fred Hughes); Brooks Gard-ner (Bushrod); Ken Jenkins (Captain); Omri Katz (John Ross); Joshua Harris (Christopher)
Subject: J.R. works the chain gang.

Cast Notes Ken Jenkins appeared as Beckstead on *Wiseguy*, starred as Mike Sloan Sr. on David Jacobs's World War II drama *Homefront* and plays Dr. Kelso on NBC's sitcom *Scrubs*. ★ Beth Toussaint starred in the 1990s Aaron Spelling night time soap opera *Savannah*.

Trivia Weekly rating: number 30. ★ This episode includes a friendly scene be-tween Patrick Duffy and Ken Kercheval, who "liked Patrick a lot. He had a marvelous sense of humor and was extremely witty. He is a bright fellow and had quite a lot of acting skills. I've done scenes with him where he has just pulled out all the stops, which is great for an actor to play off of." ★ Cathy Podewell enjoyed her scenes with Larry Hagman and "can't say enough wonderful things about [him]. He is such a great person and took me under his wing and made me feel a part of the show, even when I was only going to be on for a few episodes. He invited me to dinner with Maj and him and he made me feel so welcome."

287. "War and Love and the Whole Damn Thing"

Written by Leonard Katzman; Directed by Russ Mayberry; Airdate: December 9, 1988
Starring: Steve Kanaly (Ray)
Guest Stars: Ken Swofford (Sheriff Billy Jo Burnside); Cliff Potts (Boaz Harper); Sherman Howard (Japhet Harper); Gerrit Graham (Fred Hughes); Warren Kemmerling (Sheriff Hanks); William H. Bassett (Attorney Gurney); Omri Katz (John Ross); Joshua Harris (Christopher)
Subject: A range war at Southfork.

Cast Notes Ken Swofford was in the cast of *Switch; Fame;* and *Murder, She Wrote,* on which he played Lieutenant Perry Catalano of the San Francisco Police Department. ★ This is the first of five consecutive episodes in which Steve Kanaly returns as Ray.

Trivia Weekly rating: number 27. ★ Writer Arthur Bernard Lewis thought the J.R.-Cally storyline was not accepted by some of *Dallas's* audience. Lewis felt the storyline "affected a lot of female viewers. It's a nightmare for some women [that] their husband is going to leave them for a young girl!" ★ At the time she was cast as Cally, Cathy Podewell's appearance on *Dallas* was to end with this episode. Podewell explains, "Initially, the part was for a couple of episodes. I was going to come in, have the shotgun wedding. . . . [After] we went on location in Dallas, they said to me, 'Are you available?' And it was extended to seven episodes."

288. "Showdown at the Ewing Corral"

Written by Mitchell Wayne Katzman; Directed by Michael Preece; Airdate: December 16, 1988
Starring: Steve Kanaly (Ray)
Guest Stars: Ken Swofford (Sheriff Billy Jo Burnside); Cliff Potts (Boaz Harper); Sherman Howard (Japhet Harper); Gerrit Graham (Fred Hughes); Bill Wiley (Norm Peterson); Deborah Rennard (Sly)
Subject: Miss Ellie confronts McKay.

Cast Notes Featured actor Sean Hennigan, who plays Cowboy #2 in this episode, played Dave Colquit in *J.R. Returns* and John Savory in *War of the Ewings.*

Trivia Weekly rating: number 26.

289. "Deception"

Written by Arthur Bernard Lewis; Directed by Irving J. Moore; Airdate: January 6, 1989
Starring: Steve Kanaly (Ray)
Guest Stars: George O. Petrie (Harv); Gerrit Graham (Fred Hughes); Deborah Rennard (Sly); Omri Katz (John Ross); Joshua Harris (Christopher)
Subject: Wendell plots against the Ewings.

Cast Notes John Hoge played Ratagan in sixteen episodes during Seasons 11 through 13 and in *J.R. Returns* and *War of the Ewings*. ★ The role of Mason, one of Bart's security men, is played by extra Sean McGraw, who found that, on *Dallas*, "sometimes you get to do more than just be an extra." McGraw played one of John Ross's kidnappers in Episode 79, Pam's divorce lawyer in Episode 135, and a policeman investigating Charlie's disappearance in Episode 171 before getting a credited role as Mason in this episode.

Trivia Weekly rating: number 35.

290. "Counterattack"

Written by Leonard Katzman; Directed by Michael Preece; Airdate: January 13, 1989
Starring: Steve Kanaly (Ray)
Guest Stars: Irena Ferris (Tammy Miller); Ken Swofford (Sheriff Billy Jo Burnside); Gerrit Graham (Fred Hughes); Robert King (Dr. Proctor); Omri Katz (John Ross); Joshua Harris (Christopher)
Subject: The range war escalates.

Trivia Weekly rating: number 36.

291. "The Sting"

Written by Mitchell Wayne Katzman; Directed by Irving J. Moore; Airdate: January 20, 1989
Starring: Steve Kanaly (Ray)
Guest Stars: Irena Ferris (Tammy Miller); George O. Petrie (Harv); Warren Kemmerling (Sheriff Hanks); Deborah Rennard (Sly); Omri Katz (John Ross); Joshua Harris (Christopher)
Subject: Wendell is set up.

Cast Notes This is Smithers's last appearance as Jeremy Wendell, a Ewing nemesis since Season 3. Katzman described Wendell as "a man apparently invulnerable, who has no weaknesses, is to the best of our knowledge asexual, who cannot be blackmailed, bribed, and who has more money and power than J.R." With regard to his exit from *Dallas*, Smithers recalls, "One day on the set Larry Hagman took me aside and said, 'You know, more fan mail comes in about you than about any other guest star on the show. You ought to do something about that.' Since it had been clear the producers of *Dallas* thought well enough of the character to make him almost a series regular, and since I had been paid a minimal sum for my services up to then, my agent initiated a contract renegotiation when [Season 11] began. The producers raised their offer to within $2,500 per episode of what we were asking. My agent was convinced they would meet our price. They didn't and wrote Jeremy out of *Dallas*." ★ This is Andrew Stevens's final *Dallas* episode. Sheree J. Wilson recalls that Stevens "loved the show. He was into furthering his career into directing, which he did." ★ Leigh Taylor-Young reprises the role of Kimberly Cryder, which she played in Season 10.

Trivia Weekly rating: number 31. ★ William Smithers found George Kennedy "a nice guy and I certainly enjoyed working with him, even though the rat took over as J.R.'s arch enemy." ★ Cathy Podewell's contract was extended a second time prior to the filming of this episode. First, her four-episode contract was extended to a seven-episode contract, ending with Episode 290. After that extension, her storyline was going to end with "my character going to go to Dallas and claim [J.R.,] and then they would buy me off." The producers then decided they wanted to further explore J.R.'s relationship with Cally, and told Podewell "they wanted to keep me for the whole season."

292. "The Two Mrs. Ewings"

Written by Arthur Bernard Lewis; Directed by Michael Preece; Airdate: January 27, 1989
Guest Stars: Irena Ferris (Tammy Miller); George O. Petrie (Harv); Jonathan Goldsmith (Bruce Harvey); Eric Poppick (Jeff Salem); Omri Katz (John Ross); Joshua Harris (Christopher); Fern Fitzgerald (Marilee Stone)
Subject: Cally moves onto Southfork.

Cast Notes Costar Sally Bartunek, who appears as "Young Woman," played Elektra on the syndicated show *American Gladiators*.

Trivia Weekly rating: number 23. ★ The horsewhip incident is seen in *The Early Years*. ★ This is the seventh and final Oil Baron's Ball on *Dallas*.

293. "The Switch"

Written by Leonard Katzman; Directed by Irving J. Moore; Airdate: February 3, 1989
Guest Stars: Irena Ferris (Tammy Miller); Jonathan Goldsmith (Bruce Harvey); Omri Katz (John Ross); Joshua Harris (Christopher)
Subject: Sue Ellen advises Cally.

Cast Notes This is the first of three consecutive episodes in which Barbara Bel Geddes and Howard Keel do not appear. Their characters' absence is explained by a trip to Europe to visit the Krebbses.

Trivia Weekly rating: number 27. ★ This is the last episode of *Dallas* with scenes filmed on location in Dallas. ★ Cally's interaction with John Ross and Christopher in this and other episodes gave Cathy Podewell her first opportunity to work with child actors. She found Omri Katz and Joshua Harris to be "good and well adjusted boys. I was surprised how sweet they were."

294. "He-e-e-e-re's Papa!"

Written by Louella Lee Caraway; Directed by Patrick Duffy; Airdate: February 10, 1989
Guest Stars: Joseph Campanella (Joseph Lombardi); Jonathan Goldsmith (Bruce Harvey);
Omri Katz (John Ross); Joshua Harris (Christopher); Deborah Rennard (Sly); Donald
Craig (Massey); Anthony Peck
Subject: Nicholas's father arrives.

Cast Notes Chazz Palminteri, who appears as Frank, costarred in the 1999 Robert
DeNiro–Billy Crystal mafia comedy *Analyze This*.

Trivia Weekly rating: number 31. ★ Cathy Podewell enjoyed acting under
Patrick Duffy's direction and also admired his talent for learning his lines. "Patrick
always had lunch with Larry, and they'd invite me, so we'd have lunch in Larry's
trailer," she recalls. "Patrick was such a nice man, and has a great sense of humor.
And he can memorize on a dime! He'd look at his lines before the scene and
memorize them and I was always amazed at that because I would have been up all
night memorizing mine." ★ Under his initial contract, this would have been
George Kennedy's last episode on *Dallas*. "The network liked the strength Carter
McKay offered against J.R. Ewing," explains Kennedy, "so they renewed the fire-
works twice more [after Season 11]." Kennedy was happy to have his contract renewed, as he found *Dallas* "a marvelous company." He also enjoyed playing the
resident villain, noting, "There were lots of people out there who enjoyed seeing
J.R. 'get as good as he gave.' I got my start in films playing heavies, so I enjoyed it,
too."

295. "Comings and Goings"

Written by Mitchell Wayne Katzman; Directed by Larry Hagman; Airdate: February 17,
1989
Guest Stars: Jonathan Goldsmith (Bruce Harvey); Newell Alexander (Senator Hunsacker);
Omri Katz (John Ross); Joshua Harris (Christopher); J. Eddie Peck (Tommy McKay)
Subject: McKay's son arrives.

Cast Notes This is British actor Ian McShane's first appearance as Don Lockwood. McShane appeared in American and British movies in the 1960s and early
1970s. He played Sir Eric Russell in *Roots* and costarred in *Dallas* imitator *Bare
Essence*. He also stars in HBO's Emmy award–winning western series *Deadwood*,
which premiered in 2004. Linda Gray found McShane "a treasure! He is a great
actor—comedic, drama—he could act across the board." ★ J. Eddie Peck was a
veteran of daytime soaps. He reprised the role of Tommy in five episodes in Season 12.

Trivia Weekly rating: number 30. ★ Don Lockwood has the same name as Gene
Kelly's character in the classic musical *Singin' in the Rain*.

296. & 297. "Country Girl" (Parts One and Two)

Written by Arthur Bernard Lewis (Part One); Howard Lakin (Part Two); Directed by Patrick Duffy (Part One); Larry Hagman (Part Two); Airdate: February 24, 1989
Guest Stars: Newell Alexander (Senator Hunsacker); Omri Katz (John Ross); Joshua Harris (Christopher); Aaron Lustig (Henry Gyster); Stephen Bradley (Dr. Feffer); Deborah Rennard (Sly); J. Eddie Peck (Tommy McKay)
Subject: J.R.'s and Cally's wedding.

Trivia Weekly rating: number 17. This was Season 11's highest-ranked episode. ★ In syndication, Part One remained "Country Girl" while Part Two was renamed "Wedding Belle Blues." ★ Linda Gray was so close to Larry Hagman that she often teased Maj Hagman that they were both Hagman's wives. With J.R. marrying Cally, Gray now joked that Hagman's spouses numbered three "and he needs every one of us." ★ Cathy Podewell found that "she felt like a real bride" during the filming of the wedding scenes, which took place at Culver City. "It was as big as a real wedding day would be," recalls Podewell. "It had that magical quality."

298. "The Way We Were"

Written by Louella Lee Caraway; Directed by Patrick Duffy; Airdate: March 3, 1989
Guest Stars: Don Starr (Jordan Lee); Jonathan Goldsmith (Bruce); Robert O'Reilly (Patrick O'Riley); Richard Erdman (Mr. Willis); Deborah Rennard (Sly); Omri Katz (John Ross); Joshua Harris (Christopher); J. Eddie Peck (Tommy McKay)
Subject: Sue Ellen's movie.

Cast Notes Richard Erdman was a regular on The Ray Bolger Show in the 1950s.

Trivia Weekly rating: number 26.

299. "The Serpent's Tooth"

Teleplay by Arthur Bernard Lewis and Howard Lakin; Story by Mitchell Wayne Katzman; Directed by Larry Hagman; Airdate: March 10, 1989
Guest Stars: Don Starr (Jordan Lee); Jonathan Goldsmith (Bruce); Christopher Neame (Gustav Helstrom); Bo Brundin (Holgar Kuhn); Robert O'Reilly (Patrick O'Riley); Deborah Rennard (Sly); Omri Katz (John Ross); Joshua Harris (Christopher); J. Eddie Peck (Tommy McKay)
Subject: J.R. plots against Gustav.

Trivia Weekly rating: number 36.

300. "Three Hundred"

Written by Leonard Katzman; Directed by Patrick Duffy; Airdate: March 17, 1989
Guest Stars: Jonathan Goldsmith (Bruce); Deborah Rennard (Sly); J. Eddie Peck (Tommy)
Subject: J.R. and Bobby are stuck in an elevator.

Trivia Weekly rating: number 39. This episode, Dallas's three hundredth, earned one of the series' lowest rankings to date. ★ In recognition of the three hundred mark, Leonard Katzman wrote a script in which J.R. and Bobby are trapped in an elevator and reflect on their lives. Patrick Duffy, who directed the episode, felt that "Bobby Ewing was whatever J.R. wasn't, except the common thing that they both believed about themselves is that they were doing the best thing for their family. They took absolutely polar approaches to it. . . . I had a moral compass I would not deviate from and J.R. broke his compass, I think, at birth. And Bobby was whatever was necessary to counterbalance the character of J.R. in the family and everything else fell . . . from that relationship." Duffy liked this episode because it focused on his interplay with Hagman and because it incorporated a hobby of his and Katzman's. "Lenny and Larry and I always joked that it would be so much easier to do one show with just us two in a room," recalls Duffy. "Len and I for many years collected and drank French wines. I can't remember whose idea the elevator was but when the red (first draft) [script] came out we knew it was going to be fun. The wine was real and the work went truly very fast as Haggy and I work well as a team. I actually always wished that the entire episode would have been just the elevator but in reality I know we had to advance all the other stories as well." ★ As for the formal celebration of the three hundredth episode, the cast and crew had a party that featured a banner reading "300 Episodes" and three cakes in the shape of the numbers 3, 0, and 0. In attendance were original and current stars Patrick Duffy, Linda Gray, Larry Hagman, Ken Kercheval, and Charlene Tilton. Original cast member Steve Kanaly, now sporting a mustache, was also in attendance. Other cast regulars in attendance were Joshua Harris, Omri Katz, Howard Keel, and Sheree J. Wilson and recent cast additions George Kennedy, J. Eddie Peck, Cathy Podewell, and Beth Toussaint.

301. "April Showers"

Written by Howard Lakin; Directed by Irving J. Moore; Airdate: March 31, 1989
Guest Stars: Jonathan Goldsmith (Bruce); Christopher Neame (Gustav Helstrom); Bonnie
Burroughs (Alison Kincaid); Deborah Rennard (Sly); Lee Ryan (Doctor); J. Eddie Peck
(Tommy McKay)
Subject: Tommy assaults April.

Trivia Weekly rating: number 31. ★ The beating April receives in this episode is an example of the tribulations the character went through once she became Bobby's love interest. Sheree J. Wilson "liked going from vixen to victim. As an actress, it was great fun to play. . . . Making me a victim made me more vulnerable, and that fit with my relationship with Bobby." Despite his character's brutal treatment of April, Wilson found actor Eddie J. Peck "a doll, just the sweetest guy." ★ Cally's efforts to transform herself into a lady gave Cathy Podewell the chance to do scenes with Barbara Bel Geddes and Howard Keel. Podewell is a "big old time movie fan" and was thrilled to work with a "legend" like Keel. As for Bel Geddes, Podewell recalls, "Barbara was as sweet to me in real life as her character was to Cally. I remember one time, she gently brushed my hair off of my collar, like a mother would. It was such a sweet and loving gesture." In reality, Podewell had to add an accent to her portrayal of Cally. She explains, "My accent was not real. If I had a dime for every time someone asked me [if it was real]! That was a big compliment to me. Everyone thought I was from the Texas-Arkansas border. I would get letters from that region and people would ask me where I grew up there and what high school I went to there!"

302. "And Away We Go"

Written by Arthur Bernard Lewis; Directed by Steve Kanaly; Airdate: April 7, 1989
Guest Stars: Don Starr (Jordan); Jonathan Goldsmith (Bruce); Christopher Neame (Gustav Helstrom); Bonnie Burroughs (Alison Kincaid); Deborah Rennard (Sly); Conroy Gedeon (Detective Rigg); Sandra Kronemeyer (Pearl); J. Eddie Peck (Tommy McKay)
Subject: The Ewings travel to Europe.

Cast Notes Audrey Landers returns for an eight-episode appearance as Afton.

Trivia Weekly rating: number 30. ★ This was the last of three episodes directed by Steve Kanaly, who by the time of this episode had left the cast. Kanaly feels his best work as director got left on the editing room floor. "My great camera moves and very creative stuff never made it onto the show," he said. "They were looking for a certain type of scene and knew what they wanted." Of the scenes that were not cut, however, Kanaly's favorites are the bar scenes from this episode. He found filming those scenes "a lot of fun." ★ Sheree J. Wilson claims, "The reason Cathy [Podewell] and I got to go along on the [Europe] trip was they decided who was the most fun to travel with." Wilson describes Podewell as "the salt of the earth. . . . She was vulnerable, gullible, sweet, smart and really talented." Podewell admits that she was naïve, and that that trait, in part, led to her friendship with Wilson. "Sheree is such a good person," says Podewell. "I love her. She was such a fun, dynamic person. We got really close in Europe. We would go jogging in the morning and her boyfriend and my husband joined us. We had a great time. I was pretty naïve, just like Cally. I was in Europe for the first time and had never been on a series. And she was this worldly woman and I just ogled her. But we became really good friends, and I later got to work on *Walker, Texas Ranger* with her, too."

303. "The Yellow Brick Road"

Written by Leonard Katzman; Directed by Cliff Fenneman; Airdate: April 14, 1989
Guest Stars: David Healy (Chick Harvard); Kathryn Leigh Scott (Bunny Harvard); Gunnar Hellstrom (Rolf Brundin); Ken Swofford (Sheriff Billy Jo Burnside); Bonnie Burroughs (Alison Kincaid); Leon B. Stevens (Dr. Unger); Lillian Lehman (the Nanny); Omri Katz (John Ross); Joshua Harris (Christopher)
Subject: The Ewings in Munich and Salzburg.

Cast Notes Bunny Harvard was played by Kathryn Leigh Scott, who in the late 1960s starred as Maggie Evans in the gothic soap opera *Dark Shadows*. Scott also appeared on *Knots Landing* and *Dynasty* and in the Robert Redford movie *The Great Gatsby*. Since the 1980s, Scott has run her own publishing company, Pomegranate Press, which has published, among other TV and movie related works, several books on *Dark Shadows*. *Dallas* was one of Scott's "most enjoyable filming experiences." David Healy, who played Bunny's husband, Chick, appeared in Season 3 of *Dallas* as a state senator. Healy was an "old friend" of Scott's from her years in London in the early 1970s. She recalls, "The moment I discovered David would be playing my husband, I knew exactly how to play 'Bunny,' and we worked off one another with complete abandon. We were instantly 'married,' and just let it rip! We spoiled several takes for Larry, who couldn't keep a straight face; Bunny's walk especially got to him. . . . Everyone in the company was great, and I loved working with Larry, Patrick, and George and the gals. Cathy and Sheree were gorgeous and completely down-to-earth."

Trivia Weekly rating: number 31. ★ This was the first of four episodes featuring scenes filmed on location in March of 1989 in Salzburg, Vienna, and Moscow. As of February, Larry Hagman still had not learned the details of the European storyline. "I don't think we'll know," he said, "until Leonard finishes scouting the locations." The scenes for the characters who remained stateside were filmed in Culver City in Hollywood by the credited directors of these four episodes, Cliff Fenneman, Irving J. Moore, Linda Gray, and Michael Preece. Leonard Katzman accompanied Hagman, Patrick Duffy, Cathy Podewell, Sheree J. Wilson, George Kennedy, and the guest stars to Europe, where he directed, without credit, the on-location scenes. According to Kathryn Leigh Scott, Katzman was a "very supportive" director and "easy to work with." ★ The scenes at Brundin's estate were filmed on the grounds of Leopoldskron Castle, an eighteenth-century castle on a lake outside Salzburg. Several scenes from the 1965 Best Picture Oscar winner, *The Sound of Music*, were filmed at the nearby Bertelsmann estate on a terrace set copied from the grounds of Leopoldskron. Other Salzburg locations seen in this episode were also seen in *The Sound of Music*. ★ Says Kathryn Leigh Scott about her character's double identity, "David and I never gave a thought to the fact that we were actually spies masquerading as Ugly Americans; therefore, I think that our scene with George Kennedy as our 'spymaster' was more effective and came as a total surprise."

304. "The Sound of Money"

Written by Arthur Bernard Lewis; Directed by Irving J. Moore; Airdate: April 28, 1989 Guest Stars: David Healy (Chick Harvard); Kathryn Leigh Scott (Bunny Harvard); Gunnar Hellstrom (Rolf Brundin); Lillian Lehman (the Nanny); Alan McRae ("J.R."); Omri Katz (John Ross); Joshua Harris (Christopher); Gayle Hunnicutt (Vanessa Beaumont) Subject: The Ewings travel to Vienna.

Cast Notes Gayle Hunnicutt makes the first of thirteen appearances that last through Season 13. She starred in American and European movies in the 1960s and 1970s. Kathryn Leigh Scott found Hunnicutt "great fun."

Trivia Weekly rating: number 32. ★ Of April's and Bobby's scene in the Alps, Sheree J. Wilson explains, "Patrick was a great equestrian and I grew up with horses in Colorado. We said, 'We have to ride across those Alps.' I ad-libbed the Julie Andrews spin. It was like, 'I'm here, this is the moment.'" ★ George Kennedy recalls that "Austria was like going back in time; the music, the romance, the sense of happy harmony was everywhere." ★ Kathryn Leigh Scott found *Dallas* "an extravagant show in every respect: the wardrobe transported to Vienna and Salzburg could have stocked an entire floor of Saks Fifth Avenue. Like Old King Cole, Larry Hagman was a merry, old soul who does not know the meaning of the word moderation; we ate, drank, laughed, and partied prodigiously. We traveled from Vienna . . . to Salzburg . . . on a private train—with Larry the engineer bringing it into the station. . . . We were mobbed while filming in the streets, and we were wined and dined like American Movie Star Royalty." On a day off in Vienna, Scott and Healy rode the giant ferris wheel seen in the classic film *The Third Man*. "The ancient wooden cabin we were in would shudder to a stop and creak. . . . We both suffered terrible vertigo and claustrophobia and . . . spent the entire ride shaking and sweating until we were safely on the ground."

305. "The Great Texas Waltz"

Written by Howard Lakin; Directed by Linda Gray; Airdate: May 5, 1989
Guest Stars: David Healy (Chick Harvard); Kathryn Leigh Scott (Bunny Harvard); Gunnar Hellstrom (Rolf Brundin); Ron Canada (Dave Wallace); Omri Katz (John Ross); Joshua Harris (Christopher); Gayle Hunnicutt (Vanessa Beaumont)
Subject: A Viennese ball.

Cast Notes Ron Canada played Coach Corley on *Hangin' With Mr. Cooper*.

Trivia Weekly rating: number 32. ★ Sheree J. Wilson, like the other *Dallas* actors included on the Europe on-location shoot, found it a highlight of her time on *Dallas*. "I liked being the bad girl at the beginning [of my time on *Dallas*]," says Wilson, "but my favorite storyline was really the trip through Europe. It was the most joyful life experience. It was romantic to be in Vienna and Salzburg, being Julie Andrews—the cobblestones and majesty of those old buildings. It was like a fairy tale. And we'd wear those fur coats. It was my first love scene." ★ Kathryn Leigh Scott called the on-location shoot a "paid luxury vacation money could not buy. We were filming in historic libraries, guild halls, ball rooms, and state buildings that are closed to the public; I climbed a ladder in the library and held in my hands rare first editions hundreds of years old!" ★ Larry Hagman did not like the scene where J.R. rebuffs Vanessa's advances. "I thought that was kind of dumb, to tell you the truth," he said later. "Everybody says, 'What is the purpose of *Dallas*?' The purpose is to entertain. It's for entertainment and we don't do it for any morality plays or anything like that." ★ Cathy Podewell recalls that George Kennedy, who was a close friend of Leonard Katzman's, "was like this big teddy bear. He was always rubbing my head."

306. "Mission to Moscow"

Written by Leonard Katzman; Directed by Michael Preece; Airdate: May 12, 1989
Guest Stars: Ron Canada (Dave Wallace); Lillian Lehman (the Nanny); Alan McRae
("J.R."); Richard Minchenberg (Jerry Zeigler); Omri Katz (John Ross); Joshua Harris
(Christopher); Gayle Hunnicutt (Vanessa Beaumont)
Subject: The Ewings in Moscow.

Trivia Weekly rating: number 34. ★ Hagman believed that *Dallas*'s popularity in
the Eastern Bloc countries helped bring down the Soviet Union and end communism. "I think the opulence, the consumerism, the food, the cars—these things
made [people] want more than their governments provided them," he said. "You
take people who don't have any food to a goddamned supermarket, they're going
to want to stay." Hagman recalled that "a director from [the Soviet Union] . . . .
used to come over and we would trade a big tin of Beluga caviar for a TV, VCR,
and fifty tapes of *Dallas*. He would take them there and show them to all his
friends, and they would clone the tapes and circulate them all over Russia and so
forth. And people would see those things and say, why can't we live like that?
Why can't we have all those things that people have on *Dallas?* And . . . I honestly
believe . . . the information that there was a different way of life going on in the
world helped a lot." ★ Katzman did not feel that *Dallas* had a political agenda,
however. "All we were ever trying to do," he said, "was entertain the audience.
There was never any real deep meaning to it. We weren't trying to do a documen-
tary every week." ★ While in Moscow, the *Dallas* stars stayed at the Sovietskaya
Hotel, an ornate hotel used by state guests of Lenin's, but one without room service or elevators. Patrick Duffy, who recalled that the crew "certainly had to get
used to doing without having our every creature comfort met," observed that
Americans "come waltzing in here in our cowboy hats and mink coats and we
don't exactly meld into their society." ★ Cathy Podewell describes the shoot in
Europe as "awesome. I had never been to Europe before. Just to be in Red Square
on Larry Hagman's elbow, wearing these big fur coats—you don't get a better situation than that." George Kennedy, however, found Moscow "gray—gray weather,
gray faces, gray souls. You couldn't escape it." ★ The real Culver City Southfork
living room and kitchen sets are seen in this episode's movie studio scenes.

307. "Reel Life"

Written by Arthur Bernard Lewis and Howard Lakin; Directed by Irving J. Moore; Airdate:
May 19, 1989
Guest Stars: Andrew Prine (Harrison Van Buren III); Alan McRae ("J.R."); Ron Canada
(Dave Wallace); Deborah Rennard (Sly); Omri Katz (John Ross); Joshua Harris (Christo-
pher)
Subject: Sue Ellen leaves Dallas.

Cast Notes This was Linda Gray's last episode of *Dallas* until her guest appearance
on the series finale two years later. She also reprised the role of Sue Ellen in both

Dallas TV movie sequels and in the 2004 cast reunion. In the early 1990s, Gray played Heather Locklear's mother on *Melrose Place*, a role she continued on the short-lived spin-off *Models, Inc.* She also starred with Sylvester Stallone in the comedy *Oscar* and later appeared on Broadway and in London's West End in the stage version of the Mike Nichols film *The Graduate.* ★ Andrew Prine is a veteran of several TV series, including the western *The Road West*, on which he costarred with fellow *Dallas* cast member Glenn Corbett. ★ James Newell and Nora Masterson make their first appearances as Weststar vice presidents, roles they reprised in Season 12.

Trivia Weekly rating: number 22 with a 14.1 share. ★ CBS interrupted this episode for several minutes so CBS news could air a live report on the democratic uprisings in China's Tiananmen Square in Beijing. Several CBS affiliates repeated the episode at a later date after irate viewers complained about the interruption. ★ April's move onto Southfork enabled Sheree J. Wilson to witness firsthand the underside of filming Ewing family dinner scenes. Says Wilson, while "the set was very relaxed . . . we had to stay serious enough to get our scenes out. Patrick and Larry were like a stand-up comedy routine. Food fights, food flying everywhere— acting like immature little children—it was so funny!" ★ Sue Ellen's movie was not the first time a family member did an exposé on the Ewings. On *Knots Landing*, early in the 1982–83 season, Valene published a book based on the Ewings called *Capricorn Crude.* ★ Howard Lakin recalled that, despite the fact that Leonard Katzman did not particularly enjoy working with assertive women, he respected Linda Gray and wanted Sue Ellen to go out on top. "Len hated women who were forceful, feminist, and difficult—hated them," Lakin said. "Linda might have made his life hard but he appreciated what she brought to the show. Without Sue Ellen, J.R. was much less. . . . The way she exited . . . with her own company and, I think, millions in the bank and a handsome English guy on her arm . . . in the end, Len gave her what she wanted. It was a good thing for the viewing women of *Dallas*." ★ "Linda Gray," according to Cathy Podewell, "is absolutely one of the most genuinely sweet people I have ever met in my life. She was so gracious, but she was ready to go. It was kind of bittersweet. Her last scene filmed was with me, so it was like she was passing the reins to me. Her last scene was at Southfork. She was saying goodbye and good luck to Cally. After it was over, everyone hugged her. People swarmed all over her, and even Leonard Katzman came down" to the set. ★ Gray appeared in more than 300 of *Dallas*'s 357 episodes, which was more than any other female cast member. ★ Although aspects of Sue Ellen's character bothered Linda Gray, she acknowledged that the part "was fabulous for me. I loved it. It was my favorite part. Then it got a little old because I went to the producers and said, 'I'm drinking, having an affair. Having an affair, drinking. Drinking, having an affair. I have two things to do.' And they—I'll never forget what they said. They said, 'Yes, but you do it so well.'" Nevertheless, Gray enjoyed the freedom of life without the grind of filming a weekly series. After leaving the show, she "found I didn't want to wear makeup. I didn't want anyone touching my hair, putting a powder puff near my face. It was kind of like shedding skin. . . . It was like being dropped from another planet back on earth. . . . Buildings literally had sprung up—new restaurants—I mean, I know it sounds silly and very bizarre, but that's the way it was. . . . There's a big world out there. There's galaxies out there. What do you want to do? And, you know, how exciting to play in your garden or how exciting to do a play in Vienna. I did all of those things." ★ Two years after Gray's departure from the cast, Larry Hagman wrote that she "was the best leading lady an actor could ever ask for." Hagman also told an interviewer that Gray was "attractive, hardworking, so damned nice." Gray returned the compliment, saying, "He was the man you loved to hate, but I loved to love."

SEASON 12
1989–90—"Paradise Lost"

IN ITS PENULTIMATE SEASON, DALLAS added several young adult characters in an attempt to spice up its storyline. Former Calvin Klein model Sasha Mitchell joined the cast as J.R.'s twenty-something illegitimate son, and Kimberly Foster, who had a bit part in Season 10, won the role of April's sister, Michelle. British actress Lesley-Anne Down, who had starred in *Upstairs, Downstairs* and movies such as *A Little Night Music* and Sean Connery's *The Great Train Robbery*, was another Season 12 addition. CBS announced at its affiliate meetings that Linda Gray would return for several episodes during the year, but these appearances never occurred. CBS had a good reason to try to reinvigorate *Dallas* since it had taken the unusual step of renewing the show for two years at the end of Season 11. As a result, CBS was committed to the series through the 1990–91 season, *Dallas*'s thirteenth.

Season 12 did not get off to a good start, as *Dallas*'s two-hour season premiere not only earned an unimpressive rank of number 45, but was outperformed in the ratings by both ABC's sitcom lineup and the NBC movie *The Nasty Boys*. The dismal ratings caused Leonard Katzman to comment, "Very disappointing. Very disappointing." *Variety*, which reviewed the premiere, was slightly more impressed with the show than were viewers. Its review found that "the two-part season opener displayed promise, but, as always, Hagman steals the show with his Cheshire cat sleaziness." Any promise shown by the season premiere, however, was unfulfilled, as the ratings slid even further as the season progressed.

Season 12 marked the first time a season of *Dallas* did not include scenes filmed on location in Texas. A Lorimar spokesman confirmed early in the summer of 1989 that Lorimar Productions made the decision to stay in California as part of an effort to keep the series' costs down. Joe Pope, owner of Film Productions Services in *Dallas*, which had worked on the show's on-location shoot each summer, estimated that he lost $1 million in billings as a result of Lorimar's decision. "It means a lot," Pope said. "It's like being told you're not going to see a good friend again. It's more than economic, it's emotional." Leonard Katzman confirmed that Lorimar saved $1.5 million in production costs, but added that there were other reasons for the decision. "A lot of people got tired of uprooting their lives for two months of on-location shooting. After twelve years, some of the thrill is gone."

The thrill was also apparently gone for Barbara Bel Geddes and Charlene Tilton, who both left the show for a second and final time at the end of Season 12. According to Howard Keel, Bel Geddes' departure was the result of boredom.

"She was always nudging me, saying, 'Why don't you get with Leonard Katzman and see about the writing they've given us in this scene?'" Keel agreed that "they just wouldn't give us good scenes; we didn't get to be actors." But Keel would resist Bel Geddes' suggestion that they complain, saying, "No, that's none of my business." Keel was disappointed that Bel Geddes left, since he "hated to see somebody quit a pretty good role, especially where others are depending on the ensemble." Keel felt Bel Geddes "could be adorably cute and . . . amazing to work with," but "found her to be a complete enigma at times and wide open at others." Keel thought Bel Geddes believed Keel did not like her, but he did, writing that she "had a quality all her own and was a marvelous Miss Ellis."

For most of the year, Dallas followed Snoops on CBS and competed against Perfect Strangers and Just the Ten of Us on ABC and Hardball on NBC. It finished the season at number 55 with a 12.4 rating. CBS continued to support Dallas, however, because it was still one of the network's most-watched shows, although the network was slowly improving in the ratings. During the 1989–90 season, the number of CBS shows in the top twenty-five doubled to four: 60 Minutes; Murder, She Wrote; Designing Women; and the CBS Sunday Night Movie. Larry Hagman commented mid-way through the season, "Here we are, number 30 or 40 [in the ratings]. And we're still hot for CBS. Pretty bizarre."

SEASON 12 EPISODE GUIDE

Regular Cast

Starring:
Barbara Bel Geddes as Miss Ellie
Lesley-Anne Down as Stephanie Rogers
Patrick Duffy as Bobby
Kimberly Foster as Michelle Stevens
Larry Hagman as J.R.
Howard Keel as Clayton
George Kennedy as McKay
Ken Kercheval as Cliff
Sasha Mitchell as James Beaumont
Cathy Podewell as Cally
Charlene Tilton as Lucy
Sheree J. Wilson as April
Also Starring:
Karen Kopins as Kay
Audrey Landers as Afton
Denver Pyle as Blackie Callahan
Alexis Smith as Jessica Montfort
Beth Toussaint as Tracey

Technical Credits
Supervising Producer: Howard Lakin
Executive Producers: Leonard Katzman,
    Larry Hagman
Co-Executive Producer: Ken Horton
Producer: Cliff Fenneman
Co-Producer: Mitchell Wayne Katzman
Associate Producers: Frank W. Katzman,
    John Rettino
Executive Story Consultant: Lisa Seidman
Music: Jerrold Immel, John Parker, Richard
    Lewis Warren, Lance Rubin, Angela
    Morley

Unit Production Manager: Wayne Farlow
First Assistant Directors: Richard R.
    Johnson, Amy Rosenbaum Jacobson
Second Assistant Directors: W. Alexander
    Ellis, Keri L. McIntyre
Director of Photography: Rick R. Gunter
Art Director: David K. Marshall, Stewart
    Campbell
Editors: Fred W. Berger, A.C.E., John
    Arthur Davies
Executive in Charge of Casting: Barbara
    Miller, C.S.A.
Casting: Irene Mariano, C.S.A.
Set Decorator: Phillip Snyder
Property Master: Kerry Scott Knerr
Costumers: Laurie Riley, Lyn Paolo
Makeup: Joe Hailey, Bob Jermain
Hair Stylists: Generio Gugliemotto, Lola
    "Skip" McNalley, Laura Lee Grubich
Production Sound Mixer: Andrew Gilmore
Post-Production Sound: Thomas Gillis
    Burke, Kimberly Harris, Larry Porche,
    Catherine H. LeBaigue
Sound Operators: Larry Porche, Catherine
    H. LeBaigue, Paul Fontana
Music Supervisors: Richard Berres, Gregory
    Sill
Music Editor: Patricia Peck
Main Title Design: Cliff Fenneman
Executive Coordinator: Louella Lee
    Caraway
Executive-in-Charge of Production:
    R. Robert Rosenbaum

308. & 309: "Phantom of the Oil Rig" (Parts One and Two)
*Written by Howard Lakin (Part One), Leonard Katzman (Part Two); Directed by Irving J.
Moore (Part One), Michael Preece (Part Two); Airdate: September 22, 1989
Guest Stars: Michael Wilding (Alex Barton); Andrew Prine (Harrison Van Buren, III);
Ron Canada (Wallace); Fern Fitzgerald (Marilee Stone); Joey Aresco (Boomer); Cliff
Bemis (Mr. Shaughnessy); Jack Rader (Pete Reuther); Craig Richard Nelson (Lee Miller);
Deborah Rennard (Sly); Paul Eiding (Father Thomas Mallory); James Harper (Walter Kaz-*

mayer); Gerald Castillo (Manuel Ramirez); Omri Katz (John Ross); Joshua Harris (Christopher); J. Eddie Peck (Tommy)
Subject: J.R.'s business deals.

Cast Notes Kimberly Foster joins the cast as April's sister, and remained on *Dallas* until its penultimate episode in Season 13. Foster described herself as being from a "'one-stoplight town' in Arkansas," and told *USA Today*, "I was screaming" when she learned from her agent that she won the role of Michelle. Sheree J. Wilson says her on-screen sister was like "a little fox. We got along great, but I couldn't tell if it was acting. She'd say, 'I'd like that trailer.' And I'd say, 'That's mine.'" Foster, as well as returning cast members George Kennedy and Cathy Podewell, were added to the main title as of this episode. ★ Cliff Bemis played Paul on *Newhart*. ★ Craig Richard Nelson was a regular on *Carol Burnett & Company*, a 1979 summer variety series that brought Carol Burnett back to TV the year after her classic CBS variety show went off the air. ★ The hotel clerk is played by Reuben Grundey, who played Ernest on *A Different World*, a spin-off of *The Cosby Show*. ★ Michael Wilding is the son of movie legend Elizabeth Taylor and British actor Michael Wilding.

Trivia Weekly rating: number 45 with a 12.8 rating and 23 share. ★ In syndication, Part Two of this episode was renamed "The Leopard's Spots." ★ Producer Cliff Fenneman reworked the format of the show's main title for Season 12, and the result was also used in Season 13 and in both TV movie sequels. Prior to Season 12, the split-screen clips of the regular cast members in the main title were usually updated annually, but the format of the main title otherwise remained the same from the pilot through Season 11. Fenneman's version abandoned the split-screen clips of the cast in favor of full-screen clips. ★ This episode also marks Howard Lakin's promotion to supervising producer, a position he would hold until the show ended. Lakin wrote or co-wrote twenty-three episodes during Seasons 3 through 5 and 11 through 13. ★ Ken Horton was the co–executive producer for Season 12. He also wrote Episodes 328 and 352.

310. "Cry Me a River of Oil"

Written by Lisa Seidman; Directed by Dwight Adair; Airdate: September 29, 1989
Guest Stars: Michael Wilding (Alex Barton); Lance LeGault (Al Halliday); Gunnar Helstrom (Rolf Brundin); Don Starr (Jordan Lee); Joey Aresco (Boomer); Cliff Bemis (Shaughnessy); Thom McFadden (Doug Snyder); Jack Rader (Pete Reuther); Deborah Rennard (Sly); Joshua Harris (Christopher); Ben Rawnsley (Patterson); J. Eddie Peck (Tommy)
Subject: J.R. purchases a tanker.

Cast Notes Lance LeGault appeared as Colonel Roderick Decker on *The A-Team*. He also played Colonel Green on *Magnum, P.I.*

Trivia Weekly rating: number 49. ★ Lucy's interest in Cally's paintings and her friendship with gallery owner Alex gave Cathy Podewell the opportunity to act with both Charlene Tilton and Michael Wilding. Says Podewell, "I loved Charlene. She was so funny and was a little ball of fire. . . . Michael was very nice and very charming. You would never guess he was Elizabeth Taylor's son. He had no pretensions at all." ★ Writer Lisa Seidman wrote thirteen episodes during Seasons 12 and 13.

311. "Ka-boooom!"

Written by Louella Lee Caraway; Directed by Michael Preece; Airdate: October 6, 1989
Guest Stars: Michael Wilding (Alex Barton); Lance LeGault (Al Halliday); Joey Aresco (Boomer); Gloria Henry (Mrs. Ona Evander); Jeri Gaile (Rose Daniels); Deborah Rennard (Sly); Omri Katz (John Ross); Joshua Harris (Christopher); J. Eddie Peck (Tommy)
Subject: Tommy stalks Bobby.

Cast Notes Gloria Henry played Dennis's mother, Alice Mitchell, on the TV classic *Dennis the Menace*.

Trivia Weekly rating: number 43. ★ Sheree Wilson's golden retriever, Ilsa, is seen in the jogging scene. Wilson frequently brought Ilsa to the set, and she previously appeared on *Dallas* in a park scene, catching a frisbee.

312. "Sunset, Sunrise"

Written by Howard Lakin; Directed by Dwight Adair; Airdate: October 13, 1989
Guest Stars: Michael Wilding (Alex Barton); Lance LeGault (Al Halliday); Fern Fitzgerald (Marilee); Cliff Bemis (Shaughnessy); Joey Aresco (Boomer); Art Koustik (Police Captain); Deborah Rennard (Sly); J. Eddie Peck (Tommy)
Subject: James arrives.

Cast Notes Sasha Mitchell, who makes his first appearance as J.R.'s son, was a Calvin Klein blue jeans model who had appeared on *St. Elsewhere*. Mitchell was added to the main title as of this episode. Immediately after *Dallas* was canceled in 1991, Mitchell joined Patrick Duffy in the cast of *Step by Step*, a sitcom produced by Lorimar. Mitchell appeared on *Step* from 1991 to 1996 and in 1998 and, as on *Dallas*, played Duffy's nephew. In one episode of *Step by Step*, Duffy wonders aloud whatever happened to his brother, Mitchell's character's father. This was an inside joke about J.R.'s fate in the *Dallas* series finale. Duffy's and Mitchell's success made them two of only three *Dallas* regulars to appear on a long-running series after leaving Southfork. The third, Sheree J. Wilson, appeared on the Chuck Norris–Leonard Katzman show *Walker, Texas Ranger*.

Trivia Weekly rating: number 41. ★ Tommy's death in his father's arms is George Kennedy's favorite *Dallas* scene. "Eddie and I worked hard on it, and [the director] gave us freedom to let all the pain and grief show. Our reward? The network top floor brass, individually, came to the set and gave us both hugs and quiet words of admiration. Unheard of? Yes. And very much appreciated." Kennedy missed Eddie Peck after Tommy was killed off. Kennedy also "grew to be close friends" with

Beth Toussaint, who made her last appearance as his daughter Tracey in this episode. "When [Tracey and I] parted company the last time," Kennedy recalls, "the tears stung our faces, our hearts were in our boots."

313. "Pride and Prejudice"

Written by Leonard Katzman; Directed by Michael Preece; Airdate: October 20, 1989
Guest Stars: Michael Wilding (Alex Barton); Thom McFadden (Doug Snyder); Tedd Wilson (Clem); Deborah Rennard (Sly); Joshua Harris (Christopher); David Wiley (Sparks); Gayle Hunnicutt (Vanessa)
Subject: Miss Ellie's trip to Pride.

Cast Notes The Pride gas station attendant is played by Tedd Wilson, who was a regular on *Good Times* and starred in *Sanford Arms*, the successor show to the Redd Foxx classic *Sanford and Son*.

Trivia Weekly rating: number 36.

314. "Fathers and Other Strangers"

Written by Lisa Seidman; Directed by Irving J. Moore; Airdate: November 3, 1989
Guest Stars: Hank Rolike (Neal); Bea Silvern (Sarah Ewing); Deborah Rennard (Sly); Joshua Harris (Christopher); Gayle Hunnicutt (Vanessa)
Subject: J.R. is James's father.

Trivia Weekly rating: number 40.

315. "Black Tide"

Written by Howard Lakin; Directed by Michael Preece; Airdate: November 10, 1989
Guest Stars: Lance LeGault (Al); Jack Rader (Pete); Fred Holliday (John Atherton); Deborah Rennard (Sly); Gayle Hunnicutt (Vanessa)
Subject: J.R.'s tanker crashes.

Cast Notes Fred Holliday appeared as Dr. Barnes on *Medical Center*.

Trivia Weekly rating: number 40.

316. "Daddy Dearest"

Written by Mitchell Wayne Katzman; Directed by Irving J. Moore; Airdate: November 17, 1989
Guest Stars: Michael Wilding (Alex); George O. Petrie (Harv); Fern Fitzgerald (Marilee); Craig Littler (Senator Polkinghorne); Fred Holliday (Atherton); Omri Katz (John Ross); Deborah Rennard (Sly)
Subject: A letter from Jock.

Trivia Although she did not know it at the time, this was Fern Fitzgerald's final appearance on *Dallas*. Explains Fitzgerald, "The writers never discussed where they were going with a storyline. None of us knew when we were filming our 'last episode.' I don't think the writers knew, either!" Fitzgerald found it "a great joy to be a part of TV history, as *Dallas* was the first nighttime soap opera of its kind."

317. "Hell's Fury"

Written by Lisa Seidman; Directed by Patrick Duffy; Airdate: December 1, 1989
Guest Stars: Michael Wilding (Alex); Lee de Broux (Jack Bouleris); J. Jay Sanders (George
Middleton); Deborah Rennard (Sly); Ellen Geer (Mrs. Bouleris); Omri Katz (John Ross);
Joshua Harris (Christopher); Leslie Bevis (Diana Farrington)
Subject: Cally's suspicions about J.R.

Cast Notes Leslie Bevis returned to *Dallas* as Jeanne Lawrence in the series finale.

Trivia Weekly rating: number 44. ★ Not long before this episode aired, Larry
Hagman, "dressed in a brown pinstripe suit and jogging shoes, . . . slipped away
from the *Dallas* set at Lorimar studios" and met TV reporter Daniel P. Puzo, who
was working on a profile of Hagman, for lunch. Puzo found Hagman "in the best of
moods . . . alternately jocular, optimistic and witty." Hagman told Puzo that, earlier that morning, he and Duffy taped on the *Dallas* set a "bawdy video message" to
be played at the upcoming bar mitzvah of Omri Katz. Said Hagman, "It's a real
close family on the show."

318. "Cally on a Hot Tin Roof"

Written by Howard Lakin; Directed by Larry Hagman; Airdate: December 8, 1989
Guest Stars: Michael Wilding (Alex); J. Jay Sanders (George Middleton); Tom Fucello
(Dave Culver); Deborah Rennard (Sly); Leslie Bevis (Diana Farrington)
Subject: Cally turns to Alex.

Cast Notes Weststar publicist Maggie is played by costar Marla Maples, the former
wife of New York real estate mogul Donald Trump.

Trivia Weekly rating: number 40.

319: "Sex, Lies and Videotape"

Written by Leonard Katzman; Directed by Cliff Fenneman; Airdate: December 15, 1989
Guest Stars: Lee de Broux (Jack Bouleris); Jeri Gaile (Rose Daniels McKay); J. Jay Sanders
(George Middleton); Deborah Rennard (Sly); Robert Pierce (Medic #1); Danny Goldring
(Dick Attelsley); Omri Katz (John Ross); Joshua Harris (Christopher); Leslie Bevis (Diana
Farrington)
Subject: McKay blackmails Cliff.

Trivia Weekly rating: number 34. Excluding the season finale, this was *Dallas*'s
highest-ranked episode of the season.

320. "A Tale of Two Cities"

Written by Arthur Bernard Lewis; Directed by Leonard Katzman; Airdate: January 5, 1990
Guest Stars: Jeri Gaile (Rose Daniels McKay); Gloria Henry (Ona Evander); John Mahon
(Captain Holgar); Gregory Walcott (Commander Jedediah Joyce); Leslie Bevis (Diana Far-
rington)
Subject: The Gulf oil spill hearing.

Trivia Weekly rating: number 40. ★ George Kennedy liked being directed by Leonard Katzman, who Kennedy says "was Dallas. Without his consideration, his expertise, his selflessness, his ongoing brilliance, the show would have been nothing more than a cowtown cartoon." ★ About the time this episode aired, CBS threw a party for the casts and crews of Dallas, Knots Landing, and Falcon Crest at the Campanile Restaurant in Los Angeles. Larry Hagman attended with, as he called them, "all my blondes," his wife, Maj; TV wife, Cathy Podewell; and Sheree J. Wilson, who he called "one of my better ex-mistresses."

321. "Judgment Day"

Written by Amy Tebo; Directed by Patrick Duffy; Airdate: January 12, 1990
Guest Stars: Jeri Gaile (Rose McKay); George O. Petrie (Harv); Teddy Wilson (Clem); J. Jay Saunders (Middleton); Fred Halliday (John Atherton); Deborah Rennard (Sly); Leslie Bevis (Diana Farrington)
Subject: The Gulf oil spill hearing concludes.

Trivia Weekly rating: number 40. ★ Digger's grave is also seen in Episode 54. ★ The oil tanker spill storyline brought Ken Kercheval's character back to politics, with which he was involved in the Dallas pilot and Season 1. Kercheval won the 1990 Soap Opera Digest Award for Outstanding Prime Time Supporting Actor.

322. "Unchain My Heart"

Written by Jackie Zabel and Bryce Zabel; Directed by Irving J. Moore; Airdate: January 19, 1990
Guest Stars: Margaret Michaels (Jeanne O'Brien); Jeri Gaile (Rose McKay); Matthew Faison (Stanton Drake); Charles Stratton (Clarence Melville); Jack Rader (Pete Reuther); Fred Holliday (John Atherton); Omri Katz (John Ross)
Subject: Bobby thinks he sees Pam.

Cast Notes Lesley-Anne Down, the British actress who starred as Georgina Worsley in the miniseries sensation Upstairs, Downstairs, makes her Dallas debut and is added to the main title as of this episode. Down, a Golden Globe nominee, starred in the movies A Little Night Music, The Great Train Robbery, The Betsy, and The Pink Panther Strikes Again. She also appeared in the miniseries North and South and both of its sequels and on the soap opera The Bold and the Beautiful, alongside former Dallas cast members Susan Flannery, who, like Down, played a publicist on Dallas, and Linda Gray. Down recalls that she got the role of Stephanie Rogers after the producers "called and offered me the part. They wanted me for ten episodes, and I met with Len [Katzman], who told me they had me in mind when they came up with the part. He asked me for my ideas about the role. We talked, and I decided to do it. At that time, doing a scene with J.R. was a bit like dancing with Fred Astaire." ★ Margaret Michaels, whose physical resemblance to Victoria Principal landed her the role of Pam in Episode 282, returns in this episode as Pam look-alike Jeanne O'Brien. A year after her appearance as Pam, Michaels got a call from Leonard Katzman who asked her if she wanted to come back and play another character for a few episodes since the show was "closing out Bobby's love interests." Michaels said, "Sure," making it the easiest casting job of her career.

Trivia Weekly rating: number 46.

323. "I Dream of Jeanne"
Written by Lisa Seidman; Directed by Cliff Fenneman; Airdate: February 2, 1990
Guest Stars: Margaret Michaels (Jeanne O'Brien); Jeri Gaile (Rose McKay); Matthew Faison (Stanton Drake); Bruce Gray (Richard Mertz); Charles Stratton (Clarence Melville); Jack Rader (Pete Reuther); Fred Holliday (John Atherton); Omri Katz (John Ross)
Subject: Bobby pursues Jeanne.

Cast Notes Denver Pyle appeared on such TV shows as *The Life and Legend of Wyatt Earp*, *The Andy Griffith Show*, and *The Doris Day Show*. He starred as Uncle Jesse on *The Dukes of Hazzard*, which preceded *Dallas* in the CBS Friday night lineup from *The Dukes'* premiere in January 1979 until it was canceled at the end of the 1984–85 season.

Trivia Weekly rating: number 43. ★ Pam's middle name was Jean. ★ The title of this episode comes not only from the name of Pam's look-alike, but also from Larry Hagman's previous hit TV show, *I Dream of Jeannie*.

324. "After Midnight"
Written by Howard Lakin; Directed by Ken Kercheval; Airdate: February 9, 1990
Guest Stars: Margaret Michaels (Jeanne O'Brien); Claude Earl Jones (Duke Carlisle); Shawn Modrell (Melinda Carlisle); Richard Narita (Eugene Inagaki); Leslie Neale (Sheryl Thompson)
Subject: J.R. strikes oil.

Cast Notes Richard Narita made several appearances on *Magnum, P.I.*

Trivia Weekly rating: number 52, tying Episode 328 as the season's lowest ranked. ★ Director Ken Kercheval was the fifth *Dallas* cast member to work behind the camera, joining the ranks of Larry Hagman, Patrick Duffy, Linda Gray, and Steve Kanaly. Kercheval recalls that he "had never directed before. I didn't know lenses and camera angles and all that. I went to the crew, because our crew was pretty savvy, and said, 'I don't know what lens or what shot to use. That's not my forte. I'll work with the actors, and you set the shot up.' They were very appreciative of that. The crew really bent over backwards for me." Of the two episodes Kercheval directed, this episode contains his favorite scene, one between Patrick Duffy and Margaret Michaels. "They were in the living room. Patrick was to kiss her and pick her up and carry her into the bedroom and close the door. I went to Patrick and said, 'Patrick, is there any chance that you can pick her up while your hands are on her waist—just pick her straight up?' And he said, 'Sure.' And I said, 'And can you keep kissing her and carry her into the bedroom while you're carrying her like that?' And he said, 'Sure.' And so the kiss came and he carried her into the bedroom. And I had said to the crew, 'When they get into the bedroom, can you give it a count of five and then have the lights go out?' And that required them to redo the lighting. I said, 'No big deal if you can't.' And they said, 'No, Kenny, we can do it.' And they did! And that was the shot. I thought it was clever, and it worked." Margaret Michaels found the scene "particularly creative and tasteful."

325. "The Crucible"

Written by Leonard Katzman; Directed by Larry Hagman; Airdate: February 16, 1990
Guest Stars: Margaret Michaels (Jeanne O'Brien); Claude Earl Jones (Duke Carlisle); John Larch (Arlen/Atticus Ward); Charles Cooper (Curley Morrison); Eddie Firestone (Robert "Rabbit" Hutch); Shawn Modrell (Melinda Carlisle); Richard Narita (Eugene Inagaki); Omri Katz (John Ross); Joshua Harris (Christopher)
Subject: Bobby says goodbye to Pam.

Cast Notes John Larch played Wallace Windham in Season 7. He died in 1994.

Trivia Weekly rating: number 46. ★ According to Margaret Michaels, as a director, Larry Hagman "was so strong on where the characters were going—their heart and soul. But he would not interrupt too much." Michaels admits, however, that Hagman the director was not above the practical jokes played by Hagman the actor. "I realized when Larry was directing that he only wanted to redo certain shots so he could play one of his jokes. I was set up on a regular basis!"

326. "Dear Hearts and Gentle People"

Written by Louella Lee Caraway; Directed by Irving J. Moore; Airdate: February 23, 1990
Guest Stars: K Callan (Amy Stevens); John Larch (Arlen Ward); Eddie Firestone (Robert "Rabbit" Hutch); Stephanie Blackmore (Serena); Deborah Rennard (Sly); Daryl Roach (Detective Marshall)
Subject: Bobby visits April in Ohio.

Cast Notes K Callan starred in two projects involving *Dallas* creator David Jacobs, *Married: The First Year* and *Lois and Clark—The New Adventures of Superman.* Both shows costarred *Dallas* cast members. Leigh McCloskey played Callan's son on *Married.* Tracy Scoggins and Lane Smith costarred on *Superman,* in which Callan played Clark Kent's mother.

Trivia Weekly rating: number 50.

327. "Paradise Lost"

Written by Lisa Seidman; Directed by Patrick Duffy; Airdate: March 9, 1990
Guest Stars: K Callan (Amy Stevens); Don Galloway (Patrick Knelman); John Larch (Arlen Ward); Lisa Sloan (Beth Rutgers); Eugene Robert Glazer (Phil Rogers); Stephanie Blackmore (Serena); Deborah Rennard (Sly); Joseph G. Medalis (Rand); Jerry Potter (Ken Morton); Barney McFadden (Bruce Burns); Daryl Roach (Detective Marshall); Len Way-

land (Lefty Simmons); Omri Katz (John Ross); Joshua Harris (Christopher)
Subject: Bobby returns to Dallas.

Cast Notes Don Galloway played Detective Sergeant Ed Brown on *Ironside*.

Trivia Weekly rating: number 49.

328. "Will Power"

*Written by Kenneth Horton; Directed by Larry Hagman; Airdate: March 16, 1990
Guest Stars: K Callan (Amy Stevens); Don Galloway (Patrick Knelman); John Larch
(Arlen Ward); Claudette Nevins (Lizzie Burns); Taaffe O'Connell (Honey North);
Stephanie Blackmore (Serena); Deborah Rennard (Sly); Patrick Cronin (Al Iudecello);
Daryl Roach (Detective Marshall); Mary D'Arcy (Nancy Ann); Eric Poppick (Dave);
Frank Papia (Reynolds); Omri Katz (John Ross); Joshua Harris (Christopher)
Subject: Clayton's friends are killed.*

Trivia Weekly rating: number 52.

329. "The Smiling Cobra"

*Written by Howard Lakin; Directed by Cliff Fenneman; Airdate: March 30, 1990
Guest Stars: Don Galloway (Patrick Knelman); John Larch (Atticus Ward); Stephanie
Blackmore (Serena); Jerry Potter (Ken Morton); Tony Rizzoli (Schmidt); Len Wayland
(Lefty Simmons); Omri Katz (John Ross); Joshua Harris (Christopher)
Subject: Atticus Ward is found.*

Trivia Weekly rating: number 39. ★ As of this episode, *Dallas* moved back to the
10:00 p.m. timeslot it held prior to *Falcon Crest*'s premiere on December 4, 1981.

330. "Jessica Redux"

*Written by Leonard Katzman; Directed by Irving J. Moore; Airdate: April 6, 1990
Guest Stars: Richard Narita (Inagaki); Daryl Roach (Marshall); Omri Katz (John Ross);
Charles Kahlenberg (Dr. Kohler)
Subject: Jessica's return.*

Trivia Weekly rating: number 45. ★ Lesley-Anne Down filmed restaurant scenes
with Larry Hagman for this episode as well as Episodes 326 and 327. Down recalls
that one of these scenes "was filmed at a place in Malibu near both our homes. It
was the first scene of the day. We filmed it about 8:30 in the morning. Larry pours
us some wine, which on a movie or TV set is usually grape juice. When I picked
up the glass and took a sip, I practically spit it all out—Larry liked having the real
thing! I told Larry, 'I don't think I can do this this early in the morning!' And he
was fine with that." ★ When Alexis Smith appeared on *Dallas* in Season 6, the
credits listed her character as "Jessica Montford." Beginning with this episode,
however, her Seasons 12 credits list her as "Jessica Montfort." ★ This is the last
Season 12 appearance of Kimberly Foster, whose character left Dallas during this
episode.

331. "Family Plot"

Written by Lisa Seidman; Directed by Patrick Duffy; Airdate: April 13, 1990
Guest Stars: Don Galloway (Dr. Patrick Knelman); Richard Narita (Inagaki); Stephanie Blackmore (Serena); Daryl Roach (Marshall); Deborah Rennard (Sly); Omri Katz (John Ross); Joshua Harris (Christopher)
Subject: Jessica's arrest.

Cast Notes This is Lesley-Anne Down's last episode on Dallas. Most of Down's scenes on the show were with Larry Hagman and Ken Kercheval. Down says that "Ken Kercheval was nice, and Larry was lovely. I liked Larry a lot. And I loved his wife." Down regretted that her time on Dallas did not overlap with Linda Gray's, who Down knew socially in Malibu and liked very much. In March 2004, however, the two actresses got to work together when Gray joined the cast of The Bold and the Beautiful, which costarred Down. Gray found it "fantastic" to finally work with Down as well as former Dallas guest star Susan Flannery, another Bold cast member.

Trivia Weekly rating: number 40.

332. "The Southfork Wedding Jinx"

Written by Howard Lakin; Directed by Irving J. Moore; Airdate: April 27, 1990
Guest Stars: K Callan (Amy Stevens); George O. Petrie (Harv); Jay Gerber (Rosemont); Jeri Gaile (Rose); Stephen Mendel (Walter Berman); Ag Pugliese (Orderly); Deborah Rennard (Sly); Anne Gee Byrd (Nurse Richardson); Omri Katz (John Ross); Joshua Harris (Christopher); Barbara Stock (Liz Adams)
Subject: April and Bobby marry.

Cast Notes This episode includes Barbara Bel Geddes' and Charlene Tilton's last appearances as Miss Ellie and Lucy (although Tilton returned to Southfork for the 2004 cast reunion, for which she also served as a co-executive producer). For the remainder of the season, and through Season 13, Miss Ellie's and Lucy's absence was explained by their travels in Europe. This is Howard Keel's last Season 12 episode, although his character visited Dallas during four Season 13 episodes. In reflecting on this episode, Tilton recalled, "When I was shooting my last closeup, then it hit me: 'Wow. This has been almost half my life, doing this show.'" Tilton lives in Los Angeles and continues to act. Bel Geddes opted not to return for Season 13 after she and Lorimar failed to negotiate a satisfactory contract renewal. By the end of Season 12, Bel Geddes had appeared in almost 290 of Dallas's 357 episodes, more than any other female cast member except for Linda Gray. After finishing her final episode, Bel Geddes retired to her wooded farm in upstate New York. Bel Geddes had shared the 200-year-old farmhouse and its fifty-five acres with her late husband, Wind Lewis, for twenty years prior to his death in 1972. "He always said I married him for the farm," Bel Geddes once told a reporter. She explained, "I come here and open the windows, listen to the birds and watch my geese, and it's a great comfort to me." Bel Geddes also liked to feed the wild geese and sit near the pond. She had long claimed that her desire was to "quit [acting] and just play, which I have never been able to do my whole life. I've just worked. Now I want to read and bird-watch and do my drawing." Bel Geddes' retirement, however, was not a reflection of her feelings about *Dallas*. Bel Geddes' granddaughter explains, "My grandmother really loved *Dallas*. . . . She often spoke about her love for the show. . . . She saved everything relating to [*Dallas*] and has shown me her scrapbook about it. She loved everything about the show." ★ This is Barbara Stock's first appearance as Liz Adams, although she appeared in a minor role in Episodes 85 and 92. She became a regular cast member in Season 13. Stock played Robert Urich's girlfriend on the first and third seasons of *Spenser: For Hire*.

Trivia Weekly rating: number 42. ★ Sheree J. Wilson recalls that by the time this episode's wedding scenes were filmed, she was "seven or eight months pregnant with my first child. I had the biggest bouquet of flowers that was hollowed out to hide me."

Episode 333. "Three-three-three" (Part One)

Written by Leonard Katzman; Directed by Leonard Katzman; Airdate: May 4, 1990
Guest Stars: Harold Gould (Dr. Wexler); Mitch Pileggi (Morrisey); Shannon Wilcox (Anita); Jeri Gaile (Rose); Liam Sullivan (Mark Allen); Michael P. Keenan (Keller); Zane Lasky (Donia); Hugh Maguire (Goldman); Arthur Malet (Ryan); Marty Schiff (Del Greco); Deborah Rennard (Sly); Barbara Stock (Liz)
Subject: James and Cally plot against J.R.

Cast Notes Harold Gould is a veteran of such movies as *Marnie* and *The Sting* and such sitcoms as *Rhoda*, on which he played Valerie Harper's father, and *The Golden Girls*, on which he played Betty White's boyfriend Miles Webber. ★ Michael P. Keenan played Mayor Bill Pugen on the Emmy-winning *Picket Fences*. ★ Zane Lasky played Bob Phillips on *Knots Landing*. ★ Except for one scene in this episode in which Bobby telephones from his overseas honeymoon, neither Patrick Duffy nor Sheree J. Wilson appear in Episodes 333 and 334.

Trivia Weekly rating: number 43. ★ Cathy Podewell did not like her Season 12 storyline as much as her Season 11 scenes, although she enjoyed working with Sasha Mitchell. "Sasha is a really nice guy," says Podewell. "He was sort of serious. I couldn't believe it when I saw him on *Step by Step* playing a *Fast Times at Ridgemont High* kind of character. I hadn't perceived him as a comedic actor because he was a serious person. I didn't like [my Season 12] storyline as much as I liked working with Larry. It was fun trying to trick Larry, but I could feel my storyline moving away." ★ Several days after this episode aired, TV columnist Ed Bark of the *Dallas Morning News* wrote about Leonard Katzman's efforts, in the face of *Dallas*'s declining ratings, "to work harder, try[ing] to think of things that will titillate the audience. But once you lose people, it's awfully tough to get 'em back. Outside of the real hard core, the old faithful don't care much about the show anymore. I'd certainly like to say something different but I don't think I can. We're going to go out doing the show just the way we've always done it. And if next year is the last year, we're going to prepare for a fitting ending."

Episode 334. "Three-three-three" (Part Two)

Written by Leonard Katzman; Directed by Leonard Katzman; Airdate: May 11, 1990
Guest Stars: Harold Gould (Dr. Wexler); Stephen Mendel (Walter Berman); Shannon
Wilcox (Anita); Mitch Pileggi (Morrisey); Ken Foree (Howard); Liam Sullivan (Mark
Allen); Michael P. Keenan (Keller); Zane Lasky (Donia); Hugh Maguire (Goldman);
Arthur Malet (Ryan); Marty Schiff (Del Greco); Deborah Rennard (Sly); Barbara Stock
(Liz)
Subject: J.R. is committed.

Trivia Weekly rating: number 30. This was Season 12's highest-ranked episode, and the only one of the year to make the top thirty. ★ Larry Hagman felt this episode's scene in which J.R.'s "bastard son put me in the loony bin" was fair given J.R.'s similar treatment of Sue Ellen in Season 1. ★ Leonard Katzman believed this cliff-hanger was "one of the most unique and compelling episodes" of *Dallas*. "We think this episode is not only representative of what *Dallas* has been doing all season long but is also as divergent and innovative as [*Dallas's*] original [cliffhangers]."

SEASON 13
1990–91—"Terminus"

SEASON 13 TURNED OUT TO be the unlucky one for *Dallas*. It was cancelled at season's end after 357 episodes and one three-hour movie or, as *TV Guide* calculated it, at least with regard to J.R., "106 love scenes, 133 reconciliations with 'mama,' 53 Stetsons, 212 business deals gone bad and 16 dunkings in the Southfork pool." *Dallas* premiered in the second year of Jimmy Carter's presidency, remained a critical and popular hit almost to the end of the twelve Reagan-Bush years, and aired its last episode five months to the day before Bill Clinton announced his bid for the presidency. In that time, *Dallas* won Emmy and Golden Globe Awards, among dozens of other awards; made the cover of hundreds of magazines, including *Time*; was crowned by Nielsen as TV's number 1 show at the end of the 1980–81, 1981–82, and 1983–84 seasons, and finished in the Nielsen top ten at the end of four other television seasons. It inspired a genre that includes such long-running serials as *Dawson's Creek; Beverly Hills, 90210; Melrose Place;* and *The Gilmore Girls*, let alone *Dynasty, Knots Landing,* and *Falcon Crest*. Its trademark season-ending cliff-hanger was borrowed by almost all forms of television, even situation comedies like *Cheers* and *Friends*. And, decades later, the "Who Shot J.R.?" whodunit remains a cultural touchstone for 1980s America.

While *Dallas*'s many accomplishments would be recalled in the media build-up that accompanied its final episode, during most of Season 13, *Dallas* was a show in decline. Both Barbara Bel Geddes and Charlene Tilton opted not to return after Season 12, so Katzman was now left with only three original cast members, Larry Hagman, Patrick Duffy, and Ken Kercheval. As Katzman had done in the recent past, he turned to outside stars and an overseas locale to help the show keep an audience. Daytime soap opera queen Susan Lucci, an Emmy winner for the role she played on ABC's *All My Children* since 1970, appeared in a storyline with Duffy and Sheree J. Wilson that was filmed in Paris, and Hagman's *I Dream of Jeannie* costar, Barbara Eden, came to *Dallas* to trigger J.R.'s final downfall. Even before the new season began, however, the cast and crew knew that Season 13 could be the show's last. Two months before the Season 13 premiere, Larry Hagman told a reporter that renewal for a fourteenth season depended

> on the ratings. . . . We happen to be in a unique position where we're in the top six [shows] at CBS, so they're in a strange position where our ratings aren't terribly good—I think we came in forty-third last year—but it's still better than anybody else. . . . I'm sure they'd like to get rid of us,

just because we're an old show and they would like to experiment, and they probably will next year. But let's face it, if you're in their top ten at CBS, you're still in a viable position.

Despite Katzman's efforts, and those of the cast and crew, it was apparent from the Season 13 premiere that *Dallas*, in the words of *Variety*, was "running out of gas." *Variety*'s review of the episode entitled "April in Paris" stated, "Mercifully, *Dallas* hasn't lost its sense of humor, which is especially good news considering the preposterousness of one of its storylines. . . . Most of the acting is dreadful . . . [but] Hagman is so good—he not only knows the material is outrageous, he revels in it. . . . The J.R. storyline is completely absurd, but Hagman can probably pull it off."

Later in the season, Barbara Eden's character set in motion a series of events that would provide the set-up to the season's final episode, in which J.R., having lost everything, contemplates what Dallas would have been like had he not been born, as in the classic Frank Capra movie *It's a Wonderful Life*. Because CBS had not made a firm renewal decision prior to the time that production for the 1990–91 season wrapped on February 8, 1991, most of the cast and crew did not know for certain when it filmed the season finale whether the show would return for a fourteenth season in the fall of 1991. Therefore, the two-hour Season 13 finale was designed to give the audience a cliff-hanger in the event the show was renewed and, at the same time, provide a fitting farewell if the show were canceled. The final episode, "Conundrum," featured Oscar- and Tony-winning guest star Joel Grey and return appearances by former regulars Linda Gray, Steve Kanaly, Mary Crosby, and Jack Scalia and, from *Knots Landing*, Ted Shackelford and Joan Van Ark.

When Katzman phoned Linda Gray about appearing as Sue Ellen, Gray readily agreed, saying she "wouldn't have missed it for the world." Steve Kanaly was also happy to return, explaining that the incredible bond that developed among the *Dallas* cast and crew survived the various hirings and firings over the years. Mary Crosby found her return to *Dallas* "lovely—sort of like old home week, being back and seeing a lot of the people that were still there." Joel Grey recalls that "longtime friend" Larry Hagman "suggested me to the writers to play Adam. . . . and luckily I got to do it." Katzman also hoped that Victoria Principal would give fans closure with regard to Pam's and Bobby's relationship, but Principal declined to participate when the producers could not guarantee her that the episode would be the final episode of *Dallas* ever produced.

On April 3, 1991, almost two months after production for Season 13 wrapped, and exactly one month before the season's final episode aired, CBS announced that it was canceling *Dallas*. The show's decline in ratings and its expensive cast and production costs were factors in CBS's decision, as was the fact that the network finally had a growing stable of other hit shows providing the ratings that *Dallas* once did. By 1991, CBS now had six top-twenty-five shows, including *60 Minutes; Mur-*

der, She Wrote; Murphy Brown; Designing Women; the CBS *Sunday Night Movie;* and *Major Dad.* CBS entertainment president Jeff Sagansky released a statement about *Dallas*'s cancellation saying, "Fourteen years ago, when *Dallas* premiered on CBS, it turned the traditional one-hour dramatic format on its ear. . . . *Dallas* made a difference for CBS and left a major mark on prime-time television."

A few members of *Dallas*'s inner circle later revealed that they knew about the show's cancellation around the time that shooting was completed on February 8. Leonard Katzman learned the news just before filming *Dallas*'s final scene. Katzman told a reporter not long before the series finale aired in May, "Nobody knew [the show was cancelled] but me during the last week of shooting. But everybody had a little premonition it was coming." Katzman shared the news with Patrick Duffy. Duffy recalled that Katzman "whispered in my ear, he said, 'I got the word.' The day that we filmed the last scene, he got the word that the show was being canceled but he didn't want to tell anybody yet." According to *People* magazine's story on *Dallas*'s final days, Katzman called Larry Hagman at home in Malibu with the news just after filming ended. Hagman told TV critic Ed Bark he "pretty well expected" the news, and confirmed that Katzman told him "it was over" the week after production ended.

Said Katzman about the final scenes filmed, "On the last day of shooting, Larry and Patrick and I said, 'We have to make this end the way *Dallas* should end. . . . The ending will generate a lot of conversation.'" Hagman recalled the final days in an article he wrote for *TV Guide.* Hagman was

> on the set . . . sitting there reminiscing with my friend, Joel Grey. . . . It was a cold day. . . . I walked off the stage and shut the door, but I just couldn't stay away. And so I kept going back for a couple of days. Picking things up. On the third day I walked back onto Stage 23, the *Dallas* set, and everything was gone. Everything. The entire set: the house, the whole back part, the terrace where we used to have breakfast, the garden. They'd taken everything down in three days. Finished. Gone. It had been there for thirteen years and now it was a big empty hole in the stage."

A few weeks after *Dallas*'s cancellation was announced in April, Katzman told a reporter, "It was sad, very sad, . . . the thought of it ending." Katzman also said that *Dallas* "got too costly for its own good. The longer a show is on, the more money everybody makes. And it's not as if we're number 1 anymore." Hagman told the same reporter, "I've been getting up at 5 a.m. for this show for a quarter of my life. It'll be bizarre doing something else. This is the first year my future has been in doubt." Years later, Hagman told Larry King that the cast "knew it was going to end sometime. We were just dragging it out as long as we could, you know. And people were losing ideas, but I think the energy was always there."

Time magazine published a tribute to the show during the week the final episode aired in May. In the article, written by TV and movie critic Richard Corliss, the Ewings of *Dallas* were recognized as

> the most glamorously backstabbing clan since the house of Atreus, . . . a dozen wealthy Texans living, fighting, snarling under one ranch-house roof, a catalog of venality that included every vice but coprophilia and a leading character (J.R.) with the morals of a mink. . . . The public chose well. For here, in 356 episodes of primal prime time, were the central conflicts of American life. Country (the Ewing home at Southfork ranch) fought with city (the Ewing Oil building in downtown Dallas). Cowboys corralled oil slickers. Sons (J.R. and Bobby) double-crossed each other for their father's love. Daughters-in-law ached for the approval of a family that would always eye them suspiciously. Add myriad business rivals, mistresses, children and newly discovered relatives, and the conflict could keep roiling in a never-ending story, with cunning and variations on the time-honored themes of sex, money, power and family. . . .
>
> Even the ebullient Hagman had trouble keeping track of J.R.'s misdeeds: "I really can't remember half of the people I've slept with, stabbed in the back or driven to suicide." . . . Like the show he anchored, the aging Texan is again in fine form. He might have been speaking of *Dallas* when, in a recent episode, he mourned, "The world I know is disappearin' real fast." But it was left to his stalwart brother to put the series in perspective. "J.R.," Bobby said, "you and I have spent our entire lives tryin' to win Daddy's approval by fightin' with one another. Neither one of us givin' up until we were sure we were his favorite. Well, I've given up the fight. You are Daddy's son. The oil business is all yours, big brother. You've earned the right to Daddy's throne."
>
> In the royal family of American melodrama, *Dallas* is Daddy on the throne.

Meanwhile, the media interest that the cast and crew knew so well returned, as supermarket tabloids reported that the series would end with J.R. getting shot and a Lorimar spokesman predictably fanned the speculation by responding, "It's a typical *Dallas* secret, where the last pages of the script were torn out. So nobody knows anything." As the day of the finale approached, CBS ran promotions for the show claiming, "*Dallas:* Trust us, it ends with a bang."

The millions of fans who had followed *Dallas* since it premiered thirteen years earlier returned in droves on May 3, 1991, to say goodbye to their favorite Texans. The *Dallas* series finale earned a 22 rating and 38 share, and was the number 2 show for the week, *Dallas*'s first number 2 ranking since Episode 190 (the episode before Bobby died), aired six years earlier. The only other prime-time soap opera still on the air by the time of *Dallas*'s demise was its spin-off, *Knots Landing,* which completed its fourteen-year run two years later, in May of 1993. *Dynasty* had been canceled at the end of the 1988–89 season, and *Falcon Crest* met the same fate in the spring of 1990.

About halfway through *Dallas's* run, Leonard Katzman attempted to explain the show's appeal, writing that

> Jock and Miss Ellie and their two sons, Bobby and J.R., were hardly the average clan next door. They were light years removed from the 1950s family—and just about every other family who'd ever been invited into the living rooms of TV-viewing America.
>
> Ultimately, that's what made *Dallas* a hit. We dared to be different—we dared to portray human beings who were both weak and strong; loving and ruthless—and audiences responded enthusiastically. Our cast is perhaps the most three-dimensional group of characters ever assembled. Each one is an intriguing mixture of sinner and saint; no one is perfect, but everyone is human.
>
> In fact, human triumph mixed with human frailty is the thread linking everything that happens in *Dallas*. The Barneses and the Ewings play for high stakes and often pay a high price for their follies, but through it all they remain fighters. Even when we can't applaud their motives, we admire their spirit.

Several years later, not long before the end of the series that he considered his own, the self-proclaimed "Duke of *Dallas*" summed up, "I'm not sure we contributed anything to the advancement of mankind. But we did what we did better than anyone else ever did it. And that's pretty good!"

SEASON 13 EPISODE GUIDE

Regular Cast

Starring:
Patrick Duffy as Bobby
Kimberly Foster as Michelle
Larry Hagman as J.R.
Howard Keel as Clayton
George Kennedy as Carter
Ken Kercheval as Cliff
Sasha Mitchell as James
Cathy Podewell as Cally
Barbara Stock as Liz Adams
Sheree J. Wilson as April
Also Starring:
John Harkins as Control
Gayle Hunnicutt as Vanessa Beaumont
Clifton James as Duke Carlisle
Jared Martin as Dusty

Technical Credits

Supervising Producer: Howard Lakin
Executive Producers: Leonard Katzman,
   Larry Hagman
Producer: Cliff Fenneman
Co-Producer: Mitchell Wayne Katzman
Associate Producers: Frank W. Katzman,
   John Ernest Rettino
Executive Story Consultant: Lisa Seidman
Music: Jerrold Immel, John Parker, Richard
   Lewis Warren, Lance Rubin
Unit Production Manager: Wayne A.
   Farlow

First Assistant Directors: Richard R.
   Johnson, Amy Rosenbaum Jacobson,
   Joseph Paul Moore
Second Assistant Directors: Cary Gordon,
   John G. Behm
Director of Photography: Rick F. Gunter
Art Director: Archibald J. Bacon
Editors: Fred W. Berger, A.C.E., John
   Arthur Davies, Sean Michael Connor
Executive in Charge of Casting: Barbara
   Miller, C.S.A.
Casting: Irene Mariano, C.S.A.
Set Decorator: Phillip Snyder
Property Master: Kerry Scott Knerr
Costumers: Ed Johnson, Lyn Paolo
Makeup: Joe Hailey, Norman Leavitt, Will
   Mackenzie, Don Angier
Hair Stylists: Generio Gugliemotto,
   M. Georgina Williams
Production Sound Mixer: Andrew Gilmore
Post-Production Sound: Lee Drago
Prelay Sound: Catherine H. LeBaigoe, Paul
   Fontana, Edward Barton, Nick Kypros,
   Rob Navrides
Music Supervisor: Gregory Sill
Music Editor: Patricia Peck
Main Title Design: Cliff Fenneman
Executive Coordinator: Louella Lee
   Caraway
Executive-in-Charge of Production:
   R. Robert Rosenbaum

335. "April in Paris"

Written by Leonard Katzman; Directed by Leonard Katzman; Airdate: November 2, 1990
Starring: Susan Lucci (Sheila Foley)
Guest Stars: Chelcie Ross (Dr. Wykoff); Mitch Pileggi (Morrisey); Don Starr (Jordan Lee);
Michael P. Keenan (Keller); Hugh Maguire (Goldman); Arthur Malet (Ryan); Zane Lasky
(Donia); Marty Schiff (Del Greco); Ken Foree (Howard); Deborah Rennard (Sly Loveg-
ren); Shannon Wilcox (Anita)
Subject: April is kidnapped.

Cast Notes Susan Lucci starred as Erica Kane on the daytime soap opera *All My*
Children beginning in 1970, and won the Best Actress Daytime Emmy for the role

in 1999 after famously being nominated and losing eighteen times. The role of Sheila Foley was written specifically for Lucci, who "liked the show very much at the time." After the *Dallas* producers contacted her about appearing, Lucci "read the scripts and thought it would be fun to do." Lucci's favorite memory of *Dallas* was the on-location shoot in France. "I loved shooting in Paris," she recalls. "It was really fun. . . . [although] it was a demanding schedule as television always is with shooting a lot of material in a short amount of time. But the French food was wonderful!" Lucci also found Patrick Duffy "a real nice guy. He had his family with him, and he was extremely relaxed, which made it very enjoyable." ★ The role of Duke Carlisle, played by Claude Earl Jones in Season 12, is taken over by Clifton James, a character actor who appeared on stage, TV, and films. His movies include *Cool Hand Luke*, *Live and Let Die*, *The Man with the Golden Gun*, and *Bonfire of the Vanities*. ★ Barbara Stock was added to the main title as of this episode, becoming the twenty-first and final actor to appear in the *Dallas* main title between the pilot and Season 13. The other twenty are: Barbara Bel Geddes, Jim Davis, Patrick Duffy, Larry Hagman, Victoria Principal, and Charlene Tilton (starting with the pilot); Linda Gray and Steve Kanaly (starting with Season 1); Ken Kercheval (starting with Season 2); Susan Howard (starting with Season 4); Howard Keel, Priscilla Presley, and Donna Reed (Season 7); Dack Rambo (Season 9); Sheree J. Wilson (Season 11); and Lesley-Anne Down, Kimberly Foster, George Kennedy, Sasha Mitchell, and Cathy Podewell (Season 12). Seven additional actors were added to the main title in the two TV movie sequels. Rosalind Allen, Christopher Demetral, Omri Katz, Deborah Kellner, Audrey Landers, and Tracy Scoggins were added to the main title in *J.R. Returns* and Michelle Johnson was added to the main title in *War of the Ewings*.

Trivia Weekly rating: number 41, with a 12.2 rating. ★ This was the first of five episodes filmed on location in Paris, France. ★ Larry Hagman's mother, Mary Martin, died of cancer at age seventy-six the day after this episode aired. Her family placed photographs of themselves with her ashes, and Hagman included a photo of Linda Gray, who he said his mother "adored." Hagman reportedly took the news hard. Said his longtime friend Joel Grey during filming of the show's final episode six months later, "I think he's still dealing with it." ★ Given the possibility that Season 13 would be *Dallas*'s last, its premiere episode was widely reviewed. The *Los Angeles Daily News* wrote that "Lucci . . . comes across like one of those supervillains on the old *Batman* series. She seems perfectly capable of acting like a respectable person for spells, but she is ultimately pushed by inner failings. . . . *Dallas* is simply solid, old-fashioned storytelling, with the accent on the telling. Rarely does it surprise you with where that story is headed, the occasional cliffhanger notwithstanding. The fun comes in how it ultimately gets there." Ed Bark of the *Dallas Morning News* found that "Sue Ellen-less, Cliff-less, Pam-less, Rayless, Clayton-less, Lucy-less, and Miss Ellie-less, . . . [the] season premiere also is pulse-less and Southfork-less. . . . Ms. Lucci waits until the end of the episode to expose her claws. . . . *Dallas* portrays asylum patients with all the nuance of a two-year-old child scrawling on his first wall. All that's missing is the Looney Tunes theme. . . . I've written too many premature obituaries for *Dallas* to say with certainty that this season will close the curtain. . . . [but] it's long past time to pull the plug." In *USA Today*, Tom Green wrote, "Whoa! Don't hit the zapper. There are plenty of reasons to welcome back television's most durable prime-time soap. . . . *Dallas* is a classic, still a show worth shouting about!"

336. "Charade"

Written by Howard Lakin; Directed by Irving J. Moore; Airdate: November 9, 1990
Starring: Susan Lucci (Sheila Foley)
Guest Stars: Chelcie Ross (Dr. Wykoff); Don Starr (Jordan Lee); Mitch Pileggi (Morrisey); Michael P. Keenan (Keller); Hugh Maguire (Goldman); Arthur Malet (Ryan); Zane Lasky (Donia); Marty Schiff (Del Greco); Shannon Wilcox (Anita)
Subject: Sheila impersonates April.

Cast Notes Patrick Duffy's son, Padraic, makes the first of four appearances as Mark Harris, named after Patrick Duffy's character in his prior series, *Man from Atlantis*. Duffy admits that he "was a little nervous for my son when he was on the show. I needn't have been as he was already quite a good actor [on the] stage within his school. Leonard and Irving were more than protective of him and made his debut as smooth as possible. However, I did later see the footage Irving did of Padraic riding his bike all over the streets of Paris in the traffic with very little protection and realized I should have worried a little more than I did. [It is a] great feeling of pride to be in a scene with your son and feel the continuity."

Trivia Weekly rating: number 49. ★ Susan Lucci recalls, "It was so brutally hot when we shot in Paris. We were shooting in the summer but it was not going to air until the fall. And there was Patrick in his cowboy boots and wool jackets—at least I got to wear cocktail dresses! And they had to turn off the air conditioning because it was too noisy. . . . I remember that we were there during the Tour de France and it was so hot we were worried they weren't going to finish the last lap."

337. "Last Kiss"

Written by Lisa Seidman; Directed by Leonard Katzman; Airdate: November 16, 1990
Starring: Susan Lucci (Sheila)
Guest Stars: Chelcie Ross (Dr. Wykoff); Don Starr (Jordan Lee); Michael P. Keenan (Keller); Hugh Maguire (Goldman); Arthur Malet (Ryan); Zane Lasky (Donia); Marty Schiff (Del Greco); Deborah Rennard (Sly Lovegren); Shannon Wilcox (Anita)
Subject: Bobby's rescue attempt.

Trivia Weekly rating: number 55, tying Episode 349 as the season's lowest ranked. ★ Another thing Susan Lucci enjoyed about filming *Dallas* in Paris was that it coincided with the fashion show season there. Lucci "got to go to one show, which was thrilling. Patrick had his two teenage boys and his wife with him, and it was something for those boys to see those gorgeous models!" ★ As Cally softened her stance on J.R.'s commitment to the sanitarium, Cathy Podewell could tell that her storyline was winding down, and that *Dallas* itself "had sort of run its course. You could feel it slipping away."

338. "Terminus"

Written by Mitchell Wayne Katzman; Directed by Irving J. Moore; Airdate: November 23, 1990
Starring: Susan Lucci (Sheila)
Guest Stars: Don Starr (Jordan Lee); Omri Katz (John Ross); Deborah Rennard (Sly);
Ramy Zada (Johnny Dancer)
Subject: April's murder.

Cast Notes Ramy Zada played Detective Kung in *Second Chances*. ★ This is Don Starr's last appearance on *Dallas*. He first appeared in Episode 13, which aired twelve years earlier. Starr died in 1995.

Trivia Weekly rating: number 45. ★ Sheree J. Wilson won the 1992 *Soap Opera Digest* "Best Death Scene" Award for April's violent death scene from this episode. According to Wilson, she "asked for my exit. I wanted to go out in grand fashion; no sickness or car accident. . . . By our hiatus [after Season 12], we knew [Season 13] was our last season—everyone's contract was up. I [wanted to be at home with my new baby and] told Leonard, 'Give me the most amount of money for the least amount of shows.' I was never going to be a first-time Mom again, and I didn't want to be on the set twelve hours a day. Leonard said, 'We can't kill you off at your wedding [at the end of Season 12], we have to have you come back [in Season 13].' He said, 'We'll have to kill you off on your honeymoon.'" Wilson returned to *Dallas* in dream sequences seen in Episodes 345 and 346. ★ Wilson found Lucci "sweet and polite" and "very professional and precise."

339. "Tunnel of Love"

Written by Howard Lakin; Directed by Michael Preece; Airdate: November 30, 1990
Guest Stars: Peter White (Breslin); Jeri Gaile (Rose McKay); Deborah Rennard (Sly);
Ramy Zada (Johnny Dancer)
Subject: April's funeral.

Cast Notes The owner of the garage is played by Fred Stromsoe, who was Officer Woods on *Adam 12*.

Trivia Weekly rating: number 46.

340. "Heart and Soul"

Written by Lisa Seidman; Directed by Nick Havinga; Airdate: December 7, 1990
Guest Stars: Peter White (Breslin); Jeri Gaile (Rose McKay); Deborah Rennard (Sly);
David Gale (Gerhardt); Omri Katz (John Ross); Joshua Harris (Christopher); Ramy Zada
(Johnny Dancer)
Subject: April's will.

Cast Notes Episodes 340 and 341 are the first two of four Season 13 episodes in which Howard Keel appeared. This episode also marks the return of Kimberly Foster's character, who returns to Dallas in the wake of April's death.

Trivia Weekly rating: number 48.

341. "The Fabulous Ewing Boys"

Written by Leonard Katzman; Directed by Michael Preece; Airdate: December 14, 1990
Guest Stars: Buck Taylor (Detective Bussey); Jeri Gaile (Rose McKay); Deborah Rennard (Sly); Omri Katz (John Ross); Joshua Harris (Christopher)
Subject: Bobby's investigation of Sheila.

Cast Notes Buck Taylor played Newly O'Brien on *Gunsmoke*. ★ Ken Kercheval does not appear in this episode—the first *Dallas* without Kercheval since the show's early years. Kercheval, along with Hagman, was the only cast member to stay with the show as a regular cast member through the pilot and all thirteen seasons. (By virtue of his appearance in the final seconds of the Season 8 cliff-hanger, Patrick Duffy can also claim to have appeared in each season of *Dallas*, but Duffy was not a regular cast member during Season 8). Kercheval also appeared in one of the two TV movie sequels. Other than Hagman, who appeared in all 357 episodes of *Dallas*, Kercheval appeared in more episodes (more than 340) than any other cast member. Kercheval was adamant about staying with *Dallas* to the end. "I wanted to be there," he said a short time after the show was cancelled. "I just believe in finishing things I started." According to Kercheval, working on *Dallas* was "fun" and "luxurious," and afforded him the ability to reach a much wider audience than he reached during his years in the theater. He observed, "Of the twenty years total of all of the audiences that came to the theater, the Broadway outlets, where there were 1,200 or 700 or whatever, . . . more people saw me in one episode of *Dallas* than had seen me for twenty years of performing." Playing J.R.'s nemesis even changed his mind about originally wanting to play Ray Krebbs, and Kercheval concluded that he "was glad they overruled me. I've had a lot of fun being Cliff." Nevertheless, Kercheval had some professional regrets about his long-running association with Cliff Barnes. "I didn't put in all that time, in all those parts in New York, just to be remembered as Cliff Barnes," he said. He later expounded, "[I] didn't study for as long as I studied in New York and go to theatrical school and professional school to say, 'Well, let's see, now. Let me pick out a character here. And then I am going to perfect this character. This is the character that I will use for my career.' No. . . . It was to play anything that came down the pike. And so, I'm still interested in doing that!"

Trivia Weekly rating: number 49.

342. "The Odessa File"

Written by Howard Lakin; Directed by Nick Havinga; Airdate: December 21, 1990
Special Guest Appearance: Barbara Eden (LeeAnn De La Vega)

Guest Stars: George O. Petrie (Harv Smithfield); Peter White (Breslin); Jeri Gaile (Rose McKay); Richard Narita (Inagaki); Deborah Rennard (Sly); Susan Krebs (Toni); Nick Eldredge (Dr. Banoff)
Subject: Bobby sells Ewing Oil.

Cast Notes Barbara Eden costarred with Larry Hagman in the classic sitcom *I Dream of Jeannie* from 1965 to 1970. Eden believes that the role of Lee Ann was created for her. She "had a great time doing this. We didn't need any inside jokes, but so many of the lines are wonderful. [J.R.] asks [LeeAnn], 'Haven't we met before?' The first day on the stage, everyone was watching us. Larry looked at me and said, 'Isn't this the strangest thing? It's like we've never stopped working together.'" Eden says that "Larry was wonderful to work with again," and she "enjoyed working with Patrick very much. He was a dream."

Trivia Weekly rating: number 52.

343. "Sail On"

Written by Lisa Seidman; Directed by Michael Preece; Airdate: January 4, 1991
Special Guest Appearance: Barbara Eden (LeeAnn De La Vega)
Guest Stars: Buck Taylor (Detective Bussey); George O. Petrie (Harv Smithfield); Jeri Gaile (Rose McKay); Tom Fucello (Sen. Dave Culver); Omri Katz (John Ross); Joshua Harris (Christopher)
Subject: J.R. courts LeeAnn.

Trivia Weekly rating: number 40. Excluding the last two episodes of the season, which aired after CBS announced *Dallas's* cancellation, this was the highest ranked episode of Season 13. ★ This episode gave Cathy Podewell one of her few scenes with Gayle Hunnicutt, who Podewell describes as "such a lady, . . . soft spoken and gracious." ★ According to Barbara Eden, "It was an inside joke to have my [character's] maiden name be Nelson." Hagman's character on *I Dream of Jeannie* was Tony Nelson. ★ This episode marks the last timeslot change for *Dallas*. CBS moved the show back to the 9:00 p.m. slot, where the show would remain until it was canceled fourteen episodes later.

344. "Lock, Stock, and Jock"

Written by Mitchell Wayne Katzman; Directed by Nick Havinga; Airdate: January 11, 1991
Special Guest Appearance: Barbara Eden (LeeAnn De La Vega)
Guest Stars: Michael Alldredge (Ray King, Esq.); Joseph Malone (Assistant District Attorney J. J. Carter); Buck Taylor (Detective Bussey); Peter White (Breslin); Deborah Rennard (Sly); Patricia Barry (Janine)
Subject: LeeAnn plots against J.R.

Cast Notes Patricia Barry played Jack Klugman's wife on the 1964–65 sitcom *Harris Against the World*. ★ Joe Malone was a regular on Tracey Ullman's Fox variety show (1987–90).

Trivia Weekly rating: number 45. ★ The day after this episode aired, the *Soap Opera Digest* Awards were announced at the Biltmore Hotel in Los Angeles. *Dallas* did not do as well as it had in prior years, although it received several nominations in the prime-time categories, including Outstanding Serial (the award went to *Knots Landing*), Cathy Podewell as Outstanding Lead Actress (the award went to Michele Lee of *Knots*), Ken Kercheval as Outstanding Supporting Actor (the award went to Larry Williams of *Knots*) and Sheree J. Wilson as Outstanding Heroine (the award went to Nicollette Sheridan of *Knots*).

345. "S Is for Seduction"

Written by Howard Lakin; Directed by Michael Preece; Airdate: January 18, 1991
Special Guest Appearance: Barbara Eden (LeeAnn De La Vega)
Guest Stars: Michael Alldredge (Ray King); Joseph Malone (J.J. Carter); Buck Taylor (Detective Bussey); Jeri Gaile (Rose McKay); Ramy Zada (Johnny); Deborah Rennard (Sly); Dorothy Parke (Jill); Charles Frank (Paul Keats)
Subject: LeeAnn frames J.R.

Cast Notes Charles Frank, who plays Susan Lucci's Savings & Loan partner, was Lucci's longtime costar on *All My Children*. Frank also starred in *Young Maverick*, an updated version of the James Garner western from the 1960s.

Trivia Weekly rating: number 48. ★ Barbara Eden says, "One of the good memories I have of *Dallas* is the beautiful clothes. It's not often that an actress gets to wear designer clothes on a show."

346. "Designing Women"

Written by Lisa Seidman; Directed by Irving J. Moore; Airdate: February 1, 1991
Special Guest Appearance: Barbara Eden (LeeAnn De La Vega)
Guest Stars: Joseph Malone (J.J. Carter); Peter White (Breslin); Jeri Gaile (Rose McKay); Richard Eastham (D.A. Frank Hillson); Joshua Harris (Christopher)
Subject: Vanessa leaves J.R.

Cast Notes Richard Eastham played General Blankenship on the Linda Carter series *Wonder Woman* and was a regular on *Falcon Crest*. ★ This episode, which includes Sheree J. Wilson's final appearance on *Dallas*, is the second of two consecutive episodes in which Wilson appears in a dream sequence.

Trivia Weekly rating: number 45. ★ Of her scenes as LeeAnn De La Vega, Barbara Eden's favorite "was when I finally revealed who I was—and I pretty much ruined J.R. . . . What did I think about getting the better of that infamous villain, J.R.? Well, I would say I did feel I was in a very enviable position—and I must admit, I enjoyed every minute of it." Eden also enjoyed her scenes with Gayle Hunnicutt and Kimberly Foster, who she thought "did their jobs well. They were gorgeous and profound."

347. "90265"

Written by Leonard Katzman; Directed by Leonard Katzman; Airdate: February 8, 1991
Guest Stars: Deirdre Imershein (Jory Taylor); Deborah Rennard (Sly); Kelly Rowan
(Dana); Shari Shattuck (Kit); Joshua Harris (Christopher)
Subject: Bobby travels to Malibu.

Cast Notes Guest star Kelly Rowan, who makes her first of three appearances as
Jory's friend, Dana, stars as Kirsten Cohen in the hit serial The O.C., which premiered on Fox in 2004.

Trivia Weekly rating: number 51.

348. "Smooth Operator"

Written by Lisa Seidman; Directed by Larry Hagman; Airdate: February 15, 1991
Guest Stars: Deirdre Imershein (Jory Taylor); Charles Bateman (Senator Daniel Garrity);
Shari Shattuck (Kit); Deborah Rennard (Sly); Anthony Addabbo (John); Kelly Rowan
(Dana); Nancy Warren (Kinsey Richards); Joshua Harris (Christopher); Barbara Luna
(Carmen Esperanza)
Subject: J.R. plots against Kimberly.

Trivia Weekly rating: number 52.

349. "Win Some, Lose Some"

Written by Mitchell Wayne Katzman; Directed by Patrick Duffy; Airdate: March 1, 1991
Guest Stars: Deirdre Imershein (Jory Taylor); Deborah Rennard (Sly); Kelly Rowan
(Dana); Padraic Duffy (Mark Harris); Shari Shattuck (Kit); Eva La Rue (DeeDee);
Joshua Harris (Christopher)
Subject: Hillary's daughter.

Cast Notes Eva La Rue, who appears as James's date, DeeDee, played Annette Funicello in the 1995 TV version of Funicello's autobiography, A Dream Is a Wish
Your Heart Makes: The Annette Funicello Story.

Trivia Weekly rating: number 55.

350. "Fathers and Sons and Fathers and Sons"

Written by Arthur Barnard Lewis; Directed by Larry Hagman; Airdate: March 8, 1991
Guest Stars: Buck Taylor (Detective Bussey); Joseph Malone (J. J. Carter); Chris Weather-
head (Meg Callahan); Deborah Tucker (Debra Lynn); Mary Watson (Stephanie); Omri
Katz (John Ross); Joshua Harris (Christopher)
Subject: The Ewings' cattle drive.

Cast Notes Deborah Tucker was in the Who's the Boss? spin-off, Living Dolls, along
with The Waltons's Michael Learned and Oscar-winning actress Halle Berry. ★
William Marquez takes over the role of Raoul.

Trivia Weekly rating: number 52, with a 9.6 rating and 16 share, Dallas's worst
rating and share ever.

351. "When the Wind Blows"

Written by Louella Lee Caraway; Directed by Patrick Duffy; Airdate: March 29, 1991
Guest Stars: Deirdre Imershein (Jory Taylor); Deborah Tucker (Debra Lynn); Deborah
Rennard (Sly); Bruce Gray (David Stanley); Omri Katz (John Ross); Joshua Harris
(Christopher)
Subject: James's wife arrives.

Cast Notes This is Barbara Stock's final appearance on Dallas.

Trivia Weekly rating: number 50.

352. "Those Darn Ewings"

Written by Kenneth Horton; Directed by Dwight Adair; Airdate: April 5, 1991
Guest Stars: Deirdre Imershein (Jory Taylor); Deborah Tucker (Debra Lynn); Tony Miller
(Dr. Kessler); Omri Katz (John Ross); Joshua Harris (Christopher)
Subject: J.R.'s grandson.

Cast Notes Edson Stroll, costarring as John Kane, played Virgil Edwards on
McHale's Navy. ★ Jimmy Beaumont is played by twin brothers Chuckie and
Kenny Gravino. ★ Dallas's cancellation was announced by CBS a few days before
this episode aired. In an article about CBS's announcement, the Los Angeles Daily
News reported Victoria Principal's comment that she left Dallas four years earlier
because she "didn't feel the show was continuing to live up to what it did the first
five years. And I wanted to produce. I have no regrets."

Trivia Weekly rating: number 50.

353. "Farewell My Lovely"

Written by Lisa Seidman; Directed by Patrick Duffy; Airdate: April 12, 1991
Starring: Susan Lucci (Hillary Taylor)
Guest Stars: Deirdre Imershein (Jory Taylor); Michael Bell (Pat Connors); Deborah Tucker
(Debra Lynn); Deborah Rennard (Sly); Shari Shattuck (Kit); Omri Katz (John Ross);
Joshua Harris (Christopher)
Subject: J.R.'s search for Cally.

Cast Notes Howard Keel returns in this episode, the third of four Season 13
episodes in which he appears. ★ With the exception of the series finale's fantasy
sequence, this was Cathy Podewell's last appearance as Cally. The man playing
Cally's boyfriend in the scene where J.R. finds Cally in Florida is Podewell's real-
life husband, with whom she has three young children. Podewell "loved every
minute" of her time on Dallas, saying, "It was magical to be on a show that was an
institution."

Trivia Weekly rating: number 42. With CBS having announced Dallas's cancellation about ten days earlier, the ratings began to rise as fans came back to the show
for its final episodes. This episode's ratings pushed Dallas into the top forty-five for
the first time in seven weeks. ★ Writer Lisa Seidman's script does not reveal the

name of Cally's and J.R.'s son, nor was it revealed by the time *Dallas* went off the air three episodes later. Podewell recalls that her favorite comic strip, *Cathy*, drawn by award-winning artist Cathy Guisewite and syndicated nationwide by United Press Syndicate, "showed Cathy screaming that she couldn't believe *Dallas* was over after thirteen years of turmoil and she'd still never know the name of Cally's baby!"

354. "Some Leave, Some Get Carried Out"

Written by Leonard Katzman; Directed by Leonard Katzman; Airdate: April 19, 1991
Starring: Susan Lucci (Hillary Taylor)
Guest Stars: Deirdre Imershein (Jory Taylor); Deborah Tucker (Debra Lynn); Bruce Gray
(David Stanley); Shari Shattuck (Kit); Omri Katz (John Ross); Joshua Harris (Christopher)
Subject: Hillary's death.

Cast Notes This episode includes Howard Keel's last appearance as Clayton and Sasha Mitchell's last appearance as James.

Trivia Weekly rating: number 43. ★ Susan Lucci was not bothered by her character's murder, joking that "I didn't see how gruesome it was because I had my eyes closed!" Lucci flew to Los Angeles to film her final *Dallas* scenes on the Culver City Southfork set. Although it was apparent that *Dallas* was down to its last few episodes, Lucci found that the cast and crew did not act that way. "No one acted like it was the end," Lucci recalls. "No one seemed somber, although since I was not part of that company I might not have known if they were. But it was very pleasant and everyone was cordial." ★ Leonard Katzman was Keel's favorite *Dallas* director. According to Keel, Katzman "would say very little to you, and just listen. If he liked what you were doing, you knew he liked it, and he'd let you just keep going."

355. "The Fall and Decline of the Ewing Empire"

Written by Lisa Seidman; Directed by Ken Kercheval; Airdate: April 26, 1991
Also Starring: Jared Martin (Dusty Farlow)
Guest Stars: Deirdre Imershein (Jory Taylor); Buck Taylor (Detective Bussey); Jeri Gaile
(Rose McKay); Richard Eastham (D.A. Frank Hillson); Deborah Rennard (Sly); Omri
Katz (John Ross); Joshua Harris (Christopher)
Subject: Cliff gets full control of Ewing Oil.

Cast Notes This episode includes Kimberly Foster's final appearance on *Dallas*.

Trivia Weekly rating: number 36. This was the second-highest-ranked episode of Season 13. ★ The producers asked Jared Martin to return for this episode, Martin's final appearance as Dusty. Although Martin "was fully involved in another part of my life at that time . . . there didn't seem to be any reason to say 'no,' and I admit I was curious. I'd been away for so long I was surprised to be remembered at all." Martin enjoyed his final scene, in which George Kennedy and he out-fox J.R. one final time. Martin found Kennedy "a professional man in the twilight of a long career. He was very dialed into his character and there was little question of acting 'with' but mostly in acting 'to' him." As for the show itself, Martin says that, on the set, "there was a mood of conclusion and sadness, of loss and moving on; almost as if what was being done wasn't so important any more." Martin says he owes the show "an international B-movie notoriety in the '80s, and a Canadian TV series in the early '90s. . . . I've often wondered why I didn't try harder to capitalize on the sizeable platform of opportunity that *Dallas* offered. . . . I wanted more for Dusty but realized in the pecking order of a burgeoning new show with a half dozen emerging stars my calls for juicier scenes for my character would fall on deaf ears. Dusty was an appendage, tied to Sue Ellen and J.R. as surely as the string that ties the rim of a headlight onto an old jalopy. The show, more than my performance or presence, was responsible for what another actor might've enjoyed as a peak moment in a career. And my ambivalence about joining in the experience must've shown, and was probably resented, if noticed at all, by other cast members. . . . I was becoming best known as a Hollywood cowboy at almost the precise moment the western was dying as a cultural icon—tied to a multi-show contract that kept me unavailable for roles in films that might break the tightening net of association. I looked around for things that would cut this pattern. *Dallas* was powerful enough to make one famous and make one disappear at the same time. I felt sucked into the show's vortex. During the '80s I spent almost a year on Broadway and L.A. performing in the play *Torch Song Trilogy*; I lived in Rome doing Italian films for companies who were willing to build a film around 'Senor Doosty.' But everything radiated back to *Dallas*. . . . Looking back I realize I wasn't alone. The show tended to gobble its children, and *Dallas* stars usually took a step down after the show was over. Was there a *Dallas* curse? Or was it a case of a runaway hit carrying a lot of talented performers to heights they never would have climbed otherwise? . . . . I'll never know whether *Dallas* affected my career for good or bad. I didn't think about it at the time, and haven't thought much about it since. I did become a pretty good horseback rider by the end of the '80s; and maybe that's the best thing that came out of the whole experience."

356. & 357. "Conundrum" (Parts One and Two)

Written by Leonard Katzman; Directed by Leonard Katzman; Airdate: May 3, 1991
Starring: Mary Crosby (Kristin Shepard); Linda Gray (Sue Ellen Shepard); Joel Grey (Adam); Steve Kanaly (Ray Krebbs); Jack Scalia (Nicholas Pearce); Ted Shackelford (Gary Ewing); Joan Van Ark (Valene Wallace)
Guest Stars: Kim Johnston Ulrich (Bootsie Ewing); Leslie Bevis (Jeanne Lawrence); Patrick Pankhurst (Jason Ewing); Barbara Rhoads (Judy); Richard Lineback (Eb); Joseph Callahan (Mr. Smith); Anthony Addabbo (Jeff Peters); Katherine Justice (Alice Kingdom); Tricia O'Neil (Barbara Barnes); Rosalind Allen (Annie Ewing); Denise Gentile (Courtney); Katherine Cannon (Beth Krebbs); Teri Ann Linn (Kimberly Kavanaugh)
Subject: J.R. contemplates suicide.

Cast Notes   Linda Gray found recreating the role of Sue Ellen a challenge. While Gray "thought I got [Sue Ellen] back in my every cell, I hadn't. She was a Sue Ellen who had a different life. That was what was intriguing to me." Gray recalls that it was "my idea to bring in Jack [Scalia for the series finale]. I remember talking to Mr. Katzman. And he said, 'What are we going to do with Sue Ellen? Who would she be with?' And I said, 'Why not Jack?' And he said, 'Okay. Good idea.' . . . If it hadn't been Jack, it would have been Ian McShane, but he was in London." ★ Joel Grey, a close friend of Larry Hagman's, won the 1966 Tony Award and the 1972 Oscar for his stage and screen portrayals of the Emcee in *Cabaret*. Despite his friendship with Hagman, however, Grey "had never worked with [Hagman] but had always been a great fan and we had an excellent time together" filming this episode. Grey's favorite scene is the one "by the swimming pool where I really got to tell J.R. off." Cathy Podewell, who returned for this episode, was a musical comedy fan who was thrilled to meet Joel Grey. "He and Larry were really good friends," Podewell recalls. "It was such a kick to watch them. They were hysterical together." ★ Joan Van Ark loved returning to *Dallas*, and doing so as a new version of Valene. "They called me and said they'd like Ted and me to come on as different characters with a different look," recalls Van Ark. "And boy did Val have a different look! I was in a white, sleek, tight Thierry Mugler suit and had curled my hair to within an inch of my life! Val finally got to dress, and I loved it. There I was with Ted, my acting soulmate, playing this totally new character who came to him for legal advice. I got to be this whole other silhouette, and it was fabulous." ★ Katherine Cannon costarred on *Father Murphy*, a spin-off of *Little House on the Prairie*. She also played Tori Spelling's mother on *Beverly Hills, 90210*. ★ Christine Taylor, featured as Cliff's daughter Margaret, played Marcia Brady in the 1995 movie *The Brady Bunch Movie* and its sequel and is married to movie star Ben Stiller. ★ Several actors seen in this episode made other appearances on *Dallas*: Leslie Bevis played Diana Farrington in Episodes 317–21; Barbara Rhodes played Lila Cummings in Episode 185; Rosalind Allen played Bobby's love interest in *J.R. Returns*; Anthony Addabbo played John in Episode 348; Edson Stroll played John Kane in Episode 352; costar James Newell (Walter Kingdom) played a Weststar vice president in Episodes 307, 314, and 318; costar Tony Auer (Ted) played The Man in Episode 277; costar Dan Livingston (Edgar) was featured as Reidel in Episode 316. ★ Featured actor Conor Duffy, who plays Little J.R. in this episode, is the second of Patrick Duffy's children to appear on *Dallas*. Conor's brother Padraic appeared in Episodes 336–37, 339, and 348. Patrick Duffy recalls that Conor "was in the last scene in the park . . . with the irresponsible Bobby. . . . I then told him (as a director, although Lenny directed that one . . .) to look out the back of the car window as they drove away. Always try and get in the last shot!!!" ★ Featured actor David Katzman is the grandson of Leonard Katzman and the son of Frank Katzman. ★ Only five of the ten actors seen in the Season 13 main title appear in *Dallas*'s final episode: Patrick Duffy, Larry Hagman, George Kennedy, Ken Kercheval, and Cathy Podewell.

Trivia   Weekly rating: number 2, with a 22 rating and a 38 share. This was the first time that *Dallas* made: the top twenty since a two-hour episode featuring Cally's and J.R.'s wedding in February 1989; the top ten since Pam vanished from the hospital in October 1987; the top five since Victoria Principal's final episode in May 1987; and the top two since Bobby solved Naldo's murder in the penultimate Season 7 episode in May 1985. ★ This episode began with clips from the final pilot episode and the cliffhangers from Seasons 1 through 12. According to Patrick Duffy, Leonard Katzman decided to end this episode with a shot of Bobby since the show began with Bobby and Pam. Says Duffy, "Lenny knew long before the last episode that we were not going to be picked up for a fourteenth season so he knew that would be the last shot of the series. . . . He told me he did the last shot [of Bobby] that way to be the perfect bookend to the first shot of the show in [1978] where Pam and I are driving to Southfork. So I had the first and the last shot of the show. And thank goodness Larry had most of the stuff in between." ★ The finale of *Dallas* was not critically acclaimed. For example, the *Los Angeles Daily News* claimed that *Dallas* went out with "a whimper" instead of a bang. ★ "Frankly," says Larry Hagman, "I was ambivalent about [this episode]. When I first read it and when I subsequently saw it, it wasn't the best ending for the series but I couldn't think of a better one. And I always did what Mr. Katzman told me to do anyhow." ★ According to his widow, La Rue, Katzman was "crushed" and "very unhappy" when he learned *Dallas* was canceled. Howard Lakin recalled "walking around the empty sound stage with [Katzman]—it was like being in the band on the *Titanic*, you know? He was going to be the last man standing. He was." ★ Looking back, Larry Hagman thought the show's originality was what made it a hit. He observed, "Everybody [in the show] was pretty sleazy and there was nothing on TV like that." ★ Duffy thought that the show's success was a matter of destiny but was rooted in its similarity to Greek tragedy. "Everything was so mystical," he said, "in the sense that it was meant to be and you could never nor should you want to escape from that family of *Dallas*." Duffy claimed that *Dallas* was "the first show of that time period to be so opulent and so denigrated at the same time in terms of our moral structure. It was like some of the great Greek tragedies. We were the classic dysfunctional family but it's one thing to be a dysfunctional family in a housing development. Its another thing to be the royal dysfunctional family. And we were America's royal dysfunctional family." ★ Steve Kanaly feels the show's success was, in part, due to the fact that in 1978 "the country was experiencing double-digit inflation, high unemployment, a gasoline crunch and a hostage crisis, and a show about wealthy oilmen and pretty women gave Americans an escape from their current troubles." ★ According to Leonard Katzman, "Entertaining the audience, . . . that's our number-one aim, to keep the show entertaining. . . . We feel that we have stayed . . . totally consistent with the characters. They have grown, they have changed, they have moved around. But the basic characters have always been consistent." ★ And as for David Jacobs, who created it all? He concluded that "*Dallas* is just plain fun."

Part V

THE TV MOVIES

THE PREQUEL
The Early Years—March 23, 1986

DALLAS: THE EARLY YEARS WAS a prequel movie that aired on CBS during *Dallas*'s eighth season. It focused on the exploits of the show's central senior characters forty-five years before they hit prime time, giving the back story of Digger, Jock, and Miss Ellie and explaining how the Barnes-Ewing feud began. The origins of *The Early Years* date back to the early 1980s. In the wake of the worldwide *Dallas* craze inaugurated by the "Who Shot J.R.?" phenomenon, Lorimar considered making a movie version of *Dallas*. Series creator David Jacobs thought Jock's and Ellie's back story would make a great movie. Jacobs had already written the outline of that back story when he created *Dallas* in 1977. "I always write a back story," Jacobs explained. "I just enjoy it. It's more realistic, and it helps me to know where everyone came from." As for giving Jock's and Ellie's back story a movie treatment, however, Jacobs recalls, "Nobody liked that idea, and it just sort of fell through," as did the plan for a *Dallas* feature film in general.

By 1983, Jacobs thought of doing his prequel as a TV movie, and he pitched the idea to CBS. The network gave the proposal a green light, but Jacobs had to put the project off because NBC had optioned another one of his ideas, a short-lived serial called *Berrenger's*, which premiered in January 1985, and featured among its cast *Dallas* cast members Jack Scalia and Art Hindle. In the meantime, CBS considered having someone else write the script for a *Dallas* prequel. But Jacobs responded, "If anybody does [a prequel,] it'll be me." While Jacobs never felt responsible for *Dallas*'s success since he returned to *Family* almost immediately after creating the Ewings, the prequel restored his "proprietary feelings" about the show. Once *Berrenger's* was cancelled in March of 1985, Jacobs turned to the *Early Years* script, which followed his 1977 outline. "I knew Digger Barnes grew up on Southfork with Ellie," Jacobs explained, "and that he loved her, but she married Jock. I knew she chose Jock over Digger in a calculated way—to save the ranch." As for the business side of Jock's and Digger's relationship, Jacobs's back story provided that "Digger and Jock had been partners; Jock had the business sense and Digger knew where to dig. Digger was totally self-destructive—a drunk."

As he turned to the script, Jacobs wanted to address a criticism of *Dallas* with which he agreed. There was, Jacobs recognized, a "scarcity of black and brown faces [on *Dallas*], except in servant roles—a scarcity I found not only sociologically embarrassing but inaccurate in the modern city of Dallas." As a result, Jacobs wanted to include "a black Texan in the birth of Ewing Oil." Initially, Jacobs

332

decided to make the sharecropper family who tilled the land on which Digger senses the presence of oil a black family.

While reading a 1930s sharecropper agreement that he purchased in a dime store, Jacobs noticed that the mineral rights were excluded.

Jacobs also read about numerous incidents in which tenants were evicted after oil was discovered on their farms, suggesting a second plot device that could be incorporated into a sharecropper family's subplot. Jacobs explains, "With this information in hand—and with *Dallas: The Early Years* being, after all, a fiction, I felt it was reasonable to tell a story about two white wildcatters partnering with a black sharecropper in a racist environment to drill for oil on the sharecropped farm." Jacobs felt that by "making the courage of the sharecropper an indispensable part of the founding of the Ewing fortune, . . . I'd sort of done a little to compensate for the shortage of black characters in the series."

Jacobs was satisfied not only with the sharecropper aspect of the story, but with the details of what had been missing from the back story he created for the *Dallas* pilot many years earlier: "the actual details of the partnership and the breakup." Indeed, Jacobs recalls that "*Early Years* is the single work I most liked writing, had the most fun producing, and was most pleased with when it was done." Although his late 1980s western, *Paradise*, is Jacobs's favorite "and most personal" of all the series he has done, *Early Years* "was and remains my personal favorite of all the work I did in television."

In January 1985, press accounts reported that Jacobs was considering an entire series based on Jock's adventures as a young wildcatter. But in September of 1985, CBS confirmed that it was producing a TV movie about the origins of the Barnes-Ewing saga. In early November, *Dallas* location casting director Rody Kent, who had done location work during Seasons 3 through 11 and had appeared in several episodes of the show, was hired to find actors to fill forty-two parts for the $2.5 million three-hour movie, which was scheduled to be filmed over twenty-eight days in November and December in and around Dallas. Cast in the three leading roles were relative unknowns Molly Hagan as Miss Ellie, Dale Midkiff as Jock, and David Grant as Digger. Hagan had appeared in small roles in *Knots Landing* during the 1983–84 season, although Jacobs "wasn't crazy about her" at first. He initially favored another actress, but Hagan impressed him as a "young Katherine Hepburn" and she "just took the role away." Jacobs felt Hagan had "a fabulous screen presence" and a "persona" that held "the film together." Hagan went on to costar with Cloris Leachman in the Mel Brooks sitcom *The Nutt House* and as Angel in the Fox sitcom *Herman's Head*. She was also seen in the 1999 film *Election*, which also featured Colleen Camp, the original Kristin Shepard.

Midkiff played Elvis Presley in a TV movie and starred in two series: *Dream Street*, a blue-collar version of *thirtysomething* from the producers of that show, and *Time Trax*, a science fiction time travel show costarring *Dallas* alumnus Peter Donat. Grant costarred in the 1996 miniseries *A Season in Purgatory*, based on Dominick Dunne's roman à clef about the Kennedys, and in the film version of the John Grisham best-seller *The Chamber*. The only recognizable cast member was Hoyt Axton, the famed country music singer who had branched out into acting as early as the 1960s. Axton appeared on *Bonanza* and in the 1984 movie *Gremlins*. He was cast as Miss Ellie's father, Aaron Southworth.

Since the original script for *The Early Years* focused on events from the 1930s and the 1950s, none of the *Dallas* cast members had roles in the movie. CBS, however, asked Jacobs to work some of the *Dallas* stars into the project to ensure audience familiarity as well as high ratings. Jacobs responded that he "didn't want any of the present people in it, because I didn't want it to be another episode of *Dallas*. I wanted it to be a true 'back story.'" He ultimately acquiesced, writing an introduction featuring Miss Ellie and Pam. "I did have at one point Miss Ellie telling the story to Pamela," he said. "But Barbara Bel Geddes was ill and Pamela, Victoria Principal, had a bad back. So we have Larry as J.R. talking to a writer who's doing some research about the Ewings in the early years, and then the story starts." As a result, Larry Hagman emerged as the only *Dallas* cast member to appear in the prequel. Shooting for *The Early Years* commenced in Dallas on November 21, 1985. According to the *Houston Chronicle*, tabloid photographers "descended" upon the cast and crew in an effort to get an advance look at the young Ewings and Barneses. Filming continued until the day after Christmas to ensure that CBS had the movie in time for a spring airdate.

The Early Years aired from 8:00 p.m. to 11:00 p.m. on Sunday, March 23, 1986, two days after Episode 217 of Season 8. Ironically, while *Dallas* was at that time in a ratings slump, *Dallas: The Early Years* was a huge hit, finishing the week at number 9, with a 21.3 rating and 33 share. CBS reran the movie on May 16, 1987, the day after the series' Season 9 cliff-hanger aired. In its second showing, the movie earned an 8.7 rating and 17 share. *The Early Years* was nominated for two Emmy awards: Outstanding Achievement in Costuming for a Miniseries or Special and Outstanding Sound Editing for a Miniseries or Special.

In addition to high ratings, *The Early Years* received great critical claim. According to *Variety*, this movie "makes it on its own terms" and its "imaginative teleplay . . . commands attention." It was a "coup" with "strong commercial appeal." Ann Hodges, TV critic for the *Houston Chronicle*, wrote:

> I never thought he'd pull it off—but a tip of the Texas hat to the man who made *Dallas*. . . . Whether you're a *Dallas* fan doesn't matter. You don't want to miss this one. . . . The flashbacks are the best part. . . . The story is a dandy, and so is the cast. You'll have no trouble at all believing that these young actors might have grown up to be their TV counterparts of today. Molly Hagan is a strong-willed, sweet-faced Ellie, and Dale Midkiff is a handsome, stalwart and honorable Jock. David Grant's Digger is every inch the playboy-loser you'd expect Cliff Barnes' daddy to be . . . *Dallas: The Early Years* is a thoroughly entertaining TV movie that

could stand on its own anytime. David Jacobs does his TV creation proud.

Ed Bark of the *Dallas Morning News* raved:

It's been a long wait, but *Dallas: The Early Years* turns out to be every-thing *Dallas* seldom is. It's a three-hour "prequel" with richness of charac-ter and atmosphere. It beautifully recaptures a rural, rambunctious Texas, where dreams of big oil were free to roam. . . . Hagman is used well here. His J.R. is a little less obvious, conducting himself in a manner that befits a movie of distinction. . . . Grant and Hagan, who have the showier roles, make their characters animated but never cartoonish. . . . Grant has Dig-ger well thought out, and the depth of his preparation shows in a charac-terization that is touching, pathetic, and ever-genuine. Hagan is equally impressive as Ellie, and Midkiff is a solid rock on which to build Jock. . . . [The movie] sets a standard that *Dallas* the series isn't in a position to match. The prequel is too rich for *Dallas'* bad blood, and has the advan-tage of being set in a Texas that will always look and feel better on screen.

Bark found the movie "graced by a number of memorable scenes," including Ellie's overtures to a drunk Digger, the poker game, and an overhead shot of Dig-ger driving down a country road.

The week that *The Early Years* aired, David Jacobs penned a clever article for *TV Guide* about fictional recently discovered letters from Jock to Digger that Ja-cobs supposedly read in preparation for *The Early Years*. In "Just Discovered! The *Dallas* Papers," Jacobs wrote that, while "gathering source materials" for *Dallas: The Early Years*, J.R. denied Jacobs's request to see Jock's personal papers, but Miss Ellie overruled her son. According to Jacobs, Miss Ellie let him see the letters in an effort to set the record straight on the Barnes-Ewing feud, which she thought was "nothing but a lot of exaggerated insults and wrongheaded grudges. . . . Maybe exposing the feud will help get rid of it." Jacobs wrote that, in Jock's thin files, he found receipts, warrants, instruction books, and travel brochures. He also found four letters from Jock to Digger. Three were dated: November 21, 1951 (written ten days after Digger tried to kill Jock, an incident seen in *The Early Years*); No-vember 25, 1963 (just after President Kennedy's assassination); and April 12, 1978 (the week after Pam and Bobby eloped). The fourth, apparently written during Jock's and Digger's later years, was undated.

The 1951 letter informed Digger that Jock was not pressing charges for the shooting, and asked Digger what he thought about "coming around and sitting down and having a drink and talking it all out . . . . I know you've got reason to hate. Maybe, in your shoes, I'd hate me, too." The 1963 letter was inspired by JFK's murder. Jock wrote, "You see now, we all see now, what hate does. . . . It's un-bearable to me; isn't it unbearable to you? Or are you too filled with it to see how ugly it is and how stupid it is?" The 1978 letter wondered, "who the hell would've expected this [Barnes-Ewing marriage]" and asked Digger, "what happens now?" The undated letter lamented that he and Digger were "stubborn, stupid boys" who turned into "stubborn, stupid old men. Why does that sound so much sadder? It's too late. Sorry." After reading the letters, Jacobs pressed Miss Ellie about them. Her view of them was "they mean that Jock really mourned the loss of his and Digger's friendship but didn't know how to restore it. Jock loved Digger. He missed him every day of his life." When Jacobs wondered why the letters weren't mailed, Miss Ellie replied, "Because he was Jock and Digger was Digger."

THE EARLY YEARS CAST AND PLOT

Starring: David Grant (Willard "Digger" Barnes); Dale Midkiff (Jock Ewing); Molly Hagan (Ellie); David Wilson (Jason Ewing); Hoyt Axton (Aaron Southworth)
Introduced by: Larry Hagman (J.R. Ewing)
Also Starring: Bill Duke (Seth Foster); Geoffrey Lewis (Ed Porter)
Guest Starring: Diane Franklin (Amanda); Marshall Thompson (Dr. Ted Johnson); William Frankfather (Newman); Wendel Meldrum (Honey); Joe Rainer (Sam Culver); Marjie Rynearson (Barbara Southworth); Liz Keifer (Cherie Simmons); Matt Mulhern (Garrison Southworth); Davis Roberts (the Preacher); Kevin Wixted (Young J.R.)
With: Joe Berryman (Roscoe); Angie Bolling (Deborah); Blue Deckert (Card Player); Cynthia Dorn (Jeanne); Bob Hannah (the Sheriff); Norma Moore (Maggie); Randy Moore (Hotel Manager); Karen Radcliffe (the Hooker); Terrence Riggins (Benjamin Foster); Norma Allen (Townswoman); Jesse Baca (Driver); Ryan Beadle (Young Bobby); Frank Bell (Sharecropper); Terry Evans (Young Man); Johnny Felder (Young Cliff); Lee Gideon (Haskins); Max Harvey (Farmer); Rhashell Hunter (Priscilla Foster); Joyce Ingle (Townswoman); George Leverett (Dance Caller); Bernie Moore (Young Benjamin Foster); Tony Morris (Ranch Hand); Chuck Page (Townsman); Peyton Park (The Justice); Jim Ponds (Farmer); Ray Redd (Townsman); Debra Lynn Rogers (Joanne Haskins); Rose Mari Roundtree (Girlfriend); Mike Shanks (Hobo); Gena Sleete (Townswoman); Louanne Stephens (Woman); Fred Vest (Ranch Hand); Woody Watson (Legionaire); Andrea Wauters (Young Pam); Bethany Wright (Laurette); Joel Allen (Young Gary)
Subject: Jock Ewing meets Willard Barnes and Ellie Southworth.

THE EARLY YEARS TECHNICAL CREDITS

Written by David Jacobs
Directed by Larry Elikann
Produced by Joseph B. Wallenstein
Executive Producers: David Jacobs and Malcolm Stuart
Music by Jerrold Immel
Film Editor: Harry Kaye, A.C.E.
Production Designer: W. Stewart Campbell
Director of Photography: Neil Roach
Unit Production Manager: Robert P. Schneider
First Assistant Director: Fredric B. Blankfein
Second Assistant Director: Joseph B. Wallenstein
Executive in Charge of Casting: Barbara Miller
Casting by: Irene Mariano, C.S.A.

Texas Casting: Rody Kent & Associates
Special Visual Effects: Syd Dutton and Bill Taylor of Illusion Arts, Inc.
Set Decorator: Jack Marty
Property Master: Marty Wanderlich
Women's Costumer: Winnie Brown
Men's Costumer: Dan Lester
Makeup: Jimi White
Hairstylist: Bonnie Clevering
Special Effects: Bill Myatt
Production Sound Mixer: Skip Frazee
Sound Effects Editing: James Troutman & Associates
Music Supervisor: Dick Berres
Music Editor: Pat Peck
Executive Production Supervisor: Edward O. Denault

Cast Notes Molly Hagan hoped to meet Barbara Bel Geddes during the filming of *The Early Years*. Hagan told a reporter, "I was supposed to, but she wasn't around." ★ Larry Hagman was not just the only *Dallas* cast member to appear in *The Early Years*, he was also the only cast member to appear in every episode of the series and both TV movie sequels. As a result, Hagman has the distinction of being the only actor who has appeared in every *Dallas* episode and every *Dallas* movie ever made. (He also appeared in the 2004 cast reunion special.) Ken Kercheval, the only other series regular for all thirteen seasons, did not appear in *The Early Years* or *War of the Ewings*, nor did he appear in all of the series' episodes. ★ Matt Mulhern played Second Lieutenant Gene Holowachuck on *Major Dad*. ★ Bill Duke played the blacksmith on the Norman Lear drama *Palmerstown, U.S.A.* ★ Geoffrey Lewis played Earl on the *Alice* spin-off *Flo*. ★ Wendel Meldrum played P. K. Kelly on *Knots Landing*. ★ Several minor roles in this movie were played by actors who appeared on *Dallas*, including Joe Rainer, who played Barton in Season 9 and Dr. David Gordon in Season 11; Karen Radcliffe, who played a waitress in Season 5, Sue Ellen's sanitarium friend in Season 8, and nurses in Seasons 7 and 10; Lee Gideon, who played a Washington lobbyist in Season 9, John Cate in Season 10, and the Oil Baron's Ball Emcee in Season 11; Blue Deckert, who played a Ewing helicopter crewmember in Season 9, Grub in Season 10, and Ace Hendricks in Season 11; and Peyton Park, who was seen in minor roles in Seasons 2, 4 through 6, and 10, and played Caleb in Season 11. Other *Dallas* veterans appearing in *The Early Years* include Joe Berryman, Randy Moore, Fred Vest, and Woody Watson. ★ Eighteen-year-old Chicago native Kevin Wixted was cast as the young J.R. Wixted appeared in the Charlie Sheen movie *Lucas*. His mother thought his eyes were too sweet for him to play J.R. After Wixted landed the role, he became such a target of tabloid photographers that he had to move out of his Hollywood apartment.

Trivia This movie was the most-watched of the three *Dallas* TV movies. ★ Jason Ewing was not originally a character in this movie. When David Jacobs wrote about Jock's and Digger's early ventures, they had a third partner, but it was not Jason. As part of Jacobs's efforts to conform his script to the events on *Dallas*, he turned the third partner into Jason once he learned that Jock's brother had been mentioned during Season 7 of *Dallas*. ★ Jacobs enjoyed the opportunity *The Early Years* gave him to write about Digger. Jacobs thought "the real sloth of *Dallas* was Digger. He was a drunk, but beyond that, he was totally self-destructive." But Jacobs believed Digger was "a terrific character" who was able to present a different side in *The Early Years*. "Everyone knows Digger is a down-and-out drunkard, but in this story he's a strong character," he said. "It's his picture more than anyone else's. *Dallas* viewers know him as a loser, but I made him the luckiest man in the world. He wins at cards but gives it all to a hooker. He buys a car for cash and wrecks it after he forgets to get insurance. . . . I had a lot of fun with him." ★ TV critic Ed Bark thought that other aspects of Digger's life, most notably his marriage to Rebecca, would have made an interesting sequel to the prequel. "Scriptwriter Jacobs intentionally has left the 1940s wide open," Bark wrote. "Somewhere in there, Digger found himself a bride." ★ Said actor David Grant about Digger, "People a lot of times try to find a little courage in the bottle. And that's definitely one of the reasons behind his drinking." ★ The exterior Southfork scenes set in the 1950s were filmed at Duncan Acres, but a different ranch (not the Box Ranch used in the 1978 pilot episodes, but a different ranch, the name of which David Jacobs cannot recall) was used for exterior Southfork scenes set in the 1930s. ★ The Duncan Acres pool is covered up by the band's stage in the 1951 barbeque scene. ★ Fort Worth's Stockyards Hotel was used as the Pride Hotel and Forth Worth itself stood in for Pride's Main Street. Classic 1930s roadsters collected from all over Texas were parked along Exchange Street in the stockyards to ensure authenticity. The town of Regal was created on the grounds of the Big D Ranch. The vintage Texas State Railroad was found in Palestine, Texas. ★ Jacobs hired a linguist-dialectician from a Dallas college to help the cast with their accents. ★ director Larry Elikann directed Episode 125 in Season 5 of *Dallas*. ★ Several crewmembers from the series and the other *Dallas* movies worked on *The Early Years*, including: Dick Berres (music supervisor for Seasons 8 through 12); Edward O. Denault (executive production supervisor for Seasons 1 through 10); Skip Frazee (sound mixer for *J.R. Returns* and *War of the Ewings*); Rody Kent (location casting for Seasons 3 through 11; Kent also appeared in several episodes of *Dallas* and in *The Early Years*); Irene Mariano (casting for Seasons 1 through 13); Jack Marty (set decorator for Season 2 and production design for *J.R. Returns* and *War of the Ewings*); Barbara Miller (executive in charge of casting from the pilot through Season 13); and Pat Peck (music editor for Seasons 5 through 7 and 9 through 13).

THE SEQUEL
J.R. Returns—November 15, 1996

EVEN THOUGH DALLAS ENDED ITS original run in 1991 with a highly rated two-hour series finale which featured the return of several former cast members, fans of the show felt the final episode was more of a glorified season cliff-hanger than a true conclusion to the series. Viewers wondered whether J.R. survived and sought closure on the long-term fate of the other characters as well. After the ratings success of *Dynasty: The Reunion*, a TV movie that aired in 1991, a core group of *Dallas* alumni, including producers Leonard Katzman and Lee Rich, writer Arthur Bernard Lewis, and original cast members Larry Hagman and Patrick Duffy, pushed for a *Dallas* TV movie sequel. Within three years, they convinced CBS to greenlight the project. Katzman and Lewis penned a script that picked up several years after the series finale and resolved the question of J.R.'s apparent suicide.

Casting for the movie was done by Rody Kent, who did location casting for the series and *The Early Years*. Besides Hagman and Duffy, two other original cast members, Linda Gray and Ken Kercheval, agreed to appear. Neither Barbara Bel Geddes nor Victoria Principal agreed to participate. Bel Geddes was uninterested in coming out of retirement and leaving her quiet New England existence. Says Bel Geddes' granddaughter, "She now lives in Maine, where she loves watching the birds and living a peaceful life. She prefers to stay out of the spotlight. She has strong feelings about that. . . . She has lived a life full to the brims. She has raised a family, nurtured a career, and has now also found time to live in peace." Principal explains that she "did not join the [sequels] of *Dallas* for the same reason there should not have been a sequel to *Gone With the Wind*. . . . It was perfect the way it was."

Charlene Tilton and Steve Kanaly were not asked to be in the movie since it consisted of only ninety minutes of airtime, which limited the number of characters and storylines the writers could include. Linda Gray confirmed that "it was too hard to get all this information and everybody's back story into two hours and still make it entertaining. To have everybody back would have been impossible." Others who reprised characters they played during *Dallas*'s thirteen-year run were Audrey Landers as Afton, Omri Katz as John Ross, George Kennedy as McKay, Deborah Rennard as Sly, George O. Petrie as Harv Smithfield, and John Hoge as Ratagan. Landers "was so excited" to participate and felt "the storyline had so much potential, emphasizing the next generation" of the Ewings and the Barneses. Newcomer Christopher Demetral, who appeared in the 1995 Fox series *Dream On,* replaced Joshua Harris as Christopher. The new character of Pamela Rebecca Cooper, Afton's daughter, was played by Deborah Kellner.

Filming was to begin in July of 1995, but was delayed when Larry Hagman, who suffered from cirrhosis of the liver, learned one month earlier that he had a malignant liver tumor. Hagman underwent a fifteen-hour liver transplant operation on August 22, 1995, at Cedars-Sinai Medical Center in Los Angeles. Hagman spent the next nine days recovering in the hospital, where Linda Gray visited him almost every day.

Duffy recalled that Hagman finally took his problem seriously when it became a real health risk. "Doctor said, 'Larry, you having a drink?' And Larry said, 'Of course I'm having a drink.' He says, 'Well, when you finish that one, you can't have another because you're going to die.' So, he put down his drink and never had another drink. Never wanted one. Doesn't care. Didn't change his personality. Didn't go through withdrawals. Nothing! . . . [Later,] we were fishing in Canada together and he was probably—not probably—he was the weakest and most fragile I'd ever seen him. He was dying. And . . . I thought at that point, 'This could be the last time that I see him. This could actually be the end of the friendship.'"

Filming was delayed until the spring of 1996 to give Hagman time to recover. Hagman knew the movie could not be done without him. "I certainly based my negotiations on that," he laughingly told a reporter. "It wasn't unreasonable. I just charged 'em what I think I'm worth—a fortune." The cast and crew finally made it to Texas, where the entire movie was shot under Katzman's direction during March of 1996. Duncan Acres, now officially known as Southfork, was used for exterior filming, as it had been since Season 1, and the Calder home was once again used for interiors. Although Hagman said he "didn't miss J.R." because he "did thirteen years of him," he conceded that "it was wonderful to put that hat back on and play him again." During filming, there was no sign of Hagman's drinking, which had been a part of *Dallas* folklore both on screen and off. Audrey Landers confirmed that Hagman "definitely was not drinking. I mean, he was really . . . very, very straightforward about it. And even on the set, which was so much a part of *Dallas,* everyone was always going to the bar and pouring a drink. I don't think we did that in [*J.R. Returns*]."

TV reporter Ed Bark visited the set of *J.R. Returns* on Tuesday, March 19, 1996, a blustery day during which a funeral scene was filmed near the Southfork pool. Bark found Hagman in the real Southfork's kitchen, where he was taking the medication required by his liver transplant. Hagman told Bark that the movie was "like a dream. It really is. I mean, what's real, and what's not real?"

Leonard Katzman told Bark, "The characters are as they were, but some of the attitudes have changed a little. The '80s were the 'conspicuous consumption' decade. But I think the audience should be ready for the Ewings again." Had J.R.

become a wimp? Katzman answered, "The early drinking did J.R. a lot of harm. So he doesn't drink anymore in the show, and we make a point of saying that. Otherwise he's still ruthless. Kindlier, gentler, nondrinking and as tricky as ever." Hagman later wrote that making the movie was "vintage *Dallas*. . . . I was constantly busy running my lines while Patrick only had to glance at his script to memorize his dialogue. Eighteen years after I first saw him do that it still impressed me."

On the set, Duffy told Bark, "Everyone who watches this show is going to be vividly aware of Larry's personal history and his liver transplant. So it's the appropriate thing for Larry to say as J.R., 'Well, the doctor took me off the booze. He said it was killing me.' But Bobby still pours himself a bourbon. So it's not like we're going to all of a sudden beat the Prohibition drum. It would be a mistake to try and 'MTV' this up a little bit to make it more appropriate for a younger crowd. Because it's not what this show is about." As for his infamous 1985–86 defection from the show, Duffy told Bark that *Dallas* was "too much a part of my life now. I can only walk away from it one time, and I did that. Now I'm lock-stepped in."

Gray, the last cast member to agree to appear, discussed with Bark her initial rejection of the script. "It wasn't a ploy," she said. "It wasn't anything other than I wanted Sue Ellen to be stronger and no longer a victim of anything. I've done that, and done it well, in the past. I didn't want to have them do it without me. I couldn't stand for them to do it without me." Kercheval, who also experienced health problems by the time of *J.R. Returns*—he lost half a lung in 1994 after being diagnosed with lung cancer—commented that the characters "are probably indelibly etched in our psyches. So it's not that tough to get back to where we were."

On the last day of the shoot, Katzman told a reporter, "This has been wonderful, a real family reunion. Being here was like coming home." Four months later, Katzman recalled that he had trouble writing the script for the movie "but once I started, the characters took over . . . just as they did for so many years on the show. It's who they are." In April, after filming was complete, Hagman hosted a dinner party during which he volunteered that he would gladly do several *Dallas* movies each season, and Gray and Duffy agreed.

By the time *J.R. Returns* aired on November 15, 1996, cable's TNN (The Nashville Network) had been showing *Dallas* reruns for about six weeks. A whole new generation of viewers were falling under the Ewings' spell, although at least one of the cast members found the reruns hard to watch. Quipped Kercheval, "You can't look at those [reruns]. Those are sad because we were so young." CBS, which owned TNN, heavily promoted *J.R. Returns* on both networks. While most high-profile TV movies air on Sunday night, CBS decided to run *J.R. Returns* in *Dallas*'s Friday night timeslot, and the show's viewers responded. The movie finished at number 14 for the week with a 13.4 rating and 23 share, and was the second-highest-rated TV movie of the 1996–97 TV season. Excluding the *Dallas* series finale in May of 1991, these were *Dallas*'s best rating numbers since Sue Ellen shot J.R. in the Season 10 cliff-hanger in May of 1988.

J.R. Returns also garnered some very favorable reviews. *Entertainment Weekly* found it a "thrillingly faithful reunion of one of prime time's greatest soap operas. This 1980s ode to greed works surprisingly well in the kinder, gentler '90s. . . . Hagman still radiates the rapscallion charm that made him TV's quintessential love-to-hate character. . . . [The movie] is replete with classic *Dallas* cornball humor, pleasantly basic relationship drama, and complicated corporate scheming." *Variety* called the movie "delicious" and declared it a "welcome" show. It praised Hagman's acting, the producers' sense of continuity from the series, Arthur Bernard Lewis's "snappy" script, Katzman's able direction, and the production and costumer designers' "elegant opulence." Another critic found it "amusing," and even one reviewer who found it "bland, flat, and contrived" nonetheless suggested viewers "overlook that and just be glad Hagman's back." *Houston Chronicle* TV critic Ann Hodges, who reported on *Dallas* for many years, wrote, "Ah, J.R., you've been gone too long. . . . *Dallas: J.R. Returns* is just what deprived *Dallas* fans have pined to see. . . . This movie hits it: the *Dallas* its fans know and love, and the hero its fans love to hate."

J.R. Returns turned out to be Katzman's final work. He died of a heart attack at the age of sixty-nine on September 5, 1996, just over two months before *J.R. Returns* aired. Audrey Landers felt that it was "Leonard [who] made [the movie] happen, and his sudden and tragic death felt like the end of *Dallas*." In postproduction, the cast and crew agreed that the movie should be dedicated to him. To Patrick Duffy, "Leonard was probably the closest thing to a surrogate father that I had. His name, besides Leonard, was Uncle Lenny. He was the force behind *Dallas*. He was the quality control. He directed. He produced. He did everything but clean up the chairs after the cast had lunch. This [movie] is his monument." To Larry Hagman, Katzman "WAS *Dallas*. He wrote and directed and produced and did everything but act in them."

J.R. RETURNS CAST AND PLOT

Starring: *Rosalind Allen (Julia Cunningham); Christopher Demetral (Christopher Ewing); Patrick Duffy (Bobby); Linda Gray (Sue Ellen); Larry Hagman (J.R.); Omri Katz (John Ross); Deborah Kellner (Pamela Rebecca Cooper); George Kennedy (Carter McKay); Ken Kercheval (Cliff); Audrey Landers (Afton); Tracy Scoggins (Anita Smithfield)*
Guest Stars: *Deborah Rennard (Sly); Buck Taylor (Steve Grisham); George O. Petrie (Harv)*
Costarring: *Blue Deckert (Detective Markham); Lee Gideon (Judge Hooker); Sean Hennigan (Dave Colquit); William Earl Ray (Male Nurse); Ellen Lucy (Debbi); John William Hoge (Ratagan); Kevin Page (Officer #1); Maria Arita (Reporter); Stacy Hogue (Tammy); Katie Gratson (Wanda); Brent Anderson (Limo Driver)*
Subject: *J.R. returns to Dallas.*

J.R. RETURNS TECHNICAL CREDITS

Written by Leonard Katzman and Arthur Bernard Lewis
Directed by Leonard Katzman
Executive Producers: Lee Rich, Leonard Katzman, Rich Heller
Co-Executive Producers: Larry Hagman, Patrick Duffy
Music by Jerrold Immel
Based on Characters Created by David Jacobs
Story by Arthur Bernard Lewis
Director of Photography: Don Reddy
Production Designer: Jack Marty
Edited by Fred W. Berger, A.C.E.
Unit Production Manager/ Line Producer: Wayne Farlow
First Assistant Director: Frank Katzman
Second Assistant Director: Terri Martin
Associate Producer: Mitchell Wayne Katzman

Costume Designer: Janet Lawler
Casting by Rody Kent, C.S.A.
Sound Mixer: Skip Frazee
Set Decorator: Terri Raith
Property Master: Brad Breitbarth
Location Manager: Nanette Farlow
Production Advisor: Joe Pope
Key Make Up: Joe Hailey
Key Hair: Rachel Dowling
Assistant to Mr. Katzman: Louella Lee Caraway
Supervising Sound Editor: Burton M. Weinstein, M.P.S.E.
Re-recording Sound Mixers: John F. Reiner, C.A.S., David M. Weischaar, C.A.S., Craig M. Otte
Music Editor: Helena Lea

Cast Notes Linda Gray recalls, "A funny thing happened to me when I was in the makeup chair the first day [of filming for *J.R. Returns*]. A young man approached me and said, 'Miss Gray, can I get you some coffee?' But he just stood there! And I was staring at him, and he just stared at me. And then I realized: it was John Ross—Omri Katz—all grown up! And the entire trailer just fell down laughing." ★ Katz and Audrey Landers were two series regulars added to the main title for the first time in *J.R. Returns*. Ken Kercheval found Landers, his longtime *Dallas* leading lady, to be "a lovely person. Very career driven and determined and just a very nice lady." Also added to the main title were two actresses who had appeared on *Dallas* in other roles, Rosalind Allen and Tracy Scoggins. Allen played Bobby's ex-wife in the *Dallas* series finale fantasy sequence. Scoggins appeared as Bobby's date in Season 6 and costarred on *Dynasty* and its spin-off, *The Colbys*. She also was a regular on *Lois and Clark—The New Adventures of Superman*. The main title for *J.R. Returns* also included newcomers Christopher Demetral and Deborah Kellner. ★ Other *Dallas* veterans appearing in *J.R. Returns* include Buck Taylor, who played Detective Bussey in Season 13; Sean Hennigan, who played a cowboy in Season 11; Maria Arita, who played a restaurant hostess in Season 11; and Lee Gideon and Blue Deckert, who each appeared in several episodes from Seasons 9 through 11 as well as in *The Early Years*.

Trivia *J.R. Returns* was the second-highest-rated of the three *Dallas* TV movies, behind *The Early Years*. *Returns* earned a 14th ranking, 13.4 rating and 23 share, while *Early Years* won a 9th ranking, 21.3 rating and 33 share. ★ Larry Hagman calls *J.R. Returns* "the best" of the two *Dallas* movie sequels. ★ In addition to the Calder home and the Southfork Ranch, the movie was also filmed in Irving, Texas, and, in Dallas, at Cityplace, Mary Kay Cosmetics offices, NationsBank Tower, Crescent Court Office Building, the Dallas/Fort Worth International Airport, The Palm, Wishbone's Soundstage in Plano, and on Preston Road. ★ Cliff got a new secretary since Katzman's daughter, Sherril Lynn Rettino, who played secretary Jackie Dugan on *Dallas*, died the year before *J.R. Returns* was filmed. ★ In one scene, Hagman's and Kennedy's characters have lunch at The Palm, the real Dallas restaurant that was seen in the series. Drawings of Larry Hagman and Patrick Duffy on the wall of The Palm are visible in this scene. ★ Audrey Landers thought that it "was a fascinating moment when Cliff realized that he had a teenage daughter." ★ The enlarged version of Jock's portrait that currently hangs in the real Southfork Ranch living room is seen in *J.R. Returns* in the Ewings' living room. The smaller original was kept by Hagman after *Dallas* went off the air. ★ A Mercedes with EWING 3 tags is seen as J.R.'s car in this movie, as it was in the series. ★ Even Larry Hagman was unsure if J.R. survived the series finale. "I didn't know if he was dead," he said. "I didn't know they were going to do [a movie]. The way we ended [the series] left it open." ★ *Dallas* co-producer Mitchell Wayne Katzman was associate producer of this movie, which was edited by longtime *Dallas* editor Fred W. Berger, A.C.E. Wayne Farlow reprised his role as unit production manager, and former *Dallas* associate producer Frank Katzman was the first assistant producer of *J.R. Returns*. Louella Lee Caraway resumed her role as Leonard Katzman's assistant. ★ In the movie's atypical, pre-main title prologue scene, limo drivers waiting at the airport hold up signs reading "Heller" and "Frazee." These are references to Rich Heller, one of the movie's executive producers, and Skip Frazee, the movie's sound mixer. ★ The movie's main title was the one designed by Cliff Fenneman for Seasons 12 and 13 of the series. ★ Executive producer Richard Heller thought *J.R. Returns* might pave the way for a new series. "We'd all like to see *Dallas: The Next Generation*," he told a reporter two days before this movie aired. "It would be a logical offshoot to have the next generation. It would be an interesting slant on it if Bobby's son was like Bobby and J.R.'s was like J.R." ★ Whatever the prospects for a new series or more films, the cast members were happy to be back among old friends. Hagman felt that his costars "are dear, dear friends—like family. . . . It was so great being back together again." George Kennedy describes the cast as "a happy group. Larry was a (very talented) nut and Patrick Duffy was as nice a human being as God ever put among us. I was lucky to have been with them." Gray agreed that the movie "truly was a reunion, and that was the best part of all. I thought it would take me long to get into it, but the minute I was on the set, it came right back."

Duffy loved the script, which he thought "read to me like one of the real good episodes of *Dallas*. It was like fitting into a pair of comfortable old shoes." And he, too, felt that the project was "just like seeing your family again. . . . You put on those clothes and you step in front of that camera and it was like, . . . 'This is wonderful.'" Kercheval agreed that "it was like we never stopped."

THE TWENTIETH ANNIVERSARY
War of the Ewings—April 24, 1998

AFTER THE RATINGS TRIUMPH OF *J.R. Returns*, CBS realized that the *Dallas* phenomenon did not end with the show's cancellation in 1991. Indeed, the *Dallas* reruns shown on TNN in the late 1990s were so popular that TNN aired *Dallas* three times a day for four years and showed the entire catalogue of episodes more than twice. TNN even ran a *Dallas* marathon, hosted by Linda Gray, on New Year's Day, 1999. As *Dallas*'s twentieth anniversary approached, CBS considered the idea of doing a retrospective. Ultimately, the network decided in favor of another TV movie, and Arthur Bernard Lewis came up with a story that picked up where *J.R. Returns* left off. With Leonard Katzman gone, veteran *Dallas* director Michael Preece agreed to helm the new movie, called *Dallas: War of the Ewings*. Larry Hagman and Patrick Duffy signed on as executive producers along with Richard M. Heller, who served in that capacity with Leonard Katzman and Lee Rich on *J.R. Returns*.

Reprising their roles for *J.R. Returns* were Hagman, Duffy, Linda Gray, George Kennedy, Tracy Scoggins, and John Hoge. *War of the Ewings* also starred one original cast member who was not in *J.R. Returns*, Steve Kanaly, who credits co-executive producers Hagman and Duffy with giving Ray a "wonderful" storyline. Michelle Johnson, who had appeared in a minor role in Season 7, replaced Rosalind Allen as Bobby's love interest. The new story by Lewis did not include Cliff, Afton, or the Ewing and Barnes offspring, so Ken Kercheval, Audrey Landers, and the young adults who played the next generation in *J.R. Returns* were not asked to participate. Longtime *Dallas* chronicler Ed Bark found it "amazing" that *War of the Ewings* "goes into combat without Ken Kercheval's much-trampled Cliff Barnes character."

War of the Ewings was filmed at Southfork in the fall of 1997. For the very first time during on-location filming, a single residence was used for both exterior and interior Southfork scenes. In the pilot, the Box ranch and the Swiss Avenue home were used as the outside and inside of Southfork, respectively. From Season 1 through *J.R. Returns*, what was then called Duncan Acres (and is now called Southfork) and the Calder home were used. In *The Early Years*, Duncan Acres was used for exteriors in the 1950s scenes and another ranch (not the Box ranch) was used for exteriors and interiors for the 1930s scenes. For *War of the Ewings*, however, all Southfork scenes, both inside and out, were filmed at the former Duncan Acres. As a result, viewers saw the interior of that ranch for the very first time (and got a second look when 2004's *The Return to Southfork* was filmed both inside and outdoors at the ranch). Kanaly found it "great to be back in the saddle again. It was something like déjà vu. . . . Half of the crew was our old *Dallas* crew at the same locations, the same ranch. It was as if time stood still."

CBS aired *War of the Ewings* on April 24, 1998, just over twenty years after the first *Dallas* pilot episode aired on April 2, 1978. The network highlighted the anniversary in its promotion of the movie. Like *J.R. Returns*, *War of the Ewings* was scheduled for a Friday night, where the series had fared so well. In the end, though, the network did not promote this second sequel as heavily as it did the first, perhaps because *War of the Ewings*, unlike *J.R. Returns*, did not air during May, a Nielsen ratings "sweeps" month. *War of the Ewings* was a ratings disappointment, finishing in 42nd place in the ratings, with a 7.8 rating and 14 share, although its ratings were a 10 percent increase over those earned by the CBS series *Unsolved Mysteries* and Don Johnson's *Nash Bridges* in that same timeslot the previous week.

War of the Ewings also took a critical drubbing. The *New York Times* wrote that the movie "starts out strong but goes downhill fast. The plot . . . is as boring as dishwater. . . . All in all, it's a poor tradeoff for the sexual and social tensions of the show's early years." The *Dallas Morning News* quipped, "originality takes a holiday" in the movie's "rent-a-plot." *Entertainment Weekly* thought the pared-down size of the Ewing family undermined *War of the Ewings*. "What made 1996's *Dallas: J.R. Returns* so great," wrote Kristen Baldwin, "was its blending of the old Ewing clan with the family's next generation, like J.R.'s lothario son, John Ross, and Bobby's goody-two-shoes spawn, Christopher. *War* regrettably leaves the kids by the wayside." David Bianculli complained in the *New York Daily News* that *War of the Ewings* "plays more like a cartoon than a soap opera."

Reflecting on *War of the Ewings*, Larry Hagman notes that it "was produced by Patrick Duffy and Larry Hagman. I don't think either of us would want to do that again." Whether it was the loss of Katzman, the failure of CBS to publicize it better, or the simple fact that *J.R. Returns* sufficiently satisfied fans' curiosity about the fate of the Ewings, *War of the Ewings*, in Patrick Duffy's words, "never felt right all the way through. And I think for that reason, we're as close to . . . positive as you can say that that is the last . . . movie of *Dallas* that'll be done."

WAR OF THE EWINGS CAST AND PLOT

Starring: *Patrick Duffy (Bobby); Linda Gray (Sue Ellen); Larry Hagman (J.R.); Michelle Johnson (Jennifer Jantzen); Steve Kanaly (Ray); George Kennedy (Carter McKay); Tracy Scoggins (Anita Smithfield)*
Guest Star: *Philip Anglim (Peter Ellington)*
Costarring: *Mark Dalton (Rustler); Sean Hennigan (John Savory); Sonny Franks (Cowboy); Brad Leland (Deputy Sheriff); Amanda Welles (J.R.'s secretary); Jerry Cotton (Detective Murphy); Constance Jones (TV Reporter); John Williams Hoge (Ratagan); Paul Pender (J.R.'s bodyguard); Matthew Tompkins (Drunk); Jerry Jones (Himself); Vernon Grote (Foreman); Zach Hope (Bellman); Alfred Biernat (Doorman); Russell Towery*
Subject: *J.R. plots to regain Ewing Oil.*

WAR OF THE EWINGS TECHNICAL CREDITS

Teleplay by Arthur Bernard Lewis and Julie Sayres
Directed by Michael Preece
Produced by Elliot Friedgen
Based on Characters Created by David Jacobs
Story by Arthur Bernard Lewis
Executive Producers: Larry Hagman, Patrick Duffy, and Richard M. Heller
Music by Jerrold Immel
Director of Photography: Karl Kases
First Assistant Director: George Fortmuller
Second Assistant Director: Larry Lerner
Art Director and Production Design by Jack Marty
Location Casting: Rody Kent
Costume Design by Janet Lawler
Edited by Bud Freidgen, A.C.E.
Assistant Editor: Timothy Board

Set Decorators: Terri Raith
Makeup: GiGi Coker, Keith Sayer
Key Hair Stylist: JoJo Guthrie
Property Master: Bradley E. Breitbarth
Sound Re-recording Mixers: Neil Brody, Joseph D. Citarella
Production Sound Mixer: Skip Frazee
Supervising Sound Editors: Mike Lawshe, Catt LeBaigue
Music Editor: Chris McGeary
Boom Operator: David A. Smith
Special Effects: Jack Bennett
Stunts: Jim Henry
Location Manager: Janis Burkland
Location Stage Manager: Joseph Crisalli
Key Grip: John Knight
Production Consultant: Joe Pope
Gaffer: Darryl Tawney
Production Management: Dennis Judd

Cast Notes Michelle Johnson appeared as J.R.'s cohort Rhonda Cummings in Season 7 of *Dallas*. ★ Tracy Scoggins's character, Anita Smithfield, becomes J.R.'s attorney in *War of the Ewings*. George O. Petrie, who played Ewing lawyer Harv Smithfield from Season 2 through *J.R. Returns*, died on November 16, 1997, his eighty-fifth birthday, just after filming for *War of the Ewings* was completed. ★ Sean Hennigan played Dave Colquit in *J.R. Returns*. Other *Dallas* veterans who appear in *War of the Ewings* include Jerry Cotton, who appeared in Season 11, and Vernon Grote, who appeared in Seasons 7 and 10. ★ Jerry Jones, the owner of the Dallas Cowboys, appears as himself.

Trivia *War of the Ewings* was the least-watched *Dallas* TV movie. ★ In recognition of *Dallas*'s twentieth anniversary, *War of the Ewings* was preceded by clips from the *Dallas* pilot and Seasons 1 through 13. ★ On-location filming was once again done at The Palm restaurant, as it was for *Dallas* and *J.R. Returns*. ★ Former crew members who returned for *War of the Ewings* included music composer Jerrold Immel, who scored the pilot and episodes in all thirteen seasons of *Dallas* as well as all three *Dallas* movies; production designer Jack Marty; costumer Janet Lawler; location casting director Rody Kent, and sound mixer Skip Frazee. Joe Pope, who had provided location production consulting for *Dallas* and *J.R. Returns*, also returned for *War of the Ewings*. ★ Steve Kanaly is frequently asked why Ray is a brunette in *War of the Ewings* after so many years with a Jock-like silvery head of hair. Kanaly admits he felt funny about changing Ray's look so drastically, but explains that his hair was colored brown for another TV project he worked on and he could not undo it in time for the filming of *War of the Ewings*. ★ While the *New York Times* was lukewarm about the movie, it thought the cast looked good, especially a blonde Linda Gray. The *Times* also thought the opening shower gag would "be worth it" to any viewer familiar with Pam's season-long dream. And the *Dallas Morning News*, which also panned the movie, found Jerry Jones's scene and the scene featuring Patrick Duffy and Michelle Johnson by the sculpted cattle herd outside the Dallas Convention Center "priceless." ★ As a result of the movie's disappointing ratings, Larry Hagman acknowledged that "the bloom is off the rose for [another sequel], I think." ★ Kanaly recognized the difficulty of recreating an earlier success. "When it's magic," said Kanaly, "and when it's approaching perfection, how do you come back and copy that eight or ten years later? I think its very difficult." ★ The only three original cast members who appeared in both movie sequels were Patrick Duffy, Linda Gray, and Larry Hagman.

Part VI

THE CAST REUNION

THE REUNION
The Return to Southfork—November 7, 2004

IN LATE OCTOBER 2003, FIVE years after *War of the Ewings* aired, several *Dallas* cast members traveled to New York for two *Dallas*-related events. First, Larry Hagman, Patrick Duffy, Linda Gray, and Charlene Tilton met at SOAPnet cable network's New York studio for an appearance on the talk show *Soap Talk*. *Dallas* reruns had premiered on SOAPnet the previous month. The appearance, taped before an ecstatic studio audience, was billed as a "*Dallas* Reunion" and aired in early November in conjunction with SOAPnet's airing of the "Who Shot J.R.?" episodes from Seasons 2 and 3. The entire show was devoted to the cast reunion. The four original cast members gamely answered familiar questions from the show's hosts and audience members about *Dallas*, and clips from a number of episodes were shown.

Second, a few days later on Sunday, November 2, Hagman, Duffy, and Gray, at CBS's request, represented *Dallas* at the network's 75th anniversary gala held at the Hammerstein Ballroom in New York's Manhattan Center. The event was televised live as *CBS at 75*, and the three former *Dallas* costars were seen at the start of the show walking the red carpet together and during the show sitting together.

Tribute was paid to *Dallas* three times during *CBS at 75*. The "Who Shot J.R.?" phenomenon was recognized as one of CBS's classic moments through clips of J.R. being threatened by several suspects and shot by Kristin. In addition, the scene from Episode 54 in which J.R. calls Sue Ellen a "slut" was shown, to much mock horror and laughter from the audience. Finally, a clip of Bobby hugging Miss Ellie was seen during a tribute to various CBS series. Tina Louise, who, in addition to *Dallas*, appeared on CBS's *Gilligan's Island* (which was also represented at the gala by Dawn Wells) asked CBS to place her at the *Dallas* table and she was seen during the broadcast sitting with Duffy, Gray, and Hagman. Representing the *Dallas* spin-off, *Knots Landing*, were Michele Lee, Donna Mills, and Joan Van Ark.

Meanwhile, the wild cheering and standing ovation that she and her costars received at the SOAPnet taping made Charlene Tilton realize that *Dallas* still stirred the faithful. Tilton began to conceptualize a new *Dallas* project, but one that was very different from the last *Dallas* outing, *War of the Ewings*. Tilton—who was hurt when she was not asked to participate in either *J.R. Returns* or *War of the Ewings*—knew that *War of the Ewings* received a lukewarm reception from TV viewers and critics alike.

But given the rousing reaction of the *Soap Talk* audience to the *Dallas* reunion, Tilton concluded that, while the *Dallas* TV movies may have run their course, a retrospective of *Dallas* by its full cast was a project worth pursuing. Tilton took the idea to her agents, twin brothers Anthony and Terry Anzaldo, and together they pitched to producer (and former *Happy Days* star) Henry "Fonzie" Winkler the idea of a cast reunion and clip show. Winkler and his partner, Michael Levitt, loved the idea, and by mid-December 2004, CBS, which had experienced huge ratings successes with its 2001 cast reunion of *The Carol Burnett Show* and its 2003 cast reunion of *The Andy Griffith Show*, green-lighted the *Dallas* reunion project.

Tilton was signed to act as a co-executive co-producer of the special (along with the Anzaldos), which she, Winkler, and Levitt decided should be filmed at Southfork, resulting in the show's title, *Dallas Reunion: The Return to Southfork.* Chief among Tilton's responsibilities was lining up her former cast members to participate in the project. Those cast members who had appeared in *J.R. Returns* and *War of the Ewings* and otherwise remained within the *Dallas* fold—Larry Hagman, Patrick Duffy, Linda Gray, Steve Kanaly, and Ken Kercheval—readily agreed to Tilton's proposal.

To Tilton's surprise and delight, one *Dallas* cast member who had not stayed as close to the show or to the other cast members, Victoria Principal, also signed on for *The Return to Southfork.* Tilton phoned Principal and explained to her the concept of an on-location reunion in which the original cast would sit down together and share recollections about their landmark show. Winkler also made a personal pitch to Principal, telling her the project would be like a "high school reunion." Eventually, Principal agreed, leaving her former costar Duffy "stunned and pleasantly surprised that she's coming down."

With Principal unexpectedly on board, Tilton was left with one surviving original cast member to pursue: Barbara Bel Geddes, who had distanced herself from *Dallas* even more than Principal, and who continued her quiet retirement at her home in Maine. (For some reason—perhaps because she was in only three of the five pilot episodes or because her character was killed off in the second of her only two Season 1 appearances—Tina Louise does not seem to have been recognized by the *Dallas* family as part of the show's original cast, despite her "Also Starring" billing in both the pilot and Season 1). Tilton phoned Bel Geddes and lobbied her to appear, while Winkler worked on Bel Geddes' manager. In the end, however, Bel Geddes told Tilton, "I'd love to do it. I just can't. I know it sounds boring, but this is my life right now. I read and sit here and look at my lake."

Thus, it came as no surprise when Bel Geddes "respectfully declined the [producers'] invitation to leave her home in Maine but sent the cast her best wishes." Tilton had envisioned Bel Geddes' appearance at the ranch as a surprise to both the other cast members and the viewing audience. Although it would not be made by Bel Geddes, Tilton still liked the idea of a surprise cast member appearance. It occurred to her that, absent Bel Geddes, the logical choice for such a segment was

Mary Crosby who, as Kristin, was J.R.'s would-be assassin and fired the shot heard around the world. Crosby agreed, and became the only cast member who was not seen in the Dallas pilot to appear in The Return to Southfork.

David Jacobs, who had been at Southfork with some of the cast two months earlier to promote Dallas's premiere on DVD, did not attend the taping of The Return to Southfork, which he says was "really about the cast and their memories of the experience of making the series." Jacobs explains that he

> wasn't invited and shouldn't have been, since this really was a reunion of those who were at Southfork together over the years. I was only around for the shooting of the first five episodes, which . . . were filmed on a different ranch, and after that I wasn't around. . . . I was kind of like a parent who gave up the baby for adoption, and when it grew up to be notable, my pleasure was slightly guilty—though of course I DID take credit for the genes.

There was "curious excitement" at the Dallas/Fort Worth International Airport as the plane from Los Angeles carrying Larry Hagman, Patrick Duffy, Linda Gray, and Mary Crosby landed shortly before the October 5 and 6, 2004, taping of The Return to Southfork. Hagman, Duffy, and their wives were seen tending to the baggage claim while Gray and Crosby chatted with each other, then limousines took the cast to the Mansion on Turtle Creek, where a number of them had stayed during Dallas's annual on-location filming.

After checking into the hotel, the travelers had a dinner of tortilla soup in the Mansion's dining room. As they reminisced, Duffy left the table to call upstairs to the suite of Victoria Principal, who initially declined to join the party since she had already gone to bed. A few minutes later, however, Principal called Duffy back and asked, "Can I still come?" Principal explained, "After I hung up, it felt so wrong. I had to go down and see them all."

While the reunion was Tilton's project, it was also Principal's Dallas homecoming. All of the other original cast members participating in the reunion had been at the ranch in recent years, most of them as recently as two months earlier. Except for Tilton, they had reprised their famous Dallas roles in two late 1990s TV movies, and Tilton had played Lucy Ewing as late as 1990.

Principal, however, had not been seen on Dallas since 1987, and had not been to the city or the ranch since the summer of 1986, when she and the cast filmed exterior scenes that picked up after Bobby appeared in Pam's shower. At the time she left the show the following spring, she realized that continuing to play Pam "wouldn't [just] be my job anymore. It would be my entire career. So I did have to distance myself [from Dallas]." In a telephone interview with TV critic Ed Bark after The Return to Southfork was taped but before it aired, Principal explained that she distanced herself from the series not because she was "unappreciative," but out of self-preservation; she "just did what was necessary to go forward."

While Principal recognized that "people were mad at me for leaving *Dallas*," she responded by forging ahead with her production company (and the eleven TV movies she starred in between the late 1980s and the late 1990s) and her prosperous skin care products company. By the time she spoke with Tilton and Winkler about *The Return to Southfork* almost two decades after her last visit to *Dallas*, she realized, "I don't need to distance myself from *Dallas* anymore. I'm so far beyond that now."

What Principal did not realize, however, was how emotional an experience her return to the *Dallas* family would be. When Principal landed in Dallas and drove through the city, she was

startled to find myself crying. I didn't know that I had missed Dallas. I didn't know the skyline was imprinted in my heart. One memory kept bumping into another. I was a freight train of emotions. . . . I cried at the drop of a hat. It was just a flood of wonderment and memories, and finally, for me, something that I didn't know I needed, which was closure.

Filming began on Tuesday, October 5, at the Southfork Ranch. During the two-day shoot, the cast and crew were mobbed by fans and reporters from such outlets as *Entertainment Tonight* and CBS as they filmed in and around the ranch grounds. The script called for filmed conversations between various cast couples, including Duffy and Principal (seen outside the ranch's main house), Hagman and Duffy (in a conference room), Tilton and Kanaly (in the barn), Principal and Kercheval (at a patio table near the pool), and Hagman and Gray (in one of the ranch bedrooms). The entire cast donned black tie and gowns for a segment filmed in the Southfork living room, under the portrait of Jim Davis that was seen on *Dallas* from Season 4 through Season 13 and a photograph of Barbara Bel Geddes. Duffy read a telegram sent by Bel Geddes, who he referred to as "Bullets," which read, "Dear Friends, My dearest wishes on this memorable occasion. I shall always treasure the time we shared and the fun we had together. With love to you all, Barbara Bel Geddes."

The shoot culminated in an "Oil Baron's Ball" sequence filmed in the ranch's conference center ballroom. An audience that included pre-selected fans asked questions of the stars, and bloopers and some of Hagman's home movies were shown as well. This sequence was to have taken place outside, in front of Southfork, but heavy rains forced the crew inside. In order to fill the conference center ballroom, the producers needed extras, and they made last minute requests that were broadcast over local Dallas radio stations.

As the Sunday, November 7, 2004, airdate approached, the *Dallas* cast actively promoted their latest *Dallas* project. On Friday, October 29, Larry Hagman and Linda Gray participated in a conference call with reporters. A reporter noted that the first hour of the two-hour *The Return to Southfork* would air at 9:00 p.m., directly against ABC's new smash prime-time soap, *Desperate House-*

wives, which included among its stars Nicolette Sheridan, who was a regular on *Knots Landing* from 1986 to 1993. Gray joked that Sue Ellen was "the first desperate housewife" and said she found *Housewives* an "interesting" show that addressed the problem of prime-time soap fans that "there isn't that much to see anymore. People who used to watch *Dallas* don't have anything to watch." Gray was glad *The Return to Southfork* gave her the opportunity to reunite with Victoria Principal, who was "the only one I hadn't seen in that long a time." Hagman admired Principal's career as a producer, adding, "I doubt she has [had] time for any [previous *Dallas* projects]."

While the possibility of a disputed presidential election led CNN's *Larry King Live* to cancel the interview with Hagman that it had scheduled for Friday, November 5, various cast members appeared in other media outlets to promote *The Return to Southfork*. Hagman, Gray, and Patrick Duffy appeared on Barbara Walters's talk show *The View* on November 2 (although Walters was away and missed the taping). CBS's *The Early Show* had a "*Dallas* Week" of sorts, devoting segments to *The Return to Southfork* throughout the week before it aired, much like CBS's prime-time lineup devoted several nights of programming to *Dallas* during the week of the series' Season 3 premiere in 1980. On Tuesday, November 2, Gray appeared on *The Early Show* and was interviewed by its co-host, Rene Syler. On Thursday, November 4, Syler gave a behind-the-scenes look at *The Return to Southfork*, showing footage she and *The Early Show* crew filmed at Southfork during the special's taping a month earlier. Finally, on Friday, November 5, Hagman and Duffy appeared with Syler. That same day, Charlene Tilton, along with the author of this book, appeared on the Fox News Channel's *DaySide* with Linda Vester.

Howard Keel, who, like other cast members who were not part of the original cast, was not asked to participate in the reunion, died unexpectedly on the morning of November 7, just hours before *The Return to Southfork* was scheduled to air. Keel, who was eighty-five, died from colon cancer at his home in Palm Desert, California. While most of the press coverage focused on Keel's legendary career in movie musicals, Keel's decade-long contribution to *Dallas* was recognized with a quote Keel gave during a 1995 interview, in which he stated,

> The show was enormous. I couldn't believe it. My life changed again. From being out of it, I was suddenly a star, known to more people than ever before. Wherever I went, crowds appeared again, and I started making solo albums for the first time in my career.

Keel, who had sung for Larry Hagman at Hagman's seventieth birthday party in 2001 (a party attended by several *Dallas* alumni including Victoria Principal and Charlene Tilton), had agreed to sing again for Hagman and Hagman's wife at their fiftieth wedding anniversary party, which was scheduled for December 18, 2004. Hagman told the Associated Press that Keel "had a difficult role to play, having to replace Jim Davis, and he just fit in with our group so well."

Hagman and Gray both posted statements about Keel on their Web sites. Hagman wrote,

It is with great sadness that I say good bye to an old friend and colleague, Howard Keel. He is one of the nicest men I have ever worked with . . . a real trooper, a fine actor, a great singer, and a wonderful friend. My family will miss him VERY much.

Gray stated,

As a little girl I would go to the theatre in Culver City, California, where I grew up and watch Howard Keel in all the musicals he starred in. When I met Howard for the first time on the set of *Dallas*, I told him of how I watched him growing up as a child and he told me that many of those musicals were filmed on the same stage we were filming *Dallas* on. I have very fond memories of Howard, and he will be missed.

Keel's death was not the only surprise experienced by the producers of *The Return to Southfork* on the day the reunion was set to air. The entire CBS prime-time line-up was delayed almost three-quarters of an hour due to the running times of the National Football League games that aired on CBS late in the afternoon. As a result, *60 Minutes* aired at 7:41 p.m. instead of 7:00 p.m., and the following show, the detective hit *Cold Case*, went on at 8:41 p.m. instead of 8:00 p.m. Thus, viewers looking for *The Return to Southfork* at 9:00 p.m. did not find it. The much anticipated and heavily promoted reunion did not get on the air until 9:41 p.m. and ran until 11:41 p.m., meaning that the last third of the show did not even air during prime time.

Meanwhile, as Tilton, Winkler, and the others waited for the Nielsen ratings reports that would arrive by mid-week, the reviews were in, and a majority of critics seemed to like *The Return to Southfork*. Ray Richmond of the *Hollywood Reporter* wrote that the reunion was

[A] sweet and reasonably entertaining trek down memory lane, if overlong at two hours. . . . If you're a fan of this show that ran for an astounding 356 episodes, you'll find plenty to enjoy here. . . . *Return to Southfork* works best when it features key moments in the show's history accompanied by discussion with the players themselves, particularly the gang that participated in the legendary "Who Shot J.R.?" madness that provided a cultural phenomenon in November 1980. . . . Seeing all of this replayed in today's reality-obsessed primetime environment underscores just how far we've traveled from the era when a fictional soap could so galvanize the national consciousness.

Richmond, however, did complain that the "forced interactions of the castmates . . . tends toward the awkward."

Ed Bark of the *Dallas Morning News* called *The Return to Southfork* "smoothly entertaining." The *New York Post's* Linda Stasi found that it was "fun to see the old cast" and "nice to hear their stories," while suggesting that viewers might have preferred "a reunion not of the cast, but of the characters." According to the *South Florida Sun-Sentinel*, *The Return to Southfork* was "a pleasant nostalgia trip. . . . For *Dallas* devotees, the cavalcade of clips rates as one of this season's 'don't-miss-it' events." The *Arkansas Democrat-Gazette* called the show "well-done" but "mushy." TV critic Frazier Moore felt it would "stir amusing memories" and that, although it was "predictable and, at two hours, padded," it "doesn't matter. For its fans, *Dallas* was as big as the Texas outdoors, and going back briefly is fun."

Some critics did not enjoy the reunion, however. *The Return to Southfork* tied with a *Brady Bunch* reunion as the fifth of *Entertainment Weekly's* five worst TV shows of 2004 (it "should have been the camp blast of the year [but] felt overdone in all the wrong ways, like wearing shoulder pads with a tube top"), and tied with a *Dick Van Dyke Show* reunion as the *Hamilton Spectator's* most ill-advised reunion special (it was "a contrived cash grab that reaches its emotional zenith when surviving cast members gaze reverently at a cheesy portrait of deceased grandpappy Jock . . . and turn on the waterworks. And where the heck was Miss Ellie?").

Despite its delayed airing, *The Return to Southfork* made the top twenty-five when the Nielsen ratings were reported the week after it aired. It earned an 8.5 rating and 14 share, falling short of the high numbers won by *The Early Years* and *J.R. Returns* but its 21st place ranking was a marked improvement over the 42nd place logged by the most recent *Dallas* outing, *War of the Ewings*, which had aired six years earlier.

ABC's new phenomenon, *Desperate Housewives*, which was two-thirds over by the time *The Return to Southfork* got its delayed start, was second for the week with its largest audience to date: 25 million viewers, slightly more than double those who tuned in to catch up with the folks from Southfork. Ironically, *The Return to Southfork* lost out in the ratings to a show that was one of *Dallas's* progeny. TV critic David Bianculli, in a late October article that discussed the evolution of *Desperate Housewives* (and other serials such as *Dynasty; Twin Peaks; Beverly Hills, 90210; Melrose Place; The O.C.;* and *One Tree Hill*) from *Dallas*, was correct when he predicted that, in the Nielsen ratings, "against those ladies [from *Desperate Housewives*], Larry Hagman's J.R. may end up getting killed."

CBS re-ran *The Return to Southfork* on Saturday, November 13. During this second airing, CBS paid tribute to Howard Keel before the show's final segment by showing a photograph of Keel, complete with cowboy hat, with the words, "Howard Keel, 1919–2004." *Return to Southfork* ran behind its competition, Fox's *Cops*, NBC's *Men in Black*, and a Harry Potter movie on ABC. The reunion was 83rd for the week, with a 3.2 rating and 6 share. Nevertheless, the 21st-place ranking the reunion achieved in its first airing six nights earlier helped propel CBS to its first victory in the November ratings "sweeps" period since 1980, when, in the words of *USA Today*, "the mystery of who shot J.R. captivated *Dallas* fans"—and indeed the world.

THE RETURN TO SOUTHFORK CAST

Starring: *Patrick Duffy, Linda Gray, Larry Hagman, Steve Kanaly, Ken Kercheval, Victoria Principal, Charlene Tilton*
And: *Mary Crosby*

THE RETURN TO SOUTHFORK TECHNICAL CREDITS

Executive Producers: Michael Levitt, Henry Winkler
Co-Executive Producers: Anthony Anzaldo, Terry Anzaldo, Charlene Tilton
Supervising Producer: Gregg Sills
Produced by Gary Tellalian
Directed by Michael Dempsey
Written by Stephen Pouliot
Coordinating Producer: Linda Giambrone
Associate Producer: Paula D. Frank
Production Designer: James Yarnell
Lighting Designer and Director of Photography: Jerry Watson
Associate Director: Leslie Wilson
Production Manager: Michael Hofferth
Production Coordinator: David Hayward
Talent Coordinator: Terry Merrill
Talent Clearance: Jeanne-Marie Bremer
Post-Production Supervisor: Dave Oberg
Post-Production Coordinator: Chad Cohen
Script Supervisor: Bennett Webber
Edited by David Gibrick, Jen Gillaspy, Shawn Logue, Sharon Polito
Assistant Editors: Jeanne-Marie Bremer, Pete Fuller, Sean Humphries
Production Accountants: Adam Hutson, Martina Mikula
Production Staff: Creth Davis, Steve Dooher, Chard Foster, Xaque Gruber, Joy Kurtz, Paul Smith

Audio Mixer: Klaus Landsberg
Audio Assists: Dennis Mays, Casey Hooks
Post Audio Mixer: Mark Bauserman, Kim Beltran
Gaffer: Bill Davis
Best Boy: Jason Kallen
Camera Operators: Ken Dezendorf, Dave Eastwood, Hector Ramirez, Danny Webb, Kris Wilson
Camera Assist: Mike Wilson
Video Engineer: Terry Cooke
Cue Cards: Whitney Brown
Teleprompter: Speak Easy Prompters, Inc.
Additional Music Composed by Wil Anderson
Graphics by REZN8
Wardrobe: Warden Neil, Susan Mayes, Karina Watts
Hair and Makeup: David Babaii, Wafaa Ghannam, Alice Mansurian, Tracey L. Miller, Laura Mohberg, Jeannia Robinette, Laurie Schakosky, Patrick Tagaielle
Helicopter Provided by Air Center Helicopters
Very Special Thanks to Sherry Haughwout and Sally Peavy and To All Our Friends at Southfork Ranch, Parker, Texas

Cast Notes The producers' decision to limit *The Return to Southfork* to the original cast of *Dallas* meant that longtime regulars like Susan Howard, Howard Keel, and Priscilla Presley, as well as cast members like George Kennedy and Sheree J. Wilson from the show's final seasons, were not asked to participate. ★ Neither Susan Howard nor Donna Reed were seen in the episode clips shown during *The Return to Southfork*. Howard did not provide the producers with the permission necessary to show scenes in which she appeared, and the producers never got a reply to their inquiries made to Reed's estate. ★ Principal's suite at The Mansion on Turtle Creek during filming of *The Return to Southfork* was, by coincidence, the same suite she and her husband, Harry Glassman, stayed in during their honeymoon after their June 1985 Southfork wedding.

Trivia While the audience response to the SOAPnet *Dallas* reunion was the main factor in Charlene Tilton's decision to develop *The Return to Southfork*, she was also motivated by her realization that the special would appeal to the newest generation of *Dallas* fans, which includes her daughter, Cherish. "My daughter and her friends have *Dallas* Fridays," Tilton explained. "She says to me, 'Mom, this show is genius! This is better than *The O.C.*!'" ★ During *The Return to Southfork*, various cast members announced the results of CBS's on-line poll asking viewers to rank their top ten favorite *Dallas* cliffhangers. The results were: 1. "A House Divided" (J.R. is shot); 2. "A Blast from the Past" (Bobby in Pam's shower); 3. "Conundrum" (J.R. considers suicide); 4. "End Game" (Bobby is shot); 5. "The Fat Lady Singeth" (Sue Ellen shoots J.R.); 6. "Swan Song" (Bobby dies); 7. "Fall of the House of Ewing" (Pam's car crash); 8. "Ewing Inferno" (Southfork catches fire); 9. "John Ewing, III" (Part Two) (Sue Ellen in a coma); and 10. "Ewing-Gate" (body in Southfork pool). ★ *The Return to Southfork* begins with some of the stars arriving at the ranch in familiar Ewing cars such as Bobby's red Mercedes convertible (although Larry Hagman arrived by helicopter). ★ The special includes a scene in which Tilton complains that Lucy was never thrown in the Southfork pool. Patrick Duffy, Steve Kanaly, and Ken Kercheval quickly remedy the oversight. It also includes two scenes that spoof classic *Dallas* episodes. In one such spoof, Mary Crosby lurks near the house with a gun. In the other, Patrick Duffy wakes Victoria Principal, who feigns that the reunion was a dream. ★ Just as Dallas led to *Knots Landing*, the *Dallas* reunion led to a *Knots Landing* reunion. In June 2005, the producers of *The Return to Southfork* (Henry Winkler, Michael Levitt, Gregory Sills, and Gary Tellalian) teamed up with co-executive producers David Jacobs and Michael Filerman and taped the CBS fall 2005 special *Knots Landing Reunion: Together Again*, with William Devane, Kevin Dobson, Julie Harris, Lisa Hartman-Black, Michele Lee, Donna Mills, Don Murray, Michelle Phillips, Ted Shackelford, and Joan Van Ark.

Epilogue

WHILE 2004'S *THE RETURN TO SOUTHFORK* may prove to be the last original *Dallas* programming ever produced for network television, the *Dallas* phenomenon has not ended. In November 2004, the Bravo channel ranked J.R. Ewing as number fifteen on its list of "The 100 Greatest TV Characters" (behind, among others, Archie Bunker, Ralph Kramden, Lucy Ricardo, Arthur "The Fonz" Fonzarelli, and Mary Richards). In December 2004, *TV Guide* and the TV Land channel ranked "A House Divided," the episode in which J.R. was shot, as number 10 on its list of "The 100 Most Memorable TV Moments" (behind such historical events as the September 11, 2001, terrorist attacks; the 1969 moon landing; the *Challenger* disaster; Martin Luther King's "I Have a Dream" speech; and John F. Kennedy Jr.'s salute of his father's casket; and behind such entertainment programs as the Beatles' 1964 American debut on *The Ed Sullivan Show*, an episode of *Roots*, the M*A*S*H series finale, and an episode of *I Love Lucy*).

As of this writing, *Dallas* continues, years after its 2003 premiere on the SOAPnet cable network, to air in reruns that are highly rated and winning new generations of fans. Not long before *Dallas*'s fall 2003 premiere, SOAPnet obtained from Lorimar's successor entity, Warner Brothers, the exclusive rights to all thirteen seasons of the series. By that time, SOAPnet had acquired, in addition to many daytime soaps, *Dynasty*, *Falcon Crest*, and *Knots Landing*. *Dallas* reruns have proven so popular that SOAPnet continues to air them even though the network has completed its initial run of the entire catalogue of *Dallas* episodes.

On August 24, 2004, Warner Brothers Home Video released on DVD the first twenty-nine episodes of *Dallas*, billed as *Dallas: The Complete First and Second Seasons*. The five-disc set included the complete, unedited episodes from *Dallas*'s pilot and 1978–79 season. It also included the SOAPnet reunion and commentary by Larry Hagman, David Jacobs, and Charlene Tilton on "Digger's Daughter," "Reunion" (Part One), and "Reunion" (Part Two). With its August 2005 release of *Dallas* episodes from the 1979–80 season, Warner Brothers signaled its plan of releasing one season of *Dallas* on DVD each August—meaning all of *Dallas* should be available on DVD by 2016.

On August 19, 2004, Hagman, Jacobs, and Tilton, along with Linda Gray, Patrick Duffy, and Ken Kercheval, traveled to Southfork to help launch the DVD. Jacobs and the cast posed for photographers on a newly installed red carpet and chatted about *Dallas* with reporters, including longtime *Dallas* chronicler Ed Bark of the *Dallas Morning News*. Being at Southfork, Gray told Bark, makes "all the history come back, the whole déjà vu of it all. We were family. There were deaths and births, divorces, and marriages."

Tilton, just seventeen when *Dallas* was cast twenty-seven years earlier, told Bark, "I'm more aware of how big the show was and is now than when we were working on it." Duffy joked with the reporters that "the fact that you guys can even fake this kind of interest [in *Dallas*] is amazing to me." Kercheval explained, "You get used to" living with a phenomenon and being forever linked with a long-running role, but said that at least "my kids call me by my right name."

Reviews of the *Dallas* DVD were favorable. The *Reno Gazette-Journal* gave the DVD an overall grade of A- (with the episodes earning an A grade and the extras earning a B grade) and found that "*Dallas* has a way of getting under your skin. Like any good soap opera, there's sex, money, business, government corruption and lies. . . . Why didn't someone shoot J.R. sooner?" The *Contra Costa Times* rated the DVD a B+, stating that "it's interesting to look back at [J.R.'s] roots, especially before wife Sue Ellen . . . developed her own backbone and became one of his main foes." And the *Buffalo News* liked the "fun" commentary provided by Hagman, Jacobs, and Tilton, which "will seem like you're listening to private conversations between three old friends who have been reunited." Warner Brothers Home Video released *Dallas: The Complete Third Season* on August 9, 2005. The five-disc set included Episodes 30 through 54 from the 1979–80 season, the second full season of *Dallas*. It also included commentary by Patrick Duffy and Linda Gray on "Sue Ellen's Choice" and "A House Divided" and a new "Who Shot J.R.?" featurette with interviews with David Jacobs and the cast.

In late 2004, while ABC stalled in its development of the TV movie about the behind-the-scenes story of *Dallas* that *Variety* had reported almost two years earlier, New Regency Productions, a production company associated with Twentieth Century Fox, continued to make progress on the long-awaited big screen version of *Dallas*, an idea that was first proposed over twenty years earlier, in the wake of the "Who Shot J.R.?" craze.

According to David Jacobs, who is producing the *Dallas* movie but declined to write the script because he "thought it would be more interesting for somebody else to retell the tale," New Regency signed Australian director Robert Luketic, of *Legally Blonde* fame, to direct the film. Jacobs finds Luketic to be "an obvious leader" who "will be great" on the other side of the camera from the Ewings.

Writer Robert Harling, who penned the script for both the stage and screen versions of *Steel Magnolias*, was hired to write the screenplay. Harling, a fan of 1980s television, claimed that "*Knots Landing* was Balanchine, as far as I'm concerned." While Harling has remained mum about his script, he has confirmed that the Ewings still live at Southfork, but J.R. runs Ewing Energy, not Ewing Oil. "It's *Dallas* on acid," according to Harling. "Every woman in the cast is Lady Macbeth and every man is Macbeth."

Harling's script was completed by the fall of 2004, although Jacobs imagines that, as with any movie, "there will be many incarnations [of it] between now and the beginning of filming." Not long after the script was finished, Harling met with Luketic to discuss casting, which Jacobs calls the "most fun" part of producing the *Dallas* movie and official casting meetings began in June 2005. While Harling refused to confirm that the role of J.R. might go to Brad Pitt, he told one reporter that, in addition to J.R., the storyline includes, at least, Miss Ellie, Sue Ellen, and Lucy, saying, "They're all coming to a big screen near you!"

According to Jacobs, "New Regency and Fox would like to release the *Dallas* movie in the spring of 2006," just a few months before the scheduled release of Universal's remake of *Miami Vice* starring Colin Farrell and Jamie Foxx, and not long after the August 2005 big screen version of *The Dukes of Hazzard* with Burt Reynolds and Jessica Simpson. But what do the original Ewings have to say about their successors? Patrick Duffy has stated, "It's one thing to have a new James Bond. But to have to duplicate hundreds of people's [idea] of 'Who is Sue Ellen? Who is Pam? Who is J.R.?' That's a lot to ask an audience to do." To Linda Gray, "Hollywood has kind of run out of original ideas. They are just doing remakes of everything that was very famous awhile ago, and I don't sort of applaud that. I think we should play those roles." Larry Hagman agrees. While Hagman conceded that his friend Bruce Willis would make a good J.R., Hagman replied to Gray, "I applaud it if they hire me, for God's sake!"

NOTES

Preface

President Jimmy Carter "TV's *Dallas*: Whodunit?" by Richard Corliss, reported by James Willwerth, *Time*, August 1980, 61; "What Are Larry (J.R.) Hagman & the *Dallas* Producers Feeling from the Shots Cheered Round the World? Absolutely No Pain," Sue Reilly, *People*, July 14, 1980, 90.

The Queen Mother "*Dallas* at 10" by Larry Hagman, *People*, April 4, 1988, 102.

Former President Gerald E! *True Hollywood Story: "Dallas,"* E! Entertainment Network, airdate August 13, 2000.

Jimmy the Greek Corliss (August 1980), 63; "Now It Can Be Told: Shedunit," Richard Corliss, reported by Martha Smilgis, *Time*, December 1, 1980, 79; "She Had to Learn to Act Evil," Carol A. Crotta, *TV Guide*, August 30, 1980, 12; "How I Kept J.R. Alive," Larry Hagman, *TV Guide*, November 15, 1980, 14; *The Complete Book of "Dallas;" Behind the Scenes at the World's Favorite Television Program*, Suzy Kalter, Harry N. Abrams, Inc., New York, 1986, 237; Author's Interview with Steve Kanaly, July 31, 2002 (Kanaly Interview No. 5).

Finally, on November Kalter (book), 237.

That episode was The results of this poll were announced at the 1998 National Academy of Arts and Television Sciences Emmy Awards.

It inspired analytical *Het Geval Dallas: Populaire Kultuur, Ideologie en Plezier*, Ien Ang, Amsterdam, 1982; *Alles Uber Dallas*, Tom Fisher, Bertelsman Club, 1982; *Dallas: Skabelan Og Struktur i den Moderne TV-Serie*, Peter Kofoed & Tove Arendt Rasmussen, Aalborg Universitets Centr, 1986; *The Export of Meaning: Cross-Cultural Readings of Dallas*, Tamar Liebes, Elihu Katz, Oxford University Press, 1990; *Why J.R.?: A Psychiatrist Discusses the Villain of Dallas*, Lew Ryder with Bill Keith, Huntington House, 1982; *A Est Di Dallas: Telefilm USA Ed Europei A Confronto*, Alessandro Silj with Manuel Alvarado, Torino, 1988.

The Bonn Municipal; Restaurant business in; Turkish parliamentary meetings; In Johannesburg, theaters; The only country Corliss (August 1980), 61–63; *TVacations*, Fran Wenograd Golden, Pocket Books, New York, 1996, 176; Kalter (book), 239; "Who Shot That Nice Mr. Ewing?" Harry F. Waters, with Janet Huck, Jeff B. Copeland, and Lea Donosky, *Newsweek*, November 17, 1980.

The Southfork Ranch "Tourists Keep *Dallas* Mystique Alive," Lee Hockstader, *Washington Post*, August 19, 2002, A03.

and Warner Brothers "DVD release by end of '04," Gord Lacey, TVShowsOnDVD.com, January 7, 2004.

"Hollywood is abuzz "A Big-Screen Shot for *Dallas*," Liz Smith, *Los Angeles Times*, August 2, 2002.

Major news outlets "*Dallas* to Be Remade for Big Screen," *Variety*, October 10, 2002; "Hollywood to Make *Dallas* as Movie," www.cnn.com, October 10, 2002; "*Valley of the Dolls, Dallas* Will Return," Roger Friedman, www.foxnews.com, October 11, 2002.

PART I: THE EARLY YEARS

The Pilot

The pilot was *Entertainment Tonight: "Dallas:* Secrets of Southfork," February 5, 2000.

Before joining *Family Larry Hagman*, Leon Adams, St. Martin's Press, New York, 1987, 56.

At the time "The Cut-Rate John Wayne Changes His Luck," Dwight Whitney, *TV Guide*, February 17, 1979, 22.

"I wanted to; Jacobs and Filerman Kalter (book), 11.

Filerman, however, had *E! True Hollywood Story: "Dallas."*

Jacobs recalled that; Jacobs and Filerman; As Jacobs explained Kalter (book), 11.

CBS liked the; The network told *E! True Hollywood Story: "Dallas."*

Jacobs credited Richard; A dramatic saga Kalter (book), 36–37.

Initially, the show "Hagman Proud of Texas Roots and PBS *Lone Star* Special," Ann Hodges, *Houston Chronicle*, December 12, 1985.

In an interview Whitney (1979), 22.

Almost 10 years Kalter (book), 37.

Over 20 years *E! True Hollywood Story: "Dallas."*

Jacobs decided that; He decided to Kalter (book), 12.

So Jacobs created; The central character Kalter (book), 37.

Jacobs then wrote; What Jacobs ended; But Jacobs felt Corliss (August 1980), 64; "Reaching Back for Something Extra," Lee Margulies, *Los Angeles Times*, March 13, 1986.

When the script; Jacobs remembered that *E! True Hollywood Story: "Dallas"; Entertainment Tonight: "Dallas:* Secrets of Southfork."

CBS liked the Kalter (book), 38.

Signed to produce; He also produced "The Duke of *Dallas:* Interview with Leonard Katzman," Marsha F. Cassidy, *Journal of Popular Film and Television*, vol. 16, no. 1, spring 1988, 14.

He later said "The Baron of *Dallas:* Producer Reminisces on 10th Anniversary," Diane Haithman, *Los Angeles Times*, April 1, 1988.

While Jacobs's intent; He wrote the; The script for *Entertainment Tonight: "Dallas:* Secrets of Southfork"; Kalter (book), 13, 20, 38.

Lewis found it *E! True Hollywood Story: "Dallas."*

prompting producer Leonard; "Then," Katzman explained "A Decade of *Dallas:* Success of Steamy Soap Is No Dream," Tom Green, *USA Today*, April 1, 1988.

"Digger Barnes, who's *E! True Hollywood Story: "Dallas."*

Katzman credited the; "First you have Cassidy, 19.

Although, according to Kalter (book), 39.

Bel Geddes felt she; She was "crushed; In 1966, Bel Geddes; Lewis' illness left "To Wildlife and *Dallas* Lowlife, Barbara Bel Geddes Gives the Milk of Human Kindness," Toby Kahn, *People*, June 28, 1982, 43.

When asked not *E! True Hollywood Story: "Dallas."*

had known Katzman "The *Dallas* Cast Remembers the Good Times But Regards Its Patriarch, Actor Jim Davis, as Irreplaceable," Sue Reilly, *People*, May 11, 1981, 130.

According to costar; "By the time *E! True Hollywood Story: "Dallas."*

David Jacobs agreed Whitney (1979), 22.

One week after; He was ultimately *Patrick Duffy*, Lee Riley, St. Martin's Press, New York, 1988, 38, 62.

Leonard Katzman explained "It Was Rotten While It Lasted," Ellen Torgerson Shaw, *TV Guide*, May 9, 1981, 28.

Linda Evans was Kalter (book), 36.

Principal landed the Kalter (book), 39.

appeared on *Days Aloha Magnum: Larry Manetti's Magnum, P.I.*, Memories, Larry Manetti with Chip Silverman, Renaissance Books, Los Angeles, 1999, 209.

Aaron Spelling lured; Not long after; Principal set out "This Woman Is a Trained: Chiropractor, Agent, Stock-Car Driver, Actress. Victoria Principal's Answer Is: All of the Above," Bill O'Hallaren, *TV Guide*, June 16, 1979, 12.

Principal got the *Entertainment Tonight: "Dallas: Secrets of Southfork."*

Principal acted as; Her reputation from; Explained producer Lee "If the Eyes of Texas Bug These Days, Blame It on Those Three Sexy Wildcats from *Dallas*," Sue Reilly, *People*, December 17, 1979, 128.

Jacobs confirmed that; "Victoria, of all; "She wanted to *Entertainment Tonight: "Dallas: Secrets of Southfork."*

Michael Filerman agreed *E! True Hollywood Story: "Dallas."*

Principal's reading left O'Hallaren (1979), 12.

Duffy knew that; He read with; He recalled that *The Life and Times of "Dallas,"* TNN, April 24, 2000.

Ironically, the selection; won the role Kalter (book), 38–39.

Jacobs, without confirming *E! True Hollywood Story: "Dallas."*

received the *Dallas*; At the time "So Long, *Dallas*," Larry Hagman as told to Mary Murphy, *TV Guide*, May 4, 1991, 5; *"Hello Darlin': Tall (and Absolutely True) Tales About My Life,"* Larry Hagman with Todd Gold, Simon & Schuster, New York, 2001, 181.

"Two scripts had; "One was *Dallas* Hagman (1988), 100.

Hagman "heard a Hagman (1991), 5.

Maj Hagman recalled "Sunset at Southfork" by Mark Goodman and Todd Gold, *People*, May 6, 1991, 48.

Hagman "read the Hagman (1988), 100.

Hagman "didn't find "You think J.R. Is Mean? Why, Darlin,' the Pleasure's All His!" Dwight Whitney, *TV Guide*, March 8, 1980, 24.

Initially, David Jacobs; Jacobs thought, "'Larry *Entertainment Tonight: "Dallas:* Secrets of Southfork."

Hagman was interested; Once Hagman committed; "So this didn't; "I figured to Whitney (1980), 26.

The producers originally; Tilton, however, knew; "I read about; "She was described "Charlene Tilton Opens in La Mirada Play While Negotiating *Dallas* Role," Barry Koltnow, *Orange County Register,* November 3, 1987; *Entertainment Tonight: "Dallas:* Secrets of Southfork."

Gray won the; The part of; The scene involved Kalter (book), 39, 60; "Give Her the Simple Life," *TV Guide (Canada),* January 24, 1979.

As she went *The Linda Gray Story,* Mark Bego, St. Martin's Press, New York, 1988, 37.

While still in; "I just knew; According to Michael *CNN Larry King Live:* "Larry Hagman and Linda Gray Share Their Memories of *Dallas,*" June 20, 2000; *E! True Hollywood Story: "Dallas."*

31-year-old Steve; Although he had; He learned about; Since the producers; At the casting; Kanaly knew one; When Kanaly read Author's Interview with Steve Kanaly, February 20, 2000 (Kanaly Interview No. 1).

He thought, "I "If *Dallas* Folded, It Could Be the Last You See of Steve Kanaly," Susan Littwin, *TV Guide,* October 17, 1987, 35.

Kanaly met with; They invited Kanaly; Kanaly was offered Kanaly Interview No. 1.

trained in New; It was Capice "Swat This *Dallas* Gadfly?" Bill Davidson, *TV Guide,* April 24, 1982, 32–33.

Kercheval wanted to; "I read the; "Cliff is the Kalter (book), 56.

But Kercheval still "Cliff Is Still Trying to Be J.R.'s Worse Half," Jerry Buck, *San Diego Union-Tribune,* December 23, 1984.

Kercheval felt he *E! True Hollywood Story: "Dallas."*

But, said Kercheval Davidson (1982), 33.

because she "liked Author's Interview with Tina Louise, October 27, 2003 (Louise Interview).

The castmembers signed; Filerman recalled that *E! True Hollywood Story: "Dallas."*

Within a week; The producers, director; Larry Hagman brought; Kanaly arrived late; He was nervous; Kanaly recognized Victoria; He also recognized; He saw a; He thought, "Wait Kanaly Interview No. 1.

Patrick Duffy recalled; Said Duffy, "We *E! True Hollywood Story: "Dallas."*

Kanaly credited Katzman *E! True Hollywood Story: "Dallas."*

Katzman had flown; "I flew down; "I was coming; The Box Ranch; Interior Southfork scenes Kalter (book), 39, 71, 228–29; *Dallas: The Complete Ewing Family Saga, Including Southfork Ranch, Ewing Oil, & the Barnes-Ewing Feud, 1860–1985,* Laura Van Wormer, Doubleday & Co., Garden City, New York, 1985, ix.

The cast was Riley, 49.

On February 1; Kanaly did so; When Kanaly walked; This posed a; By the next; While the crew; The lake scene Kanaly Interview No. 1.

Meanwhile, the first "*Dallas* Milestones," *Dallas Morning News,* March 27, 1988.

The rewritten snow; CBS, however, refused; After the snow Kanaly Interview No. 1.

In looking back Van Wormer, ix.

Duffy credited Katzman's; "We were like; "And we were E! True Hollywood Story: "Dallas."

Hagman found the CNN Larry King Live: "Larry Hagman Talks About His Career, His New Series, Orleans, and His Liver Transplant Operation," January 7, 1997.

Charlene Tilton said Reilly (1979), 132.

As Principal explained Entertainment Tonight: "Dallas: Secrets of Southfork."

Tilton caught pneumonia; Recalled producer Lee; Tilton joked that; Principal noted that Reilly (1979), 131.

Some of the O'Hallaren (1979), 12.

Duffy linked Principal's; "She had a; Katzman confronted Principal; The confrontation occurred; Katzman recalled that "She's Risen Above—But Can't Ever Forget—Her Troubled Years," Michael Leahy, TV Guide, March 14, 1987, 36.

For instance, she O'Hallaren (1979), 12.

Hagman owned a; While Kanaly and E! True Hollywood Story: "Dallas."

Hagman would "drive Goodman, 46–47.

in late February Kanaly Interview No. 1.

Jacobs worked on; CBS had green Kalter (book), 13, 39.

The actors also E! True Hollywood Story: "Dallas."

Kanaly felt "that Kanaly Interview No. 1.

As Jacobs pointed; "The response to; "The critics were E! True Hollywood Story: "Dallas."

Variety reviewed the Variety, April 5, 1978.

Another Variety critic "Where Are They Now? The Original Cast of Dallas," Courtney Bond, Texas Monthly, September 2002, 170.

According to the; Three of the; More importantly, the; These ratings were Kalter (book), 39–40.

Hagman thought, "Well Entertainment Tonight: "Dallas: Secrets of Southfork."

The Pilot Episode Guide

Episode 1—Hagman and Wayne Kanaly Interview No. 1.

Hagman flew on Whitney (1980), 26.

This episode, which "Dallas Milestones."

according to author; The Renaissance Tower Golden, 173–74.

Explained Katzman, "Jim Kalter (book), 42.

Larry Hagman and; At the end; Gray was devastated; She and Hagman; Years later, when; She asked Hagman; When Gray reminded "How Larry Hagman Got Angry and Forced Some Changes in Dallas," Michael Leahy, TV Guide, May 24, 1986, 41.

according to Victoria Entertainment Tonight: "Dallas: Secrets of Southfork."

Charlene Tilton recalled; Tilton also recalled E! True Hollywood Story: "Dallas;" TNN, The Life and Times of "Dallas."

According to Kanaly; Kanaly also found Author's Interview with Steve Kanaly, August 1,

2000 (Kanaly Interview No. 2).

Hagman, a longtime; Hagman complained that; Hagman carried a Hagman (book), 207; "There's Peace (For Now) in *Dallas* as Larry Hagman Mulls Over J.R.'s Fate—and His Own," Bob Lardine, *People*, April 14, 1980, 95.

seven years after; Principal also wrote "Life Without Bobby," Victoria Principal, *TV Guide*, October 12, 1985, 36.

Episode 2—Moore liked the Corliss (August 1980), 64–65.

Moore was Victoria Author's Interview with Victoria Principal, January 7, 2004 (Principal Interview).

because the snow; The gypsum, however; After the color Kalter (book), 210.

according to the; This letter was; Jacobs published excerpts; According to Jacobs'; In the letter "Just Discovered! The *Dallas* Papers," David Jacobs, *TV Guide*, March 22, 1986, 20.

Episode 3—There was only; "I remember the; "The director called Hagman (1991), 6.

Hagman's favorite mistress Hagman (1988), 100.

Hagman wrote, "Of "*Dallas*—My Way," Larry Hagman, *TV Guide*, March 27, 1982, 2.

Episode 4—When asked to Author's Interview with Linda Gray, February 23, 2004 (Gray Interview).

As for the; Katzman acknowledged that Adams, 68.

Victoria Principal had; The man, Ed; "The indications are; After getting on *Entertainment Tonight: "Dallas*: Secrets of Southfork."

She recalled, "It "The Eyes That Turned *Dallas* Upside Down" by Bill Davidson, *TV Guide*, December 29, 1984, 29.

Confirmed pilot casting Bego, 37–38.

Gray listened to Bego, 38.

Specifically, Gray decided Kalter (book), 60.

Part of Gray's "Meaner and Crazier All the Time," Dick Russell, *TV Guide*, October 6, 1979, 9.

David Jacobs recalled Kalter (book), 39, 60.

Episode 5—David Jacobs originally; He recalled, "When; Indeed, Leonard Katzman; Jacobs did so Kalter (book), 34, 38.

Patrick Duffy recalled TNN, *The Life and Times of "Dallas."*

during filming of Kalter (book), 228.

Victoria Principal thought Principal Interview.

the barbeque scenes Kanaly Interview No. 1.

the scene where Principal (1985), 38.

Season 1

When CBS optioned; Although Texas was; This change was Kanaly Interview No. 1.

After Katzman drove Kalter (book), 230.

he and his; Duncan Acres' location; It was built; The main building Golden, 171, 173; Hockstader; Kalter (book), 229; "Where J.R. Is Shot: Visitors Get Look, *Dallas*' Locale" by George L. Rosenblatt, *Houston Chronicle*, August 17, 1986.

Joe Duncan and; Duncan recalled that "Here's the Real Dirt on Southfork," Jane Hall, *TV Guide*, January 24, 1981, 45.

Interior Southfork scenes Kalter (book), 229; "Film and Outtakes," Jane Sumner, *The Dallas Morning News*, November 15, 1996.

Once the on-location Whitney (1979), 26.

At the studio Kalter (book), 229.

This began what Author's Interview with Mary Crosby, December 4, 2003 (Crosby Interview).

Typically, after the; The crew would; Upon returning to; The remainder of Crosby Interview; Author's Interview with Sheree J. Wilson, November 4, 2003 (Wilson Interview).

Stage 23 at; During Season 8; The Southfork foyer; Stage 18 was; In later years; The cast's unmarked Kalter (book), 212, 224, 226, 229; "Bobby Ewing's Life After Death," Suzy Kalter, *People*, September 29, 1986, 47–48.

According to Bruce Kalter (book), 229.

As noted by TNN, *The Life and Times of "Dallas."*

As a result; As Season 1; While the producers; Katzman and his Kanaly Interview No. 2.

Justice starred future "Dack is No Rambo-Come-Lately," Jerry Buck, *San Diego Union-Tribune*, July 10, 1985.

Variety reviewed the; The review was; *Variety* claimed that *Variety*, September 27, 1978.

As Leonard Katzman Cassidy, 17.

CBS, like Lorimar Kalter (book), 42; Waters, 70.

"The audience," noted Haithman (April 1988).

Katzman explained that Kalter (book), 26, 28.

Season 1 Episode Guide

Episode 6—Van Ark recalls that; "It all happened; "They sent me; Van Ark thought David; Van Ark found Ackroyd Author's Interview with Joan Van Ark, December 30, 2003 (Van Ark Interview).

According to Charlene Author's Interview with Charlene Tilton, November 14, 2003 (Tilton Interview).

Victoria Principal confirms; Principal recalls that Principal Interview.

Texas actor Oliver; Seale went on; Seale recalls that; Seale loved being; "They're such warm; "Larry and Patrick *"Dallas"* Family Gathers for Dress-up Ball," Ann Hodges, *Houston Chronicle*, July 29, 1985.

Larry Hagman found "Bridegroom Revisited," Sue Reilly, *People*, December 6, 1982, 43.

Linda Gray recalled CNN King/Hagman & Gray Interview.

while appearing on Kanaly Interview No. 5.

Some of the Golden, 170.

The ranch was; Its name was; Now a 41-acre; It draws 400,000; According to a; Visitors can tour; While the interior "New 'Back to Kansas' Sitcom Stirs Up a Whirlwind," Jayne Clark, *USA Today*, June 20, 2003, 1D; Hockstader; Golden, 171–72, 174; TNN, *The Life and Times of "Dallas."*

The former has Kalter (book), 229, 231–32.

Episode 7—Victoria Principal recalls Principal Interview.

Joan Van Ark enjoyed; "Says Van Ark, "I Van Ark Interview.

Jacobs explained, "I Kalter (book), 16.

"Very early in; "I . . . . have always Haithman (April 1988).

However, Jacobs noted; As *Dallas* writer *E! True Hollywood Story: "Dallas."*

Episode 9—who Jim Davis Whitney (1979), 26.

Davis described himself Corliss (August 1980), 64.

Katzman saw Jock Cassidy, 19.

The Store was Kalter (book), 100; Author's Interview with Barbara Babcock, November 3, 2003 (Babcock Interview).

Ironically, "not a "How Dallas Feels About *Dallas*," C. W. Smith, *TV Guide*, November 1, 1980, 14.

Steve Kanaly recommended; Allen was a; Allen, however, never; According to Kanaly Kanaly Interview No. 1.

Dallas biographer Suzy Kalter (book), 215.

Episode 10—Leonard Katzman explained Russell, 9.

Katzman conceded that Davidson (1984), 29.

David Jacobs agreed Kalter (book), 60.

Linda Gray told Corliss (August 1980), 65.

Gray also thought; "The magic that; "When they said; Gray and Hagman; "Larry and I Rosen, 9.

David Jacobs felt; "I think from Kalter (book), 29.

the cast joked; Steve Kanaly and; For the blooper Kanaly Interview No. 1.

Episode 11—when David Jacobs; Both Patrick Duffy Waters (1980), 70.

According to Jacobs; As a result "The Soaps Steam Into New Season," Robert P. Laurence, *San Diego Union-Tribune*, September 25, 1985.

Duffy also became; At about the Shaw, 28, 30.

Several years later Kalter (book), 51.

of the episodes; "My favorite one Kalter (book), 20.

Episode 13—As explained by Kalter (book), 56.

Episode 14—Barbara Babcock recalls Babcock Interview.

Principal recalls this Principal Interview.

Episode 15—According to Steve Kanaly Interview No. 1.

Victoria Principal told Corliss (August 1980), 64.

The writers' motto Walters, 70.

When asked where Cassidy, 21.

Ken Kercheval enjoyed Author's Interview with Ken Kercheval, October 2, 2003 (Kercheval Interview).

Episode 16—Steve Kanaly thought Kanaly Interview No. 2.

Leonard Katzman initially; It was the; After Howard turned "She Chose *Dallas* Over Congress," Bill Davidson, *TV Guide*, May 10, 1986, 14.

"I could not; "It just didn't Author's Interview with Susan Howard, December 2, 2003 (Howard Interview).

Howard thought Kate Davidson (1986).

Ray slowly became; Kanaly recalls that; Kanaly "loved such; Kanaly believes his Kanaly Interview No. 1.

Kanaly explained Ray Kalter (book), 61.

Episode 18—this episode is Kercheval Interview.

Episode 19—Like Miss Ellie; Bel Geddes' father separated; "I didn't see; "He was a; Once when Bel Geddes Kahn.

on January 3 Reilly (1979), 128.

Episode 20—*Dallas* was not; "I had a; "I told a "Martha Scott Plays Mysterious Grandmother on *General Hospital*," Jerry Buck, Associated Press, January 24, 1986.

At the time Author's Interview with Fern Fitzgerald, October 20, 2003 (Fitzgerald Interview).

Said Leonard Katzman Cassidy, 17.

Explained Larry Hagman CNN King/Hagman Interview.

Duffy agreed: "At Riley, 49.

Bobby's friendship with; Recalls Gray, "Patrick Gray Interview.

Episode 21—Costar Kenneth White; White does not Author's Interview with Kenneth White, October 30, 2003.

veteran actor Richard Author's Interview with Richard Roat, October 30, 2003.

Explained Katzman, "In Van Wormer, x.

David Jacobs credited *E! True Hollywood Story: "Dallas."*

this episode includes; Louise found Les Louise Interview.

As a result Fitzgerald Interview.

Episode 22—According to Louise; But Louise enjoyed; Louise admired Leonard Louise Interview.

which Kercheval recalls; In real life; Kercheval produced "Kenny's; Leonard Katzman was Kercheval Interview; Davidson (1982), 32; "Ken Kercheval: He Stands By His Man," Ed Bark, *Dallas Morning News*, July 4, 1985.

Episode 24—Jim Davis thought; "Don't you think; "Why we're all Kalter (book), 18.

Episode 25—She studied acting Davidson (1984), 30.

but grandmother Mary Adams, 45.

Heidi also played Lardine, 96.

Heidi's younger brother Adams, 45.

Larry Hagman, Patrick Kanaly Interview No. 1.

looking back on Hagman (1991), 6.

Episode 26—says Charlene Tilton Tilton Interview.

Larry Hagman was Lardine, 95.

Episode 27—Katzman tried to; Later, Katzman tried; "About a month Davidson (1986), 14.

Katzman told Howard; Howard recalls that; Susan Howard found Howard Interview.

upon learning that Russell, 9.

Episode 28—Larry Hagman says Author's Interview with Larry Hagman, October 31, 2003 (Hagman Interview).

Linda Gray, however CNN King/Hagman & Gray Interview.

Gray described Sue Russell, 9.

Charlene Tilton told Reilly (1979), 127.

Episode 29—and Katzman recalled Kalter (book), 28.

during the summer; In the review "Texas Raunch," Dave Kehr, *Film Comment*, July/August 1979, 67.

Season 2

To the surprise *TV Facts*, Cobbett Steinberg, Facts on File Publications, New York, 1985, 260–61.

A mid-November; Writer Gerald Clarke; While Clarke thought; Exceptions, however, included "The Big House on the Prairie," Gerald Clarke, *Time*, November 12, 1979, 117.

According to *People* Reilly (1979), 124.

Wayne declined to Kanaly Interview No. 1.

After producers Lee; They held the Crotta, 12.

Crosby—who had; Although she recognized Crosby Interview.

Crosby "thanked [the; However, Crosby explained; "The first few Crotta, 12.

Ackroyd was unavailable; Joan Van Ark, who Van Ark Interview.

In Leonard Katzman's Kalter (book), 39.

Patrick Duffy believed; "Without a single *Entertainment Tonight: "Dallas:* Secrets of Southfork."

Charlene Tilton sought; As Jim Davis Whitney (1980), 26.

Davis found Hagman Lardine, 95.

As for Hagman; Hagman even seemed; Simon wrote that "USA Network's Contribution to TV's Sleazefest," Jeff Simon, *Buffalo News*, February 2, 1997, 1–2.

When *Dallas* ended Hagman (1991), 6.

At the same time; Steve Kanaly recalls Kanaly Interview No. 1.

Writer Arthur Bernard; "Camille Marchetta, Leonard *E! True Hollywood Story: "Dallas."*

Katzman recalled that; The creative team; While Sue Ellen; Sue Ellen returns; According to Capice; Katzman recalled, "We Corliss (August 1980), 66.

Lewis could not *E! True Hollywood Story: "Dallas."*

Katzman said, "We; Capice thought a Corliss (August 1980), 66.

and, in Katzman's Kalter (book), 28.

As for the *E! True Hollywood Story: "Dallas."*

"the public went Kalter (book), 28.

Season 2 Episode Guide

Episode 30—with *Dallas* now; Explained Phil Capice Corliss (August 1980), 64.

By 1986, the; Katzman called it Kalter (book), 40.

Episode 32—As for why Crosby Interview.

Ken Kercheval recalls Kercheval Interview.

Victoria Principal found Principal Interview.

prior to *Dallas*; During her ride; "I thought, 'How; Hagman noted that Crotta, 12–13.

Episode 33—says Joan Van Ark Van Ark Interview.

"Uncle Lennie," as Kalter (book), 205.

was a "walking Riley, 62.

Duffy also called; Susan Howard felt *E! True Hollywood Story: "Dallas."*

Steve Kanaly calls; He made the Kanaly Interview No. 1.

Episode 34—Mary Crosby recalls Crotta, 13.

Offscreen, Crosby became Crosby Interview.

Episode 37—Almost a decade Goodman, 47.

Prior to playing; *Journey* was cancelled; At the wrap Author's Interview with Jared Martin, November 3, 2003 (Martin Interview).

despite their on-screen; Crosby describes Gray Crosby Interview.

Gray explains, "I Gray Interview.

Wayne Farlow was; As Steve Kanaly Kanaly Interview No. 1.

Jared Martin recalls Martin Interview.

Episodes 38 & 39—Mary Crosby recalls Crosby Interview.

according to her Author's Interview with Hannah Lerman, January 22, 2004 (Lerman Interview).

who was asked; She replied, "They *E! True Hollywood Story: "Dallas."*

Nevertheless, Bel Geddes found Kahn.

Linda Gray found; "[But] Barbara," said "Give Her the Simple Life."

Patrick Duffy commented TNN, *The Life and Times of "Dallas."*

Charlene Tilton was *E! True Hollywood Story: "Dallas."*

Episode 40—Charlene Tilton won Reilly (1979), 131.

Episode 42—who Steve Kanaly Kanaly Interview No. 5.

Hagman's favorite *Dallas* Hagman Interview.

in a *TV* Russell, 8.

Elsewhere, Katzman called Cassidy, 20.

Gray, however, enjoyed "Give Her the Simple Life."

Gray found that Russell, 8.

Around the time; In the same Reilly (1979), 127, 132.

Charlene Tilton maintained; "I know the; "That the women *Entertainment Tonight: "Dallas: Secrets of Southfork."*

Today, Gray confirms Gray Interview.

Episode 43—Of her two; Van Ark feels that Van Ark Interview.

This episode was; "It was absolutely; CBS asked him; Since *Knots* was *E! True Hollywood Story: "Dallas;"* Kalter (book), 43.

while it has TNN, *The Life and Times of "Dallas."*

Joan Van Ark recalls; "The network," says; Nevertheless, Van Ark "used Van Ark Interview.

Tilton claimed that Kalter (book), 43.

Joan Van Ark particularly; Says Van Ark of Van Ark Interview.

When Hagman directed Adams, 118.

Shackelford and Steve Kanaly Interview No. 5.

Episode 44—Susan Howard's return; "I knew from; "That was Leonard's Howard Interview.

According to Steve Kanaly Interviews Nos. 2, 5.

Corbin recalls that Author's Interview with Barry Corbin, January 3, 2004 (Corbin Interview).

Said Corbin about TNN, *The Life and Times of "Dallas."*

Episode 46—Said Harris of Whitney (1980), 22–23.

Leonard Katzman said; "Among other things Cassidy, 21.

Arthur Bernard Lewis agreed *E! True Hollywood Story: "Dallas."*

According to Phil Kalter (book), 34.

While Hagman now Hagman Interview.

Hagman once recognized CNN King/Hagman Interview.

Charlene Tilton attributed; "As ruthless as TNN, *The Life and Times of "Dallas."*

Hagman prepared for; Although Hagman was; The second take; Hagman was happy Whitney (1980), 26.

CBS received over Ryder, 14.

this episode's final; Said Jacobs, "To *E! True Hollywood Story: "Dallas."*

this episode makes Fitzgerald Interview.

Episode 48—Leonard Katzman explained; "Early on," said Cassidy, 16.

Jared Martin enjoyed; "I loved working; "It spoiled me Martin Interview.

As for Gray Gray Interview.

Episode 49—Skinner and Principal; Explained Principal the Reilly (1979), 128.

Principal and Skinner; They divorced after *Soap Opera Babylon,* Jason Bonderoff, Pergee, New York, 1987, 96–97.

The producers, however; Like a number Davidson (1982), 30.

As a result; "It's just not; "You don't have Bark, July 1985.

Episode 50—Mary Crosby felt Crotta, 13.

who Barry says Corbin Interview.

Episode 52—Principal recalls that Principal Interview.

Elliott got the; Around the time; Elliott and Hirson Author's Interview with Stephen Elliott, November 26, 2003 (Elliott Interview).

in 1964 "Stephen Elliott, 86; Veteran Stage, Film and TV Actor Known for Role in *Arthur*," Valerie J. Nelson, *Los Angeles Times*, May 24, 2005

the week after Whitney (1980), 22.

same name as Van Ark Interview.

Episode 53—Kenney was about; He had a; Kenney "remember[s] filming; As they played; Kenney thought the Author's Interview with Ed Kenney, October 28, 2003 (Kenney Interview).

this episode's scenes; She explains that Crosby Interview.

said Larry Hagman Whitney (1980), 22.

A few years Kalter (book), 54.

Episode 54—It was seen *E! True Hollywood Story: "Dallas."*

Larry Hagman watched Hagman (book), 195.

Leonard Katzman's original; When this episode; Katzman used his Kanaly Interview No. 5.

Katzman reflected that Cassidy, 14.

Phil Capice recalled Kalter (book), 28.

Larry Hagman addressed; Hagman stated then; "The way I; When asked about "TV Update," Frank Swertlow, *TV Guide*, April 19, 1980, A-3, A-4.

Two months after "How I Kept J.R. Alive," Larry Hagman, *TV Guide*, November 15, 1980, 11.

Meanwhile, Hagman told Lardine, 88.

Fern Fitzgerald "wasn't Fitzgerald Interview.

Meanwhile, Ed Kenney; Kenney explains, "I; Needless to say Kenney Interview.

according to Mary; Crosby recalled that Crotta, 12.

This episode includes; "I saw [this; "She always brought Author's Interview with Patrick Duffy, November 20, 2003 (Duffy Interview).

when *Time* magazine Corliss (August 1980), 63, 65–66.

PART II: PHENOMENON

Season 3

As Leonard Katzman Kalter (book), 28.

New storylines were; Phil Capice said Corliss (August 1980), 66.

Hagman, in an Kanaly Interview No. 5.

When it was Hagman (1980), 12.

Even before J.R. Whitney (1980), 27.

Hagman's original *Dallas*; Since then, Hagman; On one occasion; Lorimar balked, saying; Hagman offered to Hagman (1991), 6, 9.

By the show's Lardine, 88.

Once J.R. was Hagman (1991), 10.

Patrick Duffy, who TNN, *The Life and Times of "Dallas."*

recalled that, "So *E! True Hollywood Story: "Dallas."*

Hagman acknowledged that; Hagman knew he; Hagman's "good sense Hagman (1980), 12.

Thus, at the; While he was; Hagman was at Hagman (1980), 12; Hagman (book), 196.

where the scripts; Pages of key; In Hagman's absence; Katzman had the Kanaly Interview No. 5.

The "heavy-duty dickering; By June 20 Hagman (1980), 12, 14.

In the June "TV Update," Frank Swertlow with Dwight Whitney, *TV Guide*, June 21, 1980, A-55.

While in London; Recalled Duffy, "I; The days passed; His costars wanted; They did not Kanaly Interview No. 5; *Entertainment Tonight: "Dallas: Secrets of Southfork."*

Duffy explained that *Entertainment Tonight: "Dallas: Secrets of Southfork."*

And, Duffy said *E! True Hollywood Story: "Dallas."*

Despite Lorimar's claim Reilly (July, 1980), 88.

Hagman, too, "knew *Entertainment Tonight: "Dallas: Secrets of Southfork."*

Hagman also knew Hagman (book), 196.

Hagman listened to; O'Connor told Hagman Hagman (1991), 11.

On June 21 Hagman (1980), 14.

Hagman left England; Hagman wanted to Hagman (book), 199.

Duffy, who found *E! True Hollywood Story: "Dallas."*

Eventually, as the "TV Update," Frank Swertlow, *TV Guide*, July 5, 1980, A-1.

and Hagman, in; "Of course I; "We went on *Entertainment Tonight: "Dallas:* Secrets of Southfork."

Even at the Reilly (July 1980), 88.

Two years later Reilly (December 1982), 45.

who was under Howard Interview.

thought Hagman was *E! True Hollywood Story: "Dallas."*

By the time "So Who Plugged J.R.? Sue Ellen Swears She Doesn't Know, but *People* Kibitzers Think They Do," Sue Reilly, *People*, November 10, 1980, 115.

only one year Reilly (1979), 132.

There were salary Kanaly Interview No. 5.

Hagman spent June Hagman (1980), 14.

still in the Hagman (book), 199.

Hagman made it; in a spectacular Hagman (1991), 11; Hagman (book), 201.

Hagman later said Hagman (1991), 11.

the crew felt Kanaly Interview No. 5.

Time recounted that Corliss (August 1980), 61, 63.

The editor of "*Dallas* Is Emptying the Pubs and Streets of London," Alan Coren, *TV Guide*, July 26, 1980, 11.

The University of Reilly (November 1980), 113.

Dallas was nominated; Hagman received his; When the awards Steinberg, 267–68, 270.

Dallas also won Adams, 66h.

By the time; But before the; Because of the; The strike was; During the strike; The entire SAG; Weeks went by Kanaly Interview No. 5.

Duffy commented that *E! True Hollywood Story: "Dallas."*

Katzman admitted that; "When you do Corliss (December 1980), 79.

As the additional; Bookies in Las Vegas Kanaly Interview No. 5.

The character of Hagman (1980), 14.

People magazine conducted Reilly (November 1980), 116, 118.

Most lists of Waters, 66.

Fern Fitzgerald, who Fitzgerald Interview.

were clamoring for Kanaly Interview No. 5.

For example, Linda; "We wouldn't tell; Gray also said; Gray described filming Bego, 67–68.

Ken Kercheval said; Kercheval claimed he *E! True Hollywood Story: "Dallas."*

and felt that Corliss (December 1980), 79.

Kercheval also made Corliss (August 1980), 64.

Mary Crosby claimed "Mary Crosby's Hot as a Pistol, Says Larry Hagman, But Not in a Way to Worry Dear Old Dad," Sue Reilly, *People*, December 8, 1980.

Time magazine reported Corliss (December 1980), 79.

Leonard Katzman told "Hollywood's Cover-Up! Mum's the Word on Killers and Arsonists," Kenneth Turan, *TV Guide*, November 26, 1983, 50.

Dallas biographer Suzy Kalter (book), 238.

For example, Hagman Hagman (1988), 102.

Linda Gray also; Shortly before the; "They said, 'Do *Entertainment Tonight: "Dallas: Secrets of Southfork."*

Mary Crosby recently *E! True Hollywood Story: "Dallas."*

she herself "had; "The producers knew Crosby Interview.

Katzman told *People*; Hagman joked that; CBS News' Dan; Republican Presidential candidate Reilly (July 1980), 90.

A Lorimar insider; Katzman admitted, 'The Swertlow/Whitney, A55.

Tabloids and mainstream; *People* magazine reported; Katzman vowed that Reilly (July 1980), 87–88; Waters, 67.

The worldwide obsession; After Dusty Farlow Martin Interview.

Mary Crosby also; "If it was Turan, 49–50; Crosby Interview.

Hagman was also Ryder, 7.

Ken Kercheval wished; Victoria Principal remembered *Entertainment Tonight: "Dallas: Secrets of Southfork."*

According to one Turan, 49.

Dallas writer David; "Jim Davis [said] *E! True Hollywood Story: "Dallas."*

There was a; The producers scrambled; The season's first Kanaly Interview No. 5.

Three days before; Hagman and his; After the show; Even though by Hagman (book), 201–02.

businesses in South; For years to; Duffy recalled being; Steve Kanaly recalls *E! True Hollywood Story: "Dallas;"* Kanaly Interview No. 5.

the Turkish parliament Goodman, 46.

Kanaly was at; He believed that; Kanaly and his; His table included; Kanaly commented politely; The executives' wives; The crowd at Kanaly Interview No. 5.

Approximately 350 million Kalter (book), 237.

Kanaly recalls that Kanaly Interview No. 5.

At the party Corliss (December 1980), 79.

Time magazine's review Corliss (December 1980), 79.

Newsweek wrote that Waters, 67.

Patrick Duffy predicted *Entertainment Tonight: "Dallas:* Secrets of Southfork."

Indeed, the whodunit The results of this poll were announced at the 1998 National Academy of Arts and Television Sciences Emmy Awards.

and *Texas Monthly* Kalter (book), 237.

He realized that; But by then; Katzman called the "H-o-l-d On for the TV Cliffhangers," Yardena Arar, *San Diego Union-Tribune*, April 28, 1986.

Season 3 Episode Guide

Episode 55—Parkland Hospital, where Golden, 170.

a substitute for Kanaly Interview No. 5.

a number of Reilly (July 1980), 88.

prior to the Swertlow/Whitney, A55.

the cast found; Katzman was approachable Kanaly Interview No 5.

Crosby says that Crosby Interview.

Episode 56—McCloskey was cast; but casting director; While McCloskey had; "The phenomenon of; McCloskey recalls that; At the time Author's Interview with Leigh McCloskey, December 20, 2003 (McCloskey Interview).

McCloskey is an Kanaly Interview No. 5.

according to Patrick; J.R.'s shooting, said Riley, 74–75.

Episode 57—ultimately, Linda Gray; Even as Sue; "When I first Bego, 68, 102.

She told *Time* Corliss (August 1980), 65.

the cast was; If Moore knew; All of the; His light sarcasm; which is still; It was a Kanaly Interview No. 5.

Episode 58—Its 53.3 rating "TV Update: *Dallas* Fever Hypes CBS' Ratings and Ad Revenues," Frank Swertlow, *TV Guide*, December 6, 1980, A1.

the record set Steinberg, 116.

The next most Nielsen Ratings Chart, *New York Post*, August 25, 2000, 5.

in Chicago, 76%; In New York Corliss (December 1980), 79.

advertising for this Bego, 68.

according to *Time* Corliss (December 1980), 79.

eight years after Hagman (1988), 102.

and was postponed Swertlow/Whitney, A55.

the outdoor patio Crosby Interview.

Mary Crosby recalls Crosby Interview.

Fern Fitzgerald remembers Fitzgerald Interview.

Ray Krebbs, however; Jokes Kanaly, "I Kanaly Interview No. 5.

Katzman said later Kalter (book), 28.

in an effort; While each episode Turan, 50.

originally, the pregnancy Waters, 66.

Mary Crosby later *Entertainment Tonight: "Dallas:* Secrets of Southfork."

when recently asked Hagman Interview.

Episode 59—Patrick Duffy recognized; "By holding out *E! True Hollywood Story: "Dallas."*

Katzman confirmed that; Katzman frequently put Leahy (May 1986), 38, 45.

Hagman, however, says Hagman Interview.

Mary Crosby knew; At the time Crotta, 14.

As for reporters Corliss (December 1980), 79.

Later, once she; "What more can Goodman, 47.

Now, Crosby says; Crosby explains, "I Crosby Interview.

Episode 60—Cassidy was not; Cassidy got the; Cassidy "loved being; Cassidy found E.J. Author's Interview with Joanna Cassidy, December 4, 2003 (Cassidy Interview).

Windom was Steve; The two played; "In fact, I; Kanaly found Windom's Kanaly Interview Nos. 2, 5.

Woodward was a; According to Woodward; Woodward "thought Punk; In fact, Woodward; "After Jim had Author's Interview with Morgan Woodward, October 24, 2003 (Woodward Interview).

the actors enjoyed Kanaly Interview No. 5.

not long after; Cassidy thought J.R. "Joanna Cassidy: Is She the Female J.R.?" Mark Tunnell, *US,* February 17, 1981.

Episode 61—Steve Kanaly considers; It is also; Kanaly recalls that; By the end; Kanaly thought there; Davis felt the; One day, after; Hagman tried to Kanaly Interview No. 1.

"Then [Hagman] turned Bonderoff, 48–49.

Kanaly also thought Kanaly Interview No. 1.

Phil Capice, however Bonderoff, 49.

As a result "After Years as a *Dallas* Also-Ran, Steve Kanaly Is Finally Over the Hump," Sue Reilly, *People,* May 10, 1982, 111.

according to Leonard Cassidy, 19–20.

Kanaly recalls that Kanaly Interview No. 1.

Lakin felt that; "Every character in *E! True Hollywood Story: "Dallas."*

Joanna Cassidy enjoyed Cassidy Interview.

Episode 62—Susan Howard's earlier Davidson (1986), 14.

Ken Kercheval was Kercheval Interview.

Episode 63—Pointer got the; Pointer and Wynn; Pointer recalls that; According to

Pointer Author's Interview with Priscilla Pointer, October 12, 2003 (Pointer Interview No. 2).

Pointer had never; What Pointer "remember[s] Pointer Interview No. 2.

Pointer has a; Pointer jokes that Author's Interview with Priscilla Pointer, October 10, 2003.

McCloskey recalls that McCloskey Interview.

Episode 64—Smithers recalls that Author's Interview with William Smithers, October 4, 2003 (Smithers Interview).

who McCloskey says McCloskey Interview.

Episode 65—Landers auditioned for; The following evening "Audrey Landers: Just an Old-Fashioned Girl," Pat Sellers, *US*, February 1981.

She quickly became "Rise of a Sex Symbol," Carolyn See, *TV Guide*, May 28, 1983, 28.

Leigh McCloskey enjoyed; "Anne Francis and McCloskey Interview.

J.R.'s favorite drink Golden, 177.

According to Hagman Hagman (1988), 101.

Davis and Kanaly; Later, while Shore; Shore looked over; At that point; "You can imagine Kanaly Interview No. 5.

Said Hagman, "We Hagman (1988), 101.

Audrey Landers "got Author's Interview with Audrey Landers, October 31 2003 (Landers Interview No. 1).

Anne Francis "enjoyed; Francis found Barbara Author's Interview with Anne Francis, December 13, 2003 (Francis Interview).

Episode 66—Markham did not; "We had all; Although Markham did; "He was doing; "I remember him; Markham had also; "You had the Author's Interview with Monte Markham, December 2, 2003 (Markham Interview).

Charlene Tilton was; "My marriage to TNN, *The Life and Times of "Dallas."*

all that Leigh McCloskey Interview.

Audrey Landers recalls Landers Interview No. 1.

Landers believed that See, 26.

three days after *Prime Time Network Serials: Episode Guides, Cast and Credits for 37 Continuing Television Dramas, 1964–1993*, Bruce B. Morris, McFarland & Company, Inc., Jefferson, North Carolina, 1997, 60.

Episode 67—Noble Willingham, who Author's Interview with Noble Willingham, November 16, 2003.

Upon his death "Noble Willingham, A Supporting Actor in Dozens of Films, Dies, 72," Associated Press, January 20, 2004.

Landers explains, "The Landers Interview No. 2.

Episode 69—Anne Francis recalls Francis Interview.

Episode 70—Keel sang a Kanaly Interview No. 2.

Susan Howard loved Howard Interview.

Linda Gray also; "I adore Howard; "I grew up Gray Interview.

Keel regaled the; According to Kanaly Kanaly Interview Nos. 2, 5.

He was cast; He then "got; "I went over; Keel met with Author's Interview with Howard Keel, October 9, 2003 (Keel Interview).

given Dusty's apparent; Martin explains, "Dusty Martin Interview.

Episode 71—Steve Kanaly was; Kanaly found Howard; Kanaly thought Howard; She became a; Her addition to Kanaly Interview Nos. 1, 2.

Says Howard about Howard Interview.

Howard also liked; She explained, "I E! True Hollywood Story: "Dallas."

Victoria Principal "admired; While acting on Principal Interview.

Steve Kanaly found Kanaly Interview No. 2.

Hagman recalls that Hagman Interview.

As for Duffy Duffy Interview.

Prior to directing; "I enjoy all; "Let's say there; Several months later Shaw, 30.

In particular, Duffy's; But once Duffy "Patrick Duffy Bids Bye-Bye to Bobby in the Hottest Dallas Cliffhanger Since J.R. Got Shot," Michelle Green, People, May 13, 1985, 59.

Principal agreed that; "Whenever Patrick directs Principal (1985), 35.

Steve Kanaly knew; Martin's return kept Kanaly Interview No. 5.

Monte Markham was; "I kept doing; "I'd say, 'I; Markham describes Linda Markham Interview.

Episode 72—Priscilla Pointer heard; Pointer enjoyed playing; "Fortunately, I liked; "Victoria was extremely Pointer Interview No. 2.

Principal also held; When asked about Principal Interview.

Barbara Babcock recalls Babcock Interview.

Monte Markham and; Markham recalls, "Larry Markham Interview.

Episode 73—Preece was a Kanaly Interview No. 5.

Pointer "had seen Pointer Interview No. 2.

Audrey Landers, who Author's Interview with Audrey Landers, November 1, 2003 (Landers Interview No. 2).

Landers recalls that Landers Interview No. 1.

Episode 74—John Randolph was; He was a; Randolph died in "Obituary: John Randolph" by Tom Vallance, The Independent, March 3, 2004.

during Season 6; "Craig says if; "So he tells "Alexis Smith Is Still a Lady, Even in Dallas," Jerry Buck, San Diego Union-Tribune, April 1, 1984.

Episode 75—According to Leigh McCloskey Interview.

Markham thought that Markham Interview.

Episode 76—Ken Kercheval thought; "You want to Kalter (book), 56–57.

It is also Kercheval Interview.

favorite scene of; "It is also Pointer Interview No. 2.

for such scenes; He recommended his; After suggesting she Davidson (1982), 30.

Episode 77—an actor Kanaly Kanaly Interview No. 2.

Woodward says "Steve Woodward Interview.

this episode includes Cassidy, 17.

while her character Sellers.

the week this Shaw, 30.

after filming his; "It came as; The producers thought; "Jim was too; Instead, they asked; "It was such; "I was not Keel Interview.

Season 4

In late 1980; Despite the diagnosis; His cancer was Kanaly Interview No. 5.

The chemotherapy made; But Davis never *E! True Hollywood Story: "Dallas;" Entertainment Tonight: "Dallas:* Secrets of Southfork;" Kanaly Interview No. 5.

Leonard Katzman recognized Kalter (book), 212.

In early April Reilly (1981), 130.

The cast gathered; Davis died a *Life and Times of "Dallas;"* Riley, 67.

He was sixty-five *"Dallas* Milestones."

Larry Hagman called; Hagman was traveling; and released a; Katzman found Davis; To Charlene Tilton Hagman (1988), 101; Reilly (1981), 130.

While an airport *"Dallas* Milestones."

he sent a wreath; Hagman called Davis Hagman (1988), 101.

Victoria Principal, who; Although Principal "knew; Principal had bonded *Entertainment Tonight: "Dallas:* Secrets of Southfork."

Hagman loved their Hagman (1988), 101.

Hagman wrote in Hagman (book), 209–10.

Principal recounted that; Linda Gray remembered Reilly (1981), 130.

To Ken Kercheval; And for Susan *E! True Hollywood Story: "Dallas."*

Steve Kanaly was; "He came back; Kanaly also admired; Kanaly considered Davis; Davis recounted for; Davis felt *Dallas* Kanaly Interview No. 5.

"The loss of Haithman (April 1988).

Phil Capice explained Bonderoff, 51.

Writer Arthur Bernard; "We really agonized; "It would have "Beware of the Phone-Call Trick and the Plastic Surgery Ploy," Bill Davidson, *TV Guide,* July 30, 1983, 34.

"People couldn't suddenly Kalter (book), 212.

And, as Lewis; Even if Lewis Davidson (1983), 34.

Katzman considered the Kalter (book), 212.

Lorimar felt it Davidson (1983), 34.

Although Katzman described Kalter (book), 212.

Davis received a; The cast and crew; Lead acting nods; The show failed Steinberg, 282–83, 286.

Kercheval thought it Bark (July 1985).

and Steve Kanaly felt Kanaly Interview No. 5.

In early 1982; This time, however Steinberg, 367.

It also earned Steinberg, 349.

Season 4 Episode Guide

Episode 78—**Barbara Babcock explains** Babcock Interview.

The season premiere; To keep the; Mary Crosby recalls Crosby Interview; Turan, 50.

The following scene; He recalls that Corbin Interview.

the ranch used; That ranch was "Brite and Brief," Associated Press, February 24, 1988; Kalter (book), 125.

despite her character's E! True Hollywood Story: "Dallas."

Episode 79—**When she was** Goodman, 47.

according to Ken Goodman, 46.

In another interview Bark (July 1985).

Once, when rehearsing Goodman, 47; Martin Interview.

Episode 80—**who Martin calls** Martin Interview.

Bel Geddes indeed attended; Bel Geddes was amused Kahn.

Linda Gray also Gray Interview.

Episode 81—**Recalls Brittany, "When** Author's Interview with Morgan Brittany, January 27, 2004 ("Brittany Interview).

Nelson also co-starred Kahn.

based on Morgan Pointer Interview No. 2.

Episode 82—**of her scenes** Pointer Interview No. 2.

Episode 84—**although Susan Howard** Howard Interview.

Howard respected Hagman E! True Hollywood Story: "Dallas."

Episode 85—**Jared Martin liked** Martin Interview.

The J.R./Afton falling See, 26.

Landers found that Landers Interview No. 1.

Episode 86—**CBS promoted its** Morris, 61.

Episode 87—**One of the; Martin found Keel** Martin Interview.

Episode 88—**Barbara Bel Geddes and; Hagman called Bel Geddes** Hagman (1988), 102; Adams, 27.

Episode 89—**Leonard Katzman felt** Cassidy, 19.

while Clayton was; "The cast was Keel Interview.

while Morgan Brittany's; As for her Brittany Interview.

Episode 90—**Morgan Woodward, like; Woodward explains, "Jim** Woodward Interview.

This painting now Hagman (book), 209–10.

Leonard Katzman thought; "The most effective; "The camera has Cassidy, 21.

Katzman thought "Jim "Dallas: 10 Years Old," Jerry Buck, Boston Globe, March 20, 1988.

Episode 91—**He was recommended** Kanaly Interview No. 1.

Episode 93—**According to Audrey; "Even after he; "You really could** E! True Hollywood Story: "Dallas."

Fern Fitzgerald calls Fitzgerald Interview.

Episode 95—**she believes her; "The night I** Babcock Interview.

Principal wrote the; In 1984, she "The Principal Work-Out: Improve Your Fitness While Watching TV," Victoria Principal, *TV Guide*, June 2, 1984, 10.

Susan Howard may; Howard recalled, "Victoria E! True Hollywood Story: "Dallas."

Barbara Babcock recalls; Duffy was in; "I remember we Babcock Interview.

Episode 97—while Steve Kanaly Reilly (May 1982), 111

Episode 98—Morgan Brittany felt; Hagman "was very; "He wasn't really TNN, *The Life and Times of "Dallas."*

Howard Keel was; "I really enjoyed; "She was so Keel Interview.

Episode 100—the falling out; Howard recalls that Howard Interview.

Episode 102—Leonard Katzman thought Kahn.

Initially, McCloskey had; Toward the end; McCloskey asked the; He recalls, "Phil; McCloskey describes his; "The people were McCloskey Interview.

this episode's scene; Woodward found Barbara Woodward Interview.

Cliff's embezzlement and; Producer Phil Capice; Kercheval summed up Davidson (1982), 29–30.

Episode 103—despite Lucy's ordeal *Entertainment Tonight: "Dallas:* Secrets of Southfork."

a few weeks; In researching the; Prior to the; While an assistant; Katzman pretended not; During rehearsal of; Kercheval told his; While "Capice and; When it was Davidson (1982), 30, 32–33.

Landers says that; She explains that Landers Interview No. 2.

Irving J. Moore, who Kercheval Interview.

Season 5

Patrick Duffy found TNN, *The Life and Times of "Dallas."*

People magazine reporter; As the wedding; Patrick Duffy quipped; Hagman replied, "No; Linda Gray reacted; Reilly wrote that; Charlene Tilton "sat; The wedding scenes; Someone handed the; After vows were; Gray replied, "Sure; Hagman, whose wife; The cast and Reilly (December 1982), 43, 47.

Although *Dallas* was; *Dallas* lost in Steinberg, 301–02.

As Phil Capice Kalter (book), 29.

Season 5 Episode Guide

Episode 104—Chiles was from "Texas Stars Form Minigalaxy in Hollywood and New York," Bruce Spinks, *Houston Chronicle*, August 4, 1985.

Chiles had never; "They dug up; "I went down "Lois Chiles Sets the Fur Flying on *Dallas* as J.R.'s Sexy Temptress, Holly Harwood," Susan Peters, *People*, April 18, 1983, 117.

Recalled Larry Hagman Hagman (1988), 100.

Although she did; "I really enjoyed; "Of course, being Howard Interview.

Lucy's pregnancy was; After Lucy's abortion Kalter (book), 210.

According to Gray; She explained, "When; Gray refused the Bego, 80–81.

Leonard Katzman thought Reilly (December 1982), 43.

Priscilla Presley, who; She recalled, "I *Entertainment Tonight: "Dallas:* Secrets of Southfork."

shortly before this; While the article "Do It Victoria's Way—or Else," Sheila Liebergott, *TV Guide*, September 18, 1982, 14.

although *People* magazine Reilly (December 1982), 43, 47.

Kercheval felt Cliff *E! True Hollywood Story: "Dallas."*

Episode 105—She was cast Author's Interview with Alice Hirson, October 16, 2003 (Hirson Interview).

Hirson's leading man Woodward Interview.

Fern Fitzgerald was Fitzgerald Interview.

Hirson calls Fitzgerald Hirson Interview.

Once, however, a; "Victoria Principal came; "Kercheval could not Davidson (1982), 32.

Episode 106—Steve Kanaly says Kanaly Interview No. 2.

Michael Preece was Hirson Interview.

Episode 107—Steve Kanaly recalls Kanaly Interview No. 2.

the mention of Golden, 177.

The ball was; *Dallas* castmembers frequently; According to Steve; Afterwards, "they tell C. W. Smith, 16.

Larry and Maj Kalter (book), 234.

Martin finds it Martin Interview.

Gray confirms that Gray Interview.

Episode 113—Sue Ellen sports Kalter (book), 141.

said Linda Gray Bego, 81.

Morgan Woodward's most; "My favorite scene Woodward Interview.

Episode 115—Alice Hirson recalls Hirson Interview.

Wrote Suzy Kalter Kalter (book), 217.

Episode 117—Beck's initial contract Author's Interview with John Beck, October 1, 2002 (Beck Interview).

composer Bruce Broughton; Also nominated was Steinberg, 319.

John Beck was; "My agent, who; Beck's first scene Beck Interview.

Episode 118—Beck calls Hagman Beck Interview.

Episode 119—said Larry Hagman Peters, 117.

Episode 120—Ken Kercheval found See, 28.

Episode 121—Priscilla Pointer recalls; Pointer does not Pointer Interview No. 2.

Episode 122—Brittany found Murphy Brittany Interview.

Episode 123—John Beck found Beck Interview.

Episode 125—on March 10; Five days later Davidson (1983), 38; Bonderoff, 50.

Episode 126—during 1983, while; She got through Davidson (1984), 30.

Gray recalls one; The Hagmans "have Gray Interview.

Hagman recalled that Hagman (1988), 100.

Episode 127—Morgan Woodward spent; "When I was Woodward Interview.

Episode 128—Leonard Katzman felt; "That's what the; "He may be Kalter (book), 45.

Chiles felt that; Chiles received only Peters, 117.

Episode 129—some of the Kalter (book), 206.

Episode 130—Corbin found Linda; Corbin points out Corbin Interview.

Episode 131—During the summer Gray Interview.

The trip was; Lewis told TV; Lewis said, "We're Davidson (1983), 38.

The five years Principal Interview.

a second Southfork; the fire blazed Kalter (book), 226.

editor Fred W. Berger Steinberg, 320.

according to Leonard Cassidy, 14–15.

Season 6

Morgan Brittany recalled TNN, *The Life and Times of "Dallas."*

Dallas director Irving Kanaly Interview No. 5.

Larry Hagman felt Hagman (1988), 103.

Ken Kercheval wondered Bark (July 1985).

Steve Kanaly claims Kanaly Interview No. 5.

TV Guide even; Author Stephen Birmingham "*Dallas* vs. *Dynasty*: Which Show Is Better?" Stephen Birmingham, *TV Guide*, October 15, 1983, 37–38.

Larry Hagman claimed Hagman (1988), 103.

went into syndication *BiB Television Programming Source Books*, 1998–99 Series Volume, Donna F. Witzleben, Editor, North American Publishing Co., Philadelphia, 1999.

As Bob Crutchfield; A *Dallas* movie; According to Crutchfield "*Dynasty* Measured for the Big Screen," *San Diego Union-Tribune*, August 17, 1984.

By the show's "*Dallas* to Be Remade for Big Screen."

Season 6 Episode Guide

Episode 132—John Beck returned; Beck found the Beck Interview.

Barbara Bel Geddes was Bonderoff, 50.

not long after; Katzman said that Turan, 49.

Episode 133—shortly before this; Patrick Duffy added "Watch Out—This Woman Is a Devious, Back-Stabbing Schemer!" Betty Goodwin, *TV Guide*, September 24, 1983, 16.

Episode 134—He joined the; "*Dallas* was at Author's Interview with Christopher Atkins, October 20, 2003 (Atkins Interview).

Bruce Broughton won Steinberg, 341.

Morgan Brittany "had; As a result Brittany Interview.

One of the; Atkins found Hagman; Atkins based Peter Atkins Interview.

Episode 135—Christopher Atkins enjoyed; "Omri was a Atkins Interview.

Episode 136—a home once Kalter (book), 158.

Episode 137—as Season 6 Beck Interview.

Atkins recalls that Atkins Interview.

Morgan Brittany also Brittany Interview.

Episode 138—Steve Kanaly recalls Kanaly Interview No. 2.

Chiles found Hagman Peters, 117.

Billy Bob's honkey-tonk Golden, 176.

Priscilla Presley's lack; "When my agent; Phil Capice explained; Capice then recalled "The Ticklish Plight of Being Priscilla Presley," Bill O'Hallaren, *TV Guide*, March 17, 1984, 13–14.

Presley recalls that; Presley "purposely never Author's Interview with Priscilla Presley, December 19, 2003 (Presley Interview).

She found the; Leonard Katzman said; Duffy thought Presley O'Hallaren (1984), 3–14.

Presley admits, however; "There were so; Presley credited Larry *Entertainment Tonight: "Dallas: Secrets of Southfork."*

recalls that her Presley Interview.

Gray thought it; "When someone like *Entertainment Tonight: "Dallas: Secrets of Southfork."*

Patrick Duffy agreed TNN, *The Life and Times of "Dallas."*

Episode 139—according to Ken Kercheval Interview.

the Oil Baron's; She won the; She recalled, "I; Presley found Larry; Presley felt comfortable; Katzman didn't think; Nevertheless, he heard O'Hallaren (1984), 14.

Christopher Atkins found Atkins Interview.

Episode 140—She later explained O'Hallaren (1984), 16.

Says Atkins, "Linda Atkins Interview.

three days before; A Gallup poll; The poll asked; Of respondents between; Of respondents between "Dallas Is Done In," Ed Bark, *Dallas Morning News*, April 4, 1991.

The assassination initially; "I may have Kalter (book), 12.

Episode 141—Priscilla Presley found Presley Interview.

the Oil Baron's Kalter (book), 206.

Episode 142—Christopher Atkins found Atkins Interview.

Episode 143—She became a Bonderoff, 49.

According to Ken; An example of Kercheval Interview.

Episode 144—Keel found acting; In over a *Only Make Believe: My Life in Show Business*, Howard Keel with Joyce Spitzer, Barricade Books, Fort Lee, New Jersey, 2005, 300–1.

Episode 145—Christopher Atkins "didn't; "But, yes, it; "I don't think Atkins Interview.

1985 *Dallas* record; the project was Author's Interview with Steve Kanaly, October 3, 2000 (Kanaly Interview No. 4); "Oh, Wow! A *Dallas* Album!" Rose O'Donnell, *Seattle Times*, July 4, 1985.

Episode 146—Larry Hagman relished; The year this; Said Hagman, "I TNN, *The Life and Times of "Dallas."*

Episode 147—Larry Hagman used; "That was the TNN, *The Life and Times of "Dallas."*

says Priscilla Presley Presley Interview.

Presley felt Bobby Kalter (book), 47.

Episode 148—Patrick Duffy recalled Michelle Green (1985), 59.

Principal agreed that Principal (1985), 36, 38.

Episode 150—Christopher Atkins found; "Peter really loved; "So close yet Atkins Interview.

although the script; Upon reading the Hirson Interview.

not long after "The TV Column," John Carmody, *Washington Post*, February 15, 1984.

Episode 151—neither Patrick Duffy Duffy Interview; Presley Interview.

Morgan Brittany recalls Brittany Interview.

Episode 152—around the time "Another Spinoff?" *San Diego Union-Tribune*, February 27, 1984.

Kanaly says, "neither; Nothing ever came Author's Interview with Steve Kanaly, September 28, 2000 (Kanaly Interview No. 3).

Episode 153—In real life Hirson Interview.

Episode 155—Says Morgan Brittany Brittany Interview.

production for Season "Atkins Leaving *Dallas*," *San Diego Union-Tribune*, March 6, 1984.

the cast and; The party featured "Will J.R. Be Shot Again? Tensions Mount in *Dallas* Finale," Jon Anderson, *San Diego Union-Tribune*, May 18, 1984.

shortly after joining; She replied that; Smith also quipped; Prior to *Dallas*; Then *Dallas* came; "I had a; "It's funny. It's Buck (April 1984).

but Phil Capice; "We differ," said Kalter (book), 201.

Episode 157—about whom he Atkins Interview.

Episode 158—These types of; Presley liked the Presley Interview.

According to Brittany Brittany Interview.

Episode 159—Alexis Smith filmed; While doing that; When Smith was; "He talked about; "He bought the Buck (April 1984).

Episode 160—"Victoria missed my; "I felt the; This episode includes; "Ken Kercheval and; "He used to Brittany Interview.

Episode 161—While Atkins has Atkins Interview.

Corbin recalls that; As for why Corbin Interview.

Time magazine, in "To Be Continued Next Fall," Richard Zoglin and Melissa Ludtke, *Time*, May 21, 1984.

Indeed, the script; The cast was Anderson (1984).

Phil Capice told Zoglin and Ludtke.

Katzman thought having Cassidy, 15–16.

making Bobby central; Duffy originally intended; He tried to get; During Season 6 Riley, 93.

Howard Keel felt; As for his; Kalter found Jock Kalter (book), 52–53.

Cliff appears to; "There came a Kercheval Interview.

Season 7

On May 22; While Bel Geddes had "Donna Reed to Be *Dallas*' Miss Ellie," Associated Press Report, *San Diego Union-Tribune*, June 6, 1984; "*Dynasty* Measured for the Big Screen."

Dallas writer David; According to Paulsen; "I know Leonard *E! True Hollywood Story: "Dallas."*

She told Howard Keel Interview.

Bel Geddes' exit shocked Hagman (1988), 101.

Hagman confirmed that; "But," he wrote Hagman (book), 211–12.

Phil Capice did Bonderoff, 51.

According to Mary *"Peter Pan;* Mary Martin's Still Flying High," Patricia Brennan, *Washington Post,* March 19, 1989, Y7.

Capice recalled that; "When Donna Reed's; "Someone said, 'I "As *Dallas'* New Miss Ellie, Donna Reed Trades the Kitchen for a Home on the Range," Michelle Green, reported by David Wallace, *People,* November 19, 1984, 91–92.

Reed later recalled "Donna Reed Steps into *Dallas* Role," Vernon Scott, *Dallas Morning News,* September 9, 1984.

When Reed met "The New Miss Ellie Isn't Afraid to Back J.R. Against the Wall," Glenn Esterly, *TV Guide,* November 24, 1984, 44.

Reed was "stunned Scott.

According to her Esterly, 44.

Reed had watched; She "liked Miss Scott.

On June 4 "Donna Reed to Be *Dallas'* Miss Ellie."

Howard Keel thought Keel Interview.

According to Katzman "Life and Death Alter Course of 5 TV Series," Morgan Gender, *L.A. Times,* April 1, 1985, 3.

Katzman approached the Esterly, 44.

Because the producers; Reed, who was; "It was a fearsome; "I thought perhaps "Donna Reed to be *Dallas'* Miss Ellie;" Scott.

Reed then joined "Donna Reed to Be *Dallas'* Miss Ellie;" *"Dynasty* Measured for the Big Screen."

Howard Keel easily; While Keel found Esterly, 47–48.

Shortly after Reed's; Tilton learned the; "Leonard Katzman called; "And he started *E! True Hollywood Story: "Dallas."*

A press agent; A Lorimar spokesman *"Dallas* Gives Lucy Her Walking Papers," *Northern New Jersey Record,* November 18, 1984.

At a press; At the same; Larry Hagman agreed *"Dallas* at a Crossroad: 7 Season Itch," Ed Bark, *Dallas Morning News,* January 15, 1985; "Surf's Up in *Dallas:* A Visit to J.R.'s," Gus Stevens, *San Diego Union-Tribune,* February 1, 1985.

To make matters "Patrick Duffy to Quit *Dallas,*" *San Diego Union-Tribune,* November 20, 1984.

The producers tried; Capice acknowledged that; Lorimar offered Duffy; Duffy turned the Michelle Green (1985), 56; Riley, 94.

Duffy explained, "I; In other interviews; To Duffy, Bobby; Duffy, saying he Michelle Green (1985), 56, 59; Riley, 93–94.

Duffy felt strongly; "I didn't want; "I would feel Michelle Green (1985), 56.

Duffy himself recognized *Entertainment Tonight: "Dallas:* Secrets of Southfork."

Like Duffy, Katzman; But by 1984; While Katzman agreed; Moreover, Katzman had; Katzman and Capice; Katzman emerged from; Larry Hagman explained; Katzman himself concluded Haithman (April 1988).

Years later, Katzman's E! *True Hollywood Story: "Dallas."*

Season 7 Episode Guide

Episode 162—Landers "never felt" Landers Interview No. 2.

with the start; "I feel very; "I REALLY LIKE "Actress Balances Two Roles This Season in *Dallas* and the New Series *Glitter*," Mark Dawidziak, *Dallas Morning News*, August 26, 1984.

on September 5; Lorimar sponsored the; Castmembers, including Steve; The exhibit included; The exhibit traveled "A Bit of Southfork Coming to Town," Gus Stevens, *San Diego Union-Tribune*, August 30, 1984; "People," *Dallas Morning News*, September 5, 1984.

Ken Kercheval enjoyed; Kercheval recalls that Kercheval Interview.

Episode 164—Phil Capice found; Shelton thought her "The Eyes of Texas Are Upon Her," Tom Nolan, *TV Guide*, April 20, 1985, 28.

Larry Hagman described Hagman (1991), 6.

Shelton had "the Goodman, 46.

When asked about Kercheval Interview.

although it was; "When Lenny [Katzman] Brittany Interview.

While Christopher Atkins; Atkins was under; Nevertheless, Atkins felt Atkins Interview.

Episode 165—Harrison was cast; "He saw me Author's Interview with Jenilee Harrison, October 16, 2003 (Harrison Interview).

Brittany explains that Brittany Interview.

TV investigative journalist; Safer claimed that "Who Shot Bobby Ewing?" Morley Safer, *TV Guide*, September 1, 1984, 14–15.

Episode 166–The absence was; Smithers won a "Hagman Family Makes Mary as *Dallas* Lassos on Location," Ann Hodges, *Houston Chronicle*, July 30, 1985.

Smithers explains that Smithers Interview.

It was Larry; "*Dallas* brought me; Hagman "liked what Hodges (July 30, 1985).

"In years since Smithers Interview.

this episode includes Harrison Interview.

Episode 168—Donna Reed, who; Nevertheless, Reed was Michelle Green (1984), 91–92.

Reed felt "Miss; Reed found the Esterly, 44; Scott.

After her first Esterly, 44.

According to Reed's E! *True Hollywood Story: "Dallas."*

when Reed joined Bego, 101.

Steve Kanaly thought Kanaly Interview No. 2.

this episode's airport; "I'd been warned; "Sure enough, when Scott.

Patrick Duffy told Esterly, 43.

Hagman later wrote Hagman (book), 212.

said director Gwen Esterly, 47.

Episode 169—*People* magazine reported; Hagman returned the Michelle Green (1984), 92–93.

as for the Hagman Interview.

Phil Capice told; "She has assumed; "When she first Nolan, 28.

three days after "Patrick Duffy to Quit *Dallas*."

Not long after Buck (December 1984).

William Smithers found Smithers Interview.

Episode 170—Reed found that Esterly, 47.

Episode 172—In real life Harrison Interview.

Fern Fitzgerald "loved; Fitzgerald "always felt Fitzgerald Interview.

Episode 174—*TV Guide* reporter; Despite attempts to; Leonard Katzman told Davidson (1984), 27, 30.

Kercheval notes that Kercheval Interview.

Episode 176—Stephen Elliott was Elliott Interview.

Episode 177—shortly before this; "Cliff has enormous; "He has wealth Buck (December 1984).

Jenilee Harrison describes Harrison Interview.

Episode 178—Stephen Elliott's Texas Elliott Interview.

as *Dallas* coped; Like the previous; Guests were brought; Other castmembers attending; Neither Patrick Duffy; At the party; (for $125,000 per; Linda Gray also; "They fought me; "They didn't want; As for Duffy's; Donna Reed acknowledged; "The mail, I'm; Reed found her; Hagman, who said Bark (January 1985); "Cosby: No Danger of Starvation," Gail Shister, *Northern New Jersey Record*, July 23, 1986; Stevens (1985).

Around the time; While there, he; "I spent too "Actor Says Bobby Ewing Leaves When He Does," Associated Press, January 18, 1985.

Episode 179—Donna Reed gave; In the interview; Reed, however, liked; "I feel comfortable "Donna Reed Admires Miss Ellie's Character," Associated Press, February 1, 1985.

Episode 182—Leonard Katzman accompanied Kalter (book), 206.

In late 1981; Unlike every other "Military Brat Victoria Principal Revisits Her Birthplace to Sell Tokyo on *Dallas*," Jan Condon, *People*, December 14, 1981, 46.

Episode 183—Sue Ellen's and Pam's; Gray was getting Bego, 102.

Episode 184—the trial scenes "Son of Migrant Worker to be Norwalk's Mayor," Ralph Cipriano, *Los Angeles Times*, February 7, 1985.

There were lots Elliott Interview.

Episode 185—prior to receiving; "I really don't; "They don't tell "Priscilla Presley's Character Facing Verdict in Murder Trial Friday," Jerry Buck, Associated Press, March 5, 1985.

Episode 187—Rambo was initially; Rambo was happy Buck (July 1985).

Steve Kanaly felt Kanaly Interview No. 2.

production for Season *"Dynasty* Measured for the Big Screen."

Several days later; Her two and one-half Associated Press report (April 9, 1985).

Episode 188—according to Leigh; McCloskey also found McCloskey Interview.

by this point; He told *TV* Davidson (1984), 29.

Episode 189—Ken Kercheval says Kercheval Interview.

Episode 190—Said Dack Rambo Kalter (book), 67.

Linda Gray was Bego, 102.

Ken Kercheval thought; "The motivating factor; "The issue I'm Kalter (book), 56.

Martin recalls that Martin Interview.

Episode 191—300 million viewers Kalter (article), 47.

shortly before this "Nice Guy Bobby Ewing Is Finished," Jon Anderson, *San Diego* Union-Tribune, May 17, 1985.

Priscilla Presley denied Kalter (book), 47.

Leigh McCloskey's return; McCloskey thought Barbara McCloskey Interview.

Academy Award-winning fashion; Travilla designed clothes Kalter (book), 220.

this episode's quip "The Best and Worst of the 1984–1985 Season," *TV Guide*, June 29, 1985.

the day this Adams, 661.

the deathbed scene; Said Patrick Duffy; After the last Michelle Green (1985), 59.

According to Patrick; "Leonard couldn't cut; "He actually couldn't E! *True Hollywood Story: "Dallas."*

Morgan Brittany was Brittany Interview; Kalter (book), 210.

the year after "When Bobby Does His Love Scenes with Pam, He Brings Along a Frog or a Mannequin," Mary Murphy, *TV Guide*, October 18, 1986, 30.

Charlene Tilton's release Reilly (1979), 132.

Hagman "could never Hagman (1988), 103.

Susan Howard felt Davidson (1986), 17.

Duffy liked the; He thought that; Duffy "really felt TNN, *The Life and Times of "Dallas."*

the scene in; "I can't forget; "[P]am starts laughing Principal (1985), 54.

Leonard Katzman finished; "Swan Song," he Cassidy, 12.

just before this; The article declared Michelle Green (1985), 54.

Hagman found Duffy's; "It was the Hagman (1988), 102.

PART III: THE DREAM AND THE MORNING AFTER

Season 8

According to Leigh McCloskey Interview.

Lorimar announced Bel Geddes'; According to Lorimar "Bel Geddes Returning to *Dallas*," *San Diego Union-Tribune*, April 12, 1985.

Another statement released "Bel Geddes' Return Will Help *Dallas*," *Dallas Morning News*, April 15, 1985.

Indeed, in October "The TV Column," John Carmody, *Washington Post*, May 29, 1985.

Although it has Bonderoff, 51–52.

***Dallas* writer Arthur; Lewis claimed that** *E! True Hollywood Story: "Dallas."*

Howard Keel agrees; "I think Barbara Keel Interview.

A lawyer for "Bel Geddes' Ex-Manager Sues for $80 Mil," Kathleen O'Steen, *Daily Variety*, March 30, 1993, 10.

According to Hagman Hagman (book), 212.

Larry Hagman noticed; "As much as Hagman (book), 212.

Howard Keel agreed Keel, 305.

***People* magazine reported** Michelle Green (1984), 92–93.

According to Jared; Reed's husband conceded; "When Donna saw; "She was in *E! True Hollywood Story: "Dallas."*

by then Reed Carmody (May 1985).

Susan Howard, who; "We spent some; "She did not Howard Interview.

Reed was in; Milnick signaled to; "I really don't; "It's still up; Reed was "terribly; Reed felt she; "After 44 years Carmody (May 1985).

On May 24; Although Reed lost "Reed Sues to Remain Miss Ellie on *Dallas*," *San Diego Union-Tribune*, May 25, 1985; "The Television Generation Mourns Its Favorite Surrogate Mother, Tough But Tender Donna Reed," *People*, January 27, 1986, 86.

When Katzman spoke "Oscar-Winning Actress Dies of Cancer, 64," Sue Manning, Associated Press, January 14, 1986.

Even Bel Geddes commented Bonderoff, 52.

Hagman claimed that "Bobby Ewing Is Deader Than a Mackerel, Hagman Laments," Ann Hodges, *Houston Chronicle*, June 10, 1985.

Years later, Hagman Hagman (1988), 101–02.

Ken Kercheval was Bark (July 1985).

Susan Howard agreed *E! True Hollywood Story: "Dallas;"* Howard Interview.

Shortly after her; On December 10; During the surgery "Donna Reed Fighting Cancer," *Newsday*, December 21, 1985.

While in the "The Television Generation Mourns Its Favorite Surrogate Mother, Tough But Tender Donna Reed," 86.

Reed was released Manning.

In early January; On January 12 "The Television Generation Mourns Its Favorite Surrogate Mother, Tough But Tender Donna Reed," 86.

Two days later; Leonard Katzman, who Manning.

amid reports that; Tilton's agent turned "Bye-Bye, Lucy," *Dallas Morning News*, June 1, 1985.

Steve Kanaly told; Linda Gray was Hodges (July 30, 1985).

As for Duffy's Bego, 111–12.

Howard Keel thought Hodges (December 1985).

Ken Kercheval did; Cliff was effectively Riley, 97.

Only Hagman, who Hodges (July 30, 1985).

Despite the ratings; Capice reflected that *"Dallas* Movie Strikes It Rich," Ed Bark, *Dallas Morning News*, March 23, 1986.

who later called Hagman (1991), 11.

As writer David *E! True Hollywood Story: "Dallas."*

Hagman blamed Capice; Hagman felt Capice Hagman (1991), 11, 13.

Lee Rich, the; Rich felt that; But the Season 8; Hagman, claiming that; Hagman vowed to Leahy (May 1986), 38, 44.

According to actress; In the meantime Wilson Interview.

Katzman acknowledged that "The *Dallas* of Old Will Be Back in Fall," Ed Bark, *Dallas Morning News*, August 4, 1986.

In April of; responded that, "Hagman Leahy (May 1986), 44–45.

While Katzman conceded; "Phil and I; "I think Larry Bark (August 1986).

In time, he Cassidy, 14.

Hagman, with the "Bobby Might Be Dead, But That Can't Stop Patrick Duffy from Jumping Back in the *Dallas* Saddle," Jane Hall, *People*, May 19, 1986, 181.

Duffy biographer Lee; although *TV Guide* Riley, 107; Murphy, 27.

During the call; Duffy met Hagman; As they drank; Duffy replied, "I; Hagman pressed on; "I miss you; Duffy told Hagman; Hagman asked Duffy Murphy, 27–28.

Duffy later acknowledged; His first reaction; However, during his Kalter (article), 52, 55.

Moreover, such opportunities; "I didn't just; "That wasn't the *E! True Hollywood Story: "Dallas."*

Indeed, during his Morris, 66.

After his lunch Riley, 108–09.

Duffy agreed to Murphy, 28; "Mum's the Word on Bobby's Return," Robert P. Laurence, *San Diego Union-Tribune*, June 16, 1986.

On April 9; Lorimar confirmed the; Said Lorimar spokesman "The TV Column," John Carmody, *Washington Post*, April 10, 1986.

Lee Rich stated; Duffy himself had; He was in "Patrick Duffy is Coming Back to TV's *Dallas*," Ed Bark, *Dallas Morning News*, April 10, 1986.

Although "out in; "They thought anybody Murphy, 28.

Shortly after Duffy's; Hagman summed up Hall (1986), 181.

Season 8 Episode Guide

Episodes 192 & 193—Patrick Duffy felt TNN, *The Life and Times of "Dallas."*

NBC Entertainment President "The TV Column," John Carmody, *Washington Post*, October 3, 1985.

Linda Gray, although Bego, 109.

Playing a "down; She explains, "I Gray Interview.

Victoria Principal wrote Principal (1985), 38.

Larry Hagman recalled Hagman (1988), 102.

Recalls Martin, "There Martin Interview.

Episode 194—the Krebbses' plan; We "began to; "We said, 'Donna; Steve Kanaly recalls Davidson (1986), 17; Kanaly Interview No. 5.

Priscilla Presley felt Kalter (book), 49.

Jared Martin "thought Martin Interview.

Episode 195—Although his character Beck Interview.

Jimmy Darst who; It was Darst Kalter (book), 228.

about the time; In "Life Without; While admitting that; Principal recalled how Principal (1985), 34–35.

this episode includes Harrison Interview.

Episode 196—According to costar "Barbara Eden Takes *Jeannie* Out of Bottle for TV Movie," Jerry Buck, Associated Press, October 16, 1985.

Episode 197—It was to; "I guess I'm; "But I'm also; Scott "loved it Hodges (July 29, 1985).

Off-screen, Priscilla Presley; "I loved Priscilla; "I liked her Howard Interview.

Episode 198—Not long after; Phil Capice found "Barbara Carrera Plays the Mystery Woman for All It's Worth . . . On Screen *and* Off," Michael Leahy, *TV Guide*, January 1986, 36, 38.

this episode marks Howard Interview.

Patricia's home, supposedly Kalter (book), 206.

Deborah Shelton, who; "[Mandy] thinks she's; "She has a Kalter (book), 66.

Barbara Bel Geddes' beaded Kalter (book), 222.

some of the Kalter (book), 235.

Houston Chronicle reporter; Hodges wrote about; Hodges also wrote; Barbara Bel Geddes told; Larry Hagman nailed; Gray—"the darling; Gray quipped, "At; Victoria Principal spent; Barbara Carrera, on; Carrera told Hodges; Later, she told; Jenilee Harrison approached; Don Starr joked; Extra Jim Thompson; Thompson was a; Director Corey Allen; Hodges also spoke; Miguel proudly told Hodges (July 29, 1985).

Episode 199—Barbara Carrera found Kalter (book), 62–63.

Jenilee Harrison hopes Harrison Interview.

Episode 200—The episode was "White in *Dallas* Acting as Governor," *Houston Chronicle*, July 27, 1985.

The crew built; 500 extras were Hodges (July 30, 1985).

There was talk Buck (July 1985).

Larry Hagman found Leahy (January 1986), 38–39.

as originally written; Susan Howard, however; "We've had two; "Why can't we; Capice, who found; Howard recalls, "I; Howard, however, still; "No five-months pregnant; Howard learned from Davidson (1986), 13, 17.

Arthur Bernard Lewis; "It became socially; "It was like *E! True Hollywood Story: "Dallas."*

this episode includes; "I'll never forget Beck Interview.

Episode 202—the week this; Writer Stephen Birmingham "Is *Knots Landing* Now Better Than *Dallas* and *Dynasty?*" Stephen Birmingham, *TV Guide*, November 30, 1985, 5; Birmingham (1983), 37–38.

According to Joan Van Ark Interview.

Episode 203—The on-location shoot "Bel Geddes Returns to *Dallas*," Jay Sharbutt, *Los Angeles Times*, April 13, 1985.

A real-life Southfork "Bye-Bye, Lucy."

While Larry Hagman Hodges (July 30, 1985).

Once when Hagman Bond.

While on location Hodges (July 30, 1985).

Episode 204—She told TV; Scott liked roles; Scott also enjoyed Buck (January 24, 1986).

once, when filming Golden, 170–71.

Episode 206—According to The "V star joins *Dallas* cast," *Toronto Star*, October 30, 1985, B3.

Deborah Shelton felt Kalter (book), 66.

five days after; Keel was released; Keel's illness did "Howard Keel Recovering From Heart Operation," Associated Press, January 10, 1986; "Keel Leaves Hospital," *San Diego Union-Tribune*, January 28, 1986; "People," *Twin Cities Star-Tribune*, January 10, 1986.

Episode 207—Susan Howard was Davidson (1986), 13.

Jamie's injuries, like; "It was a Harrison Interview.

Episode 210—John Beck was; "When I first Beck Interview.

this is the; To explain Principal's; When Principal healed Kalter (book), 210.

Principal's back troubles "Portrait of the Ewings as a Young Clan," Ed Bark, *Dallas Morning News*, December 5, 1985.

the Lorimar call; The call sheet; The crew and; The actors involved; To prepare for; Van Kamp was scheduled; Hagman did not; The company was; At 10:45, the; By then, Gray; The company was; After lunch, the; Scene 3, (a; Merrill Leighton, who; Ken Kercheval, Jenilee; After the scene; That scene was; As for other; Cast members not needed; Victoria Principal was; The call sheet; Scheduled for filming; Also scheduled for; Scheduled for filming Kalter (book), 209.

Episode 212—In September of "TV Dial," *St. Petersburg Times*, September 28, 1986.

the week this; He found the "Review," Don Merrill, *TV Guide*, February 15, 1986, 39.

several scenes from Davidson (1986), 13.

Episode 214—according to Lee Riley, 107.

TV Guide, however Murphy, 27.

Howard recalls that; "From the beginning Howard Interview.

Episode 215—John Beck recalls Beck Interview.

Episode 216—Linda Gray directed; While renegotiating her; Explains Gray, "It; Gray "was terrified; "I did a Gray Interview; Bego, 106–08.

according to Gray; "If a hairdresser; When Lorimar executives Leahy (May 1986), 38, 41.

Steve Kanaly recalls Kanaly Interview No. 2.

John Beck thought; "It was something Beck Interview.

Episode 217—in a telephone; "We haven't addressed; "In television, I Bark (April 1986).

towards the end Davidson (1986), 13.

Episode 218—Five days after Carmody (April 1986).

Episode 219—Almost two weeks "NBC Knocks Off CBS," Drew Fetherston, *Newsday*, April 23, 1986.

Nine days after "Personal Mention," *Houston Chronicle*, April 20, 1986.

By the end; "It's going to; "The return of Arar.

Episode 220—Forrest explains that Author's Interview with Steve Forrest, October 9, 2003 (Forrest Interview).

Episode 221—three days after; Grant stated that "The TV Column," John Carmody, *Washington Post*, May 13, 1986.

as Season 8; "Lenny Katzman . . . walked Beck Interview.

When asked about Principal Interview.

Episode 222—From the start Leahy (January 1986), 40.

CBS' press release "Chaos Erupts as Soaps End Another Year," Jeff Borden, *Dallas Morning News*, May 15, 1986.

prior to this "*Dallas* Aims for 'Who Shot?' Ratings as Duffy Returns," Jerry Buck, *Houston Chronicle*, May 16, 1986.

on the day; "Nobody on the; Because Bobby's return; the week this; Katzman stated that; Katzman added, "We're; *People* surmised that; As for the Hall (1986), 179, 181.

in accordance with; In the version; Duffy recalls, "Victoria *E! True Hollywood Story: "Dallas."*

John Beck recalls; For Beck, it; "It was the Beck Interview.

As for Duffy's Hall (1986), 180.

Katzman, Duffy and Riley, 110–11.

Recalled Duffy, "We; Katzman "cut out *Entertainment Tonight: "Dallas:* Secrets of South-fork."

Duffy discussed his; Said Duffy, "I; Duffy did not; Duffy said he Buck (May 1986).

One *Dallas* cast member; Bel Geddes had clothes Kalter (book), 220.

Ironically, fifteen months "Actor Says Bobby Ewing Leaves When He Does."

Season 9

The one exception Bark (August 1986); "NBC Tries New Sitcoms and Juggles Schedule," Bill King, *Atlanta Journal-Constitution*, May 29, 1986.

As *TV Guide* "Solving the Mystery of Bobby's Return to *Dallas*," Elaine Warren, *TV Guide*, August 30, 1986, 4.

According to Duffy Kalter (article), 55.

Katzman said, "Here's TNN, *The Life and Times of "Dallas."*

Duffy and his Kalter (article), 55; TNN, *The Life and Times of "Dallas."*

While the "dream; He felt Duffy's Bark (August 1986).

Moreover, "Bobby versus Murphy, 32.

Katzman thought that; When Katzman rejoined Bark (August 1986); Kalter (article), 52.

Katzman acknowledged that; He thought, however; "The basic story Bark (August 1986).

Katzman also felt Kalter (article), 52.

He did not; The writers, said; J.R. "was never; But during Season Bark (August 1986); Murphy, 32.

Writer Howard Lakin E! True Hollywood Story: "Dallas."

on April 22 Fetherston (April 1986).

NBC Entertainment President; but CBS Research "NBC Introduces Eight New Series," Fred Rothenberg, Associated Press, May 14, 1986.

Larry Hagman predicted "Bobby Is Making the Ultimate in Comebacks," John Carman, Atlanta Journal-Constitution, June 16, 1986.

Hagman told another; Duffy agreed that Kalter (article), 52.

Hagman stoked the; In the article; Hagman complained about; "This show could; When the author Leahy (May 1986), 36.

Bob Crutchfield of; Said Crutchfield, "We "Hagman Puts a Little J.R. Into Remarks," Ed Bark, Dallas Morning News, May 22, 1986.

Katzman jokingly confirmed; Katzman filmed three; Photographs of Hagman; People magazine tried Riley, 111–13.

CBS threw a; Cast members in; One of the; Duffy commented that; Duffy explained that; Duffy thought, by; Victoria Principal agreed; "The show was; Priscilla Presley commented; When asked about "A Network Miracle: Bobby Ewing Comes Back From the Dead," Ann Hodges, Houston Chronicle, June 18, 1986; Laurence (1986).

While there, Katzman; Katzman summarized that Bark (August 1986).

Several years later "Hagman is Comfortable in his J.R. Role," Daniel P. Puzo, St. Petersburg Times, December 3, 1989.

Half-way through Season; Initially, Principal's departure "TV Spots" by Ben Kubasik, Newsday, January 29, 1987.

Even after Principal's; It said through "Dallas to Drop Pam in Contract Squabble," Jerry Buck, San Diego Union-Tribune, February 3, 1987.

Sheree J. Wilson recalls Wilson Interview.

According to Principal; Not long before; "We had discussions; Principal claimed that Leahy (1987), 36.

Principal later elaborated Entertainment Tonight: "Dallas: Secrets of Southfork."

Leonard Katzman telephoned; The next day; While Hagman admitted "Hagman Not Happy That Victoria Principal Is Leaving Dallas," Ann Hodges, Houston Chronicle, January 30, 1987.

One year later; While Hagman felt; "The only person; "She wanted out Hagman (1988), 101–02.

Just days before Buck (1987).

Howard had hinted; According to Howard; Howard began to Hodges (January 1987).

Season 9 Episode Guide

Episodes 223 & 224—In the summer of "The Low-Down on Low-Down J.R.," Paul Rosenfield, *Saturday Evening Post*, November 1985, 61.

Hagman's family tradition Hodges (July 30, 1985).

CBS' promotions for *"Dallas, Vice* Face Showdown," Noel Holston, *Twin Cities Star-Tribune*, September 26, 1986.

Katzman thought the Haithman (April 1988).

Indeed, in the Riley, 115.

In a June "CBS Detectives Will Take on the Slumping Ratings Case," Drew Fetherston, *Newsday*, June 14, 1986.

That same month; Duffy also said; Duffy admitted that; At the same Laurence (1986).

In August, Katzman; Bark guessed from Bark (August 1986).

Shortly before "Return; *People* reporter Suzy; Kalter reviewed the; She also visited; She witnessed the; The scene took; Victoria Principal appeared; Jenilee Harrison, whose; Harrison received word; Principal and Harrison; Further, John Beck; Kalter took the; Katzman called the; Hagman told Kalter; Howard Keel thought; Kanaly just wanted; Hagman also told Kalter (article), 47–48, 51–52, 55.

Beck told another "People," *Dallas Morning News*, July 17, 1986.

TV Guide solicited Warren, 6–7.

TV critic David; But, he admitted *"Dallas* Awakens From a Nightmare Season," David Bianculli, *St. Petersburg Times*, October 17, 1986.

The resolution was Riley, 115.

writer David Paulsen *E! True Hollywood Story: "Dallas."*

according to Suzy Kalter (book), 238.

Susan Howard commented; Said Linda Gray; Priscilla Presley responded Riley, 116.

Explains Joan Van Ark Van Ark Interview.

Kanaly felt that; Hagman stated, "We; Said Harrison, "Patrick's Riley, 117.

Victoria Principal claimed Murphy, 32.

as for Katzman Tom Green (1988).

And Duffy, who; Duffy only watched; Duffy agreed that; "You make a; He noted that; Once he returned Riley, 105–07, 115.

Indeed, Duffy was, "I can swear *Entertainment Tonight: "Dallas:* Secrets of Southfork."

As Duffy explains Duffy Interview.

Episode 225—which he described *"Saturday Night* Fever," *People*, October 4, 1999, 72.

when Leonard Katzman; Explained Gray, "I Bego, 124–25.

The Valentine storyline; Says Gray, "I Gray Interview.

Katzman insisted, however Cassidy, 16–17.

TV critic David; "This season's second Bianculli (1986).

Episode 226—the Trammel Crow Golden, 174.

In Culver City Kalter (book), 224.

a new building; The Interfirst Plaza "People," *Toronto Star*, August 24, 1986.

"We had fun; "She and I Forrest Interview.

The white house Howard Interview.

parts of the Author's Interview with George Kennedy, October 29, 2003 (Kennedy Interview).

Episode 227—TV columnist John "Dallas Is Leaving Vice in Ratings Dust on Fridays," John Horn, Orange County Register, October 23, 1986.

while Steve Forrest's; Forest "knew Jim; He recalls that; Forest felt he Forrest Interview.

Episode 228—After Honor was; "I was told; Katzman went on; Katzman then told; Wilson "first played Wilson Interview.

Katzman told a; Duffy said Wilson; Ken Kercheval thought; Not long after; Wilson loved the; "We don't work; "You know your "Sheree J. Wilson Kisses and Tells," Bill O'Hallaren, TV Guide, March 26, 1988, 34.

while Mandy's Valentine Bark (August 1986).

Steve Forrest and; "We shot Dallas Forrest Interview.

Episode 229—According to Bel Geddes' Lerman Interview.

Episode 230—Jenna's pregnancy was; Said Presley, "It Entertainment Tonight: "Dallas: Secrets of Southfork."

Steve Kanaly admired Kanaly Interview No. 2.

despite Jamie's troubles Harrison Interview.

Episode 231—said Priscilla Presley Kalter (book), 49.

Steve Forrest recalls Forrest Interview.

late on November; Duffy traveled to; Production of Dallas; Duffy, however, insisted; Because the crew "The TV Column," John Carmody, Washington Post, November 20, 1986; "Police Say Robbery Was Motive in Slaying of Dallas Star's Parents," Faith Conroy, Associated Press, November 19, 1986.

Duffy later recalled Entertainment Tonight: "Dallas: Secrets of Southfork."

On March 19 "Convicted in Killing of Actor's Parents," San Francisco Chronicle, March 20, 1987; "Guilty Plea in Duffy Deaths," San Francisco Chronicle, May 6, 1987.

Recalled Duffy, "The E! True Hollywood Story: "Dallas."

Episode 232—Alice Hirson recalls Hirson Interview.

Episode 233—Wrote TV critic "Dynasty and Vice Still Slipping in Ratings," Ed Bark, Dallas Morning News, December 3, 1986.

Presley explains that Presley Interview.

of all her Harrison Interview.

Wilson "felt like Wilson Interview.

Episode 234—Miss Ellie's carriage Golden, 175.

Steve Forrest "had; "It wasn't too; "She had such Forrest Interview.

Episode 235—The crew began Bark (May 1986).

as for whether; Forrest, however, had; In the 1987; Forrest recalls that Forrest Interview.

Of her time; Harrison adds, "In Harrison Interview.

Episode 239—the day after; The Associated Press "Morning Ratings Fail in Dallas-Fort Worth," Ed Bark, *Dallas Morning News*, January 24, 1987; "Susan Howard's Character Dropped From TV's *Dallas*," Associated Press, January 27, 1987.

To make matters Hodges (January 1987).

Episode 241—While Keel agreed Keel, 303.

Episode 242—says Jenilee Harrison Harrison Interview.

Episode 244—Gray, who noted Bego, 129.

Episode 245—shortly before this; Principal had already Leahy (1987), 38.

Episode 246—Stephen Elliott's final Elliott Interview.

Episode 247—Hagman later wrote Hagman (book), 221.

In real life; According to *Washington* Washington, Meg Greenfield, Public Affairs, New York, 2001, xx.

Episode 248—according to Deborah "TV Scuttlebutt," *Northern New Jersey Record*, February 19, 1987.

Episode 250—*TV Guide* writer; On February 25; Littwin reported that; "Can I see; Barbara Bel Geddes was; Director Michael Preece; The assistant director; Kanaly discussed the; Patrick Duffy arrived; Bel Geddes asked Presley; Littwin found Kanaly; The actors made; "That was a Littwin, 34, 36–37.

Four days later "Priscilla Presley Gives Birth to Boy," *St. Petersburg Times*, March 2, 1987.

During the evening; Appearing on the; Those interviewed by; The segments were; The salute filled; On Friday, May; The party featured; The cast in "*Dallas* Cast Gets Morning Call on CBS," Ed Bark, *Dallas Morning News*, May 9, 1987; "The TV Column," John Carmody, *Washington Post*, April 29, 1987; TNN, *The Life and Times of "Dallas."*

Episode 251—Patrick Duffy commented Leahy (1987), 42.

Smithers remembers one; But Smithers has Smithers Interview.

one of Victoria Principal (1985), 36.

Ken Kercheval, who "Ken Kercheval, Victoria Principal's Ever-Losing Brother on *Dallas*, Has a Winning Way With Popcorn," *Chicago Sun-Times*, May 7, 1987.

Kercheval feels he Kercheval Interview.

PHOTOGRAPH INSERT

The Israeli Tourism, The cast members met "Second Best," Glenne Currie, United Press International, March 11, 1982; "Begin Regrets J.R. Stayed Home," United Press International, March 13, 1982.

PART IV: THE FINAL YEARS

Season 10

the decision was; While Lorimar did; Lorimar felt that "News Update: CBS Prime Time Soaps to Make Big Cast Cuts," Jeff Kaye, *TV Guide*, March 21, 1987, A-1, A-48.

As Howard Lakin *E! True Hollywood Story: "Dallas."*

"we would be "*Dallas* Corrals Tight Security for Cliffhanger," Tom Green, *USA Today*, May 14, 1987.

Presley explains, "I Presley Interview.

According to Kanaly; Kanaly learned his; The show had; As a result; Kanaly feels that; In his opinion; He was not; The timing of Kanaly Interview No. 1.

Larry Hagman and; Hagman was named "Knots Landing and Days of Our Lives Sweep Soap Opera Awards," Associated Press, January 18, 1988.

Season 10 Episode Guide

Episodes 252 & 253—Leonard Katzman sought; "When Lenny called; Brittany, however, had; "I knew that; Yet, when Katzman called; Brittany's return to Brittany Interview.

Says Linda Gray Gray Interview.

He found Dallas "TV Package," Lane Crockett, Gannett News Service, December 30, 1987.

Kercheval suggested that; Kercheval had worked Kercheval Interview.

Patrick Duffy cannot Duffy Interview.

Morgan Brittany believes Brittany Interview.

Morgan Brittany felt Brittany Interview.

this episode's scene Wilson Interview.

when Leonard Katzman; In a bid Tom Green (1987).

As early as; By March, Lorimar; The producers of; As a result; The on-location shoot "No Spring Vacation for Series Cast Members," Ben Kubasik, Newsday, March 31, 1987; Bego, 138; Hodges (January 1987).

during the shoot; On May 30; Among the 800; Master of Ceremonies "Hagman Receives a CoCo," Jane Sumner, Dallas Morning News, May 31, 1987.

as of this "Bringing Back Berle for a New Generation," Matt Roush, USA Today, July 7, 1987.

Episode 254—Says Brittany, "It Brittany Interview.

Not long after "TV Package," Lane Crockett, Gannett News Service, September 10, 1987.

exteriors for Bobby's Golden, 174.

around the time "Principal Masters a New Role," Pat Hilton, USA Today, October 2, 1987.

A short time "For CBS, The Shows Must Go On," Ann Hodges, Houston Chronicle, October 21, 1987.

Patrick Duffy recently Duffy Interview.

Episode 255—Said Linda Gray Hodges (October 1987).

In an interview; Kercheval conceded that "Ken Kercheval, Victoria Principal's Ever-Losing Brother on Dallas, Has a Winning Way With Popcorn."

Episode 256—a scene for; The Dallas **crew** Golden, 175.

shortly before this; To mark the; Attendees included Patrick; Taylor-Young heard the; Three years earlier "Dallas inspires men's cologne," Toronto Star, October 17, 1987, J3.

Episode 257—Sheree J. Wilson was; Initially, her Season Wilson Interview.

the Galleria is Golden, 175.

Episode 258—while Priscilla Presley; "Steve Kanaly," says Presley Interview.

Jack Scalia, like; Scalia ran in; He liked being; Scalia, who is "Marathon Countdown; As Sunday's Race in L.A. Nears, Actor Jack Scalia Eats, Sleeps and Thinks Running in Preparation," Gary Libman, *Los Angeles Times*, March 5, 1988 at part 5, page 1.

Episode 260—Taylor-Young liked working; "The bottom line; Taylor-Young also enjoyed "Snapshots: Quotes and Notes from December *Celebrity Focus* Magazine," *PR Newswire*, November 17, 1987.

Episode 262—According to Sheree Wilson Interview.

Episode 263—Gray thought the "It's Not a Dream: Linda Gray Is Leaving *Dallas*," Jeannie Williams, *USA Today*, February 22, 1989.

Jeff was interested Bego, 86.

Episode 264—Woodward "knew when; But Woodward "loved Woodward Interview.

Woodward's *Dallas* leading Hirson Interview.

Ken Kercheval notes; Bel Geddes used to Kercheval Interview.

Priscilla Presley enjoyed; "When I came; Nevertheless, Presley found Presley Interview.

Episode 265—half-way into her; Wilson also got; "Priscilla seems very O'Hallaren (1988), 34, 36.

Episode 266—Annabel Schofield was "A Morning Shakeup Call," *Dallas Morning News*, September 25, 1987.

Sheree J. Wilson says; Wilson adds, "With Wilson Interview.

Episode 268—Hirson had Paulsen Hirson Interview.

Priscilla Presley announced; Presley decided to; "I really wanted *Entertainment Tonight: "Dallas: Secrets of Southfork."*

Presley first considered Hagman (book), 221.

Episode 271—which was great; Kanaly "liked directing Kanaly Interview No. 2.

Episode 272—Alice Hirson's last; "Mavis was always; "But they never; Hirson found director Hirson Interview.

Episode 273—two days after "Tuesday's People," Adrian Shoobs, *Bergen Record*, February 2, 1988, A02; Libman.

Episode 274—Offscreen, Presley found Presley Interview.

Episode 276—this episode was; In noting the; Nonetheless, Katzman recognized Haithman (April 1988).

Katzman told another; Katzman said there Buck (1988).

Larry Hagman wrote Hagman (1988), 103.

Victoria Principal told; Principal admitted that; As to reappearing Tom Green (1988).

Episode 280—When Lorimar announced "On the Grapevine: Good Grief, Lucy's Back!" Paul Francis, *TV Guide*, January 23, 1988, A-2.

Katzman and Tilton; Said Katzman at Bark (August 1986).

Despite Katzman's efforts "*Dallas* Star Wants to Take J.R. to Russia," Jerry Buck, *Chicago Sun-Times*, February 7, 1989.

Lorimar attorneys started; Said Tilton, "They "Charlene Tilton Opens in La Miranda Play While Negotiating *Dallas* Role," Barry Koltnow, *Orange County Register*, November 3, 1987.

Episode 281—at the start; When asked how; Kanaly's years in; Said Leonard Katzman Littwin, 36–37.

Season 11

On February 21; That same day Williams.

According to Gray "Happy Ending Eludes Linda Gary," Ed Bark, *Dallas Morning News*, February 27, 1989.

Katzman responded to; Katzman phoned Larry Williams.

In another 1989 *E! True Hollywood Story: "Dallas."*

On February 24; "My contract is; "They all knew; Gray explained to Bark (February 1989).

Steve Kanaly confirms Kanaly Interview No. 1.

Almost 18 months Hodges (October 1987).

As for the Bark (February 1989).

Hagman knew that; Hagman claimed that Hagman (book), 222.

He called Gray Puzo.

Katzman also took; where Hagman "walked; The Dallas crew; Potapov, like the; Potapov had never; Katzman, who directed; Katzman loved the; "We think it's; "The Ewings go Hagman (book), 224; "Passport to Moscow: *Dallas* Brings Cowboy, Hats, Mink Coats and Shady Oil Deals to Red Square," Marsha Hamilton, *Los Angeles Times*, April 1, 1989; "*Dallas* Gives Glasnost a Shot of Glitz," *Northern New Jersey Record*, April 30, 1989.

During the second; Katzman denied that; "I'm not sure "Prime-Time Soaps to Rinse Serial Format," Diane Haithman, *St. Petersburg Times*, February 7, 1988.

It was thought Haithman (April 1988).

Katzman also liked; He thought that; As an example; Katzman suggested the; According to Barbara Haithman (February 1988).

CBS even considered "*Dallas* Could Go Soapless," Monica Collins, *USA Today*, January 18, 1988.

Season 11 Episode Guide

Episode 282—According to Kennedy Kennedy Interview.

Victoria Principal look-a-like; Michaels appeared on; Michaels got the; Although she had; One day, Michaels; Howard had to; "Patrick Duffy and; "As we got; Michaels traveled to; She recalls being Author's Interview with Margaret Michaels, October 8, 2003 (Michaels Interview).

Larry Hagman was; As a result; Hagman felt he Hagman (1991), 4, 13.

Victoria Principal's second "Bye-Bye, Lucy."

Ironically, Margaret Michaels' Michaels Interview.

the October season "A Summer Without *Dallas*," Ed Bark, *Dallas Morning News*, May 16, 1989.

Said Larry Hagman; But Patrick Duffy "Networks Rewrite Dire Predictions for Fall Lineups," Kenneth R. Clark, *Chicago Tribune*, August 7, 1988, 8C.

As a result; That scene featured Bark (May 1989).

Margaret Michaels thought; She found the; She also felt Michaels Interview.

Episode 283—Recalls McCloskey, "If McCloskey Interview.

Russ Mayberry was; He also directed Manetti, 237.

Episode 284—Podewell was cast Author's Interview with Cathy Podewell, November 7, 2003 (Podewell Interview).

Hagman found Podewell Hagman (1991), 6.

He bragged that Buck (1989).

Hagman claimed that; "I wanted to; "The reason Bobby Buck (1989).

Episode 285—Cathy Podewell "loved Podewell Interview.

Episode 286—this episode includes Kercheval Interview.

Cathy Podewell enjoyed Podewell Interview.

Episode 287—writer Arthur Bernard; Lewis felt the E! True Hollywood Story: "Dallas."

at the time; Podewell explains that Podewell Interview.

Episode 289—the role of; McGraw played one Hodges (July 29, 1985).

Episode 291—Katzman described Wendell Cassidy, 20.

With regard to Smithers Interview.

Sheree J. Wilson recalls Wilson Interview.

William Smithers found Smithers Interview.

Cathy Podewell's contract; First, her four-episode; After that extension; The producers then Podewell Interview.

Episode 293—Cally's interaction with; She found Omri Podewell Interview.

Episode 294—Cathy Podewell enjoyed; "Patrick always had; "Patrick was such Podewell Interview.

under his initial; "The network liked; Kennedy was happy; He also enjoyed Kennedy Interview.

Episode 295—Linda Gray found Gray Interview.

Episodes 296 & 297—Linda Gray was; With J.R. marrying Williams.

Cathy Podewell found; "It was as; "It had that Podewell Interview.

Episode 300—in recognition of; Patrick Duffy, who TNN, The Life and Times of "Dallas."

Duffy liked this; "Lenny and Larry; "Len and I Duffy Interview.

as for the; In attendance were; Original cast member Steve; Other cast regulars Entertainment Tonight: "Dallas: Secrets of Southfork."

Episode 301—Sheree J. Wilson "liked; Despite his character's Wilson Interview.

Cally's efforts to; Podewell is a; As for Bel Geddes; In reality, Podewell; She explains, "My Podewell Interview.

Episode 302—Kanaly feels his; "My great camera; "They were looking; Of the scenes; He found filming Kanaly Interview No. 2.

Sheree J. Wilson claims; Wilson describes Podewell Wilson Interview.

Podewell admits that; "Sheree is such; "I love her Podewell Interview.

Episode 303—Dallas was one; Healy was an; She recalls, "The Author's Interview with Kathryn Leigh Scott, September 8, 2000 (Scott Interview).

As of February; "I don't think Buck (1989).

According to Kathryn Scott Interview.

an eighteenth-century; Several scenes from *The Sound of Music: The Making of America's Favorite Movie*, Julia Antopol Hirsch, Contemporary Books, Inc., Chicago, 1993, 79–82.

says Kathryn Leigh Scott Interview.

Episode 304—Scott found Hunnicutt Scott Interview.

of April's and Wilson Interview.

George Kennedy recalls Kennedy Interview.

Scott found *Dallas*; On a day; "The ancient wooden Scott Interview.

Episode 305—Sheree J. Wilson, like; "I liked being Wilson Interview.

Scott called the Scott Interview.

Larry Hagman did; "I thought that; "Everybody says, 'What Puzo.

Cathy Podewell recalls Podewell Interview.

Episode 306—Hagman believed that; "I think the; "You take people Goodman, 48.

Hagman recalled that CNN King/Hagman Interview.

Katzman did not; "All we were "Leonard Katzman, Executive Producer of TV's *Dallas*, Dead, 69," Jane E. Allen, Associated Press, September 7, 1996.

while in Moscow; Patrick Duffy, who Hamilton.

Cathy Podewell describes Podewell Interview.

George Kennedy, however Kennedy Interview.

Episode 307—says Wilson, while Wilson Interview.

Howard Lakin recalled; "Len hated women; "Linda might have *E! True Hollywood Story: "Dallas."*

"Linda Gray," according Podewell Interview.

although aspects of; Nevertheless, Gray enjoyed; After leaving the *Entertainment Tonight: "Dallas: Secrets of Southfork."*

two years after Hagman (1991), 5.

Hagman also told Goodman, 46.

Gray returned the Rosen, 9.

Season 12

The dismal ratings "Dallas May Be Down, But It's Not Out," Ed Bark, *Dallas Morning News*, January 16, 1990.

Variety, which reviewed; Its review found *Variety*, September 26, 1989.

A Lorimar spokesman; Joe Pope, owner; "It means a; "It's like being Bark (May 1989).

Leonard Katzman confirmed; "A lot of Bark (January 1990).

According to Howard; "She was always; Keel agreed that; But Keel would; Keel was disappointed Keel Interview.

Keel felt Bel Geddes; Keel thought Bel Geddes Keel, 303–4.

Larry Hagman commented Bark (January 1990).

Season 12 Episode Guide

Episode 308—Foster described herself "Murphy Brown's *Live* mirror images," Matt Roush, *USA Today*, July 26, 1989.

Sheree J. Wilson says Wilson Interview.

Episode 310—Says Podewell, "I Podewell Interview.

Episode 311—Wilson frequently brought O'Hallaren (1988), 36.

Episode 312—Tommy's death in; "Eddie and I; Kennedy missed Eddie; Kennedy also "grew; "When [Tracey and Kennedy Interview.

Episode 316—Explains Fitzgerald, "The; Fitzgerald found it Fitzgerald Interview.

Episode 317—not long before; Puzo found Hagman; Hagman told Puzo; Said Hagman, "It's Puzo.

Episode 320—George Kennedy liked Kennedy Interview.

about the time; Larry Hagman attended Bark (January 1990).

Episode 322—Down recalls that Author's Interview with Lesley-Anne Down, January 7, 2004 (Down Interview).

A year after; Michaels said, "Sure Michaels Interview.

Episode 324—Kercheval recalls that; Of the two; "They were in Kercheval Interview.

Margaret Michaels found Michaels Interview.

Episode 325—according to Margaret; Michaels admits, however; "I realized when Michaels Interview.

Episode 330—Down recalls that Down Interview.

Episode 331—Down says that; Down regretted that Down Interview.

Gray found it Gray Interview.

Episode 332—Tilton recalled that *Entertainment Tonight: "Dallas:* Secrets of Southfork."

Bel Geddes opted not Morris, 70.

her wooded farm; Bel Geddes had shared; "He always said; She explained that; Bel Geddes also liked; She had long Kahn.

Bel Geddes' retirement, however; Bel Geddes' granddaughter explains Lerman Interview.

Sheree J. Wilson recalls Wilson Interview.

Episode 333—Cathy Podewell did; "Sasha is a; "He was sort Podewell Interview.

several days after *"Dallas* Has Lost Its Verve and Viewers," Ed Bark, *Dallas Morning News*, May 10, 1990.

Episode 334—Larry Hagman felt Hagman Interview.

Leonard Katzman believed; "We think this Bark (May 1990).

Season 13

as *TV Guide* Hagman (1991), cover.

Two months before "Is J.R. Running Out of Dirty Tricks?" Paul Colford, *Newsday*, September 2, 1990.

in the words; *Variety's* review of *Variety*, November 2, 1990.

Gray readily agreed Rosen, 9.

Steve Kanaly was Kanaly Interview No. 1.

Mary Crosby found Crosby Interview.

Joel Grey recalls Author's Interview with Joel Grey, December 8, 2003 (Grey Interview).

Katzman also hoped Goodman, 45.

but Principal declined Morris, 71.

CBS Entertainment President Bark (April 4, 1991).

Leonard Katzman learned *True Hollywood Story: "Dallas."*

Katzman told a "Farewell, Southfork: What It Would Be Like Without J.R.—And the Rest of the *Dallas* Clan," Diane Joy Moca, *Los Angeles Daily News*, April 28, 1991.

Duffy recalled that *E! True Hollywood Story: "Dallas."*

Katzman called Larry Goodman, 46.

Hagman told TV "Larry Hagman Finds Life Beyond *Dallas*," Ed Bark, *Dallas Morning News*, April 6, 1991.

Said Katzman about Moca.

Hagman recalled the; Hagman was "on Hagman (1991), 5.

A few weeks; Katzman also said; Hagman told the Moca.

Years later, Hagman CNN King/Hagman & Gray Interview.

Time magazine published; In the article "Goodbye to Gaud Almighty: After 356 Episodes and More Dirty Deals Than Even Larry Hagman Can Count, J.R. and His *Dallas* Clan Go Out in Style," Richard Corliss, *Time*, April 29, 1991.

and a Lorimar Bark (April 4, 1991).

As the day "*Dallas* Goes Out With a Bang," Ed Bark, *Dallas Morning News*, May 2, 1991.

About halfway through *The Official "Dallas" Trivia Book*, Jason Bonderoff, New American Library, New York, 1984, v.

the self-proclaimed "Duke Cassidy, 14.

summed up "I'm Bark (January 1990).

Season 13 Episode Guide

Episode 335—The role of; After the *Dallas*; Lucci's favorite memory; "I loved shooting; "It was really; Lucci also found Author's Interview with Susan Lucci, November 25, 2003 (Lucci Interview).

Her family placed Hagman (book), 228.

Said his long-time Goodman, 48.

The *Los Angeles Daily* "*Dallas* Opens to a New Season of Drawn-Out Plots," Phil Rosenthal, *Los Angeles Daily News*, November 2, 1990.

Ed Bark of "*Dallas* Needs to Put a Cap on a Dry Hole," Ed Bark, *Dallas Morning News*, November 1, 1990.

In *USA Today* "There's Still Life in Dirty-Dealing *Dallas*," Tom Green, *USA Today*, November 2, 1990.

Episode 336—Duffy admits that Duffy Interview.

Susan Lucci recalls Lucci Interview.

Episode 337—another thing Susan; Lucci "got to Lucci Interview.

as Cally softened Podewell Interview.

Episode 338—According to Wilson Wilson Interview.

Wilson found Lucci Wilson Interview.

Episode 341—Kercheval was adamant; "I wanted to; "I just believe Moca.

According to Kercheval; He observed, "Of; Playing J.R.'s nemesis Buck, December 23, 1984; *Entertainment Tonight: "Dallas:* Secrets of Southfork."

Nevertheless, Kercheval had; "I didn't put "Ken Kercheval, Victoria Principal's Ever-Losing Brother on *Dallas,* Has a Winning Way With Popcorn."

He later expounded *E! True Hollywood Story: "Dallas."*

Episode 342—Eden believes that Author's Interview with Barbara Eden, November 11, 2003 (Eden Interview).

She "had a "Hagman Reunited With His Jeannie," Jerry Buck, *Cincinnati Enquirer,* December 21, 1990.

Eden says that Eden Interview.

Episode 343—this episode gave Podewell Interview.

according to Barbara Eden Interview.

Episode 345—Barbara Eden says Eden Interview.

Episode 346—of her scenes; Eden also enjoyed Eden Interview.

Episode 352—In an article Moca.

Episode 353—The man playing; Podewell "loved every Podewell Interview.

nor was it; Podewell recalls that Podewell Interview.

Episode 354—Susan Lucci was; Lucci flew to; Although it was; "No one acted; "No one seemed Lucci Interview.

Leonard Katzman was; According to Keel Keel Interview.

Episode 355—the producers asked; Although Martin "was; Martin enjoyed his; Martin found Kennedy; As for the; Martin says he Martin Interview.

Episodes 356 & 357—Linda Gray found; While Gray "thought Rosen, 9.

Gray recalls that Gray Interview.

Despite his friendship; Grey's favorite scene Grey Interview.

Cathy Podewell, who; "He and Larry; "It was such Podewell Interview.

Joan Van Ark loved; "They called me; "And boy did Van Ark Interview.

who played Little; Patrick Duffy recalls; the grandson of Duffy Interview.

According to Patrick; Says Duffy, "Lenny Duffy Interview.

the *Los Angeles* "Last *Dallas* Episode Is True to Form," Phil Rosenthal, *Los Angeles Daily News,* May 4, 1991, 1.

"Frankly," says Larry Hagman Interview.

according to his; Howard Lakin recalled *E! True Hollywood Story: "Dallas."*

in looking back; He observed that; Duffy thought that; "Everything was so *Entertainment Tonight: "Dallas:* Secrets of Southfork."

Duffy claimed that TNN, *The Life and Times of "Dallas."*

Steve Kanaly feels Kanaly Interview No. 1.

Leonard Katzman felt Cassidy, 17.

as for David; He concluded that Kalter (book), 239.

PART V: THE TV MOVIES

The Early Years

In the wake Bark (December 1985).

Series creator David; Jacobs had already; "I always write; "I just enjoy Margulies.

As for giving Bark (December 1985).

By 1983, Jacobs; The network gave; In the meantime; But Jacobs responded "*Dallas* Movie Looks at Early Years of Feuding Oil Families," Jerry Buck, Associated Press, March 19, 1986; "The TV Column," John Carmody, *Washington Post*, January 14, 1985.

While Jacobs never Kalter (book), 16.

Once *Berrenger's* was; "I knew Digger "*Dallas* Creator Goes Back to *Early Years*," Ann Hodges, *Houston Chronicle*, March 21, 1986.

As for the Kalter (book), 41.

As he turned; There was, Jacobs; As a result; Initially, Jacobs decided; While reading a; Jacobs also read; Jacobs explains that; Jacobs felt that; Jacobs was satisfied; Indeed, Jacobs recalls; Although his late Author's Interview with David Jacobs, September 7, 2004 (Jacobs Interview No. 1).

In January, 1985 "*Dallas* Genre May Grow," Carolyn McGuire, *Chicago Tribune*, January 25, 1985.

But in September *The Houston Chronicle*, September 27, 1985.

In early November Margulies; "*Dallas* Prequel to Be Filmed in Texas," Jane Sumner, *Dallas Morning News*, November 3, 1985.

although Jacobs "wasn't; He initially favored; Jacobs felt Hagan Bark (December 1985).

CBS, however, asked; Jacobs responded that; He ultimately acquiesced Bark (December 1985).

"I did have; "But Barbara Bel Geddes "CBS Digs Deeper Into the Heart of *Dallas*," Bill King, *Atlanta Journal-Constitution*, March 23, 1986.

Shooting for *The*; According to the "In Hollywood: Sinatra, Savalas as *Kojak* Team?" Marilyn Beck, *Houston Chronicle*, November 29, 1985.

Filming continued until Bark (December 1985).

According to *Variety*; It was a *Variety*, March 26, 1986.

Ann Hodges, *TV* Hodges (March 1986).

Ed Bark of; Bark found the Bark (March 1986).

The week that; In "Just Discovered; According to Jacobs; Jacobs wrote that; He also found; Three were dated; The fourth, apparently; The 1951 letter; The 1963 letter; Jock wrote, "You; The 1978 letter; The undated letter; After reading the; Her view of; When Jacobs wondered Jacobs, 18–21.

Molly Hagan hoped; Hagan told a Bark (March 1986).

His mother thought "Kevin Does a Mean J.R.," *Chicago Sun-Times*, December 11, 1985.

After Wixted landed "Sinatra May Team With *Kojak*," Marilyn Beck, *San Diego Union-Tribune*, December 15, 1985.

When David Jacobs; As part of Margulies.

Jacobs thought "the Kalter (book), 66.

But Jacobs believed; "Everyone knows Digger; "It's his picture Buck (1986); Margulies.

TV critic Ed; "Scriptwriter Jacobs intentionally; "Somewhere in there Bark (March 1986).

said actor David Bark (March 1986).

the name of Author's Interview with David Jacobs, March 4, 2005 (Jacobs Interview No. 7).

Fort Worth's Stockyards; Classic 1930s roadsters; The town of; The vintage Texas State Bark (December 1985); Hodges (March 1986).

Jacobs hired a Kalter (book), 13.

J.R. Returns

Says Bel Geddes' granddaughter Lerman Interview.

Principal explains that Principal Interview.

Charlene Tilton and Kanaly Interview No. 1.

Linda Gray confirmed "Cast Ready to Take Another Shot at *Dallas*," Jefferson Graham, *USA Today*, November 14, 1996.

Landers "was so Landers Interview No. 1.

Filming was to begin; Larry Hagman, who; Hagman underwent a; Hagman spent the Hagman (book), 234, 239, 249, 255.

Duffy recalled that; "Doctor said, 'Larry *E! True Hollywood Story: "Dallas."*

Hagman knew the; "I certainly based; "It wasn't unreasonable "Back at the Ranch: *Dallas* Cast Reunites for TV Movie at Southfork," Ed Bark, *Dallas Morning News*, March 20, 1996.

Although Hagman said Graham.

During filming, there; Audrey Landers confirmed *E! True Hollywood Story: "Dallas."*

TV reporter Ed; Bark found Hagman; Hagman told Bark; Leonard Katzman told; Katzman answered, "The Bark (1996).

Hagman later wrote Hagman (book), 257.

On the set; As for his; Gray, the last cast; "It wasn't a; "It wasn't anything Bark (1996).

he lost half *Entertainment Tonight: "Dallas: Secrets of Southfork."*

commented that the Bark (1996).

On the last; Four months later "Back in the Saddle; *Dallas* Clan Returns in Reunion Movie," Ann Hodges, *Houston Chronicle*, November 15, 1996.

In April, after Hagman (book), 257.

Quipped Kercheval, "You "J.R. Returns," Susan King, *Los Angeles Times*, November 15, 1996.

Entertainment Weekly found "Television: This Week," Kristen Baldwin, *Entertainment Weekly*, November 15, 1996.

Variety called the; It praised Hagman's *Daily Variety*, November 15, 1996.

Another critic found "Larry Hagman Strikes Again as Oily Devil," Lon Grahnke, *Chicago Sun-Times*, November 15, 1996.

and even one "Best Bits," Mike Hughes, *Gannett News Service*, November 15, 1996.

Houston Chronicle TV Hodges (1996).

Audrey Landers felt Landers Interview No. 2.

To Patrick Duffy Susan King.

To Larry Hagman Graham.

Linda Gray recalls Gray Interview.

Ken Kercheval found Kercheval Interview.

Larry Hagman calls Hagman Interview.

in addition to Sumner (1996).

Audrey Landers thought Landers Interview No. 2.

The smaller original Hagman (book), 209–10.

even Larry Hagman; "I didn't know; "I didn't know Susan King.

executive producer Richard; "We'd all like; "It would be "Ayes of Texas? A Sequel Prime-Time TV Series Waits in the Ewings," *Dallas Morning News*, November 15, 1996.

Hagman felt that Hodges (1996).

George Kennedy describes Kennedy Interview.

Gray agreed that; Duffy loved the Hodges (1996).

And he, too; Kercheval agreed that Susan King.

War of the Ewings

Steve Kanaly, who Kanaly Interview No. 1.

Longtime *Dallas* chronicler "Still Ewing at Heart: *Dallas* Is Back," Ed Bark, *Dallas Morning News*, April 23, 1998.

Kanaly found it Kanaly Interview No. 1.

although its ratings "Few Spectators for Eye's Ewing *War*," Tom Bierbaum, *Variety*, April 27, 1998.

The New York "J.R. is Older; Pam's Still Dead," Anita Gates, *New York Times*, April 24, 1998.

The Dallas Morning Bark (1998).

Entertainment Weekly thought; "What made 1996's "Television: What to Watch," Kristen Baldwin, *Entertainment Weekly*, April 24, 1998.

David Bianculli complained "TV Film Sequel to *Dallas* Is the Dullest," David Bianculli, *New York Daily News*, April 24, 1998.

Larry Hagman notes Hagman Interview.

in Patrick Duffy's TNN, *The Life and Times of "Dallas."*

Steve Kanaly is; Kanaly admits he Kanaly Interview No. 1.

while *The New*; *The Times* also Gates.

And *The Dallas* Bark (1998).

as a result CNN King/Hagman & Gray Interview.

Kanaly recognized the; "When it's magic Kanaly Interview No 1.

PART VI: THE REUNION

The Return to Southfork

asked CBS to Louise Interview.

made Tilton realize; Tilton began to Author's Interview with Charlene Tilton, November 1, 2004 (Tilton Interview No. 2).

who was hurt *"Dallas* Revisited: Oil Is Thicker Than Water, Trouble Still Bubbles at Southfork," William Keck, *USA Today,* November 3, 2004, 3D.

Tilton concluded that; Tilton took the Tilton Interview No. 2.

Winkler and his; by mid-December 2004 Author's Interview with Steve Kanaly, December 21, 2003 (Kanaly Interview No. 6).

Tilton was signed; Chief among Tilton's; To Tilton's surprise Tilton Interview No. 2.

Tilton phoned Principal; Winkler also made "There's Big Tears for Big D: Homecoming Brings Rush of Emotions for Victoria Principal," Ed Bark, *Dallas Morning News,* November 7, 2004; Tilton Interview No. 2.

leaving her former *"Dallas* Cast Returns to Southfork: Actors Back at Ranch to Promote DVD," Ed Bark, *Dallas Morning News,* August 20, 2004.

Tilton phoned Bel Geddes; In the end Keck.

when Bel Geddes "respectfully "How the West Was Won," Ileane Rudolph, *TV Guide,* November 7, 2004, 58.

Tilton had envisioned; It occurred to Tilton Interview No. 2.

which he says Author's Interview with David Jacobs, November 2, 2004 (Jacobs Interview No. 6).

Jacobs explains that Author's Interview with David Jacobs, October 12, 2004 (Jacobs Interview No. 3).

There was "curious; Hagman, Duffy and; After checking in; As they reminisced; A few minutes; Principal explained that Keck.

At the time; In a telephone; While Principal recognized; By the time; What Principal did; When Principal landed Bark (November 7, 2004).

An audience that; This sequence was; In order to Tilton Interview No. 2.

A reporter noted; Gray joked that; Gray was glad; Hagman admired Principal's *"Dallas* Stars Back for Reunion Show," *Philadelphia Daily News,* November 1, 2004.

died unexpectedly on; Keel, who was; While most of *"Dallas* Actor Howard Keel Dead," Associated Press, November 7, 2004; "Musical Idol, TV Star Howard Keel Dies," Bruce Fessier, *Desert Sun,* November 8, 2004.

Keel, who had; Hagman told the "MGM Star Howard Keel Dies," Josh Grossberg, www.eonline.com, November 8, 2004.

Hagman wrote, It Statement on the Death of Howard Keel by Larry Hagman, www.larryhagman.com, November 16, 2004.

Gray stated that Statement on the Death of Howard Keel by Linda Gray, www.lindagray.com, November 16, 2004.

Ray Richmond of; Richmond, however, did "Review: A Return to *Dallas*," Ray Richmond, *The Hollywood Reporter*, November 5, 2004.

Ed Bark of "*Dallas* Reunion Sure to Have Drama," Ed Bark, *Dallas Morning News*, November 5, 2004.

The New York "Get Out Your Cowboy Hats and Cocktails," Linda Stasi, *New York Post*, November 6, 2004.

the South Florida "Meanwhile, Back at the Ranch . . . ," Tom Jicha, *South Florida Sun-Sentinel*, November 6, 2004.

the Arkansas Democrat "J.R. and the Gang Reunite for *Dallas* Retrospective," Celia Storey and Michael Storey, *Arkansas Democrat-Gazette*, November 7, 2004.

TV critic Frazier "TV Viewers Return to *Dallas* for Reunion," Frazier Moore, Associated Press, November 7, 2004.

with a Brady "Series of the Year," Gillian Flynn, *Entertainment Weekly*, December 31, 2004.

a Dick Van Dyke "The Most Memorable Moments of 2004 TV," Joel Rubinoff, *Hamilton Spectator*, January 3, 2005.

TV critic David "Why We Love Trashy TV Soaps: *Desperate Housewives* Marries Sex With Romance and Campy with Clever to Set a New Gold Standard" David Bianculli, *New York Daily News*, October 31, 2004.

of USA Today "CBS Trounces the Competition in Sweeps," Gary Levin, *USA Today*, December 2, 2004, 1D.

neither Susan Howard; Howard did not Tilton Interview No. 2.

Principal's suite at Bark (November 7, 2004).

While the audience; "My daughter and "We Love Lucy," Nicholas Fonseca, *Entertainment Weekly*, November 5, 2004.

EPILOGUE

In November 2004 "The 100 Greatest TV Characters," www.bravotv.com, November 2004.

In December 2004 "The 100 Most Memorable TV Moments," www.tvland.com, December 2004.

On August 19, 2004; Jacobs and the; Being at Southfork; told Bark, "I'm; Duffy joked with; Kercheval explained that Bark (August 2004).

The Reno Gazette-Journal "Disney Does *Aladdin* Right," Forrest Hartman, *Reno Gazette-Journal*, October 8, 2004.

The Contra Costa "Now Available on DVD," *Contra Costa Times*, October 15, 2004.

And the Buffalo "Second Chance: DVD Collections Provide Instant Access to Television Shows," Toni Ruberto, *Buffalo News*, September 24, 2004.

that Variety had "ABC in Bed With *Dallas*," Josef Adalian, *Variety*, March 11, 2003.

was first proposed "*Dynasty* Measured for the Big Screen."

declined to write Author's Interview with David Jacobs, September 22, 2004 (Jacobs Interview No. 2).

signed Australian director Author's Interview with David Jacobs, October 20, 2004 (Jacobs Interview No. 4); Author's Interview with David Jacobs, October 21, 2004 (Jacobs Interview No. 5).

Jacob finds Luketic Jacobs Interview No. 3.

"will be great Jacobs Interview No. 2.

Harling, a fan; While Harling has; "It's *Dallas* on; "Every woman in "Texas Tease: What's Brewing on *Dallas*' Movie Remake," Karen Valby, *Entertainment Weekly*, November 12, 2004.

Harling's script was Jacobs Interview No. 2.

Not long after; While Harling refuses Valby.

According to Jacobs Jacobs Interview No. 2.

the scheduled July 2006 "Gong Li Has Signed on to Michael Mann's *Miami Vice* for Universal Pictures," Borys Kit, *The Hollywood Reporter*, March 30, 2005

Patrick Duffy has Valby.

To Linda Gray; Larry Hagman agrees "Texas Gold: *Dallas* Reunion Hits the Memory Lode," Amy Amatangelo, *Boston Herald*, November 5, 2004.

While Hagman conceded "Hagman: 'Let Willis Play J.R.,'" *World Entertainment News Network*, October 17, 2004.

Hagman replied to Amatangelo.

BIBLIOGRAPHY

Author's Interviews

Atkins, Christopher; October 20, 2003.

Babcock, Barbara; November 3, 2003.

Beck, John; October 1, 2003.

Brittany, Morgan; January 27, 2004.

Carrera, Barbara; October 14, 2003.

Cassidy, Joanna; December 4, 2003.

Corbin, Barry; January 3, 2004.

Crosby, Mary; December 4, 2003.

Down, Lesley-Anne; January 7, 2004.

Duffy, Patrick; November 20, 2003.

Eden, Barbara; November 11, 2003.

Elliott, Stephen; November 26, 2003.

Fitzgerald, Fern; October 20, 2003.

Forrest, Steve; October 9, 2003.

Francis, Anne; December 13, 2003.

Gray, Linda; February 23, 2004.

Grey, Joel; December 8, 2003.

Hagman, Larry; October 30, 2003.

Harrison, Jenilee; October 16, 2003.

Hirson, Alice; October 16, 2003.

Howard, Susan; December 2, 2003.

Jacobs, David; September 7, 2004; September 22, 2004; October 12, 2004; October 20, 2004; October 21, 2004; November 2, 2004; and March 4, 2005.

Kanaly, Steve; February 20, 2000; August 1, 2000; September 28, 2000; October 3, 2000; July 31, 2002; and December 21, 2003.

Keel, Howard; October 9, 2003.

Kennedy, George; October 29, 2003.

Kenney, Ed; October 28, 2003.

Kercheval, Ken; October 2, 2003 and November 6, 2003.

Landers, Audrey; October 31, 2003 and November 1, 2003.

Lerman, Hannah; January 22, 2004.

Louise, Tina; October 27, 2003.

Lucci, Susan; November 25, 2003.

Markham, Monte; December 2, 2003.

Martin, Jared; November 3, 2003.

McCloskey, Leigh; December 20, 2003.

Michaels, Margaret; October 8, 2003.

Podewell, Cathy; November 7, 2003.

Pointer, Priscilla; October 10, 2003 and October 12, 2003.

Presley, Priscilla; December 19, 2003.

Principal, Victoria; January 7, 2004.

Roat, Richard; October 30, 2003.

Scott, Kathryn Leigh; September 8, 2000.

Smithers, William; October 5, 2003.

Tilton, Charlene; November 14, 2003 and November 1, 2004.

Van Ark, Joan; December 30, 2003.

White, Kenneth; October 30, 2003.

Willingham, Noble; November 16, 2003.

Wilson, Sheree J.; November 4, 2003.

Woodward, Morgan; October 24, 2003.

Note: The author requested an interview from all surviving, located *Dallas* actors who received a "Starring," "Also Starring," "Special Guest Star" or "Special Guest Appearance" credit (although some additional interviews were done with cast members who received a "Guest Star," "Co-Star" or other credit). Cast members who declined the author's interview requests are Karen Kopins, Ian McShane, Brad Pitt, and Ted Shackelford. Barbara Carrera spoke about her time on *Dallas* but did so off the record. The remaining "Starring," "Also Starring," "Special Guest Star," and "Special Guest Appearance" cast members who could be located did not respond to the author's interview requests.

Books

Adams, Leon. *Larry Hagman*. New York: St. Martin's Press, 1987.

Ang, Ien. *Het Geval "Dallas": Populaire Kultuur, Ideologie en Plezier*. Amsterdam, 1982.

Bego, Mark. *The Linda Gray Story*. New York: St. Martin's Press, 1988.

Bonderoff, Jason, with an introduction by Leonard Katzman. *The Official "Dallas" Trivia Book*. New York: New American Library, 1984.

Brooks, Tim and Earle Marsh. *The Complete Directory to Prime Time Network and Cable TV Shows, 1946–Present*, Sixth Edition. New York: Ballantine Books, 1995.

Fisher, Tom. *Alles Uber "Dallas."* Bertelsman Club, 1982.

Golden, Fran Wenograd. *Tvacations*. New York: Pocket Books, 1996.

Greenfield, Meg. *Washington*. New York: Public Affairs, 2001.

Hagman, Larry, with Told Gold. *Hello Darlin': Tall (and Absolutely True) Tales About My Life*. New York: Simon & Schuster, 2001.

Hirsch, Julia Antopol. *The Sound of Music: The Making of America's Favorite Movie*. Chicago: Contemporary Books, Inc., 1993.

Kalter, Suzy. *The Complete Book of "Dallas": Behind the Scenes of the World's Favorite Television Program*. New York: Harry N. Abrams, Inc., 1986.

Keel, Howard, with Joyce Spizer. *Only Make Believe: My Life in Show Business*. Fort Lee, NJ: Barricade Books, 2005.

Kofoed, Peter, and Tove Arendt Rasmussen. *"Dallas:" Skabelan Og Struktur i den Moderne TV-Serie*. Aalborg Universitets Centr, 1986.

Liebes, Tamar, and Elihu Katz. *The Export of Meaning: Cross-Cultural Readings of "Dallas."* Cambridge: Oxford University Press, 1990.

Manetti, Larry, with Chip Silverman. *Aloha Magnum: Larry Manetti's Magnum, P.I. Memories*. Los Angeles: Renaissance Books, 1999.

Morris, Bruce B., with a foreword by Michele Lee. *Prime Time Network Serials: Episode Guides, Cast and Credits for 37 Continuing Television Dramas, 1964–1993*. Jefferson, NC: McFarland & Company, Inc., 1997.

Riley, Lee. *Patrick Duffy*. New York: St. Martin's Press, 1988.

Ryder, Lew, with Bill Keith. *Why J.R.?: A Psychiatrist Discusses the Villain of "Dallas."* Huntington House, 1982.

Silj, Alessandro, with Manuel Alvarado. *A Est Di "Dallas:" Telefilm USA Ed Europei A Confronto*. Torino, 1988.

Steinberg, Cobbett. *TV Facts*. New York: Facts on File Publications, 1985.

Van Wormer, Laura, Introduction by Leonard Katzman. *Dallas: The Complete Ewing Family Saga, Including Southfork Ranch, Ewing Oil, & the Barnes-Ewing Feud, 1860–1985*. Garden City, NY: Doubleday & Co., 1985.

Witzleben, Donna F., Ed. *BiB Television Programming Source Books, 1998–99 Series Volume*. Philadelphia: North American Publishing Co., 1999.

Articles

"A Morning Shakeup Call," *Dallas Morning News*, September 25, 1987.

"Actor Says Bobby Ewing Leaves When He Does," Associated Press, January 18, 1985.

Adalian, Josef. "ABC in Bed with *Dallas*," *Variety*, March 11, 2003.

Allen, Jane E. "Leonard Katzman, Executive Producer of TV's *Dallas*, Dead at 69," Associated Press, September 7, 1996.

Amatangelo, Amy. "Texas Gold: *Dallas* Reunion Hits the Memory Lode," *Boston Herald*, November 5, 2004.

Anderson, Jon. "Will J.R. Be Shot Again? Tensions Mount in *Dallas* Finale," *San Diego Union-Tribune*, May 18, 1984.

———. "Nice Guy Bobby Ewing Is Finished," *San Diego Union-Tribune*, May 17, 1985.

"Another Spinoff?," *San Diego Union-Tribune*, February 27, 1984.

Arar, Yardena. "H-o-l-d On for the TV Cliffhangers," *San Diego Union-Tribune*, April 28, 1986.

Associated Press report on Charlene Tilton Wedding, April 9, 1985.

"Atkins Leaving *Dallas*," *San Diego Union-Tribune*, March 6, 1984.

"Ayes of Texas? A Sequel Prime-Time TV Series Waits in the Ewings," *Dallas Morning News*, November 15, 1996.

Baldwin, Kristen. "Television: This Week," *Entertainment Weekly*, November 15, 1996.

———. "Television: What to Watch," *Entertainment Weekly*, April 24, 1998.

Bark, Ed. "*Dallas* at a Crossroad: 7 Season Itch," *Dallas Morning News*, January 15, 1985.

———. "Ken Kercheval: He Stands By His Man," *Dallas Morning News*, July 4, 1985.

———. "Portrait of the Ewings as a Young Clan," *Dallas Morning News*, December 5, 1985.

———. "*Dallas* Movie Strikes It Rich," *Dallas Morning News*, March 23, 1986.

———. "Patrick Duffy Is Coming Back to TV's *Dallas*," *Dallas Morning News*, April 10, 1986.

———. "Hagman Puts a Little J.R. Into Remarks," *Dallas Morning News*, May 22, 1986.

———. "The *Dallas* of Old Will Be Back in Fall," *Dallas Morning News*, August 4, 1986.

———. "*Dynasty* and *Vice* Still Slipping in Ratings," *Dallas Morning News*, December 3, 1986.

———. "*Morning* Ratings Fail in Dallas-Fort Worth," *Dallas Morning News*, January 24, 1987.

———. "*Dallas* Cast Gets Morning Call on CBS," *Dallas Morning News*, May 9, 1987.

———. "Happy Ending Eludes Linda Gray," *Dallas Morning News*, February 27, 1989.

———. "A Summer Without *Dallas*," *Dallas Morning News*, May 16, 1989.

———. "*Dallas* Needs to Put a Cap on a Dry Hole," *Dallas Morning News*, November 1, 1990.

———. "*Dallas* May Be Down, But It's Not Out," *Dallas Morning News*, January 16, 1990.

———. "*Dallas* Has Lost Its Verve and Viewers," *Dallas Morning News*, May 10, 1990.

———. "*Dallas* Is Done In," *Dallas Morning News*, April 4, 1991.

———. "Larry Hagman Finds Life Beyond *Dallas*," *Dallas Morning News*, April 6, 1991.

———. "*Dallas* Goes Out With a Bang," *Dallas Morning News*, May 2, 1991.

———. "Back at the Ranch: *Dallas* Cast Reunites for TV Movie at Southfork," *Dallas Morning News*, March 20, 1996.

———. "Still Ewing at Heart: *Dallas* Is Back," *Dallas Morning News*, April 23, 1998.

———. "*Dallas* Cast Returns to Southfork: Actors Back at Ranch to Promote DVD," *Dallas Morning News*, August 20, 2004.

———. "*Dallas* Reunion Sure to Have Drama," *Dallas Morning News*, November 5, 2004.

———. "There's Big Tears for Big D: Homecoming Brings Rush of Emotions for Victoria Principal," *Dallas Morning News*, November 7, 2004.

Beck, Marilyn. "In Hollywood: Sinatra, Savalas as *Kojak* Team?" *Houston Chronicle*, November 29, 1985.

———. "Sinatra May Team With *Kojak*," *San Diego Union-Tribune*, December 15, 1985.

"Begin Regrets J.R. Stayed Home," United Press International, March 13, 1982.

"Bel Geddes' Return Will Help *Dallas*," *Dallas Morning News*, April 15, 1985.

"Bel Geddes Returning to *Dallas*," *San Diego Union-Tribune*, April 12, 1985.

Bianculli, David. *"Dallas* Awakens From a Nightmare Season," *St. Petersburg Times*, October 17, 1986.

———. "TV Film Sequel to *Dallas* Is the Dullest," *New York Daily News*, April 24, 1998.

———. "Why We Love Trashy TV Soaps: *Desperate Housewives* Marries Sex With Romance and Campy With Clever to Set a New Gold Standard," *New York Daily News*, October 31, 2004.

Bierbaum, Tim. "Few Spectators for Eye's Ewing *War*," *Variety*, April 27, 1998.

Birmingham, Stephen. *"Dallas* vs. *Dynasty:* Which Show Is Better?" *TV Guide*, October 15, 1983, 36–39.

———. "Is *Knots Landing* Now Better Than *Dallas* and *Dynasty?"* *TV Guide*, November 30, 1985, 4–8.

Bond, Courtney. "Where Are They Now? The Original Cast of *Dallas*," *Texas Monthly*, September 2002, 170.

Borden, Jeff. "Chaos Erupts as Soaps End Another Year," *Dallas Morning News*, May 15, 1986.

Brennan, Patricia. *"Peter Pan*; Mary Martin's Still Flying High," *Washington Post*, March 19, 1989, page Y7.

"Brite and Brief," Associated Press, February 24, 1988.

Buck, Jerry. "Alexis Smith Is Still a Lady, Even in *Dallas*," *San Diego Union-Tribune*, April 1, 1984.

———. "Cliff Is Still Trying to Be J.R.'s Worse Half," *San Diego Union-Tribune*, December 23, 1984.

———. "Priscilla Presley's Character Facing Verdict in Murder Trial Friday," Associated Press, March 5, 1985.

———. "Dack Is No Rambo-Come-Lately," *San Diego Union-Tribune*, July 10, 1985.

———. "Barbara Eden Takes *Jeannie* Out of Bottle for TV Movie," Associated Press, October 16, 1985.

———. "Martha Scott Plays Mysterious Grandmother on *General Hospital*," Associated Press, January 24, 1986.

———. *"Dallas* Movie Looks at Early Years of Feuding Oil Families," Associated Press, March 19, 1986.

———. *"Dallas* Aims for 'Who Shot?' Ratings as Duffy Returns," *Houston Chronicle*, May 16, 1986.

———. *"Dallas* to Drop Pam in Contract Squabble," *San Diego Union-Tribune*, February 3, 1987.

———. *"Dallas:* 10 Years Old," *Boston Globe*, March 20, 1988.

———. *"Dallas* Star Wants to Take J.R. to Russia," *Chicago Sun-Times*, February 7, 1989.

———. "Hagman Reunited With His Jeannie," *Cincinnati Enquirer*, December 21, 1990.

"Bye-Bye, Lucy," *Dallas Morning News*, June 1, 1985.

Carman, John. "Bobby Is Making the Ultimate in Comebacks," *Atlanta Journal-Constitution*, June 16, 1986.

———. "The TV Column," *Washington Post*, February 15, 1984.

————. "The TV Column," *Washington Post*, January 14, 1985.

————. "The TV Column," *Washington Post*, May 29, 1985.

————. "The TV Column," *Washington Post*, October 3, 1985.

————. "The TV Column," *Washington Post*, April 10, 1986.

————. "The TV Column," *Washington Post*, May 13, 1986.

————. "The TV Column," *Washington Post*, November 20, 1986.

————. "The TV Column," *Washington Post*, April 29, 1987.

Cassidy, Marsha F. "The Duke of *Dallas*: Interview With Leonard Katzman," *Journal of Popular Film and Television*, Volume 16, Number 1, Spring 1988, 12–21.

Cipriano, Ralph. "Son of Migrant Worker to be Norwalk's Mayor," *Los Angeles Times*, February 7, 1985.

Clark, Jayne. "New *Back to Kansas* Sitcom Stirs Up a Whirlwind," *USA Today*, June 20, 2003, 1D.

Clark, Kenneth R. "Networks Rewrite Dire Predictions for Fall Lineups," *Chicago Tribune*, August 7, 1988, 8C.

Clarke, Gerald. "The Big House on the Prairie," *Time*, November 12, 1979, 117.

Colford, Paul D. "Is J.R. Running Out of Dirty Tricks?" *Newsday*, September 2, 1990.

Collins, Monica. "*Dallas* Could Go Soapless," *USA Today*, January 18, 1988.

Condon, Jan. "Military Brat Victoria Principal Revisits Her Birthplace to Sell Tokyo on *Dallas*," *People*, December 14, 1981, 46–47.

Conroy, Faith. "Police Say Robbery Was Motive in Slaying of *Dallas* Star's Parents," Associated Press, November 19, 1986.

"Convicted in Killing of Actor's Parents," *San Francisco Chronicle*, March 20, 1987.

Coren, Alan. "*Dallas* Is Emptying the Pubs and Streets of London," *TV Guide*, July 26, 1980, 11–14.

Corliss, Richard, reported by James Willwerth. "TV's *Dallas*: Whodunit?" *Time*, August, 1980, 60–66.

Corliss, Richard, reported by Martha Smilgis. "Now It Can Be Told: Shedunit," *Time*, December 1, 1980, 79.

Corliss, Richard. "Goodbye to Gaud Almighty: After 356 Episodes and More Dirty Deals Than Even Larry Hagman Can Count, J.R. and His *Dallas* Clan Go Out in Style," *Time*, April 29, 1991.

Crockett, Lane. "TV Package," *Gannett News Service*, September 10, 1987.

————. "TV Package," *Gannett News Service*, December 30, 1987.

Crotta, Carol A. "She Had to Learn to Act Evil," *TV Guide*, August 30, 1980, 12–14.

Currie, Glenne. "Second Best," United Press International, March 11, 1982.

"*Dallas* Actor Howard Keel Dead," Associated Press, November 7, 2004.

"*Dallas* Gives Glasnost a Shot of Glitz," *Northern New Jersey Record*, April 30, 1989.

"*Dallas* Gives Lucy Her Walking Papers," *Northern New Jersey Record*, November 18, 1984.

"*Dallas* Inspires Men's Cologne," *Toronto Star*, October 17, 1987, J3.

"*Dallas: J.R. Returns* Review," *Daily Variety*, November 15, 1996.

"*Dallas* Milestones," *Dallas Morning News*, March 27, 1988.

"*Dallas* Review," *Variety*, April 5, 1978.

"*Dallas* Review," *Variety*, September 27, 1978.

"*Dallas* Review," *Variety*, September 26, 1989.

"*Dallas* Review," *Variety*, November 2, 1990.

"*Dallas* Stars Back for Reunion Show," *Philadelphia Daily News*, November 1, 2004.

"*Dallas: The Early Years* Review," *Variety*, March 26, 1986.

"*Dallas* to Be Remade for Big Screen," *Variety*, October 10, 2002.

Davidson, Bill. "Swat This *Dallas* Gadfly?" *TV Guide*, April 24, 1982, 29–33.

———. "Beware of the Phone-Call Trick and the Plastic Surgery Ploy," *TV Guide*, July 30, 1983, 34–38.

———. "The Eyes That Turned *Dallas* Upside Down," *TV Guide*, December 29, 1984, 26–30.

———. "She Chose *Dallas* Over Congress," *TV Guide*, May 10, 1986, 12–17.

Dawidziak, Mark. "Actress Balances Two Roles This Season in *Dallas* and the New Series *Glitter*," *Dallas Morning News*, August 26, 1984.

"Donna Reed Admires Miss Ellie's Character," Associated Press, February 1, 1985.

"Donna Reed Dies of Cancer at 64," *Seattle Times*, January 14, 1986.

"Donna Reed Fighting Cancer," *Newsday*, December 21, 1985.

"Donna Reed to be *Dallas*' Miss Ellie," Associated Press, *San Diego Union-Tribune*, June 6, 1984.

"*Dynasty* Measured for the Big Screen," *San Diego Union-Tribune*, August 17, 1984.

Esterly, Glenn. "The New Miss Ellie Isn't Afraid to Back J.R. Against the Wall," *TV Guide*, November 24, 1984, 43–48.

Fessier, Bruce. "Musical Idol, TV Star Howard Keel Dies," *Desert Sun*, November 8, 2004.

Fetherston, Drew. "NBC Knocks Off CBS," *Newsday*, April 23, 1986.

———. "CBS Detectives Will Take on the Slumping Ratings Case," *Newsday*, June 14, 1986.

Flynn, Gillian. "Series of the Year," *Entertainment Weekly*, December 31, 2004.

Fonseca, Nicholas. "We Love Lucy," *Entertainment Weekly*, November 5, 2004.

Francis, Paul. "On the Grapevine: Good Grief, Lucy's Back!" *TV Guide*, January 23, 1988, A-2.

Friedman, Roger. "*Valley of the Dolls*, *Dallas* Will Return," www.foxnews.com, October 11, 2002.

Gates, Anita. "J.R. Is Older; Pam's Still Dead," *New York Times*, April 24, 1998.

Gender, Morgan. "Life and Death Alter Course of 5 TV Series," *Los Angeles Times*, April 1, 1985.

"Give Her the Simple Life," *TV Guide* (Canada), January 24, 1979.

Goodman, Mark, and Todd Gold. "Sunset at Southfork," *People*, May 6, 1991, 44–49.

Goodwin, Betty. "Watch Out—This Woman Is a Devious, Back-Stabbing Schemer!" *TV Guide*, September 24, 1983, 14–16.

Graham, Jefferson. "Cast Ready to Take Another Shot at *Dallas*," *USA Today*, November 14, 1996.

Grahnke, Lou. "Larry Hagman Strikes Again as Oily Devil," *Chicago Sun-Times*, November 15, 1996.

Gray, Linda. Statement on the Death of Howard Keel, www.lindagray.com, November 16, 2004.

Green, Michelle, reported by David Wallace. "As *Dallas*' New Miss Ellie, Donna Reed Trades the Kitchen for a Home on the Range," *People*, November 19, 1984, 91–92.

———. "Patrick Duffy Bids Bye-Bye to Bobby in the Hottest *Dallas* Cliff-Hanger Since J.R. Got Shot," *People*, May 13, 1985, 54–59.

Green, Tom. "*Dallas* Corrals Tight Security for Cliffhanger," *USA Today*, May 14, 1987.

———. "A Decade of *Dallas*: Success of Steamy Soap Is No Dream," *USA Today*, April 1, 1988.

———. "There's Still Life in Dirty-dealing *Dallas*," *USA Today*, November 2, 1990.

Grossberg, Josh. "MGM Star Howard Keel Dies," www.eonline.com, November 8, 2004.

"Guilty Plea in Duffy Deaths," *San Francisco Chronicle*, May 6, 1987.

Hagman, Larry. "How I Kept J.R. Alive," *TV Guide*, November 15, 1980, 10–14.

———. "*Dallas*—My Way," *TV Guide*, March 27, 1982, 2–6.

———. "*Dallas* at 10," *People*, April 4, 1988, 98–103.

Hagman, Larry, as told to Mary Murphy, "So Long, *Dallas*," *TV Guide*, May 4, 1991, 4–13.

"Hagman: 'Let Willis Play J.R.,'" *World Entertainment News Network*, October 17, 2004.

Hagman, Larry. Statement on the Death of Howard Keel, www.larryhagman.com, November 16, 2004.

Haithman, Diane. "Prime-Time Soaps to Rinse Serial Format," *St. Petersburg Times*, February 7, 1988.

———. "The Baron of *Dallas*: Producer Reminisces on 10th Anniversary," *Los Angeles Times*, April 1, 1988.

Hall, Jane. "Here's the Real Dirt on Southfork," *TV Guide*, January 24, 1981, 44–45.

———. "Bobby Might Be Dead, But That Can't Stop Patrick Duffy From Jumping Back in the *Dallas* Saddle," *People* magazine, May 19, 1986, pages 178–80.

Hamilton, Marsha. "Passport to Moscow: *Dallas* Brings Cowboy, Hats, Mink Coats and Shady Oil Deals to Red Square," *Los Angeles Times*, April 1, 1989.

Hartman, Forrest. "Disney Does *Aladdin* Right," *Reno Gazette-Journal*, October 8, 2004.

Hilton, Pat. "Principal Masters a New Role," *USA Today*, October 2, 1987.

Hockstader, Lee. "Tourists Keep *Dallas* Mystique Alive," *Washington Post*, August 19, 2002, A3.

Hodges, Ann. "Bobby Ewing Is Deader Than a Mackerel, Hagman Laments," *Houston Chronicle*, June 10, 1985.

———. "*Dallas*' Family Gathers for Dress-up Ball," *Houston Chronicle*, July 29, 1985.

———. "Hagman Family Makes Mary as *Dallas* Lassos on Location," *Houston Chronicle*, July 30, 1985.

———. "Hagman Proud of Texas Roots and PBS *Lone Star* Special," *Houston Chronicle*, December 12, 1985.

———. "*Dallas* Creator Goes Back to Early Years," *Houston Chronicle*, March 21, 1986.

————. "A Network Miracle: Bobby Ewing Comes Back From the Dead," *Houston Chronicle,* June 18, 1986.

————. "Hagman Not Happy That Victoria Principal Is Leaving *Dallas,*" *Houston Chronicle,* January 30, 1987.

————. "For CBS, The Shows Must Go On," *Houston Chronicle,* October 21, 1987.

————. "Back in the Saddle; *Dallas* Clan Returns in Reunion Movie," *Houston Chronicle,* November 15, 1996.

"Hollywood to Make *Dallas* as Movie," www.cnn.com, October 10, 2002.

Holston, Noel. "*Dallas, Vice* Face Showdown," *Twin Cities Star-Tribune,* September 26, 1986.

Horn, John. "*Dallas* Is Leaving *Vice* in Ratings Dust on Fridays," *Orange County Register,* October 23, 1986.

Houston Chronicle Report on *Dallas: The Early Years,* September 27, 1985.

"Howard Keel Recovering From Heart Operation," Associated Press, January 10, 1986.

Hughes, Mike. "Best Bits," *Gannett News Service,* November 15, 1996.

Jacobs, David. "Just Discovered! The *Dallas* Papers," *TV Guide,* March 22, 1986, 18–21.

Jicha, Tom. "Meanwhile, Back at the Ranch . . . ," *South Florida Sun-Sentinel,* November 6, 2004.

Kahn, Toby. "To Wildlife and *Dallas* Lowlife, Barbara Bel Geddes Gives the Milk of Human Kindness," *People,* June 28, 1982, 43.

Kalter, Suzy. "Bobby Ewing's Life After Death," *People,* September 29, 1986, 46–55.

Kaye, Jeff. "News Update: CBS Prime Time Soaps to Make Big Cast Cuts," *TV Guide,* March 21, 1987, A-1, A-48.

Keck, William. "*Dallas* Revisited: Oil Is Thicker Than Water, Trouble Still Bubbles at Southfork," *USA Today,* November 3, 2004, 3D.

"Keel Leaves Hospital," *San Diego Union-Tribune,* January 28, 1986.

Kehr, Dave. "Texas Raunch," *Film Comment,* July/August 1979, 66–68.

"Ken Kercheval, Victoria Principal's Ever-Losing Brother on *Dallas,* Has a Winning Way With Popcorn," *Chicago Sun-Times,* May 7, 1987.

"Kevin Does a Mean J.R.," *Chicago Sun-Times,* December 11, 1985.

King, Bill. "CBS Digs Deeper Into the Heart of *Dallas,*" *Atlanta Journal-Constitution,* March 23, 1986.

————. "NBC Tries New Sitcoms and Juggles Schedule," *Atlanta Journal-Constitution,* May 29, 1986.

King, Susan. "J.R. Returns," *Los Angeles Times,* November 15, 1996.

Kit, Borys. "Gong Li Signed On to Michael Mann's *Miami Vice* for Universal Pictures," *The Hollywood Reporter,* March 30, 2005.

"*Knots Landing* and *Days of Our Lives* Sweep Soap Opera Awards," Associated Press, January 18, 1988.

Koltnow, Barry. "Charlene Tilton Opens in La Mirada Play While Negotiating *Dallas* Role," *Orange County Register,* November 3, 1987.

Kubasik, Ben. "TV Spots," *Newsday,* January 29, 1987.

————. "No Spring Vacation for Series Cast Members," *Newsday,* March 31, 1987.

Lacey, Gord. "DVD release by end of '04," TVShowsOnDVD.com, January 7, 2004.

Lardine, Bob. "There's Peace (For Now) in *Dallas* as Larry Hagman Mulls Over J.R.'s Fate—and His Own," *People*, April 14, 1980, 88–96.

Laurence, Robert P. "The Soaps Steam Into New Season," *San Diego Union-Tribune*, September 25, 1985.

Laurence, Robert P. "Mum's the Word on Bobby's Return," *San Diego Union-Tribune*, June 16, 1986.

Leahy, Michael. "Barbara Carrera Plays the Mystery Woman for All It's Worth . . . On Screen *and* Off," *TV Guide*, January 18, 1986, pages 35–40.

———. "How Larry Hagman Got Angry and Forced Some Changes in *Dallas*," *TV Guide*, May 24, 1986, 34–45.

———. "She's Risen Above—But Can't Ever Forget—Her Troubled Years," *TV Guide*, March 14, 1987, pages 34–43.

Levin, Gary. "CBS Trounces the Competition in Sweeps," *USA Today*, December 2, 2004, 1D.

Libman, Gary. "Marathon Countdown; As Sunday's Race in L.A. Nears, Actor Jack Scalia Eats, Sleeps and Thinks Running in Preparation," *Los Angeles Times*, March 5, 1988, part 5, 1.

Liebergott, Sheila. "Do It Victoria's Way—or Else," *TV Guide*, September 18, 1982, 14–17.

Littwin, Susan. "If *Dallas* Folded, It Could Be the Last You See of Steve Kanaly," *TV Guide*, October 17, 1987, 34–37.

Manning, Sue. "Oscar-Winning Actress Dies of Cancer at 64," Associated Press, January 14, 1986.

Margulies, Lee. "Reaching Back for Something Extra," *Los Angeles Times*, March 13, 1986.

McGuire, Carolyn. "*Dallas* Genre May Grow," *Chicago Tribune*, January 25, 1985.

Merrill, Don. "Review," *TV Guide*, February 15, 1986, 39.

Moca, Diane Joy. "Farewell, Southfork: What It Would Be Like Without J.R.—And the Rest of the *Dallas* Clan," *Los Angeles Daily News*, April 28, 1991.

Moore, Frazier. "TV Viewers Return to *Dallas* for Reunion," Associated Press, November 7, 2004.

Murphy, Mary. "When Bobby Does His Love Scenes With Pam, He Brings Along a Frog or a Mannequin," *TV Guide*, October 18, 1986, 27–32.

Nelson, Valerie J., "Stephen Elliott, 86; Veteran Stage, Film and TV Actor Known for Role in *Arthur*," *Los Angeles Times*, May 24, 2005.

Nielsen Ratings Chart, *New York Post*, August 25, 2000.

"Noble Willingham. A Supporting Actor in Dozens of Films, Dies at 72," Associated Press, January 20, 2004.

Nolan, Tom. "The Eyes of Texas Are Upon Her," *TV Guide*, April 20, 1985, 26–31.

"Now Available on DVD," *Contra Costa Times*, October 15, 2004.

O'Donnell, Rose. "Oh, Wow! A *Dallas* Album!" *Seattle Times*, July 4, 1985.

O'Hallaren, Bill. "This Woman Is a Trained: Chiropractor, Agent, Stock-Car Driver, Actress. Victoria Principal's Answer Is: All of the Above," *TV Guide*, June 16, 1979, 10–12.

———. "The Ticklish Plight of Being Priscilla Presley," *TV Guide*, March 17, 1984, 12–16.

———. "Sheree J. Wilson Kisses and Tells," *TV Guide*, March 26, 1988, 33–36.

O'Steen, Kathleen. "Bel Geddes' Ex-Manager Sues for $80 Mil," *Daily Variety*, March 30, 1993, 10.

"Patrick Duffy to Quit *Dallas*," *San Diego Union-Tribune*, November 20, 1984.

"People," *Dallas Morning News*, September 5, 1984.

"People," *Dallas Morning News*, July 17, 1986.

"People," *Toronto Star*, August 24, 1986.

"People," *Twin Cities Star-Tribune*, January 10, 1986.

"Personal Mention," *Houston Chronicle*, April 20, 1986.

Peters, Susan. "Lois Chiles Sets the Fur Flying on *Dallas* as J.R.'s Sexy Temptress, Holly Harwood," *People*, April 18, 1983, 117.

Principal, Victoria. "The Principal Work-Out: Improve Your Fitness While Watching TV," *TV Guide*, June 2, 1984, 10–14.

———. "Life Without Bobby," *TV Guide*, October 12, 1985, 34–38.

"Priscilla Presley Gives Birth to Boy," *St. Petersburg Times*, March 2, 1987.

Puzo, Daniel P. "Hagman Is Comfortable in his J.R. Role," *St. Petersburg Times*, December 3, 1989.

"Reed Sues to Remain Miss Ellie on *Dallas*," *San Diego Union-Tribune*, May 25, 1985.

Reilly, Sue. "If the Eyes of Texas Bug These Days, Blame It on Those Three Sexy Wildcats from *Dallas*," *People*, December 17, 1979, 124–32.

———. "What Are Larry (J.R.) Hagman & the *Dallas* Producers Feeling from the Shots Cheered Round the World? Absolutely No Pain," *People*, July 14, 1980, 87–90.

———. "So Who Plugged J.R.? Sue Ellen Swears She Doesn't Know, But *People* Kibitzers Think They Do," *People*, November, 10, 1980, 113–18.

———. "Mary Crosby's Hot as a Pistol, Says Larry Hagman, But Not in a Way to Worry Dear Old Dad," *People*, December 8, 1980.

———. "The *Dallas* Cast Remembers the Good Times But Regards Its Patriarch, Actor Jim Davis, as Irreplaceable," *People*, May 11, 1981, 130–31.

———. "After Years as a *Dallas* Also-Ran, Steve Kanaly Is Finally Over the Hump," *People*, May 10, 1982, 111.

———. "Bridegroom Revisited," *People*, December 6, 1982, 42–47.

Richmond, Ray. "Review: A Return to *Dallas*," *The Hollywood Reporter*, November 5, 2004.

Rosen, Gary Alan. "Linda Gray: No Malice in Her Memories of *Dallas*," *TV Guide*, May 4, 1991, 9.

Rosenblatt, George L. "Where J.R. Is Shot: Visitors Get Look at *Dallas*' Locale," *Houston Chronicle*, August 17, 1986.

Rosenfield, Paul. "The Low-Down on Low-Down J.R.," *Saturday Evening Post*, November 1985.

Rosenthal, Phil. "*Dallas* Opens to a New Season of Drawn-Out Plots," *Los Angeles Daily News*, November 2, 1990.

———. "Last *Dallas* Episode Is True to Form," *Los Angeles Daily News*, May 4, 1991.

Rothenberg, Fred. "NBC Introduces Eight New Series," Associated Press, May 14, 1986.

Roush, Matt. "Bringing Back Berle for a New Generation," *USA Today*, July 7, 1987.

———. "Murphy Brown's *Live* Mirror Images," *USA Today*, July 26, 1989.

Ruberto, Toni. "Second Chance: DVD Collections Provide Instant Access to Television Shows," *Buffalo News*, September 24, 2004.

Rubinoff, Joel. "The Most Memorable Moments of 2004 TV," *Hamilton Spectator*, January 3, 2005.

Rudolph, Ileane. "How the West Was Won," *TV Guide*, November 7, 2004, 57–60.

Russell, Dick. "Meaner and Crazier All the Time," *TV Guide*, October 6, 1979, 8–9.

Safer, Morley. "Who Shot Bobby Ewing?" *TV Guide*, September 1, 1984, 14–15

"*Saturday Night* Fever," *People*, October 4, 1999.

Scott, Vernon. "Donna Reed Steps Into *Dallas* Role," *Dallas Morning News*, September 9, 1984.

See, Carolyn. "Rise of a Sex Symbol," *TV Guide*, May 28, 1983, 26–29.

Sellers, Pat. "Audrey Landers: Just an Old-Fashioned Girl," *Us*, February 1981.

Sharbutt, Jay. "Bel Geddes Returns to *Dallas*," *Los Angeles Times*, April 13, 1985.

Shaw, Ellen Torgerson. "It Was Rotten While It Lasted," *TV Guide*, May 9, 1981, 26–30.

Shister, Gail. "Cosby: No Danger of Starvation," *Northern New Jersey Record*, July 23, 1986.

Shoobs, Adrian. "Tuesday's People," *Bergen Record*, February 2, 1988, A02.

Simon, Jeff. "USA Network's Contribution to TV's Sleazefest," *Buffalo News*, February 2, 1997.

Smith, C. W. "How Dallas Feels About *Dallas*," *TV Guide*, November 1, 1980, 13–16.

Smith, Liz "A Big-Screen Shot for *Dallas*," *Los Angeles Times*, August 2, 2002.

"Snapshots: Quotes and Notes from December *Celebrity Focus* Magazine," *PR Newswire*, November 17, 1987.

Spinks, Bruce. "Texas Stars Form Minigalaxy in Hollywood and New York," *Houston Chronicle*, August 4, 1985.

Stasi, Linda. "Get Out Your Cowboy Hats and Cocktails," *New York Post*, November 6, 2004.

Stevens, Gus. "A Bit of Southfork Coming to Town," *San Diego Union-Tribune*, August 30, 1984.

———. "Surf's Up in *Dallas*: A Visit to J.R.'s," *San Diego Union-Tribune*, February 1, 1985.

Storey, Celia, and Michael Storey. "J.R. and the Gang Reunite for *Dallas* Retrospective," *Arkansas Democrat-Gazette*, November 7, 2004.

Sumner, Jane. "*Dallas* Prequel to Be Filmed in Texas," *Dallas Morning News*, November 3, 1985.

———. "Hagman Receives a CoCo," *Dallas Morning News*, May 31, 1987.

———. "Film and Outtakes," *Dallas Morning News*, November 15, 1996.

"Susan Howard's Character Dropped From TV's *Dallas*," Associated Press, January 27, 1987.

Swertlow, Frank. "TV Update," *TV Guide*, April 19, 1980, A-3–A-4.

Swertlow, Frank, with Dwight Whitney. "TV Update," *TV Guide*, June 21, 1980, A-1, A-55.

Swertlow, Frank. "TV Update," *TV Guide*, July 5, 1980, A-1–A-2.

———. "TV Update: *Dallas* Fever Hypes CBS Ratings and Ad Revenues," *TV Guide*, December 6, 1980, A-1.

"The 100 Greatest TV Characters," www.bravotv.com, November, 2004.

"The 100 Most Memorable TV Moments," www.tvland.com, December, 2004.

"The Television Generation Mourns Its Favorite Surrogate Mother, Tough But Tender Donna Reed," *People*, January 27, 1986, 84–86.

Tunnell, Mark. "Joanna Cassidy: Is She the Female J.R.?," *US*, February 17, 1981.

Turan, Kenneth. "Hollywood's Cover-Up! Mum's the Word on Killers and Arsonists," *TV Guide*, November 26, 1983, 48–52.

"TV Dial," *St. Petersburg Times*, September 28, 1986.

TV Guide. "The Best and Worst of the 1984–1985 Season." June 29, 1985.

"TV Scuttlebutt," *Northern New Jersey Record*, February 19, 1987.

"V star joins *Dallas* cast," *Toronto Star*, October 30, 1985, B3.

Valby, Karen. "Texas Tease: What's Brewing on *Dallas*' Movie Remake," *Entertainment Weekly*, November 12, 2004.

Vallance, Tom. "Obituary: John Randolph," *The Independent*, March 3, 2004.

Warren, Elaine. "Solving the Mystery of Bobby's Return to *Dallas*," *TV Guide*, August 30, 1986, 4–7.

Waters, Harry F., with Janet Huck, Jeff B. Copeland, and Lea Donosky. "Who Shot That Nice Mr. Ewing?" *Newsweek*, November 17, 1980, 66–77.

"White in *Dallas* Acting as Governor," *Houston Chronicle*, July 27, 1985.

Whitney, Dwight. "The Cut-Rate John Wayne Changes His Luck," *TV Guide*, February 17, 1979, 22–26.

———. "You think J.R. Is Mean? Why, Darlin,' the Pleasure's All His!" *TV Guide*, March 8, 1980, 22–26.

Williams, Jeannie. "It's Not a Dream: Linda Gray Is Leaving *Dallas*," *USA Today*, February 22, 1989.

Zoglin, Richard, and Melissa Ludtke. "To Be Continued Next Fall," *Time*, May 21, 1984, 96.

Broadcast Interviews

E! True Hollywood Story: "Dallas," E! Entertainment Network. Airdate August 13, 2000.

Entertainment Tonight: "Dallas: Secrets of Southfork." Airdate February 5, 2000.

CNN Larry King Live: "Larry Hagman Talks About His Career, His New Series, *Orleans*, and His Liver Transplant Operation." Airdate January 7, 1997.

CNN Larry King Live: "Larry Hagman and Linda Gray Share Their Memories of *Dallas*." Airdate June 20, 2000.

The Life and Times of "Dallas," The Nashville Network (TNN). Airdate April 24, 2000.

ACTOR INDEX

Note: Each episode in which an actor appears is noted by the episode number. The TV movies are abbreviated as follows: EY for *The Early Years*; JR for *J.R. Returns*; and WE for *War of the Ewings*. The cast reunion, *The Return to Southfork*, is abbreviated by RS.

DIRECTOR INDEX

Note: Each episode directed is noted by the episode number. The TV movies are abbreviated as follows: EY for *The Early Years*; JR for *J.R. Returns*; and WE for *War of the Ewings*. The cast reunion, *The Return to Southfork*, is abbreviated by RS.

WRITER INDEX

Note: Each episode written is noted by the episode number. The TV movies are abbreviated as follows: EY for *The Early Years*; JR for *J.R. Returns*; and WE for *War of the Ewings*. The cast reunion, *The Return to Southfork*, is abbreviated by RS.

* indicates "Written by" credit shared with another writer
** indicates "Story by" credit
*** indicates "Teleplay" credit shared with another writer